A Popular History of France from the First Revolution to the Present Time: 1832-1881

Abby Langdon Alger, Henri Martin

A POPULAR

HISTORY OF FRANCE,

𝔉rom t𝔥e 𝔉irst 𝔅ebolution to t𝔥e 𝔓resent 𝔗ime.

BY

BON LOUIS HENRI MARTIN,

SENATOR OF THE FRENCH REPUBLIC, AUTHOR OF "ITALIAN UNITY," "EUROPEAN RUSSIA,"
"THE GENIUS AND DESTINY OF FRANCE,"
ETC., ETC.

A POPULAR

HISTORY OF FRANCE,

FROM

The First Revolution to the Present Time.

By HENRI MARTIN.

Translated

By MARY L. BOOTH AND A. L. ALGER.

WITH CONCLUDING CHAPTERS

By FREDERICK MARTIN.

FULLY ILLUSTRATED

WITH WOOD AND STEEL PLATES BY A. DE NEUVILLE, LEOPOLD FLAMING, G. STAAL, VIOLLAT, PHILLIPPOTEAUX, LIENARD. AND OTHERS.

VOL. III.

BOSTON:

DANA ESTES AND CHARLES E. LAURIAT,

301 WASHINGTON STREET.

1882.

COPYRIGHT, 1882.
BY ESTES AND LAURIAT.

CONTENTS.

———•———

CHAPTER I.

CHAPTER II.

CHAPTER III.

CHAPTER IV.

CHAPTER V.

CHAPTER VI.

CHAPTER VII.

CHAPTER VIII.

CHAPTER IX.

CHAPTER X.

CHAPTER XI.

CHAPTER XII.

CHAPTER XIII.

CHAPTER XIV.

CHAPTER XV.

CHAPTER XVI.

CHAPTER XVII.

CHAPTER XVIII.

CHAPTER XXIII.

CHAPTER XXIV.

CHAPTER XXV.

LIST OF STEEL ENGRAVINGS.

VOL. III.

LIST OF ILLUSTRATIONS.

Vol. III

A POPULAR

HISTORY OF FRANCE

FROM 1789 TO THE PRESENT TIME.

CHAPTER I.

CONSTITUTIONAL MONARCHY OF JULY (*continued*). — LEGITIMIST RISING MADE BY THE DUCHESS DE BERRI. — REPUBLICAN REVOLT OF JUNE 5 AND 6. — ST.-SIMONIANS. — GENERAL PROGRESS OF LITERATURE, SCIENCE, AND ART.

April to October, 1832.

AT the time of Casimir Périer's death the situation of France was most threatening and critical. The government, as we have said, persisting in maintaining what it called the system of March 13, the deputies of the opposition issued a protest, May 28. They set forth their grievances against a government which, they said, "was constantly receding from the Revolution which created it." As a whole, however, the language of this protest was vague, and designated no clearly defined form of government as desirable. The Left, with much show of reason, desired more firmness towards foreign powers and a different attitude with respect to other nations; but it was rather hazardous to claim that "this was the only means of keeping the peace."

This protest was known as the Compte Rendu, and was drawn up by Odilon Barrot and Cormenin. Its vagueness was caused by the very diverse opinions held by the signers, many of whom still believed in constitutional monarchy, while others were aiming at a republic. The Compte Rendu had no element of popularity, and was soon stifled by important occurrences; for just as this manifesto of legal opposition appeared, civil war was attempted by the legitimists and threatened by the republicans.

It was neither Charles IV., nor his son, nor the grave and sad Duchess d'Angoulême, who urged the partisans of royalty to rash deeds. The ex-royal family had retired to Edinburgh, and the Bourbons were sheltered at Holyrood, in the palace of those Stuarts whose misfortunes and faults they had renewed. One member of the family, however, did not share the resignation of the rest. The Duchess de Berri, an active and imaginative woman, of little judgment and great will, had never ceased to conspire since the July revolution. She obtained from Charles IV. a paper ordering royalists to recognize her as the regent of the kingdom in her son's name; she then left Great Britain, and established herself in Italy, at Massa, a city belonging to that Duke of Modena who betrayed the Italian patriots and refused to recognize the supremacy of Louis Philippe. There for some months she held a court which at once called to mind Coblentz in the time of the emigrants and Paris in the days of the Fronde, and at which plot after plot was hatched amidst jests and laughter.

All the foreign powers save England wished these conspiracies well, but had little faith in them, and were unwilling to compromise themselves in their behalf. The duchess, however, hoped to reconquer France by French aid. The reports sent her from the interior excited brilliant hopes, and she felt that the throne of July was ready to crumble at a touch. She was assured that not only the West and South, but Paris itself, would rise at her word; legitimist agents scattered money broadcast, and enrolled in their ranks, with the ex-servants of the Restoration, adventurers and workmen embittered by want, and even Bonapartists, among whom figured General Montholon, one of Napoleon's companions at St. Helena, side by side with the royalist Marshal Victor, Duke of Belluno. The plan was to invade the Tuileries during a ball, but discord, as usual, was rife among the royalists. Bourmont's followers were unwilling that Victor should reap the fruits of success; they thwarted the measures adopted for the evening of February 1, and amidst the discord many of the minor conspirators were captured by the police at an eating-house in the Rue des Prouvaires.

No proof existed against the leaders of the plot. The duchess's courage did not desert her, and she signed, at Massa, an order for the establishment of a provisional government at Paris, mapped out a new charter far inferior to that of 1814 and closely resembling the declaration issued by Louis XVI. which provoked the oath of the Tennis Court. April 24, she set sail with a small band of followers, among them Marshal Bourmont, who emigrated from Algiers after the July revolution, when the Bourbons left France. Such was the general chosen by the " queen regent " to restore the white flag to France.

The duchess landed on the evening of the 28th of April, not far from Marseilles, which the legitimist townsmen had promised to capture for her during the night of the 29th. Crowds gathered, bearing the white flag, and the alarm bell began to ring; but the authorities were forewarned, the national guard and liberal youth marched against the mob, singing the Marseillaise, and dispersed them without bloodshed. The duchess, finding that she had failed at the South, refused to re-embark, and secretly journeyed into Toulouse and La Vendée, traversing those places in the disguise of a peasant, and concealing herself on a small farm, where she was found by a few of the leaders of her party. Elements of hostility to the new government yet lingered in La Vendée, Brittany, and Maine, but still the West was greatly changed, as its inertia in July, 1830, clearly proved. Royalism was not extinct, but the flame burned low; prejudices had diminished, and new interests had sprung up. The duchess listened only to ultras, and planned an uprising for the 24th of May.

Just as she issued this order, M. Berryer arrived, having been sent by the chief legitimists of Paris to dissuade her from civil war. The eloquent orator wrung from her a promise to renounce her schemes, but the next day she resumed her manœuvres. Meantime Bourmont, the future general of the insurrection, who was lying in concealment at Nantes, sent a counter order to the leaders of troops, after an interview with the Queen, the 3d of June being fixed upon for the attack. Owing to this confusion, the movement lost the little chance it might have had, not of success, but of being something more than a mere affray. Some of the troops never received the countermanding order, and rose in revolt, May 24, only to be ignominiously put down, which was also the fate of their friends, the correspondence of the duchess having fallen into the hands of the military authorities. The insurgents fought bravely, and the defence of Castle de la Pénissière has remained memorable. Forty-five Vendeans made such stout resistance that their foes were forced to fire the building to dislodge them, and many escaped through the flames.

The duchess fled to Nantes, where a few trusty friends concealed her from the active pursuit of the police.

At the very time that the legitimists' revolt was crushed in the West, Louis Philippe's monarchy was struggling with a more formidable foe in Paris.

The republican party was daily waxing bolder; the presence of foreign refugees, especially Poles, who swarmed into France after their country's downfall, increased the irritation of young France against what they called "the government of peace at any price." To many young men the republic was less a political doctrine than a sort of fighting religion. They rallied around whatever appealed to them under the most warlike aspect, without caring much for theories. A society was formed about this time, entitled "The Rights of Man," closely allied to the "Friends of the People," led by an energetic and impassioned man, Auguste Cannes. Its object was to establish communication among the working-classes, and group them into sections, and it adopted, as its charter, the declaration of the rights of man proposed by Robespierre, but not accepted by the convention. This revival of the old political party was for a long time the principal stumbling-block in the way of the republican party, dividing its already scanty numbers and estranging many who had been disposed to join it.

CASSIMIR PERIER.

The republicans strove to hide their dissensions from others and from themselves; but, setting aside the socialistic sects formed or in process of formation, there were two opposite and very different schools, — the conventional or dictatorial school, and the school of liberal democracy, which desired institutions ruled as in America by the idea of individual freedom. The latter formed an association called the Central or Communal Council, to which La Fayette and Armand Carrel belonged, both of whom, despairing of harmonizing constitutional monarchy with the revolution, now devoted themselves to preparing for the coming of the republic. Their party desired to achieve its end by the gradual progress of enlightenment; the other school was impatient to pass from discussion to action. The occasion offered: it was seized.

General La Marque, the spokesman of the war party in 1831, had just died, and, being greatly beloved by the younger part of the population, it was resolved to give him a splendid funeral. June 5, at early dawn, a vast procession formed, headed by La Fayette, Laffitte, Clausel, and the whole Left wing of the Chambers, thousands of soldiers, and the Polish, Italian, and Spanish refugees, whose cause La Marque had upheld, the banners of these conquered nations floating in the air beside the French flag, which La Marque had striven to send to their aid. All this was calculated to excite the public mind. It seemed like a mass of tinder only waiting a spark to fall.

Sixty thousand men followed the funeral car from the Rue d'Anjou St. Honoré to the Bastille, between two lines of spectators. The throng seemed to be going to battle rather than to a funeral. The cries of "Long live Poland!" which burst forth everywhere at sight of the Polish uniform, were mingled constantly with unceasing shouts of "Long live the republic!" The excitement reached its height on the Place de la Bastille, at the sight of a large number of scholars from the Polytechnic School, who had defied their teachers, and joined the procession in spite of the commandant's orders.

A staging was erected near the Austerlitz bridge, and La Fayette, mounting it, harangued the people, spoke of 1789 and 1830, saluted the flags of oppressed nations, and begged the crowd to end this patriotic day in peace. He then entered his carriage, and a rumor was spread that he was on his way to the Hôtel de Ville to proclaim a republic. At this moment a singular-looking man appeared, riding a black horse and bearing a red flag with the words, " Liberty or death!" A great tumult ensued, and General Excelmans exclaimed, " No red flag; no flag for us but the tricolor!" The man disappeared, but left behind a vague feeling of repulsion and alarm.

The young men leading the procession now strove to prevent the removal of La Marque's body to the provinces, desiring to take it to the Pantheon. A skirmish with the mounted guards followed, in which the latter came off victorious. Meantime troops were seen approaching, upon which a cry was raised: "To arms!" "The time is ripe!" exclaimed Jules Bastide. An artillery officer from the national guard then drew his sword. Some of his men shouted " Liberty!" others left the ranks. An engagement ensued, and the cavalry was driven back by volleys of shot from the houses round about, held by insurgents, who fired the first gun.

The insurrection spread rapidly along both banks of the Seine; the rebels seized a powder-magazine and arsenal, and between three and six o'clock in the afternoon held all the ground between the Bastille and Place des Victoires, building barricades, and constantly increasing in numbers, although by no means proportionate to the space occupied or the length of the funeral procession, only a fraction of the republican party having joined the contest.

The men in power, struck by the vast extent of the revolt and ignorant of the real strength of their adversaries, were in despair. Nor was the anxiety less among the more eminent republicans, such as La Fayette and Armand Carrel. Carrel sought an interview with General Clausel, who, having personal grievances against the government, had gone over to the Left. Both hesitated, uncertain whether they could now withdraw.. Carrel then hastened to Odilon Barrot, to urge him to take the lead of the movement; Barrot refused. Carrel deemed it impossible to form a republic without aid from the Left wing of the Chambers, the existing elements of the republican party being insufficient, and at a meeting at the office of the *National* that night, he stoutly protested against the movement.

The situation became modified. Thiers showed as much decision as Soult had displayed uncertainty; he summoned his fellow-deputies to rally round him, and cheered on the national guard. Louis Philippe, on his side, was firm. He was at St. Cloud, but, unlike Charles X., he hastened to Paris, and reviewed the troops by night, meeting an ardent welcome. The troops of the line during the evening resumed the offensive, under Marshal Lobau, and drove the insurgents from most of the positions held by them. On the morning of June 6, the rebels were driven into a sort of citadel about the church of St. Merry, where they sustained a regular siege.

While the cannon still echoed through the heart of the old quarter of Paris, the King, leaving the Tuileries at noon, traversed Paris on horseback, his calm and resolute bearing winning him the hearts of many who still wavered, and impressing even his foes. An admirable saying is attributed to Louis Philippe on this occasion: when reproached with exposing himself to such perils, he replied, "I have a good shield in my five sons." The remark was true; the murder of the King would not have slain royalty. Later on, through Louis Philippe's own fault, royalty was destroyed without any attempt on the King's life, any more than on that of Charles X.

On returning to the Tuileries he found Laffitte, Odilon Barrot, and Arago, sent thither by the opposition party, "not," as Barrot expressed it, "with conditions, but with requests." They urged him to take advantage of a victory no longer doubtful, and to make an honorable change in that policy of his ministers whose sad results were evident. "The policy of my ministers," exclaimed the King; "I don't know what you mean: there is but one policy, and that is my own; convince me that I am wrong, and I shall change it; until then I will not depart from it, should you bray me in a mortar." In the intoxication of success he frankly acknowledged his personal government, which had been lauded by the *Moniteur*. He added, however, that " he had refused to declare Paris in a state of siege, as his ministers desired, wishing to rule by the law alone."

The defeat of the rebellion was insured at early dawn, yet a handful of men, barely one hundred and fifty, were still struggling at four in the afternoon, holding an army in check. This little band, led by an obscure young man named Jeanne, fought no longer for victory, but from sheer despair. Being exhausted, one of them cried, " Food !" " Food !" exclaimed Jeanne; " it is three o'clock, at four we shall all be dead !" and, in fact, the majority were soon killed or captured, Jeanne, however, escaping in the confusion with several comrades. So ended the insurrection of June 5 and 6. Two revolutions cannot occur within two years, unless the grievances be of a kind to drive a nation to the last extremity. Still the sacrifice of the brave heroes, who rushed forward uncalculatingly, in the name of the republic, was not wholly in vain. A feeling of admiration mingled with awe lingered behind them, which enhanced the glory of the republican party and impressed its enemies.

A reactionary movement naturally followed the defeat of the revolt. Two thousand arrests were made; the Polytechnic School and the artillery of the national guards were disbanded, and Gisquet, the chief of police, exceeded his luckless proclamation of the time of the cholera, by hunting up an old statute ordering medical men to denounce their wounded patients. Almost all indignantly refused.

The King broke his promise to the delegates of the opposition party, and, yielding to the entreaties of his ministers, established a state of siege, for which there was no longer either motive or excuse. In consequence, councils of war were convened, to try not only insurgents, but writers accused of instigating rebellion. The courts protested, and the newspapers, even those in government pay, upheld them in their protest. The matter was brought to a trial, and decided in favor of the courts. Louis Philippe, mindful of his promise to rule by law, bowed to the decision and instantly raised the siege, thus proving himself capable of resisting the temptations of victory. An event which occurred abroad also served to strengthen his power. The Duke of Reichstadt, Napoleon's son, died at Vienna, July 22, 1832, aged twenty-one, and the Orléans dynasty thought itself freed from the rivalship of the empire.

The prisoners captured June 5 and 6 were soon brought to trial, and suffered various degrees of punishment. The daring Jeanne, leader of the St. Merry insurgents, was captured and transported. The Southern and Western legitimists were tried simultaneously with Parisian republicans, most of them being acquitted, in consequence of a counter terror organized by the Chouans.

These political trials were enlivened at the summer's close by a case of a very different nature, which excited a lively curiosity abroad as well as throughout France. We allude to the trial of the St.-Simonians, — one episode in a vast moral and intellectual movement, for the world of ideas has its revolutions as well as the world of facts.

Henry St. Simon was a nobleman of a philosophic turn, who had hit upon a scheme for religious reform, and professed an idea set forth by more than one great thinker before him, — by Leibnitz, Turgot, and Condorcet, — namely, the doctrine of perfectibility or indefinite progress. "The age of gold," said St. Simon, "lies before and not behind us." He proposed to apply this doctrine to economic and political order, and was applying it to religion when he died. In his last work, "New Christianity," he did not invent a new religion, but desired to develop anew the Christian religion. He won numerous disciples. In reading accounts of the secret discussions of the St.-Simonians we find many dangerous errors mingled with lofty thoughts, but nothing commonplace. These errors would soon have corrected themselves, had the St.-Simonians been content to form a philosophic association, to teach, discuss, and develop the doctrine of perfectibility, as was largely done throughout France and even in Belgium. The school, however, soon deviated from its pristine purpose, led by two men named Bazard and Enfantin, who schemed, not to assist intellectual progress by gradual instruction, but to lay violent hands on civil and religious society. They dreamed of nothing less than making themselves Pope and Emperor.   Nor did they agree as to the moral and religious conditions of the society to be ruled by this theocracy. Bazard, an ex-Carbonaro, united with his false views in regard to limitless authority very pure and wholesome notions as to the regulation of human life, while Enfantin proclaimed the flesh equal to the spirit, fickle and ever-changing loves on a level with constant unions, while the part and the rights which he attributed to the future "priest" and "priestess" recall the mystic materialism of some antique creeds.

A rupture ensued; reconciliation was impossible, the break occurring on questions relative to woman and marriage.   After this rupture, which took place in November, 1831, two groups were formed, one of philosophers under the austere and moral Jean Reynaud, the other under Enfantin.   The latter retired to Mesnilmontant with his party, and formed a sort of monastic community, waiting for a woman to appear, who should join him, complete the new law, and become priestess and mother of the sect, as he was its priest and father.   He and his chief disciples were speedily indicted for "outraging public morals."   Enfantin, accustomed to rule with a glance, vainly tried to fascinate his judges by a look, and was condemned, with two comrades, to two years' imprisonment, whereupon the little church at Mesnilmontant was dissolved.   At the same period another but far less original and well-known sect was put down.   We refer to what was known as the "French Church." An Abbé Châtel, taking with him a few other priests, deserted the Roman Catholic Church and said mass in French.   They had followers in certain quarters, but soon disappeared, leaving no trace behind.

Not so with St.-Simonism; on its dissolution new sects sprang up.   Fourier and his phalanstery were revived; Communism, so alarming after the terror, and stifled in the blood of Babœuf, reappeared.   St.-Simonism was like the preface of a book yet to be completed.

Bazard and his followers returned to the bosom of the Catholic Church.   Unable to found a new papacy, they went back to the old one. Enfantin and his comrades, although ceasing to live in common, retained their community of ideas, their social and pantheistic philosophy. They plunged headlong into the great industrial and financial movement; unable to gain possession of society, to guide it in the path of material progress, towards which they struggled, they at least did their part to help it on. In Egypt they were the forerunners of De Lesseps, and bequeathed to him assistants in the cutting of the Suez Canal; and from their tarry in Egypt came one of the masterpieces of modern music, Félicien David's "Desert Symphony."

While those St.-Simonians, who had striven to realize their Utopia, returned to active life, a new school sprang up, based on the early theories of St. Simon, enlarged and altered to suit religious feeling. This was the Positivist school, founded and led by Auguste Comte. This learned mathematician and physicist worked to establish the fact that the human mind was first governed by theology (religious, based on miraculous revelation), then by metaphysics (rational, idealistic, and spiritualistic philosophy); that the reign of metaphysics must be finally followed by the reign of science, that is, of positive knowledge based on observation and experience; all that could not be attained by observation and experience was unworthy to occupy the human mind. But he did not long hold true to his theory; sentiment claimed its due, and he even took sentiment for the principle of social organization, and, like St. Simon, returned to the idea of one religion, the religion of humanity without a God, in place of whom Comte put humanity, as if that were a being, a person. The Positivists have lasted, increased, and multiplied, and joined the scientific movement, which has long prevailed and still prevails; for the constant progress of physical science, that is, physiology, is the prevalent characteristic of our age. Physiology is not philosophy, but it prepares priceless material for it. Auguste Comte in France, like Hegel in Germany, ended in a policy of absolution. He dreamed of a sort of double papacy, whereof he was to be the spiritual, and the Czar Nicholas the temporal head.

The ideas of Comte were refuted from a lofty standpoint by the

St.-Simonian school in 1830, previous to the rupture caused by Enfantin, and this refutation was taken up and stoutly maintained in 1831 by Jean Reynaud and his followers, who, like the Positivists, though in another sense, shared in the modern scientific movement. Reynaud, seeking the laws of life and its progressive development in nature and mankind, adopted, in so far as natural history goes, the theories of one of the most illustrious naturalists of our age, Étienne Geoffroy St. Hilaire, then engaged in a famous contest with Cuvier. Cuvier maintained that the earth had been the scene of a series of revolutions in which everything was suddenly destroyed, and renewed by successive and separate creations; that God created all species of plants and animals as they now exist, and that they have never varied.

Geoffroy St. Hilaire, on the contrary, believed in progressive development from the lowest to the highest stage. This conception, which excited the admiration of Goethe, the greatest writer and clearest thinker in Germany, seemed to Reynaud more accordant with reason and religious philosophy.

We cannot now even attempt to indicate the series of scientific discoveries which marked the nineteenth century, and but briefly refer to some of the scholars who were the glory of France. Modern science took up the tradition of bygone heroes, for Geoffroy St. Hilaire was the heir of Buffon. Arago and Fresnel returned to Descartes, who advanced the theory that heat, light, and sound are phenomena produced by motion, which these scientists now triumphantly proved. Perhaps no scientific man has ever won such popularity in France as Arago. Together with Fresnel, he greatly advanced the cause of physics, and brought astronomy within the reach of all by his lucid and attractive method. Among other scholars of the period were Fourier, the great physicist, not to be confounded with Fourier the Utopian; Lussac, Thénard, Poisson, and Biot, busy in physics and chemistry; Ampère, stamping every science with the imprint of his genius; and Blainville and Serres, laboring in the departments of natural history and comparative anatomy.

We have shown the uniting link between the religious doctrine of perfectibility and the natural sciences. They were bound less plainly but yet more closely to historical science, and to those Oriental studies destined to reveal to us the language, ideas, and religions of the ancient races of Asia and Egypt. Voltaire, often unjust towards the past, still felt that something great would yet come to us from the East. Later on, French soldiers admired the vast monuments of Egypt, though ignorant of their meaning and of the characters graven and painted upon them, whose secret was revealed to us by Champollion, who laid bare six thousand years of history, and through these, thousands of years before them, while Champollion's successors, chief among them Rougé, went still further.

A Frenchman unveiled the mysteries of Egypt, and a Frenchman, Eugene Bournouf by name, rediscovered the language and religion of Zoroaster, the apostle of Bactria and Persia, and gave us the religious books of Buddhist India.

Side by side with these scientific discoveries progressed the literature of the imagination and the fine arts, gloriously continuing the career opened under the Restoration. The young Romantic school was deeply stirred by the July revolution. Victor Hugo wrote superb farewells to the past, and went over to the tricolor, fated to lead him to the republic later on. Lamartine slowly followed in his footsteps, and a still more wonderful change excited the minds of men. Lamennais, the great ultramontane author, who had waged such hot war on modern society, left Rome to espouse the cause of revolution.

The success of the new school, despite its brilliant qualities and strong effects, is still contestable as regards the theatre, at least in comparison to the great dramatic era of the seventeenth century; its lyric superiority may be the cause of its dramatic inferiority. The century has been more successful in romance than in drama. A woman, born a great writer, George Sand, in our day has moved all souls by her revelations of society as it is, while her truth and poetry show her to be the heiress and daughter of Rousseau. Close beside her stands another author, Balzac, whose style and taste may be audacious, but whose power, subtle observation, and fertile imagination are incontestable.

We have already mentioned the progress of the fine arts under the Restoration, which went on increasing. Eugene Delacroix, Ingres, and Ary Scheffer gathered scholars and competitors about them, and, without being on a level with these masters, Horace Vernet was very popular, Decamps painted the men and scenery of the East, and Rousseau raised landscape painting to a height hitherto unknown. Sculpture, that thoroughly French art, flourished amain. David and his rivals multiplied their elegant and vigorous efforts. Rude, a man who, like Rouget de l'Isle, had his day and was touched by the finger of immortal inspiration, revived the spirit of 1792 in his group of " The Departure," as did the author of the Marseillaise in word and song.

Architecture was the only art which stood still, seeming to have exhausted its creative faculty, and to be no longer an art but a science. Music pursued a bright career. Two foreign artists of the first water now allied themselves to the native composers of France, namely, Meyerbeer and Rossini.

We have endeavored to sum up briefly the chief features of this stormy period, which fired as well as troubled the spirit of man. Extraordinary intellectual progress is the essential characteristic of the epoch. Some of the ideas then prevalent were doomed to fade out of sight; others, of great import, will not at once ripen. One or even many generations are but a brief space for the incubation of an idea; our century is a century of preparation.

Taken as a whole, the period which we are retracing is at once superior in breadth of horizon and depth of meaning to the liberal age preceding, and inferior in its authoritative and socialistic tendency, which tends to weaken the spirit of individual liberty, and which produces, as we shall see, most dangerous consequences from the standpoint of political liberty.

CHAPTER II.

CONSTITUTIONAL MONARCHY OF JULY (*continued*). — MINISTRY OF OCTOBER 11. — REPUBLICAN INSURRECTION IN APRIL. — FIESCHI PLOT. — SEPTEMBER LAWS. — DISSOLUTION OF THE MINISTRY OF OCTOBER 11.

October 11, 1832, to February, 1836.

HAVING striven to give a brief abstract of the great forward movement in literature, art, and science at the period of history of which we write, we must once more take up the course of political events after the defeat of the republican insurrection of June 5 and 6.

The King was anxious to retain the ministry, which, since Casimir Périer's death, obeyed him blindly, yet he felt that the Chamber of Deputies would not long tolerate the personal will of an irresponsible monarch; they were still too severely constitutional, and demanded a ministry endowed with actual power. The June crisis gave Louis Philippe a brief respite, but with the autumn he must act. He first offered the ministry to M. Dupin, but could not make terms with him. He then turned to De Broglie and Thiers, the former of whom insisted that Guizot should be added to the number. Louis Philippe was reluctant to yield, apparently foreseeing that Guizot was destined to be fatal to him. Marshal Soult, the minister of war, was made president of the council; the Duke de Broglie took charge of foreign affairs; Thiers at first had the interior, and afterwards the department of commerce and public works united; while Guizot was appointed minister of public instruction, D'Argout took the interior, Humann the finances, and M. Barthe became minister of justice. The ministry formed October 11, 1832, was full of talent, but in point of intellect was far behind the majority of the Chamber.   The cabinet began by creating a batch of new peers to insure the support of the peerage.

A few days later, the Duchess de Berri, who had been concealed at Nantes for some months, was discovered, arrested, and sent prisoner to Castle Blaye in the Gironde (November 6).   She was betrayed for a large sum of money by a Jewish convert to Catholicism, who had been introduced to the Pope and afterwards to the duchess during her stay in Italy.   Her capture freed Louis Philippe, if not from serious danger, at least from a cause of anxiety.   Toward the close of the year the government had a still greater triumph.

The Belgian question had been dragging along for two years without effecting a definite arrangement between Belgium and Holland.   Louis Philippe married his eldest daughter to King Leopold, August 3, 1832, hoping thus to recover influence in Belgium, but the King of Holland persisted, in spite of the decision of the conference at London, in holding the citadel of Antwerp.   Russia, Austria, and Prussia, though blaming his course, refused to take part in the quarrel.   The conference broke up, and France and England agreed together to insure the evacuation of those territories illegally held by Holland and Belgium.   Belgium readily yielded to the demands made, but Holland refused to stir from Antwerp, the king hoping that Prussia would come to the rescue.

A French army, led by Marshal Gérard, already skirted the Belgian frontier, but at the decisive moment the English ministry faltered, offended by the thought that the French and Belgians would once more fraternize under arms.   The French ministry declared that no time was to be lost.   Louis Philippe yielded, and forbade his son-in-law, Leopold, to take the field with France. The Belgians, who had made great efforts to organize their army and regain their military reputation, were hurt and mortified, and the expedition intended to unite two nations only estranged them from each other.

November 15, seventy thousand French, under Gérard, accompanied by the King's two elder sons, entered Belgium, marched on Antwerp, and attacked the citadel from without.   Gérard warned the governor of the place, General Chassé, that if the town were bombarded he should hold him personally responsible, and Antwerp, still grateful to Carnot, her first French governor, in 1814, now owed her preservation from a great catastrophe to a French soldier. The siege lasted until December 14, when the French carried the outpost of St. Laurent by storm, and ten days later Chassé capitulated.

Shortly after the military entrance of Belgium, November 19, 1832, the opening of the Chambers was marked by a grave event. As the King was riding toward the Chambers, over the Pont Royal, a shot was heard. No one was wounded, and it was at first supposed that a soldier's gun had gone off by chance; but a pistol was soon picked up discharged, and a girl who fainted near the spot, declared, on reviving, that she saw a young man fire at the King. Louis Philippe calmly went his way, but while making the opening speech before the Chambers the news spread through the assembly, and cries of "Long live the King!" burst forth. That evening the deputies thronged to the Tuileries. "Well," said the King to Dupin, "so they fired on me!" "Sire," replied Dupin, "they fired upon themselves." No one was arrested at the time, but a few days later several young men were seized, who were, however, acquitted. This attack on the King united the ministry more closely than ever, and weakened the opposition. Various important laws were passed during this legislative session, the elective principle was introduced into the General Councils, and a million francs were appropriated to the cause of public education, at the suggestion of Guizot. Free schools were also established, and those departments of the French Institute suppressed by the Empire were restored. A professorship of constitutional law was created, and the publication of a vast mass of unpublished papers, relative to the history of France, was undertaken by Guizot.

While Guizot labored in the cause of education, Thiers applied himself to progress of another sort. Although a partisan of protection in trade, he caused the reduction of many of the exorbitant and really prohibitive tariffs which prevented any foreign commerce, obtained a special grant of one hundred millions for public works, and spent them wisely on roads, canals, and lighthouses. He also secured the passage of a law to facilitate grants for the establishment of railroads, — a vast scheme inaugurated by the United States, and now beginning to excite universal interest.

The Chamber of Deputies was almost unanimous in regard to these peaceful questions, but continued to dispute over political differences. The Duchess de Berri was an embarrassing prisoner. What was to be done with her? The ministry claimed that no member of a royal family could be brought to trial. The opposition protested stoutly. No one desired bloodshed, but the Left could not admit the principle of the impunity of princes. De Broglie and Thiers enlarged on the dangers of trying the duchess, painting them in blacker colors than were presented at the trial of Charles X.'s ministers, and the Chamber, in alarm, voted that the ministry should be left free to choose its own course (January 5, 1833). The legitimists gloried in the fears which they created, but matters soon turned to their confusion. A rumor spread that the prisoner was about to give birth to a child, and bitter recriminations passed between the journals of both parties. A dozen successive duels resulted, but the pride of the legitimists in their heroine was destined to a fall, for the duchess, finding that she could no longer conceal her condition confessed (February 22) that she had secretly married a Sicilian gentleman during her stay in Italy. She was held prisoner until the birth of her daughter (May 10), the government of Louis Philippe taking the same precautions to insure the authenticity of the birth as the government of Louis XVIII. had in the case of the Duke de Bordeaux. In June the captive was set free; nothing more was to be feared from her, but she had cost the dignity of the royal family dear. Louis Philippe had gained his point; the legitimists were abashed and put out of countenance.

The republicans, on the contrary, were more active than ever, and by no means discouraged by their defeat in June. Their chief organ, the *Tribune*, even styled the Chamber of Deputies "a prostituted assembly," upon which the editor was condemned to three years' imprisonment and ten thousand francs' fine (April 16); but the

DUCHESS DE BERRI.

republican papers were neither alarmed nor repressed. The society of the "Friends of the People," and an association to preserve the liberty of the press, were also brought to trial and acquitted. The former was, however, dissolved, and gave place to the "Rights of Man." To these societies belonged many eminent republicans, — La Fayette, Armand Carrel, Garnier Pagès senior, Cormenin, etc.

A question now arose which caused much dissension, namely, the question of fortifying Paris. Vauban conceived the scheme under Louis XIV., and Carnot under the Republic; Napoleon took it up too late, and the memory of two invasions was enough to revive it. Unfortunately, when Louis Philippe undertook to execute this vast work, soon after the June insurrection, it was considered rather as a plan for ruling and restraining than for defending Paris. The first works ordered by Marshal Soult were regarded with distrust, even outside the republican party, and a decree was passed forbidding the work until a special law should be adopted for its completion. Soult, nevertheless, continued his labors, and protests from the departments arrived daily; the Society of the Rights of Man eagerly strove to foment another rebellion, and this time discontent invaded the middle classes and national guard. The government recognized the danger, and surrendered in time, suspended the works, and diverted public attention from the matter by a brilliant celebration of the third anniversary of the July Days. Napoleon's statue was solemnly restored to its column, July 28, 1833, thus imprudently associating memories of the Empire with those of the Three Days' Revolution.

The Society of the Rights of Man was doing its utmost to stir up Paris and France. The working classes were struggling for less time and higher wages in various cities, and in Paris strikes occurred on a large scale, sixty thousand men being engaged in the movement. Many interesting documents were published, setting forth genuine grievances and lawful desires, such as "wages sufficient to permit men to economize for the dull season, and resting space sufficient for health and education." From the extent and fervor of the movement in October, Paris might have feared a renewal of the

Lyons insurrection, but there was not the same unity of action. Numerous concessions were made, the public authorities interfered and arrested many of the Society of the Rights of Man, and the uproar gradually subsided.

Much of the trouble was attributed to the newspaper venders, who cried the contents of their journals through the streets, and an attempt was made to silence them. The Society of the Rights of Man then issued various revolutionary manifestoes, which brought down upon them an attack from the opposition and dynastic as well as the official journals, and the government lost through the exaggeration of its friends the benefit of the excesses of its foes. A sort of congress of republican associations was held, Cavaignac supporting the manifestoes and Carrel contesting him. A memorable discussion followed, soon after which twenty-seven members of the Society of the Rights of Man were brought before the courts on a charge of conspiracy. They were acquitted, having merely prepared for action by procuring arms, but not having any fixed plan of conspiracy.

Foreign questions were again mingled with domestic policy in the course of the year 1833. Great emotion was excited throughout Europe by the Polish, Italian, and German refugees assembled in France and Switzerland, and sympathizing in thought and deed with the French republicans. The German universities were in a ferment; the notion of Germanic unity was then associated with the idea of liberty and revolt. A revolutionary movement was attempted at Frankfort in April, and easily quelled; but later on, at a festival held at Hambach by students from all parts of Germany, alarming manifestations occurred.

The three powers of the Holy Alliance now renewed their martial preparations, and in September, 1833, the Emperors of Russia and Austria and the King of Prussia met at Munich-Graetz in Bohemia. The czar again urged war with France, but the other sovereigns, although not refusing to take part with Nicholas in case of actual war, were averse thereto. It was, therefore, decided to wait the result of the struggle which seemed imminent between the French

government and the various societies. Each monarch despatched a
note to the French cabinet, declaring that "if France failed to
thwart the machinations of the unruly spirits within her territory
against foreign nations, and any intestine trouble therefrom ensued,
then allies would come to their succor." The French minister
of foreign affairs, Duke de Broglie, replied that "France would permit no armed intervention in Belgium, Switzerland, or Piedmont,
and that elsewhere she would act as her interest might dictate."

Although the conference of Munich-Graetz made a great noise in
Europe, nothing came of it, but meantime something of far greater
importance was taking place in Germany. The Prussian government had attained a long-sought end, and effected the commercial
unity of the greater part of Germany in a way most profitable to
itself. The compact of the "Zollverein" (Customs Union), signed
December 5, 1833, annexed to Prussia fourteen German states,
among them two chief states of Southern Germany, Bavaria and
Würtemberg; nearly twenty-four million Germans being thus com-
mercially allied. The Zollverein, which Metternich, that would-be
great politician, tranquilly permitted to take root, was aimed at
once against Austria and against France. Prussia, loath to engage
in a doubtful trial of arms with France, began a war of tariffs by
raising the import duties on all French products.

The French legislative session reopened December 23, M. Dupin
being re-elected president of the Chamber of Deputies. The Chambers seemed inclined to pacific measures, but the course of events
did not favor these desires. Foreign refugees continued to plot, and
Mazzini, a man destined to fame, now organized in Paris a society
known as "Young Italy." He was possessed at once by a great
and a chimerical idea. The great idea, since accomplished under
another form, was Italian Unity; the chimera was a plan to revo-
lutionize Europe, taking Italy for the head and front of this revolution. The first conspiracy was discovered and severely repressed at
Turin, but Mazzini persevered and strove to stir up Switzerland
and Lyons. Their inhabitants, however, refused to act, and his
bands of refugees retreated in discouragement. The triple alliance

sent threatening notes to Switzerland, reproaching her with tolerating revolutionists. They also alluded to French revolutionary agents, but France was prepared to give satisfaction on this point, having formed a plan of offensive warfare against the republican party and all political societies.

There was still much tumult at Paris, and even more at Lyons, where the working classes had joined the republicans, and the manufacturers were bent on vengeance for their defeat in November, 1831. The workmen finally sued for peace, but the government nevertheless pursued its course of action, and caused the passage of a law to prevent the existence of all societies (March 25). Protests at once burst from societies all over France, notably from the Mutuals of Lyons, and the July Union, headed by La Fayette. Two plans were mooted: one being for passive resistance, meeting as hitherto and letting the case be brought into court, when the multitude of suits would be very embarrassing to the government. The other plan was armed resistance, but on the eve of the crisis an unforeseen event changed the views of the ministry. The Chambers were summoned to pay twenty-five millions indemnity money to the United States of America for debts of the Empire, whose justice Napoleon had acknowledged, but whose payment the Restoration had eluded and deferred. The treaty signed under Casimir Périer's ministry was now to be executed, which assured great advantages to the French trade in silk and wine. The payment was, however, refused by a slight majority. The Duc de Broglie indignantly resigned, and it was surmised that the King schemed against him, offended by his independence and obstinacy. He was replaced by Admiral de Ligny, a good sailor but no politician, whom the King hoped to govern, as he had Sebastiani. Thiers was called to the ministry of the interior in lieu of D'Argout, and the ministry of justice was given to Persil. This was a bold step toward reaction (April 4).

Disturbances but too well foreseen now broke out at Lyons. Certain workmen were pursued, in consequence of trifling threats and violences committed during a recent strike, and no attempt was made to avoid a conflict. The garrison was increased; ten thousand soldiers and sixty cannon being held in readiness. The committee of the Society of the Rights of Man felt that the situation was quite unlike that of 1831, and would fain have postponed the contest, but the frantic mutualists urged them on. April 9, barricades were erected, shots were heard, and the struggle opened and continued furiously for five days, fire being added to the horrors of carnage. On the 13th of April, the insurgents were forced to lay down their arms, and thus ended the second revolt in Lyons, under Louis Philippe.

On hearing of this uprising, the Parisian government, anxious to prevent a similar outburst in Paris, arrested most of the committee of the Society of the Rights of Man. Upon this the remaining members were fired to action, and during the afternoon of the 13th, barricades were raised in Rue Maubée and the neighborhood, also around the famous church of St. Merry. Thiers displayed great energy, himself marching under fire at the head of a column of troops. The insurgents issued a proclamation calling the people to arms, but the offices of the *Tribune* being in the hands of the law, it did not appear in that paper, and Armand Carrel, who opposed the insurrection of June 5, was even more bitter against this one, and declined to print it in the *National*.

The next day the struggle was renewed, but the barricades were feebly defended, and the conflict of April 14 would have made little mark in history had it not been followed by a bloody scene which gave it a sinister fame. Among the regiments employed to put down the revolt was the 35th Line, which an unfortunate incident at Grenoble had made exceedingly unpopular. Its unfriendly reception on all sides imbittered and incensed this regiment, and one of its detachments being fired upon from a barricade, or perhaps a neighboring house, it invaded the latter, and finding no rebels, slew the occupants, including women and children, nineteen in all. This odious episode of civil war, known as the "massacre of the Rue Transnonain," left a lasting impression behind, and in some measure robbed the government of the moral benefits of victory.

Soon after this affair the republican party met with a serious loss in the death of La Fayette, May 20, 1834. His funeral rites were brief and simple, circumstances forbidding the solemn obsequies due him. The first and the last, as we may say, of the glorious figures of 1789 vanished with him. He appeared before the dawn of the Revolution, and quitted the earth when its fate was still doubtful. He was not a man of genius, but remains greater in history than many such; his was the true grandeur, — that of character. He devoted himself from his earliest youth to the cause of justice, and never departed therefrom. During sixty years but a single grave mistake, not of intention but of act, can be imputed to him, — that of 1792. It is unjust to reproach him for not having established the republic in 1791 or 1830; he only obeyed then what he considered the national wish. Soon convinced, after 1830, that the experiment of constitutional monarchy would be unsuccessful, he predicted and called for a liberal republic. Time was destined to justify his perseverance; it is his republic that has prevailed, and become the only possible hope of France.

At the moment of his death, the new monarchy seemed much strengthened by the mistakes of its foes. Louis Philippe skilfully profited by the industrial exhibition opened, May 1, in a temporary building on the Place de la Concorde. The exhibition was far superior to its predecessor, which progress the King ascribed, in his inaugural address, to the peace which he had maintained, and he spared no pains to make himself popular with the exhibitors.

An important question for France, as well as other nations, was solved with the opening of the exhibition. France had held her own and gradually extended her sway in Algiers since its capture, but there, as in Belgium, the government policy was weak and vacillating; the same dread of English jealousy made Louis Philippe hesitate to adopt broader and bolder measures to assure his possession of Algiers. A long and fiery debate ensued in the Chambers, and in April, 1834, Marshal Soult declared, in the name of the ministerial council, that France would keep her conquest, come what might. This was a bold step, from which there was no appeal.

LAFAYETTE.

There was some merit in this resolution, coming as it did at a time when Spanish and Portuguese affairs were drawing the English more closely to France.

Very grave events had occurred in these latter countries during 1833. The tyranny of Don Miguel, who had been troubled but not crushed by France in 1831, now crumbled to ashes before the force of a national movement. The ex-Emperor of Brazil, Don Pedro, Miguel's eldest brother, having abdicated in his son's favor, came to Europe to emancipate the land of his forefathers. Landing in Portugal and taking the lead of the liberal party, he entered Lisbon, July 28, 1833, and proclaimed a liberal constitution, in the name of his daughter, Queen Maria. Miguel, however, still made a stand in the provinces.

In Spain, strange to say, it was through Ferdinand VII. that the liberals gained an opportunity. He had taken for his second wife the young Princess Christina of Naples, who had brought him a daughter to whom she wished to secure the throne. Ferdinand, ill and worn out, was torn hither and thither by his wife and his brother, Don Carlos, in whose favor the absolutists desired to set aside the princess, in virtue of the ancient Salic law excluding women from the throne, and introduced into Spain by Philip V. The moderates, rallying round Queen Christina, claimed the privilege of the old Castilian law acknowledging women, and already recognized by Charles IV., Ferdinand's father, and the Cortes of 1812. His wife finally prevailed over his brother. Ferdinand declared his daughter Isabella his heiress, and died September 29, 1833, leaving the regency to his widow, who, under the pressure of public opinion, made the constitutionalist Martinez de la Rosa her prime minister, and gave Spain a species of charter, under the title of "royal statute." Don Carlos and his followers rebelled, and the regent was unable wholly to quell the insurrection. France and England recognized the infant queen, Isabella II., which the three absolutist nations refused to do.

This grave difference seemed naturally to lead to the formation of two opposite factions in Europe, — the absolutist East and constitutional West. The public thought this fact accomplished when it suddenly learned of a quadruple alliance between France, England, Portugal, and Spain.

The new Spanish minister, Martinez de la Rosa, finding that Don Carlos and Don Miguel had joined forces, announced to England his intention of sending a Spanish army into Portugal to aid Don Pedro. The English cabinet, always ready to interfere in Portuguese affairs, thereupon concluded a treaty with the Spanish ambassador and an envoy from Don Pedro, promising to send an English fleet to Portugal. France had nothing to do with the matter, and was only asked to join as an afterthought, upon which the French government demanded a consent to a counter scheme, which Lord Palmerston reluctantly gave, and the triple alliance became the quadruple alliance, with this difference, that England agreed to aid in the expulsion of Don Carlos and Don Miguel, while France was to take no part unless it should be judged necessary by her allies and herself (April 22, 1834).

The Chamber of Deputies was dissolved May 25. The government deemed the time ripe for the elections, which occurred June 21, and were unfavorable to the republicans. A fresh change took place in the ministry in July. Soult, who was on bad terms with his colleagues, resigned in consequence of a difference relating to Algiers, and was replaced by Marshal Gérard, through Thiers. This seemed a good omen on account of the liberal opinions of the new minister, who belonged to the third party and was anxious to appease the people by a general amnesty rather than to irritate them by trying the prisoners of April.

At the opening of the session (July 31) the speech from the crown did not allude to the question of amnesty. The third party carried the day, and the Chambers were adjourned until December 29. Soult's retirement did not restore union, and Gérard soon followed his example and withdrew. Thiers suggested De Broglie as a substitute, but the King refused, unwilling to renew the "triumvirate" of Broglie, Guizot, and Thiers. The two last then resigned, and a ministry was made up from the third party, composed of men of no great political note, — Marat, Duke of Bassano, an ex-imperial minister, Persil, and others, — but they could not agree, and resigned within three days. The King recalled Thiers, who preserved his alliance with Guizot, and the presidency of the council was given to Marshal Mortier, Duke of Tréville. It was to be purely nominal (November 22).

The reopening of the Chambers (December 29) was signalized by a remarkable debate between Dupin and Thiers, on the amnesty question, Thiers taking the opposition. On this occasion the great poet Lamartine revealed his rare powers as an orator, advocating clemency and conciliation. Soon after, Mortier, mortified at his lack of actual power, resigned, and Guizot put forward De Broglie as a candidate for the presidency. The King and Thiers were finally unwillingly brought to accept him, and the ministry was established March 12, De Broglie declaring that he must have full power to call together the council and exclude the King, as Casimir Périer had done. He instituted many beneficent laws and measures, took steps to abolish slavery in the French colonies, and again brought up the subject of American indemnity, which had caused his resignation the previous year.

The time of trial for the April insurgents was now at hand. Out of more than two thousand people arrested, the court held one hundred and twenty-one on various charges; forty-three had escaped. These one hundred and twenty-one were brought to Paris and distributed through the various prisons. Each prisoner chose his advocate from the flower of the republican party, but such a brilliant array alarmed the court, and they forbade all pleading save by professional advocates. Against this the prisoners loudly protested, and their protest was made more effective by the publication of "Words from a Believer," by Lamennais, who made himself the prophet of the Revolution, and with fiery poesy united religion and democracy.

The trial opened May 5. The majority of the prisoners refused to answer any questions unless they could choose their own defenders, and for several days scenes occurred exceeding in violence

the great trials of the Revolutionary Tribunal. The Court of Peers
finally decided to remove the recalcitrant prisoners and try them in
their absence, contrary to the law which requires the presence of
the accused. Some few of the insurgents yielded, but the rest
steadfastly refused to submit, and on the 11th of May a letter appeared in the republican papers, written in the name of the chosen
advocates, urging the prisoners to persist in their course. "France,"
it said, "will never acknowledge judges where there is no counsel.
The Court of Peers, having put it out of your power to defend
yourselves, will doubtless have the courage to condemn you. . . . .
The infamy of the judge is the glory of the accused!" The authors
of this insulting letter were summoned to court. Among them
were two deputies, M. de Cormenin and Audry de Puyraveau. The
former declared his signature a forgery, and it was ascertained that
one Michael de Bourges had drawn up the paper, and signed it in
the name of many who were absent from the meeting at which
it was adopted. De Bourges and Trélat, the chairman of this meeting, bravely assumed all responsibility in the matter, and were sentenced, the former to ten thousand francs' fine and one month's
imprisonment, and the latter to the same fine but three years in
jail. Those who simply disavowed their signatures were dismissed.
Some who acknowledged them in an insulting manner were condemned to a month in prison; among these was the philosopher
Jean Reynaud.

After this incident the Court of Peers resumed the original trial,
only to call forth still more scandalous scenes than marked former
sessions, the prisoners being dragged before the court by force, and
often appearing before the bar with their clothes torn to rags in the
struggle. Amidst these scenes, it was discovered that Cavaignac,
Guinard, Marrast, and twenty-five others, the most violent of the
Parisian prisoners, had escaped from St. Pelagie during the night of
July 12. The trial of the Lyonnese rebels then followed, marked
by an eloquent plea for one of the accused by Jules Favre. Before
sentence was passed, a tragic event filled Paris with horror, and
diverted public attention from the trial.

Rumors of plots against the King's life had long been rife. The air was filled with sinister stories, for which there was but too much foundation, and which disquieted the public mind. It was now announced, in France and abroad, that the King would be attacked at the annual review in July. July 26 the police were notified that an infernal machine had been made, and would be exploded near the Boulevard du Temple. All search was, however, vain, and as the royal procession reached the fatal spot the King observed a puff of smoke issuing from a window. He turned quickly to one of his sons, riding beside him, and exclaimed, "Joinville, that is meant for me!"

A loud explosion followed, and the ground was strewed with dead and wounded. More than forty persons fell, among them Marshal Mortier, who had escaped in so many battles only to perish in Paris by a blow meant for another. Five other generals were wounded, and the horses of the King and the Prince de Joinville were hurt, though they themselves escaped unscathed. Amid the universal terror and confusion, Louis Philippe said with the utmost coolness: "Come, gentlemen, let us proceed!" and finished the review amid cheers from the national guard and the indignant multitude. The police hastened to the scene of the explosion,—a small, mean-looking house, No. 50 Boulevard du Temple, — where they found a machine composed of twenty-four gun-barrels arranged like organ-pipes. The house was deserted, but a man was arrested in a court-yard close by who had clambered down from a roof with the aid of a rope. He was bleeding profusely, having been wounded by his own machine, several barrels of which had burst. He gave his name as Girard, but he was soon discovered to be a Corsican, called Fieschi.

The general feeling was one of horror at this attack, which, as in the case of the infernal machine used against Bonaparte, had stricken down so many lives without reaching the one for whom it was designed. The reaction was favorable to the King. The public shared with emotion in the solemn obsequies of the victims of July 28, and, as was the case after the murder of the Duke de Berri, liberal institutions suffered for the assassin's crime. August 4, following the example of the royalist ministry of 1820, Louis Philippe's ministers presented to the deputies a scheme for restrictive and reactionary laws. It was not surprising that the utmost pains should be taken to protect the royal person, but these measures went far beyond protection. They forbade not only any offensive allusion to the King's person, but all discussion of his rights to the throne and of the principle of his government. The jury was modified, and a bare majority allowed to pass sentence. Articles instigating insurrection, destruction of the government, or contempt of the King, etc., were subject to new and extravagant penalties, from which it was difficult to escape. The caution money for all journals was increased, and all drawings and engravings used by them were made subject to censorship, thus depriving the republican caricaturists of a most effective weapon. The object was, in fact, to restrict any expression of opinion to the King, Chambers, electives taxed five hundred francs, and electors taxed two hundred; no one outside this charmed circle was to have the right to speak.

Great opposition was made by the constitutionalists, and the veteran Royer-Collard raised his voice against these laws, but in vain. Guizot's famous colleague from the Sorbonne, Villemain, also vainly pleaded for their amelioration. They were accepted and known as the September laws, having been definitely passed on the 9th of that month. The republicans entitled them the " Fieschi laws."

The session closed two days later, having been fatal to liberty and even to the government, which won a sinister victory.

During the discussion of the press laws the trial of the April insurgents was renewed, and by August 13 seven Lyonnese were sentenced to transportation, two to twenty years' imprisonment, and forty to various periods of confinement. The court then adjourned until November, when the military prisoners were tried and condemned. Their leader, Clement Thomas, was destined to reappear in the foremost ranks of two revolutions, and meet a tragic doom in 1871.

The remainder of the prisoners were tried in January. The prodigious case came to an end on the 23d, and resulted favorably to no one, all parties seeming depressed and enfeebled. Hardly was this disposed of when Fieschi was brought to trial. His accomplices were soon discovered, for it seemed that he was no politician, but an ex-bandit, thief, and forger, intensely vain, and capable of monstrous crimes for the sake of notoriety. His only motive for hostility to the government was the fact that the police had failed to appreciate or accept his services. A fatal chance brought him in contact with a Jacobin fanatic, named Morey, to whom he mentioned his plan for a machine to be used in barricades. "Better use it against Louis Philippe!" was the reply. Morey was poor, but he applied to a grocer of the Faubourg St. Antoine, named Pepin, who, flattered at being invited to "slay the tyrant," demanded a supply of arms from Cavaignac, and on his refusal, procured them at a second-hand shop. A young workman, named Boireau, joined the plot, and his scanty and incoherent revelations furnished the police with the information they possessed.

Among all the famous political trials none is more repulsive than this. It is monstrous to see the brigand Fieschi, who dealt out death indifferently to serve passions not his own, posing as a melodramatic hero before his judges, as it is painful to see the high official who questioned him, flattering his vanity to make him confess. When it was proved to Fieschi that Morey had premeditatedly sought to rid himself of him by loading the guns in such a manner as to make them burst, he confessed everything, and gave up Morey and Pepin to death.

Morey and Fieschi were beheaded, but Boireau escaped, Fieschi having spared him in his revelations.

When the Fieschi case closed, France was passing through a ministerial crisis. It seems as if their joint participation in so important a matter as the September press laws should have cemented the union of the three ministers forming the cabinet. This was not so. Thiers, though often led away by his disposition to subordinate principles to facts, had none of the tendencies of the doctrinarians. He was and remained a child of the Revolution. Only a year before he had differed from his colleagues, as well as the King, in regard to Spain. A Spanish army, joining Don Pedro, having driven Miguel and Carlos from Portugal, the latter withdrew to England, then traversed France in disguise, re-entered Spain and stirred up the Basque provinces. The Carlist movement gaining ground in Aragon and Catalonia, the Spanish government asked for aid from France. Thiers desired to send an army at once, but De Broglie and Guizot did not favor this measure, and the King absolutely opposed it. De Broglie inquired the intentions of England, who answered that she should not interfere, but would leave the responsibility to France. Thiers was forced to yield, although some assistance was furnished Spain.

There was no break in the cabinet on this occasion, but the seeds of dissension were sown, and a singular incident paved the way for the dissolution of the ministry. When the minister of finances, M. Humann, presented the budget to the Chambers, January 14, he announced his intention to reduce the five per cents, offering to reimburse such state creditors as declined to accept the reduction. This was the same scheme which had so lamentably failed in De Villèle's hands. Humann made this declaration without consulting his colleagues, at which De Broglie, the head of the cabinet, was indignant, and Humann was forced to resign. There was, however, a strong party in favor of the reduction, made up of country proprietors, jealous of Parisian capitalists and stockholders. This party returning to question the action of the government, M. de Broglie replied, "The government can make no pledges for any set time." This arrogant answer was most irritating, and the third party profited by this feeling to make a movement in favor of the reduction of the stocks. The ministry requested the adjournment of the question, which was refused, and the ministry resigned (February 15, 1836).

It was thought, and with much semblance of truth, that the King had again secretly intrigued to break up the triumvirate. The court on the one hand, the third party, and even the Left, urged Thiers to become the head of the new cabinet, and he accepted. The ministry was formed February 22, Thiers being president of the council and minister of foreign affairs. Hippolyte Passy, Pelet (de la Lozere), and Sauzet were respectively made ministers of commerce, public instruction, and justice. Marshal Maison, who replaced Gérard in the war department, D'Argout, who succeeded Humann in finances, and Admiral Duperré, minister of the marine, re-entered with Thiers. M. de Montalivet was made minister of the interior for the second time. This showed the King's participation in the affair.

Affairs were now very complicated. The two parliamentary ministries of March 13 and October 11 were replaced by a cabinet in which the personal government of the King stood face to face with the man who uttered the maxim: "The King reigns, but does not rule." It remained to be seen whether Thiers would triumph or fall.

CHAPTER III.

CONSTITUTIONAL MONARCHY OF JULY (*continued*). — THIERS MIN-
ISTRY. — MOLÉ-GUIZOT MINISTRY. — CAPTURE OF CONSTANTINE. —
ELECTION OF 1837. — THE COALITION. — ELECTIONS OF 1839. — FALL
OF THE MOLÉ MINISTRY.

February, 1836, to March, 1839.

M. THIERS'S situation on taking possession of the ministry
was delicate and difficult. He was suspended between the
progressive and the non-progressive parties, without secure hold on
either. He avoided, as far as possible, all occasion for conflict, and
accepted the reduction of the five per cents, but contrived to have
the matter adjourned (March 22). Nothing of special note occurred
during this session, except the suppression of gaming-houses.

Vexatious events abroad coincided with the accession of Thiers to
the ministry. The French politicians who refused to fight for Poland
cheerfully testified officially to their interest in that unhappy land,
and at every legislative session alluded to it sympathizingly, and
at the same time to the re-establishment of the balance of power in
Europe.

The three powers who had spared Poland responded to these
demonstrations by trampling under foot the last shreds of Polish
independence. Cracow, the capital of old Poland, had been constituted a republic by the treaties of 1815, and thither Poles from
various provinces flocked for refuge, hoping to find there a shadow
of their country. The three powers took umbrage at their assem-
blage, and summoned the Cracovian senate to expel them, and,
as it did not obey quickly enough, Austrians, Russians, and Prussians successively invaded and occupied the town, the French

government having been apprised of the fancied necessity of not
even observing the treaties of 1815. The ministry made no protest, and Thiers lost ground thereby. He had other cares with
respect to Spain, where the government affairs were rapidly
growing worse. The queen's ministers were unable to subdue the
Carlists, who were aided by the absolutist powers, and the democratic party were incensed at the impotence of the government.
During the autumn of 1835 the queen was forced to accept as minister, Mendizabal, who represented the most advanced opinions, and
who at once seized and sold convent lands, and ordered large levies
to put down the Carlists. The result of these measures was not,
however, immediately felt, and the danger seemed imminent.

Lord Palmerston, the English minister of foreign affairs, had
opposed interference with Spain when Thiers proposed it. Now,
hoping to gain from Mendizabal concessions favorable to English
trade, he decided to send a fleet to the shores of the Basque provinces, and proposed that France should occupy Fontarabia and
other posts. Contrary to his wont, Thiers declined this scheme
(March 18), because he had yielded to the King, and entered into
his plans for union with Austria and Russia. The change in the
foreign policy of the government was now made manifest by the
journey to Germany undertaken by the King's two elder sons, the
Dukes of Orléans and Nemours. They first went to Berlin, where
they were well received by the King of Prussia, then repaired to
Vienna, where the true object of their journey came to light, being
nothing more nor less than a marriage between the Duke of Orléans
and an Austrian princess. The young prince hoped to win the hand
of a daughter of Archduke Charles, the most illustrious of the Austrian generals, and the one most esteemed by the French. He was
pleasing and accomplished, and would probably have been accepted
had not the Emperor Francis II. and M. de Metternich combined
to break off the match.

The princes set out for Italy, but were suddenly recalled to
France by news of a fresh attack on their father. June 25, as the
King was driving from the Carrousel by the Pont Royal, a shot was

fired at him almost from the muzzle of a gun cane. Two bullets were buried in the panels of the carriage, and the wad was found in his hair. The assassin made no effort to escape, and was instantly arrested. He was a young man, named Alibaud, — a handsome and interesting youth, who seemed to have been actuated solely by blind fanaticism. "I wished to kill the King because I regard him as an enemy to the people. I was wretched: the government caused my misery. The King is at its head; that is why I wished to kill him."

He also declared that he first conceived his murderous scheme when the King had ordered citizens to be massacred in the streets of Lyons and at the church of St. Merry. "His reign is a reign of blood!" he exclaimed; "I had the same right to his life that Brutus had to that of Julius Cæsar." These wild sayings and comparisons serve to give an idea of the frenzy which then had taken possession of many youthful minds; but the true cause of the hatred which Louis Philippe inspired was not his fancied cruelty, but his system of peace and compromise with European monarchies, which was in the eyes of these young hotheads a black plot to stifle revolution everywhere.

Alibaud showed no signs of contrition, and was beheaded July 11. He had no accomplice, but information received by the police concerning other analogous plots caused the annual review on the July anniversary to be omitted that year. Still July 29 did not pass unnoticed; M. Thiers inaugurated the Arc de Triomphe de l'Étoile, which was completed at last. It was intended to commemorate the glory of French arms from 1792 to 1815, and was a masterpiece of art. We have already alluded to Rude's great bas-relief of "The Departure," which forms its chief ornament, and must also refer to the admirable bas-reliefs of "Peace" and "Invasion" by Etex.

Three months later, the Place de la Concorde was the scene of another inauguration. A monument of ancient history was reared directly opposite this monument of contemporaneous history. Two obelisks, taken from the principal temple in Thebes, had been presented to France and England by an Egyptian pacha, one of which, the obelisk of Luxor, was now put in place.

Some days previous to the first of these inaugurations, the republican party met with a heavy loss in the death of Armand Carrel. He was the victim of a quality which, carried to excess, became a fault in a man whose life was so important to his country and his party, namely, that point of honor which led him to fight a duel upon every journalistic quarrel. He met his end in a duel with M. Émile de Girardin, and the republicans, in their bitter grief, did not hesitate to say that Girardin had drawn Carrel into the dispute for the express purpose of taking his life. The meeting took place at St. Mandé, near Vincennes, July 22, 1836, the weapons chosen being pistols. Both fired and fell simultaneously; Girardin was wounded in the thigh, Carrel in the groin. The latter died on the following night, aged thirty-six. His death was probably the greatest loss which France had known since that of Hoche. Even La Fayette said of him, "He is the master of us all!" Had he lived, events would doubtless have taken a different turn.

While Carrel thus prematurely vanished from sight, his former fellow-worker on the *National*, Thiers, was wielding power under very precarious conditions.

For a few years past, France had been on good terms with Switzerland, and had protected that republic against absolutist power, which would have invaded it if not restrained by fears of war with France. For some time, however, partly in displeasure at the conduct of revolutionary refugees in Switzerland, partly to please Austria, the French ambassador, Duke Montebello, had begun to exert a threatening pressure on the Swiss government to oblige it to expel all refugees. The Swiss Diet agreed to do so, but a strange accident complicated the situation. Among the French refugees whose expulsion was so imperiously demanded, was a man named Conseil, who was recognized as a spy sent by the French police, and in indirect correspondence with the French ambassador. This created great scandal; the affair occurred in August, but before the question of French refugees could be settled an important change took place in the French ministry, caused not by Swiss but by Spanish affairs.

Unhappy Spain was in perpetual turmoil. Civil war still continued, and ministry succeeded ministry. Thiers, finding any understanding with Austria hopeless, returned to his original plan of Spanish intervention, and the King reluctantly consented to send further aid. Just at this time the Carlists managed to force the blockade which held them prisoners in the Basque provinces, and to devastate the whole country. The Spanish cities responded by massacring the allies of Don Carlos and proclaiming the constitution of 1812. The troops also rose in revolt. Two regiments entered the residence of Queen Christine, near Madrid, and forced her to sign an order for the restoration of the constitution (August 12, 1836).

Upon this Louis Philippe desired to renounce all attempt at interference, however indirect. Thiers and the majority of his colleagues, finding all resistance vain, resigned (September 6).

The King then made M. Molé minister of foreign affairs and president of the council. This personage was essentially a man of the Empire, imbued with traditions of the old régime, and thus a most worthy tool of the personal government. Guizot was also restored to office upon his own terms, namely, that the ministry of the interior should be given to his friend, M. de Gasparin, prefect of Lyons at the time of the rebellion of 1834. Guizot also obtained the ministry of finance for M. Duchâtel, and that of justice for M. Persil. The other members of the cabinet were of slight importance. In fact, the ministry had two heads, and very ill-assorted ones. There was no harmony between Guizot and Molé, but this suited the King, who meant to make one counterbalance the other.

The new ministry inherited the Swiss troubles, and aggravated them by assuming that the matter of the spy Conseil was only a machination of the refugees, and demanding instead of giving reparation. The Swiss Diet quailed before the threats of the French ministry, but retained a lingering resentment, and here, as in Belgium, Louis Philippe lost all the moral benefit of the services he had rendered his neighbors.

Meantime domestic treason was at work. October 31, the ministry received telegraphic news of a Bonapartist *coup-de-main* at Strasburg. The Orléans dynasty had thought themselves rid of the Empire by the death of Napoleon's son, but the imperial family had not become extinct with the Duke de Reichstadt. The eldest son of Queen Hortense, whom Napoleon had destined as his heir, before his marriage with Marie Louise, died in 1831, of fatigues endured during the insurrection in the Romagna, but left behind a brother, Louis Napoleon, who was now (1836) twenty-eight years old. His mother, Queen Hortense, the divorced wife of the ex-King of Holland, a woman of easy reputation but of much more intellect than was commonly believed, educated her sons as claimants to the throne, and inspired the one left to her with a blind faith in his own destiny. This is not the place to examine into the complex character of the man doomed to be so fatal to France. Suffice it to say that his fixed idea inspired him with an inflexible will and obstinacy which atoned, in a measure, for his lack of quick apprehension and prompt decision.

Educated in Switzerland, he returned thither on the failure of the Italian movement in 1831, in which he had shared, and strove to enter into relations with French republicans and ex-imperialists. He appreciated the advantage to be derived from the union cemented under the Restoration, between the Bonapartists and liberals. He also endeavored, in emulation of his uncle, to endear himself to the army, and published various military treatises. During the summer of 1836 the irritation caused, not only in Switzerland but in Eastern France, by the Conseil affair, led him to suppose that the time for action had come, and he prepared proclamations inviting the people and the army to rise against Louis Philippe, offering the imperial eagle as the symbol alike of liberty and glory.

He gained allies in the Strasburg garrison, chief among them Colonel Vaudrey of the 4th Artillery, at whose quarters he appeared early on the morning of October 30. The colonel then informed his

men that Louis Philippe was no longer king, but that the Emperor's
nephew would lead them on to battle, and regain the heritage of
his uncle. Other officers were less easily led away; they declared
Louis an impostor, and he and Colonel Vaudrey were arrested.

When the government of Louis Philippe gave the Duchess de
Berri into the hands of justice the opposition showed great displeasure. There were serious excuses to be pleaded then in regard
to the relative position of younger and older branches of one family.
Not so now, and yet the government resolved to pursue the same
and even a gentler course. Louis Napoleon was taken through
France incognito, and sent to America.

A few days after the failure of this attempt at a Bonapartist
restoration, the representative of legitimate restoration died in
exile. Charles X. and his family had left Scotland for Austria, and
the old King died peacefully at Goritz, November 6, 1836. His
death made little impression in France, nor was public opinion, outraged as it was at the liberation of Louis Napoleon, affected when the
government opened the prison doors to the ministers of Charles X.
De Polignac was banished, and his colleagues allowed to retire to
the provinces.

The opening of the Chambers (December 27) was marked by
another attack on the King. No one was injured, and the assassin,
a young man named Meunier, was mercifully pardoned by Louis
Philippe, and was sent to America. This humane act produced
favorable impressions towards the King, but had no influence on
parliamentary debates. The discussion relative to Spain was not
disadvantageous to the government, contrary to that on the Swiss
question, and the Strasburg-Louis-Napoleon affair proved yet more
fatal to the government. Instead of sending Prince Louis's accomplices before the Court of Peers, who would infallibly have condemned them, they were handed over to the Jury of the Upper
Rhine, who acquitted them.

Unfortunately, the character of this acquittal, which might be
taken as a well-merited reproof, was impaired by the seditious outbreak which followed it, — a banquet and oration being given to

men whom, though materially acquitted, all should morally condemn. The French government, in alarm, at once presented several new laws for the repression of political crimes and offences, one of which ordained separate trials for military men and civilians, accused of the same acts of treason, the latter being sent to a court-martial. This was vehemently opposed by jurists, especially by M. Dupin, as subversive of the rule and spirit of the French Code.

The law called "Disjunction" was rejected by two hundred and eleven votes against two hundred and nine (March 7, 1837). The ministry did not at once resign, but a rupture ensued between Molé and Guizot. Molé sought, but did not obtain, the aid of Thiers and Dupin to form a new cabinet, and Guizot attempted to reconstruct the ministry of October 11. The King, forced to choose between a doctrinarian ministry under Guizot and a Molé ministry, naturally chose the latter. He restored M. de Montalivet, with colleagues of slight importance, unconscious that a feeble ministry made a feeble state (April 15). Molé, far from ruling the Chambers, quite effaced himself before the majority, and party leaders scornfully tolerated the ministry. And yet the weak Molé ministry accomplished one important act, and one requiring a certain amount of resolution, but the resolution was all on the part of the King. We refer to the amnesty granted to all political offenders (May 8). Louis Philippe desired to rule in person and yet to conciliate, without inquiring if that were possible. We may accuse him of guile, but never of violence.

The Orléans dynasty failed to obtain a marriage alliance with any of the great powers, and therefore fell back upon the petty German principalities, and, through the medium of the Prussian king, the Duke d'Orléans married Princess Helena of Mecklenburg, sister of the Grand Duke of Schwerin, an amiable and excellent woman.

The wedding was celebrated with great splendor at Fontainebleau, which Louis Philippe had restored, and was followed by the inauguration of the Versailles Museum. The King had been working for years to convert the palace of Louis XIV. into a great historical museum, and now called together the literary, political, and artistic world to approve the completion of his idea (June 10). Next day, during a review at Versailles, he presented, with his own hand, a banner to the military school of St. Cyr, exhorting them to uphold the honor of the tricolor, and quoting a stanza from the Marseillaise, which was received with shouts of " Long live the King! Long live liberty!"

The effect of this scene was very good, but to what end, if the next day the King failed to carry out his words, and persisted in a weak foreign policy?

A melancholy event soon put an end to the marriage rejoicings for the crown prince. On the evening of June 14 an exhibition was given on the Champ de Mars, representing the capture of Antwerp. The crowd was so great at one of the gates of the Military School that twenty-four persons perished in the crush and many were seriously injured. A gloomy impression lingered behind, and called to mind a similar accident at the wedding of Louis XVI. and Marie Antoinette. The Duke d'Orléans instantly put a stop to all festivities, and took upon himself the care of the sufferers and their families.

The legislative session was of no special interest during the summer, save from an economic point of view. The financial situation was fair. An attempt was made to introduce railroads, which met with but partial success. October 11, an order for the dissolution of the Chambers was issued, and Molé, mortified at the part he had played, struggled to gain a majority, relying greatly on the effect of the amnesty act, and also on a victory won in Algiers.

Matters had been greatly mismanaged in that country, where a new and dangerous power had sprung up in the person of a brave and intelligent young Arab chief, the descendant of a family of hereditary religious influence. Abd-el-Kader presented himself to the Mussulman tribes as the man chosen by Mahomet to free them from the Christians. General Desmichels imprudently treated him as an equal, and recognized him as the emir or prince of the region (February 25, 1834). Abd-el-Kader was thus imposed by French

TLEMCEN.

authority even upon those who had hitherto refused to submit to him.   Not content with ruling the province of Oran, he undertook to subdue Algiers, whereupon an inevitable rupture took place, and at the skirmish of Malta French troops under Trézel met with severe losses (June 26, 1835).

The French government finally decided to send Marshal Clausel and the Duke of Orléans to Algiers, where they at once took the offensive, gained a victory at Mascara, the residence of the emir, and occupied Tlemcen, the two chief cities of Oran.

Clausel's forces were, however, insufficient, and Abd-el-Kader, assisted by the Bey of Constantine, who ruled in Eastern Algeria, harassed him greatly.   Clausel returned to Paris for reinforcements. Thiers saw the folly of half-measures, and was prepared to assist Clausel on a large scale, but, unfortunately, he fell from power, and his successors did not inherit his broad views.   Clausel felt that his resources were inadequate to march against Constantine.   The weather was bad and the season far advanced; nevertheless, time pressed, and he decided to risk the expedition.

Leaving Bora, November 8, with about nine thousand men, Clausel reached Constantine on the 21st.   The bey Ahmed was unpopular, and the French hoped that many of the Kabyles and Arabs would join them, but, seeing the scanty numbers of the French, they preferred to stand by the bey.   Clausel's only chance was to try a bold stroke, which he did at two points and under most difficult conditions.   Constantine is built on a high plateau, surrounded on three sides by a deep ravine, the bed of the Rummel. The town can be approached only by a Roman bridge, spanning the river, or by a narrow tongue of land which joins the plateau to other hills.   Heavy winter rains had long been falling, and the ground was so soaked that cannon could not be brought over this semi-isthmus called Coudiat-Aty.   The double attack failed; food and ammunition gave out, and the French were forced to retreat to Bora, forty leagues away, constantly pursued and harassed by the Arab cavalry.   Changarnier finally ordered his men to form a hollow square and stand their ground.   The Arabs threw themselves upon them and were cut down on all sides. Dismayed by the charge, they fell back and contented themselves with firing at a distance. This incident made the military fortune of Changarnier.

Clausel was at once recalled, and succeeded by General Damrémont, General Bugeaud being sent to Oran. The latter was esteemed a brave and active officer, but he soon fell a prey to the diplomatic wiles of Abd-el-Kader, and signed a new treaty with him worse than that of his predecessor, Desmichels. In return for a vague recognition of the sovereignty of France, Bugeaud acknowledged Abd-el-Kader as emir, not only of almost all Oran, but of Titery, and even granted him part of Algiers! The ministry approved his action, and the wretched treaty of Tafna gained a precarious peace, which gave the emir time to strengthen his forces.

Damrémont had about the same number of men as Clausel, that is, ten thousand, but he set out much later in the season, well provisioned and provided with siege artillery. He reached Constantine, October 6, in fine condition, and established batteries on the Roman bridge and at Coudiat-Aty. The autumnal rains now began to fall, in spite of which the breach was opened October 11. The next morning, Damrémont approached to reconnoitre the breach. An officer, seeing that he was exposed to the enemy's fire, ran to warn him, but the next instant a bullet struck him dead. The loss of this brave leader, instead of discouraging the troops, spurred them on. General Valée, of the artillery, took command, the attack was instantly begun, and, after a hot fight, the Mussulman authorities yielded. Many of the inhabitants, while endeavoring to escape, were hurled down the precipices into the bed of the torrent.

The conquest of the ancient capital of Numidia insured France a firm foothold in the interior of Algeria. But the ministry did not profit as they expected in the elections, either by the amnesty or by the capture of Constantine. The legislative session reopened December 18. M. Molé, who was of no party, hoped to break up factions by gaining to himself secondary personages, but only succeeded in incensing the party leaders and uniting them against himself. He postponed the peril by proposing no political laws, and suggested but one important measure,——in regard to the railroads. Nine great lines were to be laid by the state, the ministry having excellent reasons for keeping the monopoly in their own hands. This the Chambers could not comprehend, and there was a general protest against the law. The republican press alone defended the course of the state, for once setting aside party interests. The scheme was rejected by an enormous majority (May 10, 1838), and the offers of various railroad companies were accepted. After this lamentable decision, which left France so far behind England, America, and even Belgium, the session closed (July 12).

Shortly before, a person who had played a long and active, if not a glorious, part in the annals of France, vanished from the earth. Talleyrand died May 18. April 24 the Duchess d'Orléans presented Louis Philippe with a grandson, who received the title of the Count of Paris. The dynasty now numbered three generations of kings.

Trouble with Switzerland was renewed during the summer, through Louis Napoleon, who had been recalled from America by the illness of his mother, Queen Hortense, who died at Aremberg. Once in Switzerland, he resumed his conspiracies, quickly oblivious of the gratitude he had expressed for the clemency of the King, towards whom he acknowledged himself, in a letter to Odilon Barrot, "to have been very culpable." One of his acquitted accomplices, Lieutenant Laity, now published a pamphlet to prove that in his former attempt the prince had ninety chances in his favor to ten against him, and had failed only through a fatality,——clearly showing his readiness to begin anew. Laity was tried by the Court of Peers, and sentenced to five years' imprisonment and ten thousand francs' fine, and the French ambassador was ordered to demand the expulsion of Louis Bonaparte from Switzerland. It was doubtful whether France had a legal right to require the expulsion of a refugee, and public opinion was much excited against the government of Louis Philippe. The Diet resisted the demand. The question grew more aggravated, and French troops were ordered to assemble on the frontier. Louis Bonaparte finally saw that there was but one course to take, and voluntarily retired to England (October, 1838).

Another important event, immediately following this, aroused universal discontent against the government. Ever since the time of Casimir Périer, France had continued to occupy Ancona, and, although this had caused no amelioration in the papal government the Italians still hoped to profit by the presence of the tricolor.

The Emperor of Austria, Francis II., had just died. Pope Gregory XVI. persuaded his nephew and successor, Ferdinand II., to remove from Bologna the Austrian troops, which had been stationed there since 1831, and then demanded that the French should also evacuate Ancona, as an agreement, signed in April, 1832, had stipulated that they should do, whenever the Austrians quitted the Papal States. Now it had always been understood that this double evacuation should not occur until certain modifications had been made in the papal administration, the necessity of which was recognized by the absolutist powers themselves. However, the reign of Gregory XVI. was the worst known in the Roman States from time immemorial, and Thiers accordingly wrote to the French ambassador at Rome, " The fact of the withdrawal of the Austrians does not necessarily entail that of the French." Molé took no notice of this important reservation, and withdrew the French garrison (October 25).

Italy was distressed and France indignant at this surrender of all transalpine influence.

The ministry next hoped to atone for its unwise European policy by successes in America. Many complaints had been made of acts of violence committed upon the French in Spanish America. A tyrannical demagogue, named Rosas, ruling at Buenos Ayres, carried matters to such an excess that a French flotilla was sent out, under Admiral Leblanc, who adroitly captured the fortified island of Martin Garcia, just outside Buenos Ayres (October 11). Hostilities were prolonged for years with no decisive result. It was there that Garibaldi, then commanding a Genoese merchant vessel, won his first laurels, as an ally of the French.

· Another and more famous military exploit took place in Mexico. The Mexican government refusing to give satisfaction for injuries done French residents, a squadron, under Admiral Baudin, was sent against Vera Cruz, the chief seaport of Mexico. The fortress of San Juan d'Ulloa was taken November 28, the young Prince de Joinville, Louis Philippe's third son, distinguishing himself greatly in the action, and entering the city at the head of his sailors in triumph a few days later. The Mexican government granted the required satisfaction, and peace was restored..

No news came from Mexico until after the reopening of the Chambers, nor if it had would it have affected the position of affairs at home, which was most unfavorable for the ministry. Molé, as we have said, had alienated all the party leaders. The government and its allies were weak in action and foolhardy in speech. The opposition party was displeased at the concessions made by the authorities, and the liberals were deeply enraged by an insolent publication, in which a Bordelais pamphleteer, named Foufiède, attacked the parliamentary government in behalf of the royal pre- rogative. A bitter conflict ensued in the legislature, which assumed a character more and more formidable to Louis Philippe.

The Chambers opened December 17. The coalition appeared in full force, and, in answer to the royal speech, the ministry drew up an address which they strove to impose on the government and the King. A hot discussion ensued, in which Molé displayed unex- pected oratorical power. He was upheld by one eminent auxiliary, more eloquent than influential, — the poet Lamartine. The ministry finally struck out the more hostile parts of the address, but it was accepted by a very small majority, and, in consequence, the ministers resigned (January 22, 1839).

The King applied to Marshal Soult to frame a new cabinet. Soult was unsuccessful in the attempt, whereupon the King recalled his former ministers, and declared the session closed (February 3).

This made two general elections in fifteen months, — a serious matter. The watchword of all factions of the opposition was: " War on personal government ! " The King was directly engaged in the struggle. The ministry was outvoted and once more resigned, this time definitively (March, 1839).

Personal government was conquered, and yet Louis Philippe did not despond. He saw how difficult it would be for the victorious coalition to agree together in governing, as they had agreed to overthrow the ministry, and bided his time.

CHAPTER IV.

CONSTITUTIONAL MONARCHY OF JULY (*continued*). — DIVISION IN THE
COALITION. — INSURRECTION AND MINISTRY OF MAY 12. — EASTERN
QUESTION. — SECOND THIERS MINISTRY.

March, 1839, to October 22, 1840.

THE coalition were unable to agree upon a successor to Molé, —
Thiers, Guizot, and Odilon Barrot being successively suggested. After various combinations had been vainly tried, the King
formed a ministry, *ad interim*, and the Chambers opened (April 4).
It was now for the deputies to solve the question. General agitation and irritation prevailed; it was felt that public interests were
suffering, and popular opinion held the King responsible. He was
not alone to blame for this crisis, in which the individual obstinacy
and pretensions of more than one politician had had their share.

The prevalent anxiety and discontent at last persuaded the Chambers to consider a suggestion, by Mauquin, of an address to the
Crown, asking the King to appoint a skilful, patriotic, and honest
ministry, which should not be provisional (May 10). But, before
this address was drawn up, a bloody distraction came to the King's
aid, which alike terrified Paris and the Chambers. An insurrection
broke out (May 12).

The laws of April, 1834, against political associations, and the
September laws of 1835, had forced republican societies to remain
in the shade, without suppressing them. From public, they were
transformed into secret societies, and the mystery that surrounded
them and the diminution of their numbers impelled them to constantly increasing excesses. The " Family " society, the successor
of the famous Society of the Rights of Man, had already issued cir-

culars urging a "social revolution," the destruction of the "government of the rich," which made the fate of the working-man no better than that of a serf or negro. This society, being broken up by the police in 1837, reorganized under the name of the "Seasons," and advocated the most extreme socialism. It had three great leaders, — August Blanqui, a gloomy and opinionated conspirator; Armand Barbès, as expansive and generous as Blanqui was reserved and hard, belonging to the opulent and cultivated classes and overflowing with sympathy for the poor and suffering; and Martin Bernard, a journeyman printer, brave and self-sacrificing, and carried away, like Barbès, by sincere feeling.

In the spring of 1839 the society, formed into three groups under these three chiefs, numbered barely one thousand members. The leaders, conscious though they were that their forces were insufficient, were unable to restrain the impatience of their men. On the afternoon of May 12 they gathered in small bands in the quarters of St. Denis and St. Martin, about the Rue Bourg-l'Abbé. They numbered but six or seven hundred, who dreamed that thousands would join them, and that illustrious personages would lead them on to battle. On seeing their error they faltered, but Martin Bernard cheered them on. They broke open and plundered the shop of an armorer, named Le Page, and formed into two parties, one marching toward the Place du Châtelet, and the other and larger, under Barbès, to the Palace of Justice, whose guard rushed out on hearing the noise. The officer in command was ordered to surrender. "I will die first!" he exclaimed. One of the insurgents instantly shot him dead. Several soldiers were killed or wounded, and the rest disarmed. The rebels then hastened to the prefecture of police, hoping to take it by surprise.

Although they failed in this attempt, they succeeded in capturing the Hôtel de Ville and holding it for a time. Barricades were built in the quarters of St. Denis and St. Martin, but the mass of the people refused to rise, and between nine and ten o'clock that night the fire ceased, and various efforts to renew the struggle next day were promptly suppressed. Barbès, covered with wounds, was arrested at midnight; Bernard was taken a few days later, but Blanqui eluded the vigilance of the police for a considerable time.

The first result of this mad insurrection was the instant formation of a ministry. Not one of the men whom the King called upon dared refuse. Marshal Soult was made president of the council and minister of foreign affairs; M. Duchâtel was minister of the interior; M. Passy, of finance; Villemain, of public instruction; and M. Dufaure, of public works. Some of these men were of high distinction, and one, Dufaure, was destined to play a prominent part in French politics; but the great parliamentary influences of the time were lacking, and the King again gained control of foreign affairs under the protection of Soult. The situation enforced a truce on parliamentary factions, and little of note occurred during the session.

Industrial expositions were now held every five years. That of 1834 was brilliant; that of 1839 showed fresh progress, especially in Parisian manufactures. During this summer M. Arago announced to the Academy of Arts and Sciences that two scientists, Daguerre and Niepce, had found a way to fix reflected images upon a metallic plate, thus drawing and engraving, as it were, by sunlight. This was the origin of the daguerrotype. Railroads made but little progress. The Versailles road was inaugurated August 2, and a vote was passed to give government aid to the company. Forty-four million francs were also granted for the improvement of harbors, and twelve millions to finish canals.

Upon the conspirators of May 12 being brought to trial, much sympathy was shown for them. Barbès was condemned to death, whereupon the workmen and students in a body presented a petition for his pardon, and his sister, surrounded by her family, pleaded with the King for her brother's life. Supported by the Duchess d'Orléans, Louis Philippe listened to her and changed the sentence to transportation (July 17, 1839). This was one of the most honorable acts of his life.

Bernard was also sentenced to be transported, but neither he nor Barbès was sent to the colonies; both were imprisoned at Mont St. Michel, where Blanqui joined them a year later, having been arrested and found guilty.

Matters in Algeria again assumed importance. French rule still prevailed throughout the vast province of Constantine, but meantime the rival power of Abd-el-Kader, raised against France by her own hands, grew daily stronger in Oran and Algiers, and strove to gain ground in Constantine. Abd-el-Kader profited by a peace, which was really a badly kept truce, to build fortresses and reinforce his army with European deserters. During the autumn of 1839 the French, having rebuilt the old Roman seaport of Russicada, under the name of Philippeville, and occupied another position at Djidjeli, between there and Bougie, marched under Marshal Valée and the Duke d'Orléans through the mountainous district peopled by the Kabyles, and seized Hamza with slight opposition.

Abd-el-Kader thereupon determined to reopen hostilities, and the struggle lasted throughout 1840, one famous feat of arms occurring iu February. A company of one hundred and twenty-three foot-soldiers, under Captain Lelièvre, with one small cannon, defended the little fort of Mazagran, for four days and nights, against thousands of Arabs, who were at last forced to retreat. No check discouraged Abd-el-Kader, who continued to harass the French with unfailing ardor. During the spring Marshal Valée and the Duke d'Orléans achieved many victories, but the war still continued its course.

Public interest in 1839 was divided between Algeria and events that were occurring at the other extreme of the Mediterranean. In 1840 France was on the eve of a European war, on account of Turkey and Egypt. In July, 1839, the Chambers, before separating, voted a grant of ten millions to increase the navy, — a sign of the gravity of the situation.

Here we must go back for a few years to explain the origin of the crisis that agitated France and Europe in 1839 and 1840.

Two men, of similar ideas but different capacity and conduct, were rivals in the Mohammedan East, — Sultan Mahmoud, and his vassal, Mehemet Ali, the Pacha of Egypt. Both were, or desired to be, reformers, to the advantage, of course, of their own absolute power, but the Pacha had a better balanced mind than his sovereign, and fortune had hitherto favored him in the struggle. Mahmoud's defeat by the Russians in 1829, following hard upon the reforms considered by old Mussulmans as opposed to their religion, deprived him of all moral authority, while Mehemet Ali daily gained popularity.   He was a Turkish soldier, born in Macedonia, and had been a most successful general during various Egyptian wars.

The too successful vassal soon excited the jealousy of his vanquished and humiliated master, who secretly influenced the Pacha ruling in Central Syria, at St. Jean d'Acre, against his rival. Mehemet's son, Ibrahim, conquered the Pacha and seized St. Jean d'Acre.   An open rupture between Sultan and vassal ensued.   Ibrahim drove Mahmoud's troops from Syria, invaded Asia Minor, and defeated the Grand Vizier at Konieh, December 22, 1832, upon which Mahmoud invoked Russian aid.

This was a decisive moment in Oriental history.   From the point of view of French, and indeed of European interests, Russia excepted, it was desirable that Mehemet Ali should push on to Constantinople, dethrone the Sultan, and rule the Ottoman Empire in the name of Mahmoud's infant son.   But the man who swayed the foreign policy of England, Lord Palmerston, was hostile to Mehemet, and the government of Louis Philippe dared not uphold the Pacha. Mahmoud accordingly yielded to Egypt and Russia, gave up a large part of his domains to Mehemet, and, on the arrival of a Russian squadron with troops, concluded with Russia the treaty of Unkiar-Skelessi, which, in case of war, closed the Bosphorus to all military vessels save those of Russia (May – July, 1833).   Half of the Ottoman Empire was, therefore, in the hands of the Pacha of Egypt, and the other half under the jurisdiction of the Czar.   France and England protested against this treaty, the English ministry advising the Sultan to retract it, if possible.

In 1838, Mehemet Ali demanded the hereditary rule of Egypt and Syria for his son, Ibrahim, and his family, thus transforming the government of a province into an hereditary principality.   Mahmoud dared not refuse with respect to Egypt, but he demanded the immediate surrender of Syria, and entered that province with an army (April 21, 1839).

The first thought of the French government was to prevent the Russians from entering the Bosphorus, or to follow them. The first thought of Lord Palmerston was to force the Turks and Egyptians to suspend hostilities, by the simultaneous despatch of a French and an English fleet to the Syrian coast. He was more jealous at heart of France than of Russia. France would not consent to this union of forces, but, at the urgent entreaty of Austria and Prussia, Soult sent two aides-de-camp—one to Mehemet Ali at Alexandria, the other to the Turkish general—to arrest hostilities. At the same time the French and English cabinets agreed upon eventual measures for the entrance of the two fleets into the Bosphorus.

France thus assumed a serious responsibility. Louis Philippe was possessed by strange illusions in regard to his influence in Europe, imagining that he had gained Austria and Prussia, despite the conduct of Austria in the matter of the Duke d'Orléans's marriage. He even proposed to the English cabinet that a congress should be held at Vienna to settle the Eastern question, not seeing that a congress, if one were held, would turn against him if he did not agree with England. These illusions, however, were shared by the Chamber of Deputies and a great majority of the people, as was proved by a report offered by Jouffroy, upon the loan of ten millions for the navy. Thiers, however, had no faith in them.

While the Chamber voted on this report, events in the East were progressing with alarming haste. June 24, the Turkish army was utterly routed at Nézib by Mehemet's son. July 1, Mahmoud died, worn out by work, anxiety, and the excesses in which he sought oblivion. He left his crumbling empire to a son of sixteen, Abd-ul-Medjid. A few days later the Turkish admiral left the Bosphorus with his fleet, and surrendered to Mehemet Ali in the port of Alexandria. It was evident that should Ibrahim, the victor of Nézib, advance, he would sweep before him the whole Mussulman population from the Euphrates to the Bosphorus. Three days after the battle, however, Soult's messenger entered the camp, bearing Mehemet's orders to halt the troops. Ibrahim dared not disobey an order which his father would never have issued had he known of the victory, and saw the fruits of his brilliant successes wrested from his hands.

Louis Philippe still clung to the idea of a Viennese congress, to which Russia was loath to consent. The conduct of the French government was imprudent; that of the French ambassador at Constantinople was absurd. Admiral Roussin was a good sailor, but a wretched diplomatist. He joined the cause of Mahmoud against Mehemet, contrary to the public opinion and interests 'of France; he was led by the Austrian ambassador to draw up a note to the Ottoman Porte, announcing that the five great powers were agreed upon the Eastern question, and that no final resolve must be taken without their knowledge (July 29). The English ambassador signed this paper eagerly; the Russian, hesitatingly.

Now, this statement was utterly false. The French government, in consequence, recalled the ambassador, but the mischief was done. The Czar Nicholas, at first indignant with his ambassador, soon forgave him, when he found there was a chance of embroiling France and England. Lord Palmerston had made advances to him, to which he now replied by sending M. de Brunow to London, where he effected an agreement between England, Russia, Austria, and Prussia, against France. However, Russia and England were not wholly harmonious. One great question remained to be settled: Nicholas could not yet submit to give up the exclusive right to enter the Bosphorus. Lord Palmerston's colleagues obliged him to offer France a concession for Mehemet Ali, in the shape of the pachalic of St. Jean d'Acre, — the seaport excepted. Louis Philippe would have accepted, but public opinion forbade his cabinet to yield. As France persisted in claiming for Mehemet all Syria, with Arabia and Crete, which were already in his possession, Palmerston hastily withdrew the concession, so reluctantly made, and Nicholas yielded his sole right to the Bosphorus, the four powers thus coming to a peaceful agreement, leaving France out of the question. During these negotiations the latter country was represented in London by

General Sebastiani, who was now succeeded by Guizot, a man less dependent on the King. Louis Philippe agreed to the change, because he had a request to make of the cabinet, namely, an annual allowance of five hundred thousand francs for his second son, the Duke de Nemours.

There was a complete want of tact in this demand. Louis Philippe was no miser, as his foes pretended; his published accounts prove this, and, from the monarchial point of view, the claims made in favor of his children were wholly justifiable, but they were a great political mistake. A bitter and sarcastic pamphlet by M. de Cormenin ridiculed the demand, which was voted down by the Chambers by two hundred and twenty-six votes against two hundred (February 20, 1840). The ministry at once resigned. The last act of the cabinet of May 12, among whom was a great literary critic, M. Villemain, deserves honorable mention; it was voting a monument to Voltaire, which was erected near the Théâtre Français.

The King recalled Thiers, who was by no means anxious to resume the reins of power. There was no longer any trouble about the Spanish question, which had twice caused his rupture with the King. Events seemed to have justified Louis Philippe's negative policy. The government of the Spanish Queen had succeeded, unaided, in expelling the pretender, Don Carlos, and the Carlist chiefs, finding their struggle vain, for the most part submitted to treat with the ministers of Isabella. Thiers, however, found the Eastern question in a very unsatisfactory condition, and sought to lighten the responsibility thereof by transferring the burden to Soult or De Broglie. Both refused, and he was forced to assume the presidency of the council, with the foreign affairs. M. de Rémusat was minister of the interior, M. Cousin of public instruction, and the other ministers were members of the Left Centre or special men. The ministry went into office March 1.

The position of affairs was perilous abroad and uncertain at home. There was no immediate danger for the cabinet, but its footing was insecure. Thiers was anxious for a truce between political parties, that he might have time to gain adherents. Guizot agreed to retain the English embassy and to persuade his friends to support the new ministry, on two conditions: first, that no change should be made in the September laws; second, that there should be no electoral reforms. Thiers proposed to put off the latter question. Odilon Barrot and his allies were disposed to give him sufficient time, but there had latterly been warm discussions on the subject of parliamentary as well as electoral reform in the Chamber of Deputies. The legitimists, who made reform merely a machine for war, demanded universal suffrage of several degrees, hoping in this way to gain control of the rural population. Enlightened republicans did not deem their country ripe for universal suffrage, but claimed a vote for the national guards, which would confer the electoral right on the petty bourgeoisie, farmers, and settled mechanics. The extreme Left fused with the republicans in the "radical party." The dynastic Left was not so advanced in its ideas of reform, and advocated restricted suffrage.

The Eastern question afforded a specious pretext for postponing so important a discussion. Thiers inaugurated his ministry by a conciliatory address, in which he declared his desire to maintain both the Ottoman Empire and the power of Mehemet Ali. To him electoral and parliamentary reform was a subject for future study. The extreme Left, through Garnier-Pagès, protested against this desire to postpone everything, but the ministry gained a strong majority, and proposed no important laws, save one for the regulation and restriction of juvenile labor in manufactories, and one for the construction of a line of Transatlantic steamships.

The ministry, however, could not ward off political discussion. Parliamentary reform was taken into consideration, though no results were achieved. Electoral reform, eagerly demanded by the extreme Left, was not thoroughly debated, although demanded by two hundred and forty thousand petitioners.

Thiers then made an effort to divert attention from domestic policy in a way which threatened to revive perilous memories. Some years previous, Napoleon's statue had been restored to its column, and Thiers now proposed to bring back the Emperor's body from England.   The Duke d'Orléans warmly supported the scheme. The King accepted it, as did the Chambers and public opinion, blind to coming danger (May, 1840).

The return of the " Emperor's ashes " — a menacing presage of the return of the Empire — was the inevitable sequence of what had occurred under the Restoration.   It was a national error, and not the fault of the few.   In celebrating Napoleon in verses as resplendent as the Pyramids and Austerlitz, Victor Hugo, like Béranger, was only the organ of the popular infatuation.   The excitement was great throughout the land when General Bertrand, the most popular of Napoleon's fellow-exiles, placed in the King's hands the sword worn by Bonaparte at Austerlitz (June 4).   Louis Bonaparte at once issued in England a violent protest against the act by which Bertrand had robbed the Emperor's heirs of the only heritage left them by fate.   He closed with menaces, proving that he had already forgotten Louis Philippe's imprudent generosity.

England consented to restore Napoleon's body to France, and the Prince de Joinville was sent for it to St. Helena.   Under the influence of these stirring events, Louis Philippe reviewed the troops (June 14), and was greeted with shouts of " Long live the King! Long live reform! "   Carried away by the excitement of the moment, he promised reform, but, unfortunately for himself, soon forgot his pledges.

A few days later a festival was held at Strasburg, on the occasion of the inauguration of a statue of Gutenberg, the inventor of printing, by David d'Angers.   Scientists, artists, and authors met together as the guests of the Alsatians, and no subject was broached save that of peace and harmony between nations, especially between Germany and France.   Germany responded badly to these advances, and the French were soon aroused from their dream of international fraternity.   The legislative session closed July 13, and two days later a diplomatic event of the utmost importance was accomplished at London against France.

Upon the accession of the ministry of March 1, Louis Philippe, despite the ill-will displayed by Palmerston, was still blindly confident that England would do nothing without his cognizance. Thiers was more clear-sighted, and tried to gain time, but, alas! it was too late. Meantime, the Eastern question dragged its slow length along, no conclusion being reached, until, finally, a palace revolution broke out at Constantinople, and the grand vizier, Khosrew, the personal enemy of Mehemet Ali, was overthrown. Mehemet Ali, then, satisfied that he could sway the new Ottoman ministry as he pleased, announced his intention of treating with the young Sultan on amicable terms.

A short-lived joy reigned in Paris. The English ambassador at Constantinople shared, if he did not exceed, the prejudices of Palmerston, and prevented the Turks from settling matters with Mehemet. Palmerston next instigated, through his agents in Syria, a long-planned insurrection against the Egyptian government, although he denied all complicity to the English Parliament, with his usual contempt of truth. Meantime, he hurried on the quadruple alliance. Guizot, without sharing the strange illusions of the King, did not thoroughly penetrate the motives of Palmerston, although his correspondence betrayed his anxiety. .

July 15, a treaty was signed between the four powers and Turkey. The Sultan offered Mehemet Ali the hereditary rule of Egypt and the pachalic of St. Jean d'Acre during his lifetime; the offer to remain open for ten days. The treaty, contrary to all diplomatic usage, was at once put into execution, although the Prussian ambassador had not yet received his letters of credit from Frederick William IV., successor to Frederick William III., who had died on the 7th of the previous June. Guizot knew nothing of the treaty until two days later, nor was he then informed of its context. This mystery and haste were designed to enable the English fleet to capture the Egyptian squadron cruising on the Syrian coast, but M. Thiers, divining the treaty, by a happy inspiration sent Mehemet Ali word to recall his fleet to Alexandria, and thus saved his ships.

Palmerston attempted to appease France with hackneyed excuses, which Thiers received with calm dignity. The King gave way to an outburst of rage, which showed in what dreams he had persisted until this rude awaking, and made the Queen, in alarm, close the doors of the apartments, lest his angry voice should be heard outside.

General indignation prevailed in France. For the first time in ten years all parties seemed united. The idea of vengeance for 1814 and 1815 was universal, and the Marseillaise resounded in the French theatres, as in 1830. France once more turned its eyes towards the Rhine, and accused Austria and Prussia as the authors of this insult. A violent revival of the anti-French spirit responded to this national movement from the other side of the great river. This spirit, indeed, had never been really lulled to sleep since 1813. Every method was now employed to excite the German people against France, and Becker's famous song, "The German Rhine," recalled the war lyrics of 1813. Alfred de Musset's glowing pen flung back defiance, and Edgar Quinet, one of the loftiest and deepest spirits of this generation, raised his voice to warn France of her peril.

Precautionary measures were instantly taken, recruiting-offices were opened, and a royal order was issued for loans to increase the navy. July 28, the anniversary of the revolution of 1830, solemn ceremonies were held on the inauguration of a bronze column, surmounted by a figure of Liberty, which was erected on the site of the Bastile in commemoration of the Three Days. The remains of the victims of July 27, 28, and 29, 1830, which had been temporarily interred here and there in Paris, were carried to the church of St. Germain l'Auxerrois, where magnificent obsequies were celebrated, after which the coffins were transferred to vaults, prepared below the July Column. The King saluted the coffins as they passed, and was well received by the crowd on account of his patriotic demonstrations. He went directly after the ceremony to the Château d'Eu, where he was to meet Guizot and Thiers to discuss Eastern affairs. There he received startling news: Louis Bonaparte had landed at Boulogne (August 6).

During his stay in England, young Bonaparte had been busy with the same intrigues as in Switzerland, — bribing journals, circulating pamphlets, and seducing subaltern officers. He had suborned the commander of the Department of the North, General Magnan, afterwards one of his chief accomplices on December 2, and had renewed his correspondence with Clausel. His plan was to seize the garrison of Boulogne, with the arms stored in the castle, and thence proceed to Paris. He had prepared harangues, promising the soldiers "glory, honor, and fortune," and telling them that the shade of Napoleon spoke to them through his voice. His plans thus made, he set out from London with General Montholon, a handful of officers and men, and an eagle, destined to play the part of a living symbol in the coming drama. On landing at Boulogne he gained entrance to the barracks through a subaltern, and addressed the soldiers, who had been told that Louis Philippe had ceased to reign. They were on the point of yielding, when a captain rushed in and ordered the men and under-officers to rally round him. Louis Bonaparte fired his pistol at the brave fellow, but missed him, and was forced to escape, hurriedly followed by his fellow-conspirators. Being pursued by the troops, they fled to the sea-shore and swam to a boat, in which they attempted to regain their ship.

The troops fired on the fugitives, wounding several. The boat capsized, and a spent ball touched Louis Bonaparte, who was taken, and brought, with his accomplices, before the Court of Peers, who sentenced him to imprisonment for life at the Castle of Ham, where he was placed in the room once occupied by Polignac. This abortive attempt rendered him ridiculous in the eyes of the cultured classes, who read the newspapers and knew the details of his adventures. The mistake was thus made of thinking him no longer dangerous, and forgetting that the majority did not read.

Louis Philippe, reassured with regard to Louis Bonaparte, held a lengthy conference at Eu in regard to the Eastern question. The discord between King and ministers was only held in check by the fact that both parties considered Mehemet Ali strong enough to withstand the quadruple alliance. The husband of Louis Philippe's eldest daughter, Leopold, King of the Belgians, tried to compromise matters, and bring about a reconciliation between France and England, but in vain. Lord Palmerston rudely expressed his conviction that Louis Philippe would yield, saying, "I will make him pass through the eye of a needle."

In proportion as the chances of war increased, democracy flourished. Petition followed petition for electoral reform, and there was a general ferment among the laboring classes. Various books and pamphlets were published on social questions, chief among which were one by Dr. Villermé, on the condition of artisans, and one by Louis Blanc, upon the "Organization of Labor." Blanc, though still very young, was well known in the political world as a man of sincere truth and convictions.

The movement proceeded rather from the old trades-unions. Some claimed higher wages, some less work; many demanded the abolition of middlemen, and strikes ensued in several cities. In Paris they assumed vast proportions, more than one hundred thousand men taking part in them. The government at first held aloof, but was finally obliged to interfere and make various arrests, which only added fuel to the flames. The storm, however, cleared without doing any serious damage, although it left but too well-founded apprehensions for the future.

At the very time that Paris was shaken by these strikes, the government solved an important question in regard to the fortification of the city, — a subject naturally revived by the possible approach of another coalition. Public opinion was divided, some favoring and some opposing the project. Thiers considered that both detached forts and a wall around the city were necessary, and that one could not be had without the other, in which belief he was upheld by the leading newspapers, and has been justified by events. The system adopted enabled Paris, thirty years later, to defend herself for four months without external aid, and would have saved Paris and France had it not been for the crime and misfortune which betrayed the army of Metz.

The works were begun in September, under the direction of General Dode de la Brunerie, of the engineers, and were conducted with vigor, intelligence, and economy, considering the vast proportions of the task, which was to cost one hundred and forty millions.

The English journals that supported Palmerston at once broke into insolent menaces, regarding this as the preface to a general war. On the other side of the Rhine, the "Teutomaniacs," the anti-French party, redoubled their violence. The French government replied by issuing an order for the levy of fresh regiments (September 29).

French diplomacy, meantime, persuaded Mehemet Ali to inform the Ottoman Porte that he would accept Syria for life, giving up all the rest, and even, finally, submit to the decision of the young Sultan. England prevented the latter from treating directly with the Pacha, and urged him to insist on the downfall of Mehemet Ali at the expiration of the date fixed by the quadruple alliance. The Anglo-Austrian fleet had already opened hostilities. It was supposed in France that Mehemet's son and general, Ibrahim, would not attempt to defend the sea-board towns from the English navy, but would retire into the heart of Syria and there defy the coalition, thus embarrassing them and gaining time. Ibrahim, however, had the temerity to defend the coast, in which he did not display the vigor to be expected from the victor of Nézib. Beyrouth, bombarded by the English, was captured September 11, and Sidon, containing large stores of arms and ammunition, capitulated on the 22d. On hearing this, Thiers's first thought was to protest against Mehemet's downfall, send a French fleet to the aid of the Egyptian squadron, and put the French army on a war footing.

The cabinet discussed the matter with the King (October 3). The latter differed from Thiers, upon which the ministers offered their resignation. This was not accepted, and a compromise was made. It was decided to declare an attack on Egypt a *casus belli*, to recall the fleet from the Levant to the Hyères, and to continue military preparations, convoking the Chambers October 28. The recall of the fleet in the eyes of the public was the surrender of Thiers to the King and a concession to the enemy.

Thiers notified Palmerston, through Guizot, that France refused to acknowledge the downfall of Mehemet Ali in Egypt (October 8). France vibrated with indignant patriotism and a spirit of national pride. On the other hand, many were heard to say: "We did not go to war for Poland or Italy! What sense is there in braving a European coalition for the Pacha of Egypt?" October 15, Lord Palmerston advised the Sultan to permit Mehemet to keep Egypt for himself and his family, provided he evacuated all the rest.

On the same day, another attempt was made on Louis Philippe's life. A shot was fired at his carriage from the quay of the Tuileries, but the gun was too heavily loaded, and burst, wounding no one but the assassin, who proved to be a *frotteur*, named Darmès, belonging to a communist society. He declared that he had no accomplices, and that he had sought "to kill the greatest tyrant of ancient or modern times"! He was tried and condemned a few months later.

The political opponents of Thiers took advantage of this attack to decry the ministry, accusing Thiers of unchaining revolution by appealing to warlike passions. Stocks fell from 119 in July to 104 in October, and foreign governments became more and more hostile. Public opinion wavered, and the situation of enlightened patriots was cruel indeed. France had been rashly launched upon a question unworthy to imperil a nation's existence. It was not certainly a national question of the first importance whether Syria should belong to the Sultan or the Pacha.

Discord ruled both in the cabinet and in the royal family itself. M. Cousin, the minister of public instruction, went over to the King, declaring that war would entail revolution. The Duke of Orléans sided with Thiers, and on being warned that he was imperilling the dynasty, replied, "Well, better fall on the Rhine than in the gutter of the Rue St. Denis!"

October 20, Thiers presented to the King the draft of a speech from the Crown, firmly setting forth the necessity of taking vigorous measures to prevent the disturbance of the balance of power in Europe. Louis Philippe rejected this address, which implied the resolution to put the nation on a war footing. The ministry, thereupon, again sent in its resignation, which was now accepted. Thiers had returned to power unwillingly, and retired without regret. The King at once recalled Marshal Soult to the presidency

of the council, Guizot was summoned from London to take the port-
folio of foreign affairs, Humann that of finances, and Duchâtel and
Villemain also re-entered the cabinet.   In point of fact, this was a
renewal of the Guizot ministry (October 29), and the association of
Guizot and the King was not again interrupted until the fall of the
July monarchy.

CHAPTER V.

CONSTITUTIONAL MONARCHY OF JULY (*continued*). — GUIZOT MINISTRY. — RIGHT OF SEARCH. — DEATH OF THE DUKE D'ORLÉANS. — AFFAIRS IN TAHITI AND MOROCCO.

October 29, 1840, to January, 1845.

THE new ministry entered office under painful circumstances. Guizot's opinions naturally rendered him unpopular, and he was made even more so by the peculiar conditions of his accession; — the ambassador, thus succeeding the minister, whose agent he had been, seemingly must have betrayed his chief, in order that he might supplant him. We say seemingly, but, in reality, Guizot had been much more deeply involved than Thiers in Egyptian politics, and had cherished more illusions than he before the ministry of March 1, although he now advised the King to abandon his past course of action. Both felt that they were doing France a great service in thus avoiding war; but the irritated national feeling gave them no credit for their good intentions, and regarded their inconsistency as treachery.

The speech from the Throne, on the opening of the Chambers (November 5, 1840), denied any intention, on the part of European powers, to injure or insult France, and declared that the latter should side, not with revolution against Europe, but with Europe against revolution. One phrase, intended to be conciliatory, proved most offensive. In it the King said, "Let any one touch Strasburg, and we shall see what will happen!" Public opinion was loud in its invectives against a king who could imagine that Strasburg might be threatened; it was reserved for the baleful reign of Napoleon III. to show that this wild threat might prove a reality. The discussion of this speech necessarily led to recriminations between the past and present cabinet, which could not fail to be prejudicial to Guizot and to the King, who, though not mentioned, was felt to be behind the ministers.   In view of the attitude of the Chambers, the committee on the address was obliged to amend it, and to introduce the affirmation that " France would suffer no attack on the balance of power in Europe."   The ministry accepted this amendment, as they did Thiers's reservation in regard to Mehemet Ali's retention of Egypt.

This reservation seemed far from compromising, and yet Lord Palmerston refused to agree to it, declaring that " the Sultan alone had the right to decide to which of his subjects he would intrust such or such a part of his territory."   This signified that Egypt, as well as Syria, might be taken from Mehemet.   Louis Philippe received this message meekly.   In a letter to his son-in-law, King Leopold, who still served him as mediator, he accepted the situation, and expressed an eager desire for the speedy conclusion of some arrangement to which the "five powers" might subscribe.   Guizot urged the King to be less hasty, were it only for appearance' sake.

Just at this time important news came from the East, where the English were busy.   November 2, the English fleet bombarded and destroyed the chief seaport of Syria, St. Jean d'Acre, which had resisted many a siege only to fall into the hands of England.   Three weeks later, the squadron appeared at Alexandria.   Mehemet Ali was ready for battle, but English gold had done its work; he met with discouragement and defection everywhere, and was forced to yield.   November 27, he signed an agreement with Commodore Napier, binding himself to evacuate Syria at once, and dismiss the Ottoman fleet, in return for the hereditary government of Egypt, with the guaranty of the quadruple alliance.   When it was known that Mehemet had capitulated, they breathed more freely at the Tuileries.

The Alexandria agreement, however, did not put an end to all difficulties.   The English ambassador at Constantinople, backed by Palmerston, urged the Sultan to withdraw with one hand what he offered with the other. In granting hereditary rights to Mehemet, the Sultan reserved the privilege to choose a successor among the Pacha's sons, and to impose upon him conditions which wholly deprived him of military or maritime power. The continental powers opposed the policy of England, and the Sultan was obliged to grant better terms, on the acceptance of which an agreement was signed at London, July 13, 1841, by the "five powers." France simply agreed to facts accomplished in spite of her, and acknowledged the Sultan's right to close the two straits — the Bosphorus and the Dardanelles — to all ships of war.

Lord Palmerston had now achieved his ends. Russia had yielded the privilege, given to her navy by the treaty of Unkiar-Skelessi, and France had suffered Mehemet Ali to be humbled. The English ministry bought its success at the price of renewed hostility from France, for although the King and Guizot might forget, France would not, being rather disposed to exaggerate than to blot out her wrongs.

Another event, well calculated to kindle popular imagination, made the situation of the French government still more difficult. The remains of the man who had been war incarnate were solemnly brought back to France, at the moment when the King and Guizot proclaimed that "peace everywhere and forever," which the opposition dubbed "peace at any price."

We have mentioned the mission of the Prince de Joinville to St. Helena. On reaching the island (October 8), the remains of Napoleon were brought on board with great ceremony, by the English authorities, in presence of General Bertrand and other companions in exile of the Emperor. The body was found intact, and the face still retained its melancholy beauty. The body was placed upon a catafalque, between decks, on the frigate "Belle-Poule." They arrived safely at Cherbourg (December 8), and the coffin was transferred to a steamboat, which conveyed it up the Seine to Paris, where it was landed (December 14), and placed on a magnificent funeral car nearly fifty feet high, drawn by sixteen horses splendidly caparisoned. The cortege entered the city by the Arc de

NAPOLEON'S FUNERAL PROCESSION.

Triomphe, amidst the firing of cannon, ringing of bells, and huzzas of the people. In spite of the most severe cold experienced for years, multitudes passed the night on the Champs Élysées, waiting to see the funeral procession pass. All the harm which Napoleon had done was forgotten, and only the memory of his glorious deeds remained.

The King received the body beneath the dome of the Invalides, and caused the sword of Austerlitz to be placed on the coffin by General Bertrand. A solemn service was celebrated by the Archbishop of Paris. The listening crowd drew sad comparisons between the grandeur of other days and the present state of abasement. The anger excited by the ministerial attitude found vent in cries of "Down with Guizot!" and the result of this homage paid by the "King of peace" to the "Emperor of war" was a dangerous revival of imperialistic traditions, and an additional weakening of the régime of 1830.

M. Guizot had carried out his plans in regard to foreign affairs, — he had achieved a reconciliation with European monarchies, — while in his domestic policy he returned to the system of resistance exemplified by constant attacks on the press, but, at the same time, he accepted the legacy of Thiers in one important point, — the completion of the Paris fortifications. In regard to these there were singular complications. The Russian Czar occasionally relaxed his sullen attitude, and sought to interfere in French affairs. Considering Guizot too English, he entered into correspondence with Molé, who was plotting to revenge the coalition on the ministry of October 29. Soult, the nominal president of the cabinet council, cared little for Guizot, and opposed the plan adopted for the fortifications, — a combination of detached forts with a continuous wall. Molé accordingly laid a scheme for Russian alliance, and a return to the exclusive system of detached forts, hoping in this way to overthrow Guizot. His intrigues came to naught.

While the Chambers were discussing the fortifications, a legitimist journal, the *France*, published three letters from the King, relating successively to Algiers, Poland, and the detached fortresses.

This affair proved very injurious to Louis Philippe. In the first he agreed with England to conform to the very letter of the promises made by Charles X. in regard to Algiers, which promises the legitimists denied, throwing all responsibility upon the present King.

The second letter was addressed to a French ambassador, and Louis Philippe vaunted therein of having, through his policy, stripped Poland of all means of defence, and complained of the ingratitude of Russia, Prussia, and Austria, in return for this prodigious service.

In the third letter the King protested that "the forts, far from being meant to repel foreign invasion, would become, in case of need, a triumphant instrument for controlling the turbulent population of Paris and its amiable faubourgs. To this project" (the construction of the forts), he added, "is in some sort attached, not the duration of constitutional monarchy, but the perpetuity of my dynasty, which is far more important to France."

The scandal was immense. The opposition was indignant, while the King's friends' made feeble protests. It was soon discovered that these documents came from London; that the originals, with many more of the same sort, were in the hands of an intriguing French woman; and that some of them, at least, were from M. de Talleyrand's portfolio. The first letter was prefaced by a few lines to Talleyrand, warning him not to lay too much stress on the words, but to regard the understanding between them, which seemed to prove that Louis Philippe was deceiving England rather than France, and was by no means decided to renounce Algiers. However this might be, the King did not come off with honor. The editor of the paper which published the letter was tried for forgery, and, although unable to produce the original, was acquitted. This was equivalent to condemning the King (April 24, 1841). A painful impression lingered in the Chambers. The discussions which ensued with respect to the finances gave the deputies cause for reflection. The state of the treasury had been good only in seeming for the last ten years. There was in reality a deficit of a thousand million francs, which the minister of finances, M. Humann, charged to the account of the ministry of March 1 and its military preparations.

Thiers made a vigorous defence, and showed that there was a deficit of two hundred and fifty-five millions in 1830, and proved that out of the present thousand millions his cabinet had expended but one hundred and seventy-five millions in putting the army and navy on a respectable footing. The ministry then proposed a temporary loan of four hundred and fifty millions, to cover a part of the deficit, until fresh resources should enable them to employ this sum on the public works now being executed; for the rest of the deficiency they would use the reserves of the sinking fund. The tax laws were made more productive by levying them more stringently. This led to angry remonstrance in many places, Toulouse being the scene of serious outbreaks during the early part of July. The resistance was so general that the prefect sent for instructions how to meet it. He was at once recalled, and a new prefect, M. Mahul, sent to take his place. He was received with a prodigious hubbub, upon which he called out the troops, to which the people responded by raising barricades. The national guards then assembled; they were also opposed to the new measures, and the government authorities were forced to leave the city.

The government could not imitate its agents without abdicating. It accordingly sent to Toulouse a commissioner extraordinary, Maurice Duval, ex-prefect of Isères, with a large number of troops, who put down the disturbances, and matters proceeded peacefully. These scenes were repeated in other cities, and left rankling resentment behind.

During these troubles the republicans lost the best man left them since the death of Carrel. Garnier-Pagès died, June 28, under forty, and was replaced in the Chambers by a man of less subtlety but more brilliancy, Ledru-Rollin, who was destined to play a foremost part in the revolutionary annals of France. In his address to his electors, he far exceeded the most radical deputies, thus irritating not only the dynastic Left, but many of the republicans as well, who deemed his professions premature. His prosecution by the

government restored him to favor, Odilon Barrot, Arago, Berryer,
and Marie uniting to defend him in the name of the entire opposition.   The case was referred from one court to another; Ledru-
Rollin was finally acquitted, while, strange to say, the editor of the
paper in which his speech was printed, M. Hauréau, was condemned (November 23, 1841) as the chief offender.

September 13, 1841, the young Duke d'Aumale returned to Paris
with the regiment at whose head he had distinguished himself in
Algeria, and his brothers, the Dukes of Orléans and Nemours, went
to meet him with a brilliant staff.   As the procession passed through
the Faubourg St. Antoine a pistol-shot was heard, and a bullet, intended for the princes, struck the horse of an officer.   The author
of the attempt — an old soldier, named Quénisset, condemned for
insubordination — was at once arrested.   He confessed that a plot
had been formed by a remnant of one of the secret societies still
existing in Paris.   Several arrests followed, and one of the men implicated wrote to a republican paper, the *Journal du Peuple*, begging
the editor, M. Dupoty, to join with the *National* in defending his
cause.   Dupoty was instantly charged with complicity, and, despite
the protests of Ledru-Rollin and Cousin, he was sentenced to five
years' imprisonment.   Quénisset was condemned to death.   There
was a general outburst of indignation, which augured ill for the government, although it retained a majority in the Chambers in regard
to domestic policy.   Abroad, it had enjoyed a short-lived satisfaction in the downfall of Lord Palmerston at the height of his
great military and diplomatic triumph.   His arrogance and pride
won him many enemies in his own country as well as in France,
and he lost his seat during the autumnal elections of 1841.   The
Whigs were succeeded by moderate Tories, very different from those
of other days, the new ministry being made up of Sir Robert Peel,
Lord Aberdeen, and Lord Wellington.   Louis Philippe and Guizot
were delighted to exchange Palmerston for Aberdeen, and yet the
first serious troubles of the Guizot ministry came from England,
against the desire of Aberdeen, who had no personal enmity to
France.

The annoyance arose from the famous question of the Right of Search, which dated back to the time of the Restoration. The Congress of Vienna passed an order for the abolition of the slave-trade, upon which England proposed to the other nations to grant their armed vessels a mutual Right of Search over merchant-vessels, in order to detect and prevent the transportation of slaves. England had a double interest in the matter: that of naval predominance, — her navy being much larger than that of other nations, and able to exercise the right on a larger scale than they, — and that of religion and humanity, which was felt by a majority of the people, who were opposed to slavery. The ministers of the Restoration declined the proposition, but Louis Philippe, soon after his accession, accepted it, and Casimir Périer seemed blind to the consequences. The first treaty was signed November 30, 1831, new clauses being added in 1833. The smaller states followed the example of France, and the larger powers agreed to subscribe to it in 1838, on condition of framing a new agreement. England took advantage of this to aggravate the first conditions, extending the right of search indefinitely beyond the thirty-second degree of latitude, and thus subjecting all commerce between Europe and the United States to this maritime inquisition, and removing all limits to the number of cruisers of each nation. Negotiations continued between the nations until the treaty of July 15 cut them short. They were resumed by Guizot and Aberdeen, who signed a compact at London (December 20, 1841).

The July treaty, which restored France to the European alliance, had been ill received ; with this one it was much worse. The maritime populations of France were incensed to learn that their ships were subject to English inspection on all the African and American coasts. The press became the mouthpiece of popular indignation. France was humiliated at the attitude of her government compared with that of the United States. Lord Aberdeen having said that, in case of the United States' refusal to agree to the treaty, England would not let herself be stopped by a bit of bunting (the flag), the American representative at London replied that, in case of need,

the United States would cause this bit of bunting to be respected.
February 13, 1842, the American minister to France sent a letter to
Guizot, expressing his regret that France should agree to such a
course, and inquiring whether, like England, she claimed the right
to verify the nationality of American vessels, in which case peace
between the two countries would inevitably be endangered.

This incident put the finishing stroke to the popular displeasure,
and the question was brought before the Chambers. Guizot was
defeated, but did not retire, although his position was far from envi-
able. The French government refused to ratify the treaty signed
by their ambassador at London, and proposed certain changes, which
Aberdeen felt bound to refuse. Matters thus remained in suspense.

The Guizot ministry sustained this serious check early in 1842.
The personal policy of the King experienced another shock during
the previous year in Spain. General Espartero, a strong ally of
England, was made regent (May 8, 1841), upon which the "Chris-
tinos," or partisans of Queen Christine, rebelled against him, but
were soon suppressed.

Algeria alone afforded some compensation to France, General
Bugeaud appearing in a new light on becoming governor of the
French possessions in Africa. Vulgar and violent in the Chambers,
and unskilful in his negotiations, he now justified the good opinion
which Thiers had of him from a military point, and formed an excellent plan of action against Abd-el-Kader, capturing Tekedempt,
Boghar, and Mascara in the spring of 1841, conquering almost the
whole province of Oran, and finally occupying Tlemcen in January,
1842. Abd-el-Kader was driven into Morocco, with a mere handful of men, but was still hopeful. He preached the holy war in
Morocco, where the traditions of Islam were far more piously preserved than in the Ottoman Empire, although the Emperor Abd-el-
Rahman's seat was but insecure. Abd-el-Kader resumed his incur-
sions into Oran, but had neither strongholds nor regular troops; he
was reduced from a sovereign prince to a mere partisan leader.

The Guizot ministry had hitherto met with no serious difficulty
save from abroad, but it now began to be alarmed at the state of

affairs at home. The conservatives discerned the necessity of progress, and there was a fresh outcry for reform. Deputies Ganneron and Ducos, early in 1842, made a motion to obtain admission to the franchise for the second list of the jury, and to restrain deputies from accepting salaried positions during their term of legislative office. This was very modest, but Guizot refused to grant it, declaring that there was no necessity for reform. Lamartine indignantly exclaimed that to govern in such fashion there was no need of a statesman; a milestone was sufficient. This epigram clung to the majority that rejected the motion, and they were thenceforth known as the "milestone conservatives."

Yet this ministry of resistance and negation lent a willing ear to those who asked it to work for material interests. A law was passed for the construction of a net-work of railroads, made up of six great lines from Paris to the frontiers and coasts of France,—an effort being thus finally made to put France on a level with other countries in this respect.

The financial administration of France contrasted painfully with that of England, where Sir Robert Peel had recently accomplished reforms at once bold and sagacious. He lowered all the taxes levied on articles of consumption which oppressed the poor, and re-established the income taxes for the wealthy classes. England, like France, had an annual deficit, but the income tax soon covered the temporary losses brought about by the decrease of the tax on consumption.

Ill assured of the Chamber of Deputies, and indignant at its opposition to the Right of Search, the government dissolved it (June 13, 1842). The moral situation grew constantly worse, the government continuing to bribe juries to execute its pleasure in various trials of newspaper editors, etc. The elections occurred July 12, and a new Chamber was returned, containing very much the same elements as the preceding one.

The day after the elections (July 13), the Duke d'Orléans was going from the Tuileries to Castle Neuilly, in a light carriage, when the horses took fright and ran. The prince, who was agile and a

practised gymnast, jumped from the carriage, but, wrongly calcu-
lating his distance, he lost his balance, was thrown backwards, and
fell unconscious on the ground. He was carried into a grocer's
shop, the royal family was summoned, and, a few hours later, he
died without regaining consciousness. He was thirty-two years
old, and was universally mourned. Had he lived, the course of
affairs might have been very different. His views were wholly
unlike those of his father. It is doubtful whether he was very liberal, but he was certainly very national, and eager for the honor
of France and the army. His chief endeavor would have been to
atone for 1814 and 1815, and he would doubtless have made Thiers
his minister. France would have been spared, in all probability,
the revolution of 1848 and the second empire, and the transition
to democracy and a definite republic would have been quite different. He left a remarkable will, desiring that his son, the Count
of Paris, whether he became king or remained the obscure and
unknown defender of a cause to which all belong, might be, first
and foremost, a man true to his age and nation, the exclusive and
zealous partisan of France and the Revolution. He added, "and
a Catholic," feeling that, from a political point of view, it was
desirable for the head of the nation to belong to what was called
" the faith of the majority."

His widow, while she lived, strove to carry out his wishes, but
his family did not follow in her footsteps.

For a time this great misfortune strengthened the government,
by allying to it the Left Centre and even the dynastic Left; but a
serious question soon divided them once more. It was important
to settle to whom the regency would fall in case of the King's
death previous to the majority of the elder son of the Duke
d'Orléans. His will designated his eldest brother, the Duke de
Nemours. Barrot preferred his widow, the duchess, while Thiers
upheld Nemours, and the latter was finally chosen by the King
and his ministers.

The Guizot ministry was strengthened by the very event which
was later to result so fatally to the July monarchy. The cabi-

E. RONJAT.

THE DUKE OF ORLEANS.

net continued to abuse its power, and failed to seize a signal occasion to act for the advantage of the state against a coalition of private interests. For several years negotiations had been going on between France and Belgium, with a view to a Customs Union between the two countries. In October, 1842, Louis Philippe's son-in-law, King Leopold, visited Paris to consummate the arrangement, which was most advantageous to France, but prejudicial to private manufacturers and property holders. A sort of industrial congress protested, the ministry shrank back in dismay, and the scheme fell to the ground, much to the delight of England, Austria, and Prussia, who were loath to see France profit by this union.

The ministry could not resist the conservative deputies, whether right or wrong, and now gave up the Right of Search treaty of December 20, 1841, gaining the tolerance of the tory ministry in England, to the credit of that body, for popular opinion was against this action on the part of France.

The session of 1843 was marked by long-needed economic measures, and equal taxes were laid on colonial (cane) sugar and domestic (beet-root) sugar. This measure was most beneficial to home manufacture.

Louis Philippe's policy was successful, during the year, in Spain, where the regent, Espartero, had gradually alienated the progressive party by his illiberal spirit, the industrial region of Catalonia by his submission to the commercial influence of England, and the Basque provinces by his constant threats to abolish their privileges. The Cortes quarrelled with the regent, who twice declared them dissolved. Insurrection broke out on all sides. Espartero bombarded Barcelona and Seville, thereby only hastening his fall. Assailed on every hand, he embarked for England (August, 1843). The government did not long remain in the hands of the progressive party; reaction was inevitable in this fickle country. The party of the queen-mother soon gained the ascendency, recalled Christina, and gave her, not the regency, the young queen having been declared of age, but the actual power (December, 1843).

In Algeria, Abd-el-Kader, despite his heroic efforts, failed to recover his former position. He stirred up the native tribes, but Bugeaud soon drove them back to the mountains, and, on the 16th of May, 1843, the young Duke d'Aumale surprised and captured the encampment of the Emir, who escaped with great difficulty. The insurgent tribes surrendered, and Abd-el-Kader again sought refuge in Morocco. Bugeaud was made Marshal of France.

Louis Philippe was well satisfied with the triumph of his son, for whom he destined, a little later, the government of Algeria. Erelong he had a pleasure of another kind. Early in September the Queen of England visited him at the Château d'Eu, accompanied by Lord Aberdeen, her minister of foreign affairs, — an event which was regarded as a confirmation of amicable relations between the two countries. This, however, was only so in seeming, for France was really on the brink of serious difficulties with England.

The first subject that came up between the French and English cabinets, after Victoria's visit to France, did not give rise to these difficulties. The Duke de Bordeaux having arrived in London in October, Louis Philippe induced the queen not to receive him at court. The Duke de Nemours, on the contrary, was officially received by the queen at London and Windsor. Meantime, the exiled heir of Charles X., under the title of " Henry V.," took up his abode at a mansion in Belgrave Square, where he received homage from a large number of French legitimists, among them M. de Chateaubriand and M. Berryer, as well as certain deputies, who thus gave in their adherence to another government than the one to which they had sworn allegiance. This conduct was rebuked in the speech from the Crown at the opening of the Chambers (December 27, 1843). Berryer made but a feeble defence, while Guizot warmly discussed the subject, denying the principle of legitimacy, and appealing to the Revolution for support.

Berryer, in turn, reproached Guizot with visiting Ghent, in time of civil war, to give political counsel to Louis XVIII. A frightful tumult followed, amidst which Guizot stood firm, and demanded a quiet hearing, which was finally granted, and the next day the paragraph in the address which censured the visit of the deputies to

London was accepted. It cost the government and Guizot dear. All the deputies implicated resigned, and were re-elected with the aid of the opposition.

The question of the Right of Search again arose, and Guizot was forced to promise that he would labor for the total abolition of the treaty, and was, in fact, negotiating with Lord Aberdeen to abolish this right, without putting an end to the abolition of the slave-trade, when a new event seriously disturbed the relations between France and England, namely, the occupation by the French of the island of Tahiti. A brief retrospect is necessary to fully understand this important question.

For some years the French government had felt the necessity of having, in these remote waters, if not colonies, at least ports, where their vessels could put in for supplies. In 1841 and 1842 France occupied the islands of Nossi-Bé and Mayotte, between the eastern shores of Africa and the large island of Madagascar. A company was formed to colonize New Zealand, but was forestalled by England. It is difficult to admit that the occupation of certain points of that vast region sufficed to insure to the first holder complete sovereignty, but Guizot was reluctant to contest the matter with England. This was in 1840. In 1842, Admiral Dupetit-Thouars proposed and effected the occupation of the Marquesas Islands, the native chiefs readily submitting to French rule. These little islands formed a good naval station and place of transportation for French criminals, but were too small for a settlement of any magnitude. Dupetit-Thouars next turned to the Society Islands, of which Tahiti was the largest. Both climate and soil were delightful, and the mild and gentle natives were feebly ruled by Queen Pomaré, who gave much cause for complaint to French merchants and missionaries. The admiral demanded reparation, and the terrified queen signed a treaty accepting the French protectorate (September 9, 1842). Certain English and Protestant missionaries had long exercised a civilizing influence in these islands, and were naturally loath to be displaced by French Catholic priests. One of them, named Pritchard, who was also the English consul, unceasingly instigated

Queen Pomaré and her followers to rebel, and finally persuaded the former to hoist an independent flag. Dupetit-Thouars hauled it down, and, in conformity with his warning to the queen, took possession of the Society Islands in the name of France (November 6, 1843).

The news of this event reached Paris in February, 1844. The King and cabinet were much alarmed, fearing a storm of indignation from England. The King wished to disavow the admiral's conduct on the spot. The ministry obtained a brief delay, but on the indignant protest of the English cabinet and people finally agreed to abandon all thoughts of the protectorate. The French press and popular opinion were incensed, and the Chamber of Deputies loudly blamed Guizot's course, although a motion to pass a vote of censure was defeated (March 1). The Chamber thus fell a victim to the same public displeasure with the ministry.

The concession which angered France appeased England, but fresh embarrassments arose abroad. The weak and anarchical government of Morocco permitted Abd-el-Kader to plot against France, and he soon managed to draw the Emperor of Morocco into the quarrel. An engagement took place near Ouchda, between the natives and General Lamoricière, who routed his foes. England anxiously watched the contest from the rock of Gibraltar, and, through consideration for her, the French cabinet hesitated to declare war. The natives of Morocco renewed their aggressions, however, when Marshal Bugeaud vigorously took the offensive. The ministry, meanwhile, determined to send an ultimatum to the Emperor of Morocco, and to despatch a squadron, under the Prince de Joinville, to cruise along the coast.

The English cabinet was disturbed, only half trusting Guizot's assurances that France desired no further conquests, and ordered the English consul at Tangiers to urge the Emperor of Morocco to satisfy the French government and avoid war. It was, however, too late; the French had already begun operations by land and sea. Just at this time the news from Tahiti rekindled the passions in England that had been calmed by the disavowal of Dupetit-Thouars.

A VIEW IN MADAGASCAR.

Pritchard, after renouncing his consular office, had excited an insurrection in the Society Islands. While the French governor, Bruat, repressed the outbreak on a neighboring island, his second in command arrested and imprisoned Pritchard, who was liberated on the governor's return, on condition that he should leave the archipelago on an English ship in the harbor. Pritchard gone, the other English missionaries joined with Bruat in suppressing the revolt. These facts were exaggerated by distance into a papist attempt to expel the Bible from the Pacific archipelagoes. There was a general outburst in the English Parliament; even Sir Robert Peel expressed himself with unwonted heat, declaring that "a gross outrage had been committed on England in the person of her agent," and demanding immediate reparation from France. The legislative session in France was drawing to a close, and Guizot hastened to dissolve it (August 5), that he might be free to settle with England, unfettered by the Chambers.

At the same time cannon were rumbling by land and by sea in Africa. The Emperor of Morocco not replying to the ultimatum, Prince Joinville (August 5) bombarded Tangiers, in presence of the men-of-war of various other nations, which looked quietly on. In two hours the defences were levelled, and resistance ceased. Out of respect to England the prince did not occupy Tangiers, which was opposite Gibraltar, but, proceeding to Mogador, one of the commercial centres of Morocco, he destroyed its ramparts, and captured and garrisoned a little island commanding the entrance to the harbor (August 15). The Kabyles, meanwhile, came down from the mountains, drove out the imperial garrison, and pillaged and burned Mogador, not as allies of France, but on their own account.

The evening before the French descent on Mogador there occurred, at the other end of Morocco, the most important military action that had been seen in Africa since the taking of Algiers. The son of the emperor, Abd-el-Rahman, appeared on the Isly River, near the Algerian frontier, with a large body of troops, and summoned Bugeaud to surrender Lalla-Maghrenia, and withdraw beyond the Tafna. The marshal replied by marching straight upon the enemy. On the morning of August 14, the battle took place, and proved, as Bugeaud expected, a mere repetition of the famous Egyptian victories. The enemy was utterly routed. The action was so rapid that the French loss was almost nothing, and the enemy's only from two to three thousand men.

These events excited a lively joy in France and a corresponding displeasure in England. To the French, the victory over Morocco seemed a victory over England, while the English inveighed against the ambition of France, which strove to capture the whole African coast and the archipelagoes of Oceanica to establish "papacy." The English cabinet ordered large naval armaments, and talked of reinstating Pritchard at Tahiti, if necessary, by the cannon.

In the situation brought about between the two countries, by the unfortunate policy of Lord Palmerston, everything served to incense one against the other. On calmly studying the history of the time, after the lapse of years, it is evident that it would have been madness for France and England to come to blows for such trifling grounds. Unhappily the government of the time did not sufficiently respect the dignity of France, the King himself expressing his passionate desire for peace in terms often humiliating to national honor.

Guizot felt that France could not permit the restoration of Pritchard or the recall of the officer who had arrested him, and wrote to that effect to the English government, but offered to grant an indemnity to Pritchard.

At the same time that this offer was made, and, of course, accepted by England, peace was concluded with the Emperor of Morocco, who had sued for it after his defeat. No change was made in the conditions offered previous to the victory, namely, the punishment of the authors of the aggressions which caused the war; the expulsion of Abd-el-Kader from the territory of Morocco; and the recognition, by the Emperor of Morocco, of the French title to the old Algerian frontier (September 10). No indemnity was demanded. Prince Joinville could not disguise his dissatisfaction at this conclusion of such brilliant military and maritime triumphs,

and the *Journal des Débats* tried to explain this strange generosity
by saying that "France was rich enough to pay for her glory."
The English laughed heartily at this fine maxim, but France did not
take it so lightly, and there was a general outcry of indignation.
Matters were settled as well as might be with England, but popular
opinion looked with little favor on the course of the French government, and was ill pleased with Louis Philippe's visit to Queen
Victoria in October.   At another time the honors paid him would
have been esteemed marks of respect; now Louis Philippe was
reproached with being too kindly received in England.

M. Guizot had rid himself of the Chambers that he might regulate
foreign affairs as he liked, but the day of reckoning was only postponed.   During the discussion of the address, in January, 1845, he
was attacked by Molé, who still aspired to regain power.   Molé's
speech was adroit, but it would have come better from other lips,
and Guizot, in his reply, took advantage of the false position of the
ex-cabinet leader overthrown by the coalition.   Thiers, in turn,
attacked Guizot's foreign policy.   The ministry gained a victory
almost equivalent to a defeat, and the petty majority received the
nickname of "the Pritchardists."   The régime declined daily;
scandalous affairs in which various high officials were concerned
gave rise to a feeling of the prevalence of immorality in the governing classes, and the clear-sighted friends of the King held their
breath in alarm.   M. de Montalivet, who was sincerely attached to
the royal family, implored Louis Philippe to make some concessions,
and to approach the Left Centre, but the King was deaf to all
warning.   Neither he nor Guizot would see the signs of the coming
storm on the horizon.

CHAPTER VI.

CONSTITUTIONAL MONARCHY OF JULY (*continued*). — GUIZOT MINISTRY (*continued*). — STRUGGLE BETWEEN THE CLERGY AND THE UNIVERSITY. — ELECTIONS OF 1846. — SPANISH MARRIAGES. — FESTIVITIES. — AFFAIRS IN SWITZERLAND AND ITALY.

1843 to December 28, 1847.

ALTHOUGH order reigned in the streets, and there had been no popular disturbance since the census riots in 1841, the moral and social situation of France was more serious than at the time when the July government defended itself, arms in hand, against insurrections not sustained by public opinion. Socialism was rife among the working-men in the towns and a part of the young bourgeoisie. Among the socialists, some aspired to revolution; others contented themselves with discussion, and waited for time to accomplish the changes that they desired. To the latter class belonged the Fourierist or Phalansterian School, led by Victor Cousin and the communistic followers of Cabet. Since the grand intellectual movement, of which we gave a brief summary, between 1830 and 1832, we have had occasion to mention the appearance of a distinguished publicist in the ranks of socialism, Louis Blanc, who had recently published a brilliant and caustic book, "The History of Ten Years" (1830 – 1840), in which he handled the July monarchy without gloves. In 1840, a new champion noisily entered the arena, — Prudhon, with his famous saying, "Property is theft." In another work he uttered a second and yet more extraordinary maxim: "God is incarnate evil!" Thus, according to Prudhon, property should be abolished to attain equality and justice, and men should stray from God to arrive at virtue. He thus began, like Rousseau, with paradoxes, but much worse and with less excuse, for, since Rousseau's time, the Revolution had shown how words are translated into deeds, and what is the responsibility of writers. The double result of his words was to draw the violent and vulgar into dangerous excesses, and to terrify the timid into reaction. So little of a communist was he in practice that he held aloof, not only from communists proper, but from socialism in general, while proclaiming himself the only true socialist. Absolutely opposed to the immoral ideas of Enfantin and Fourier, he was firm in his austere devotion to family life and good morals. He maintained the inferiority of woman, and despised chivalrous ideas and sentiments. From the hard and narrow rationalism which he made his boast, he might be thought a stranger to the Gallic spirit and the French spirit of modern times, as well as to that of the Middle Ages. But with all his lack of delicacy, he had much nobleness of soul. The moral law of which he dreamed for man was not the satisfaction of passion, but the satisfaction of conscience and duty.

One of the marked characteristics of the period in which Prudhon lived (1840 – 1848) was the direct intervention of the working-classes in journalism. They had more than one paper and magazine of their own. The ideas disseminated by Prudhon and many inferior doctrinaires, although they sowed the seeds for future evils, had no immediate effect. Clericalism, on the contrary, acted directly upon the government and the Chambers. The ultramontane party, which had long been kept in the background, now raised its head anew.

During the early part of Louis Philippe's reign the great body of professors and teachers at the University flourished and labored, untrammelled by oppression; but by degrees the government strove to reconcile the clergy, and to detach them from the legitimist party. In 1841, Villemain, then minister of public instruction, proposed a law to prevent clerical encroachment in educational matters. The law was defeated, and thenceforth the clerical party clamored boldly for liberty, and the performance of the Charter's promise respecting freedom of instruction. What they desired, in reality, was not liberty, but the freedom to substitute one monopoly for another. There were some, however, who truly wished for the union of liberty and Catholicism, such as the brilliant Dominican orator, Lacordaire, — a man of sentiment rather than logic, but a sincere and generous spirit.

The person who played the principal part in the clerical campaign now entered upon was a young layman, a peer of France, Count de Montalembert,—a bold and aggressive spirit with an ardent and mobile imagination, and a remarkable author and orator, more artistic and polemical than sectarian at heart. The clergy warmly attacked the professors of the lyceums and colleges, declaring that the present system of education was destructive to faith and morality; that it was infected with scepticism, pantheism, etc., and dangerous to family ties.

The Jesuits were the real inspirers and leaders of the warfare. They knew that, if the clergy triumphed, the victory would profit, not the Gallicans, but themselves. Forced, in 1828, to give up the ostensible charge of the seminaries, they had never quitted France, but for some years had worked quietly in secret. Instead of the twelve houses which they had under the Restoration, they now had twenty-seven, and numerous other monasteries and lay associations of clerical tendency were under their direct guidance. The Society for the Propagation of the Faith labored in foreign countries, and took no interest in intestine dissensions; but the Society of St. Vincent de Paul, founded by a praiseworthy writer, M. Ozanam, and other true Christians, soon fell under the influence of those who sought to centralize religious power.

The violence and extent of ultramontane aggression produced its inevitable result in a revival of the liberal spirit and a strong reaction. In proportion as the assault on the University was prolonged, the resistance of the professors grew in strength and determination. The College of France soon entered the lists, and took a foremost rank, with three men of diverse gifts but equal popularity among the young men of France, — Edgar Quinet, Michelet, and

Mickiewicz. All three were widely known in the literary world, and when they saw the renewal, under Louis Philippe, of the ultramontane war of the Restoration, they boldly took the field. Michelet launched forth his book, "Priesthood, Woman, and the Family," — a terrible polemic, in which he declared sacerdotal influence incompatible with the true family spirit. He then joined Quinet in publishing "The Jesuits and Ultramontanism," the fiercest attack which that formidable society had known since Pascal (June, 1843). Quinet followed this, two years later, with another doctrinal work on "Christianity and the French Revolution," a book whose title indicates its spirit.

The two friends contended simultaneously against the Jesuits, who were striving to subordinate France to ultramontane cosmopolitanism; the socialists, who wished to absorb it into a humanitarian cosmopolitanism; and the doctrinarians, who humbled France before monarchical Europe. The Gallic spirit in them rebelled against German fatalism imported into France by the Hegelian school. Meantime the struggle between the liberal and the clerical party passed from books and papers into the legislative Chambers early in 1844. A monument to Molière was inaugurated on the 15th of January of that year, to the great scandal of the Jesuits and their friends, and, some days later (February 2), the government, yielding to religious pressure, presented a law to give over secondary instruction to the clergy. Cousin, who had hitherto been reproached for his moderation and reticence, now broke forth in defence of the inalienable right of the State to authorize and watch over all institutions of learning. The Chamber of Peers passed the law, with amendments in favor of the clergy, but the deputies regarded it so unfavorably that the discussion of it was postponed for a time.

M. Villemain, anxious and ill, resigned the ministry of public instruction, and was replaced by Salvandy, — an honest and generous man, who was soon circumvented and led astray by the clerical party. At this time, however, there was too strong a reaction against the pretensions of the clergy for the government to yield to them.   May 2, 1845, M. Thiers moved that all enactments against the Jesuits should be enforced.   The motion was adopted by a large majority, and the ministry, daring neither to resist the Chambers nor to obey and enforce the laws, sent an Italian, named Rossi, one of the board of public instruction, to treat directly with Pope Gregory XVI.   The Holy Father, although a violent despot in his own States, now listened to the voice of prudence, and directed the General of the Jesuits to close all their houses in France, without waiting to be compelled to do so.   They changed their residences and names, and bided their time, as they had done in 1828.

The clerical party was not disheartened.   " If the vanguard have laid down their arms, the main body of the army remains," said Montalembert, and the clericals made up for their defeat by urging on the new minister of public instruction against the University and College of France.   Edgar Quinet was forced to resign his professorship, at which the rage of young France knew no bounds.

Political progress was at a complete stand-still in the government of France, but commercial progress advanced daily, as was proved by the Exposition of 1844.   Justice was here rendered to Philippe de Gérard, the long-neglected inventor of flax-spinning and other useful machines of the highest importance in manufactures.   France now succeeded in making her own locomotives, and in 1845 the electric telegraph was introduced.   In 1844 a commercial treaty was concluded with China, which opened the extreme East.   The very government which refused to make any reform at home lent willing aid to important changes in the colonies, a law being prepared and presented for the abolition of slavery.

In 1845 the republicans met with a fresh loss in the death of Godfrey Cavaignac.   The hopes of his party turned upon his brother, General Eugene Cavaignac, who had not hitherto entered the political arena, but had spent his youth in Africa, where he won high renown for his services and noble character.

The legislative session closed July 21, 1846, after the rejection of various projects for reform, presented by Ledru-Rollin, Rémusat, and Crémieux.   The Left issued a manifesto in view of fresh elec-

tions. The governing powers did not, however, try the experiment
of renewing the Chambers as soon as had been expected, foreign
events affording an unhappy diversion from intestine quarrels.

Late in February, 1846, an insurrection broke out in Austrian
Poland (Galicia), and Cracow was captured by Polish patriots.
A rumor was soon circulated that all Poland shared in the movement, and that it was the uprising of 1830 on a larger scale; and as
the rumor spread, one hundred and sixty-five deputies opened a subscription for the Poles, declaring that all political divisions faded
before the common feeling of sympathy. Unhappily these brilliant
illusions were but transitory. The rebellion, led by a mere handful
of heroes, was soon stifled in the blood of its authors, and only
served to make Galicia the scene of horrors comparable alone to
those enacted in San Domingo during the negro insurrection. The
powers which had shared Poland unceasingly strove to efface
national traditions, and sow dissension between social classes. German officials were instructed to excite to the utmost the hatred of
the peasants against the noble land-owners, whom they depicted
as their oppressors, and to favor the circulation of communistic
pamphlets among them. When, therefore, a party of young nobles
and students took up arms, the Austrian government was prepared
to let loose the peasants against them. Messengers rode through
the country, crying, "The nobles are murdering your brothers!
Rise and arm!" The credulous peasantry hastened to the castles
and slew the inmates, — masters, servants, and workmen. The massacre lasted for several days and nights, a reward being given by
the Austrians for every head brought in. A certain Jacques Szela,
who had been imprisoned for infamous crimes, was freed on the eve
of these events, and far outdid the wishes of his liberators, for he
gathered a horde of ten or twelve thousand assassins about him,
and spread murder and pillage through the land. The Austrian
government negotiated on equal terms with this brigand, and, in
August, 1847, he received from Emperor Ferdinand, nephew and
successor to Francis II., the large gold medal, in reward for "his
wholly justifiable conduct in Galicia."

Public opinion held, not the Austrian emperor, but the real head of the Austrian government, responsible for this slaughter. The prime minister, Metternich, who had hitherto been only unpopular, now became execrable. When these frightful events came up for discussion in the French legislature, it was too late to save the victims, and naught remained but to brand the murderers. Guizot, however, refused to express any opinion or to utter a word of blame against "a foreign government." What had occurred did not lead Louis Philippe's government to renounce its attempts at reconciliation with Austria.

At this same time a warm discussion arose on the subject of electoral corruption. No reform was accomplished, but large sums were granted for the navy, for canals, railroads, etc. The Chambers were dissolved July 3, 1846.

The dissolution of the Chambers was preceded by an event to which little importance was attached at the time. Louis Bonaparte escaped from Ham, May 25, disguised as a mason. On reaching London he wrote to the French ambassador to England, begging him to inform his government of his "peaceful intentions." His conduct, however, had never justified any one in believing that he had renounced his ambitious dreams. He spent his time in issuing pamphlets, prepared by abler pens than his, and in forming relations with republicans and dynastic opponents. The imperial pretender seemed transformed into a democrat with socialistic tendencies. From London he kept a sharp watch on what was going on in France.

The month of July was spent in electoral excitement. Thiers drew up a letter to his electors, setting forth the situation so frankly and clearly that his friends dissuaded him from publishing it, as it would have rendered impossible any further relations with the King or any return to power. This document, which was not known until long after, is of much interest as elucidating the character and views of Thiers. It is a true political monument.

The ministerial majority was notably increased, a private combination of interests carrying the day (August 1, 1846). There was a general demand for reform, to which Guizot replied by saying that every political party promised reform, but none save the conservatives would give it. The Chambers reopened, August 19, M. Sauzet being chosen president by a vast majority against Barrot. This victory turned the heads of the cabinet. Guizot forgot his promises, and as for the King, he only laughed at them. A new and hitherto unknown deputy, destined to too much notoriety in the annals of France, M. de Morny, telling the King that if the crown would but carry out the promises of the ministry the opposition party would disappear, Louis Philippe answered, with a scornful smile, "You do not know this country."

A movement of an economic and not political character now appeared in the Chambers, resulting from an important change lately effected in England. A great industrial crisis was threatening England, and, at the entreaty of Cobden and Bright, — two active, eloquent, and popular economists, — Sir Robert Peel and the tory ministry removed the prohibition laws and introduced free trade. French economists strove to follow this example, and a Free Trade League was formed at Paris by a group of distinguished writers, — Frederic Bastiat, Adolphe Blanqui, Michel Chevalier, Wolowski, and others, — which was soon neutralized by a counter-league among the great land-owners, cattle-dealers, manufacturers, etc. Public opinion was not ripe for free trade, and the hostility to England, which had revived since 1840, did the protectionists good service, although even now France was feeling the inconveniences of the protective system. The harvest of 1845 was not good, and a potato blight increased the consequences of lack of grain. The crop for 1846 was still worse, and commerce demanded that the duties should be removed from foreign cereals. When this was finally granted, frightful floods prevented the circulation of the wheat received from Odessa. Vast speculations ensued, and the Russian government, unfriendly as it was, rendered France a service by buying her stock to the amount of fifty million francs, an operation which it found advantageous through the vast purchases by the French of Russian grain.

The winter was a hard one, and public charity was severely taxed. Starving mobs robbed wagons, boats, and storehouses of their wheat, or forced the owners to sell at a nominal price. Riots occurred, and troops of beggars scoured the land and forced the farmers to feed them. The government, having taken no precautionary measures, now resorted to severity. Troops were sent out; prisons were filled to overflowing; many were sentenced to death or hard labor for life. The state of affairs slowly improved upon better prospects for the harvest of 1847.

While France suffered thus at home, her embarrassments and troubles recommenced abroad. The question arose of the " Spanish marriages," which made so much noise at the time, and revived her differences with England with more bitterness than ever. The two nations were still rivals in Spain; England, even under a tory ministry, favored the Spanish progressionists, while France held a middle course, which was more or less reactionary. The little Queen Isabella was growing up, the time for marriage was approaching, and French and English jealousy now centred on this point. The husband of Queen Victoria, Prince Albert of Saxe-Coburg, wished her to marry one of his Coburg cousins, while the French government, through Guizot, protested against any attempt to remove the Spanish throne from the house of Bourbon (March 2, 1843). Louis Philippe informed Lord Aberdeen that he did not wish Isabella to wed one of his own sons, which would have involved France in the inextricable Spanish quarrels and embroiled her with England. What he and Guizot desired was that she should marry a Neapolitan Bourbon, and that Louis Philippe's youngest son, the Duke de Montpensier, should espouse her younger sister, thus reserving chances for the future without risking the present.

The Regent of Spain, the queen-mother Christina, had other plans. Herself a Neapolitan, she also would have preferred a Neapolitan prince, but she saw that such an alliance would be ill received in Spain. Not believing in half-way measures, she wished for her daughter either Montpensier, — that is, an intimate alliance with France, — or, if Louis Philippe refused, the Prince of Coburg,— an alliance with England.

In September, 1845, Queen Victoria and her minister of foreign affairs made a second visit to Eu, to discuss Montpensier's marriage with Isabella's younger sister. It was settled that this should not take place until Isabella was a wife and mother, and, in return, that the English government should support the claim to the queen's hand of no suitor that was not a Bourbon. The English ambassador at Madrid, however, urged Christina to make overtures to the Coburgs, and a constant succession of complaints and explanations ensued. These troubles were interrupted by a serious piece of news. The tory ministry, defeated on the Irish question, gave way to a whig ministry, headed by Lord John Russell. He intrusted the charge of foreign affairs to Lord Palmerston (June 29, 1846), who took a very different position from that of Lord Aberdeen, informing the French ambassador that there were but three possible claimants for Isabella's hand, — Prince Leopold of Coburg and two Spanish princes, the sons of her uncle Don Francisco.

Before this communication reached Paris, Palmerston met with an unexpected rebuff from Spain. Christina, who considered him her especial foe, broke off all relations with the Coburgs, and declared that since her uncle Louis Philippe would not give Montpensier to her daughter, the young queen should marry her cousin, the Duke of Cadiz, and her sister, Montpensier, but that she insisted the two marriages should be concluded on the same day. The offer was accepted, after some hesitation, and the double marriage contract was signed at Madrid, August 28, the ceremony taking place October 10. The whole blame belonged to England, which first broke faith. Palmerston, however, enlarged on the "boundless ambition" of France, and on the broken promises of the King and his ministers. Public opinion was taken captive, and Queen Victoria felt wounded and aggrieved. Many Frenchmen, also, were disposed to misinterpret every official act, and the French government, which had alienated itself from popular favor in 1840 by its concessions to England, was now embroiled with England without regaining ground in France. Louis Philippe was accused of sacrificing the English alliance to family interest, after sacrificing the national dignity to that alliance.

England was hostile, France dissatisfied; as for the continental powers, they held aloof, ready to turn the quarrel to their own advantage. The fatal consequences of the Franco-English quarrel first appeared abroad. The Czar of Russia had long desired to destroy the last vestige of Polish nationality, — the wretched little republic of Cracow. Austria and Prussia had hesitated hitherto, fearing the protests of France and England; but the Cracow insurrection of February, 1846, of which we have spoken, furnished Nicholas a fresh pretext for offering that city to Austria, to which nation it was finally delivered (November 11, 1846). It was the recompense for the Galician massacres.

Guizot felt the impossibility of preserving silence in face of this daring violation of the treaties of 1815, and proposed to Palmerston that they should act in concert. The offer was declined, and the two nations sent separate protests. Guizot's message contained a phrase which would have made a deep impression from any other source: "No power can cease to respect treaties without thereby freeing the other parties to the compact."

The legislative session of 1847 opened amidst the commotion caused by the grain riots in France, and by Spanish and Polish troubles abroad. The Crown speech announced the protest of the French government against "the breach of treaties by the incorporation of Cracow with Austria," whereupon Odilon Barrot asked explanations concerning the conclusions to be drawn from this violation of European rights. Guizot replied, that the government simply noted this infraction with a view to the future policy of France; this reservation made, it considered the treaties still good, and was resolved to observe them loyally.

Thiers then broached the subject of the Spanish marriages, censuring that of Montpensier as of little political utility, and not worth a quarrel with England. The government had not yet heard the last of this affair. Guizot defended himself ably with respect to the negotiations previous to the double marriage, but blundered as regarded his conversation with the English ambassador, Lord Normanby, hinting that he had not reported it accurately. The English cabinet instantly took part with their envoy, and the *Morning Chronicle*, Palmerston's organ, insultingly styled Guizot a " convicted impostor." The Austrian minister to Paris finally effected a reconciliation, Guizot making a semi-apology to Normanby, which must have been most painful to his pride.

Meantime, Guizot was unceasingly reminded of his promises to bring about reform, the ministerial policy, as Deputy Desmousseaux de Givré aptly expressed it, being summed up in one word: " Nothing! nothing! nothing!"

Hitherto, however, the conservative progressionists had voted with the ministry; but at the election of a vice-president of the Chambers, — to replace M. Hébert, made minister of justice, — they voted against it, and the *Press*, Émile de Girardin's journal, threatened the cabinet with fresh defeats if they admitted second-class jurors to electoral rights. On the day of the election referred to (March 22), M. Duvergier de Hauranne laid before the Chambers a new scheme for électoral reform, which produced animated and prolonged debate, but was negatived by a majority of nearly a hundred. Guizot still declared the demand for reform to be a forced and artificial one, and refused to yield to it. The fact is, that the ministers obtained this majority by privately promising to introduce another and more acceptable scheme for reform. When the King heard this he exclaimed: " Ah! my ministers made promises, did they? For my part, I promised nothing. I will never agree to reform!"

The opposition was not discouraged, and other debates ensued, one being based on the incompatibility of being both placeman and deputy. On this the majority fell from one hundred to fifty. The most harmless economic reforms, such as a uniform tax of twenty centimes on letters, etc., were, however, set aside. All this only inflamed the public the more, and proved that material reforms were essentially allied to political reforms. Corruption and disorder were rife; contractors and their employees combined to rob the state, and too often the high functionaries set to watch them shut their eyes, either from negligence or complicity. The newspapers of the period are filled with scandalous revelations in regard to official dishonesty and criminality, De Girardin, editor of the *Press*, being first and foremost in the work. He was finally summoned before the Chamber of Peers, to answer for his printed statement that a peerage had been offered for sale for eighty thousand francs. Being a deputy, the Chamber of Deputies authorized his trial by the Chamber of Peers, and, his story not having been proved false, he was acquitted, — a grave rebuke to the ministry (June, 1847).

Two ex-ministers — General Cubières, minister of war in the cabinet of March 1, and M. Teste, minister of public works in the cabinet of October 29 — were next brought to trial, the former charged with bribing others for his own interests, the latter with taking bribes. They were condemned to lose all rights of citizenship, Teste being also sentenced to three years' imprisonment (July, 1847). The effect produced on the people may be easily imagined. In the present state of the popular mind everything was turned against the government. During the summer of 1847 a lugubrious event re-echoed throughout France. A peer of France, belonging to a noble family of the old régime, the Duke de Praslin, killed his wife, a daughter of Marshal Sebastiani. This crime had no connection with politics; but, the culprit having poisoned himself to escape the scaffold, the government was accused of aiding this great lord to escape the punishment of common criminals.

The lack of respect for the ruling power was deeply rooted. Strong and intact in appearance; it was hollow to the core. People were disgusted with a rule accused on all sides of humiliating the country without and debasing it within; and, the moderate party having disappointed public hopes, men looked back to the memories of the great and terrible revolutionary epoch. As Lamartine expressed it, "France was profoundly bored." This great author had recently issued his dramatic work on the "Girondists," idealizing all the personages of the Revolution, from the Girondists to

Philippoteaux del

Gouttière sc

LOUIS-PHILIPPE

BOSTON, ESTES & LAURIAT.

Robespierre. About the same time appeared the first two volumes of Louis Blanc's "History of the Revolution," which, while it condemned terrorism, rehabilitated the political and social ideal of Robespierre and the Jacobins. Michelet then brought to light the first volumes of another history of the Revolution, for which he interrupted his "History of France previous to 1789." He was in haste, foreseeing the coming revolution. The February crisis was at hand.

The issue of the legislative session of 1847 convinced the parliamentary opposition that there was nothing to be gained from either government or legislature. The government jeered at the opposition to an indifferent and silent country, and the opposition resolved to take up the defiance hurled at them. Its first appeal to the country was made in 1832 in the Compte Rendu, to which appeal France made no reply; but fifteen years had brought about many changes, and the opposition party did not doubt that France was now ready to use her influence against the great body of privileged egotists. An alliance was made between the dynastic Left and the radicals, including all classes, from Thiers to Garnier-Pagès, Jr., Carnot, and Armand Marrast of the *National*. Their common object was to carry the most necessary reforms by a national pressure foreboding revolution. Reflective spirits,—ever among the warmest believers in a republic,—however, desired to retard rather than to hasten the downfall of the July government. They felt that the country was not prepared for universal suffrage,—the inevitable result of a republic,—and that a gradual transition was most eminently desirable. They were sincerely bent on profiting to the utmost by the charter of 1830, and leaving the completion of the work to another day, perhaps another generation.

A petition was sent about, demanding electoral reform in such general terms as might appeal to liberals of every shade; and a more direct means of stirring public sympathy was adopted in the shape of a series of public banquets, at which reform was preached. Thiers approved the plan, but took no personal part, while Odilon Barrot entered into it heart and soul.

The first of these banquets took place in Paris, July 10, at
Chateau-Rouge, in the Rue de Rochechouart, and was largely attended; one of the speakers — Count de Lasteyrie, of a liberal
family, closely allied to Lafayette — asking the grave question,
" Will the blind obstinacy of our government and of the conservative party provoke a third revolution ?"   The leader of the dynastic
opposition, Odilon Barrot, and the ex-doctrinarian, now the bitterest
foe of Guizot, M. Duvergier de Hauranne, fairly equalled republican
orators in their severe judgment of the reigning policy; but, on the
other hand, the radicals, Pagnerre, Marie, etc., setting aside the
future, kept within the same legal bounds as the constitutionalists.
The effect of this meeting was very great, and not even the journalistic invectives lavished upon it were able to destroy its influence,
which extended from city to city.   Lamartine made a speech at
Mâcon far more radical than any uttered at Chateau-Rouge.   He
predicted the downfall of royalty if the present fatal policy were
continued, and, recalling the recent scandals which made France
blush, declared that "the revolutions for liberty, and the counter-
revolutions for glory, must be followed by the revolt of the public
conscience and the revolt of shame and contempt."

Banquet followed banquet from one end of France to the other.
The ministry had been lately modified, quite unnoticed by the
public, — the nominal president of the council, Marshal Soult,
sending in his resignation, worn out and alarmed by the progress of
affairs.   The king then made Guizot president in name, as he had
long been in fact; thus replying to public opinion by a bit of bravado.   The enemies of the government hailed this nomination with
ironic glee.

Hitherto there had been perfect harmony at these banquets; but
at Lille, where M. Ledru-Rollin and Barrot were both present, the
latter was unable to carry his point and toast the king, as was
usually done as a pledge that the limits of the law should be observed.   He therefore withdrew, leaving the field to Ledru-Rollin.
This unfortunate mischance, however, did not bear the fruit expected
by the foes of reform, Ledru-Rollin being less violent than Barrot
had feared.

Meantime foreign affairs divided public interest with these domestic struggles for reform. Italy and Switzerland were the scene of events whose influence was felt in France soon after. November, 1847, witnessed the close of a prolonged contest in Switzerland, much to the chagrin of the French government, but to the delight of the general public.

Switzerland always felt the effect of every crisis in France. The French Revolution cost her the abolition of the régime which divided her into ruling and subject districts; but the Directory imposed upon her a military constitution as foreign to her natural tendencies as to her traditions. Later on, Bonaparte, then First Consul, laid his interfering finger upon her laws; and so it went on. After 1830, Switzerland began to look up again; several revolutions in the cantons resulted favorably to the democrats, who were, however, prevented from gaining due advantage by the reactionary element. Still, they were not discouraged, and strove to attain a federal republic similar to that in the United States of America, the chaos of twenty-two petty sovereignties being replaced by federal order. The task was as dangerous as it was needful. Religious quarrels complicated political quarrels, and there seemed to be a vast gulf between the Vaudois democrats, the Protestant conservatives of Geneva, the old Bernese patricians, and the ultra-Catholic mountaineers of the smaller cantons. There were the most various ideas, morals, and tongues among these populations, who spoke German, French, and Italian. Louis Philippe and his party deemed the task hopeless, but many brave and intelligent men reckoned securely on bringing out of the confusion a Swiss nation which would refuse foreign intervention.

If the French government had preserved the spirit of 1830, it would not have been thus deceived as to the truth; it would have sustained the men who represented French ideas against the champions of the past, upheld by the foe to all progress, Austrian despotism. Guizot did just the reverse, — allying himself with Austria to maintain the treaties of 1815, which guaranteed the sovereignty of the cantons, while Austria was destroying these very treaties in Poland.

The Swiss parties were grouped as follows: on one hand, the Catholics and conservative Protestants; on the other, the radicals and ardent democrats. The former had their head-centre in the convents; the latter, in the Corps Francs, an armed association. The two parties were in constant warfare: now one canton closed all convents, then another opened them; Valais revised its constitution, and absolutely forbade the exercise of Protestantism. This was a great triumph for the Jesuits, who pushed their advantage and entered Lucerne, which was at once attacked by eight thousand men of the Francs Corps, who were routed (April, 1845). Seven Catholic cantons then united in a league called "Sonderbund" (December 11, 1845), for the defence of their cantonal sovereignty. The radicals next effected a revolution at Berne, the most important canton (January, 1846), which was imitated at Geneva in October and in May. The radicals gained the majority in the elections, and avenged themselves by making the leader of the attack on Lucerne president of the Diet (May 27).

Swiss affairs were the subject of a stormy debate in the French Chamber of Deputies, June 24, 1847. As early as March, 1845, Guizot had entered into negotiations with the three absolutist powers in regard to Switzerland. Metternich and himself were alike hostile to the radicals, although he perceived the perils of armed interference. He finally protested in favor of the sovereignty of each canton, through the French ambassador; and was answered by the president of the Diet, M. Ochsenbein, that if the great powers ventured to interfere with Swiss affairs, they would meet a people ready to sacrifice their last drop of blood to defend their independence (July 5). The Diet decided to dissolve the Sonderbund, and adjourned till October 18, to consider the means of executing this decision.

At all the French political banquets, great sympathy was expressed for the Swiss, and the "treachery" of the French government towards the principles of the French Revolution was loudly denounced. Guizot meantime, unable to send French troops to the aid of the Sonderbund, sent arms, which were seized midway.

As for the English government, Guizot, sacrificing his self-love to his system, strove to gain the support of Lord Palmerston for his views in regard to Switzerland. Palmerston replied evasively, and made advances to the president, Ochsenbein, hoping to gain favor at the expense of the French government.

When the Diet met in October, they at once set in motion an army of fifty thousand men, under General Dufour, a Genevese officer of great merit, with a reserve of thirty thousand. All attempts at conciliation failed, and the representatives of the seven leagued cantons left the Diet (October 29), addressing an appeal to the three great powers, guarantees of the treaties of 1815. Dufour seized Friburg without opposition, captured Lucerne (November 24), and on the 29th, the conflict ceased. Instead of the interminable civil war predicted by Guizot, the federalist majority won a complete and final triumph after a far from bloody campaign of a fortnight.

Guizot, so fine an analyzer of past events in his great historic works, could not grasp things going on before his eyes; he saw them as he would have them, not as they were. Neither could he bow to facts; and early in 1848, two statesmen, Austrian and Prussian, were sent to Paris, to plot against Switzerland. They were sure of the support of Russia, if any blow were to be aimed at revolution; and England was to be left out of the question. The admission of Louis Philippe, the July King, to the alliance of the three absolutist powers was a great step, and a new 1823 was to result, Switzerland replacing Spain. We learn from Guizot's Memoirs that Austria was to invade Switzerland from the east, and France from the west, despite Louis Philippe's sincere aversion to armed interference.

The 24th of February was soon to sweep away these schemes with those who conceived them, alike in Austria and in France.

The federal transformation of Switzerland took but a fortnight, notwithstanding foreign threats. The enfranchisement of Italy was to cost long and painful efforts, and only to succeed at last, with outside aid, after fearful reverses and redoubled oppression. At this point of our narrative, towards the close of 1847, Italy had passed through two hopeful years, although France and her own government were still at odds.

Many and various had been the emotions of the dwellers beyond the Alps since the unfortunate attempts of 1831. While the more ardent spirits aspired, with Mazzini, to achieve Italian unity by revolution and war, many distinguished men, members of the clergy among them, tried to provoke, by peaceful means, such progress as was compatible with the existing government of Italy, if not with the foreign government, Austria. While hoping to introduce the institutions of modern civilization, they dreamed that they might win the papacy to the cause of reform and national independence.

Nothing could be done with Gregory XVI., the incarnation of reaction; but he died June 1, 1846, and the Sacred College, feeling the necessity of more liberal measures, replaced him by a very different man. Pius IX. took his seat with a desire to conciliate his subjects, and to remedy the horrible abuses with which the Holy See was environed. He marked his accession by an amnesty (July 16, 1846). Fifteen hundred exiles returned, and all Italy flamed with enthusiasm, nor was the effect less in France and throughout Europe. Even those least favorable to the papacy were touched, and Pascal's question was revived, " Shall we see a Christian pope in St. Peter's chair ? "

But the boundless hopes which he inspired were the new Pope's peril. Guizot and his ambassador at Rome, Rossi, at first gave Pius IX. most sensible advice, urging him to reform in the finance and administration. Pius IX. hesitated; with more mind than Louis XVI., he had much of his character. Some months passed unmarked by any serious reform. The Pope was coldly received in Rome (November 7). Anxious and alarmed in his turn, he hastened to fit out three commissions of reform on the very next day. But they delayed, and accomplished little; the patriot party urged and directed public outcry, and fanned the flame of opposition against Austria, accused of paralyzing the Pope's good intentions, and a project was formed for making Pius IX. head of an Italian confederation.

The Pope took fright, and his minister, Cardinal Gizzi, published a decree blaming all "desires and hopes incompatible with the lofty and peaceful character of the Vicar of Jesus Christ," etc. This was ill received. The Pope yielded again in a certain degree, announcing the establishment of a national guard and a Roman municipality. A festival was arranged for the anniversary of the amnesty (July 16, 1847), but a rumor spread that a conspiracy planned by the Austrians was to break out on that day. A national guard was eagerly improvised in Rome, to withstand the foe, the actual power being placed in the hands of this guard. Gizzi was replaced in the ministry by Cardinal Ferretti, kinsman of the Pope, and of acknowledged liberal tendencies.

The French ambassador Rossi renewed his advice to the Pope to carry out his reforms at once, and thus arrest revolution; but it was too late. The movement set on foot in the Roman States soon spread throughout Italy. Austria responded by advancing a body of troops upon the Roman frontier, driving out the national guard, and capturing Ferrara (August 10).

All Italy trembled with rage, and a loud cry of "Long live Italian independence!" was uttered. The fears of France were verified; the question, from being merely liberal, became purely national, and the papal government protested bitterly against Austrian violence. The French government blamed the publicity of the protest; but it was inevitable, for the papal government would have been lost, had it not resented Austrian aggression. Tuscany and Piedmont shared the universal enthusiasm, the Piedmontese king, Charles Albert, declaring that "his sword should be drawn in the sacred cause of Italy." In his youth he led the Piedmontese patriots against Austria, then turned against the vanquished liberals, but always retained a lurking hatred for Austria, and a spark of national ambition. October 30, 1847, he published a list of reforms, which gladdened Turin, Genoa, and all Sardinia.

The Pope, in his turn, assembled a State Council at Rome, November 15, while Louis Philippe and M. Guizot were doing their utmost to restrain the Italian governments from colliding with

Austria, thus making themselves even more unpopular in Italy.
The French government were well aware that they must defend
the Pope, if need were, against revolution, or even against Austria,
nor could they permit the invasion of Austria; but this feeling was
so cleverly disguised that every one, without exception, believed
France the unconditional ally of Austria.

Lord Palmerston took large advantage of these errors on the part
of France, both in Italy and in Switzerland. His agents covered
the land, noisily applauded all popular demonstrations, extolled
English sympathy, and even strove to kindle an insurrection in
Sicily. A distinguished English statesman, Lord Minto, was sent
to Italy by Lord Palmerston, ostensibly to study the situation, and
his presence was esteemed a pledge of English aid. Palmerston's
course was certainly more blameworthy than that of Guizot, but
this is no excuse for the latter. The French ambassador at Naples,
M. Bresson, the same who arranged the Spanish marriages, spoke
his mind so plainly on this point that the king reproached him
severely. This distressed him so greatly that he committed suicide,
which melancholy event so disturbed one of the king's sons, Prince
de Joinville, then commanding a squadron stationed on the Italian
coast, that he wrote a memorable letter to his brother, Duke de
Nemours (November 7, 1847). He said: "We are being hurried
into revolution. . . . . The king heeds no advice; his will must be
omnipotent. There is no longer a ministry; its responsibility is
null; all rests with the king, who has reached a point where he
will bear no remark: he is used to govern; he desires it to be
known that he governs; his vast experience, courage, and other fine
qualities lead him to affront danger insolently; but the danger
none the less exists. . . . . The situation of France is a fearful one,
at home and abroad. And all this is the king's single-handed
work. . . . . The worst of it is, that I see no remedy. . . . . I had
hoped that Italy might provide the cure. We can now do nothing
there, but leave the country; for if we remain, we must of necessity
make common cause with the retrograde party. . . . . To sum up the
whole: in France, a wretched financial condition; abroad, France

must choose between an apology to Palmerston in regard to Spain, or join Austria, in playing the spy in Switzerland and struggling in Italy against her own principles and her national allies: all this due to the king, the only king who has violated the constitutional institutions of France."

Thiers, Odilon Barrot, and many who had long supported the *juste milieu* against the dynastic opposition, shared the prince's fears, which also alarmed the queen, unwonted to meddle with politics; and she begged De Montalivet, the most zealous friend of the Orleans family, to explain the true state of public opinion to the king. Louis Philippe refused to listen to him, to Marshal Gérard, or to old Marshal Sebastiani, so cruelly wounded by the murder of his daughter, the luckless Duchess de Praslin, and yet stifling his personal grief to enlighten his king. Nor had the king's sister, Madame Adelaide, a woman of much sense, better success. She died during the winter (December 31), and her death was taken by the royal family as an evil omen, although the government of Louis Philippe gained an important victory in Algiers soon after.

The Emperor of Morocco had never carried out his treaty in regard to expelling Abd-el-Kader from his states, not from ill-will, but from impotence. Abd-el-Kader, sustained by the fanaticism of the native tribes, roamed about the borders of Algeria and Morocco with a band of followers, continually preaching the "Holy War," and threatening to destroy the Mohammedan monarch who made peace with Christians and "infidels." During 1845 he managed to stir up various insurrections, two episodes of the campaign retaining a melancholy fame, — the incident of the Dahra Grottos and that of the Column Montagnac. A tribe of mountaineers were accustomed to take refuge in an impenetrable cave, whence they harassed the passing French troops, who could not lay a finger on them. Colonel Pélissier, commanding a French corps, having vainly ordered them to surrender, piled fagots at the entrance of the cave, and set fire to them. The flames were once extinguished, in the hope that the natives would yield, but they again fired on the troops and such of their own number as strove to escape.   The fire was rekindled,·and eight hundred wretched beings perished, victims of their fanatic courage; the soldiers were overwhelmed with horror on entering the cavern, and finding all these calcined corpses, women and children among them (June, 1845).

The other affair, which occurred a few months later (November, 1845), was the total destruction of a small column of French troops, under Lieutenant-Colonel Montagnac, by a body of Arabs and Kabyles led by Abd-el-Kader himself.   Nearly three hundred French were killed or captured after stout resistance, the prisoners being, with few exceptions, strangled, not by Abd-el-Kader's order, but in spite of it, he being quite incapable of so savage an act.

These Arab revolts only drew down fearful evils on the rebel tribes.   Abd-el-Kader was driven from point to point, and finally hemmed in by General Lamoricière, to whom he surrendered on condition of being taken to Egypt or Syria.   He was taken before the governor-general (December 23, 1847).   Marshal Bugeaud had been replaced in this office by the Duke d'Aumale, son of Louis Philippe; and this young prince agreed to Abd-el-Kader's terms, which the royal government, however, refused to grant, and held him captive in France for some years, when, another government coming into power, he was allowed to retire to Syria, where his dignified attitude and lofty character won him universal respect.

The capture of Abd-el-Kader preceded the fall of Louis Philippe, as the taking of Algiers came before the ruin of Charles X.   Checks in France coincided with this foreign triumph.   The government was defeated in various elections; the political banquets were renewed with fresh energy; and the Chambers opened, December 28, 1847, amid these threatening auspices.   It was to be the last legislative session of the July government.

THE INVALIDES.

CHAPTER VII.

CONSTITUTIONAL MONARCHY OF JULY (*close*).—FEBRUARY REVOLUTION.

December 28, 1847, to February 24, 1848.

WHEN the legislative session opened, the king was greeted with cold silence. He pronounced his speech in a voice less firm than usual, but his words were imprudently irritating. He declared that one thought supported and cheered him on amid the distress bred by blind and hostile passions, namely, the fact that the constitutional monarchy and the unity of the great powers of the state provided the most secure means for crushing every obstacle. This was the only portion of the speech which lingered in the memory of men. " Hostile passions " referred to the republicans; " blind passions " to the dynastic opposition.

Stocks went down, and it was very evident that some unusual event was close at hand. The ministry seemed to strive to increase the public displeasure. The lectures of Edgar Quinet, Mickiewicz, and Michelet were cut short by official order, and the students marched in a body to the Chamber of Deputies to demand freedom for the higher education; thence they proceeded to the offices of the republican newspapers, thus inaugurating the stormy year 1848 (January 3).

The discussion of the address to the crown opened under very unpleasant circumstances for the ministry. M. Guizot was suspected, undoubtedly correctly, of permitting the bribing of members of the Court of Accounts to resign, that their places might be used to reward parliamentary services. It is sad to see a statesman of lofty intellect and undoubted personal probity brought to believe corruption the necessary tool of a constitutional government. Guizot made but a feeble defence before the House of Lords; and one young peer, D'Alton-Shée, hurled a republican speech in the teeth of the astounded assembly, while De Montalembert, who had hitherto mixed liberalism with Catholicism, reproached the government for failing to uphold the Sonderbund in Switzerland, and inveighed against radicalism, the Revolution, and all the institutions of the nineteenth century. The House applauded, but nevertheless introduced into the ministerial address congratulations to the Italian princes who had granted their people reforms.

The discussion had a very different result in the House of Deputies, where it was opened January 17. Odilon Barrot delivered a scorching invective upon Guizot, who vainly wore a mask of indifference, pleaded old custom, and finally made a desperate appeal to his majority, who gave him a vote of confidence, which, far from saving him, only involved the Chamber in his downfall.

Thiers made a grand speech upon the financial question, proving the state expenses to be enormous, and the debt constantly increasing. He only exposed the material dangers of the situation; but a man of genius and penetration, hitherto known as a writer, not an orator, De Tocqueville, described its moral dangers. He had won laurels by one of the greatest works of political economy in the French language, "Democracy in America." Removed from democracy by birth, his study of facts, his reason and reflection, had led him to adopt it; thus setting an example which Thiers was one day to follow with rare renown and incalculable results.

M. de Lamartine next attacked the subject of foreign affairs. Thiers spoke like a statesman, De Tocqueville like a philosopher, and Lamartine like an inspired tribune. "Through you," he cried to the ministers, "France, contrary to her nature, contrary to the law of centuries and of tradition, became Austrian at Rome, sacerdotal at Berne, Austrian again in Piedmont, Russian at Cracow, French nowhere, counter-revolutionary everywhere!"

Guizot replied by vaunting the moderation of Austria, — Austria, even then invading the duchies of Parma and Modena, and bathing in Italian blood, her hands yet red with the blood of Poland, while Sicily burst into insurrection to the cry of "Long live the Constitution!" and the troops of the Neapolitan king bombarded Palermo.

Thiers replied to Guizot next day in terms far more excessive than those of Lamartine.

"The acts of Austria," he said, "seem those of an executioner, not a king. . . . . The men slain in Italy are noble imitators of those revolutionists who took the Bastille in 1789, and overthrew in 1830 a government which violated the laws. . . . . It is said that France has moved the world for fifty years, ... for more than three hundred years! Yes, Frenchmen were those great criminals who proclaimed the freedom of thought with Descartes, ecclesiastical independence with Bossuet, and who restored the rights of humanity with Montesquieu and Voltaire. I own it with a glow of pride! . . . . It is, therefore, in imitation of France that Italy now demands reform from princes of liberal mind, and rises in revolt against execrable tyrants!"

Such words from such lips profoundly stirred the whole assembly. He continued in the same vein, was supported by Thiers and Barrot, who further insisted that if Austria renewed the attack on Ferrara, in the Roman States, France must perforce intervene with armed force.

Guizot was silenced.

The debate on the Swiss question was even more fatal for the ministry, their conduct in this affair having been yet more base. Thiers, who advanced daily, made a brilliant speech, avowing himself a revolutionist, though not a radical, and was greeted with thunders of applause. Thiers kept his solemn promise never to forsake the cause of revolution, if not in the troubled period which ensued, at least in the last and most glorious part of his career, that by which history will judge him.

This discussion was alike the most impassioned and the most impressive which had stirred France since the beginning of the July government. Just at this time a political banquet was forbidden by the police, M. Duchâtel, the minister of the interior, insisting that the government, having suffered for its tolerance in this matter, was justified in forbidding any assembly where entrance money was taken. "If you think," he cried, "that the government will yield to any manifestations whatever, you are vastly mistaken!"

"You talk like Charles X.!" cried the Left, while the Centre applauded the minister. Hébert, Keeper of the Seals, then set forth and eagerly maintained the strange theory that all which is not expressly permitted is forbidden; there are no rights save those written in the Charter. "Not even the right to breathe!" shouted some one. "They go beyond the Restoration!" exclaimed Barrot; "Polignac and Peyronnet never used such terms!" The entire opposition rose, glaring menacingly at the ministerial bench; the Centre responded to the Left by furious clamor. President Sauzet disappeared, and the deputies separated noisily (February 9).

No such scene had been seen in the Assembly since 1830, and the impression was tremendous throughout Paris. The more intelligent conservatives were terrified, and urged the ministers to make terms; but Guizot was immovably obstinate. No reconciliation was possible between the two sides of the Assembly, but some progressive conservatives still strove to unite the government and the country. Guizot refused to make any concession for the present, or any promise for the future, insisting that he would resign rather than yield.

When the vote was taken, the opposition carried the day, and there was no address to the crown. But it is very doubtful whether this extraordinary hiatus opened the king's eyes. He had recently received very ill a sort of petition for reform presented by certain progressive conservative deputies, and on their departure trampled the paper under foot in senile rage.

The February crisis was at hand, had burst upon France in very truth; and the incident destined to be the direct cause of the catastrophe had already stirred the popular mind for a month. We alluded just now to a political banquet which was interdicted by the police. Since the stormy argument held on the subject, the question had remained in litigation.

January 14, the police prefect forbade the banquet planned for the 19th, and a large number of eminent lawyers, consulted by the committee, declared this prohibition illegal. Émile de Girardin wrote to Odilon Barrot, February 8, urging him to resign if the obnoxious law were passed, telling him that the whole opposition party would follow suit. On the other hand, he invited the ministry, through the public press, to propose a law to the Chambers which should set at rest all doubt on the point of the legality of these meetings.

The ministry scorned the advice. Armand Marrast proposed that the whole Left should resign, and that their journals, the large majority of the press, should put the Chambers under a veto, and replace the reports of their sessions by those of the electoral meetings; but this proposition was finally set aside. It is worthy of note that two of the republican leaders suggested most peaceful means, while the greater part of the dynastic opposition persisted in a course which led to strife. Thiers, however, their greatest statesman, was for peace, but he was unheeded. Girardin persevered, and sent in his solitary resignation.

February 14, it was announced that a committee of deputies was to arrange, in concert with the central committee of the Parisian electors, a banquet to be given as a protest against tyranny. All Paris was in a ferment, and business was quite suspended.

The king and his first minister were equally blind. "Reform," said Louis Philippe, "is war; it is the beginning of the end! As soon as the opposition takes the reins of government, I shall take my leave!" But he did not dream that such an event could come to pass; never doubting that armed force would easily scatter any assembly.

Meantime Marrast declared to the ministry, in the *National*, that if they wanted a riot they would not get it, but instead an immense and peaceful manifestation, whose very calm would make them tremble. To avoid any occasion for conflict, Tuesday, February

22, was fixed for the banquet, instead of Sunday or Monday, days when the masses are most active; and it was decided that it should be held, not in the twelfth district, at the mouth of the crowded faubourgs St. Jacques and St. Marceau, but in the deserted street leading to Versailles, near the Arc de Triomphe de l'Étoile.

At this news the progressive conservatives made a vain attempt to persuade the opposition to give up the banquet. Lamartine angrily replied: "We stand between shame and danger. . . . . Shall we place the neck of France beneath the feet of the ministry? Never! We should be less than men!" The committee issued a request that Paris would, by her calmness and firmness on the 22d, give the strongest of all proofs of the progress of political morality.

The alarm felt by the conservative body now spread to the ministry, and even Guizot ceased to oppose the universal desire that the quarrel should be referred to the law. It was agreed that the deputies of the opposition should enter the banquet-hall, despite the warning to be given by a police agent; that the latter should testify to this violation of the law, and summon the meeting to disperse. M. Odilon Barrot would then protest, and declare that they only desired the question to be tried by the courts, and beg the assembly to yield to force, reserving their rights. The question would thus be brought before the Court of Appeal (February 19).

The storm seemed averted, this expedient being acceptable to all; but an unforeseen event destroyed this prospect of a legal and peaceful solution. On the morning of the 21st, the opposition journals published the programme of the "reform manifesto," drawn up by Marrast in the name of the sub-committee charged with the preservation of order. It gave the marching order of the procession which was to form in the Place de la Madeleine, and also a list of subscribers, among whom were the national guards, who were begged to form in a particular manner, to preserve order and prevent any outbreak.

This publication startled the public, surprised and alarmed the

constitutional opposition, and caused a violent reaction among the
conservative party. The government had been warned of a vast
demonstration, but were not prepared for this kind of order for
the day issued to the national guard, who were not to be armed,
it is true, but would be in uniform and in a body. The ministry
would have dreaded a vast outbreak less than this concourse of
one hundred thousand men meeting and parting in perfect order
at a word from the opposition.

Louis Philippe and Guizot had consented with reluctance to an
attempt at a compromise, the king declaring that he would not do
as the elder branch had done. "I will not be taken by surprise,
not I!" he said; "I will not commit the mistakes of Charles X.;
I will take wiser precautions and defend myself better!" King
and ministry seized this occasion for rupture. MM. de Morny and
Vitel were sent to Barrot to withdraw the promise given; and
although De Morny protested, neither the king nor Guizot would
listen, — the minister, because he was resolved on civil war; the
king, because he had no faith in civil war.

On the eve of the day fixed for the banquet, Barrot interviewed
the ministry in regard to the withdrawal of the agreement made
between the government and the opposition. Duchâtel replied
that the ministry had never agreed to allow any processions or
assemblies in the public streets. The opposition then retired to
consider their course. If the banquet were given, a collision was
inevitable on the Place de la Madeleine, and yet they could not
consent to suppress the great manifestation which Paris had prepared, and to which reformers from every department were flocking.
They must therefore give up the banquet altogether. The committee and the press representatives were indignant, but were finally
appeased by a promise that the ministry should be impeached. A
deputation was sent from the schools to reproach Barrot with what
the young men called "a desertion to the enemy"; but, the first
explosion over, the various political groups recoiled from the vast
responsibility of a conflict. The representatives of the most fiery
republican party met at the office of the *Reform*, where Ledru-

Rollin and Louis Blanc argued with all who urged insurrection. In face of the force at governmental disposal, victory seemed impossible.

The opposition felt very gloomy, as after a mortifying retreat. At the Tuileries all exulted; the king constantly repeated, "I knew it! I knew it!" But at the office of the *Siècle* an event occurred to change the general feeling. It was announced that the government had summoned the national guard to appear next morning. Cries of joy went forth. All seemed right again. "Here is our manifestation!" they exclaimed; "here we have it, and in the best form!"

The ministry had indeed intended to hold Paris next day with the troops of the line and the national guard; but when it was known that the banquet was given up, this plan seemed useless, the imprudence of giving the opposition a chance for a demonstration was perceived, and a counter-order was sent to the troops. The leaders of the opposition also issued counter-orders for the movement, as far as their influence went, but it was too late!

During the first years of Louis Philippe's reign, the national guard, the middle class, repressed republican movements by force of arms, and the popular masses did not aid them. Now the national guard was opposed to the reigning power; and the masses, which all parties had hitherto failed to stir, acted for themselves. They had prepared for a grand manifestation; they meant to carry it out.

The movement began with the youth of the middle classes. The students met, as originally proposed, on the morning of the 22d, on the Place de la Panthéon, regardless of their deputies, who strove to restrain them, but who were carried along with them, singing the Marseillaise. Three thousand strong, mixed with laborers, they marched to the Chamber of Deputies, shouting, "Long live reform! Down with Guizot!" No precautions had been taken. The gates of the Palais-Bourbon were scaled, but, the Chamber not being in session, the aimless invaders retired before the troops which hastened to the spot; still this beginning showed the current of events.

THE SURPRISE OF FIESCHI.

The king watched the tumult from the Tuileries. Soon shouts were heard close by, and the gates were closed. Louis Philippe kept his imperturbable calm, and said that he would drive them all like dust before the wind.

The crowd increased; quarrels occurred between the people and the municipal guards. Showers of stones were hurled at the latter, and barricades were started in the Rue de Rivoli, almost under the king's windows, then in the Rue St. Honoré, and near the markets.

In the afternoon, Barrot came to the Chamber to deliver the articles of impeachment against the ministry, and President Sauzet closed the meeting before a word could be uttered concerning the condition of Paris.

The movement spread rapidly. Paving-stones were torn up and the armories pillaged. There was nothing of the suddenness or precision of a preconcerted insurrection; but to a careful observer it was all the more formidable. No signal had been given, yet everybody rose.

Means of defence were not lacking. The government had triple the force that Charles X. had; more than thirty thousand soldiers, reinforcements hard by, artillery, and a long-considered plan of Marshal Gérard for the occupation of Paris in case of trouble; and finally, as a last resource, those detached fortresses, which had caused so much discussion, and which girt the capital as with a belt of iron.

But who was to use all these instruments of warfare, and how were they to be handled? The troops of the line were led by General Tiburce Sebastiani, brother of the marshal; the national guard by General Jacqueminot, father-in-law of Duchâtel, — both brave soldiers; but the former was timid, and the latter, though bold, did not understand the spirit of his men. The king had placed over them the future regent, Duke de Nemours, but without titulary command, rather as an umpire than a chief. Cold, reserved, and uncertain, he had certain valuable qualities, but lacked just those which were indispensable under existing circumstances.

It was but too plain that supreme power was trembling in the grasp of a veteran, who spent his feeble strength in words; the King of June, 1832, no longer lived.

The day was spent in hesitation and half-measures, and towards five o'clock it was agreed to summon the national guard. Had they been called the night before, as first proposed, the men would have appeared at dawn to shout for reform. Now that they were wanted to put down revolt, they refused to stir, but very few answering the summons.

The importance of the situation increased; by nightfall several barriers were set on fire; the first shots were exchanged, and the first blood shed in an attack near the barrier Monceaux. At one in the morning the handful of the national guard which had assembled, was dismissed, and at three the troops were ordered to their barracks, as the barricades were not strenuously. defended.

The king and ministry felt themselves masters of the situation. During the evening the queen questioned the officer of the national guard on duty at the palace, and was told that the men would not fight against the people, and that it would be advisable to change the ministry that very night; but the king treated the advice with scorn.

No sooner had the soldiers begun to take a little rest than they were again called out. Revolt was renewed at dawn; no sooner did the troops open a passage through the narrow, crooked streets of the heart of Paris than barricades sprang up behind them.

After long hesitation a fresh appeal was made to the national guard, — a doubtful attempt, which turned against its authors. The reformers among the guards assembled, while those who took part with the government stayed at home. The men sang the Marseillaise as they marched, and shouted for reform beneath the very windows of the king; farther on, they protected a body of workmen against the municipal guard, and drove the latter back to their quarters.

Similar incidents occurred on every hand. Five hundred men of the Fourth Legion, headed by a number of officers, carried to the

Chambers a petition for the impeachment of the ministry. Their road was blocked on the Bridge de la Concorde by a conservative battalion, and a conflict was imminent, when some deputies of the Left interposed, and took charge of the petition. In various quarters the troops shielded the people from the municipal guard and the cavalry legion, the most aristocratic and monarchic of the national guard, and begged their colonel, M. de Montalivet, to warn the king of the impossibility of saving the monarchy unless speedy concessions were made.

The issue of the crisis might yet be reform, and not revolution; but there was not an hour to be lost.

The king at last opened his eyes: the defection of the national guard, so easily foreseen, and yet to him so startling, struck like a thunderbolt; but his present sense of danger lent him no spark of manly decision. He could not see that he must either yield at once or fight to the death. He clung to a vain hope, and hoped to escape by substituting one minister of his own choosing for another. Hard pressed by his queen, whose feminine and maternal heart showed her the extent and imminence of the peril, he held a prolonged council with Guizot and Duchâtel, and expressed his "bitter regret" at parting with them; "necessity and the safety of the monarchy," he said, "required the sacrifice;" and he informed them of his intention to intrust the ministry to M. Molé, which intention was instantly communicated to the Chamber by M. Molé.

The Centre was struck with rage and consternation, while there was a lively feeling of joy among the people and the army when they learned that Guizot was no longer minister, and that citizens and soldiers would no longer be exposed to mutual murder; some even cried, "Long live the King!" But the name of Molé soon chilled this ardor among politicians, who queried whether Louis Philippe were making a mock of the country. The most ardent republicans and the remnants of secret societies resolved to do their utmost to carry out and complete the revolution. The struggle was generally suspended, but the situation remained insecure.

From the point of view of order and the government, there were
two measures to be taken instantly, — to dismiss the troops, and
proclaim a change of ministry, with serious reform. Neither was
adopted. To tell the truth, there was no longer a government.
The retiring ministry did nothing, and the king thought it prudent
not to bind himself by public promises.

Molé advised the king to call upon Thiers and Barrot, and, after
long resistance, obtained permission to form a cabinet with Thiers.
At a time when moments were so precious, hours were lost in
delay. Molé and Thiers could come to no understanding, the latter
demanding parliamentary reform, electoral reform, and the dissolution of the Chambers, the last of which Molé knew that the king
would never grant.

At this very instant matters were growing suddenly and fearfully
worse. During the evening the aspect of Paris was strange, but
not alarming. A nervous excitement seized upon the masses, who
crowded the streets; an impromptu illumination made the city as
light as day. Public offices and the ministerial dwellings were
lighted willy-nilly; the crowd fed the hungry troops, and every
sign of civil war disappeared, only a handful of obstinate and
irreconcilable spirits still lurking in corners and byways, whom the
proclamation of a ministry from the Left would have inevitably
silenced; even then the mob were cheering Barrot and Thiers
beneath their windows.

A torchlight procession passing near the ministry of foreign
affairs was stopped by an infantry detachment guarding the
mansion, which had been threatened during the last few days.
Neither party felt any hostile intentions, but the crowd swayed
forward, and officers of the national guard urged the commander
of the infantry to open his ranks and let the people pass; he
replied that he had his orders, and that it was impossible. Meantime, the ever-increasing throng pressed forward, and the first line
of the soldiers gave way before them. A shot was fired, although
not by order, some say by an unlucky chance; according to a
recently published account, a sergeant fired, contrary to his cap-

tain's order, upon a man who was flourishing a torch, and threatening the lieutenant-colonel with it.

It was like a match set to a train of powder. Shots were fired, unordered, on every hand. A hundred men fell dead or wounded. The crowd fled with cries of fright and fury. The soldiers, terrified at their own deed, also disbanded and fled.

This unfortunate accident entailed incalculable consequences. The maddened mob took it as a crime, a trap, a treason; the corpses were lifted, placed upon a cart, and borne through the streets with shouts of "Vengeance!" Some hurried to the churches, and from eleven till midnight peal after peal of the alarm bell cast a gloom over Paris, and predicted a dread to-morrow.

During this melancholy night ministerial negotiations were continued slowly and confusedly, with neither candor nor haste. Nothing could determine the king to take a decided stand. He summoned to the Tuileries, on the one hand, Thiers, the representative of compromise, and, on the other, Marshal Bugeaud, representative of resistance; at the same time he recalled Guizot and Duchâtel, seeking their advice. Bugeaud accepted the command-in-chief, and addressed his staff, boasting that he had never been beaten on such an occasion, and that he would soon put an end to the revolutionists.

Thiers arrived at two in the morning; the king, with ill grace, granted the very moderate electoral reform, and permitted Barrot to join Thiers in the cabinet, but persisted in refusing to dissolve the Chambers; and Thiers left to seek his colleagues, unsatisfied on this main point, and disturbed at the choice of Bugeaud, whom he knew to be most unpopular.

Bugeaud set to work to restore some semblance of unity to the troops, and planned to announce the Thiers-Barrot ministry to calm such of the citizens as could be won over, and then boldly to attack the rest. This plan would have succeeded the day before, but would it answer next day? It was not a question of days, but of hours now.

The people, on their side, were hard at work. More than fifteen hundred barricades were erected with rare skill, many being regular fortresses, some reaching to the second-story windows, the principal ones being cannon proof. Bullets were cast, cartridges made, and the attitude of the national guard inspired perfect confidence. Nevertheless, neither masses nor politicians were yet irrevocably bent on revolution. On the morning of the day destined to such fame, February 24, the *National* named terms of peace, and the *Reform* admitted that, by the use of certain measures not involving governmental ruin, order might be speedily restored. No question had yet arisen of forfeiture or of republic.

The news of Bugeaud's nomination greatly excited the mob and discouraged the friends of compromise. He was hated less for his reactionary and aggravating conduct in the legislature than for a crime of which he was innocent, the massacre of Rue Transnonain.

Thiers more conscientiously than confidently labored at the reconstruction of the cabinet, going to the house of Barrot with two chosen colleagues, De Rémusat and Duvergier de Hauranne. Barrot cried out against the choice of Bugeaud and the royal refusal to dissolve the Chamber, and only accepted office conditionally upon seeing the king, nor did Thiers intend to accept unless on certain terms. They would fain have sought the Tuileries at once, but the king, feeling the need of rest, had fixed their meeting for eight, next morning, and so the rest of the night was lost in efforts to complete this problematic ministry.

Armand Marrast notified Thiers that the king must abdicate before noon. This message was not taken with sufficient gravity. It showed that the republicans might still accept a regency.

Thiers, Barrot, and their chosen colleagues set out for the Tuileries, and were nowhere allowed to pass without giving their names and errand. "You are being deceived!" was the universal cry. "Louis Philippe has combined with Bugeaud to slaughter us!" The eventual ministers reached the Tuileries by half past eight, and the king persisted in his refusal to dissolve the Chambers. Logically there was nothing to be done but to decline office and withdraw. But Thiers and his friends could not make up their minds to yield and let the catastrophe come without straining every nerve to prevent it. The king begged them to appease the people, and everything could be settled afterwards.

Settled! and how? Still equivocating, at a moment when the greatest frankness and most stringent promises might be too late!

With more generosity than prudence, Barrot undertook to harangue the people, and forced Thiers, who would have followed, to remain with Bugeaud, who had been busy, as aforesaid, with perfecting his plans. Troops had been sent in various directions, but, their destinations once reached, they found their communications cut off, and themselves in the position of garrisons in a besieged city; barricades rose around them; the barracks of the municipal guard were attacked, and they were obliged to surrender; the national guard joined the people, and were joined in turn by the students from the Polytechnic School, despite the master's orders. Thus the marshal's plan was an utter failure! His courage fell before the evil tidings which poured in on every hand. Struck by the vivid picture painted him of the situation, he ordered the firing to cease, and wrote to General Bedeau: "Utter conciliating words, and fall back on the Carrousel."

General Bedeau, an excellent officer, has since been most unjustly accused. If, instead of pausing, he had forced his way to the Place de la Bastille, he would have found it deserted, and would speedily have been blocked and reduced to impotence like the rest.

Thiers now returned to make a last plea with the king, and, the Duke de Nemours adding his entreaties, Louis Philippe finally agreed to let his ministers announce the dissolution, providing his name were omitted, — a puerility, whether urged by obstinacy or reserve. The proclamation was hastily drawn up; it is dated ten A. M. But there was no printing-press at hand, they were forced to carry it to the newspaper offices, and before it was issued, far other things than dissolution were to be considered.

While Thiers talked to the king, Barrot talked to the people. His attempt to sway the vast population of Paris by his eloquence was a heroic feat, but an impossible one.   He was listened to, as he went from point to point, and received with cheers, but these cheers were mingled with cries of " Down with Bugeaud!" and occasionally even " Down with Thiers!"   Thiers had supported the *juste milieu* too long not to be suspected and disliked by ardent republicans. As he advanced, some shouted: "We know you, Barrot! you are a brave man, you defend the people; but they are cheating you, as they did in 1830!"   Then came shouts of "Down with Louis Philippe!" and when Barrot and his friends reached the St. Denis gate, they beheld a regular fortification barring the way, crowned with red flags, — a dreadful omen!   In place of the banner of 1789, the banner of the French Revolution, behold the banner of an anonymous revolution.

"Those who held this barricade," says Barrot in his Memoirs, "only replied by their deathlike silence to the cheers of the mob, which surrounded me."

He was forced to retrace his steps, with anxious heart and exhausted body.   The crowd continued to show sympathy for him, but cries of "Down with Louis Philippe!" and "Down with Thiers!" increased, mingled with a yet louder yell: "To the Tuileries! to the Tuileries!"

Barrot saw that if he returned to the Tuileries escorted by this mob, it would enter with him and at least force the king to abdicate.   He therefore turned aside to his own house in the Rue de la Ferme des Mathurins.

The experiment was complete.   Thiers, Barrot, Bugeaud, — the statesman, orator, and soldier, — all three summoned too late, were alike impotent.   The king had let slip, one by one, every chance of safety without trying one betimes.

The army continued to fall apart, amid countless minor events into which history cannot enter.   There was nothing like the great struggles of July, 1830, and June, 1832.   Scattered engagements reaped a few victims, the soldiers fighting now on one side, now on the other.   Amid all these disorderly scenes the drama still preserved its unity and advanced to its conclusion.   Revolution progressed hour by hour, moment by moment, now holding possession of the people's palace, the Hôtel de Ville, and threatening the royal palace.

A number of politicians, republicans, and dynastic oppositionists assembled at the house of Barrot, on his return from his dangerous excursion. Garnier-Pagès, Pagnerre, and their friends declared that the king must abdicate; Barrot and the dynastics protested. Although no conclusion was reached, the former went with Barrot to the ministry of the interior, of which they took precarious possession. Duchâtel and Guizot had just escaped, the latter in feminine disguise, to escape attack,—a strange and mournful close for the cabinet which had ruled France for seven years and more.

Once at the ministry of the interior, Barrot was obliged to own that those who demanded abdication were right, and he begged Dupin to explain the painful necessity to the king.

The gunshots on the Place de la Concorde caused terror in the Tuileries, and when order was restored, it was felt to be but a brief respite. Thiers proposed to retire to St. Cloud, and reconstruct an army to re-enter Paris. Bugeaud approved, but the king would come to no decision. Four thousand men, sixteen cannon, and several detachments of national guards still lingered on the Carrousel, and to assure himself of their sentiments, Louis Philippe mounted his horse and rode out. Scattering cries of "Long live the king!" were drowned by eager shouts for "Reform!" "You have reform!" exclaimed the king with an effort; but there was no response. The king turned bridle, saying to Thiers, "I see it clearly, all is over!"

When he returned to his cabinet, and "rather fell into than seated himself in a chair," to use the expression of Garnier-Pagès, the conversation turned on abdication and a regency. "Let Helen [Duchess d'Orléans] be regent!" said the Duke de Nemours, renouncing his rights, to grasp at the chance for the preservation of the dynasty. But no one could deny that the chance was very slight. De Nemours respectfully and timidly pronounced the fatal word to the king, who hesitated, but, soon animated by the queen, declared that he would hold his crown dear as his life! At the entreaty of M. Crémieux, a deputy from the Left, who brought information and sincere advice, he agreed to make Barrot president of the council, Thiers no longer being feasible.

At this instant a sharp discharge of musketry was heard. There was a reservoir on the Place du Palais-Royal, used as a guard-house and occupied by two detachments of municipal guards and infantry. An unlucky chance, of which there were so many during this period, prevented the guard from being punctually relieved; they remained alone in the midst of the throng, and a few shots, perhaps accidentally fired, caused a desperate struggle between them and the people. Generals Lamoricière and Perrot, and others equally daring and humane, risked their lives to close the mad carnage; but neither side would listen, and the conflict lasted two hours. The armed mob growing ever more frantic, every hope of compromise died.

M. Crémieux's success in gaining Barrot the presidency no longer availed. Émile de Girardin, hurrying to the Tuileries, begged the king to abdicate and announce the Duchess d'Orléans as regent. The king's youngest son, Duke de Montpensier, warmly supported this entreaty. Louis Philippe, after a pause, uttered these words: "I have always been a peace-loving prince, — I abdicate!"

Louis Philippe, nevertheless, long delayed signing his surrender. The queen and his daughters protested, sobbed, and embraced the unhappy king; the queen, carried away by grief and by the very extent of the danger, exclaimed that death were preferable to abdication! She and her daughters accused every one of treason, especially the Duchess d'Orléans, who was quite unconscious of the use made of her name.

The king asked the generals present whether it would be possible to defend the Tuileries. The majority said, "No!" The Duke de Montpensier laid a paper before the king, and with feverish impatience urged him to sign. Louis Philippe opened wide his arms, said in a hollow voice, "Well, if it must be so!" and wrote slowly, "I resign the crown which the voice of the people called me to assume, in favor of my grandson, Count de Paris. May he succeed in the great undertaking which devolves on him this day!"

"It was quarter past twelve. At ten, Louis Philippe still declared that he would never agree to dissolve the Chambers; at eleven, he exclaimed that his life should be the price of his abdication; at twelve, he no longer reigned!" (Garnier-Pagès.)

The greater part of the crowd that thronged the Tuileries — generals, officers, deputies, and courtiers — left, heedless alike of fallen king, heir, or mother of the child to whom his grandfather had bequeathed a broken crown. Thiers and Bugeaud remained. The Duke de Nemours recalled the troops from the Carrousel to the courtyard of the Tuileries, and ordered the gates to be closed. The struggle at the reservoir continued, shots were fired on the Carrousel, and M. Crémieux rushed in, breathless, to tell the king that the mob was on the point of attacking the Tuileries.

Louis Philippe changed his uniform for citizen's dress, and left the Tuileries by a back entrance, with the queen and royal family, minus the Duchess d'Orléans, her children, and the Duke de Nemours, who remained to protect his sister-in-law. The sad procession crossed the deserted garden, whose gates were still guarded by a few soldiers, and went out, the Duke de Montpensier crying to the guards, "We sacrifice ourselves to prevent bloodshed!"

The court carriages, which had been ordered, were stopped by the crowd on the Carrousel, and nothing could be found but three wretched one-horse vehicles, into which the king, queen, part of the royal family, and a few of the household were crowded; two of the princesses, who were left behind, sought shelter with friends. The troops on the Place de la Concorde looked on with surprise. The carriages set off, escorted by a body of cavalry, and proceeded to St. Cloud, — Louis Philippe leaving Paris, never to return.

He had always declared that he would not do as Charles X. had done, and now his end was far worse! Monarchy grew baser and more base. Louis XVI. closed his life with one of the greatest tragedies known to history. Charles X. preserved a certain dignity on his road to exile; but Louis Philippe slunk from the palace of kings, stripping off the insignia of his rank, and soon put on the robes of deceit, and fled from France. He did not lack personal courage, but he lost all resolution and strength of mind when he saw the fragile basis of his power crumbling beneath him. He uttered a remarkable saying in his exile: "There is no possibility of attack or defence in the case of moral insurrection. It is said that I issued an order forbidding a shot to be fired. It is false. But such an order was unnecessary; it was in the air!"

Thiers and Bugeaud did not leave the Tuileries until after the king was gone. "All is lost!" said Thiers, and he went home without stopping at the Chambers, convinced that nothing more could be done for the dynasty or for constitutional monarchy.

The Duchess d'Orléans also left by the garden, with her two boys, a few friends and followers, scarcely knowing whither she went. The Duke de Nemours protected her retreat with a body of infantry.

The gates of the Tuileries were now opened; the mob rushed in; one man took his seat upon the throne, and gravely saluted the crowd, amid roars of laughter; then the throne was removed, hoisted into a cart, and burned on the Place de la Bastille.

Meantime another band discovered three hundred municipal guards who had taken refuge in a pavilion near the gallery of the Louvre. Their uniforms were removed, blouses substituted, and they were set free, instead of being killed, as they expected. The 24th of February was far removed from August 10 and its bloody vengeances. The contestants from the reservoir next poured into the Tuileries, having won a victory by firing the building, and the soldiers, suffocated by smoke, surrendered. They broke and tore busts and portraits of the king, and every token of royalty; but no one thought of following Louis Philippe. He was forgotten, and the mob marched to the Chambers to proclaim a republic. Those left behind, drunk with wine from the palace vaults, tricked themselves out from the royal wardrobe, and parodied royal receptions and court festivals. The crown jewels were carefully laid away and guarded; the apartments of the Duchess d'Orléans were spared, as was the queen's oratory, her large crucifix being taken to the church of St. Roch. The Palais-Royal was sacked from top to bottom, the picture gallery being destroyed.

THE DUCHESS OF ORLEANS AND HER CHILDREN IN THE CHAMBER.

Barrot advised the Duchess d'Orléans to go to the Hôtel de Ville, and she was inclined to this courageous course; but Dupin dissuaded her from what he called madness, and persuaded her to go to the Chambers. This "madness" was her only hope, if one yet remained. She was almost popular, being respected, as had just been proved at the Tuileries. If it were daring but magnanimous to present herself to the people at the Hôtel de Ville, it was chimerical to beg the deputies to protect the dynasty, when they were evidently incapable of protecting themselves.

While Louis Philippe and the widow of his eldest son were leaving the Tuileries, the one in flight, the other in the hope of saving the future of a child and a dynasty, Marrast and other republicans were consulting with Lamartine in one of the offices of the legislative department. Marrast had long watched the course of the great poet-orator, convinced that he would fill an important place in the future. Lamartine insisted that the monarchy was worn out, that a feminine regency could not outlast three months, and that France needed something definite. It was agreed that he should propose or support the formation of a provisional government. This conversion to a republic was not the work of a day. As early as 1831 Lamartine predicted the approach of universal suffrage.

Marrast left him to return to the *National* office, where he found a crowd discussing the same point, and declaring that the republic existed in point of fact as in point of right. He hastened to the Palais-Bourbon. A list was made out, composed of Dupont de l'Eure, Arago, Marie, Garnier-Pagès, Ledru-Rollin, and Marrast, Barrot being added to win him to the republic, and this list was sent to the deputies, while some one was despatched to seek the members of the new government, and lead them to the Hôtel de Ville. The delegates bearing the list and the Duchess d'Orléans reached the Chambers simultaneously. The duchess and her elder son were loudly cheered as they passed through the streets, and her hopes revived.

Barrot, appearing a moment later, refused to join the provisional government, declaring that it was his duty to do his utmost to

establish the regency. During this debate the duchess and her
children entered the hall of session, amid applause from the majority
of the deputies. Dupin had announced the king's abdication, the
accession of Count de Paris, and his mother's regency. Cries of
" Give us a provisional government" were heard amid the tumult.
President Sauzet declared the meeting adjourned " until the Duchess
d'Orléans and the new king should withdraw."

This was an odd way of defending their cause, but he had lost
his head. The duchess hesitated, but remained, feeling that, her
son once out of the hall, all was over.

Neither could Sauzet force the national guard and the crowd who
thronged the corridors to retire. Speeches were made for and
against. Many deputies left the hall. Ledru-Rollin and Lamartine
protested against the regency; but so great was the uproar that
Sauzet again adjourned the meeting, and disappeared, followed by
the greater part of the deputies, only a few of the Left remaining.
The duchess, feeling that all was lost, withdrew with her children,
who were separated from her in the crowd; and she spent an hour
of cruel anguish, after which they were brought back in safety.

In the legislative halls confusion knew no bounds. The list of
names for the new government was read amid indescribable uproar,
and the mob then rushed to the Hôtel de Ville, where events of a
similar nature seemed to prove that the Duchess d'Orléans would
have been no more successful there. The proclamation of abdication
was read, and was hailed with shouts of " No abdication ! Downfall!
Republic !" The members of the new provisional government
finally forced their way through the throng, and were received with
applause, but also with a demand for the instant proclamation of a
republic. They then withdrew to deliberate, drew up a statement
that the republic had been adopted for the time being by the people
of Paris and the provisional government, but that the primary
meetings must decide on the final form of government. The ministerial portfolios were next distributed, — Dupont de l'Eure being
made president of the cabinet; Lamartine, minister of foreign
affairs; Ledru-Rollin, secretary of the interior; Crémieux, of justice;

Marie, of public works; and Arago, of the navy. The other offices were given to non-members of the government.

What more singular situation than that of this council, improvised hastily to bring order out of chaos, driven from town to town, and stifled, as it were, by the pressure of the vast wave of human beings that thronged the building.

There was some doubt as to the proclamation of the republic; Dupont de l'Eure, Arago, and Marie questioning their right to forestall the decision of the sovereign people, taken as a whole. While this was in discussion, Marrast, Flocon, and Louis Blanc appeared, whose names were added to the government, together with that of a workman named Albert. This was the first time that a workman had figured in such a position, nor was there anything in the man to justify the step. Their deliberation was interrupted by the clamor of the impatient crowd without, and this form was hastily agreed upon: "The provisory government desire a republic, dependent on the ratification of the people." They dissolved the Chamber of Deputies, forbade the reassembly of the Chamber of Peers, and ordered the convocation of a National Assembly as soon as the necessary measures for regulating the polls could be taken. Every citizen was to belong to the national guard, have a vote, and be entitled to bear arms.

Thus the Second Republic was born. Under existing circumstances, the government could not do otherwise. Not the government brought together by the storm of February 24, but Louis Philippe and Guizot, were responsible for this leap into an unknown future, sudden and unprepared for as it was.

CHAPTER VIII.

SECOND REPUBLIC. — PROVISIONAL GOVERNMENT.

February 24 to May 8, 1848.

THE new government came into office amid a most singular state of affairs; hanging, as it were, on the brink of an abyss. The Convention was born, indeed, amid most tragic conjunctures; but it was based on national suffrage: it had a right of command. The provisional government, chosen by a handful of men under the spur of necessity, had no foundation, no point of support, and stood face to face with problems darker and more profound than those of 1793. Then the crisis was political; now it was social. No longer the form of society, but its very foundations were shaken.

In the first hour of its existence the government was forced to a tremendous and inevitable step, which was now irrevocable, — the proclamation of universal suffrage, predicted by Lamartine in 1831 and eloquently claimed by Ledru-Rollin in 1847.

But what was the state of the nation when called upon to realize the perfect republican ideal? As we said, it was utterly unprepared; not only was the politic spirit immature, but the nation had retrograded, or rather deviated from the right path. As the wise De Tocqueville foresaw, the towns-people had grasped at socialistic ideas, ignorant that the social improvements to which the working class may legitimately aspire can only be the result and gradual development of a republican rule. In the country, on the other hand, people hated the old régime, were indifferent to the July monarchy, and dreaded the name of republic, which recalled 1793 and the Terror. Their only kindly feeling, as regarded revolution, was for Napoleon, whom they still lauded in opposition to the Bour-

LAMARTINE.

bons. The rural districts were Bonapartist to a man. In these dangers and embarrassments the ex-government and its party had no share. Louis's downfall was more rapid, if not more complete, than that of Charles X. No fresh expedition to Rambouillet was requisite to force the fallen king into exile. Louis Philippe and the queen sailed from Havre, under assumed names, March 2, in an English vessel, which landed them at Newhaven. The majority of the royal family assembled at Claremont Castle, an estate of the King of Belgium, a few miles from London. The Duchess d'Orléans and her two sons went to Germany. While this fallen royalty, filled with horrid memories of the Revolution, were a prey to terror until they left French soil, the provisional government was only anxious to facilitate and protect their flight; but the first duty was to lift Paris from her chaotic condition. All authority, all police, had vanished. The government was aided in its task by a throng of willing assistants, the best of whom were the people themselves, who would not permit pillage or personal violence. Two thieves caught in the act were shot, and the motto "Death to thieves!" was the watchword even at the worst moment. The barricades remained, lest the ex-government should make some fresh attempt; all public buildings were protected by armed crowds, men in rags and tatters guarding the bank and its treasures. Not an excess was committed, nor a threat uttered. The popular feeling was fine; the danger lay in imagination.

The Hôtel de Ville was still encumbered by a never-ending stream of people, and on the morning of February 25, one workman rushed into the council chamber and laid a petition on the table, crying for work, "the right to labor, *in an hour!* Such is the will of the people!"

These words explain, with terrible precision, the crisis which was at hand. The government was obliged to agree to guarantee the laborer's existence by work, and to provide work for every citizen. A formidable promise! Doubtless society should not permit one of its members to starve; but can a government be certain of always having work to give to every one who comes and demands it as a right?

The poor provisional government had not time to breathe. No sooner was the proclamation on the labor question published, than a tremendous tumult broke forth in the square below. Guns were fired, and shouts were heard of, " The red flag ! the red flag !" and a mob rushed in, red flag at their head.

This was a decisive moment. The question was whether the standard of modern France and the Revolution should disappear before a sectarian flag; whether all tradition should be set aside, and society be plunged into unknown depths.

Lamartine forced his way to the top of the great staircase, and made heroic efforts to gain a hearing, entreating the men not to force the insignia of civil war upon the government. " The government," he cried, " will die sooner than degrade itself by obedience. . . . . The red flag has gone no farther than the Champ de Mars, steeped in the people's blood in 1791; the tricolor has gone around the world, with the name, the glory, and the freedom of your country."

The mobile and impassioned mob burst into applause, and furled their bloody banner. The honor of the day belonged to Lamartine alone; and similar scenes, repeated again and again, make Lamartine one of the grandest and most original figures in French history, more like an orator of antiquity than of the Revolution.

The government at once announced that their insignia should be the Gallic cock and the tricolor.

The importance of this incident has not been exaggerated, but its real character has been often misinterpreted. A very small number brought to bear fierce feelings and evil purposes. The majority who demanded the red flag never thought of it as the ensign of vengeance and terrorism, and nothing could be more unjust than to accuse Louis Blanc, who urged his colleagues to yield to the will of the people, of a desire to re-erect the scaffold and the gallows. To its partisans the red flag was the emblem of Utopia, not of blood.

The government made good use of every moment left them by this ceaseless tumult. It was found necessary to leave the police department in the hands of the Lyonnese ex-insurgent Caussidière, who had seized it and surrounded himself by his comrades, all members of former secret societies; as he said, he "brought order out of disorder"; but no one knew, nor did he himself know, to what use he might at any instant turn his "mountaineers," as they dubbed themselves, and their blue blouses and red sashes were anything but comforting to the ordinary citizen.

Lamartine conceived a happy thought, which was eagerly acted upon.   Thousands of gaunt laborers without work thronged the streets, and they were enlisted as a guard mobile, and gradually converted from an element of anarchy into a potent instrument of order in the hands of a brave African campaigner, General Duvirier. Their fathers and elder brothers were also idle, trade having been at a low ebb during the last years of Louis Philippe's reign, and the revolution closing abruptly the few industries which existed.   February 26, the government ordered the establishment of national workshops, and the resumption of all public works.   Capital punishment for political offences was also abolished, together with the political oath, which never protected any power, and which even now did not prevent officials pledged by this oath to Louis Philippe, from offering their services to the republic.

February 27, the government solemnly renewed the proclamation of the republic on the site of the Bastille.   The barricades were removed at the close of the ceremony; the Court of Appeals and military officials were present.   The judicial, administrative, and commercial bodies then visited the Hôtel de Ville, and the various marshals sent in their allegiance to the new government, Bugeaud doing so in terms of great dignity and patriotism.   The clergy eagerly gave in their adherence, and the papal nuncio expressed his "deep sense of satisfaction at the respect paid to religion by the Parisians, amid such important events."   Even the legitimists promised to support the provisional government.

It would be a calumny on human nature, especially French human nature, to regard this universal adherence as a vast lie. The first impulse is always sincere with the Gallic race.   February 27 was a glorious day, but what would the next day be?

Among the earliest promises of allegiance sent in, were those of Napoleon's last surviving brother, Jerome, ex-king of Westphalia, his son, Lucien Bonaparte's son, and the Strasburg and Boulogne pretender, Louis Napoleon Bonaparte; the latter hurried from London to Paris, "to enlist," as he said, "under the flag of the republic, with no other motive than to serve his country." The government, deeming his presence dangerous, ordered his instant departure. He obeyed.

The press of every shade of opinion preached harmony and concord, and a touching scene occurred (March 2) at the grave of Armand Carrel, a long procession of national guards and students going to salute his remains. His unfortunate assassin, Girardin, expressed his bitter regret, and begged that government would forbid all duels, Armand Marrast accepting this expiation in the name of the illustrious dead.

We have now seen the dawn of the Second Republic from its sympathetic side; but while certain parties were hoping for a future of unknown and boundless comfort to be reached through social reform, others brutally retrograded, and strove to repel by violence the progress which interfered with their interests. They destroyed machinery, tore up rails, destroyed Louis Philippe's castle at Neuilly, and sacked the Rothschild mansion at Suresnes, shouting, "Down with monopoly!" Rothschild's monopoly consisted in importing foreign grain during a famine, and thus lowering the price of bread. However, these outrages were soon repressed.

February 28, fresh popular pressure was brought to bear on the government, the mass of the people being seized with a species of delirium, and fancying that the state could do anything and everything that they asked. This time they demanded a "Ministry of Progress," the very thing which Louis Blanc and his colleagues had desired should precede the organization of labor. The majority of the council replied that it already existed in the Ministry of Public Works. Louis Blanc, unable to gain his point, resigned, and, as a compromise, was made head of a committee to consider the labor question in general. This step was soon followed

by an order for the reduction of the hours of labor and the abolition
of middle-men. It is a difficult question whether the state has a
right to limit the hours for labor for any save children, the strongest
practical argument in favor of such right, being its existence in
England, where the feeling of individual rights is strongest.

The government, yielding to the pressure of circumstances on this
point, was firm in other respects, refusing to confiscate the goods of
the Orléans family, and boldly attacking the question of taxes.
The customs had gradually disappeared, and nothing could be done
until the National Assembly met, when a reform budget was to be
presented. The stamp-tax was, however, abolished on the spot,
owing to the great outcry made by the press.

Louis Philippe left the treasury in a wretched state. The deficit
for 1848 was two hundred and forty-five million francs, the
funded debt had increased eight hundred millions in seven years,
and the floating debt was eleven hundred and thirty millions. In
the face of these vast liabilities, but sixty millions would remain in
the treasury when the interest on the funds was paid, nor did the
government know where to turn for help in the general confusion.

March 3, a meeting was held to consider the terrible situation,
and the secretary of the treasury, having settled that the interest
must be paid a fortnight in advance, to show their determination to
avoid bankruptcy at any price, resigned. His office was then given
to Garnier-Pagès, who handed over the mayoralty of Paris to Marrast. Garnier-Pagès was as great an optimist as his predecessor
was a pessimist, which goes for a great deal.

The electoral meeting, now composed of the entire nation, was
fixed for April 9, and the meeting of the National Assembly for the
20th. This Assembly was to consist of nine hundred representatives chosen by the departments in proportion to their population,
each representative to receive twenty-five francs per day. All titles
of nobility were abolished, and the order of the Legion of Honor
retained.

The government, having provided for the first necessities at home,
began to consider their attitude towards foreign countries. March 5,

Lamartine published a pamphlet, adopted by the council, and addressed to the diplomatic agents of France. He declared that the various forms of government were equally legal, relative to the state of development of each nation, and that there was no need of war between the French republic and European monarchies. "If France," he added, "considers that the time has come to reconstruct certain oppressed nationalities, she cannot do otherwise than aid them." He also advised the formation of armies to protect the frontier. A committee was appointed to attend to the matter, and a loan of one hundred and fourteen millions was voted, despite the financial distress of the country.

Some alarm had been felt regarding Algeria, on account of the presence of the Duke d'Aumale and Prince de Joinville; but they expressed great patriotism with thorough dignity and manliness. The duke left Algeria, which the provisional government transferred to General Cavaignac, and embarked with his brother (March 3) for England by way of Spain.

But Paris was still in a state of ferment; the people were like a river which has overflowed its banks and refuses to return to its former limits. There was a great scarcity of work, nor was it easy to find occupation for the hands in the national workshops upon this sudden demand. A similar state of affairs prevailed in the departments; Emanuel Arago barely repressed civil war in Lyons, where the memory of the bloody strife waged in Louis Philippe's time still lingered. Club after club was formed, where every imaginable question of politics, morality, and social rights was nightly discussed. The universal allegiance proffered the government was of brief duration. The clubs were already opposing and crying out against it, aided and abetted by the newspapers, one of the latter finally putting to the government the question, "What would you do if the Assembly refused to proclaim the republic?" This was like a match to gunpowder. The clubs and revolutionary papers were in a fury. Girardin, the editor of the journal in question, was loudly threatened; but the government protected him from violence, and respected the liberty of the press even in the case of this enemy.

LOUIS PHILIPPE AT THE HOTEL DE VILLE.

March 15, the paper published by the minister of the interior demanded the postponement of the elections, on the plea that a year was requisite to prepare the people to throw off the influence of the aristocracy and to learn to use the suffrage. It was too true that the people were unprepared for universal suffrage; but the best and only chance for the republic was to have the elections at once, while the land still felt the impression of February 24, and before anti-republican factions had had time to act. Lamartine, Garnier-Pagès, and the majority of their colleagues felt assured of this; but Louis Blanc differed from them. He was in the minority, however, and the clubs might have failed to execute their threats of bringing one hundred thousand men into the field if another manifestation of an opposite nature had not occurred.

The government was, at this time, reorganizing the national guard, and made the mistake of disbanding the picked companies, which had been a special feature, and scattering the men in other companies. They complained, and justly; but the manifestation which ensued was far from reasonable. Urged on by the conservative press, thirty thousand national guards went (March 16) to the Hôtel de Ville, to demand the withdrawal of the offensive measure.

Students and workmen, thinking the government threatened, hastened to the spot and blocked the way, so that the troops were obliged to disperse, contenting themselves with sending delegates to the government. This demonstration of the "fur caps," as it was called, from the head-dress worn by these picked bodies of men, bore important fruits, very different from those expected by the instigators, the government issuing a reproof to the troops for breaking the public peace, and a proclamation written by Lamartine, declaring that government would commit an usurpation by retaining the power, that is, adjourning the elections for an unnecessary hour.

More processions and petitions were the result; but the government stood firm, and the result was favorable to it and to the republic, although these manifestations had a lamentable effect in lowering stock. The secretary did not attempt to stem the current, knowing that it would be in vain. Unable to lend the money frantically begged by the whole of industrial and commercial France, he strove to find new branches of industry, which were seized as saving planks in the general shipwreck. The courts of bankruptcy were thronged by men, whose paper was good but the day before, and whose shops were filled with goods that they could not sell.

Ably assisted by Duclerc, under-secretary of state, and Pagnerre, the secretary of the provisional government, Garnier-Pagès formed two institutions destined to be, not merely the resort of a moment of distress, but valuable and durable establishments. I refer to the banks of discount and general warehouses. At the latter, the merchant or manufacturer could deposit his goods and receive a receipt, enabling him to discount his notes at the former. The state, the bank, chambers of commerce, and, finally, individuals furnished the capital. This helped individuals, but was of no avail to the state; the provisional government staggered under the huge debt bequeathed by Louis Philippe, and the bank was almost empty. An heroic remedy was requisite, and the ministry declared that bank bills must take the place of currency. Paper money reappeared, but it was not the signal for former catastrophes. Still even this did not fill the gaping treasury. Bankruptcy was imminent. Amid the many counsels thrust upon him, Garnier-Pagès and his intelligent assistants saw but one available resource, — to levy a direct tax. The government agreed to increase the four regular duties forty-five per cent, which would produce one hundred and ninety-two million francs. Public opinion at first approved, and it was not till later that party zeal dubbed the action a crime. Other taxes were also altered; some being abolished, others increased.

Meantime, Carnot, minister of public instruction, was also straining every nerve; primary instruction was made free and obligatory; and for the higher education he desired to found a new school, embracing institutions for the education of teachers, lawyers, doctors, engineers. As there was no money to carry out such a scheme, the College of France was enlarged and improved to meet the deficiency. The study of history from 1789 to the present time was introduced into the schools, it being inadmissible, under a republic, to leave the

rising generation in ignorance of the great events which had renewed
and reinvigorated their country.   The use of arms and military drill
were also to be taught, academic libraries were established in every
parish, courses of public lectures by the most distinguished men
were given in Paris, and it was hoped that this happy innovation
would spread throughout France.   The office of schoolmaster was
declared honorable and to be esteemed of all men, and the interests
of education looked bright and hopeful.

In the matter of religion, we have already described the eager
adhesion of the clergy to the February revolution; not only such
moderate spirits as the Archbishop of Paris, or men urged by generous zeal to approve brilliant novelties, like Lacordaire, but those who
had been and were again to be leaders of the most extreme ultramontanism offered their services freely to the republic.   M. de Falloux,
famed for his ultramontane and legitimist books, wrote a letter
(February 25) to one of the papers, lauding the Parisians, who, he
said, "had given their victory a sacred character."   Many other
examples might be quoted.   In the face of such a movement, apparently sincere to such a degree that the Pope was alarmed, Carnot and his friends returned to the hopes of 1789, and deemed it
possible to make the lower ranks of the clergy the allies of the revolution, striving to conciliate schoolmaster and priest, clergy and
university.   This attempt to gain the Catholic clergy was unsuccessful; but events have justified the educational system inaugurated
in 1848: the third republic has taken up and will complete the
work of the second, as that took up the tradition of the first.

The fine arts also flourished, being confided by Ledru-Rollin to
an artist of much merit, M. Jeanron, who rendered an inestimable
service to France by cataloguing the collections of the state;
countless treasures, hidden or lost, were brought to light, and the
Louvre was, as it were, renovated by the careful classification of its
contents.

Great improvements were made in the workings of the law, and
all unjust judges were removed from office.   It is worthy of mention here, that crime had been on the decrease since the 24th of

February. The same fact was noticeable in Paris during the calamities of 1870. Political and social passions and preoccupations divert men from selfish passions which lead to crime.

In regard to public works, a less satisfactory report must be given. It was no easy task to improvise work for the ever-increasing throngs who demanded labor and food from the state. By the end of April, the list of laborers numbered nearly one hundred thousand, and although their wages were very small, they reached the sum total of fourteen millions in about four months. The danger lay in the undignified and anxious attitude of these workers, who did no work, for they were simply occupied in aimless digging in and around Paris and the Champ de Mars, and who could be neither used nor dismissed.

Louis Blanc desired to substitute a system of universal partnership for the present system of competition, and suggested that the state should buy all the factories which could be purchased, and put them in the hands of companies of workmen. His scheme was fallacious, and the government would assuredly have failed under the existing state of trade ; and he was stoutly opposed by the economic school, prominent among whom was the ex-St.-Simonian, Michael Chevalier, upheld by Lamennais and Buchez. The labor question was eagerly discussed by group after group, until Prudhon finally gave the world his solution of the social problem. He denied alike the rights of ownership and of possession in common, and his system was, perhaps, the most chimerical of all. He accomplished his end, — notoriety ; but it profited neither democracy nor republic, and he shared with Blanc and Cabet, the apostle of communism, the dangerous honor of spreading panic among the middle classes, and endangering interests that he should have protected.

We have attempted to show the efforts made by the provisional government to provide for the dread necessities of the present, and to prepare for the future. Meantime, other cares — foreign troubles — disputed public interest with domestic problems. The February revolution shook Europe even more profoundly than its predecessor in July ; most remarkable events occurred daily, every state, great and small, from the Irish Sea to the Baltic, being stirred as by a volcanic eruption.

The first consequences were felt beyond the Juras, in the little Swiss canton of Neufchâtel, which was also the property of the Prussian king by right of heritage. This small domain established itself as a democratic republic, on the same footing as its neighbors (February 29 to March 1).

In Italy an explosion was inevitable. A revolt against the King of Naples, in Messina and Calabria, came to naught; but the movement soon spread through the Neapolitan provinces, and the king was forced to grant a constitution based on the French charter of 1830 (February 11). His example was followed in Sardinia and Tuscany, and even the Pope was finally obliged to grant a constitution and two legislative chambers, the Jesuits being meantime driven from Naples and Sardinia, where they had exercised tremendous tyranny. The Italian provinces subject to Austria fretted hourly under foreign rule, and their demonstrations were becoming daily more alarming, when startling news from Vienna reached Venice and Lombardy.

There had been political and national disturbances in Austria, as in Italy, before the February revolution, liberal aspirations coming to light in Hungary, Bohemia, and Vienna itself, in consequence of Metternich's despotism; and when, upon the news of the French revolution, the Austrian government assumed a hostile attitude, the public wrath was such that the government was forced to refrain from interfering with France (March 10). But this was not enough; the minister who had so long oppressed the empire was not longer to be endured, and an insurrection broke out (March 13) in Vienna, to the war-cry, "Down with Metternich!" He was obliged to resign, and joined Guizot and Louis Philippe in England. Emperor Ferdinand then promised to bestow a constitution on his people, and was loudly cheered by the Viennese mob, in which Poles, Hungarians, and Tzechs were mingled with Germans.

But it was national independence, not a constitution, that his Italian subjects demanded; they had been working towards that end for years.   Venice had the good fortune to possess a politician of the first water, not an aristocrat, but a man of the middle class, and Daniel Manin persistently roused public spirit by such legal means as foreign sway permitted.   The Austrian government, dreading these tactics far more than street riots, imprisoned him; but on hearing what had happened in Vienna, the terrified governor set him free, thus giving the movement a head, instead of. arresting it.   Manin formed a National Guard, seized the arsenal, and proclaimed a republic (March 19 – 22).   The governor surrendered, and Venice was freed by a plebeian named Manin, having been sold into captivity by an aristocrat of the same cognomen.

Liberty cost a greater price in Milan, the seat of the viceroy and of military command.   Old Field-Marshal Radetzki had an army in his control, while the Milanese were almost unarmed; but they were led by men of wonderful intellect and rare courage.   The name of one is well known in France,— Henri Cernuschi.   The cathedral used by the Austrians as a fortress was captured by the insurgents, who were aided by the peasants of the environs, and after four days' bloody fight, Radetski evacuated the city, marking his retreat by atrocities which only increased the popular fury (March 18 – 21).

The glorious news of the freedom of Venice and Milan was hailed with enthusiasm in France; and the fires of liberty, once kindled, soon spread throughout Germany, where various concessions were enforced.   The Prussian king, who but a year before had protested that he would maintain sovereign and traditional authority, and never yield to the modern constitutions resulting from revolution, now declared that he felt called to save liberty and German unity. The humiliation which Frederic William now endured was but a temporary trial, from which he was one day to rise stronger than ever.   He declared that he would take charge of Germany in these perilous days.   " Prussia," he said, " now becomes Germany "; and he summoned the German princes and states to meet the Prussian Diet to decide upon the foundation of a new Germany, united, yet not uniform, — united in diversity, and united in liberty.

Prussia, in the future, failed to keep to this programme, for she respected neither liberty nor diversity.

But Prussian ambition threw down its mask too soon. Austria and Bavaria angrily protested. In certain cities Frederic William was burned in effigy, and he was forced to retract, and disavow the meaning put upon his words (April 2).

What he unsuccessfully attempted in the name of Prussian monarchy was next essayed in the name of German democracy. A great meeting of German delegates was held at Frankfort, where universal suffrage was proclaimed, and a national assembly convened for the first of May.

Poland woke from her slumber, and Czar Nicholas resumed the hostile attitude toward France which he held upon the accession of Louis Philippe. Even England was violently shaken by the democratic party of the chartists, and Ireland dreamed of an Irish republic in imitation of France.

Amid all this European revolution, the offspring of French revolution, what course was proper and possible for the new authorities?

The question was put most urgently by the foreign refugees and residents of Paris; Poles, Germans, Belgians, and Swiss all demanded arms and aid. The Poles demanded more, — they required the formal intervention of France to set their country free. But the situation was no longer what it was in 1831. A war for Poland in the time of Louis Philippe would have been war with Prussia and Russia as well; in 1848, the people of Berlin set Polish political prisoners free, and led them through the streets in triumph; Austrian agents suggested the Austrian emperor for king of Poland, and hostile manifestations to Russia prevailed in Germany.

Still the provisional government dared not trust to appearances, and could only give the Poles words of sympathy, and wait for the result of the movement in Germany, while they refused, and with greater show of reason, to aid the groups of German revolutionists assembling in Paris and elsewhere.

Belgium wavered an instant on receiving the news of February 24, but the skill of King Leopold averted the storm. He declared

himself ready to abdicate: he was begged to remain. Liberal and
progressive laws satisfied public opinion, and the government at
Brussels received Lamartine's assurance that the French republic
would respect Belgian independence and neutrality.

Nevertheless a number of Belgian refugees residing in Paris
were determined to carry the republic into their own country. They
organized as best they could, and set off. Ledru-Rollin would fain
have assisted them, but felt that he ought not to do so. After much
hesitation he sent a despatch to that purport to M. Delescluze, the
Belgian commissary, who, not receiving it, armed and sent to
Belgium a body of twelve hundred men, who were put to flight at
a place with the strange name of Riskall. The French government
disavowed all part in the expedition, and there was no quarrel
between the two governments.

A similar incident occurred in Savoy, where a republic was proclaimed in consequence. Nor could France recover Savoy from the
Sardinian king by force, as he was esteemed her probable ally.
King Charles Albert was now involved in war with Austria,
greatly against the will of the English minister, Lord Palmerston,
once so revolutionary, but anti-French before anything else. The
French government, on the contrary, deeming war inevitable, offered
to send an army into Italy by way of Savoy, which offer was declined, the king uttering the speech, which became more famous
than it was truthful, "God made Italy sufficient unto herself"
(March 23), — a proud speech, dictated by his dread of a republic
rather than his doubtful patriotism. Almost the same words were
used at the same time by the most celebrated of Italian republicans, Mazzini, to Lamartine, the French minister of foreign affairs.
"Italy," he said, " we hope, can work out her own salvation ! . . . .
We count on your *moral* support."

This refusal of French aid cost Italy cruel reverses, and ten years
more of oppression; it cost France civil war and its fatal results,
from which foreign war would doubtless have saved her.

France had now offered to uphold Italy, and in vain. She had
refused to assist insurrection in Germany, Belgium, and Savoy. She

must now take her stand in regard to England, where there was a double disturbance: the English were struggling to get a democratic charter; the Irish, for what they called "Repeal." When the great Irish "agitator," Daniel O'Connell, recently dead, roused his country in favor of repeal, it meant the restoration of an Irish parliament in Dublin; now it meant something else, — like the old "United Irishmen," they aspired to be set free from the English crown. They sent deputies to Paris, who received sympathy, but were told that the French republic could not possibly interfere with domestic matters in the British Islands. This reply won the public gratitude of England, without offending Ireland, where the popular movement was soon stifled.

Nor were the English chartists more successful: the government used none but legal means to oppose them, and made no attack on liberty; public opinion ceased to favor the movement, and England came triumphantly out of her double crisis. The contrast offered by the issue of popular outbreaks in Vienna and Berlin, as opposed to London and Brussels, was entirely to the advantage of liberal governments.

Meantime, excitement increased in France instead of being allayed. Countless newspapers sprang up, rivalling each other in scandal and exaggeration. The revolutionists cried out against the sloth and inaction of the government, the reactionists against its tyranny. There were three hundred clubs in Paris, and the partisans of Louis Bonaparte began to scheme in favor of the pretender of Strasburg and Boulogne, promulgating the book he had written, while a prisoner at Ham, on "The Extinction of Pauperism." He himself proposed the formation of a great labor association, to which waste lands should be given; but later, when he was in a position to execute the scheme, nothing was said of it.

Amid all these revolutionary, socialistic, and Bonapartist rumors, an incident burst upon the world which caused a great noise. We refer to the discovery at the ministry of foreign affairs of an exact and complete account of the most secret actions of the secret societies before the insurrection of May 12, 1839. This anonymous revelation could only have been dictated by one of the leaders of the movement headed by Barbès, Blanqui, and Martin Bernard. On its publication, Blanqui protested without waiting to be accused, and on being summoned to appear before a jury from the revolutionist clubs, refused to do so, and plunged deeper than ever into plots and counter-plots.

A fresh crisis seemed at hand. The labor party were determined to carry out their object, and enforce the system of Louis Blanc, Blanqui conspiring to make himself dictator. What would the minister of the interior do? Ledru-Rollin was drawn in contrary ways, — by Caussidière and the club leaders, on the one hand; by Jules Favre and his friends, who favored a less hasty policy, on the other.

The labor demonstration was fixed for April 16. Ledru-Rollin still hesitated. The danger was great. Even the staff of the National Guard wavered, and felt the influence of the labor party at the Luxembourg. The leaders of the manifestation disagreed as to what should be done if they succeeded, but none the less each man worked for himself. All depended on Ledru-Rollin.

The movement began on Sunday morning, April 16. From thirty to forty thousand men met on the Champ de Mars, Blanqui among them, breathing fire and flame. The hour was decisive. Pressed by his friend Carteret, Ledru-Rollin no longer hesitated. His loyalty dissipated the images of dictatorship which had dazzled his sight. "The riot must be put down," said Carteret, "by the unanimous action of the National Guard." "You are right!" replied Ledru-Rollin. He went to Lamartine, the drums were beaten to summon the national guard to arms, and Lamartine took command of the small body of Garde Mobile at hand.

Despite the ill-will of the staff, the summons was obeyed. The troops reached the Hôtel de Ville before the mob. The people of Paris, like Ledru-Rollin, decided for the government. One hundred thousand bayonets protected the Hôtel de Ville. The whole city flocked to the spot. Blanqui's labor was lost, and the day ended with a great review of the National Guard, lasting till eleven at

GALLERIES OF VERSAILLES.

night, amid cries of, " Long live the Provisional Government ! " and
" Down with the Communists ! "

This was a very noteworthy event : the theories of communism
had been loudly preached ; but when the masses, accessible to many
a vain delusion, saw the dream take shape in communism, they
turned away in anger, that being radically opposed to the French
spirit of individuality.

The 16th of April confirmed March 17 ; but the popular wisdom,
displayed twice in one month, gave birth to hopes cruelly belied two
months later !

April 20, the government distributed the new colors to the troops,
and four hundred thousand men marched in order through the Arc
de Triomphe de l'Étoile.

April 27, the government proclaimed the abolition of slavery, the
Second Republic thus repairing, in the remnant of distant colonies,
the evil done by First Consul Bonaparte. The new colony in the
Mediterranean, Algiers, was included in the decree, which is one of
the titles of the provisional government to the gratitude of posterity.

The vast electoral movement assumed intensity as the important
day (April 23) drew near. The words *republic* and *progress* were
everywhere, but what meaning did they hide ? While workmen
struggled against masters, tenants against landlords, disinterested
feelings were most touchingly displayed. M. de Lamennais quoted
(March 10) the noble words of a laborer : " We have given three
months of misery tò the service of the republic ! " The same generous impulse prompted many to carry their trifling savings, their
ornaments, and even their honorary medals, as patriotic offerings,
to the Hôtel de Ville. The people also respected the law, a rarer
virtue than generosity, and the love of peace and concord survived
the many shocks it had received in countless souls.

Both ex-liberals and constitutionalists protested their unreserved
allegiance to the republic. Partisans of the dynastic opposition
published professions of loyalty. Thiers announced his willingness
" to establish the republic on lasting foundations," and Odilon
Barrot dubbed any one who dreamed of restoring monarchy, a crimi-

nal. Even legitimists clung to the republic. All the candidates — among them, bishops, priests, and monks — declared their acceptance of the republic.

The labor party from the Luxembourg and the revolutionists from the clubs attempted to gain by the elections what they had vainly striven to win through a popular demonstration. They published a list of "people's candidates." Twenty out of thirty-four were work-men; they omitted, on the one hand, the moderate majority of the government, and, on the other, Blanqui and Cabet. Even here communism was rejected.

In Paris, the election went off most quietly. When universal suffrage was discussed under Louis Philippe, even republicans granted the material difficulties in the way of permitting such vast numbers of men to vote, but they vanished on the first trial. The only requisite was to provide enough districts. The result could not be proclaimed until the evening of the 28th, owing to the immense number of ballots to be counted. Lamartine headed the list, then came the other moderate candidates. Ledru-Rollin and Louis Blanc came last. The Luxembourg ticket was thoroughly defeated. The labor party experienced the consequences of their rout on April 16, and working-men would not vote for labor candidates.

The elections were, for the most part, equally peacefully con-ducted throughout France, the results being very various. Lamar-tine was elected in ten departments. There were but two exceptions to the universal order, — one at Limoges, where there were quarrels between the National Guards and the working-men, when the latter found that their candidates were defeated, but peace was soon re-stored. At Rouen, the results were more serious; there, too, the storm rose from the same source. Class divisions were strongly marked in Rouen, and the riot went so far as street fights and bar-ricades, cannon being employed. The victory of the government was followed by a violent reaction of the middle classes. The gov-ernment did its utmost to restore peace and good-will; but the first blood had been shed since the establishment of the republic, and it was an evil omen.

The opening of the National Assembly (May 4) in the Palace of the former Chamber of Deputies seemed to wash out the memory of this sad augury. The provisional government, through its president, Dupont de l'Eure, gave up its authority to the Assembly, which renewed, amid cheers, the proclamation of the republic, again repeated outside the palace, before the people and the troops. Those who witnessed this glorious scene, can never forget it.

Two days later (May 6), Lamartine read, before the Assembly, in the name of the president, Dupont de l'Eure, the provisional government's account for its actions ; then the ministers read their individual reports. May 8, the Assembly, with scarcely a dissenting voice, voted that the provisional government merited the thanks of the country. Posterity will confirm the vote. No government ever struggled against greater difficulties with more courage and honesty.

CHAPTER IX.

SECOND REPUBLIC (*continued*). — SECOND CONSTITUENT ASSEMBLY. — EXECUTIVE COMMITTEE. — MAY 15. — MEMORABLE DAYS IN JUNE, 1848.

May 4 to June 28, 1848.

WE have already hinted at the many varying elements in the Assembly which now ruled the destinies of France. Neither ardor, honesty, nor talent was wanting, but there was no clear sense of what was possible and desirable. The new Constituent Assembly was marked throughout by vacillation and indecision. The first president was Buchez, author of the Parliamentary History of the Revolution. His panegyric of Robespierre and the Jacobins caused him to be shunned by the moderate party, but his religious views and severe morality won him the preference of conservatives and New Right. The session opened with a discussion, by the fifteen bureaus or committees into which the Assembly was divided, of the form to be adopted by the executive power. Numerous schemes were suggested, the Old Left finally triumphing. The executive power was vested in a committee of five, who were to choose the ministers. This committee consisted of Lamartine, Ledru-Rollin, Arago, Garnier-Pagès, and Marie, — Dupont de l'Eure, the venerable dean of the provisional government, having withdrawn from candidacy, May 10.

This executive committee then formed a ministry composed of Crémieux, Duclerc, Bastide, Recurt, Carnot, Trélat, Flocon, Bethmont, and Admiral Casy ; the department of war fell to General Cavaignac, governor of Algeria ; Marrast and Caussidière were retained as heads of mayoralty and police ; Pagnerre continued his position as secretary general to the government.

These nominations were no sooner confirmed than the foreign question and the social question became involved and required immediate investigation.

The news from Poland was most gloomy. The natives of Galicia, who had hardly dared breathe since the massacres of 1846, took courage on hearing that Vienna was in a state of revolution and that the notorious prison at Spielberg was empty; but the Austrian government, although it suppressed statute labor to curry favor with the peasants, soon took arms against the Polish patriots, who were only put down when Cracow was bombarded (April 26).

Prussia made many promises to Poland, and the Frankfort Assembly, as aforesaid, issued a proclamation against the division of Poland; but these fair hopes were fleeting.

The spirit of invasion and national egotism promptly replaced the first impulse of sympathy and equity. Schleswig, despite its Danish population, and Posen and Western Prussia, despite their Polish citizens, were declared a part of the German confederacy. It was declared that "Germany must maintain her ancient limits," this comprising the Austrian states formerly dependent on the German Empire. Nor was this all: Germany laid claim to a part of Holland and Switzerland, and to Alsace and Lorraine (April 12). France then perceived how mistaken was her idea of the character to be assumed by German revolution, though she still strove to delude herself with flattering prospects.

The storm burst in the province of Posen, on the occasion of a royal decree allotting more than half the province, including the capital, to Germany. The Poles tried to vindicate their rights by force of arms, but were overcome by numbers and forced to surrender (May 8).

In Italy the movement was vast, but lacked concentration. The people flung themselves eagerly into what was called "the crusade" against the stranger; the Grand-Duke of Tuscany, although an Austrian archduke; the Pope, in spite of his scruples as common father of the faithful; and the Neapolitan king, the most anti-revolutionary of princes, were drawn into "the Italian league." But the league had no head.   Charles Albert, who entered bravely on the campaign and drove Radetzki back to Verona, had no idea of submitting his plans to the supervision of other princes; the King of Naples thought only of escaping from the obligations he had undertaken; and Pius IX., his conscience ill at ease, threatened with schism by German prelates, torn by his conflicting duties as an Italian prince and as head of the Church, withdrew the blessing conferred on the Italian crusaders, April 29, declaring that nothing was further from his intentions than to wage war with Germany; then, May 4, alarmed by the anger of the Romans, he rejoined the national party, without recovering his original prestige.

In spite of the early victories of Charles Albert, the success of the Italian cause was very dubious.   A strong feeling against Italy appeared not only in German Austria, but throughout Germany, where pride of race and thirst for dominion stifled all sense of international right.   Austria accordingly prepared for a tremendous effort to recapture Italy.

All France felt a lively interest in events beyond the Rhine and the Alps.   Two deputies questioned the committee, immediately upon its formation, in regard to Poland and Italy.   Lamartine replied that the French flag would advance at the hour and to the extent appointed by legislative wisdom and foresight, but, once advanced, it would not turn back as in 1831.   The subject was then adjourned till May 15, upon which Louis Blanc introduced the domestic question in its most trenchant form, by renewing the proposition to create a ministry to attend to the promotion of industry and progress.   This scheme was almost unanimously vetoed, a committee to inquire into agricultural and industrial interests being substituted. The delegates of the Luxembourg, upon this, published a declaration, refusing to assist in the Peace Jubilee to be held in celebration of the assembly of the representatives of the people at Paris.

The Assembly was already a butt for the attacks of reactionists and ultra-revolutionists; and this before any action had been taken, save the very reasonable decision in regard to the executive power. Still more bitter was the hostility felt towards all members of the government. The agents of the various factions united to prevent the continuation of the present situation.

The state of foreign affairs afforded too favorable an opportunity to be let slip by these agitators, and a central committee of clubbists, led by one Huber, a man connected with the police under Louis Philippe, appealed to the barricade chiefs and the delegates of democratic clubs. It was by them decided that a manifestation to claim aid for Poland should occur May 15. No armed force was to be employed, and it was believed that the people would respond in large numbers.

An advance demonstration in favor of Poland took place on the 13th, thousands of men marching along the boulevards from the Bastile to the Madeleine. A law had been passed the day before forbidding the direct presentation of petitions at the bar; this was intended to prevent any such invasion of the Assembly as occurred during the Revolution. The crowd respected this law, and sent its petition through delegates, who conveyed it to a deputy; the throng then dispersed in good order, thus assuaging public opinion but too securely.

Meantime, revolutionary factions were in a state of chaos and tumult, some anxious to have recourse to arms, some distrustful of the result. Barbès, seeing that Blanqui was preparing to lead the movement, dissuaded his club from taking part in it, his example being followed by several other republican clubs. Various protests were made, but in vain. Every precaution was taken by the Executive Committee and the president of the Assembly, and at eleven o'clock the procession started from the Place de la Bastille, being joined on the Boulevard du Temple by Blanqui and his club, who took the lead and marched forward with extreme rapidity, thus reaching the Madeleine long before the time expected.

The National Guard, wearied of being so often troubled in vain, responded but languidly to the present appeal; still, the danger might have been faced by concentrating the forces in hand. Instead of this, General Courtais hoped to arrest the progress of the procession by fair words. The mob refused to hear him, and swept on to the doors of the Assembly, where Lamartine and Ledru-Rollin attempted to address the people, who continued to batter the gates and to cry, "Away with the bayonets!" The gates were set ajar to admit twenty delegates; many more followed on the heels of Blanqui, and when Barbès and his men learned of his admission they insisted upon their right to enter likewise. A terrible struggle ensued; the crowd forced its way into the Assembly, where a discussion of the Polish and Italian question was going on. Amid the tumult, Louis Blanc took the floor and demanded silence for the reading of the petition in favor of Poland, which was granted. The petition having been read, President Buchez requested the mob to leave. Barbès, seeing Blanqui in the front ranks, pressed forward and exclaimed: "Citizens, you have done well to come hither to exercise your right of petition, and it is the duty of the Assembly to comply with your desire, which is that of France; but, that it may not seem to yield to force, you must retire."

Great confusion followed. The crowd outside increased every moment. The drum was beat to call the National Guard to arms. Barbès assumed the leadership and declared that they must vote on the spot for the despatch of an army to Poland, and a tax of a thousand million francs on the rich, and that the call to arms must be rescinded, otherwise the representatives should be declared traitors.

The tumult grew louder as the sound of drums approached. Armed men with threatening looks surrounded President Buchez, who sat motionless, with Vice-President Corbon by his side. The president was called upon to forbid the beating of the call to arms. Knowing that it could have no effect at this late hour, and that a refusal would inevitably bring on a catastrophe, he hesitatingly agreed, thus doubtless preventing crime, but not quelling the storm. Huber leaped to the platform and declared the National Assembly dissolved. The president was hurled from his seat by a knot of fanatics. He left the room at once, followed by the vice-president and the majority of the representatives.

The invaders, masters of the hall, were quarrelling over the names for a new provisional government, when a drum was heard close by. "The Garde Mobile!" shouted some one. Panic-stricken, they rushed forth, shouting, "To the Hôtel de Ville!"

This political orgy lasted nearly four hours. Shortly before five, the troops entered and finished clearing the hall; the vice-president reopened the meeting, while the president hastened to the Luxembourg to confer with the Executive Committee. Clément Thomas, colonel of the Second Legion, took the place of Courtais, arrested as a traitor by the National Guard. He was not a traitor; he was only weak. Lamartine ordered a vote of thanks to the troops, and declared that the place of the government at such a moment was not in the council room, but in the street at the head of the army. He then mounted his horse and rode to the Hôtel de Ville, where some of the insurgents still lingered, wrangling over the choice of a government.

Barbès, and Albert, the workingman, who was a member of the provisional government, played at dictatorship in one wing of the building, while Mayor Marrast occupied the other, holding communication with the Executive Committee. Lamartine and Ledru-Rollin soon came up with troops, arrested Barbès and Albert and dispersed their men without bloodshed. Garnier-Pagès meanwhile proceeded to report to the Assembly what the Executive Committee had done and intended doing. "We have decided," said he, "to lend energy to power. We all desire an honest, firm, and moderate republic!"

This was the origin of a phrase whose meaning was strangely changed within a brief space, and which became the countersign of men who desired no republic at all.

A contrary breeze now set in, as was but natural after such excess and extravagances. The very next day, deputies from the Left attacked the Committee which they had applauded in the hour of danger. The trouble was in the prefecture of police, which was a hot-bed of sedition. On the morning of the 16th the building was surrounded by troops, and the deputies of the House reproached the government for its criminal delay in attacking the factionists in

their last retreat. The Executive hoped to gain the day without loss
of blood. Caussidière, being summoned before the Assembly, succeeded better than Louis Blanc in obtaining a hearing. He made an
able defence, then resigned, promising to persuade his men to disband
quietly, and he kept his word. The police force was reorganized with
new elements. There was, nevertheless, no real harmony or confidence between the two branches of the government, and the Peace
Jubilee, May 21, an effort to renew the great festivals of the Revolution, ill accorded with the state of popular feeling. Nothing was
omitted in the way of decoration, the sun shone, the procession was
fine, but beneath the official joy lurked a chill of anxiety.

It was now time to return to the foreign question, which had
furnished the pretext for invading the Assembly. Europe was one
vast scene of chaos. Germany was striving to wrest Schleswig from
Denmark, which called Sweden to the rescue, and at the same time
was attempting to drag the Slavs and Tcheks into the German union,
which the Germans were endeavoring to organize at Frankfort.

In Italy, while Radetzki withstood Charles Albert on the Adige,
a fresh Austrian army, reinforced by German volunteers, entered
Venice. At the other end of Italy, Sicily had rejected the concessions
of Ferdinand of Naples and decreed his downfall. War, therefore,
existed between Sicily and Naples. It broke out next in Naples
itself, between the Liberals and royal troops, composed for the most
part of Swiss regiments. May 15, the very day that the French
Assembly was invaded, Naples was ravaged by fire and bloodshed ;
the royal troops prevailed, and the first use which ·Ferdinand made
of his sad victory was to recall the fleet and the army, which he had
been forced to send to aid Lombardy and Venice against Austria.

Even before receiving this melancholy news from Naples, Lamartine had again laid the question of intervention in Italy before the
Executive Committee (May 19–21). The French squadron was
already in the Adriatic, and his plan was to dispatch an army across
the Alps at once. The Committee preferred to await an appeal from
Italy, and he could only obtain an order for the organization of 300
battalions of Gardes Mobiles, thus gaining 800,000 additional men.

CHURCH OF ST. EUSTACHE

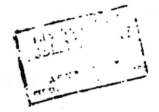

May 23, Lamartine made a fresh effort in behalf of Italy, and read the correspondence between France and Prussia relative to Poland, maintaining the opinion that Poland could only be set free with the support of Germany. The Assembly and the press in general agreed; and on the following day, May 24, the Assembly requested the Executive Committee to carry out the following measures to the best of their ability: a friendly compact with Germany, the restoration of Poland, and the liberation of Italy.

The German Constituent Assembly, which met at Frankfort, May 18, responded warmly to the advances of the French government, but it was in question to know whether their deeds and words corresponded, and their deeds, alas! were already opposed to the wishes of the Assembly.

May 22, the United States Minister in Paris presented a decree from the Senate and House of Representatives congratulating the French nation, in the name of the people of America, upon the establishment of a republic in France. The sympathy of America had a high moral value, but could not materially influence the progress of events in Europe.

The entire Assembly agreed in regard to the foreign question. Dissensions were renewed the next day with respect to home affairs. This was indicated by the formation of several clubs, composed of the various representatives; one of which remained celebrated, — the club of the Rue de Poitiers. All the Reactionists, Conservatives, and Alarmists, from the Legitimists and clerical party to the Liberals of the old dynastic Left, were members. Odilon Barrot, Berryer, De Falloux, and Thiers were of the number. Thiers, however, no more than Barrot and their friends aimed at this time at re-establishing a monarchy, as is proved by his famous speech of this epoch: "The republic is the form of government least calculated to divide us." To appreciate his motives and those of many others, it is necessary to read a letter quoted by Garnier-Pagès in his History of the Revolution of 1848, in which Thiers explains that he supports the clergy through fear of socialism. Clerical instruction, which he dislikes, seems to him better than that

of sectarian demagogues (an allusion to Blanqui.) The historian of
the Revolution for an instant lost faith, but not in the principles
of 1789, nor in their power of resistance: he was destined later to
return gloriously to that cause of the Revolution which he had a
right to call his own.

Various other clubs were formed besides that of the Rue de
Poitiers; one at the Palais National, and another socialist club, in
the Rue des Pyramides. This latter (which was the smallest),
although attacking the actual condition of society, warmly protested
its respect for property.

One important event followed another in the Assembly. May 26,
the law of April 10, 1832, by which the government of Louis
Philippe forbade the elder Bourbon branch to set foot on French
soil, was applied to Louis Philippe himself and his family; this
being a protest on the part of the Assembly against all monarchical
claims. The next day, certain representatives presented a request
for the abrogation of that article of this law exiling the Bonaparte
family. This petition was signed by Louis Blanc, which was
logical if not politic, on his part, as he had voted against the ban-
ishment of the Orleans family. As a matter of fact, this clause was
already void, three members of the Bonaparte family being members
of the Assembly.

At the very time that Louis Blanc was working for the abolition
of this law, he was in serious danger himself. Barbès and Albert
were prisoners at Vincennes. Blanqui had just been arrested in his
hiding-place. May 31, Attorney-General Portalis petitioned the
Assembly for an order to arrest Louis Blanc as an accomplice of the
invaders of May 15, but Blanc made a magnificent and successful
defence. The next step was to curtail the national workshops, by
many considered nests of rebellion. All workingmen who had
been settled in Paris for less than six months were dismissed,
and no laborer was taken who had refused work in private enter-
prises. The superintendent was also dismissed because he continued to take in new artisans contrary to orders and also favored
Bonapartist outbreaks among the men. The next manager,

M. Lalanne, soon restored order, although the shops still gave rise to much uneasiness.

The right wing of the Assembly saw no danger save from socialism and the workshops; neither of these was the chief cause of the troubles which now disturbed Paris. Public meetings were held daily at various points, being principally arranged by Bonapartists. The elections were impending, and zealous agents were at work in favor of Napoleon-Louis Bonaparte, — a friend of the people, the author of "The Extinction of Pauperism," who must be sent to the Chamber, or even be made head of the government. A body of bold and needy men soon rallied round this name; men who felt that they had no future in a republic, and who dreamed of a fortune under a new empire. No means were neglected, — newspapers, pamphlets, lithographs and medals of the Strasburg and Boulogne pretender. The old soldiers and worn uniforms of the grand army were brought forward. Street singers were paid to chant Napoleonic strains. These projects found favor with workingmen and small tradesmen; the new republican and socialistic Napoleon mingled strangely in their minds with Béranger's songs and the first Napoleon.

The party played a double game. While it preached a socialistic Bonapartism to some, to the Rue de Poitiers Club it described Napoleon's name as the watchword of order and social safety. The elections took place June 8. In Paris, Caussidière headed the lists. He resigned his deputyship with his office of prefect of police, concealing his real motives under the guise of frankness and good nature, thus continuing to unite the suffrages of ultra-revolutionists and reactionists. He was followed by Goudchaux, a moderate republican, and Changarnier, that African general who directly after February 24 had proffered his sword to the provisional government, as a man, he said, who "was accustomed to conquer." April 16, he placed himself at the disposal of the government at the Hôtel de Ville, to oppose the rioters, and his attitude upon that occasion attracted the attention of conservatives of every shade. Next came Thiers, then the socialist philosopher Pierre Leroux, Victor Hugo,

Napoleon-Louis Bonaparte, the Lyonnese revolutionist Lagrange, and Prudhon.

At the general elections of April 23, there was a strong current of public opinion in favor of the majority of the provisional government; nothing of the sort any longer existed, as this strange medley testifies. It is a significant fact that M. Thiers, who was not elected April 23, now had the votes of five departments, and Louis Bonaparte of four. The latter, to be sure, owed his quadruple nomination to the less enlightened classes; his partisans had spread a report that if he arrived at power he would abolish all taxes, being, as was said, rich enough to dispense with them and to rule with his own money. They also acted upon the army in similar ways.

Public meetings were still held daily, the object-evidently being to harass and disorganize the National Guard, thus increasing the chances of success for a sudden attack. The Executive Committee passed a new law against such assemblies, and continued to suppress the most turbulent, many arrests being made. (June 8 – 11.) The Executive Committee did not suspect the existence of a Bonapartist conspiracy, yet they determined to carry out the law of 1832, banishing the Bonapartes, and to arrest the newly elected Louis Napoleon, should he return to France. A fine speech was made to this effect by Lamartine, but when the question of the validity of the election of Louis was brought before the Assembly, a hot discussion ensued. Jules Favre and Louis Blanc took his side, being filled with generous illusions as to the solidity of a weak and tottering republic, but were stoutly opposed by Buchez, Pascal Duprat, and Ledru-Rollin, the latter of whom spoke like a true statesman. Louis Bonaparte's adherents prevailed. This was the first great error of the Constituent Assembly of 1848. As Odilon Barrot remarks in his memoirs, " the mass of the conservatives paid little heed to the perils of the republic," unaware that with the republic France was laid open to danger merely to spite the Executive Committee.

The first impulse of Lamartine and Ledru-Rollin was to resign; but the republican club at the National Palace begging the members

M. THIERS.

of the government to stand firm, the Executive Committee decided to remain in office.

June 15, the president of the Assembly read aloud a letter from Louis Bonaparte. "I learn," he wrote, "that my election serves as a pretext for deplorable scenes. . . . . *If the people impose duties upon me, I shall fulfil them;* but I disavow all who impute to me ambitious designs, which are not in my mind." He declared himself ready to remain in exile were it necessary to the happiness of France. The significant phrase in italics stands out pre-eminent. It savored of the usurper. There was a general impulse of indignation. The minister of war, Cavaignac, pointed out that the word "republic" did not once occur in the letter. Jules Favre spoke as warmly against Louis Bonaparte as he had hitherto done in his favor, and insisted that the letter should be sent to the minister of justice. It was judged due to the dignity of the Assembly to defer action in the matter until the next day.

The next day there came another letter containing Bonaparte's resignation, sent, he said, "in order not involuntarily to encourage disorder." His friends had made it clear to him that his hour had not yet come; but he remained in London, constantly busy. His purse being empty, he conceived the singular idea of borrowing from the Czar of Russia.

The Bonapartist troubles were thus indefinitely adjourned, but dissensions occurred daily in regard to economic and social questions, such as railroads, savings banks, and government stocks. All workmen between the ages of eighteen and twenty-five were desired to join the army for two years; those who refused were excluded from the national workshops. The government desired to gain time and to transform the shops into manufactories for the railroads, but the Left insisted that the purchase of railroads should be set aside and the shops closed. This party did indeed agree to vote for certain work on bridges, roads, and canals, which was wholly inadequate, however, to employ this vast body of men; nor would it accept the proposition of one of its own members, Léon Faucher, the economist, who asked for a loan of ten millions for work on the railroads.

Such a policy tended to civil war, unwittingly to most, but not to all; some asked nothing better than to see the republic wrecked in a social tempest, hoping that the *régime* which they regretted or awaited might arise from the chaos. The most active and determined in the course of conflict and reaction was M. de Falloux, chairman of the committee on finance, a man of wide influence. To many in the Assembly the national workshops were a sort of nightmare, many a republican being as eager as the adherents of the Left to see the end of so abnormal a state of affairs. June 15, M. Goudchaux, demanding for the workmen a number of new institutions, also declared that the shops "must be at once abolished."

The delegates of the national shops responded with a remarkable address. "It is not," they said, "that we lack the will to work; it is useful work that is lacking our hands! . . . . You require the instant suppression of the shops; what is to become of one hundred and ten thousand workmen, whose modest daily wages provide for the wants of themselves and their families? Shall they be given over to the evil counsels of hunger and despair? shall they be flung as a prey to the factious assassins of liberty? . . . . Organize, instruct, elevate the national workshops, but do not abolish them."

A proclamation was addressed to all laborers, entreating them not to be carried away by reaction, and not to encourage by their presence "manifestations popular only in name." — "Neither emperor nor king! — Long live the republic!"

This was between the 18th and 20th of June. These highly interesting documents prove that the ranks of the most ardent democracy began to see where the real danger, the real foe, lurked, — namely, among the socialist leaders, who inspired these allusions to recent troubles. Almost all, save Blanqui, strove to repair the harm which they had done the republic in decrying its legislators and its deeds. It was late in the day to control the passions let loose by republican socialists, and now made use of by the agents of Cæsarean demagogues.

The head men in the national workshops, then chosen delegates, for the most part seemed well disposed, and there was every reason to hope that, by closing the shops gradually, with prudence and humanity, the workmen might be restrained by Director Lalanne, while any hasty action could not fail to bring on a fatal catastrophe. Nevertheless, an outbreak of three or four hundred of these workmen took place under one Pujol, an ardent Bonapartist, and a member of the Blanqui Club. (June 22.) This mob protested against the enlistment of laborers between the ages of eighteen and twenty-five, and against the removal of workingmen from Paris, and they loudly clamored for a hearing. The minister of public works, M. Marie, received eight delegates from their number, headed by Pujol, who began a speech in an arrogant tone.

The minister interrupted him hastily, crying, "I recognize you. You were one of the first to invade the Assembly, May 15. You attacked the sovereignty of the people! You shall not speak here!"

"No one here shall speak before me," was Pujol's insolent answer.

"This man forbids your speaking!" said Marie to the other delegates: "are you his slaves?"

Murmurs arose, and after an angry debate, the delegates withdrew, Pujol exclaiming, "We know what we wanted to know; the Executive Committee never desired the organization of labor!"

On reaching the street, he addressed the crowd, declaring that Marie had called the workmen from the national shops slaves. He was answered by cries of "Down with Marie! Down with the Executive Committee! Long live Napoleon! Long live the emperor!" The throng then dispersed to rouse the national shops to revolt, agreeing to meet at six in the evening on the Place du Panthéon.

The Executive Committee, warned by Marie, ordered the arrest of Pujol, with fifty of his delegates and accomplices; but the police were demoralized and did nothing.

Pujol and his followers did not succeed in rousing the shops, but collected some thousand men before evening. When six o'clock came he talked of rearing barricades against "the new tyrants," and dismissed his audience till six the next morning. There was, therefore, ample warning, and no surprise, in the events of June, any more than in those of February. During the night, the Executive Committee requested the Minister of War to take military possession of the Place du Panthéon before the hour appointed for meeting. During the night, a number of the delegates of the workingmen sent a deputation to M. Marie, and, being content with their reception, published and distributed a letter assuring the people that the government had no intention of suddenly closing the national shops, but meant to substitute a genuine industry for an unproductive and ruinous state of affairs by redeeming the railroads. There was, therefore, still the most favorable chance for thwarting the insurrection. Unfortunately, the danger was not in the workshops, the clubs, and the streets alone, but also in the Assembly, in the government or around it. June 21, the day on which Pujol organized his plot, De Falloux renewed his demand for the dissolution of the shops, supported by M. Rouher, a man who had just made his appearance in the world of politics.

Important steps were also taken, on the evening of the 22d, by both sides óf the Assembly, to modify the executive power. The Right was still hostile to the Executive Committee; a part of the Left, without personal hostility, thought it necessary to concentrate the power in one man, — in a word, to substitute a president for a Directory. Overtures had already been made to Cavaignac. It was very dangerous for the republicans to raise such a question, as an insurrection was imminent; brave men, like the members of the Executive Committee do not resign in the hour of peril. The result was .that the Executive Committee and the minister of war were alike placed in a false position, which could not fail to embarrass and confuse their resistance to the factions.

Pujol and his band were prompt at the rendezvous on the morning of the 23d, but the troops did not appear, nor has their absence ever been clearly explained. There was a series of misunderstandings, as on May 15. The Executive Committee wished to scatter the troops and prevent the erection of barricades, while the minister of war desired to unite the government officers at the Palais Bourbon, mass the troops about that point for its defence, and attack the mob by sending strong columns against decisive points. "If a single company lays down its arms," he exclaimed, "I will blow out my brains!" The committee reluctantly yielded.

Cavaignac had been ordered to hold forty thousand men in readiness besides the ten thousand Gardes Mobiles, and twenty-five thousand Gardes Republicains; instead of which, he had but twenty-three thousand, or, as some say, twenty-nine thousand. Nor had Cavaignac his own way in all points, for Arago and Garnier-Pagès persisted in sending a part of the National Guard to hold the Luxembourg. Events proved them right; the line which they defended was never lost through the terrible days that followed. The pupils from the schools hastened to join them, as did a number of notorious socialists.

Barricades were quickly erected at various points on the left bank of the Seine, in the city, and on the Boulevards. Cavaignac's plan was good, from a strategic point of view, but the result was unfortunate. The absence of regular troops, between the Hôtel de Ville and the Boulevards, depressed the National Guard, and prevented them from rising. Murmurs arose on all sides against the Executive Committee, which was unjustly blamed for this lack of troops. Other engagements had occurred at various points. Hitherto the two parties had been nearly equal in numbers, but the Assembly's course of action soon swelled the ranks of the insurgents. Rouher made a strong effort to close the national workshops that very day, and although the minister of public works protested, and no decision was arrived at, an impression was made. The crowd took no heed of the accessory measures which accompanied the proposal to close the shops; three millions indemnity money for the workmen; three months' pay to foremen, clerks, &c. Factious spirits spread the report that the shops were to be closed within three days, and a host of laborers, hitherto uncertain, went over to the rebels.

Hot skirmishes took place during the day, barricades being built up as quickly as pulled down. The number of the insurgents grew constantly. To understand this state of affairs, we must take into account the moral condition of the poorer classes. It was not merely a question of the national shops. The famous "three months of misery," credited to the republic, had passed, and the misery still existed. The poor blamed the "ill-will of the middle class"; they declared that the latter could aid them if they would, and they gave way to a feeling of anger all the more to be feared in proportion to its blindness and vagueness. If they had any sentiment of attachment to a name, it was to that of Napoleon; but it is noteworthy that this name, which had filled the city for months, was scarcely heard now that the insurrection had begun. This was evidently due to the Bonapartist leaders, who felt that the conflict should be anonymous, to unite all the rancor in a common revolt.

Almost the whole twelfth arrondissement, and a portion of the eleventh, were in the hands of the insurgents. Arago went in person to the barricade in the Rue Soufflot, to treat with them, but to no purpose. Taking the head of a column of troops, he boldly forced his way through this barricade and several others, but was stopped in the Rue des Mathurins, where the struggle continued furiously.

At four o'clock, General Cavaignac reported the situation to the Assembly. He gave merited praise to the National Guard and the Garde Mobile, who had proved their trustworthy spirit. During the first day, Paris was really in their hands; no one knows what might have happened had they joined the revolt.

Nevertheless, the contest grew more and more bloody; General Clément Thomas of the National Guard was wounded in taking a barricade at the corner of the Rues St. Antoine and Culture-St. Catherine, and a number of other officers were dead or wounded. The ministers, deputies, and Executive Committee themselves marched with the troops to cheer them on. Cavaignac cannonaded a formidable barricade in the Faubourg du Temple. His artillerymen were killed at their guns, and he only gained his position by help of reinforcements sent by Lamoricière. Other barricades in the neighborhood were captured towards evening, but this victory

cost them dear.   Demands for help which could not be granted
came in from every side; despatches were sent to the departments
for more troops; but what might not happen before they came ?

The centre of the insurrection was now on both sides of the
bridges joining the city to the left bank of the river, near the Hôtel
Dieu.   After a desperate attack, the barricades were carried, with
great bloodshed, General Bedeau and Representative Bixio being
seriously wounded.

As the news came in to the Assembly from various quarters, a
gloom fell upon the citizens.   They felt that the Republic was bleeding from every pore.

Cavaignac persisted in his system of concentration, and did not
hold the most important positions which he had captured.   The
consequence was that the rebels instantly returned to these points,
which at daybreak were still more formidable than the night before.
Numerous prisoners were taken by the insurgents, but were not
treated with cruelty, many being set at liberty.   Another important event was the reappearance of the famous device of February
24, "Death to Thieves!" placarded in the Faubourg St. Antoine.
This showed that the enraged masses had lost neither their self-
respect nor moral sense.

The construction and disposition of the barricades showed the
participation of numerous old soldiers, most of whom were led away
by Bonapartist memories and sentiments.   There were also a number of Legitimists.

On the morning of June 24, while the newspapers, published
amidst the din of cannon and musketry, assumed a significant attitude, — the Socialistic and Republican journals denouncing the Bonapartists, and the Bonapartist press preaching insurrection, — an
important event occurred at the ministry of war.   General Rapatel,
lately made colonel of the Second Legion, brought Cavaignac a letter
which had just reached him from London, dated June 23, and signed
by Louis Napoleon Bonaparte, who named Rapatel minister of war,
and requested him to take immediate possession of the office.
Cavaignac sent the document to the public prosecutor.   This letter

has since been lost, but there can be no doubt of its authenticity. Rapatel's known discontent with the government gained him this perilous favor, which he declined.

At daybreak the discussion in regard to the military plan of action was renewed between Cavaignac and the Executive Committee. It resulted in the passage of a decree placing Paris in a state of siege, and vesting the executive power in Cavaignac. The Committee instantly resigned, thus closing that form of power which was really the prolongation of the provisional government, minus the socialist element. Posterity will be more just to these men than were their contemporaries: they yielded to extreme difficulties; and it is scarcely probable that others would have done better. Their patriotism, courage, and disinterestedness are beyond dispute. No more upright government ever existed.

The fall of the man of February was the first retrograde step of the Republic. The man given them as a successor, however, was also a true republican. He addressed the troops and the insurgents with a sympathy, sense, and appreciation which might have prevented the civil war, had they been shared by the Assembly committees. The president of the Assembly, Sérard, Buchez's successor, also issued a kindly proclamation to the working classes, and sixty delegates were chosen to go to the barricades and call upon the rebels to lay down their arms.

The reinforcements sent for the night before now began to come up, and Cavaignac ordered a renewed attack under three generals,— Damesme, on the left bank of the river; Duvivier, near the Hôtel de Ville; and Lamoricière, in the northern part of Paris. The struggle was renewed with vigor early in the day; the insurgents were driven by cannon from two high houses in the city, which served them as fortresses, and a series of strong barricades on the left bank were taken. The Law School and Pantheon were finally recaptured, after a bloody battle within the latter building. General Damesme displayed equal valor and intelligence; during the struggle he received a mortal wound, and died like a patriot.

The proclamation that the city was besieged caused more anger than alarm, and served the rebels rather than injured them. It had been stoutly opposed by a representative just beginning a great political career, M. Jules Grévy.

The National Guard and troops of the line still advanced, but with great difficulty. Victor Hugo bravely harangued the mob: they refused to listen, but did not fire on him. Towards evening Cavaignac considered himself strong enough to hold the positions that he had succeeded in recapturing; but it was plain that much more blood must be shed ere the final victory was gained. The night of June 24 was even more sinister than the preceding one. Frightful atrocities were attributed to the rebels, and these imaginary horrors gave rise to actual barbarities, which infuriated the troops, who considered themselves peculiarly an object of revenge to the insurgents, and rendered them merciless. In spite of all that the commanding officer could do, they shot ten prisoners; and this, being reported among the rebels with great exaggeration, spread terror and rage.

The third day, destined to be so fatal, began with a fresh misfortune. General Duvivier dying from the combined effects of heat and a shot in his foot, Colonel Reynaud, who took his place, was shot and killed by a prisoner. Scenes of horror followed in rapid succession. General Négrier, coming up with reinforcements, took command on the Place de la Bastille; the barricades of the Faubourg St. Antoine rained shot, and the troops faltered. The general, advancing alone to reconnoitre, was killed by a stray ball from the gun of one of his own men. A representative, M. Charbonnel, was also slain.

The Assembly and the new government strove to stop the carnage. A loan of three millions was voted to be distributed in charity throughout Paris. The new chief of the executive power and the president of the Assembly signed a proclamation protesting against the rumor that "cruel vengeance awaited the insurgents who should surrender." "Come to us," it said, "come like repentant brothers, submissive to the law, and the arms of the Republic are open to receive you."

A courageous man, Representative Galy-Cazalat, went to the

district of the Temple, where the populace were assembled, to read
the decree, and, being well received, he ventured, decree in hand,
into the Faubourg St. Antoine, where there was a brief lull.

After the decree had been carried to the insurgents, not by a
member of the Assembly, but by the Archbishop of Paris, M.
Affre, who, though cultured and kindly, was timid by nature, and
seemed little capable of an heroic deed. His feeling of duty and
Christian charity raised him above himself. He went to General
Cavaignac and informed him of his resolution, which Cavaignac
vainly opposed. " My life is of small moment," he responded, and
set out for the Place de la Bastille. The officer in command, the
fourth during the day, three having fallen, proposed a truce. The
fire was suspended, and the archbishop entered the faubourg simultaneously with Galy-Cazalat, and two other deputies. He had
not taken twenty steps when a shot was heard, followed by a general
discharge from the troops on the other side of the Place de la
Bastille. The insurgents cried, " Treason! treason!" and returned
the fire from all sides. The archbishop fell, struck down by a ball
from one of the neighboring houses. Amidst a general volley of
shot from both sides he was picked up and carried to the house of a
neighboring priest. The wound was mortal. The news soon spread,
and filled the combatants with horror: night fell, and the firing
gradually ceased. The archbishop died the next day, saying,
" May my blood be the last that is shed!"

The fearful struggle was not ended. Before this misfortune,
which was a deplorable accident, but not a crime, it had been sullied
by an odious deed.

General Bréa, who replaced Damesme, hoping to persuade the
mob to surrender, went about announcing the loan of three millions
for their succor. On reaching the barrier at Fontainebleau he was
advised not to venture in; but, generous, humane, and trusting, he
did not believe in the existence of danger; followed by four officers,
who would not leave him, he crossed the boundary line, and was
instantly surrounded and swept away. For two hours, brutally
threatened by some and shielded by others, he and his friends hung

between life and death.   He and a captain of his staff were finally killed; the rest escaped.   At the news of this crime the National Guard and Garde Mobile opened fire, and in a few moments carried the barrier and barricades, thus putting an end to the insurrection on the left bank of the river.

On the evening of the 25th the rebels retained nothing but the Faubourgs of St. Antoine and the Temple.   The result was no longer doubtful.   Fresh reinforcements constantly arrived, and many who had hitherto remained quietly at home now took up arms, and were most violent against the rebels.

The tragic events of the day forced the Assembly to abandon the policy of pacification.   An order was passed for the arrest of Emile de Girardin, whose journal, the *Press*, had contributed to provoke the conflict.   The paper was suspended with ten others, Bonapartist, ultra-revolutionary, and ultra-reactionary.

Since the death of the archbishop, the people of the Faubourg St. Antoine had seemed more willing to hear reason.   They sent delegates, with an address setting forth that " the Faubourg had always fought for the democratic republic; that the inhabitants had no wish for bloodshed, but only demanded the ratification of their rights and duties as French citizens."

The delegates were well received by President Sénard, who promised to lay their propositions before the Assembly.   Cavaignac made no objection, but Lamoricière passionately protested, declaring that their only object was to gain time for an attack on his men, while they were struggling in another quarter.   Sénard thereupon replied in writing to the delegates, that, if they wished to preserve the rights and fulfil the duties of French citizens, they must instantly destroy the barricades.   Cavaignac gave them until ten o'clock to surrender.   They could not consent to submit unconditionally.   Ten o'clock struck.   The general waited a moment.   Then the artillery thundered, and the foremost houses of the faubourg fell beneath the attack.   There was little resistance.   The majority of the people felt that it would be madness to cause the destruction of their homes and the death of their wives and children in the flames.

Meantime Lamoricière took possession of the Faubourg du Temple. At half-past one, June 26, on the resumption of the legislative session, the president announced that all was over.

This strange insurrection, without name, without avowed aim, without a flag, as we may say,—it mingled with the red flag the tricolored flags of the shops, — was the fiercest and most terrible of all the unsuccessful struggles that had been waged. It was the result of a premature revolution, which had overturned society without being able to restore it to order, and put questions that it had no power to solve.

Repressive measures followed in rapid succession. Such of the National Guard as had failed to respond to the call to arms were disarmed; all suspected clubs were closed, and a committee was formed to investigate events as far back as May 15. To a law for the transportation of any man found armed was added an order for the trial by court-martial of the chiefs and instigators of the revolt. A strange paradox! The chiefs were allowed to defend themselves before a judge, while those who only followed in their train were condemned without a hearing. But in Cavaignac's mind, transportation implied neither civil death nor stigma, and might be followed in time by full pardon. Pierre Leroux and Caussidière alone opposed this law. Caussidière, whose conduct had been so equivocal on the 15th of May, took care this time to place himself above suspicion.

The horrors of this revolt did not cease with the fighting. Numbers of prisoners were huddled together in the Abbaye du Conciergerie, the cellars of the Hôtel de Ville, and the national palaces. There were twelve or fourteen hundred in the vaults below the terrace running from the Tuileries to the Place de la Concorde. The wretched creatures were stifled in this close, fetid passage; and when they approached the air-holes to breathe, the sentries fired on them. The military authorities, on being notified, attempted to take them from this horrible prison. As the first detachment of twenty-five hundred marched along in the darkness, on the night of the 26th, escorted by the National Guard, a gun went off accidentally. A panic ensued; the soldiers, thinking themselves attacked, fired on the prisoners and upon one another, and the neighboring posts fired on all together. One hundred and seventy were left on the ground, killed or wounded!

The total list of victims of the civil war has never been correctly ascertained; nearly fifteen hundred are proved to have perished, and more than twenty-five hundred wounded to have been tended in the hospitals; but many more must forever remain unknown.

The next morning (June 27), Cavaignac issued a proclamation of victory. He announced his desire to return to the rank of citizen, and appealed to justice, protesting against the hasty executions which had unfortunately occurred. The spirit of reaction was rampant; more than eleven thousand persons were arrested, although a goodly number were soon released. With the exception of the assassins of General Bréa the rest profited by the abolition of capital punishment for political crimes.

June 28, the Assembly issued a proclamation, declaring "that, in a state of universal suffrage, rebellion against the sovereignty of the people was the greatest of crimes," and protesting that the interests of the laboring classes were sacred above all others. Soon after this Cavaignac declared that he surrendered the species of dictatorship he had exercised into the hands of the Assembly, which restored the executive power to him anew, and conferred on him the title of President of the Ministerial Council, and the right to nominate the ministry. The Right had offered to support Cavaignac, but showed great displeasure at his choice of ministers, which was too republican for the men of the Rue de Poitiers, who soon found means to break in upon it.

July 3, the new government proposed a decree for closing the national workshops, and withdrew the projected law for redeeming the railroads. This had become inevitable.

Cavaignac entered office with intentions quite as patriotic as his predecessors of the February government, and apparently the strength which they had lacked. His position, however, was in reality far worse than theirs. The evil that they strove to avert had broken

out; the class struggle, the social conflict had begun. Jean Reynaud graphically summed up the situation during the days of
June: "We are lost if we are conquered, — we are lost if we are
conquerors." It was too true; the republic had received its death-
blow. Victorious, the political world would tend in a few months to
monarchical Cæsarism by force of reaction; vanquished, it would fall
in a few days into demagogic Cæsarism by force of anarchy. Like
the fabled Janus, Bonapartism was ready to turn either of its two
faces to France, its destined prey.

CHAPTER X.

SECOND REPUBLIC (*continued.*) — SECOND CONSTITUENT ASSEMBLY (*continued.*) — GENERAL CAVAIGNAC'S GOVERNMENT. — ELECTION OF DECEMBER 10.

June 27 — December 20, 1848.

CIVIL war had seated on the pinnacle of power a man unknown to the political world but a few weeks before, and who had had no opportunity to dazzle public imagination by brilliant successes during his honorable military career. However, his sound judgment, uprightness, dignity, and calm resolution soon gained him the confidence of the whole Assembly. The Republicans felt that he was incapable of trampling the laws under foot and betraying the republic; the others, whatever might be their dreams for the future, realized the necessity, for the moment, of clinging to the man who had conquered insurrection. He was more solid than brilliant, and lacked the breadth and wealth of resource requisite for a nation so little used to self-government.

The civil war was smothered by the bloody struggle of June, but the fires it had kindled still smouldered in many hearts. During the troubles in Paris, there was no attempt at insurrection in the departments, save at Marseilles, but the same passions pervaded all the great cities of France; there was class dissension everywhere, — workmen against employers, peasants against the petty bourgeoisie. These peasants, however, jealous of the bourgeoisie as they were, were at the same time bitterly opposed to the June rebellion and to everything that savored of communism, and they continued to flood Paris for days after victory was gained, that they might aid in putting down the insurgents.

The danger that menaced the new government lay rather in the country than in the Assembly; and yet the Assembly soon showed that there were great difficulties to be contended with there. With the exception of the ministers of war and the navy,—the former of which positions had been given to Lamoricière, the latter to an admiral of no political importance,—Cavaignac had formed a Republican ministry. He gave the portfolio of the interior to Sénard, who had seconded him so well, as president of the Assembly, during the late trying days; he called Goudchaux to the department of finance, Bethmont to that of justice, Tourret to that of agriculture and commerce, Recurt to public works; Bastide had charge of foreign affairs, and Carnot of public instruction.

The Right quarrelled with his selection of Carnot, the real motive of their dislike being his desire to establish a great republican system of education. So great was the opposition that Carnot resigned, and his lofty schemes were not resumed for many years. July 5, he was replaced by Vaulabelle, author of the History of the Restoration, who remained but a short time in the ministry. The Right did not oppose the succession of Marie, an ex-member of the provisional government, to Sénard as president of the Assembly.

July 6, funeral ceremonies were held on the Place de la Concorde in honor of the victims of the recent rebellion, but the lookers-on were cold and sad. The motto, "Liberty, Equality, and Fraternity," seemed a satire on the morrow of this fratricidal struggle.

The government strove to appease the working classes by well-meant measures. The national work-shops were necessarily closed in the departments as well as in Paris, but food was distributed from house to house to the amount of the three million francs voted June 25, and three millions more were granted in favor of stock companies, composed either of workmen alone or of workmen and employers; a day's work was limited to twelve hours: yet all the good intentions and efforts of the government could not efface the sorrowful memories of the month of June. Thousands of Parisians were still imprisoned, awaiting transportation. New press-laws were passed August 9 and 11, and the newspapers suppressed in June were allowed to resume publication. Clubs were not prohibited, but were so regulated as to render them less dangerous.

PLACE DE LA CONCORDE.

The check given to the improvement of the educational system by the resignation of Carnot affected also the economic and financial movement. Goudchaux, who replaced Garnier-Pagès, attempted to restore the duties on liquors and the tax on salt, abolished by his predecessor. He also withdrew the scheme for the State redemption of railroads, and thus lost a fine opportunity for carrying out the plan of the Republican party of the time of Louis Philippe by the substitution of the State for great stock companies.

Amid these economic and political debates, a singular episode agitated the Assembly. Socialism appeared again in the lists, under the championship of the sectarian who was at war with all others, namely, Proudhon. Before the events of June, the Assembly had listened with interest and even with sympathy to the social and philosophic opinions of Pierre Leroux, whose religious feeling and broadly comprehensive views had won tolerance for his extreme ideas and his eccentricities. Proudhon, however, with his positive and irritating opinions, only excited an increasing annoyance. As he denied everything that exists and everything that others proposed, he was requested to state what he wished in his turn. He accepted the challenge, and presented a proposition which, according to him, would end in the " liquidation of the old régime, without violence, without expropriation, and without bankruptcy," — in other words, the abolition of property. This was to be effected by a law obliging all capitalists and stockholders to disburse to their tenants and debtors of every class, under the name of a loan, one sixth of their income, and to pay another sixth into the national treasury as a tax, designed to found a bank of exchange. For the first time since the February revolution, M. Thiers took the floor, and readily showed the sophistry of this scheme, as did also, not long after, the economist Frédéric Bastiat.

This discussion suggested to Thiers the idea of issuing a series of books and pamphlets against Socialism, for which a subscription was raised by the club in the Rue de Poitiers. Of these ephemeral publications, some were quite remarkable. as, for instance, Thiers's own little book " On Property."

While this tourney of economic and social questions was waging, the Assembly was preparing to discuss most important interests. The committee appointed June 26 to inquire into the causes of the June insurrection and the illegal attempt of May 15, acting upon a preconceived idea, refused to see anything in the insurrection beyond the Luxembourg and the national workshops, socialism and communism. It set to work to study the deeds and words of the provisional government during the early days of the Republic, accusing Ledru-Rollin as well as Louis Blanc and Caussidière. In this way, it entirely lost sight of immediate causes, and, troubling itself only with democrats and socialists, stopped its eyes and ears to all that concerned other parties, refusing to see the important part played in the disturbances by the Bonapartists,—so clear to-day to all who study the documents of the time. Pujol, who had set the ball rolling in the first days of the insurrection, was subjected only to trifling interrogation, and was not even summoned before a council of war.

The report of the committee was read August 3, by Quentin Bauchart, and produced a bad impression even on the moderate party of the Right. Ledru-Rollin, severely attacked in the report, took the floor, and retorted, rather than defended himself, exclaiming that this was the work of partisanship, and not of justice,— a statement which was received with loud applause, and Cavaignac shook his hand warmly. Louis Blanc and Caussidière were less successful. It was determined to prosecute them, but the government, although unwilling to oppose this step, gave them time to escape to England.

Important and unfortunate events were now occurring abroad. The Venetian province had again fallen into the hands of Austria, with the exception of Venice, which, shut in by its lagoons, determined to defend itself to the last extremity. Charles Albert, unable to profit by his advantages, was again held in check by Radetzki. Venice, not obtaining the official recognition of France, which would have been a pledge of protection, yielded to a union with Lombardy under the rule of Charles Albert, and this at a time when he was becoming less and less able to protect her.

During the first two weeks in July, the government of Cavaignac renewed the offer of intervention several times made by Lamartine, but Charles Albert refused anew. The consequences were incalculable. About this time an event occurred which was little known, and concerning which we have imperfect information, but which, if it had all the importance which it seems possible to ascribe to it, might have changed the whole aspect of Europe. Czar Nicholas, after assuming a threatening attitude toward the February republic, resumed a position of reserve and expectancy. The troubles in Austria and Prussia greatly impressed him by showing him that central Europe was unable to interfere with anything he might undertake. His ambassador at Naples, M. de Creptowich, gave the French ambassador to understand that Russia was ready to offer carte blanche to France in the west — i. e., Italy and the left bank of the Rhine — in return for carte blanche to Russia in the East.

Possibly Charles Albert's refusal led Cavaignac to seek an understanding with England. However that may be, he refused to listen to the overtures of Russia, whereupon Nicholas became the protector of Austria. Cavaignac then proposed to join England in imposing Franco-English mediation on Austria and Italy.

Just at this time, Radetzki resumed the offensive with success. After five days of fighting, the brave Piedmontese were driven back to the west of the Mincio. On hearing of this defeat, the Milanese sent to Paris for help. Charles Albert at once disavowed all part in this embassy, and not until a week later (August 3) did he submit to ask for a French army, and then only on condition that France should not claim Savoy as her reward; i. e., France was to give her blood and her money to gain a nationality for Italy, and leave besides a shred of her own nationality in the grasp of an Italian prince.

This strange communication did not reach the French government until August 7. While it was on the way a great catastrophe had taken place. The Milanese, like the Venetians, were prepared for a desperate defence. The heroes of March had reappeared at the head of the people, and among them a brave partisan leader, newly arrived from America,—Garibaldi, the genius of revolutionary war. Unfortunately the spirit of the army was not equal to that of the citizens. The Piedmontese, hotly pursued by superior numbers, were again defeated within sight of Milan. Charles Albert, deceived by evil counsellors, lost his head, and surrendered the city to Radetzki. Milan rebelled, and anarchy was let loose. The king departed by night with his troops: no preparations for defence had been made, and the next morning (August 6) half the population fled rather than die among foes. August 9, Charles Albert signed an armistice, agreeing to give up all outside of his former dominions, including Venice. The Piedmontese reactionists persuaded him to sacrifice Lombardy and Venice, to avoid French intervention, and to keep Savoy. Venice, abandoned by the king, returned to the republic, with Marino as dictator. Marino sent to France for succor. (August 11, 12.)

The French government replied, August 7, to Charles Albert's request for help that it was too late, and that France could only offer to mediàte in conjunction with England. The terms of the mediation had already been agreed upon by the French minister of foreign affairs, M. Bastide, and Lord Normanby. They were that Austria should renounce Lombardy, and Venice remain under Austrian rule, with a separate constitution and national administration, as in Hungary.

August 22, Cavaignac explained his foreign policy to the Assembly, his only object being, he said, to ensure an honorable peace to the republic. This peaceful tendency was far from being shared by all those around him. Marrast, then president of the Assembly, from a conviction that it was for the interest of the republic, Lamoricière as a military point of honor, and even Bastide, pressed him to follow a more energetic course. At one time, therefore, he consented to send the French fleet to Venice, and gave orders to that effect.

September 3, Austria accepted the proffered mediation, but said nothing in regard to Venice, notwithstanding which the order for the sailing of the fleet was revoked, although the French squadron in the Adriatic was directed to prevent a blockade of Venice. Had the troops been despatched, the occurrence of events, so fatal in their results, at Rome towards the close of the year, might have been prevented.

In September, Austria's success was but ill-assured. On the one hand, Venice was determined to resist to the last, and the event proved her powers of endurance; on the other hand, Charles Albert, incensed against the reactionary advisers who had persuaded him to a humiliating surrender, thought only of rehabilitating himself by taking up arms anew. The fresh disturbances in Austria encouraged him and revived the hopes of the Italians. The Hungarians, at last perceiving their mistake in permitting Austrian rule in Italy, broke with Austria, which roused the Slavs of Hungary against them in turn. The Croats, instigated by Vienna, invaded Hungary proper, the Magyar country. They were beaten and repulsed by the Hungarians, and a few days later a new insurrection broke out in Vienna. The Austrian emperor left the city (October 6 and 7), and the whole empire was given over to war. The Tcheks were also fighting the imperial troops in Prague.

Everything seemed to summon France to unfurl her banner. Even Lord Palmerston, reassured in regard to the designs of France, now favored Italian independence, and public opinion in England was bitterly hostile to Austria. Cavaignac still refused to move. He had no confidence in Charles Albert, whom he judged by the past; but this was not his chief motive. Being only a temporary chief, whose powers might soon expire, he did not think himself justified in engaging France in war. His scruples deserve respect, but prove that he did not understand the situation of the country. Before the June revolution, foreign war would have been the only means of preventing civil war: now it was the only hope of warding off the consequences of civil war and saving the republic, — a doubtful and dangerous chance indeed; but there was no other. The republic, prematurely established, misunderstood by the masses, shut up within itself, without outside diversion, without *éclat*, without the prestige of a glorious record wherewith to fire the popular imagination, was inevitably doomed to perish. Cavaignac did not see — what was seen clearly by those about him who had studied foreign affairs while he was serving France in Africa — that the foreign policy which Louis Philippe practised for eighteen years would destroy the republic in a few months.   Armand Carrel would not have hesitated to do what Cavaignac shrunk from; but Cavaignac's error was the error of an honest man, and his disinterestedness renders his memory honorable.   He desired peace at home as well as abroad, although he did not believe it possible at the time.   In spite of all his efforts to the contrary, the state of siege was still kept up, — a course which did not tend to strengthen the government.

The partial elections which took place in September were even more alarming than those which preceded the last of June.   The small number of voters in many departments seemed to show that many citizens were already disgusted with political life.   The result was adverse to the republic: out of fifteen nominations, thirteen belonged to the conservatives.   What was yet more serious was the fact that Louis Bonaparte, elected by four departments in June, was chosen by five in September.   Among the five figured that of Moselle, that district which the senseless policy of its candidate, when emperor, was one day to surrender, with the great military city of Metz, to the foreigner.

When the result of the elections was announced in Paris, the names of Louis Bonaparte and Raspail were received with cries of, " Long live the Emperor!" and " Long live the Social Republic!"

September 26, Louis Bonaparte took his seat in the Assembly. He protested against "the calumnies of which he had been the object," and vowed gratitude and devotion to the republic, which had restored to him his country and his rights as a citizen.   His conduct, he said, should be ever marked by loyalty to the law, and prove that no one had the interests of the republic more closely at heart than he.

The republicans responded to these reactionary elections by banquets celebrating the anniversary of the establishment of the first republic.   The effect these assemblies produced was not a happy one. In Paris, Ledru-Rollin launched into exaggerations injurious to the

cause, hoping to regain the socialists. At Toulouse, matters were
still worse. The passions of the south were blindly let loose. The
guests at a republican banquet, in presence of the authorities, hissed
the toasts to the National Assembly and Cavaignac, and rushed
through the streets, noisily threatening the rich and the priests.
This made a great scandal in the Assembly. The Right censured
the minister of the interior, M. Sénard, for the presence of office-
holders at the banquet that ended so disgracefully, whereupon he
resigned, with Recurt and Vaulabelle. These three were replaced
by Dufaure, Vivien, and Freslon (October 13), republicans of the
future. This choice caused some question, but was finally confirmed;
and the raising of the state of siege, which coincided with the entry
of the new ministers, was taken as a pledge of the conciliation and
moderation promised by the government. A fourth minister, M.
Goudchaux, next retired, and was replaced by Trouvé-Chauvel, who
made no especial mark.

The new ministry continued its policy of conciliation. The rest
of the June prisoners were transported to Algiers instead of to
remote colonies. Several weeks previous to the election of that
committee of inquiry which had only served to foment angry passions, the Assembly formed, under different circumstances and in a
very different spirit, a committee to frame a constitution for the
republic. This committee decided that the new constitution, like
those of the French revolution, should be preceded by a declaration
of principles, to be proclaimed " in presence of God and in the name
of the French nation." One article was as follows : "The French
Republic respects foreign nationalities, ... it will never employ
its powers against the liberty of any people."

The violation of this solemn pledge during the reaction of 1849
entailed results from which France still suffers.

Discussion waxed hot in the commission when social questions
and those of political organization were taken up. The members were
all distinguished men, and much was expected of them; but it was
soon evident that the strange character of the February revolution
had shaken the firmest minds. Armand Marrast, Louis Blanc's

fiercest opponent in the provisional government, now stoutly upheld the right to labor, and after much discussion the following article was introduced: "Society should furnish work for all able-bodied men who cannot procure it otherwise." Even this modified form of the proposition presented great practical difficulties.

The right to assistance did not call forth the same objections, and the clause was written down as follows: "Abandoned children, the infirm, and the aged are entitled to receive support from the State." The right to education was next recognized. When the important question, whether there should be one Chamber or two, was raised, the committee took into account neither the example of America nor that of the convention itself, which had created two Chambers immediately upon the transition from a revolutionary to a normal government. Barrot and De Tocqueville argued strongly in favor of a dual assembly, the latter declaring that the republic must either perish or accept the system of two Chambers. A single Chamber was, however, accepted by thirteen against three.

The question of legislative power was succeeded by that of executive power. No one denied the necessity of vesting it in one person; every one wished a president, not a directory. By the same superficial logic which carried the vote for a single assembly it was decided to place the presidential election in the hands of the people, on the pretext that any other course might be taken as an attack upon popular rights. The majority failed to see that, while the legislative power should be in the hands of the people, the executive power should come from the legislature; that the representatives of the people should make the laws, and choose the chief magistrate who should execute them. Even the ripest intellects were bewildered. De Tocqueville, usually so wise, caused it to be decided that the president was ineligible for re-election, thus doubling the chances of conflict and *coups d'état*.

Some of the committee being dismayed at what had been done the discussion was resumed, and it was proposed to elect the president from the Assembly. Odilon Barrot insisted that any other expedient would bring on civil war. The majority blindly persisted

(June 15) in refusing to make the royal families who had hitherto reigned ineligible for the presidency.

It was decided that the Assembly should choose a council of state, the magistrates to be chosen by the executive power, the justices of the peace to be elective, and mayors to be nominated by town councils.

The system of substitutes in the army was abolished, although it was long before this reform was put in execution. Cavaignac, strange to say, favored military reform to the point of reducing the term of service to two years, as in Prussia.

Marrast was made chairman, and presented the constitution to the Assembly, June 19. Many of the members were opposed to various clauses, but the consequences of the June rebellion caused an adjournment of their public discussion until September 4. The debate opened with the right to labor, which Thiers opposed in a remarkable speech. The article was rejected by five hundred and ninety-seven against one hundred and eighty-seven, the following formula being substituted: " The republic should, by fraternal assistance, ensure the support of its needy citizens, either by procuring them work to the extent of its means, or by giving the means of existence to those who are unable to work and have no family."

The right to education was hotly discussed, De Montalembert eagerly arguing in its favor. It was not a question of a struggle between State and individual, but between State and Church, and was finally decided in favor of the State.

The two Chambers having been rejected, the Grévy amendment alone could save the republic. M. Grévy proved with irresistible logic that a president chosen by universal suffrage would be more powerful than a king. " Are you very sure," he cried, " that some ambitious spirit raised to the *presidential throne* will not be tempted to make his term of office perpetual? And if this ambitious spirit be the scion of one of the families that has reigned in France, if he has never formally renounced what he calls his rights, if commerce languishes, if the people are suffering, if there comes one of those critical moments when want and credulity make the nation an easy prey to those who mask their plans against its liberty under fair promises, can you answer that this ambitious spirit will not succeed in overthrowing the republic ?"

This prophetic voice was unheeded. The Grévy amendment was rejected by a large majority. The danger so forcibly pointed out by Grévy was not denied by Lamartine, who, in a speech as eloquent as illogical, predicted that the people were about to desert the cause of liberty and progress and destroy themselves in the pursuit of a will-o'-the-wisp; but he closed with the exclamation, "The die is cast. Let God and the people decide!"

Since his retirement from power this great poet and orator had irretrievably lost his balance. His political career closed with a fatal error. To him belongs the sad honor, not of causing, but of swelling the majority which destroyed the republic. Six hundred and twenty-seven against one hundred and thirty voted for the election of a president by universal suffrage. (October 9.)

This vote having been passed, deputy Antony Thouret, son of the great lawyer of the Constituent Assembly, renewed the proposal to exclude from the presidency all members of the ex-royal families of France. Louis Bonaparte took the floor to defend himself against the suspicions cherished in regard to him, speaking awkwardly, and with a foreign accent which did not add to his eloquence. Thouret sprang up and cried: "I thought this man dangerous; having heard him, I acknowledge my error, and withdraw my proposition."

There was a general laugh. Louis Bonaparte made no answer; his dull eye did not kindle, and his face preserved its usual impassiveness.

The separation of Church and State desired by Lamartine was not effected, and the clause in the charter of 1830, concerning the "religion of the majority," was effaced.

It was now necessary to fix the date of the presidential election. The pretentions of Louis Bonaparte were again discussed. He had not been seen in the house since Thouret's speech, but on the 26th of October, he again took the floor with greater boldness. "Of what am I accused?" he said. "Of accepting an office which I never sought? Yes, I accept it as an honor!" And in an adroit little speech he contrived to flatter both the conservatives and the masses.

The majority wished to postpone the presidential election until the constitution was drafted, but the committee and Cavaignac thought otherwise; the latter was in haste to know his fate and that of the country. The election was finally fixed for December 10. A last effort was made to exclude the ancient dynasties. Cavaignac himself exclaimed that it was too late. It was settled that the oath of allegiance to the constitution should be limited to the president, and the constitution was accepted November 4, very few refusing to subscribe to it. Among the number was Odilon Barrot. As a whole, the constitution of 1848 was far inferior to that of the year III. Judging France by this comparison, we are forced to admit that she had rather retrograded than advanced during the half century. It was at least a striking indication that the return to a republic was premature.

November 12, the constitution was read to the people on the Place de la Concorde, and a mass, followed by a Te Deum, was celebrated by Archbishop Sibour, the successor of the martyr of June 26. The snow was falling, and the festival was as cold and gloomy as the weather.

Nothing was thought of now in France but the presidential election. Eugene Cavaignac and Louis Bonaparte were the two rival candidates. Ledru-Rollin and Raspail were also talked of, but they had no serious chance. None supported Lamartine. The great poet, lately elected to power by one million six hundred thousand votes, could not understand this sudden abandonment after such immense popularity. What he called public ingratitude filled his soul with bitterness and darkened the rest of his life.

Most of the middle-class republicans rallied round Cavaignac; as for the workingmen, defeated in June, they felt their inability to elect a candidate from their own ranks, and from resentment against Cavaignac and the bourgeoisie went over to Louis Bonaparte. The Bonapartists renewed their former manœuvres on a vast scale;

extravagant promises, popular songs, pictures, and a constant asso- ciation and confusion of "uncle and nephew" were employed. Many a peasant in the remote mountains still doubted that the emperor was dead, seeing only the name Napoleon, the name of Bonaparte being dropped, and the candidate only known as Louis Napoleon. These methods would have been impossible with a people who had had the advantages of a good common- school education and who possessed any knowledge of political affairs. They would fail to-day : they succeeded in 1848. Many of the newspapers attacked Cavaignac as a tyrant ; and the leaders of the Right, members of the old constitutional opposition, after much hesitation, went over to Louis Napoleon, as did Thiers, who was Cavaignac's personal enemy. Thiers, who did not feel the same repulsion for the consulate and the empire as does the present gen- eration, took Louis Napoleon for an inexperienced and somewhat narrow-minded man, whom he could easily restrain and direct, not guessing the determined obstinacy and prejudice hidden beneath his heavy and commonplace exterior.

Diverse and even contrary elements were thus united in favor of "the nephew of the emperor." One only of the social forces was in a state of uncertainty and division, namely, the clergy, some few members of which leaned towards Cavaignac. The Cavaignac party was wholly at a disadvantage in the struggle. To a conscien- tious and honorable man like Cavaignac, his official position was rather a hindrance than a help. His friends tried to turn the weapon of ridicule against the violent and extravagant decla- mation of his foes. The hero of Strasburg and Boulogne was an easy prey, owing alike to the memory of his two singular and abortive expeditions, his ill-proportioned features, his expressionless physiognomy, and his heavy bearing ; he only looked well on horse- back. But ridicule, effective as it is with the cultured, has little hold on the rural districts, and the workingmen of the city were moved by passions too deeply-seated to be affected by this light raillery, which did not raise a smile.

M. Dufaure, minister of the interior, issued a brief political circular to the various prefects, urging them to watch over the integrity of the coming elections and to lay the true interests of the republic before their voters, upon which Jules Favre accused the administration of interfering in the debate between the two candidates. Dufaure forcibly refuted the accusation with the Assembly's approval. (November 24.)

A much more serious and more lengthy struggle ensued between the head of the executive power and some of his predecessors in the government. The Executive Committee, abruptly dismissed during the latter days of June, had been most unjustly accused and suspected, thus causing a very natural anger among its members, which was, however, wrongly concentrated on the new head of the government. Barthélemi St. Hilaire, the former secretary of the committee, together with Garnier-Pagès, Duclerc, and Pagnerre, now published a pamphlet entitled "A Fragment of History," in which they accused Cavaignac of disobedience to orders and of fomenting the revolt in order to make himself necessary and to gain the dictatorship. Cavaignac challenged the writers to a public discussion, when he defended himself nobly, winning a renewed vote of thanks for his conduct in June. His success was equally great among the middle classes in the rural districts, and numerous deputations from the National Guard called to congratulate him.

Louis Bonaparte could not claim any such triumph. He issued an address to the people (November 29), full of dissimulation, although protesting against it, and abounding in vague and contradictory promises, which every man could interpret as he pleased.

During the month previous to the presidential elections, events had occurred abroad from which Cavaignac hoped to draw some advantage for France. As has been said, he was unwilling to send armed aid to Italy against Austria. A few days after the Austrian attack on Bologna, the pope sent to France for four thousand soldiers to protect Rome. (August 25.) Cavaignac refused, not wishing to take part against Austria or to interfere with domestic troubles in Rome. Matters, however, assumed so grave an aspect at Rome, that the French government felt obliged to abandon its neutral position.

Pius IX., once the idol of the Romans, grew daily more unpopular.
After Charles Albert's defeat, he dismissed his liberal ministry, and
took into his service Count Rossi, ex-ambassador of Louis Philippe
and of Guizot, a man of superior intellect and energy, who attempted impossibilities by resuming amidst the revolution of 1848
the doctrinarian policy of 1847. He thus, as a constitutional minister, encountered the hostility of the absolutists and the Jesuits, and,
as opposed to war, that of the patriots. November 15, at the opening of the Roman legislature, he entered the hall amid the hoots of
the mob, whereupon a man plunged a dagger into his breast.

So great was the popular frenzy that this detestable crime was
hailed by the huzzas of the mob, which the next day flocked to the
Quirinal, where the pope then resided, and ordered him to join the
alliance against Austria and to choose patriotic ministers. A skirmish followed between the Swiss papal guard and the people,
supported by the civic guard and regular Roman troops. Pius
IX. apparently yielded to force; but he expressed to the French
ambassador, Duke d'Harcourt, his desire to take refuge in France.
Cavaignac had already thought of offering an asylum to the Holy
Father. On learning of Rossi's murder, he telegraphed to the fleet
at Toulon to carry to Civita Vecchia a brigade destined for Venice,
and dispatched M. Freslon, minister of public instruction, to receive the pope at Marseilles in the name of the republic.

November 30, this step was seriously questioned by the Assembly,
Ledru-Rollin and Jules Favre looking upon the dispatch of troops
to Civita Vecchia *via* Marseilles as an attack upon Roman liberties,
contrary to the constitution. This was not the purpose of Cavaignac or his ministry, who only wished to ensure the liberty of the
pope and to protect his embarkation. The Assembly approved the
measure, although many members refused to vote.

Pius IX., meantime, instead of coming to France, took refuge with
the King of Naples, the most reactionary of Italian princes. This
indicated what was to be the end of a career which had opened so
happily. Louis Napoleon, true to his double-faced policy, blamed
Cavaignac's course in the public press, as likely to offend foreign

powers; but at the same time, he wrote to the papal nuncio in favor of the maintenance of the temporal sovereignty of the head of the church, — a sovereignty against which he had borne arms in 1831. We shall see the gradual unfolding of the terrible results of this pledge of Louis Napoleon, from 1849 to 1870. This was the beginning of the fatal " Roman question."

The presidential election was at hand and took place in an orderly manner. Louis Napoleon was chosen by a large majority. The rural districts and lower class of citizens on the one hand, and on the other, the old aristocrats and heads of the clerical party, together with many of the June insurgents, voted in his favor. December 20, the result of the election was laid before the Assembly. Cavaignac took the floor, resigned his office, and thanked the members, in simple but dignified terms, for the confidence that they had placed in him. The president of the Assembly, Armand Marrast, then proclaimed Louis Napoleon Bonaparte president of the republic until the second Sunday in May, 1852. Louis Bonaparte next came forward and took the oath of allegiance. He declared that he would consider as enemies all who should attempt to alter in illegal ways that which the French nation had established. He also paid a tribute to Cavaignac, and on leaving the stand, offered him his hand; but Cavaignac turned away, too straightforward and upright to accept the hand of a dissimulator.

December 20, 1848, began the government of that man to whom in a fit of delirium France confided her fate, and who was to preside over her destinies until September 2, 1870. This unfortunate nation, to use the language of the great historian Michelet, stabbed herself with her own hand.

CHAPTER XI.

SECOND REPUBLIC (*continued*). — SECOND CONSTITUENT ASSEMBLY (*continuation and close*). — PRESIDENCY OF LOUIS NAPOLEON.

December 20, 1848—May 29, 1849.

LOUIS NAPOLEON now took the place of Cavaignac. A man whose every plan was simple and whose every word was sincere, was succeeded by one made up of hidden thoughts and secret intrigues. We shall follow his treacherous course of flattering popular aspirations, and at the same time satisfying and reassuring the conservative party. The time will come but too soon when we shall see this double-dealing and complex personage at liberty to abandon himself freely to his own inspirations, and to apply his system of government, if such it may be called, to France.

His ministry was formed before his own official recognition. Knowing that he must make allies of men who would shield him from the general eye, and, above all, from the Assembly, he selected Odilon Barrot as head of the Cabinet; to Barrot, as to Thiers, whom he consulted about the same time, he seemed wholly absorbed with the idea "of accomplishing great things and of dazzling the public mind by the brilliancy of his government." The two statesmen to whom he unbosomed himself made the same response: that it was necessary, not to do great things, but to restore a feeling of security to the country, thus allowing of progress and improvement. Barrot added rudely that it was no time for theatrical effects, and that for his part he would not serve "a government of mountebanks."

Louis Napoleon did not give up his dreams, but he postponed them; he seemed to yield to Barrot's reasoning, and instead of a

Engraved by H.B. Hall, N.Y. from a Photograph made in Paris, 1849

NAPOLEON III.

noisy harangue he addressed the Assembly modestly, as we have said, December 20.

The Cabinet, headed by Barrot as minister of justice, was chiefly composed of men of the old dynastic opposition, with one republican, Bixio, and one legitimist, who, for a brief space, had welcomed the advent of the republic of February 24, — M. de Falloux. The latter for a long while hesitated to associate himself with a Bonaparte, but, more clerical than legitimist at heart, he yielded to the persuasions of a very influential ecclesiastic, Abbé Dupanloup, whose ruling thought was to gain the ascendancy in educational matters. De Falloux lost no time. Before accepting the ministry, he won a promise of support from Thiers for a law "for liberty of instruction," and made constant exertions to gain his point. While De Falloux worked to this end, heedless of all else, the incompatibility between a president with imperial tendencies and a parliamentary ministry was soon made evident. Louis Napoleon having requested the minister of the interior, Léon de Maleville, to send him the documents relating to his attempts at Strasburg and Boulogne, the minister refused to part with these papers, which ought never to leave the archives of his department. Louis Napoleon at once wrote De Maleville an arrogant and autocratic letter, declaring that he would not suffer the ministers whom he had appointed to treat him as if the "famous constitution of Siéyès were still in force." He alluded to the scheme of Siéyès, which General Bonaparte so cunningly replaced by his constitution of the year VIII.

All the ministers tendered their resignation, which the president refused in a letter of apology to De Maleville and his colleagues. This was one of his characteristics, — to advance suddenly, then draw back and begin again next day. No one was ever more ready to eat his words or more obstinate in accomplishing his purpose. De Maleville and Bixio insisted on resigning; the rest remained, but it was evident that Barrot and Louis Napoleon could not work together long. (End of December.) Indeed, the ministry suited neither president nor Assembly, being too parliamentary for the one, and too much given to the old school of constitutionalism for the other.

Public opinion protested loudly against the continuance of the Constituent Assembly, desiring to replace it by a legislature. The nation was like a sick man, turning and twisting in his bed, hoping to gain ease by each change of position. The question was brought before the Assembly early in January.

The situation now became most difficult. The accomplices of Louis Napoleon in the outbreaks at Strasburg and Boulogne rallied round him, and urged him to a new *coup-de-main*. General Changarnier, commander of all the military forces, showed himself ill-disposed towards the Assembly, while the Garde Mobile were quite ready to uphold the zealous republican party; and the democratic socialists, led on by Delescluze, Ledru-Rollin's former agent in the north, appeared to be preparing for action.

What were their various schemes? This has never been clearly made known. The most notable republicans seem to have been averse to aggressive measures; and on the other hand, Louis Napoleon may have invented the story that Changarnier offered to instal him at the Tuileries, and proclaim him emperor. Changarnier always protested stoutly against the statement. The events of the evening of the 28th had much the air of a nascent *coup d' état*. A number of arrests were made among leading democrats, and Changarnier occupied the palace of the Assembly with his troops. Marrast, thus besieged, demanded an explanation, which he failed to receive. This proceeding did not tend to reassure or appease the president and members of the Assembly; but Barrot protested that Changarnier's intentions were good, and offered to place the troops in and about the Palais Bourbon under the command of any general whom Marrast might choose. Time passed; the Assembly met, and Barrot explained that the government felt obliged to take these military precautions, fearing some movement planned by a part of the Garde Mobile and " the anarchists."

Great excitement prevailed throughout Paris, where the Assembly was thought in danger, and some of the troops prepared for defence.

There was no conflict, however. The same day, January 29, Rateau's proposition to dissolve the Assembly came up for discussion, and was passed by a majority of eleven. Numerous petitions combined to persuade the members to yield against their will.

What passed at Bourges, a few weeks later, was unfavorable in its moral effect on the extreme revolutionary party. While the majority of the prisoners taken in June had been set free or held for transportation, and their leaders tried by court martial, those taken May 15 were tried before the Supreme Court. Melancholy weeks ensued. Barbès again affirmed that the famous document revealing the proceedings of the various secret societies could be the work of none but Blanqui. Barbès, at least, lost no prestige on this occasion. Far from excusing himself, he called down all the rigors of the law upon his head with his wonted sincerity. He was condemned to transportation for life with Albert, ex-member of the provisional government ; Blanqui and some others were sentenced to several years' imprisonment. Barbès appeared no more on the political stage ; he gained the deep sympathy of those who most regretted his errors.   (March – April.)

Italian affairs continued to occupy the public mind. The pope, still at Gaeta, on Neapolitan soil, refused to treat with his former ministers and the Roman legislature. The constitutional party, disavowed by the pope, melted away ; and a junta, appointed by the Chamber of Deputies, declared the Roman Parliament dissolved, convening a Constituent Assembly to replace it. (Dec. 28, 1848.) February 9, this Assembly proclaimed a republic, reserving the necessary pledges for the exercise of the pope's spiritual power. The Roman republic adopted Mazzini's motto, "God and the People."

Spain, then governed by Marshal Narvaez in the name of Queen Isabella, had, some weeks previous, invited the Catholic powers to unite in restoring temporal power to the Holy Father. All the monarchic powers, Catholic and Protestant, agreed, except England and Piedmont. Charles Albert protested against foreign intervention, and offered an asylum to the pope, taking it upon himself to restore order in the Roman States, but Pius IX. refused. Piedmont then strove to come to an understanding with France.

. Louis Napoleon was much puzzled to know what part to take. The minister Drouyn de Lhuys opposed any connection between France and the Roman revolution, but declined to say in advance what steps the government might take. Upon this, Charles Albert, urged on by Italian patriots, and anxious to change the present intolerable state of affairs at any price, broke his truce with Austria, heedless of the advice of the French government.

The result of the war was speedily decided. March 20, the King of Sardinia took the field: the 23d, he lost the battle of Novara, and that very evening abdicated in favor of his eldest son, Victor Emmanuel. He left Italy, broken both mentally and physically, and went to Portugal to die. The future justified his sacrifice, for the disaster which seemed to be the ruin of Piedmont and its dynasty paved the way for its increased glory, and led its princes to a degree of power of which they had never dared to dream.

Austria did not pursue her victory to the end, lest she should tempt the French to invade Italy, but promised to make no conquest of Piedmont. Thiers dissuaded Louis Napoleon from war, showing him that the country was unprepared, and at the same time alarming the Austrian *chargé d' affaires* by allusions to the warlike intentions of France and its president. Austria, renouncing Piedmont, attempted to draw the new king into counter-revolution, and urged him to reclaim absolute power. Victor Emmanuel refused the advances and advice of Austria, although a revolt at Genoa, promptly repressed by his troops, afforded him a pretext for attacking liberal institutions. He remained true to his father's constitutional promises, and thereby paved the way for a brilliant future.

The attitude of the French Assembly aided in calming the ardor of Austria, which at first wished to impose a heavy indemnity on Piedmont. The Assembly authorized the partial and temporary occupation of Italy by the French, "the better to guarantee the safety of Piedmont and the honor and interests of France." (March 30.)

Austria shrank from war with France on account of Piedmont; but she wished to advance into Central Italy. March 30, while the French Assembly was taking measures in regard to Italy, the ambassadors of the Catholic powers held a conference on the appeal made to them by the Holy Father at Gaeta. Pius IX. demanded that they should unite in some decided action. Austria, Spain, and Naples were agreed, but the French envoy held back in accordance with his orders. Austria was already threatening Bologna and Tuscany, whither the grand duke had fled, leaving his duchy in the hands of Italian revolutionists. The Austrians announced that they should next march on Rome. As for the King of Naples, he had recovered Sicily, which had not accepted French mediation in time. Palermo alone still held out, and the King of Naples was in a position to interfere in the Roman States. Spain was also ready to send troops.

April 16, Barrot requested the Assembly to issue a loan of one million two hundred thousand francs for the "expedition to the Mediterranean." The call was urgent and was answered at once. Jules Favre presented a report on the matter, declaring that France merely intended to arbitrate between Austria and Rome, not to overthrow the Roman republic. M. Schoelcher, a member of the committee, protested against this assertion, and declared that the ministry had said that France meant to restore the pope, even against the will of the Romans. Barrot was invited to settle the question, but declined to express himself in a decided manner. There was but one man in the ministry who had any clear idea of what he was doing, and that was De Falloux. He had urged the closing of the national workshops, which led to the June revolt. He now urged the expedition to Rome, which would bring on a fierce contest between the French army and Italian patriots, and cause a counter-revolution in Rome. He wished to restore the pope unconditionally; the other ministers and the president of the republic hoped to enter Rome without a blow and to restore the pope, — the ministers, with constitutional institutions, and the president, with the Code Napoléon and a lay administration. The ministers accused those who believed in the Roman republic, of faith in chimeras, while they themselves pursued another chimera, — a pope who should be a constitutional king, as though constitutions were compatible with infallibility.

The French ambassador, by order of his government, informed the foreign envoys assembled at Gaeta that France would interfere, unassisted and alone, and that French troops were about to land at Civita Vecchia.

The expedition was intrusted to General Oudinot, son of the marshal who made that name illustrious under the empire. His instructions ordered him to treat with the triumvirs, who held executive sway in Rome, without recognizing their authority; he was to judge for himself whether to march on Rome, should he feel sure of a peaceable reception. He was charged "to prepare the way in the Roman States for the restoration of a regular order of things, on bases consistent with the legitimate rights of the people."

The instructions sent to Gaeta and to the French ambassadors at Rome and Naples were more explicit; they affirmed the double necessity of the temporal power and of free institutions at Rome, but omitted to say how this double result was to be attained.

General Oudinot embarked at Toulon with a few troops, a part of which was the brigade intended by Cavaignac for Venice. The expedition set sail for Civita Vecchia, preceded by an aide-de-camp, to announce to the governor of that place that France desired to respect the wishes of the majority of the Roman populace and would not impose upon them any form of government not chosen by themselves. Oudinot landed the next day, April 25, and was peacefully received. Notwithstanding this friendly beginning, the Roman Assembly protested "against this unexpected invasion," and announced a firm resolve to resist, "holding France responsible for the consequences."

Oudinot then changed his ground, proclaimed Civita Vecchia in a state of siege, and disarmed the Roman troops. However, he attempted to negotiate, and sent a diplomatic agent and an officer to Rome to require the triumvirs to permit Rome to follow the example of Civita Vecchia.

The triumvirate was in reality Mazzini. That great Genoese orator, adopted by Rome, was the soul of her government, and ruler of the Constituent Assembly. A foe to all compromise, he fought everywhere to the bitter end, caring little for immediate success, and assured that present defeat would lead to future victory. Two dreams were struggling for mastery in his brain : that of a constitutional papacy, and that of a unitary Italian republic, ruling the world as in the days of ancient Rome. His dreams were not all fancy, since one of them has since been realized in the national unity of Italy.

The Roman Constituent Assembly directed the triumvirs to save the republic and repel force by force. Oudinot's envoys informed him that its demonstrations were only for form's sake, and urged him to hasten to Rome, where the populace would sustain him. This was a mistaken view, for when he appeared at the head of less than five thousand men, without siege artillery or means for scaling walls, April 28, the people rose against him, and barricades were erected on every hand. April 27, Garibaldi had entered Rome with a body of volunteers, among them being a battalion of emigrants from Lombardy, who, unable to defend Milan, came to the rescue of Rome. As they drew near the city, the French encountered placards bearing Article V. of the French Constitution of 1848 : "The French Republic will respect all foreign nations . . . . . and will never use her powers against the liberties of any people."

Oudinot advanced, and was received with a volley of shot outside the Vatican. Not only did he fail in his attack upon two of the doors, but two hundred and fifty of his men were disarmed and led into the city, and he was obliged to retire to a distance with considerable loss. (April 30.)

This sad news made a serious impression in Paris. The Assembly repented of their course, and great indignation was felt by those who voted for the loan because they were led to believe, by the assertion of the government, that the Roman republic would yield without a struggle. May 9, Jules Favre, one of the committee which had supported the government on April 16, taking the floor, exclaimed,

"I was deceived and the Assembly with me. . . . . French blood has been spilt; it has been spilt for the pope, it has been spilt for absolutism!" And he closed by demanding the instant recall of Oudinot.

M. Drouyn de Lhuys, the minister of foreign affairs, protested against the recall of the troops to Civita Vecchia while the Austrians were invading the Roman States by way of Bologna. In spite of all his efforts, the measure passed.

Next day Louis Napoleon published a letter in the *Patrie*, declaring his confidence in the ministry and his belief that the military honor of France was involved. He eagerly seized this occasion to work upon the mind of the army. Changarnier copied this letter in the order of the day to the Paris army, deeming it adapted to strengthen the soldiers' attachment for the head of the government.

The president's letter and the commanding general's arrogant bravado aroused a storm in the Assembly. Ledru-Rollin demanded the impeachment of the president and ministry, and the recognition of the Roman republic. Odilon Barrot defended the ministry most eloquently, and the tempest subsided. Changarnier explained his conduct as best he might, and was not removed from office, but the minister of the interior, Léon Faucher, was obliged to resign. (May 13.) The other ministers, conforming to Barrot's wishes, seemed ready to defer to the desires of the Assembly and to resume negotiations with the Roman government. They sent an envoy to Rome in the person of Ferdinand de Lesseps, ex-consul-general to Barcelona, where he had behaved with equal energy and humanity under trying circumstances. His instructions were as vague as those given to Oudinot, although a despatch from Drouyn de Lhuys to the latter had been more explicit, the general having been directed to tell the Romans that France would not take part against them with the Neapolitans, who were at Terracina; and in fact Oudinot remained inactive while Garibaldi sallied out to drive off the Neapolitans; but the dispatch also ordered the general to make an attempt to enter Rome, by fair means or foul, when reinforcements arrived.

The ministry were at variance among themselves, even without counting De Falloux, their only point of union being their desire to gain time, as the Constituent Assembly was on the eve of dissolution. The legislative elections were to take place May 13. Guizot returned to the political arena upon this occasion, having published in April a pamphlet urging Bonapartists, Legitimists, and Orleanists to unite and form " the party of order," giving no pledges for the future. He excluded only the republicans. The opponents of the republic took his advice, but did not choose him as their candidate, thinking him likely to be too unpopular.

Opposed to the great conservative party was the democratic and socialist party,— socialist in name, but revolutionist in fact. A certain number of moderate republicans figured on the list of each party. Cavaignac was chosen in Paris and his native country; but the majority of the members and ministers of the provisional government and Executive Committee, even Lamartine, Marrast, Garnier-Pagès, and Jules Janin, were not re-elected; Ledru-Rollin was chosen by five departments, and stood second in Paris, the first on the list being Lucien Murat, son of the former King of Naples. This was the Empire, face to face with the radical Republic.

The East, Centre, and Southeast voted chiefly for the extreme Left, both in the rural districts and the cities; the peasants, who voted for Louis Napoleon, turned against the reactionary candidates of the nobility and the higher class of citizens. The election of Ledru-Rollin was significant: set aside at the presidential election, he was now taken up in preference to sectarians and utopians.

Only fatal results could be predicted from these elections. The men of worth and political experience at the head of the conservative majority found themselves engaged in a cause which threatened to overthrow instead of maintaining existing institutions, to the profit, not of their opinions but of a different rule from that of 1814 or 1830.

The Constituent Assembly was approaching its last hour. It finally forced the government to divide the command of the National

Guard and the army of Paris, illegally united under Changarnier's command, which was satisfactory to the members, but of little present significance. The tax on liquor was abolished, involving a hundred millions, for which no equivalent was found. The tax on salt was also reduced two thirds, which took more than forty millions from the budget. This was an unfortunate ending.

A final debate on foreign affairs occurred in regard to the Russian invasion of Hungary with the purpose of aiding the Austrians against the Hungarians (May 22). Monarchs assisted one another; nations afforded each other no support!

The Constituent Assembly held its last session May 27, and on the 28th the new Assembly came into office. The second Constituent Assembly had had nothing of the grandeur of the first: its honesty and sincere patriotism must plead for it in history; its insufficiency and errors were due to the obscure and uncertain condition of France in 1848. Its successor was destined to cause it to be signally regretted.

CHAPTER XII.

SECOND REPUBLIC (*continued*). — PRESIDENCY OF LOUIS NAPOLEON (*continued*). — SECOND LEGISLATIVE ASSEMBLY. — ROMAN WAR, JUNE 13. — COUNTER-REVOLUTIONS ABROAD. — DOMESTIC REACTION.

May 28 to November, 1849.

THE Legislative Assembly opened May 28, 1849. The majority did not refuse to join in the cry, "Long live the republic!" raised by the Left; but their action in the formation of the committees contrasted strongly with this exclamation. Dupin was made president, and the presidents and secretaries of committees, save Arago, were very nearly what they might have been under Louis Philippe.

Before this new state of affairs the ministry tendered its resignation. Louis Napoleon accepted it, and summoned Marshal Bugeaud, who at first hesitated and finally refused to undertake the formation of a cabinet, doubting what the army might do in case of a popular uprising against his ministry. The army was declared by its leaders to be averse to all monarchical reaction, and the great number of military votes obtained by the republican candidates at the elections had confirmed this assertion. Barrot consented to withdraw his resignation, and endeavored to form a ministry to satisfy moderate republicans by including Dufaure, De Tocqueville, and Lanjuinais.

Affairs in Rome did not favor reconciliation. Deceit and contradiction were everywhere prevalent. M. de Lesseps and Oudinot had received instructions quite at variance with each other, and each was likely to increase this difference by personal prejudices. De Lesseps went straight forward, thinking only of making a peaceful

arrangement with the Romans.   During his negotiations, Oudinot
received reinforcements and marched to Rome.   He agreed, however, to a truce and refused to permit a papal delegate to settle at
Civita Vecchia.

Lesseps finally arranged a treaty with the Roman States, pledging
the support of France to the Roman people, who were to consider
the French troops as a friendly army, ready to aid in their defence
but to take no part in the administration of the country.   This
made France the ally of the Roman republic, as the most ardent
republicans of France desired.   Oudinot, however, refused his consent, and the next day a dispatch arrived from Paris recalling
Lesseps and directing Oudinot to enter Rome by force of arms.

No compromise was possible.   The Roman government would
not resign, and the French government would never recognize it.
The ministry accused De Lesseps of misinterpreting his orders.   It
is certain that had the minister of foreign affairs told him frankly
what was wanted of him, — to gain time for Oudinot to prepare
to attack Rome, — he would unhesitatingly have refused such a
mission.

The conflict was renewed at once between the French army, numbering twenty-eight thousand, and the defenders of Rome, thirty
thousand strong, twelve thousand being civilians on duty within the
city.   It has often been said, in excuse of this war, that Rome was
then ruled by strangers : the truth is, that of these thirty thousand
armed men, scarcely a thousand were foreigners, — French, Germans,
and Poles.

·June 3, the French carried a number of outposts and began the
siege under Vaillant, a skilful general of the engineer corps, who
was greatly annoyed by Garibaldi's bold sallies.

The French government had begun the war reluctantly; it felt
obliged to continue it.   It was not Drouyn de Lhuys, but De
Tocqueville, who had recalled De Lesseps upon the resumption of hostilities.   De Tocqueville and Dufaure, who had both
eagerly rallied to the support of the republic, were drawn after
Odilon Barrot into this unfortunate affair, while the mass of the

republican party was enraged at the news from Rome. The ultras and the moderates shared this feeling alike. There was only one difference between them, but that was a grave one: the mountaineers and socialist democrats had pledged their candidates to set the example of armed resistance, should the Constitution be violated, as, in spite of all subtle arguments to the contrary, it must be owned was now the case. The deputies of the Mountain party were summoned to keep their promise, and a declaration was issued, June 11, announcing that this party " would do its duty." An address was also issued to the German democrats, now in full revolt, in and about Baden, against the Prussian king and other German princes. Other violently insurrectional documents were published, and a heavy gloom brooded over Paris. A crisis was evidently at hand which could only be fatal in its results. The cholera, which had returned and raged as furiously as in 1832, added its horrors to political anxieties; and carried off many well-known people, including Bugeaud, who had latterly displayed an unwonted moderation and sense.

Peace was far remote. On the very day that the Mountain published its declaration, Ledru-Rollin took the floor to call for the impeachment of the president and cabinet. Barrot made a reply to the effect that it was to protect Roman liberty, as well as to prevent the Austrians from entering the field, that war was made on Rome. Ledru-Rollin quickly proved the contradiction between the order of May 7, issued by the Constituent Assembly, and the order to attack Rome, given by the ministry. But what did this signify to the reactionary majority of the Legislature? Hitherto, Ledru-Rollin, from a moral point of view at least, had had all the advantage, but he let fall a fatal speech: "We will defend the Constitution from violation, even by force of arms!" which was wrung from him by the pledges mentioned above.

The Right burst into cries of rage. The extreme Left confirmed Ledru-Rollin's words. The next day the party committees and the press rivalled each other in their angry denunciations; the newspapers threatened an immediate repetition of the scenes of the

10th of August and the 31st of May. The Assembly, as was expected, refused to authorize the impeachment, and Ledru-Rollin somewhat softened his tone, feeling that an insurrection would be far less excusable now than it was on the 15th of May or the 23d of June, the circumstances being very different; a great insurrection cannot be repeated twice in a year.

The deputies of the Mountain were urged on from without by the revolutionary press and the committees, of whom Delescluze was then the most obstinate and embittered leader. A manifestation took place at the Chateau d' Eau. Twenty thousand men, members of the National Guard and others, led by officers and a few politicians, among them Jules Bastide, the minister of foreign affairs under Cavaignac, marched along the Boulevards, shouting "Long live the republic! Long live the Constitution! Long live the Roman republic!"

The government had had ample time for preparation, and its action had the unity lacked by its foes. General Changarnier, in command of the army of Paris, held the chief points of the city, and by marching three columns of troops directly across the procession, he cut it in two, and then ordered a charge to right and left.

Touching scenes ensued: citizens and national guards fell on their knees and bared their breasts, crying to the soldiers, "Would you fire on your brothers?" The men did not fire, but by the mere force of their first movement, drove the crowd before them. The manifestation was thus put down without resistance and almost without bloodshed, — an easy matter, as the men were unarmed. Some of the insurgents cried "To arms!" various armories were pillaged, and a few barricades were built.

Some of the Mountain deputies were at this moment assembled with Ledru-Rollin at their headquarters in the Rue du Hasard, near the Rue de Richelieu. Urged by the most ardent of the revolutionary leaders, they hastened to the Palais Royal garden, where Colonel Guinard of the National Guard had convened his men. The brave and loyal Guinard had even less hope of success than Ledru-Rollin, but his generosity and his conviction that the government was plotting against the republic, forbade him to resist the appeal made to him. The soldiers formed in line, the representatives in the middle, and proceeded towards the Conservatoire des Arts et Métiers (formerly the Church of St. Martin in the Fields). A few barricades were erected in the neighborhood, but the majority of the people, although sympathizing with the movement, did not rise. The conservatory was at last attacked, and an exchange of shots took place between the artillery and the National Guard, in spite of Guinard's prohibition. A detachment of infantry then made its way through the gate, which had been left open in the confusion, and several representatives were taken prisoners. There was no conflict within. The soldiers who invaded the hall, where the majority of the deputies remained, hesitated to arrest them, and Ledru-Rollin and his colleagues escaped through the garden. Guinard was the last to quit the conservatory, evacuated alike by insurrectionists and soldiers. No search was made for him, but he was afterwards arrested in his own house. Ledru-Rollin succeeded in quitting France.

This eloquent and generous orator, fitted to be the voice, but not the head of a great party, disappeared from the scene of action because he suffered himself to be led by his party, instead of restraining and guiding it. He was no statesman, but his name is nevertheless still popular. The people remember that he was, if not the first, at least one of the most zealous, among the petitioners for universal suffrage in the time of Louis Philippe.

The Legislative Assembly announced itself in permanent session. At the request of the ministry it declared Paris in a state of siege. The greater number of the mountaineers, who had not been at the conservatory, returned to the Assembly the next day, and disavowed the recent deeds of their party. This weakness was even more disastrous than the affray at the conservatory.

The majority did not choose to see that their victory would profit others than themselves. On the afternoon of June 13, Louis Napoleon traversed Paris with a military escort, and was loudly cheered. The Assembly, making common cause with the president for the moment, did not trouble itself as to his supporters.

The news of the failure of the movement in Paris allayed the ferment in the departments. There was no serious trouble, save at Lyons, where the bloody scenes of old were renewed. (June 15.) Lyons, like Paris, was declared in a state of siege.

In Paris, proceedings against the representatives arrested June 13, and many others, were authorized, thus causing a tumult in the Assembly. The remnant of mountaineers, recovering from their first depression, seemed anxious to atone for their recent weakness by redoubling their former violence. Their rage could not restrain the majority, who never found the measures proposed by government sufficiently rigorous. Great restrictions were placed upon the press; and it was on this occasion that Victor Hugo, who had hitherto voted with the conservatives, began to break from the Right.

The party of the Mountain now began to struggle desperately. The very rapidity of its defeat had prevented its dissolution or destruction, and the Alsatian mountaineer, Savoie, took it upon himself to question the government in regard to its attitude towards Germany. He reproached the ministry with hostility to German republicans, and proposed to pass a vote requesting the government to insist that the independence of Baden and the Palatinate should be respected. The German revolutionists had for some time been masters of the grand duchy of Baden, of the Palatinate, on both banks of the Rhine, and of Hesse-Darmstadt. The regular troops in these countries joined the revolutionists; but they had already met with defeats from the forces of Prussia, Bavaria, and other monarchies, and, despite their vigorous resistance, they were driven south of the Neckar and began to break up.

The government refused all compromise with German rebels, as it had done with the Romans; and the German rebellion, after a struggle of some weeks, was stifled in Baden, its stronghold.

The complementary elections, to replace the representatives who had won duplicate nominations in May, took place July 8, and the usual results of a defeat were evident. Reactionists were chosen by departments which had elected democrats and socialists in May.

PORTE ST. DENIS.

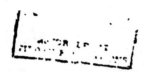

The list of the "Electoral Union," i. e. the anti-republican party, prevailed in Paris; Bonapartists won by favor of ex-constitutionalists and loyalists. Yet the republicans stood their ground, and effected, though with great difficulty, a beginning of union between moderate republicans and democratic socialists. In the departments the reactionist victory was not complete: Lamartine and Jules Favre, defeated in May, were now elected.

The Assembly thought of sitting some weeks, but the Left opposed the measure, alleging the danger of another 18th of Brumaire, or a *coup de main* by the president in the absence of the Assembly. A Bonapartist committee was even then agitating in favor of a presidency for life and a *plébiscite*. Louis Napoleon hastened to reassure the Assembly, and to protest his respect for the laws in the strongest terms. He was at this time making a journey through the departments; he visited Ham, where he had been imprisoned for six years, and there he publicly confessed that in this place he had suffered the just punishment for his "bold attack on the laws of his country"; and at Tours he eagerly denied the accusation of meditating some enterprise similar to that of Brumaire 18. "Neither *coup d'état* nor insurrection!" he cried.

The Assembly was finally prorogued from August 13 to September 30. During its stormy legislative session important events had occurred outside of France. The siege of Rome was actively carried on from the 3d of June. Since the defeat of the opponents of this war at Paris, June 13, the capture of Rome was only a question of time, and, the French army having received its siege artillery, the time could not be long. Among the besieged the volunteers fought bravely, and the Roman artillery struggled obstinately against the enemy, who began to batter in breach, June 13. On the night of the 21st an assault was made, and two bastions were carried. The defence did not falter, for Garibaldi animated all around him with his heroic fire. June 27, the French batteries succeeded in destroying the greater part of the Roman batteries, and on the next day a third bastion was taken by storm, the Roman artillerymen being killed at their guns.

· The besiegers were now masters of the Janiculine hill, overlooking St. Peter's, the Vatican, and the whole of modern Rome. It was impossible to prolong the struggle without involving the city's ruin. The Roman Assembly met that night. Mazzini insisted upon death beneath the wreck of Rome, while Garibaldi acknowledged that all hope of success was lost. The Assembly decided to surrender, unanimously, save for Mazzini. The Triumvirate resigned, and the municipality was charged to make terms for surrender. M. de Corcelles, the successor of Lesseps, as minister plenipotentiary from France, insisted upon unconditional surrender, which was finally granted.

July 2, Garibaldi left Rome with four thousand volunteers, hoping to reach Venice, but he could not cut his way through the Austrian troops occupying Bologna and the Romagna. He dispersed his followers, and narrowly escaped with his life; while his brave wife, who had never left him amid all his dangers, now died of fatigue.

July 3, the French entered Rome, the Roman expedition thus proving a material success; but it remained to be seen if it would be equally successful from a moral and political point of view.

August 6, the Roman question was again brought up for debate in the French Assembly. Tocqueville, the minister of foreign affairs, declared that it was equally necessary to restore the temporal power of the Pope, to insure liberal institutions to the people, and to prevent the return of former abuses. Although he guaranteed the Pope's good intentions, it was evident that he doubted them. M. de Falloux made an eloquent and impassioned plea for the papacy; but he quoted speeches of Pius IX. proving that the Holy Father would make no promises for the future.

· The impossibilities of the situation now became apparent to all. The Assembly's dream was a chimera. The plan had been to hold provisional power over Rome, and make terms with Pius IX. alone. Corcelles and Oudinot, influenced by him, allowed reaction to rise once more in Rome, and permitted the reinstallation of ecclesiastic government, August 1. A triumvirate of cardinals restored the Inquisition, and claimed the right to rule the police, and to force

French soldiers to act the part of sheriffs in the service of religious vengeance.

. The French government wavered, and recalled Oudinot. August 18, the president of the republic wrote an unofficial letter to Lieutenant-Colonel Edgar Ney, son of the Marshal, telling him that France had no idea of "inaugurating the Pope's return by proscription and tyranny." He bade him direct General Rostolan, Oudinot's successor, to forbid the occurrence of any act beneath the shadow of the French flag which might belie the character of French intervention. "I sum up the restoration of temporal power to the Pope as follows," he wrote: "a general amnesty, a secular administration, the Code Napoléon, and a liberal government."

This letter was copied widely, and finally appeared in the *Moniteur* (September 7), producing a tremendous effect both in France and Italy, as Louis Napoleon had hoped. The events of June 13 had pledged him to the conservatives; he thought that it was time to make a contrary movement, and arrange a reconciliation with new Italy, in whose cause he bore arms against the papacy in 1831.

The Pope, who was on the point of re-entering Rome, withdrew to Naples, where, being reassured by French diplomatic agents, he made no public protest, but made several civil and municipal concessions to the Romans, and published an amnesty with numerous exceptions (September 12).

Many other military incidents coincided with the French siege of Rome. War was rampant on the Baltic, the Adriatic, the Tiber, and the Theiss. The Prussian king and German princes, who repressed revolution on the banks of the Rhine, upheld it in the country between the Baltic and the North Sea. The insurgents of Holstein and Schleswig, made bold by this support, invaded the purely Danish countries of North Schleswig and Jutland. The Danes fought bravely against great odds, and gained a battle at Frédéricia, July 6, which was followed by an armistice and the evacuation of Jutland. Thus Germany failed, for the nonce, to crush Denmark beneath her weight, but she did not lose sight of the desired prey.

Germany was given over to discord, for a thorough comprehension of which we must go back to the autumn of 1848. At the time of her first victory over Charles Albert, in the summer of 1848, Austria quarrelled with Hungary and contended with insurrection in Vienna and Prague; but her military strength proved her safeguard. She then prepared to resume the offensive against Hungary, and to recover her influence in Germany.

The Frankfort Assembly had ever increasing cause of displeasure with Austria, which took the form of a protest against the union of any part of the German Empire in one and the same body of state with non-German countries. Austria contested the question (end of November, 1848), and the Assembly, estranged from Austria, was drawn towards Prussia, a thing to be dreaded alike by princes and democrats. After much discussion, on the 27th of March, 1849, the Assembly decided to offer the hereditary empire of Germany to the king of Prussia.

The king gave an evasive answer. Austria again protested, and recalled her deputies from Frankfort. The uncertainty and fluctuations of the Prussian king provoked troubles in Berlin, while a movement was set on foot in the petty states to force their governments to recognize the authority of the Frankfort Assembly. April 28, the Prussian king refused the imperial crown, being reluctant to receive it at the hands of decaying revolution. A few days later, a bloody revolt occurred in Dresden, the Saxon government, aided by Prussian troops, gaining the upper hand (May 6 – 9). The Prussian king, who had protested against the constitution issued at Frankfort, recalled his deputies thence, in imitation of Austria, May 14, and invited the German governments to an opposition congress. Revolution next broke out in Baden and the Palatinate, with the unfortunate results aforesaid. Prussia, triumphant over Rhenish revolutionists and rid of the Frankfort Assembly, which was destroyed by its own impotence, tried to frame a German constitution in her own favor, to which the other states were invited to adhere.

This was by no means the intention of Austria, who had no idea

·of yielding the supremacy to Prussia, and accordingly made a coun-
ter-proposition: a directory of three members, — Austria, Prussia,
and a third. The two governments, being unable to agree, made a
temporary arrangement, September 30, to hold until the 1st of May
·1850, and Austria, who seemed lost in 1848, recovered strength for
a space. Her safety was not due to herself, however, for she was
forced to the humiliating expedient of asking aid from a formidable
neighbor.

Her campaign against Hungary was successful at first, owing to
her skilful use of the party hates between Slaves, Magyars, and
Roumanians; but her victories were soon cut short. Thousands of
Polish volunteers, led by the heroic and skilful generals of the war
of 1831, hastened to join the Hungarians, and after a furious struggle, lasting two months, the Austrians were driven back to Presburg,
and forced to appeal to Russia. Czar Nicholas did not hesitate.
Hungarian victory would entail Polish rebellion. The Hungarian
diet decreed the downfall of the house of Hapsburg, thus, with
heroic imprudence, closing all possibility of compromise. It was useless to contend against the united forces of the two empires, and the
war was ended in August by the destruction, capitulation, or dis-
persion of the Hungarian army. Austria marred the inglorious and
dearly bought victory, which 'she owed to Russia, by her wonted
cruelty. Thirteen captive generals were hung in a single day!

The same month which witnessed the defeat of Hungary saw the
fall of Venice. Hunger forced her to yield, after a prolonged defence which was the admiration of Europe and the honor of Italy.
Daniel Manin, who had won unparalleled efforts and sacrifices from
the people by whom he was elected, retired to France, and the sympathy which he inspired, the influence which he exerted, were not
fruitless in later days.

The restoration of the grand-duke took place in Tuscany, in July.
Italy and Europe were once more in the grasp of reaction. The
great movement of 1848 was a universal failure.

Reaction had not yet reached its term in France, the centre of
revolution, whence the movement sprang, although there was a cer-

tain fluctuation in the government, marked by Louis Napoleon's letter to Ney, and followed, in the train of the European counter-revolution, by a second act of greater import.

A number of Hungarian and Polish leaders fled into Turkey. Austria and Russia threateningly ordered the Ottoman government to give up these refugees. Turkey refused, and claimed the support of England and France. These countries made common cause, and the French fleet was directed to join the English fleet in the Bosphorus.

Austria and Russia drew back, and France once more held a good position in Europe. Louis Napoleon and Odilon Barrot had done their duty, the former in his own interest, the latter in the interest and honor of France. The union of England and France in Italy was merely on the surface, and was barren; in Turkey it was most useful.

At the instant that France and England worked together for an important political act, science established a material link of novel character between the two nations. A submarine telegraphic cable was laid from shore to shore.

Upon the reopening of the French legislature, the Roman question was again brought up, *apropos* of loans for the French army in Rome. M. Thiers, in his report, boldly defended the papal *motu proprio*, that is, the papal decree as to administrative concessions and the amnesty; it remained for Pius IX. to complete his work. This report was the reverse side of the president's letter to Edgar Ney, although Thiers said nothing of that document, this silence being more wounding to Louis Napoleon than a fierce attack would have been.

The Left took part with the presidential letter. Even Cavaignac, who had refused to take the hand of Louis Napoleon on the 20th of December, now praised his letter. Victor Hugo went still further, and insisted that the Pope should be forced to accept a representative and civil government. This was the occasion for his lasting rupture with the majority and his union with democracy.

The ministers, Tocqueville and Odilon Barrot, strove to show that there was no essential difference between the president's idea and that of the committee, whose spokesman M. Thiers had been. The committee, they said, aspired to introduce liberal institutions in Rome, and the president merely disliked to impose them by force!

In this fashion the ministry gained its end, and obtained the desired loans by four hundred and fifty-nine votes against one hundred and eighty (October 20).

This result was far from satisfactory to the president, who thought his ministers too conciliatory, and who, at heart, did not care to agree with the majority: he would have preferred popularity at the expense of the Assembly in regard to the Roman question.

October 13, the trial of June 13 was opened before the supreme court. Guinard and sixteen others were condemned to transportation. Guinard had never attempted to evade the responsibility of his actions: his attitude was simple and noble as his life had been. He was imprisoned, not transported: popular sympathy was too much in his favor to allow him long to remain captive.

The result of this trial, which ended November 15, was the downfall, voted by the Assembly, of thirty representatives (February 8, 1850).

During the progress of this trial an event of some importance occurred. December 20, the president had accepted, through necessity, a parliamentary ministry, which he now felt strong enough to dismiss, that he might himself govern with a clerical ministry. He therefore wrote to Odilon Barrot, expressing his high esteem, and his regret that it seemed absolutely needful for him to "govern all parties" by choosing ministers who represented none. He then sent a message to the Assembly, October 31, denouncing the resurrection of bygone factions, declaring that "France was anxious to feel the hand and the will of the elect of December 10," that she required "a master who should be firm and a unit." For form's sake, he was quite ready to promise to maintain the constitution, to which he swore allegiance, but all the rest was in a most imperial tone.

The new ministry was made up of men, some few of whom had

special merit, but none of whom had any parliamentary authority. Among them were Deputy Rouher, distinguished for his rapid changes of opinion in 1848, and ready to espouse the cause of the strongest; Achille Fould, the banker, destined to be the financier of a new empire; and Deputy Parieu, whose past record was far from pointing to an entrance into such a cabinet.

The new ministry laid before the Assembly a plan of action as meagre as the president's message was emphatic. At the same time the *Moniteur* announced that the step taken involved no more than a change of names.

This, as we have already said, was a characteristic of Louis Napoleon: a clap of thunder was always followed by a silence; his wily timidity was combined with a spirit of adventure.

The majority, startled at first, did not resist; the ex-ministry was too liberal for their taste; they were not sorry to see the last of it, and, strange to say, did not seem conscious of the full import of the step taken. Nor were they roused to action by secret circulars, which they discovered, and which betrayed the fact that the government was forming an entirely Napoleonic police agency. The majority overlooked these circulars, and accepted the system of police destined to be used against them one day.

This harmony of government and majority continued on an occasion when it was far more justifiable, i. e. when the question of restoring the tax on liquor, which it was possible to modify, although not to suppress, was discussed.

November 3, the president, assisted by his new keeper of the seals, M. Rouher, solemnly restored the magistracy to the old fixed tenure of office, according to legislative decree. He announced, during the ceremony, that France had now "left behind her the epoch of revolutions."

The same prophecy had been made before, but on the morrow of a crisis which all hoped would be the last, and not on the eve of fresh revolution brought on by the very man who used these words.

A few days later, Louis Napoleon pardoned the majority of the men condemned in June, only five hundred remaining, who were

afterwards sent to Algeria, where French colonization was beginning
to thrive in spite of many obstacles. The Constituent Assembly
and General Cavaignac had been much interested in it, the former
body having voted fifty million francs in its interest, and nearly
fifteen thousand colonists having started out with enthusiasm to
found a new France beyond the sea.

The year 1849 witnessed bloody battles in Southern Algeria, at
the entrance to the Great Desert, which insured France the possession of oases, the first steps towards the dark world of the equator,
where she now hopes to open a way for commerce and civilization
through the African continent. The siege of Zaatcha is famous in
the history of the wars of France with Africa.

CHAPTER XIII.

SECOND REPUBLIC (*continued*). —LEGISLATIVE ASSEMBLY (*close*). — PRESIDENCY OF LOUIS NAPOLEON (*continued*). — EDUCATIONAL LAWS OF 1850. — LAW OF MAY 31. — STRUGGLE BETWEEN THE PRESIDENT AND ASSEMBLY.

October, 1849, to December 1, 1851.

WHEN the legislative session opened, September 30, the chief topic of debate was the new educational law, which was to be the chief domestic event of the time, as the Roman war was the great foreign event. The Carnot ministry desired to reconstruct the system of education from a free religious aspect, in harmony with the principles of the French Revolution; but the present scheme was founded on a very different basis. In December, 1848, Thiers had promised De Falloux, on the latter's entrance into the cabinet, that he would work with him in the matter of education; De Falloux and his party desiring a law which would strip the university of its privileges.

What were the motives that impelled M. Thiers in a direction so contrary to his true nature and the general tendencies of his life? We have quoted his very remarkable letter written in the spring of 1848. He now reurged the necessity of uniting against socialism, "which threatened to destroy society." It would be unjust to consider his concessions to the clergy as due only to physical fear of an overthrow, a fear which would have led him to join the priests in imposing on the people beliefs in which he himself had no faith. Many socialist sects promised to abolish suffering and want, and to bring in an era of universal happiness. Thiers thought it needful to oppose these utopias, which would overthrow and not replace social orders, with the religious sentiment, which, without enforcing inert resignation, aids man to endure inevitable ills, leads him to conform to the universal laws of order established by a Supreme Will, and renders present sufferings bearable by a faith in a life beyond the present.

M. Thiers has never wavered in this belief; but he lost sight of the fact that the Catholic clergy added to these fundamental ideas, common to all creeds, others more foreign to modern thought. Ultramontanism swept on like a rising tide: a compromise in regard to educational matters was, if not easy, at least possible, between the men who shared the views of Thiers and the old Gallican church; with the church ruled by the Jesuits, the compromise must be either a trick or an impossibility: there is no division of infallibility; it demands all or nothing. The men of the clerical party capable of making terms, such as Falloux, Dupanloup, the political Catholics, were carried off their feet and swayed by the Jesuit party, which was destined to swallow them up, twenty years later, at the council of Rome.

M. Thiers went so far at this time as to desire all primary education to be intrusted to the clergy. He considered the forty thousand lay teachers of France as the vanguard of a vast socialistic army about to devour society. It was left for the most energetic organ of the clerical party, Abbé Dupanloup, to shrink from this step. Dupanloup and Falloux wished to do nothing rashly; they knew that the clergy was insufficient for primary or for intermediate instruction; their desire, therefore, was to undermine, not to abruptly abolish, the university and lay teaching.

After long and heated arguments, a law was passed, on the 15th of March, 1850, tending to conciliate the clergy, to whom was restored much of its supremacy, especially over primary schools. The schoolmasters appointed under the influence of Carnot were found to have taught socialist rather than religious doctrines, and were accordingly dismissed, teachers being thenceforth subject to the approval of the prefect. The first result of this law was the estab-

lishment of two hundred and fifty-seven ecclesiastical schools before
the end of the year 1851. In 1853 the Jesuits had more than
twenty schools.

The educational law contributed quite as much as the Roman war
to dig the ditch which divided republicans and ex-liberals, and
events daily occurred to increase the anger and alarm of even the
most moderate partisans of the republic. Early in February the
police cut down the liberty-trees planted in Paris in 1848. This
was done in the most irritating fashion, as if expressly to provoke
outbreaks, which the higher powers felt quite sure of suppressing.

By an order issued February 12, the government had divided
France into five great military commands : the minister of war affirmed this to be a mere precaution against socialism, thus satisfying
the scruples of the Assembly. The majority scornfully declined to
celebrate the anniversary of the ratification of the republic (May 4).
The attitude of the government and Assembly seemed to result in a
union between moderate republicans and socialist democrats, such
as had been attempted the previous year.

Elections were now necessary to replace the thirty representatives
expelled for complicity in the events of June 13. The preparatory
meetings were satisfactory to all enlightened partisans of the republic, and were far less tumultuous than the clubs and committees
of 1848. Three seats for Paris being vacant, the Parisians returned
three decided socialists, — Carnot, the ex-minister of public instruction, Vidal, and De Flotte, a man of ancient family, who fought in
the fatal insurrection of June, but who now came forward in the
name of conciliation, not of vengeance.

Hope of winning the day in the coming general elections swelled
the hearts of the democracy ; and even those journals hitherto most
violent now urged order, patience, and calmness. This novel attitude alarmed the Right far more than riots had done : its members
foresaw that the popular vote would go against them, and they
planned a scheme for reforming the electoral law, which was presented by Léon Faucher, May 18, and hailed with indignation by
the Left, which did not prevent it from being passed by a large ma-

jority, on the 31st of May. For the second time this date marked
a sad epoch in the history of France. The law restored the former
term of three years' residence, instead of six months only, as requisite for the enjoyment of the suffrage. The special proofs required
to confirm residence must needs exclude very many citizens of even
longer standing. As the lower orders in Paris form a very floating
population, the framers of this law maintained that it would exclude
what they called "the rabble," — a fatal phrase, for which they
were long and bitterly blamed, — but, in point of fact, it was the
great majority of the laboring class which was excluded.

M. Vesin, a member of the Right, strikingly observed that "the
majority, anxious for victory at any cost, might well yield this victory to him who silently bides his time."

Louis Napoleon was indeed silent, although his ministers harangued.

When the Assembly thus deprived nearly three millions of citizens of the right of suffrage, they forever lost their hold upon the
inhabitants of the great cities; the consequences were yet to be
seen. Petitions with 527,000 signatures were sent in unavailing
protest, but the majority gave way to blind delight, and Louis Napoleon quietly watched the growing unpopularity of the Assembly.
He left them to triumph in their brief power, and prepared for the
morrow by continuing his Bonapartist propaganda in every direction.

There was no lack of warning. "You are working to restore the
empire," said General Lamoricière to the majority, — "the empire,
minus genius, grandeur, and glory!"

The lack of foresight in the Assembly was made the more inconceivable by the growing discord between it and the president.
Louis Napoleon, lavish, and surrounded by greedy and needy partisans, was deeply in debt, and demanded that the Assembly should
raise the dotation to three million francs yearly. This increase was
looked on with little favor, and would have been refused had it not
been for the somewhat high-handed interference of General Changarnier, who, in a measure, took the president under his protection,
at the instigation of Odilon Barrot, who considered that the time
was not ripe for a rupture between president and Assembly.

Louis Napoleon showed more wounded feeling than gratitude, and the newspapers in his pay attacked the Assembly and all assemblies in general; one of these journals, the *Pouvoir*, was tried, and condemned to pay a heavy fine, which did not, however, tend to make the others less violent.

August 9, the Assembly took a vacation. The first prorogation of the Legislature was uneventful enough; the second was followed by endless incidents.

The Left wing of the Assembly persistently refrained from urging any revolt against the new violation of the constitution, postponing everything until the general elections in 1852, greatly to the indignation of the exiles in London. The latter had formed a revolutionary committee in England, composed of Ledru-Rollin and his friends, with Mazzini and numerous German and Polish refugees, who were afterwards joined by Kossuth. The agitation stirred up by these men in London resulted in the organization of a society called the "Young Mountaineers," in the eastern and southeastern departments of France. Certain leaders were arrested on the charge of preparing an insurrection, and their plot seemed balked. But it was not so; the society flourished as a secret club, and simply adjourned action until 1852, thus siding with Paris rather than with London.

While a portion of the democrats were thus working without immediate results, the legitimist notables hastened to Wiesbaden, to greet the Count de Chambord, heir to Charles X. They were joined by a number of Orleanists, who hoped to effect a union of the two Bourbon branches, — a "fusion," as they called it. Some of the legitimists dreamed of a very different fusion with democracy by submitting the "return of the king of France" to universal suffrage, in the form of an appeal to the people; but the Count de Chambord rejected the idea as incompatible with "hereditary rights," nor was he better disposed to compromise with the younger branch.

The head of the Orléans branch, Louis Philippe, had recently died in exile at Claremont, at the age of seventy-six. He died serenely, in the full possession of his faculties, surrounded by his family. He had expressed a wish to be buried at Dreux, in the family tomb; and this desire has lately been fulfilled, twenty years after his death. France treasured no hostility to his memory; if he erred in his policy, his expiation was severe (August 26).

It was noted with dissatisfaction at the presidency, that General Changarnier had held a funeral service for Louis Philippe at the Tuileries, the residence of the staff officers of the army of Paris. Guizot and his ex-colleagues were present. The relations between the president and Changarnier were growing cold; and the latter has since said and written that Louis Napoleon offered him the office of constable if he would serve Napoleon's ambition, which he declined.

. The fusion with the elder branch failing, the hopes of the Orleanists still rested on the oldest son of the unhappy Duke d'Orléans, the Count de Paris, still a child; but neither legitimists nor Orleanists had much influence with the masses; the danger to the republic lay in another quarter. Louis Napoleon's intrigues had quite a different significance; he was playing a double game: his presidency expiring in 1852, he was aiming at two objects, — either to win the legal revision of that clause of the constitution forbidding the re-election of the president, or to supply the place of this revision by a *coup d'état*. He accordingly resolved on a tour through the provinces to probe popular opinion, traversing first Eastern France, from Dijon and Lyons to Strasburg, returning by Nantes and Rheims, being received sometimes ill and sometimes well by the inhabitants, who were mostly democrats and republicans. His public addresses were written by an able writer, M. Mocquart, who could not disguise his style.

At Lyons he declared himself "the representative of the two great national manifestations, which, in 1804 and 1848 alike, aimed to restore the grand principles of the French Revolution." He thus recalled not even Brumaire 18, and the consulate, but the date of the empire, 1804. He assured the people that the title to which he chiefly aspired, was that of an honest man; he declared himself, first and foremost, "the slave of duty."

. He next visited Normandy, where he expressed himself somewhat more freely. "If stormy days should come again," said he at Caen, "and the people attempted to impose a fresh burden upon the head of the nation, that head would be culpable indeed to desert his lofty mission !"

Having thus done his utmost in the provinces, he returned to Paris to work upon the army, holding splendid reviews and feasting the troops. Upon these occasions many of the regiments cried out, "Long live Napoleon!" and even, "Long live the emperor!" The legislative committee, in alarm, summoned General d'Hautpoul, minister of war, contrary to the advice of Barrot. But the minister refused to recognize any meaning in these cries, and called upon Changarnier to witness that it was impossible to prevent scattering cheers during a review. Changarnier boldly replied that it was perfectly possible, and that, contrary to his advice, these cheers had "not only been encouraged, but provoked."

This was serious. The head of the army was at odds with the president (October 7). When Louis Napoleon learned that Changarnier proposed to suppress these manifestations on the part of the troops, he suggested to the cabinet, through the minister of war, that the army of Paris should be divided into four, one division only to be commanded by Changarnier. The ministry, despite their devotion to the president, refused.

Louis Napoleon seemed to waver; he sent D'Hautpoul to govern Algeria, replacing him by General Schramm; but soon after, he dismissed Changarnier's brigade-major, who had questioned the advisability of the manifestations (October 31).

Conflict was in the air. Changarnier seemed on the point of attack; but he was only active in warfare and knew nothing of politics; he spent his strength in boasts; he talked of sending Louis Napoleon to Vincennes, and fancied he could obtain the authority of the president of the Assembly, M. Dupin, the most timid of men in any revolutionary crisis!

It is equally doubtful if Changarnier could have defended himself and the Assembly, had Louis Napoleon cashiered him as he had his brigade-major. Be that as it may, Napoleon postponed his schemes,

CATHEDRAL OF LYONS.

and once more strove to lull the fears of the Assembly. He ordered the dissolution of a society called "The 10th of December," which had served him too noisily, its members loudly cheering him wherever he appeared; then, upon the reopening of the session (November 12), Minister Baroche read a message from him, most comforting to all who were willing to be comforted, but full of deceit and prevarication.

The Assembly, conscious of the weakness resultant on division, thought best to feign content, and did not observe that there was no mention of the law of May 31 in this long message.

Still the reconciliation between president and Assembly did not prevent the Bonapartist press from continuing its invectives, nor was the truce of long duration. Louis Napoleon pursued a course of alternate advance and retreat, equally the result of previous calculation, which would have ruined him with a firm and united legislature, but which simply disconcerted so inharmonious a body as the present.

January 3, 1851, the president again requested his cabinet to dismiss Changarnier. The ministers resigned, and the president called a council of leaders of the majority. He declared that he would never exceed the limits of his constitutional power, but neither would he permit them to be curtailed. "Exceptional circumstances," said he, "have created an abnormal and extraordinary military command at Paris, the motive for which has ceased to exist; I have therefore determined to put an end to it, as is my right, and have assembled you, that you may assure the Assembly of the legality of my intentions."

The parliamentary chiefs had supposed themselves called in consultation; they were informed of an irrevocable resolve. They expressed their feelings with more or less warmth, Thiers being very sharp and Barrot most pathetic in his entreaty that the president should not enter on this fatal course.

Two days later (January 10), the *Moniteur* published the names of the new cabinet, containing four of the last one, who had only resigned for form's sake. These were politicians in the president's confidence, — Baroche, Rouher, Achille Fould, and the representative of the educational law, De Parieu. These old ministers showed the character of the cabinet better than the new ones, among whom was M. Drouyn de l'Huys. Changarnier was replaced in command by two insignificant generals, who, in Louis Napoleon's idea, were only chosen temporarily.

Great was the agitation in the Assembly, and M. de Remusat proposed to form a committee to take fitting measures. M. Jules de Lasteyrie, then a member of the Right, but very liberal under Louis Philippe, and yet to be an ardent republican, vigorously branded the Bonapartist intrigues; he recalled in angry terms the excesses of the "10th of December" club, — "seven or eight thousand scamps," with whom it was hoped to lead France astray. His words were memorable. Thiers also made one of those speeches which are historic events. The spirit of it was very different from that which animated him on former occasions. Thiers now saw that socialism was not the only, perhaps not the greatest, danger that threatened France, and did what he could to repair his rash remarks about the "rabble." He had recently visited the Orléans family at Claremont, and took pains to explain the visit as an homage paid to misfortune; he said that he had questioned his conscience whether the destiny of modern nations did not guide them rather towards a democratic republic than towards a constitutional royalty. .... "We must buy our experience fairly and fully. . . . . After all, the republic is the universal government."

He thus went back to his famous speech made in January, 1848, and seemed desirous of effacing his immediate past. Unluckily the republicans looked upon his change as a mere manœuvre, and had no faith in a sincerity which the future fully proved. Thiers concluded with the phrase so often quoted, "If the Assembly give way, the empire is accomplished!" (January 17.)

The proposition of the committee in favor of Changarnier not being accepted by the Left, it was changed for a vote declaring that the Assembly had no confidence in the ministry. Odilon Barrot still held aloof, persistently maintaining the Assembly's inability to carry the struggle through to the end.

The ministry resigned, and Louis Napoleon, seeing that the moment had not come to open the battle, made up a cabinet of business men, whom he described in a message to the Legislature as chosen without reference to political parties. This meant nothing more nor less than personal government.

February 3, the president made a fresh demand for money. The three millions were gone already. Doubtless, he had no hope of gaining his request, but he meant to pose as a victim. His petition was refused, and he instantly sold his carriages and horses to move compassion by the sight of the "poverty" of the head of the state.

The coalition which inflicted this blow, broke next day, the majority returning to reaction, and the Left to nurse its wrath.

The president, who had already appealed to Barrot before he made up his business cabinet, again begged him to form a ministry. Barrot made the attempt, and as he belonged to no party faction, he could study the situation more calmly than the parliamentary chiefs. He desired to revise the constitution to admit of the re-election of the president, with a view to prevent a *coup d'état*, civil war, and despotism. Louis Napoleon would never have renounced his hopes of empire, but he would have postponed his schemes, could he have been re-elected; it would have been so much time gained, with all the chances involved by delay.

Barrot, however, failed to persuade Thiers and his friends, and was forced to renounce his plans for the ministry. The president then made Léon Faucher head of a cabinet containing Rouher, Baroche, and Fould, his trusty agents of April 11.

The election of Faucher was worthy of a Machiavelli: it was done to fan the flames of discord between the Right and Left. Faucher undertook to preserve the law of May 31 intact, bugbear as it was to the Left; and the Right, knowing him to be incapable of conniving at a *coup d'état*, took heart of grace, little guessing the plots which were going on behind his back.

Meantime, the question of the revision of the constitution stirred the country as deeply as the question of dissolution in the days of the

Constituent Assembly.   Even the French exiles in London had their
scheme of revision.   Ledru-Rollin demanded the direct government
of the people by the people.   Strange that a man of his sense should
fail to see the utter impracticability of such a plan!   It was contested by Louis Blanc, who, for a wonder, defended common-sense
against utopian dreams.

In France, the republican party was opposed to any revision of
the constitution to repeal the law of May 31.   The Bonapartist
press inveighed against this law, while the ministers declared
themselves its firm defenders.   This was a warning plain enough to
any who would see it and take it (May).   The Assembly soon received a more direct one.   June 1, at the inauguration of a railroad
at Dijon, the president said openly that although the Assembly
had aided him in repressive measures, it had always refused to
sanction any of the many benevolent plans which he had prepared
in the interest of the people.

False as this was, the intention was plain.   Faucher instantly resigned.   His resignation was refused, and the obnoxious phrase suppressed in the official report of the speech ; but the Assembly was
nevertheless made aware of it, and the Right was naturally very
angry at it.   On the occasion of a question of military discipline,
when certain republicans recalled the fact that on the 18th Brumaire the passive obedience of the troops had proved to be the success of usurpation, Changarnier seized the opportunity to declare
that there was no longer the least excuse for an enthusiasm likely to
mislead the army.   " The army," said he, " is no more desirous than
yourselves to entail upon France the miseries and the shames of
Cæsarean rule. . . . . No one could force our troops to fight against
the law and the Assembly. . . . . Advocates of France, deliberate
in peace !"

These high-sounding phrases were loudly applauded.   Changarnier spoke ; Louis Napoleon acted.

It was no longer possible for the Right to deny the danger; and
yet this party went on with its reactionary and unpopular policy,
giving the president boast for boast.

The revisionary movement grew daily. On the 14th of July the signatures exceeded 1,366,000. The question had been before the Assembly for several weeks, more than two hundred members maintaining the necessity of a revision. The discussion which followed was most interesting. Victor Hugo delivered a fiery harangue, in which he asked, "Must Napoleon the Great be followed by Napoleon the Little?"

Odilon Barrot was the only speaker who gave a true account of the situation, and the real object of the revision. He showed the immense advantages which would accrue to the president were revision refused, and won a majority, though not the three-fourths majority required by law. The revision was thus lost, July 17. Barrot, the Duke de Broglie, and those who voted for revision in order to prevent a *coup d'état*, hoped to return to the question after the three months' interval exacted by law before a proposition could be renewed.

But it was too late. Louis Napoleon had decided upon armed usurpation, revision having failed. Long before the question was decided, he was at work preparing his instruments. Cavaignac and the Constituent Assembly strove to promote French colonization in Algiers, but Louis Napoleon looked thither with quite another purpose. The generals who had won renown in that country had returned to France to take part in public affairs, and many of them opposed the president, who now hoped to gain their successors in Africa to his cause. General St. Arnaud was strongly recommended to him, his irregular and adventurous life making it probable that he would readily enter into plots and schemes, while his intellect and his energy seemed omens of success. He was charged with an expedition into the country of the Kabyles to make himself a name (May, 1851), and did sufficiently well to be much talked of in the papers, and to be promoted a step. He was summoned to Paris in July, and received the command of a division. Another important change took place in the military command of Paris. General Baraguey d'Hilliers, Changarnier's successor in the command of the troops of the line, being unwilling to aid in a *coup d'état*, was replaced by General Magnan, a needy and unscrupulous man, already suspected of complicity in the Boulogne affair in 1840.

Louis Napoleon now secretly prepared a pamphlet, assisted by Granier de Cassagnac, that publicist who compromised rather than served Guizot during the latter years of his ministry. It was a plan of revision, and no legal one either. It substituted the constitution of the year VIII, or something like it, for that of 1848. Forty thousand copies were printed early in August, but were held in reserve. As the crisis approached, Louis Napoleon ceased his noisy demonstrations. His financial distress greatly contributed to urge him to action, for he could no longer obtain credit. His dreams and aspirations were now transformed into actual conspiracy. He was using as a summer residence that castle at St. Cloud, the scene of action on Brumaire 18; there he laid his plan of usurpation, August 11, with his most intimate confidants,— De Morny, De Persigny, Rouher, and Carlier, the prefect of police.

We have already alluded to Rouher, a clever orator, who joined Louis Napoleon, as he would have joined any superior power, or any government willing to make him minister.

Viator de Persigny was an old subaltern officer, with a fanatic devotion to Bonapartism and the person of Louis Napoleon, dating from the days of Strasburg and Boulogne. An odd genius, but active, inventive, and determined, he contrived to be elected in two departments in 1849, and to exert a certain amount of influence, not in the Assembly, but upon the Bonapartist groups.

M. de Morny was a very different person. He was said to be the son of Queen Hortense, and unacknowledged brother of Louis Napoleon; still it was not the ties of blood, although he boasted loudly of his descent, but mature consideration, which led him to attach himself to the president, or rather the pretender. In him, the man of pleasure masked the wily calculator. A deputy at the close of Louis Philippe's reign, he vainly gave prudent counsel to Guizot; naturally hostile to democracy, and wisely judging the impotence of legitimists and Orleanists, he had followed the banner on which he fancied fortune perched; he felt his superiority to the man whose cause he espoused, and meant to guide him to his own profit, as he might indeed have done, had not his luxurious habits and excessive scepticism made him incapable of the endless patience necessary to achieve great ends.

Louis Napoleon and his accomplices agreed not to wait for the reopening of the Assembly: they would arrest the members of the permanent committee; the president would issue decrees to be drawn up by Rouher in the spirit of the pamphlet just mentioned; Paris and some other large cities should be put in a state of siege, and the decisive blow should be struck, September 17.

The conspirators now required a military leader to execute their plans, and, knowing that they could not count on General Randon, the minister of war, Louis Napoleon offered the post to St. Arnaud. To the president's great surprise, he hesitated, and excused himself. After him, another general declined, and the prefect of police, hitherto very ardent, also refused.

This involved delay, and Louis Napoleon sought out another plan. October 14, he announced to the cabinet that he meant to propose that the Assembly should repeal the law of May 31. This was a step which the Assembly might have foreseen. Léon Faucher at last discovered that he had been used as a screen to mask the intrigues of the president; he resigned, and his colleagues needs must do the same.

Having baffled public opinion by vain negotiations with the most various men, the president announced a new extra-parliamentary ministry, in the *Moniteur* of October 27. One name was highly significant, — that of the minister of war, St. Arnaud. This time, he had accepted.

Another election was of equal importance. Carlier, the prefect of police, followed the retreat of the Faucher ministry, having too many Orleanist ties to do otherwise. He was replaced by M. de Maupas, prefect of the Upper Garonne, whom Léon Faucher had meant to dismiss. This gentleman had demanded the arrest of numerous moderate republicans, and on being told that citizens could not be arrested simply on suspicion without proof, cried, " Proof, indeed; find proof in their houses!" His action being reported at Paris, Faucher summoned him thither for a reprimand. Louis Napoleon called him to the Elysée, and put him at the head of the police. Although lacking the capacity and daring of St. Arnaud or Morny, he was ready to do his best, and Louis Napoleon at last had his forces at hand.

St. Arnaud opened the campaign by a circular addressed to the troops, insisting upon passive obedience. "The responsibility," he wrote, "rests solely with the leader who issues the order. Military law is the soldier's only law."

"Military law is the soldier's only law!" That was plain enough.

The Assembly reopened, November 4. The presidential message suggested the repeal of the law of May 31, in terms approved by the Left. Louis Napoleon's plan was evident: he had excited the Right against the Left by the reactionary ministry of Faucher; he now meant to excite Left against Right by a scheme for revoking a reactionary law. He also incited the people against the Assembly.

Odilon Barrot says truly, in his Memoirs, that there was but one sensible course to be pursued: to revoke the law of May 31, thus reconciling the Left and the ex-majority, and to vote for revision and bring in a new Constituent Assembly.

The Left did nothing of the kind, but rashly persisted in rushing into a contest with the president. The proposition was rejected, Barrot and several others, who were disposed to accept it, voting against it as a point of honor. Had they decided to join the Left, Louis Napoleon would have been disarmed, and forced to postpone his plots once more.

The questors, whose office it was to protect the safety of all Assemblies, proposed to confirm the decree of May, 1848, giving the president of the Assembly the right to summon the troops his own authority. The minister of war acknowledged that this decree was always in force, but, at the same time, he refused to recognize that the president of the Assembly had such right, on the plea of the impossibility of a conflict between the president of the Republic and the Assembly.

At the same time that he declared the decree to be still posted in all the barracks, his subordinate, Magnan, was requesting his officers to remove it.

St. Arnaud soon retracted his words, and publicly denied that he had ever said anything which could be construed into an admission that the decree of May, 1848, was still in force.

The committee replied to this audacious denial by ordering a discussion of the suggestion of the questors on the 19th of November. This debate must be decisive : if the measure was passed, the Assembly could defend itself; if not, everything was in the hands of the executive power. After a noisy argument, Colonel Charras, formerly under-secretary of state under Cavaignac, demanded the indictment of St. Arnaud. The Assembly rose tumultuously. Changarnier ordered the doors to be closed, and that no one should be allowed to leave, the vote once taken. St. Arnaud, warned, as it is said, by Rouher, and fearing lest the questors should arrest him, hastily departed with Magnan ; Morny had already gone.

All hesitation now became inconceivable to any one who studies the course of events from the distance of our times. The Left hesitated whether to vote with the legitimists and Orleanists, who seemed even more to be dreaded than the imperial pretender. The eyes of some few republicans were open, as were those of Charras ; among them were the African generals, Edgar Quinet, Barthélemy St. Hilaire, Arnaud (de l'Ariège), Bixio, Dufaure, and Jules Grévy, who strove to rescue the Second Republic, and two of whom were to become, one the minister, the other the president, of the Third.

The vast majority sided against them, and voted with the Bonapartists and the tremblers who shrank from conflict. The proposition of the questors was rejected by four hundred and three votes against three hundred.

The Assembly abdicated. Thenceforth, as Thiers had predicted, the Empire was achieved !

"The vote of November 17," says a historian of the Right (M. Victor Pierre), "assured to Louis Napoleon the support of the army ;

the repeal of the law of May 31 won him the favor of the people."

Each political faction rivalled the other in senseless imprudence, and the Bonapartists made skilful use of their follies to terrify the common people, and lead them to prefer, as one of their documents plainly says, "the reign of steel to the reign of fire." To disguise the conspiracy on foot at the Elysée palace, they accused the leaders of the ex-majority, of a plot against the person of the president.

When everything thus foretold a speedy blow, and no outsider doubted its approach, the parliamentarians accused of treason exhausted themselves in seeking means of self-defence which they could never use. Those who retained most calmness, Barrot and a few others, went on with their discussion of a municipal and provincial law, "in the hope," says Barrot, in his Memoirs, "that if this law were powerless to save the present, it might be useful in the future."

With the object of effecting a reconciliation, an amendment was proposed, reducing the term of residence requisite to the franchise to one year, and making the requisite verification less difficult to be obtained. The measure passed, the term of years being changed to two.

All this was now in vain. The ex-majority had begun to moderate its opinions too late.

Meantime, the preparations for the *coup d'état* went on. The conflict had been fixed for the 17th of November, if the proposition of the questors succeeded. Now the conspirators hoped to gain a bloodless victory. All those regiments whose officers favored the president were assembled at Paris, in charge of generals, of whom Louis Napoleon felt sure. The old municipal guard of Louis Philippe's time was restored under another name, and this vast body of troops was kept constantly busy. Reviews, distributions of crosses, and meetings of officers followed in rapid succession, the boldest spirits ever striving to confirm the wavering ones. November 9, six hundred officers went in a body to the Elysée, to assure Louis Napoleon of their devotion. A fortnight later, General Magnan announced to the general officers of the army of Paris that they would soon be called on to obey important orders blindly; that whatever happened, his responsibility would shield them.

On the other hand, Louis Napoleon was working for the favor of the working classes; he gave decorations to manufacturers as well as to soldiers. On the 21st of November, at one of these distributions, he exclaimed: "How prosperous the French republic might be if demagogic ideas and monarchic hallucinations did not disturb it on either hand!"

The Assembly had spied the danger from afar: it failed to perceive it now that it was close at hand. Its fears not being instantly justified, it rested in puerile security. If wise and active men, like De Maleville and Duvergier de Hauranne, revealed the plan of the conspiracy to their colleagues, they refused to heed it. "We have at least a month before us yet," said Changarnier; others pretended that Louis Napoleon would never alienate Parisian tradesmen by destroying the sales of New Year's day.

Everything was ready. At the last moment Louis Napoleon again began to hesitate. Bold in his schemes, uncertain in execution, a conspirator, but not a man of action, he was quite capable of letting the fitting moment pass, and yet he and his followers were quite at the end of their pecuniary resources. Persigny, who considered that his absolute devotion justified him in anything, had a violent scene with the president. Morny and St. Arnaud also told him that the time for dreaming was passed. The day and the hour were fixed.

Various factions in the Assembly, composed of Bonapartists, and men anxious from other motives to make terms with the president, were also, in these last moments, considering an unconstitutional revision of the constitution. Politicians, clerical rather than legitimist or Orleanist, like Montalembert and De Falloux, worked to this end, and a Bonapartist historian (Granier de Cassagnac) affirms that De Falloux, on the evening of December 1, suggested that Louis Napoleon should propose a prolongation of the presidential powers, to be carried by a simple majority in case of resistance from the Left.

Louis Napoleon was to answer next day. De Falloux has protested against this accusation. During the evening Morny, St. Arnaud, and Maupas arrived to make all arrangements with the president for the *coup d'état* next day. Louis Napoleon, always superstitiously observant of dates, chose that of his uncle's coronation and of the battle of Austerlitz (December 2) for this occasion.

CHAPTER XIV.

SECOND REPUBLIC (*close*). — COUNTER-REVOLUTION OF DECEMBER 2.

December 2, 1851.

ON the evening of the 1st of December there was an official reception at the Elysée, and nothing denoted the approach of any extraordinary event; no one remarked that the president said a few words, in an indifferent manner and an undertone, to the new brigade major of the National Guard. Yet this was an order to prevent the beating to arms next day, and to keep the troops out of sight.

The invited guests retired. Louis Napoleon was left alone with Morny, St. Arnaud, Maupas, and Mocquart, the head of the president's cabinet, and his private secretary. Towards midnight an aide-de-camp appeared, and took from Louis Napoleon's hand a parcel containing the manuscript of the proclamations and decrees which were to announce the *coup d'état*. Upon this package Louis Napoleon had inscribed the word *Rubicon*. Not content with copying his uncle's 18th of Brumaire, he parodied the crossing of the Rubicon by Julius Cæsar.

The aide-de-camp took the manuscript to the national printing-offices, where the printers had been kept, under pretext of a press of work. The director, a party to the conspiracy, cut the manuscript into fragments, so that the compositors could not tell what they were setting up. They were suspicious: some refused to work; the majority yielded, and worked, each under the eye of two police agents. A company of soldiers were ordered to shoot any man who attempted to leave, or to approach a window.

Morny stationed himself at the ministry of the interior, unceremoniously dismissing the lay figure who had recently filled that position. Maupas had assembled all the police at the prefecture, and between four and five o'clock in the morning he summoned the forty commissaries, and informed them of the work in store for them. They had been carefully chosen, and not one refused.

While these men traversed Paris with their underlings to effect the prescribed arrests, the palace of the Assembly was invaded. This was not accomplished without some difficulty, the two questors who lodged in the palace, General Leflô and M. Baze, being energetic fellows: they could rely on the military commander of the palace and the commander of the garrison, and had also a battery of artillery at their orders. The success of an open attack was doubtful; treachery was more convenient. A traitor was found in the person of Colonel Espinasse, whose regiment furnished the battalion guarding the palace that night; his adjutant-major opened the door to him and the rest of his regiment. The commander of the garrison, startled at this sudden invasion and recognizing Espinasse, cried out, "Colonel, you are disgracing the regiment!" and he tore off his epaulettes, broke his sword, and threw the pieces at the feet of the invader. This brave officer was named Meunier.

Espinasse and his men forced their way into the rooms of the military commandant, Lieutenant-Colonel Niel, and seized his sword. "You do well to rob me of my sword," said Niel to Espinasse; "I should have run it through your body!"

The indignation of General Leflô was still greater, when, surprised in his bed, he found himself face to face with Espinasse, who called himself his friend, and in whom he put such trust, that, but the day before, he had shown him a secret passage by which he hoped to escape, in case of need. Espinasse placed a guard at the door of this exit.

The other questor, M. Baze, made a desperate resistance, and was dragged from the palace half naked. He and his comrade were taken to Mazas prison.

Meantime, the other commissioners arrested those officers and generals who were members of the Assembly, — Cavaignac, Changarnier, Lamoricière, Bedeau, Charras, Valentin, and also M. Thiers,

and fifteen other representatives. Not one of those pointed out to
the police escaped. All had been on their guard when the danger
was yet remote; when it was at their door, they were heedless of
it! No resistance was attempted; in fact, it could only have led to
murder on the part of the executors of the president's orders; the
conspirators were resolved to shrink from no crime. The arrested
representatives joined the questors at Mazas, with a number of representatives supposed to have a certain influence over the people.

Carlier sent Louis Napoleon the following despatch: "We have
triumphed all along the line!"

Paris awoke to find the walls covered with copies of a decree
and three proclamations. By the decree, the president declared the
Assembly dissolved, universal suffrage restored, and the law of May
31 repealed. Paris was declared in a state of siege, and popular
meetings were to be held from the 14th to the 21st of December.

Two presidential proclamations were addressed, one to the people,
the other to the army.

The first accused the Assembly of having become the centre of
plots and civil war, affirmed that the constitution was framed with the
object of lessening in advance the power which the people intended
to confer on the president, and that six million votes had been cast
in protest. The president declared that it was to uphold the republic that he invoked the solemn arbitration of the only true sovereign, the people, between himself and the men who had already
destroyed two monarchies, and now hoped to overthrow the republic.

He then submitted the basis of a new constitution on the system
of his uncle, the First Consul, as follows: 1st, a responsible chief,
chosen for ten years; 2d, ministers, depending on the executive
alone; 3d, a council of state, preparing the laws and discussing them
before the legislative body; 4th, a legislative body, discussing and
voting the laws, and elected by universal suffrage; 5th, a senate,
guarding the original contract and the public liberty.

The president asked an answer, and showed that the question lay
between peace and prosperity on the one hand and anarchy on the
other.

To the army he used very different terms. Instead of speaking of the republic, he talked of national supremacy, whose legitimate representative he was; he accused both 1830 and 1848, the constitutional revolution and the republican revolution, of treating the troops like a vanquished foe, when they were, he said, the flower of the land. While thus flattering the army, he demanded its passive obedience, making himself alone responsible to the people and to posterity for measures which he deemed indispensable to public welfare.

Side by side with these proclamations, was one from the prefect of police, announcing that any attempt at revolt would be promptly and severely put down.

The first impressions of the Parisians were confused and complex. Louis Napoleon hoped that the repeal of the law of May 31 would be received with applause. This was too much to expect from so intelligent a population. Still he gained one result; the working classes, seeing the Assembly which they detested, dissolved, and universal suffrage restored, were not angered, but waited with a mixture of ironical satisfaction and surprise for further developments.

The middle classes, better disposed towards law and parliamentary institutions, understood the course of events far better, and stormed or laughed as the case might be. Many thought that the enterprise would fail, as at Strasburg and Boulogne.

The newspapers might have affected popular opinion, but every office was held by troops, and no republican journal was allowed to appear.

During the morning various groups of representatives strove to make some plan of resistance. The republicans met to proclaim the downfall of Louis Napoleon, while others tried to force their way into the legislative palace, which thirty or forty contrived to do. They passed a vote that Louis Napoleon had forfeited his office. President Dupin was brought in, and timidly made his submission, declaring that it was useless for right to struggle against might. Other meetings were held, and the National Guard was summoned to defend the place of session of the Assembly; but the call to arms was not beaten, and orders had already been issued that any member of the National Guard found bearing arms was to be shot; accordingly not a man appeared.

M. Dufaure uttered noble sentiments. "We are now," he said, "the sole defenders of the constitution, of right, of the republic, and the country. Let us not fail in our duty to ourselves, and if we needs must yield to brute force, history will record the fact that we struggled to the last."

M. Pascal Duprat then said that the only means of safety lay in an appeal to the mob: "Revolution is our only defence."

"Law, law!" was the cry, — "no revolution!"

A detachment of infantry now entered, but at the order of the president of the Assembly, the officer in command retired to consult his superiors. At the suggestion of Berryer, the Assembly then named General Oudinot commander of the army of Paris. Captain Tamisier, the only republican member of the Assembly not arrested, objected that the memory of his Roman expedition would rob Oudinot of all authority with the people. The latter accordingly offered to take him as brigade-major, as a guarantee of good faith.

Oudinot soon dispersed a second body of infantry, as the president of the Assembly had the first; it was followed by two police commissioners, who ordered the Assembly to disperse; an officer next appeared with orders from General Magnan to arrest all who remained, and take them with "all respect" to Mazas. Upon the summons of Oudinot, as the sole military and legal authority, for the troops to depart, their officer replied that he recognized no orders save those of his superiors.

The representatives were led between two lines of soldiers to the barracks on the Quai d'Orsay, without any attempt at interference from the crowd, although there were cheers for the constitution, Assembly, and republic.

While these events were occurring, another attempt at legal resistance was made at the Palace of Justice.

The constitution had invested a supreme court with the right to call upon the grand jury to judge the president of the republic in case of high treason. This court now met, but took no decided action, and postponed the choice of an attorney-general until next day. At this juncture the police discovered and invaded the room where the court was held, in the most remote part of the Palace of Justice. The magistrates were ordered to disperse, which they did, protesting that they yielded to superior force.

Next morning they reassembled, having made M. Renouard, a most respectable and enlightened man, attorney-general. No action was, however, taken, owing, as was said, "to the material obstacles to the execution of any decree that might be issued."

Although these attempts at resistance were foiled, loyal subjects failed to flock to the Elysées on the 2d of December, and Louis Napoleon's immediate followers urged him to appear in public. He therefore mounted his horse, and rode towards the Tuileries with a large military escort. The mob was not markedly hostile, but seemed cold and satirical. Occasional cheers for the republic, constitution, and Assembly were heard, and the president went no farther. In the afternoon he reviewed the troops, then shut himself up until the crisis was over, sitting for hours with his head in his hands, while his accomplices worked for him.

This was not what he had promised (November 9) to the officers who laid their services at his feet. "If the day of danger ever dawns," he said, "I shall not imitate the governments which preceded me; I shall not say, 'March, I will follow'; but, 'I lead the way, follow me!'" Unfortunately, those who were working for him were far more able than he!

In spite of the arrest of so many representatives, the Assembly had not yet heard the last of the *coup d'état*. The remnant met; a vigorous appeal to the people was drawn up by Victor Hugo, and it was decided that the representatives should proceed to erect barricades in the most populous quarters next day.

Paris began to grow warm; the middle classes were in a blaze; but what were the people to do? Indomitable courage was required to try the fate of arms against the forces wielded by the conspirators. On the morning of December 3d, sixty thousand soldiers were

PALACE OF JUSTICE

posted at the principal points of Paris, and the National Guard had been disbanded and dismissed. Never before was might so destitute of right.

On the morning of the 3d, the *Moniteur* published an order for the opening of registries to receive the votes for or against the plebiscite, December 14. Popular opinion was most adverse to this suppression of secret suffrage.

A committee of consultation was formed to act until the new constitution was accepted. The men who composed it knew nothing of it in advance, and several refused indignantly. Léon Faucher, faulty and criminal though he was, but incapable, as he said, "of aiding and abetting the violation of the law," inquired by what right he was "thus insulted." De Montalembert refused, but finally accepted, his Catholic zeal leading him to forget his love of liberty and legality in this fatal moment.

Rouher and Achille Fould accepted, as did Morny and St. Arnaud, positions in the new cabinet announced the same day.

Yet not only the public, but the inhabitants of the Elysée palace, had great doubts of final success. Many believed that this attempt would end as those of Strasburg and Boulogne had done, forgetting that now Louis Napoleon held the executive power, and had Morny and St. Arnaud on his side.

Faithful to their resolve, a small band of representatives collected in the Faubourg St. Antoine, December 3. The people seemed sad and preoccupied, and, when urged to action, they replied, "But we have no weapons; we were disarmed after June, 1848," showing that they still felt resentment to the Assemblies of 1848 and 1849. Others said, "They have restored universal suffrage!"

At this juncture carriages appeared, containing the representatives on their way to Vincennes prison. They thrust their heads from the windows, and implored the people not to attempt to free them, and the mob cried, "These fellows are good for nothing!"

Those representatives who had come thither, ready to sacrifice their lives, were good for something, however. They girt on their official scarfs, and cheered on the mob; but in vain. One workman exclaimed, "Do you suppose that we're going to be killed to save your twenty-five francs a-day?"

"You shall see," replied Representative Baudin, "how men can die for twenty-five francs!"

A feeble barricade was raised, the columns of infantry came up, the first shot was fired from the barricade, and was returned. Baudin, who stood in the front as if to offer a mark, fell dead. The soldiers crossed the barricade, and easily carried the day. Similar scenes ensued in various quarters, and strong appeals were made to the people and the army.

Towards 3 P. M. proclamations from Maupas and St. Arnaud were posted in the streets. The first announced that all street gatherings were to be instantly dispersed by force; the second declared that any person taken in the act of building or defending a barricade, or with arms in hand, was to be shot. It is said that St. Arnaud hesitated to write this last word, and that Morny added with his own hand, "Shot!" He never wavered, and his *sang-froid* never failed him, either in the execution of this great political crime or in his life of pleasure and speculation.

These atrocious acts, ordered by the refined sons of a corrupt civilization, proved that a phase of despotism was to dawn, after thirty-five years of legal rule in various forms.

Shots soon responded to these proclamations. The most resolute associations of workmen offered their services to the committee of resistance, and terrified despatches were sent from the prefecture of police to the ministry of the interior. Maupas was not of Morny's temper. Numerous brief engagements ensued, but the troops easily triumphed.

While these skirmishes were going on, sixty representatives of the Left assembled in the Rue des Moulins, and renewed the declaration of downfall. They were visited by a member of the Bonaparte family, the son of Jerome, ex-king of Westphalia. A representative of the people, he had always voted with the Mountain party, and opposed his cousin, the president. He and Emile de Girardin declared that there was no hope of success by armed force, and desired to confine themselves to protests. He was unheeded, and finally withdrew, while thirty representatives went out to distribute the decree of downfall.

The excitement increased, and during the night the generals imprisoned at Mazas were transported to the fortress of Ham, where Louis Napoleon had been imprisoned for six years. The order was to guard the prisoners and to prevent their escape at any cost, — an order easy of interpretation.

Undoubtedly Napoleon feared an attack on Mazas, for his surroundings were highly alarmist. Morny, always calm and cold, quietly remarked to the tremblers, "Yesterday you wanted barricades; now you have them, why should you complain ?"

Morny forced his plan upon a council of war held at the Elysée. It was a plan founded on the experiences of the July and February revolts, and consisted in sparing the troops, letting the insurgents work their hardest and build strong barricades, then surrounding the insurrection, hemming it in, and striking a decisive blow.

General Magnan was charged with the execution of this plan. A despatch sent him by Morny deserves quotation: "In great cities, war can only be made by cutting off the supplies and reducing the inhabitants to starvation, or by overwhelming them with terror." Every precaution was taken to prevent a dearth of food among the troops, such as occurred in 1830 and 1848, and Louis Napoleon distributed his last fifty thousand francs among the men for pocket-money.

The night of the 3d of December was spent in building barricades from the Rue du Temple to the Rue Montmartre, and in the Faubourg St. Martin. It is frequently said that the police took an active share in the work, and they certainly did not oppose it.

The next morning passed quietly, save for a fresh proclamation from Maupas: "All gatherings of foot-passengers on public streets will be dispersed without further warning. Let all peace-loving citizens stay at home ! It will be dangerous to interfere with preconcerted arrangements."

About two o'clock the troops set out, well fed and stimulated in every sense. Thirty thousand men were divided into five corps, while the little bands of insurgents, scattered here and there, scarcely numbered twelve hundred armed men. The people were constantly more hostile to the president's scheme, but their hostility scarcely extended to a desire for bloodshed.

Terrible scenes soon followed, which have left an indelible mark on the pages of history. Men were shot down like dogs, and the firing was so rapid that, in the words of an eye-witness, "it flashed along the boulevard like an undulating flame." "It seemed," said one of the wounded, "as if a water-spout were sweeping onward, carrying with it every obstacle in its path."

General, afterwards Marshal, Canrobert, who commanded certain of the troops, long afterwards declared that he not only did not give the order to fire, but that he exposed his life, among his maddened men, to force them to cease shooting. Other officers say the same of themselves, and there is no motive for contesting their statements, but the responsibility of the massacre none the less rests wholly with the leaders of the conspiracy, who had long been filling the minds of the soldiers with every imaginable slander of the Parisian people and the Assembly, going so far as to declare that the Assembly wished to deprive them of their poor bounty money.

When they set out, they expected that shots would be fired from every window and roof, as in June, 1848. The massacre was the result of a frantic panic; it was a repetition, on a grand scale, of the catastrophe of February 23, 1848, on the Boulevard des Capucines, excepting that that was a fatal accident, and this was deliberately planned to terrify the rich middle class.

The two halves of Paris on the right bank of the Seine presented a very different, though equally terrible aspect. On the west was slaughter without a battle; on the east, a brave and desperate struggle. The great barricade in the Rue St. Denis, crowned with the tricolored flag, defied the efforts of its assailants for two hours. Four cannon thundered against it, but neither destroyed it nor forced the one hundred and fifty republicans who held it to surrender; the regiment attacking it was driven back to the boulevard, but fresh troops, coming up, finally captured the barricade. Other barricades in various quarters were defended with equal valor, but the soldiers maintained their supremacy amid terrible bloodshed. The number of deaths is unknown. The figures given by apologists for the *coup d'état* are utterly unreliable. No one knows how many died that day, or how many died that night. Many credible witnesses say that they heard, on that awful night, cries, groans, explosions, and firing by platoon, at the police offices, on the Champ des Mars, about the Invalides and the Luxembourg; and an old constituent, Xavier Durreiu, declares, in a pamphlet on the *coup d'état*, that he saw prisoners murdered with tomahawks in the courts of the conciergerie.

Paris looked frightful indeed next day. Blood lay in pools upon the pavement; corpses were laid in rows, more than three hundred and fifty being taken to the northern cemetery for instant burial, — but the gravedigger left the heads out of the earth, that their families might recognize the dead!

The Parisians could no longer laugh at Louis Napoleon: he had succeeded in putting a serious face on the matter; ridicule changed to horror. The *coup d'état* was triumphant. The weak hastily rallied to the cause; the strong raged at their impotence to punish successful crime; the trembling mob was silent. All day, on the 5th of December, silent and sombre figures stalked about, breathing the concentration of fury. A few feeble attempts were made to rebuild the barricades, but they were given up almost as soon as begun. All was indeed over with Paris!

The same day a presidential decree established that when troops aided in "restoring domestic order," their services were to be reckoned as services in a campaign. Thus civil war was placed on a level with foreign war.

Another decree restored the secret ballot, as a concession to public opinion, although the army had already voted according to the first plan, within forty-eight hours after the 2d of December. There were 303,000 ayes, 39,000 nays, and some thousand non-voters.

On the 15th, Morny issued a circular recommending the observance of the Sabbath. The public works were to be closed on Sundays and holidays. The circular set forth that "the man who, despising the most venerable traditions, reserves no day for the accomplishment of his religious duties, must sooner or later become the victim of materialism!" This was characteristic of the new régime, under which every excess was to go hand in hand with every species of hypocrisy.

It was also decreed that any member of a secret society, or any one under police surveillance and breaking ban, might be transported to Cayenne or Algiers, as a measure of public safety, thus putting a vast number of people, especially in Southern France, at the mercy of the powers that be. Arrests multiplied with alarming rapidity; Bonapartist historians say that they exceeded twenty-six thousand. The prisons overflowed, and prisoners were sent to fortresses, where they were confined in damp and chilly casemates.

The crisis, stifled in Paris, continued in the provinces, where a great diversity of opinion prevailed. The North, the major portion of the East, and the Northwest still felt the Napoleonic impress of December 10, 1848. The peasants of the North and East little guessed the share of the Bonapartist party in the events of June, 1848, for which they had a sincere disgust. The democratic socialistic propaganda had made slight progress in these regions, while it flourished largely in the South and a part of Central France. There the vague term "socialism" was accepted without any tendency to communism. The people were hostile to great proprietors, although passionately attached to their small properties; they had the undefined aspirations, the wrath and instinctive impulses, of a democracy which has not yet learned to know its own nature. They determined to go in a body to the polls, well armed, in spite of the law of May 31; they hoped that a democratic renovation might result from the struggle. But exactly what the struggle would be, no one knew.

The year 1852 seemed to a vast number of the masses a sort of mystic date, a new era of liberty and prosperity. The hope of some was the terror of others. This revolution of fixed limits inspired such terror in the conservatives, that they were ready to accept anything to avoid it. To escape 1852, they plunged into the 2d of December, with scarcely an exception, abandoning their insulted, hunted, and imprisoned representatives without decent respect. And the majority of these representatives, in their inmost souls, approved this abandonment.

It is needless to say that the civil and military officials, chosen and prepared long in advance, were loyal to the *coup d'état*, with a few honorable exceptions.

In the North and East, the republicans could make but feeble resistance. In Central France, unavailing attempts at legal opposition without recourse to arms were made, but were necessarily vain. An event which occurred in the province of Ain made its mark in history. Certain French republicans, who had fled to Switzerland, attempting to enter Ain and raise the people, four of them met two custom-house officers on the frontier, who tried to stop them. A fight ensued. One of the custom-house officers was fatally wounded. One of the insurgents was drowned in an attempt to swim the Rhone. The other three were captured next day. Charlet, the one who wounded the officer, was sentenced to death by a council of war, and was guillotined some months after. His execution, under such conditions, exceeded the massacres ordered by St. Arnaud: the February revolution abolished capital punishment for political crimes or violation of the law; the counter-revolution of December restored it, to the profit of the usurper who had drowned the laws in the blood of their defenders.

Nièvre was the hotbed of democracy in Central France. The first outbreaks were repressed; then Clamecy broke out. There the authorities were unable to capture the republican leaders as they had done elsewhere. The peasants from the valley of the Yonne joined the citizens, and although there was no pillage, murders abounded. Troops were finally sent from Paris, and the insurgents, now fled to the neighboring woods, were easily tracked and taken. The insurrection of Clamecy was long dwelt upon by Bonapartist journals. There were crimes but too real; the truth was insufficient; pamphleteers, in the pay of the victors, heaped up monstrous tales to terrify the conservative classes ; murder, fire, pillage, and outrage,— nothing was wanting, and this system was speedily applied by paid journals to every provincial insurrection.

The atrocity of the repression, unfortunately, was not imaginary. Carlier, the former prefect of police, was sent as commissioner extraordinary to Nièvre and its environs. He had broken with Louis Napoleon, through aversion to universal suffrage, when the president determined to abolish the law of May 31 ; he returned to the cause, when it was a question of seeming reactionary terror. He issued a circular declaring that any one sheltering an insurgent would be considered an accomplice, and the Lyonnese council of war sentenced such an accomplice to twenty years' hard labor. There were more than fifteen hundred arrests in Clamecy, and the terrors of December, 1851, were not forgotten for many a year in that wretched region.

In the southwestern provinces some enthusiasm for Louis Napoleon was shown, December 10, 1848, and yet the democratic party had gained ground there since. The question rested with Bordeaux and Toulouse. Toulouse had too strong a garrison to attempt an uprising. At Bordeaux the garrison was weak, but the republican leaders lacked decision, and nothing was effected. The attempts made at a hundred points in the Southwest showed what the movement might have become if at least one of these two great cities had afforded a centre and a support. The democratic party was even stronger in the Southeast. Languedoc, Provence, and Dauphigny were largely connected with the Society of the Mountaineers, and multitudes of workmen and peasants, whose parents sided with the "whites" in 1815, now took part with the "reds," if we may give that epithet to the masses who were democrat and revolutionary rather than socialist and sectarian. The Society of the Mountaineers had no central point of union ; each province was a separate body. The initiatory rites were borrowed from freemasons and Carbonari, and were well calculated to strike the imagination. The neophyte, with bandaged eyes, swore upon a naked sword, by the sacred name of Jesus, to "leave father, mother, wife, and children, to fly to the defence of liberty." There were said to be sixty thousand members in the Herault; many were police agents, who played a double game, and spied their superiors for the benefit of their association.

If these societies had been as orderly and well captained as they were zealous and numerous, they must have been irresistible. Montpellier, the capital of Herault, whose citizens voted "no" to the plébiscite, was restrained by the large garrison; but Beziers rose before the secret police had any warning. The movement, being ill managed, was soon suppressed; after which more than three thousand people were arrested, two thousand of whom were transported. Many fugitives from the troops were killed.

Provence made the most determined resistance to the 2d of December; however, Marseilles, like Bordeaux and Toulouse, was passive. The leaders waited to hear from Paris, and the people, being without direction, did not rebel. Toulon was too closely watched to rise; but many little towns and villages took up arms. The *coup d'état* was victorious in every instance, the victory being marked by mournful events. One prisoner, Martin Bidouré, was shot, but not killed. He dragged himself to a farm-house, where he was taken in and nursed. Being captured, he was shot a second time! Other frightful executions were numerous, one gendarme alone killing four prisoners tied together, one of them being only seventeen years old. He showed no remorse, and had claimed the privilege of shooting these men, who had wounded him during the insurrection.

The province of the Lower Alps held out to the last. Poor and thinly peopled, it seemed the most wretched in the South; yet it was the only one where the movement was conducted with perfect unity and rare intelligence. When all hope was lost, these brave men could not bear to yield without a struggle. They marched to meet the troops; three or four thousand men held the defile of the Mées, and successfully repelled the first regiment attacking them. Honor was saved; all the leaders, but one, resigned themselves to yield the day. Aillaud, the superintendent of woods and waters in the Lower Alps, the leader of the defence of the Mées, refused to surrender; he fled to the mountains with a few hundred men, and was followed by the troops. The republicans had committed no cruelty; they were treated with ferocity. In the pursuit many prisoners were shot. Aillaud's band gradually lessened; but by great skill and daring the hero himself escaped his enemies, reached Marseilles, and was on the point of sailing for a distant point, when he was recognized, seized, tried by a council of war, and sent to Cayenne, where he died. His name and that of Buisson, the organizer of the movement in the Lower Alps, deserve to be cherished by posterity.

The republican rising in the Lower Alps was almost unanimous; even parish priests shared its dangers with true devotion. The ensuing ruin was equally general; many inhabitants fled to escape arrest, and whole villages were left deserted. The misfortunes and the patriotism of this brave and honest people merit the esteem and sympathy of France. Nowhere else were similar harmony and ability of direction witnessed, although energy was not lacking in some of the dwellers on the shores of the Rhone.

The struggle came to a final end by the middle of December. The few crimes committed by insurgents here and there cannot be compared to the atrocity of the vast reaction which spread over a very great part of France. Many brave men, whole sections of the country, did themselves honor by their bold resistance; but, as is remarked by that excellent historian of the *coup d'état*, M. Eugène Ténot, the event proved, on a great scale, the inability of secret societies to effect harmonious action which should decide the destinies of a nation, although for once the societies had right and law on their side.

It is also worthy of note that, for the first time since the dawn of the French Revolution, a great revolutionary movement occurred in Southern and a portion of Central France, while the Northern and Eastern provinces, where the spirit of 1789 was always most permanent and pronounced, were passive or almost so. This was a most striking proof of the mental trouble and confusion which had prepared France for the fatal period upon which she now entered.

CHAPTER XV.

DICTATORSHIP OF LOUIS NAPOLEON. — RESTORATION OF THE EMPIRE.

Middle of December, 1851, to December 2, 1852.

THE struggle was over: terror of the victors followed. Thirty-two departments were in a state of siege. More than one hundred thousand citizens were languishing in prison. Trial followed trial in rapid succession, the cases being classed under three heads: 1st, persons found armed, or against whom serious charges existed; 2d, persons charged with minor offences; 3d, dangerous persons. The first class was judged at once by a council of war, the second sent to various tribunals, the third transported without trial.

Many prisoners were not even questioned. Numbers were set free; but multitudes were still held.

Under these conditions the date of the plébiscite, December 20 and 21, approached. Notices were posted to the effect that "any person seeking to disturb the polls or to question the result of the ballot would be tried by a council of war." All liberty of choice was taken from the electors, many of whom were arrested on suspicion of exciting others to vote against the president of the republic.

When the lists were published it was found that the "ayes" had carried the day, although many did not vote at all.

Indubitably the figures were notably swelled by violence and fraud. No supervision of the ballots was possible. The majority of those who presided at the polls were utterly unscrupulous, while many voted in the affirmative under the influence of terror. The huge majority of ten to one which the committee proclaimed, was evidently fictitious; nevertheless, terror aside, Louis Napoleon was sure of a less majority, but still a majority; the Napoleonic fame still lingered with some; others, as was inevitable in such a case, yielded to the fear of the unknown, to the dread of a new crisis.

December 31, ex-Minister Baroche presented the result of the ballots to the prince-president, — a strange title now given to Louis Napoleon, for the time being, in lieu of another. "Prince," said he, "restore to France the principle of authority lacking for fifty years. Unceasingly contest anarchic passions. . . . . May France at last be freed from those men ever ready for murder and pillage, the horror of civilization," etc.

The prince-president did not answer this speech in the same spirit, but strove to justify usurpation by sophistry. "France," he said, "understands that I violated the law to restore the right. More than seven million votes pronounce my absolution." He said that with the aid "of all good men, the devotion of the army, and the protection of heaven," he hoped to deserve the confidence that the people would continue to place in him. He condescended to promise liberty in the future, reserving to himself the choice of a fitting moment for granting it.

The diplomatic corps, with the clergy of Paris, hastened to offer him their congratulations, and the archbishop of Paris promised to pray to God for the success of the lofty mission intrusted to Louis Napoleon.

Next day, January 1, 1852, Archbishop Sibour celebrated a Te Deum in Notre Dame, the prince-president sitting under a canopy. His cousin, Prince Napoleon, who had declared himself adverse to December 2, now rallied to the cause, and sat close by. The archbishop had also been very hostile to the *coup d'état* at first. Made archbishop by General Cavaignac, up to December 2 he was intensely republican. December 3, a democratic and Catholic laborer — a combination occasionally found — wrote, begging him to lead the clergy, the representatives of the people, and the magistrates of the supreme court, or to resist the *coup d'état* with the peaceful weapons of justice and religion. Unable to gain admission to the archbishop, he confided the letter to Representative Arnaud, a man reckless of danger; but, as he would have been arrested before he reached his destination, his young wife took the letter and set out, her child in her arms, to allay suspicion. The letter was received, but the archbishop, though honest, was weak, and his courage failed. He shrank from repeating the martyrdom of his predecessor. "It is too late!" he replied.

January 1, he received the triumphant perjurer in his cathedral, and celebrated a victory which horrified him.   Other prelates pursued the same course; and when the prince-president made a journey through the provinces shortly after, the majority of the bishops hailed him as "the Lord's anointed," a term used under the ancient monarchy.   One of the chief prelates of France did not hesitate to apply to the man of December 2, the words applied to Jesus by Simeon, "Lord, now lettest thou thy servant depart, for I have seen the salvation of the Lord!"   He was also invited to take up his abode at the Tuileries, "the only residence worthy of him."

This conduct of the Catholic party and the episcopate was destined to have enduring and terrible results. The republic of 1848, at the height of her feverish tumults and daring dreams, sought the priestly blessing for her liberty trees; the clergy now rewarded her by greeting her murderer as the envoy of God. Deep resentment rankled in many hearts, and an abhorrence of Catholicism far stronger than that of the days of the Restoration sprang to life, affecting all religious faith and favoring nihilism.

On the morning of the first day of the year, which opened a period so different from that which so many hopeful spirits had awaited in 1852, a decree substituted the imperial eagle of Rome for the cock, by which constitutional monarchy and republic alike recalled ancient Gaul. Another decree announced that the leader of state would take up his abode at the Tuileries.

While the man of December 2 lodged in the palace of kings, the chief representatives of the republic were cast into exile. The executors of the plot treated the captive representatives very differently according as they were conservative or republican. When the

The ministers, therefore, are to be dependent upon him, and may not form a responsible and jointly liable council. They are to have no connection with the deliberative bodies. The president will command the army and navy, declare war, make treaties of peace, alliance, and commerce, fill all offices, make all rules and regulations requisite to the execution of the laws. Justice will be executed in his name. He alone can issue, sanction, and promulgate a law. All public functionaries will take an oath of allegiance to him.

"The wheel within the wheel of the new organization will be a state council of from forty to fifty members, chosen and revocable by the president of the republic, discussing the laws in private session, then presenting them for the approval of the Legislature."

The legislative body was to consist of two hundred and sixty-two members (one for each thirty-five hundred electors), chosen for five years by universal suffrage. This body would vote upon the laws and taxes.

Louis Napoleon, having profited so largely by the repeal of the law of May 31, could scarcely refuse to retain direct universal suffrage, but he essentially altered its character by various modifications. He also so reduced the importance of the only great body still elective, that he had little or nothing to fear from it. Another assembly, the Senate, was to be composed of eighty members, which number might be increased to one hundred and fifty. The senators were irremovable, and were to be chosen by the president of the republic, with the exception of cardinals, marshals, and admirals, who were senators by right. The president might give each senator an income of thirty thousand francs. The Senate was the guardian of the constitution and of "the public liberty." It was to oppose the promulgation of laws contrary to the constitution, to morality and religion, etc.

The executive power chose all mayors, and was at liberty to select them outside the town council.

In fact, the constitution of 1852 surpassed the constitution of the year VIII. as a piece of monarchic reaction. It entailed no consulate, but an empire, — dicatorship and total confiscation of public liberty. Thirty-seven years after the fall of Napoleon the Great, the long struggle for French freedom resulted in the restoration of absolute power into the hands of a man destitute of genius or of glory.

The publication of the constitution was followed by the restoration of two institutions of the empire, — the ministry of state, held by a Corsican, M. Casabianca; and the ministry of police, in the hands of Maupas.

January 22, two decrees were issued, the one commanding the Orléans family to sell, within the term of one year, all goods belonging to them within the territory of the republic; this referred to the property belonging to the Orléans princes, exclusive of the gift made by Louis Philippe to his children upon his accession to the throne. The second decree annulled this gift as contrary to the old laws of France, added to the public treasury Louis Philippe's legacies to his heirs, and distributed them as follows : —

Ten millions to the mutual aid societies, established in 1850 ;

Ten millions for the improvement of lodgings for laborers in great manufacturing towns ;

Ten millions for the establishment of respectable loan institutions in the provinces ;

Five millions to establish a superannuation fund for the deserving poor.

The remaining sum went to endow the Legion of Honor.

Louis Napoleon thus tried to win the approval of the army, clergy, and working classes for his confiscation of the Orléans property. He was not restrained by the scruples which prevented the republican government of 1848 from laying claim to the gift of Louis Philippe, and he wounded the Orléans family in their purses as he wounded the republicans in their persons, while he showed no more respect for the property of the latter, who had been notably despoiled.

The council of state made a lively resistance to the two decrees. Some were deprived of office for their opposition, and several ministers resigned. Fould, Rouher, and Magne were unwilling to assist in robbing the former royal family; but their mild protest did not extend to a rupture with the new government, for they returned to its service shortly after. Even St. Arnaud, who had served under the Orléans princes, feigned withdrawal: but it was only a feint. Another minister, the most important of all, M. de Morny, actually resigned! It is improbable that such a man would care for law or moral propriety, and it is untrue, if we accept the testimony of a Bonapartist historian, well acquainted with the secrets of the empire (M. Granier de Cassagnac). He reports that Morny made the incredible claim to some official recognition of the secret tie of blood between himself and the president; nor did he shrink from alluding to it in a speech at a banquet. Louis Napoleon was naturally deeply wounded by this indiscretion, and it was this motive which caused Morny's withdrawal from the ministry. But the quarrel was of brief duration. Morny was not one of those assistants who can be dismissed when they have served once! He was too necessary! Louis Napoleon made him president of the Legislature, where he ruled with rare skill.

Fialin de Persigny replaced him in the ministry of the Interior. Duke de Nemours and Prince de Joinville protested, in a most energetic letter, against the robbery of their family. "We will not stoop," they said, "to point out the peculiar horror which it causes us to see slanders against our royal father reproduced by one who has twice been in a position to appreciate the generosity of King Louis Philippe, and whose family have never received anything but kindness at his hands.' . . . . We are happy in the assurance that these shameful decrees were only possible under a state of siege, and after the suppression of every protecting pledge of the national liberty."

The blow struck home to the conspirator so rashly pardoned by Louis Philippe.

The middle classes were alarmed at the attack on property rights, but were sensible of their impotence.

The National Guard, an institution identified with the middle classes under Louis Philippe, and radically democratized by the February revolution, was now transformed into a passive tool of the executive power. A decree, issued January 11, deprived it of its democratic character by giving the government power to limit the number of national guards for every station, and to suppress them where their aid seemed unnecessary. Despotism spread daily in every direction. On the 17th of February the liberty of the press was notably reduced, and severe penalties were affixed to any infraction. In fact, the press was made dependent on the good-will of the president.

Education was next attacked, a decree of March 9, 1852, stripping the professors of the University of all the pledges and principles granted by the First Empire. Their election and dismissal were now in the hands of the president and his ministry, and the supreme council of 1850 became a mere name, the members being chosen by the president.

Thus the emperor's heir failed to respect even the great and useful achievements of his uncle, and destroyed, through his mania for despotic uniformity, the great body of the University created by Napoleon I. More than forty professors, the flower of them all, refused to take the oath required by the constitution, and voluntarily wrecked their career rather than swear allegiance to a perjurer. A new course of studies was laid out, philosophy giving way to lectures by a chaplain upon religion and morality. The scholars were divided into two classes, the first studying literature with a view to pursuing some liberal career; the second studying the sciences with a view to a commercial or industrial career, to entering the medical or other special schools. This system of bifurcation, as it was called, this division of medicine and the literary professions, was utterly absurd, and tended only to debase the national intellect.

M. Fortoul, the minister of public education, a wise and learned man, was not the author of this wretched reform. A republican false to the republic, a philosopher faithless to his philosophy, a university graduate the willing tool of the university's foes, he did not mistake the danger and the folly of the task imposed upon him. His scepticism led him to accept it, since the ministry was to be bought at that price alone. The consequences of the bifurcation were so fatal that it was of necessity set aside during the reign of Louis Napoleon himself.

The new power, in 1852, labored to turn all the forces of the country to material interests, while it stifled all moral interests. It suppressed education and the press, and constantly stimulated the financial and industrial movement. During the first months of his rule Louis Napoleon adopted many important measures in regard to finance, social economy, and public works. Many works had been begun under the Legislature, which shortly before its fall had authorized the city of Paris to accept a loan of fifty millions to continue the Rue de Rivoli to the Hôtel de Ville and to build central markets. It is just to recall at the same time the fact that the Legislature voted large sums in the interest of science, under Léon Faucher, loans for the resumption of the excavations at Nineveh, and for the restoration of the famous temple at Memphis (the Serapeum), under the conduct of Mariette Bey, who devoted himself to the great work of restoring ancient Egypt.

Numberless railroad companies now sprang to life, and roads were rapidly built upon a grand scale. The government adopted the system of grants on a long term of years, — say ninety-nine, — plus the guarantee of a small rate of interest. In everything the cry was for instant success, at any cost.

Great financial operations followed on the heels of the first grants to railroad companies. The Stock Exchange, in spite of public storms, had thriven constantly since 1848, as had business and manufactures; still in 1851 the panic about 1852 prevented the rise of stock. When quiet was restored, all interest followed the victor; stock went above par in mid December, and was at 103 early in March. The dictator then saw fit to change the five per cents into four and one half per cent bonds, offering to reimburse such creditors of the state as were unwilling to accept the reduction. A very large majority accepted, as usual on such occasions. This saved the state about eighteen millions annually, and was very advantageous to manufactures, as it lowered the rate of interest.

The Bank of France lent the government efficient aid in various

FOUNTAIN OF ST. MICHEL, PARIS.

ways, and in return the government gave up its right of interfering with the privilege of the bank until 1867.

Louis Napoleon then founded, with great ostentation, two important establishments, the Bank Foncière of Paris (March 18), which soon became the Crédit Foncier of France; and a few months later (November 20), the Crédit Mobilier. The former was reputed to be for the support of agriculture; but it was used almost wholly for great building operations, and simply facilitated the artificial, or at least very precipitate and exaggerated movement for the reconstruction of Paris and other great cities, by which Louis Napoleon hoped to dazzle France and Europe. The Crédit Foncier was not serviceable to the agricultural interest, but its constitution was solid, and it is still a powerful and enduring institution. The Crédit Mobilier, without the bases and the security of the other, after an epoch of false splendor, died out amid much scandal.

This year's budget, like the constitution, was the work of a single man. The dictator settled it by a decree; then, having ordered the elections for his Chamber of Deputies, just before his constitution went into operation, he raised the universal state of siege (March 28). This was only a feint, for his government was a permanent state of siege. Terror, if not compression, ceased for the well-to-do class when the power was once firmly established; in ordinary times a man of any note could not be carried off and transported without causing an uproar ill according with the public peace and prosperity which the new government boasted that they had restored; but panic still prevailed among the obscure working-classes of Paris and elsewhere. The laborer was flattered and caressed, but a workman known by the police to hold advanced opinions was liable to disappear in a night, never to be heard from more. Cayenne and Lambessa alone could tell where he languished and died. This state of things continued at intervals for years.

Had the state of siege been lifted sooner, the elections, deprived of preliminary meetings and journalistic aid, would scarcely have been more free. They occurred February 29, the result being assured in advance. The official candidates presented, or rather imposed, were generally elected; the republicans failed to vote throughout a great part of the country. The *Siècle*, the only republican journal in Paris, which survived by keeping silent at first, made a bold attempt, and recommended three candidates,—Generals Cavaignac and Carnot for Paris, and Dr. Hénon for Lyons. They were all elected, and these exceptions,. pre-eminent amid these strange elections, showed that political France was not yet dead.

The Legislature was far more like a general council representing material interests only, than like a chamber of deputies. Montalembert and the three republicans already named, were the sole relics of former political assemblies. The recommendation of the official journal, *Le Constitutionnel*, had been followed: "Renounce," it said to the candidates,—"renounce all struggle after the influence that you exerted under parliamentary rule; accept a modest and busy post." To the electors it said: "You need guidance; be thankful that the government has pointed out the candidates most likely to support the president, for they will give you opportunity to vote for him again."

March 29, the prince-president proceeded to install the great state bodies at the Tuileries. It was thought that he would hint in his speech that he expected the title of Emperor, but he left that point vague, and still talked of preserving the republic. This was mere mockery of his hearers and of France; but he seemed in no haste to seize the prey which could no longer escape him.

The legislative session was opened in the two chambers by their respective presidents, chosen by the dictator. For the Senate Louis Napoleon chose his uncle, Jerome, ex-king of Westphalia, who uttered a discourse upon the return to institutions which, in his opinion, "could alone realize the union of order and liberty." He spoke of his nephew's triumph as retaliation for Waterloo.

The president of the legislative body was Billault,—an ex-deputy, semi-liberal, and semi-socialist. His speech was an attack on parliamentary rule.

In virtue of the new constitution, the two presidents directed the members of both chambers to take an oath of obedience to the constitution and of allegiance to the president of the republic. The three republican deputies wrote to the president of the Legislature that their electors desired to protest against the destruction of public liberty, not to send the elect to sit in an assembly which had no power to repair the violations of the law. Rid of these colleagues, who could but have been embarrassing, the Legislature could not fail to be a model of docility, yet it risked one timid attempt at discussion with the council of state by way of amendment, only to be gravely reminded by Casabianca, the minister of state, of the respect due to the constitution. The legislative body hastily submitted, and the budget was accepted at the first session. Montalembert undertook the part of opposition single-handed. Having accepted the 2d of December, he began somewhat tardily to talk of tyranny and perverted institutions! He found no echo, either then or later, when he attacked the decrees in regard to the Orléans property.

The prince-president declared the session closed, June 28. "The trial just made," he said, "proves that France possesses every requisite of a strong and free government!" During the session a rumor was current that Louis Napoleon was to be proclaimed emperor on the 10th of May, after the distribution of eagles to the army; but this was not carried out. The dictator had no desire to be made emperor in this fashion. He meant to do it more artfully, and to make it seem that the nation forced the accomplishment of his wishes upon him.

He therefore undertook a fresh journey through the provinces, going, first, to inaugurate the railroad between Paris and Strasburg, and receiving at Nantes a military deputation sent to congratulate him by the King of Prussia. He then traversed Central, Southern, and Western France, being well received in all quarters. He was received as a monarch at Nevers, the capital of Nièvre, the province so shaken by the republican movement in December, and so crushed by reaction. Similar imperialist demonstrations were repeated at Lyons, where an equestrian statue of the Emperor Napoleon was unveiled in the presence of his nephew. The watchword was everywhere given by the authorities and influential persons, whose example was imitated by the crowd, irreconcilable opponents keeping silent.

During the greater part of the journey, Louis Napoleon maintained a certain reserve, which he dropped at Bordeaux (October 7). The president of the Bordeaux chamber of commerce plainly demanding the restoration of the empire, the prince-president made an answer which is famous in history, borrowing for it the language of his uncle, as he borrowed his title later on. "To benefit the country," he said, "we must not apply new systems, but we must give confidence in the present, security in the future. This is the reason that France seems to be returning to the empire. There is, nevertheless, one fear to which I must respond. . . . . Certain persons say, *empire is war!* I say, *empire is peace!* It is peace, for France desires peace; and when France is at peace the world is content." And he concluded by saying that his conquests would be the reconciliation of discordant parties, the conversion to religion, morality, and prosperity of those people who had neither faith nor well-being.

The nephew of the great conqueror posed as a peacemaker and a crowned apostle.

He returned to Paris, October 16, and was received in state at the Orléans station. The official bodies greeted him with shouts of "Long live the Emperor!" The Marseillaise, the sacred song of revolution and republic, saluted this monarchic restoration : Napoleonic deceit still prevailed!. The prefect of the Seine and the municipal authorities entreated the prince-president to "resume the crown of the immortal founder of his dynasty." The procession traversed the boulevards, passing under a long line of triumphal arches, from the first of which a balloon was let off, in the form of an eagle holding a crown in his claws. Every theatre was superbly decorated. All this was very like the thing that Odilon Barrot, four years before, strenuously urged Louis Napoleon to avoid, — the Olympic circus. The clergy, also, shared in this triumphal reception, and the last triumphal arch bore the inscription, "Napoleon III., the savior of modern civilization." Various speeches were made, all demanding the restoration of the empire. But with all this theatric pomp, the festival was cold; the people looked on without laughter, applause, or song. "A change seemed to have come over the French nature," as the historian of the Second Empire (Taxile Delord) remarks.

Next day, the following paragraph appeared in the *Moniteur*: "The tremendous desire for the restoration of the empire manifested throughout France, makes it incumbent upon the president to consult the Senate upon the subject."

The Senate and Legislature were convened November 4; the latter was to verify the votes, should the Senate decide that the people must be consulted in regard to a change in the form of government, which no one doubted would be the case. The Senate received a message from Louis Napoleon, suggesting a change in the constitution to meet the popular pleasure. A committee was chosen, and a report was read by Troplong, formerly a peer of France, and first president of the royal court of Paris under Louis Philippe. He talked loudly of "providential men," who, at certain eras, are chosen to repair the evils of revolution; he then declared that France was both monarchic and democratic, and that the empire united in itself past and present, monarchy and republic. To assure the dynastic tradition in the imperial house, he proposed that the new emperor should take the name of Napoleon III. He also expressed the desire of the committee that, "in a future not far removed, a wife might present the emperor with heirs worthy this great name."

This wish recalls to us to-day the Nemesis of the ancients in its most tragic form!

The Senate, in accordance with the conclusions of the committee, passed a decree for the submission of the restoration of the hereditary empire for popular acceptance (November 7); the senators then went in a body to St. Cloud to inform the prince-president of this decision. Louis Napoleon, in his answer, recalled the fact that it was forty-eight years since the Senate came to this same palace to offer the crown to the head of his family. . . . "The spirit of the

Emperor is with me," he said; "his mind guides me, his spirit protects me."

The people were then called upon to vote for the plébiscite decreed by the Senate (November 20 and 21). Republican and legitimist protests were circulated in despite of the police, the government publishing them in the official organ, the *Moniteur*, as if in defiance, thinking that the excessive violence of the republican proscripts of London and Guernsey would alarm the peace-loving public. The result of the vote was even greater than that of December 20, 1851; the authenticity of the figures may indeed be doubted, but there is not a doubt that there was really a large majority in favor of the plébiscite. France abandoned the struggle!

On the evening of December 1, the three great state bodies, the two Chambers and the State Council, went to St. Cloud, and the president of the Legislature presented the result of the ballot to the new emperor, who sat enthroned, between his uncle Jerome and his cousin Napoleon, the ex-deputy of the Mountain party.

To the congratulations of the presidents of the two Chambers, Napoleon III. did not hesitate to reply: "The new reign inaugurated by you to-day, unlike many recorded in history, is not founded upon violence, conquest, and stratagem! . . . Will you not all assist me to establish, in this land troubled by many revolutions, a stable form of government, founded upon religion, justice, probity, and love of the suffering classes?"

Next morning, December 2, amid a chill fog far from recalling the sun of Austerlitz, the imperial procession marched from St. Cloud to the Tuileries. Napoleon III. entered between Persigny and St. Arnaud, whom he had lately made Marshal of France with Magnan, "for services rendered in December, 1851," said the decree.

The *Moniteur* published the names of the holders of the chief offices in the imperial household, — grand almoner, grand marshal of the palace, grand equerry, master of ceremonies, and all the paraphernalia of the First Empire. St. Arnaud received, on various pleas, three hundred thousand francs yearly; Magnan, two hundred thousand francs. This was a great change from the twenty-five francs a day with which the deputies of the republic were so often reproached. As for the emperor, his civil list was speedily fixed by the Senate at twenty-five millions annually, like that of his uncle, with an annual dotation of one million five hundred thousand francs for the princes and princesses of the imperial family, and a landed endowment for the crown, comprising the imperial palaces, manufactories, forests, etc.

December 2, 1852, St. Arnaud, Persigny, and Prefect Berger read the plébiscite to the army, National Guard, and people, from the balconies of the Tuileries, the roof of the royal palace, and the roof of the people's palace, as if to signify that, according to the words of the senatorial reporter, revolution and the ancient monarchy were displaced at one and the same time.

Thus opened the reign destined to end at Sedan.

CHAPTER XVI.

SECOND EMPIRE. — CRIMEAN WAR.

December, 1852, to April 16, 1856. :

LOUIS NAPOLEON was now the Emperor Napoleon III.; he now enjoyed, in name as well as in fact, the plenitude of supreme power to which he had, all his life, had a fatalistic conviction that he should attain. What would he do with it, and would he know how to use it? His partisans proclaimed him a great man in advance; some of his foes went from one extreme to the other in regard to him: they hated him no less, but they took him for a deep Machiavellian genius, after having taken him for an utterly silly fellow. His friends, and indeed some of his enemies, inferred, from his skill at conspiracy, his skill at government: they were fascinated by his first success, which was followed by other and more brilliant triumphs, due to a concurrence of unheard-of circumstances. If his eye was lifeless, his face expressionless, these were considered signs of a strong will mastering and suppressing every emotion. Louis Philippe talked well, but too much and too often; Napoleon III. listened well and seldom spoke. His silence was taken for profundity, instead of the mask of indecision, — we do not say the mask of stupidity, for Napoleon III. did not lack ideas, obstinate ideas, firmly rooted ideas; but this vague and dreamy obstinacy is not the active, practical perseverance, which can execute what the brain conceives, which can prepare, properly dispose, and carry out the means of execution. In this complex and contradictory nature there was a singular mixture of the conspirator, perfect in the art of dissimulation, and the romantic dreamer, the most dangerous combination of contrary defects which a nation could possibly find in its leader:

QUEEN HORTENSE.

Estes & Lauriat

these were the vices of a usurper without his good qualities. It was inevitable that this man should plunge France in most perilous situations from which he was unable to extricate her. If he succeeded at first, it was owing to circumstances rather than to his own deeds, and circumstances could not always be propitious.

We have seen the course in which Louis Napoleon engaged the country after the 2d of December : he excited a great financial and industrial movement to distract men's minds from politics. The general condition of Europe favored this movement: the age was one of great discoveries and brilliant innovations, such as the introduction of the electric telegraph and the great spread of the railroad; Europe, coming out of the revolutionary crisis of 1848, turned towards progressing commerce and manufactures with even more energy and entireness than in the time of Louis Philippe.

All France and Europe waited to see whether Napoleon III. would keep to his Bordeaux programme and rest in this peaceful activity. They queried if an event which occurred early in 1853, and which roused great curiosity, would favor the spirit of peace.

This event was the emperor's marriage, which followed within a few weeks of the proclamation of the empire.

Napoleon III.'s first thought was to choose a wife from some princely German family. He thought of a Princess Vasa, half Swede, half German ; then of a princess of Hohenzollern ; but the father of the former, a general in the Austrian service, at the advice of the Austrian government, hastily affianced his daughter to a Saxon prince. Napoleon III., foreseeing a similar check on the part of the Hohenzollerns, cousins of the King of Prussia, abandoned this match and abruptly took his stand. In January, 1853, the *Moniteur* announced that the emperor was to marry Mlle. de Montijo, of a grand Spanish family, " distinguished alike," as the official newspaper declared, " for the superiority of her intellect and the charms of her beauty."

January 23, the bureaus of Senate, Legislature, and State Council were summoned to the Tuileries, where the emperor informed them of his decision in a lofty speech. " The marriage which I am about to contract," he said, "is not in accord with the traditions of the ancient policy, and this is to its advantage." He affirmed that if France and monarchic Europe were to be allied, it was not "by royal alliances, which create a false feeling of security and substitute family interest for national interest. . . . . The marriage of Napoleon I. and Marie Louise was, it is true, a great event; but during the last reign, on the contrary, the national self-love could not but suffer to see the heir to the crown vainly soliciting for years the alliance of a sovereign family, and finally obtaining the hand of a princess, no doubt accomplished, but of secondary rank. . . . . When, in the sight of old Europe, one has succeeded, by the force of a new principle, in attaining the height of ancient dynasties, one cannot gain acceptance by seeking entrance to the family of kings at any cost, but rather by keeping one's origin constantly in mind, and frankly accepting, in the sight of Europe, the position of one risen from the ranks, — a glorious title when one has risen by the free choice of a great nation." He added a panegyric of the lady of his choice, and closed by declaring that once again he was "inspired by Providence!"

The civil and religious marriage rites were celebrated with great pomp, January 29 and 30. The public thought the allusion to the marriage of the unfortunate Duke of Orléans to a princess who had the esteem and sympathy of all, anything but suitable; it would have been another thing had it been known that the sovereign who used this lofty language had also solicited, without obtaining, a princely alliance " of secondary rank."

The new empress, Mlle. Eugénie de Montijo, daughter of a Spanish grandee who had served the French cause in the time of King Joseph, and of Scotch origin on her mother's side, was well known in Paris, having shone at the Elysée *fêtes* during the dictatorship. As a general thing, the marriage was regarded merely as a youthful and impulsive act, somewhat untimely for a leader of state of mature age. People were amused by the imperial romance; they would have wept over it, had they foreseen that this love-match would have more fatal political results than the marriage of Louis XVI. or that of Napoleon I.

Two women exerted a decided influence over Napoleon III., the one at the beginning, the other at the close of his career. The one was his mother, Queen Hortense; the other was his wife. The one paved the way for the empire; the other hastened its coming.

The remote consequences of the emperor's marriage were still buried in the shadows of the future. The immediate consequence was the dawn of an epoch of luxury and pleasure, of strange and extravagant fashions, in which a young and lovely queen, passionately fond of ornaments and parties, gathered around her a frivolous and restless society. This society was carried away by the double whirlwind of speculation and of pleasure. Fortunes were made, lost, and remade, as in the time of Law; there was as great an excess of gambling in stocks as there was of luxury, and the chief leader of December 2, Morny, stood forth amid the tumult as master of the revels and supreme prince of speculators.

The new reign, judging by appearances, if it were not moral, was at least pacific. The emperor opened the legislative session of 1853, February 14, by a speech in which the phrase chiefly noted and commented on was as follows: "To those who may regret that liberty does not play a greater part in the imperial programme, I would reply: Liberty never helped to found an enduring political edifice; it crowns the work when time has made it solid."

He thus postponed liberty for an indefinite period; but he promised peace. The first thing, he said, was to rule France well and to reassure Europe. He consequently announced a diminution of expenditure and of armament. The army, reduced by thirty thousand men the year before, was to be cut down twenty thousand more. March 8, a Universal Exhibition was decreed for the 1st of May, 1855; England having set the example in 1851.

This attitude of the imperial government greatly modified English opinion, at first most unfavorable to the 2d of December, and four thousand London merchants sent a deputation to express to Napoleon III. their desire for a good understanding between the two nations. The legislative session of 1853 was of little interest. We should note the changes in the system of jury, which placed the composition of every jury in the hands of the executive power, and also the changes in the councils of *prud'hommes.*[*] It is needless to say that these all tended to make the organization more liberal.

The public works were carried rapidly forward. New sections were added to various lines of railroad. A submarine telegraph was laid between France and Algiers, various reductions were made in customhouse tariffs, and the protective system was somewhat relaxed.

The industrial movement grew apace. Agriculture proved far from successful in 1853; it was a bad year both for grain and grapes; the price of wheat went up, but the alimentary crisis did not cause such cruel sufferings as it had in 1846 and 1847. The memory of those fatal days made the government more provident. The crop proving deficient, in September measures were taken to import foreign wheat to the amount of four hundred million bushels. In Paris, and some other cities, a system was arranged by which bread should be sold at an advance in times of plenty, and on lower terms in times of scarcity.

It is a notable fact that during the year 1853, in spite of the police spies who penetrated everywhere, a conspiracy was twice formed to attack the emperor, while out driving. A number of arrests were made, and the conspirators were exiled or imprisoned.

The peaceful outlook of France and Europe, in which the laboring classes began to put full trust, was purely illusory. Napoleon III., unlike as he was to his uncle, had all the latter's easy indifference in regard to keeping his promises. He meant to surprise the world by greater deeds than the opening of new boulevards and avenues in Paris, and he was well aware that France would soon demand her liberty, if her fancy were not fed with other food than industry, architecture, and festivals. Domestic shows were not enough; foreign spectacles must be provided. The impulse given to arts and manufactures proved a lasting one, but foreign affairs none the less form the chief interest of the history of the first year of the empire.

Continental monarchies beheld the event of December 2d with

---

[*] Mixed councils of master tradesmen and workmen for the decision of disputes between persons of these two classes.

a mixture of satisfaction and anxiety; they were delighted at the overthrow of the republic, but they dreaded the results which the dictatorship of a Napoleon might entail.   Lord Palmerston, the English minister of foreign affairs, soon manifested his approval of the *coup d'état*; hostile to Louis Philippe without any very legitimate cause, he felt an entirely causeless aversion to the Republic of 1848.   This minister, whom all the continental courts detested as a revolutionist, and who was constantly inspiring revolution throughout Europe, now came forward as the enemy of revolution in France, because he feared that he could not make a tool of free France.   The president-usurper, whom he had studied and knew thoroughly, struck him as capable of becoming his ally in some plot profitable to English policy, as he understood it.

An eminent colleague of Lord Palmerston, Lord John Russell, very liberal in doméstic affairs in England, but ill disposed towards liberty for other nations, was equally indulgent in regard to December 2d.   Other English statesmen, on the contrary, protested loudly, and during the first weeks that followed the catastrophe at Paris, public opinion was roused alike by moral feeling and by the fear of war and invasion which the mob deemed imminent. English newspapers eagerly cried out for a renewal of the European coalition. Lord Palmerston, against whom his colleagues, and the queen especially, had previous grounds of complaint, was forced to quit the ministry.

Louis Napoleon's peaceful protestations calmed England.   Immediately after the 2d of December, dazzled by his success, he momentarily planned a bold stroke, which would doubtless have caused a renewal of the coalition against France, and let loose the dogs of war: he signed an order for the annexation of Belgium; but Achille Fould, and other financiers about him, terrified at such an enterprise, succeeded in persuading him to retract. Upon this he turned towards England and strove to win her alliance, thus passing instantly from one extreme to the other, and from one scheme to another of the most opposite nature.

England, thus appeased, readily consented to recognize the em-

pire upon its restoration in December, 1852; she acted towards the
Second Empire as she had towards the Second Republic, without
heeding that article of the treaties of 1845 which forbade any restoration of the Bonaparte family.   The English government declined an attempt at an understanding set on foot by the Czar of
Russia, and greatly desired by the King of Prussia, between the four
great powers of the old coalition.

However, on the 16th of December, 1852, the House of Commons
overthrew the Tory ministry so favorable to Napoleon III. upon a
financial question.   A new cabinet was formed of men of various
shades of opinion.   Lord Palmerston was reinstated; but he was the
only member who passed as well disposed towards the new emperor,
and he was given the portfolio of state, not of foreign affairs, this
seeming to indicate an attitude of watchfulness and reserve in regard to the imperial government.

As for the continental powers, we must go back as far as 1850 if
we would appreciate their respective positions at the beginning of
1853.   The rivalry between Austria and Prussia increased from
1840 to 1850.   A bold and energetic man, Prince von Schwartzenberg, who governed Austria in the name of the young emperor,
Francis Joseph, aimed at a triple achievement, — to fuse the multifa-
rious nationalities of the Austrian Empire in one monarchy, more or
less constitutional, as the case might be; to re-establish the old Germanic Diet; and to bring the whole body of the Austrian Empire into
the Germanic Confederation, without distinction between the German provinces and other nationalities.   After the catastrophes which
so nearly crushed Austria, the Austrian minister cherished a hope
of gaining European supremacy for his land by placing his emperor
at the head of a confederacy of more than sixty million men.

To this daring, but clean-cut and decisive policy the King of Prussia and his minister, Radowitz, opposed nothing but shadowy and
contradictory designs.   Sprung from a race which had risen perforce
by unscrupulously breaking through all ancient law, and which was
erelong to return to this course, King Frederic William dreamed of
an ideal Christian moral claim, seeking the type of it far behind him

in the Middle Ages; he detested revolution, and France, the mother of revolution; he refused to accept the crown of the German Empire from the hands of revolution, and still he aspired towards Germany for Prussia, although he bowed to the honorary supremacy of Austria, the heir of the ancient empire.

Under these conditions Austria, once set free from Hungarian war by Russian intervention, inevitably regained her advantage over Prussia. Frederic William, after his rupture with the Frankfort Assembly, vainly strove to convene an assembly of German princes under his presidency, in place of the Revolutionary Assembly; then he fell back upon "the limited union" between the states of Northern Germany. This "limited union" speedily failed him; the principal states of Southern Germany, and Saxony with them, then tried to form a special union, to stand independently between Austria and Prussia. This feeble effort was not successful. Austria, on the contrary, marched straight onward, and convened the representatives of the former diet at Frankfort.

By one of those contradictions usual to him, the Prussian king, after stamping out revolution in the grand duchy of Baden, upheld it alike in Schleswig Holstein against the King of Denmark, and in the electorate of Hesse, where a contemned government yielded unresistingly upon the desertion of its every subject. The Elector of Hesse appealed to the Frankfort Diet restored by Austria, and the diet ordered the restoration of the fallen prince. War was imminent between Prussia and Austria, and her allies of the diet. Their troops were already face to face in Hesse. This was little more than a year before the 2d of December. Louis Napoleon saw in this an opportunity to play a great part; he made secret overtures to Frederic William for an alliance between their respective countries. The Prussian king declined the offer, and, contrary to the wishes of his parliament and people, who were ready for war, shrank back from Austria, and concluded the humiliating treaty of Olmütz (November 29, 1850). Prussia consented to the dissolution of the remnant of the "limited union," abandoning Hesse and the insurgents of Schleswig Holstein.

This was the moment for the Western powers, for France and England, to insure Denmark's future, by helping her to obtain a definite understanding suitable to the laws of Danish nationality in regard to the Schleswig question.   This was not done, and the question was left open to Prussian ambition.

This ambition, at that time, seemed crushed for a long time to come.   Prussia appeared to be very weak, and Austria very strong. Prussia resisted Austrian ascendancy on one point only, but this point was an important one.   It related to the entry of the Austrian Empire, with all her provinces, whether Hungarian, Slavic, Italian, or Roumanian, into the Germanic Confederation.   The French government supported Prussia in protesting stoutly against the claims of Austria, which were necessarily renounced (January – March, 1851).   The long German crisis resulted in the re-establishment, pure and simple, of the old diet.   To all appearances nothing remained of the revolution of 1848 in Germany ; but this restoration of the past was very superficial.

The audacious politician who had pulled Prussia down died soon after, and Austria did not find another Schwartzenberg.   In 1850 Prussia gained a success which, although quiet, afforded some compensation for her defeats.   Hanover entered the Customs Union, which opened to that commercial union the rivers opening into the North Sea.

Russian influence played a large part in the events in Germany which we have just summed up.   Czar Nicholas was the real leader of European reaction against the revolution of 1848 : he saved Austria ; he ruled Prussia by the power of his strong will over the dreamy and impressionable spirit of Frederic William IV.; the petty German princes regarded the Czar as the true and only emperor.   Nicholas accordingly supposed his supremacy thoroughly established in Central Europe, and aspired to recover it over the Ottoman Empire, where English influence counterbalanced his.   In 1849 he had seen England and France unite to confirm the Sultan's refusal to give up his Hungarian and Polish guests to Austria and Russia ; but President Louis Napoleon expressed himself less

harshly in the matter than did the English government. Still it
was not England, it was France whom Russia soon encountered as
her rival in the Orient.

This was in regard to the "Holy Places," or monuments raised
on the scenes of Christ's birth, life, and death. Russia had long protected the Greek religion, known as "orthodox," in the Holy Land,
with sincere religious fervor and ardent national ambition. The
protection of the Catholic or Latin creed has always been affected
by the French government, as a tradition of the crusades. The rights
of the Latins in the Holy Land were the occasion of divers treaties
between France and Turkey, one being in 1690, and one in 1740.
Greeks and Latins never ceased to dispute over the ancient Christian
sanctuaries, divided between them at Jerusalem, Bethlehem, and
Nazareth. Ridiculous monkish battles frequently broke in upon the
majesty of these spots; but the question was none the less serious.
The position of France in these countries was a delicate one. Her
traditional protectorate of the Latin worship and of the tribes who
professed it must needs be maintained under penalty of degradation in the opinion of the Orientals; but it was no less necessary to
exercise this patronage moderately, and not to alienate the believers
in the Greek faith, who form the great majority in the Christian
East.

Louis Napoleon, once president, saw what a good opportunity
this would be to give pledges to the clergy, whose ally he had become, and to take an effective stand. He instructed his ambassador, in 1850, to claim loudly the privileges accorded to the *protégés*
of France by the treaty of 1740, and upon which the Greeks and
Armenians had infringed. The questions in point were, who should
hold the master key of the church in Bethlehem; whose right it was
to repair the cupola of the church of the Holy Sepulchre; at what
hour Greeks, Latins, and Armenians should celebrate their worship
in turn in the sanctuaries held in common by them; and finally,
how the temples belonging exclusively to one or the other should
be divided.

The Ottoman Porte acknowledged the just foundation of the

claims presented by France, to the no small rage of Nicholas. He imperiously demanded the maintenance of the *statu quo*, that is, of the innovations favorable to the Greek religion. Turkey agreed. The French government was angry in turn. The Ottoman Porte, not knowing which party to conciliate, finally settled the matter in the gross, reasonably enough, but unsatisfactorily to all.

This dispute had been going on for eighteen months, when the empire was re-established in France. Nicholas, much vexed, wished to form another coalition, at least a diplomatic one, against the new emperor. England declined to take any part in it. The King of Prussia was more disposed to agree, but he dared not act apart from Austria. These two powers did indeed make some reservation in regard to the maintenance of the treaties of 1815, and the territorial state guaranteed by them, by claiming and receiving an official certificate of Napoleon III.'s pacific intents; but they went no further. Nicholas then resigned himself to recognize the new emperor; nevertheless he could not decide to treat him as "a brother," according to the custom among sovereigns; he therefore signed his official letter, "From your majesty's . . . . *good friend.*"

This puerility entailed terrible results. Nicholas thought that he could renew towards Napoleon III. the offensive treatment which he had used towards Louis Philippe; but insults borne by the peace-loving monarch of 1830 would not be endured by the turbulent adventurer of December 2. For once the haughty Czar's conduct cost him dear; the rival self-love of the two despots meeting and clashing, one of the two must go down, and afford the other an ephemeral triumph at the cost of hundreds of thousands of lives.

Nicholas, not succeeding in uniting the powers of Europe against the new French Empire, attempted to renew the coalition under another form, and addressed very strange proposals to the English ambassador, Sir Hamilton Seymour. Starting upon the theory that Turkey was dying out, he offered to settle the succession with England, admitting Austria to a share, but excluding France. He declared that he had no desire to occupy Constantinople permanently, without clearly explaining what he meant to do with it after his temporary occupation of it. He intended to turn the Roumanian principality (Wallachia and Moldavia), with Serbia and Bulgaria, into independent states under his protectorate; he had no idea of permitting Greece to extend and become a powerful state, or the Byzantine Empire to be reconstituted. He thus revealed how insincere was the sympathy expressed by his government for the Greeks; he had only protected Greece on condition that she ceased to grow and gave up all aspiration to live her own life. He concluded by offering Greece and Egypt to England (January–February, 1853.)

The English cabinet seemed but little tempted by these offers : it did not admit, in regard to Turkey, that the sick man was on the point of death, but proposed, on the contrary, to seek out every means to help him to live; it would not admit the exclusion of France from transactions which might take place "in the interests of Turkey."

The Czar's attempt thus failed completely, and his minister, Nesselrode, who usually tempered the violence and audacity of his master, finally declared to the English ambassador, that Russia was ready to co-operate with England to prolong the existence of the Ottoman Empire (April 15).

The monarch's acts illy accorded with his minister's words. Nicholas, for some weeks, had been sending troops to the frontiers of the Roumanian provinces, and despatched one of the great dignitaries of the court as ambassador extraordinary to Constantinople, with great pomp and circumstance. Admiral Prince Menchikof, however, was fitted, both by character and manner, to be anything rather than an ambassador of peace, and opened the campaign by a glaring affront to the Turkish minister of foreign affairs (March 2). He refused to pay him the usual visit, on the pretext that this statesman had shown himself inimical to Russia. The Turkish minister resigned his office; but the grand vizier, in consequence of the attitude assumed by Menchikof, demanded that the representatives of France and England should summon their respective fleets to the Levant.

The English minister delayed compliance with this grave demand. Napoleon III. without waiting for the action of England, hastily sent a squadron to Salamis.

However, Menchikof proved unexpectedly docile in regard to the question which had arisen between France and Russia; after some parley, the matter of the "Holy Places" was amicably settled between him and the French ambassador, M. de Lacour (May 4). Everything seemed to be finally arranged; whereas the trouble was but just beginning. The question was not definitely answered; it was only set aside. Nicholas merely moderated his demands upon this special point to make more general claims.

Menchikof called upon Turkey to give solemn pledges to the Czar, to be held as binding as a treaty. By these pledges the Sultan promised Russia that no change should be made in the rights, privileges, and immunities enjoyed by the orthodox (Greek) churches, pious institutions, and clergy in the dominions of the Ottoman Porte.

Such a promise solemnly made to a foreign power would have been a direct recognition of protection for the Greek religion, and consequently for the great majority of the Christian subjects of the Sultan. Russia thus infringed upon the European Convention of 1841, which implied the harmonious action of all the great powers in Oriental affairs.

The Ottoman Porte, encouraged by the English and French ambassadors, resisted. The English ambassador, Lord Stratford de Redcliffe, a very energetic man, used the great influence acquired by him in Constantinople to elevate the moral standard of the Turkish government, and matters assumed the aspect of a duel between Menchikof and himself, or rather between him and Nicholas in person.

Menchikof then affronted the Turkish ministers afresh by penetrating to the heart of the seraglio, to parley with the Sultan, aside from them. The Turkish ministers resigned in a body; but their successors were equally firm, nor would the Sultan yield to intimidation. Menchikof declared negotiations broken off, and re-embarked (May 18–21).

Nicholas, unable to obtain aid from England, decided to act with-out and in spite of her.   He was much deceived, on the one hand, as to what he might hope for from Austria, whose safety was due to him, and on the other hand, in regard to the strength of the peace party in England.   He thought that "that nation of shopkeepers " would never fight,—an idea which proved true later on, for a time at least, to the great detriment of England and Europe, but which was not so now.   The England of 1853 was by no means ready to accept everything which might occur without her borders, and to plunge from Lord Palmerston's turbulent policy into the contrary extreme, a policy of inaction.   The personal feeling of the head of the English cabinet, Lord Aberdeen,— a foe to war, as he showed only too plainly, — did much to delude the Czar.   Lord Aberdeen, none the less, began to be drawn towards a point which he had never wished to approach, both by Lord Clarendon, the minister of foreign affairs, who had no fear of war, and by Lord Palmerston, who favored it even more strongly than Napoleon III. himself; the course of events and the current of opinion flowed towards bellicose conclusions.

May 28, the English minister announced to Parliament that he was ready to defend Turkey.   At this stage of the proceedings news came to London, that the Russian minister, Nesselrode, had informed Turkey that Russian troops were even then crossing the frontier, "not to wage war," but to hold hostages until the Ottoman Em-pire should yield.   The English cabinet despatched a squadron from Malta to join the French fleet, and between the 13th and 14th of June the combined squadron anchored at the mouth of the Dardanelles.

The strange conduct of Nicholas produced strange and unexpected results !   When he trampled under foot the international agreement of 1841, he divided himself from all Europe ; he forced Austria and even Prussia to give him up ; he placed himself in the position which France would have occupied in 1840 if she had done battle for Egypt ; he more or less completely turned against himself the coalition which he had striven to re-form against France, and he gave Napoleon III. the marvellous good luck to be the representative

of European interests against Russia. It was an inconceivable piece
of blindness.

It would seem that the personal opinion of Guizot, communicated
to the Czar by his ambassador at Paris, M. de Kisseleff, could not
have been without influence upon Nicholas ; M. Guizot considered
an alliance between England and Napoleon III. simply impossible.

M. Drouyn de Lhuys, the French minister of foreign affairs,
skilfully took his stand by proposing to the Russian minister of
foreign affairs that a conference should be held by all the parties to
the treaties of 1841. Nicholas replied by an order to his troops
to enter the Roumanian principalities (July 3).

We can easily understand why the Czar should attempt to strike
a bold and sudden blow, and launch all his forces, naval and military,
unawares upon Turkey, before the Western powers could render
her any efficacious aid ; but by his style of action he risked all the
dangers of daring without having its favorable chances. All the
tumult which he stirred up only resulted in sending an ordinary
body of troops into Roumania to kick their heels ! Events began to
prove what insufficiency was masked beneath the imposing appearance of this haughty ruler.

We have already observed that Napoleon III. was not a man of
action, although he was a man of plots and conspiracies ; it may be
said of Nicholas, that, although a man of authority, he was no more
of a man of action than his adversary.

Unwilling to recede, and not advancing bravely, the Czar tried a
change of base in his policy. Repulsed by England, he altered his
course towards France, and made advances to Napoleon III., who
drew up a rough draft to serve as the basis of a compromise. This
scheme was modified at a congress held at Vienna by the representatives of the great powers, and the Czar accepted it (August 3).

Napoleon III. seemed satisfied. He was not absolutely bent on
war, provided he could play the leading part in peace. Nevertheless he urged the English government to consent that the combined
squadrons should enter the straits of Dardanelles to atone for the
Russian invasion of the provinces of the Danube.

The English government hesitated; but during the following month a document, emanating from the Russian ministry of foreign affairs, proved that at St. Petersburg Napoleon's scheme was in some sort interpreted to mean that the powers adhered to that ultimatum of Menchikof declined by Turkey.

It was no longer possible for Lord Aberdeen to confine his government to half-measures. The French and English squadrons entered the Dardanelles October 22. This was a direct declaration of war, the treaty of 1841 forbidding men of war to enter either the Dardanelles or the Bosphorus in time of peace. Turkey took the initiative by calling upon the Russians to quit the provinces of the Danube, and upon the refusal of the Russian commander, war was declared between Russia and Turkey (October 23).

Nicholas replied by a manifesto, appealing to the religious passions of his subjects in a style which recalled the days of the crusades.

The Turks assumed the offensive by skirmishes on the Danube and on the Asiatic frontiers. They met with severe checks in Asia, and with success on the Danube, where they were commanded by an energetic and intelligent leader, Omer Pacha, an Austrian slave, who had turned Mussulman.

Nicholas sent his Sebastopol fleet into the Black Sea against the Turks. The Turkish squadron stationed in those waters was in no state to sustain the fight, and although the French and English ambassadors might have saved it by ordering their vessels thither, they failed to do so. Both lacked the quality of decision in warfare, although Lord Stratford de Redcliffe was not lacking in it in diplomacy. November 30, the Russian fleet overwhelmed the Turkish squadron in the harbor of Sinopis; twelve men of war and four thousand men being swallowed up by the waves.

This disaster proved very irritating to public opinion in France, and even more so in England, thus destroying all hope of success for the negotiations still going on at Vienna. In September, Nicholas had had interviews with the Emperor of Austria and the King of Prussia, over whom he strove to retain his influence. The Austrian and Prussian governments, from different motives, both wished to prevent war between Russia and the West. They were notwithstanding obliged by the conduct of the Czar to ally themselves with the Western powers, Nicholas stubbornly refusing to allow Europe to interfere in his quarrel with Turkey. Before the news of the disaster at Sinopis reached Vienna, a protocol was signed there (December 5), between Austria, France, England, and Prussia. It announced a double purpose: 1st, to put an end to hostilities; 2nd, to maintain the Ottoman Empire in its integrity.

It was not without fear and reluctance that Austria thus broke with Russia; but Napoleon III. had a strong hold upon her. He showed her that she must either accept France as a friend in the Orient or as a foe in Italy. Austria followed France against her will. Prussia followed Austria in the same way.

This harmony was more apparent than real: Austria and Prussia sought to retard any action; Napoleon III. hurried it on. Just as he had urged England to send her fleets to the Dardanelles, he now persuaded her to despatch them to the Black Sea, with orders to drive back to Sebastopol every Russian ship met on the high seas. The French and English squadrons cleared the Bosphorus, January 3, 1854, and the resolve taken to forbid the Russian fleet to enter the Black Sea was announced at Sebastopol by an English frigate.

Russia suspended all diplomatic relations with France and England. Nicholas requested the Austrian Emperor to agree, with Prussia, to observe an armed neutrality. Francis Joseph refused, unless Nicholas would promise to respect the integrity of the Ottoman territory. Austria then formed an observation corps in Transylvania, on the confines of the Danubian provinces. This was a bitter blow to the Czar, who regarded the young sovereign of Austria as his ward and pupil, and could not understand how Francis Joseph could put the interests of his kingdom before services received. The King of Prussia, in spite of his personal and political attachment to Nicholas, dared not break with the potentates who signed the protocol of December 5.

Napoleon III., having pressed so eagerly forward, now desired to

CASTLE COBURG.

win the honors of moderation.   Upon the avowal of the English
cabinet, he wrote directly to the Czar (January 29, 1854), proposing
that Russia should evacuate the Danubian principalities, France
and England, on their side, evacuating the Black Sea.

Nicholas refused, with recriminations against France and England.
Austria began to grow warm, and advised the answering of the Czar
by a double despatch from Paris and London, renewing the Turkish
summons to leave the provinces of the Danube.   The presence of
Russians in that region so close to the Austrian Empire was the
chief source of annoyance at Vienna.   Having suggested this plan,
Austria stoutly upheld it, and Prussia, although far less anxious
to carry it out, nevertheless advised Nicholas to consent to the
evacuation.

Russia made no response, and the French legislative session
opened at this important juncture (March 2).   In his opening address the emperor affected an entire disinterestedness in the name
of France.   "She has," said he, "no idea of self-aggrandizement."
He loudly celebrated the English alliance, promised the Austrian
alliance, and was silent in regard to Prussia, whose attitude seemed
doubtful.

March 7, the legislative body authorized a loan of two hundred and fifty million francs.   The secretary of the treasury
(Bineau), instead of having recourse to the bankers, opened a public subscription for the loan.   The idea was excellent, and the
innovation successful.   There were nearly one hundred thousand
subscribers, and they offered almost double the amount required
(March 14 – 25).   This seemed a surprising result, but later on, we
meet with far more startling triumphs of the same nature.   To the
loan of two hundred and fifty millions the discontinuance of the
sinking fund added an unexpected resource in the shape of eighty-
seven million francs.

March 27, a double message announced to the legislative bodies
of France and England that war was declared against Russia.   The
French legislature then voted a contingent of one hundred and forty
thousand men for the year instead of eighty thousand.

April 10, a treaty of alliance between France and England was signed, followed by a declaration from the two nations in favor of the law of neutrals. England gave up her ancient claim to the monarchy of the seas; there was no longer a question of fictitious blockades, nor of confiscation to the detriment of neutral parties. This was a great step forwards in the law of nations, and was due to the attitude of the United States, which would have joined Russia in case England had ventured to apply her former maxims to merchantmen.

The officers of the French and English navy were instructed to act, in all quarters of the globe, as if they belonged to one and the same nation. This intimate union between England and the heir of the illustrious man who died at St. Helena seemed most extraordinary. Napoleon III. desired to amaze the world; he now succeeded.

On the eve of the Anglo-French compact, Prussia decided to sign a new protocol, in which the four powers were to reiterate, in more precise terms, the declaration formulated on the 5th of December in regard to the essential conditions of a compromise in the East. This, however, did not yet engage Prussia or even Austria to play any active part. King Frederic William, whose heart was with Nicholas, was divided between the military and feudal party, wholly devoted to Russia, and the party of the citizens and the House of Deputies, which held to the Western alliance. The latter party did not favor France; but it dreaded Russia extremely, and sought to lean upon England's strong arm. The House of Deputies, at Berlin, made lively demonstrations against the Russian policy, and Frederic William allowed himself to be urged into taking another step towards the Western alliance. April 20, he signed a defensive alliance with Austria, obliging him to sustain the Austrian army if it should defend what were called "German interests" on the Danube. A protocol of May 23 stated that the Anglo-French and Austro-Prussian treaties were based on similar grounds.

The anti-Russian coalition would go into effect if the question should centre on the Danube; for Austria was resolved on war in case Russia persisted in occupying the Danubian provinces. If the only object had been to secure the return home of the Russian troops and the Czar's compliance with the European agreement of 1841, the four united powers might have gained the day without coming to open contest with Russia, since the quarrel would have been so unequal and senseless a one for her. Napoleon III. might possibly have been content with this result, were he allowed to wear the laurels of victory; but it was now the English government which refused to hear of pausing where matters stood, aiming at something beyond the provinces of the Danube. In March, England had ordered a large fleet of steamships into the Baltic; this being the first time that steam had been employed on any large scale in war. National passions and ambitions were aroused in England's bosom, driving that land to the opposite extreme from the party which desired peace at any price. Lord Palmerston personified these passions and ambitions. He now urged the nation against Russia, as he had worked against France in 1840. He agitated vast schemes in his imagination, — to invade the Baltic as well as the Black Sea; to destroy, in one of these seas, Sebastopol, and in the other, Cronstadt; to annihilate the Russian navy; to drive the Russians from Circassia; etc. Lord Palmerston was enchanted to be able to use France for this great and wholly English aim. Napoleon III., therefore, was now led, rather than leading; he became the instrument of another in his turn; for if France, as all Europe, was interested in removing the Russians from Constantinople, she had not the slightest motive for destroying their navy. Had there been any way of agreement with Austria to restore Poland, there might have been both French and European reasons for accepting it; but the insinuations of Napoleon III. to this effect were not favorably received by England; he did not insist upon them, and consented to impose vast sacrifices upon France for an interest which was utterly alien.

France, then, had no clear appreciation of what was exacted of her: her imagination was seduced by the novelty of a brilliant alliance with her former foe; and the idea of retaliation for 1812 became popular throughout the land, by the error of Nicholas, who, in his imprudent boasting, constantly threw that unfortunate date in the teeth of France.

In whatever spirit and under whatever condition war was to be waged, it became steadily more probable during the entire year. Napoleon III., without absolutely deciding to take the fatal step, did all that was necessary to precipitate the shock. He had had ample time to prepare for it, and was not ready. He failed and was destined always to fail, to act up to the maxim of the true statesman: Be ready for either case. He constantly reckoned upon circumstances rather than himself, dreaming that some unforeseen chance would extricate him from his difficulty. This was a great defect in his character, which did but increase with years.

"There was," said M. Camille Rousset, the French historian of the Crimean war, "neither preparation, arrangement, nor plan of any sort."

A body of troops was hastily formed at Marseilles, in March, under the command of St. Arnaud, who resigned the ministry of war to Marshal Vaillant. This body of men numbered about thirty thousand. Everything was done quickly and ill. Ships and stores were collected at random. Marseilles was in a perfect chaos. Officers and men set off in small detachments. Lord Raglan, the leader of the English forces which were to work with the French, sailed from Marseilles, April 22, St. Arnaud following upon the 29th. The two generals joined the first convoy of French and English troops, quartered, as best they could, at Gallipolis, on the Dardanelles. The first offensive act in the Black Sea was the bombardment of Odessa by the combined squadrons (April 22).

The sight of the troops of the two allied nations, on their arrival in the East, afforded a real contrast. The French soldiers were always ready, up to a certain point, to take the field, thanks to their military habits, and to the continual petty warfare in Africa; if, however, they were not thoroughly prepared, it was through the personal fault of the leader of the state, who had not specially prepared the supplies necessary for the circumstances. In England all warlike habits were forgotten, and the troops were in no

way fit to enter into immediate action, not through the actual
error of any individual statesman, but through the permanent mistake of the whole administration ever since the close of the great
wars. French and English were equally needy on their landing in
Turkey; but the French soldier soon righted himself by his singular ability to turn his hand to anything; the Englishman, unfit for
anything not included in his trade as a soldier, suffered cruelly
when the Frenchman was not on hand to help him.

The allies did not remain long at their first station, the headquarters being transferred, in May, to the north of the Bosphorus, to
Varna, on the Black Sea. There they were on the Russian flank;
before the end of March the latter had crossed the Lower Danube
and occupied Dobroudscha, the marshy region extending between
the Danubian provinces and the sea; there they received large reinforcements, and besieged Silistria. The allies were well posted to
harass them; but the position could be turned to no account, the
troops being in no condition to march. St. Arnaud, in his letters,
complained to the emperor that every necessity was lacking.

The combined army, in fact, was not put upon any respectable
footing until the beginning of July. It then numbered about thirty
thousand French and twenty thousand English. For several weeks
there had been many discussions between the two governments in
regard to the general direction of the war, and between the military
leaders in regard to the positions to be occupied and the work to be
done. Austria showed herself more and more hostile to Russia; she
too, in her turn, imitating France and England, firmly demanded
that the Czar should evacuate the principalities; she then treated
with Turkey for the eventual occupation of those provinces by her
own troops, and opened a national loan of four hundred million
florins (June). Austria thus set seriously to work; but she could
not agree with England as to the motive for the war. Vienna
thought of nothing but the Danube; London only thought of Sebastopol and Cronstadt; Napoleon III. was divided between the two.

At this juncture the chief object at which Austria aimed was won
without her unsheathing the sword. Marshal Paskievitch, the con-

queror of Warsaw in 1831, did not succeed before Silistria ; a wound
obliging him to give up the command, his successor, after fruitless
assaults, was ordered to raise the siege (June 23).   The troops of
Omer Pacha crossed the Danube in their turn, and gained a fresh
advantage at Giurgevo.   The Russians, having the Turks in face of
them and fearing lest they should be attacked on both flanks, by the
Anglo-French on one side and by the Austrians on the other, fell
back upon Bucharest (July 9, 10), and then left the Danubian
principalities during August.

What were the political consequences of this much desired
evacuation ?

Shortly before the Russian retreat, important despatches were
sent from London and Paris to Vienna (July 22), claiming the
application of the principles set down in the protocol of April 9.
The French despatch pointed out most precisely the pledges to be
exacted : it claimed, first, that the protectorate exercised by the
Emperor of Russia over Wallachia, Moldavia, and Serbia should be
replaced by the collective protectorate of the great powers ; second,
that the navigation of the mouths of the Danube should be freed
from all obstacles ; third, that the treaty of July 13, 1841, should be
revised to limit the Russian power in the Black Sea ; fourth, that no
power should longer exercise any authority over any subjects whatsoever of the Ottoman Porte, but that the five great powers should,
in common, obtain from the Ottoman government the consecration
of the privileges of the various Christian communities.   This was
viewing the matter in a truly European light.   The despatch also
contained an article which, as it was understood, expressed an
interest very particularly English: namely, " the limitation " ; that
is, in reality, the destruction of the naval power of the Russians in
the Black Sea.   We thus see the French government prescribing
what might be called an *English* requirement ; this was the political
masterpiece of Lord Palmerston.

Henceforth, therefore, other questions were at stake than simply
to bring Russia back to the treaty of 1841 and to force her to
leave the principalities.

Some days after (July 28), Austria persuaded the secondary states of Germany, assembled at Bamberg, to agree, though very reluctantly, to the Austro-Prussian Convention of April 20. The Prussian government would much rather have withdrawn from the agreement than have urged others to engage in it.

August 8, in a communication to the Austrian government, the French and English ambassadors declared that events during the war might make certain modifications necessary in the guarantees already specified. The two documents, English and French, which were identical, did not directly imply "the limitation of Russian power in the Black Sea," but only the revision of the treaty of 1841 in the interest of European equipoise.

Austria and even Prussia approved of the pledges required by France and England, and requested Russia to accept them. They thus consented to ask something more than the mere evacuation of the principalities, which was already accomplished, and beyond the return to the treaty of 1841.

The Czar replied to Austria and Prussia that he could not accept the interpretation given by France and England to the principles laid down by the four great powers in the protocol of April 9; his adversaries, he said, obliged him to trust these questions, as they must do, to the fortunes of war. Prussia seemed to accept this answer, and did not insist. Austria took another step forward, and sent her troops into Wallachia.

Just as the Russians quitted the provinces of the Danube, they were attacked in the Baltic, where a French squadron had joined the English fleet. Not feeling prepared to carry out Lord Palmerston's dream, the destruction of Cronstadt, they fell back on the Aland islands; a French corps, commanded by General Baraguey d'Hilliers, was landed on the principal island of the group, and the forts of Bomarsund, an important position overlooking the Baltic and the Swedish coast, were attacked both by land and by sea. Nicholas had planned a vast system of fortifications at this point. The two great towers and the batteries already established were captured in three days (August 13–15). Very few men were lost by the enemy's guns; but cholera and dysentery made cruel ravages among crews and troops.

The Aland islands were formerly captured from Sweden by Russia. France and England now offered to restore them to the Swedish government, which dared not accept them, not feeling able to hold them. The fortifications were accordingly destroyed and the islands deserted. The Baltic expedition was a mere episode; the great drama of the war began in the Black Sea.

As early as June 23, a letter from Napoleon III. gave St. Arnaud his choice of two objective points: Anapa, the chief seaport of the Caucasus; or the Crimea. Here again the English mind inspired the French emperor. The unanimous cry in England was, Sebastopol. This great naval arsenal summed up in itself, to the English, the whole Eastern question.

Some days after (June 29), the English cabinet assigned Sebastopol as the goal, to their general, Lord Raglan; and this, when the Russians still occupied the principalities, and Austria was begging the support of Anglo-French troops on the Danube.

St. Arnaud resisted, alleging the insufficiency of his means. " We need a year to prepare in," he wrote back. He nevertheless decided to agree to Lord Raglan's proposal to attack Sebastopol, and twelve French and English ships of the line went to reconnoitre that harbor in the latter half of July.

At the very moment that the French ships sailed, St. Arnaud was inspired with the unlucky idea of sending an expedition into Dobroudscha, as a feigned attack, to draw away the attention of the Russians, who had not then left the Danubian provinces. St. Arnaud, by removing the troops from Varna, hoped to prevent any risk of cholera, which had sprung up at head-quarters. This hope was cruelly deceived. The French troops met no Russians, only a few Cossacks; but the cholera attacked them in the marshes of Dobroudscha. One of the three divisions, ordered thither, melted away there, and the other two, stationed in a less unwholesome region, suffered less; still the cholera ran riot, even on board ship, the squadrons being obliged to quit the coast to get rid of the epi-

demic. The month of August was a terrible one to the allied
armies. The French troops, under this painful trial, displayed a
constancy and devotion more difficult to achieve than before the
foe.

Another calamity was soon added to cholera. August 10, a fire
devoured the magazines of the allies, who considered themselves
very fortunate to save their powder.

The gaps in the French regiments had next to be filled up, and
the supplies to be renewed. French and English showed great
activity and perseverance in the task. Lord Raglan was an old comrade of Wellington, a brave soul and a ripe intellect, while St.
Arnaud's stubborn energy was capable of application to great deeds
or to great crimes. Preparations for the Crimea were carried on
at Varna without the loss of a day or an hour.

The same could not be said of London or Paris. The French
army had no siege artillery, thanks to Napoleon III., who had
decided to change the cannon in February, 1854, just on the eve of
war, — a fresh proof of his lack of common sense. It was not until
the 1st of September that twenty-four out of the fifty-six guns expected were landed at Varna.

Early in September the expedition, at last, got under sail; with
recent reinforcements, it numbered thirty thousand French soldiers,
and from twenty-one to twenty-two thousand English, to which
were added six thousand Turks. The French squadron, under
Admiral Hamelin, comprised fifteen ships of the line, four of which
were screws, five sailing vessels, thirty-five steam frigates, corvets,
and despatch boats. The English squadron only comprised ten
ships of the line, and fifteen steam frigates or corvets, the chief
English naval forces being in the Baltic; but the English had
greatly the advantage in regard to transports, their merchant service
furnishing them with one hundred and fifty magnificent vessels,
both sailing and steam ships.

The troops set out full of confidence and ardor; they forgot all
their ills on leaving the melancholy shores of Varna. They marched
joyously into the unknown, into a country whither the grand army

of the Revolution and the Empire, that indefatigable traveller, had never journeyed.   This distant region was once, if not the cradle, at least one of the principal stations of the French race; the name *Crimea* is a mere corruption of the name of the Cimmerians, one of the great branches of the ancient Celtic or Gallic family.

The Crimean peninsula is made up of two portions of entirely opposite character. The northern part, the most extensive, is a vast plain, a steppe producing nothing but grass, upon which the Tartar flocks feed. The southern part consists of a triple line of wooded mountains, interspersed with fertile valleys. The city, forts, and arsenals of Sebastopol were situated at the southeastern point of the peninsula, on the shore of a bay, cutting deeply into the country and recalling the harbor of Brest on a small scale.

Russia, not thinking Sebastopol exposed to serious danger for that year, had collected but a small portion of the vast standing army, which numbered seven hundred thousand men. Of these multitudes, scattered broadcast from Finland to the borders of Turkey in Asia, there were, at this moment, scarcely more than fifty thousand soldiers in the Crimea; less than forty thousand being within reach of Sebastopol, under the orders of Prince Menchikof, formerly the envoy of Nicholas at Constantinople.   Menchikof was far more surprised than he ought to have been when he saw the great Anglo-French fleet loom up on the horizon.

The point for disembarkation was chosen from information given by Lord Raglan, at a conference between the leaders of the two armies and two squadrons. The commander of the French army could not assist at it: illness confined him to his bed; the anxiety and fatigues of the year completed the ruin of St. Arnaud's health, long since shattered by his stormy career. Attacks of an affection of the aorta narrowly failed to carry him off during the voyage, and on the 12th of September, he dictated a letter to the minister of war, asking for a successor.

Next day a detachment of the allied troops occupied the town of Eupatoria, on the west coast of the Crimea, twenty miles or so to the north of Sebastopol, meeting with no resistance; then the rest of the men were landed to the south of the gulf of Calamata, near the place called the Old Fort. This operation consumed four whole days (September 14 – 17). The Russians made no attempt to prevent their landing, and St. Arnaud, reanimated by the approach of great contests, found sufficient strength to mount his horse. September 19, they set out for Sebastopol, the French keeping to the sea-coast, the English marching inland and more to the left. Towards noon the Russian camp came in sight, crowning a line of hills. These hills were those which border the Alma River on the south. The battle was postponed until the following day.

The position of the Russians was very favorable, since the foe must cross a river and ascend steep hills before reaching them; but their general, Menchikof, failed to profit by it, as he might have done. He did not hold the cliffs nearest the sea, on his left, with any degree of care; he thought that his troops would be exposed there to the fire of the allied fleets. This was true; but he deemed the cliffs inaccessible, and never took the pains to assure himself if they were so indeed. He was not strongly established for some distance back from the sea, opposite the road to Eupatoria, the mass of the Russian army being gathered before the English troops, and the French having little or nothing in front of them.

The allied generals agreed that Bosquet's division, placed at the extreme left, should turn the flank of the Russians by the cliff, and should be set in motion, the next day, September 20, at half past five in the morning. The main body of the two armies was not to march until seven o'clock. There was a great delay on the part of the English, whom lack of habit rendered slow to get under way. No general movement occurred until 11.30. Protected by the guns of the smaller French vessels, which drove the Russian outposts from the cliffs, General Bosquet sent the two brigades of his division across two fords, one at the very mouth of the Alma, the other, a little higher up, above the village of Almatamak. These brigades, contrary to Menchikof's expectation, succeeded in scaling the cliff, one by means of a goat path, the other without a road; the former without cannon, the latter hoisting their artillery to the summit.

There was but one Russian battalion on this side, which was quickly driven back. Menchikof, struck with amaze, was obliged to employ his whole reserve force at once, in an effort to repair his negligence. It was a decisive moment. The main body of the French troops was still on the plain below, on the other side of the Alma. Bosquet, rejoined by his cannon betimes, repulsed the Russian reserve and held his ground, the French light artillery displaying a marked superiority.

The struggle, meantime, was waged most vigorously by the English and Russians, at the top of the road to Eupatoria and the village of Bourliouk. It continued with alternating success and reverses, because Bosquet was not strong enough in numbers to push his advantage, and Canrobert, the commander of another division, which should have come to Bosquet's aid, delayed joining him. Canrobert was unwilling to go into battle without his guns, which were forced to make a long circuit.

The English, several fine Scotch regiments among them, made prodigious efforts to carry the batteries and epaulments established by the Russians on the hills above Bourliouk and the Alma. The English were several times driven beyond the river, and the works were repeatedly captured and recaptured.

When the French left and centre wheeled into line, although Canrobert was momentarily repulsed, the Russian resistance could not long be continued. Bosquet, reinforced by the Turkish division, resumed the offensive, and outflanked the enemy, upon which Menchikof ordered a retreat.

The English attribute the victory to a skilful manœuvre effected by Lord Raglan against the centre of the enemy's posts; but it seems evident that, so soon as the Russians failed to repulse Bosquet at the foot of the cliff, the battle was infallibly lost to them.

If the enemy could have been pursued, the defeat would have been a complete disaster to the Russians, for they had suffered so much and were so disorganized that their retreat changed readily into a rout; but the French had left their knapsacks behind them to scale the heights, and could pursue the foe no farther.

The city and arsenals of Sebastopol were situated midway on the long narrow bay of which we have already spoken; the north shore of the bay was protected by several forts established on the heights, which Lord Raglan proposed to attack. St. Arnaud refused. Lord Raglan then proposed to turn the flank of Sebastopol and attack the place on the south, which was agreed upon. These debates consumed two days, and the march was resumed on the 23d.

On the road loud reports were heard from the Russians, who were scuttling some of their ships to block the entrance into the harbor. Admiral Kornilof only yielded to this tragic deed, ordered by Menchikof, as a last resort. This destroyed that Black Sea fleet which formed the pride of the Russians, and which thus died a suicidal death without sharing in a single fight. Menchikof also departed with the army defeated at the Alma, leaving Sebastopol to the care of the fleet and one body of militia.

The allies advanced through a country interspersed with woods and hills, — a very dangerous region for attack, had they been dealing with an able and alert adversary. Menchikof had no military quality save courage. The movement of the allies was accomplished before the Russian general had even guessed what they were doing. The Anglo-French crossed the Tchernaïa River, and took possession of Balaklava, a place situated on a little bay in the middle of the Chersonese plain, which forms, as it were, a small peninsula within the great Crimean peninsula, between the gulf of Sebastopol, the Tchernaïa, and the sea (September 26).

St. Arnaud arrived in a dying condition. He was seized with cholera on the previous day, and the terrible disease met with slight resistance from his shattered frame. Before entering Balaklava, he gave up the command to General Canrobert, who had received authority *in posse* from the emperor on his departure from France, in case St. Arnaud broke down. The ex-commander of the Crimean army was taken on board the French ship, the Berthollet, September 29, and died a few hours after. This man, capable of much evil and much good, might have left an illustrious name behind him if he had pursued a different course in life.

At the time of St. Arnaud's death the chiefs of the two armies were eagerly discussing the question whether or no to attack Sebastopol without delay. The English generals were divided, but Lord Raglan favored immediate action. Canrobert was opposed to it, as, it seems, were most of the French generals. The attack was postponed until the breastworks, as Canrobert wrote to the minister of war, were shattered by the heavy artillery of the French. Now there were no breastworks; the Russians, not foreseeing an attack, had merely thrown up a few pieces of wall on the land side, and outlined a few bastions, without either fosses or glacis. The great military engineer, who acted as the chief defender of Sebastopol, Todleben, has since declared that an immediate assault could not have failed of success.

It is probable that the attack would have taken place, had St. Arnaud lived, in which case the capture of Sebastopol would have been announced at Paris and London very shortly after the victory of the Alma. The effect upon popular opinion would have been immense, but the positive consequences would not have been what the French and English public fancied. Serious as the loss of Sebastopol might have been to the Russians, this disaster, coming at the beginning of the war, would but slightly have impaired the Russian military power; the Russians must then have been fought upon ground far less advantageous to the aggressors, and the struggle might have been prolonged indefinitely. The course of events will show that it was for the interest of the allies to keep the Crimea as the seat of war.

The allied generals did not appreciate the value of days and hours. Sebastopol had plenty of resources, if she only had time enough to use them and men capable of directing the work; neither time nor men failed her.

Menchikof, on leaving Sebastopol with his army, fearing his communication with the mainland would be cut off, left the command divided between Admiral Kornilof, on the northern side of the gulf, and Admiral Nakhimof and General Moller, in the city and suburb on the southern side. The defenders of the place saw the necessity of unity in command, and Nakhimof and Moller, amid the plaudits of all their subordinates, tendered the supreme authority to Kornilof, whose vigor and activity inspired entire confidence in every heart Kornilof, in his turn, intrusted the direction of all the defensive works to a lieutenant-colonel of engineers, accidentally at Sebastopol as a volunteer; this was no other than Todleben, destined to such great and speedy celebrity.

These Russian officers, under the pressure of extraordinary circumstances, displayed thus suddenly a knowledge of men and a readiness which no one would have suspected to exist in a race so crushed by despotism.   The Czar was not there to impose his arbitrary will; every man was selected by his comrades in arms for the post best fitted to him.

Kornilof began by acting strongly upon the moral sense of his men.   September 29, an imposing religious ceremony was celebrated; preceded by a procession of priests singing national hymns and blessing the crowd, he made a tour of the place, passing in review soldiers, sailors, and citizens.   "Kill any man who mentions retreat," he cried, "and if I order you to retreat, kill me!"

Thus, as the historian of the Crimea (Camille Rousset) tells us, Sebastopol was less a city than a military colony.   Out of its forty-two thousand inhabitants, thirty-five thousand belonged to the army or navy; they were artisans or clerks in arsenals and dock-yards, from whom fighters could be recruited.   The sacrifice of a portion of the fleet and the forced inaction of the rest, who were withdrawn to the foot of the bay, put enormous supplies at the disposal of the officers, as well as an immense amount of marine ordnance, and eighteen thousand sailors quite ready to become bold soldiers.   Todleben demanded, and Kornilof agreed, that these potent means of defence should be transported from the ships to the shore.   Counting in a few battalions left behind by Menchikof, Sebastopol soon possessed more than thirty thousand defenders, with a tremendous supply of stores.

These defenders, and the place which they defended, must be sheltered, and as yet there was but a mere hasty outline of fortifications; it would have been a hopeless task to undertake to improvise an enceinte, or enclosure, according to the rules of military architecture. The ground in and about Sebastopol and its suburb is a mass of ravines, escarpments, and arms of the sea; it is irregularity itself. What would have been a puzzle, an obstacle, an impossibility to an ordinary engineer, became an assistance and a power to Todleben. With the greatest genius, he took advantage of the lofty positions and deep valleys. He set at work thousands of toilers, sailors, soldiers and citizens, kindled in them a portion of his own ardor, inspired them with his stubborn perseverance. In a few days he had thrown up huge masses of earth and stones, and created a line of defence. Any one who had broached such a scheme before a committee of engineers would have been deemed mad. Todleben accomplished, or at least began, one of the greatest deeds in military history; what he had already done he was destined to continue to do throughout a long siege.

Thus protected from within, Sebastopol once more found herself stoutly supported from without. Menchikof, seeing that the allies had established themselves to the south of the Chersonese, returned with his army to the heights of Belbek, at the north of Sebastopol; he held free communication with the town and sent as many as thirty battalions thither.

The allies, on their side, lost no time. The idea of a sudden attack once abandoned, they set vigorously to work in view of a regular siege. French and English shared the field-works, as they had divided the encampment. The English occupied the small port of Balaklava, and the eastern part of the Chersonese plain; the French held the western part, with their naval forces in the gulf of Kamiesch. The gulf of Sebastopol, which extends from west to east, pushes out a branch towards the south, which forms the seaport and divides the town of Sebastopol from the suburb of Karabelnaïa; in this suburb are the great naval establishments. The French directed their works against the town, and the English against the suburb.

The trenches were opened between the 9th and 10th of October, and on the 19th a general bombardment occurred both on sea and on shore.　Neither the fleets nor the French attack by land proved successful; but the English batteries, favorably situated, destroyed the defences at Karabelnaïa; the explosion of a powder-magazine completed the ruin of the Great Redan, the chief work erected on this side by Todleben.　Lord Raglan, however, seeing that the French were not prepared to storm the city, did not conclude to profit by his advantage and try to take the suburb.

This day cost the Russians dear.　Their brave leader, Kornilof, was mortally wounded by a bullet, upon one of the works protecting Karabelnaïa, the Malakof tower, destined to win tragic fame.

Kornilof's spirit lingered with those whom he commanded.　Todleben, seconded by the untiring devotion of his laborers, performed Herculean tasks during the following night, and the Great Redan was restored within twelve hours.　The bombardment was renewed for several days, without special result.

The French, far from being discouraged, vied with the Russians in pushing forward their intrenchments, and improving the chances of a siege.　Although ill established upon the arid Chersonese plain, they kept themselves in good condition, which was more than could be said for the English troops, who wasted away from the privations due to the gross ignorance of the administration as well as of the soldiers themselves; the English soldiers fought finely, but could do absolutely nothing else.

The Russians, meantime, were growing daily stronger.　The Austrians not budging from the Danubian principalities, and seeming not at all disposed to invade Russian territory, Nicholas ventured to order a part of his army of the Danube into the Crimea.

Menchikof then felt himself justified in resuming the offensive, and sent some twenty thousand men forward to the Tchernaïa. These troops advanced beyond this river, October 25, and attacked the positions held by the English between Balaklava and the Tchernaïa.　The Russians gained a few small redoubts guarded by Turkish troops; but when they tried to push farther into the plain, their cavalry was dashed to pieces against a regiment of Scotch mountaineers and an excellent brigade of heavy cavalry, made up of

Scotch and Irish. The affair would doubtless have ended there if, according to an order which was misunderstood, an English brigade of light cavalry had not rushed forward alone, and attacked the whole Russian corps single-handed.   With irresistible impetuosity, they overcame every obstacle, cavalry, infantry and artillery, and were finally swallowed up in the mob through which they passed. Not one man would have returned to tell the tale if a French regiment of African chasseurs had not descended from the heights like a thunderbolt upon the Russians, while the English heavy artillery came up to gather in the remnant of their brave comrades. This was the famous charge of Balaklava, a piece of mad heroism, which has lingered in the legendary lore of military history.

The Russians held their ground at the entrance of the Chersonese, in the redoubts captured from the Turks.   No one thought of driving them thence ; it was in the direction of the besieged city that the French redoubled their attack ; they boldly ventured to storm the town in presence of Menchikof's army, and the English helped them out.

The enemy, on the other hand, had quite recovered confidence. Menchikof had received such reinforcements that he now numbered one hundred thousand soldiers, not including sailors. The allies had only sixty odd thousand.   November 3, two sons of Nicholas, the Grand-dukes Nicholas and Michael, entered Sebastopol amid the cheers of its defenders. The allies agreed to begin the siege November 7, but Menchikof forestalled them. Before day-dawn on the 5th, four Russian columns marched out to attack the positions of the allies.

Two of these attacks, one in the direction of Balaklava, the other from Sebastopol against the French outposts, were mere diversions. The real attack was made against the camp of the English, who were besieging Karabelnaïa. The English encampments were upon a plain called Inkermann, between Karabelnaïa and the valley of the Tchernaïa, so closely compressed by two ravines as to form a species of isthmus. Two strong columns of Russians, thirty-six thousand men in all, met at this point : the first came from Kara-

VIEW OF SEVASTOPOL

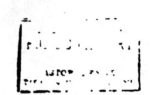

belnaïa; the second descended the hills on the opposite bank of the
Tchernaïa and crossed that stream near its mouth. They were to
meet, in order to outflank the English camp and attack it in the
rear. Their movements were ill contrived, each acted independently
of the other, instead of joining their forces. The English were,
nevertheless, in great danger. The column from Karabelnaïa surprised a division of their troops and almost overwhelmed them by
their superior numbers. Somewhat reinforced, the English disputed every inch of ground, and the contest went on through rain
and fog, until the Russian general, Soimonof, was killed. Dismay
seized his troops; they ceased to advance, then retreated, received
no more orders, and withdrew from the fight.

The column from the opposite bank of the Tchernaïa, under General Pavlof, meantime, began their attack upon the other portion of
the English camp. There were furious onsets and long alternatives
of triumph and defeat. Although the English right wing was joined
by the left, who had shaken off the column from Karabelnaïa, the
inequality of numbers was still great. The English drove Pavlof's
vanguard back to the valley of the Tchernaïa; but the bulk of his
troops, strengthened by an immense park of artillery (nearly one
hundred guns), hurled their heavy battalions forward with such
force as to remain masters of an earthwork protecting the right of
the English camp (the battery of earth-bags). Should the Russians
keep this position, the English were definitely driven from the plain
of Inkermann, and the day was lost.

The English had hitherto prided themselves upon sustaining the
brunt of battle without the aid of the French. There was not a
moment more to be lost; two of their generals were killed, several
wounded; the soldiers were exhausted. Lord Raglan summoned the
French, who were only waiting to be called.

General Bosquet, who commanded the nearest corps, hurried forward his two foremost battalions. It would have been too late if
the enemy had passed the captured earthwork and advanced
beyond the isthmus. Luckily the Russians were less active than
brave. The French foot-soldiers renewed the heroic charge of the

cavalry at Balaklava; in their onslaught they drove the main body of the Russians back far beyond the battery of earth-bags. They were in turn repulsed by the enemy; but the movement of the latter was arrested all the same. The Russian leaders could not manoeuvre rapidly enough to post themselves, as they should have done, between the English and the fresh French reinforcements.

The French troops arrived at a trot, in rapid succession, with the agility which the soldier trained by African wars had already displayed at the Alma. The Russians repulsed a second attack; they bowed beneath a third, effected with still further reinforcements. One of their regiments was hurled by French Zouaves and Turcos from the top of the cliff into a deep ravine, where it perished, and the rest of the Russian troops slowly and painfully retreated under the destructive fire of the French artillery.

This bloody day cost the Russians some twelve thousand killed, wounded, and missing. The English lost about twenty-six hundred men; the French, between seventeen and eighteen hundred. The latter, besides their decisive intervention at Inkermann, also repulsed a sortie from the garrison of Sebastopol.

According to military historians, the Russian defeat was largely due to their lack of mobility, and want of skill in manoeuvres, the pedantic and minute tactics imposed upon them by Nicholas only serving to hamper them in the face of the foe.

The allies, victorious, but exhausted by such a victory, postponed the siege, and decided to remain on the defensive until the arrival of more troops. They completed the circumvallation protecting the Chersonese, from Balaklava to Inkermann; the Russians had completely withdrawn; the French also covered themselves, in the direction of the town, by a line of vallation.

Winter now drew on, threatening to be severe. November 14, a fearful storm upheaved the sea, and swept bare the Chersonese plain, tearing up tents, carrying off barracks, destroying ships or driving them far out to sea. Many French and English vessels received great damage; one French ship, the Henry IV., was lost, with a number of smaller ones belonging to the French, English, and

Turkish. The crew of the Henry IV. was saved. The majority of French and English sailing vessels, after being repaired, left the Black Sea.

Autumn rains followed the tempest, and the rain was followed in turn by intense cold. There was no lack of warm clothing and food, but the troops had no other shelter than miserable tents, or holes which they dug in the rocky soil. No one at London or Paris had thought betimes of providing wooden walls. The French suffered much, and the English even more; but the brave fellows were not disheartened, and most cordial relations existed between the allies.

While the great siege of Sebastopol was going on, France and England renewed their efforts to draw Austria into an active alliance. The German Diet finally accepted the Four Guaranties, though with rather an ill grace. December 2, Austria pledged herself to France and England to call upon Russia to accept the Four Guaranties before the 1st of January, 1855. There was to be an offensive and defensive alliance between the three powers if hostilities broke out between Austria and Russia, and effort was made to gain the adhesion of Prussia to this alliance.

Nicholas answered the treaty of December 2d by a violent manifesto. His ambassador at Vienna was informed that the three powers had no wish to attack the integrity of Russian domains, but would take advantage of the war in regard to the Russian settlements on the Black Sea (end of December).

December 26, Napoleon III. opened the legislative session with a speech, in which he celebrated the military triumphs of France and her alliance with England, which Austria had joined in a treaty, "defensive for the time being, but perhaps soon to be offensive."

The Legislature voted a new loan twice as great as the preceding one, — five hundred million francs. The public subscription was reopened, and succeeded even better than before. The session was marked by a new law in regard to the constitution of the army. This law created an endowment for the army, and established the system of substitutes, re-enlistment, and military pensions upon a new basis. The state put itself in the place of enlisting-officer, and turned "crimp," as the term went in old times. The system of re-enlistment with bounties could not fail to injure the spirit of the army, to fill it up with bad soldiers destitute of any true military spirit, and to divide it more and more from the nation.

A ministerial crisis had recently occurred in England. The misfortunes of the army were charged to the ministry. Of fifty-three thousand men sent to the East, but sixteen thousand were left before Sebastopol. The ministers were dismissed because they had made insufficient preparations for the war. Lord Palmerston not only escaped the fate of his colleagues, but was placed at the head of the new cabinet charged with repairing the errors of the past. He lacked neither energy nor industry. He rapidly took a number of vigorous measures, which the public eagerly seconded by spontaneous individual action as well as by association. It was a true regeneration of English administration. Order, plenty, and a good use of the means at hand gradually improved the aspect of the English quarters in the Crimea, and the French ended by admiring what had been the object of their pity.

The preceding ministry, before retiring, signed a diplomatic agreement, whose scope was not thoroughly understood until later. January 25, 1855, a treaty of alliance was signed between Piedmont, England, and France. Fifteen thousand Piedmontese were to join the allies before Sebastopol. England advanced twenty-five millions to Piedmont. Being short of soldiers, she kept the Piedmontese in her pay; but the government of Piedmont had intended to join the war, not as a hireling, but as an ally. This treaty was a bold and skilful scheme on her part. The Piedmontese government had at its head the statesman who was destined to repair the errors and misfortunes of the Italy of 1848, Count Cavour. This brave and learned politician desired his country to take an active part in great European affairs at any cost, and wished to prepare points of support for her in view of future claims which might be made on her.

To carry out a scheme whose remote purpose he could not reveal to all, M. de Cavour had had many obstacles about him to overcome:

many cried out that he was selling Italian blood to strangers; his colleagues in the cabinet, the Right and Left parties in the Piedmontese Parliament, were all against him. King Victor Emanuel understood and sustained him, and he was at last allowed full liberty of action.

The Piedmontese reinforcement could not reach the Crimea until the close of spring, and, on the other hand, long delays were inevitable before the English government could effect the happy results which we have mentioned. Meantime the winter was frightful on the bleak Chersonese plain, hardened by frost and lashed by whirling snow. The remnant of English troops wasted steadily away. In mid-January they had not more than ten thousand men left before Karabelnaïa. The French, on the contrary, had received such large reinforcements that, in spite of their losses, they numbered seventy-five thousand men on January 31. They helped the English as best they could, shared everything with them, and undertook a great part of their work before the besieged place. Lord Raglan finally requested General Canrobert to allow his troops to take charge of a portion of the English outworks, that is, the trenches opposite the Malakof tower.

And yet the French, too, were a prey to most cruel sufferings. The cavalry and artillery were almost completely dismounted. Although the men bore the cold better than the horses, the hospitals were crowded; great numbers of soldiers perished or were crippled by frost-bites. A fresh misfortune also befell the army and France. A large frigate, the Sémillante, loaded with troops and siege-guns, was swallowed up by a tempest, with all on board, in the Strait of Bonifacio (mid-February).

The besieged underwent no less misery than the besiegers. Besides the losses caused by cannon, disease consumed the people confined in Sebastopol. The men who guarded the fortifications of the vast enceinte were as much exposed to the inclemency of the weather as their adversaries.

The Russians were no readier to yield than the French or English. Todleben, while constantly strengthening his outworks, assumed the offensive with counter-approaches. There were continual nocturnal skirmishes between companies of volunteers made up by both parties.

Nicholas sent regiment after regiment to fill up the awful gaps in his Crimean army. The allies, on their side, persuaded the Turkish general, Omer Pacha, to descend upon Eupatoria, in the Crimea, with twenty thousand men, which number was speedily doubled. Nicholas ordered a part of the Russian army to attack Eupatoria, and Omer Pacha repulsed them successfully (February 16–17).

Shortly after, a great piece of news was announced throughout Europe, as well as in the Crimea. The Emperor Nicholas was no more. The successive defeats of his troops by the French and English moved him deeply. This last check from the Turks completely broke him down. Rumor stated his death to be the result of suicide: this was a mistake. Already ill, the Czar, in spite of his doctor's orders, insisted upon holding a review on an icy-cold day; he returned, and never left his bed again. This man, who for thirty years had filled the thoughts of all Europe, expired on the 2d of March, 1855. One of the two contending despots thus died of his defeat; the other was fated to end yet more miserably, after inflicting upon France yet worse calamities than those drawn down on Russia by Nicholas.

Nicholas was succeeded by his eldest son, Alexander II. The new Czar was already advanced in life (thirty-seven years old); it was thought that he disapproved of the rash and haughty policy of his father. All Europe dreamed of instant peace. A truce cannot be put to so bitter a war waged under such conditions! Alexander II. began his career by a very lofty manifesto, extenuated, however, by a circular letter from Minister Nesselrode.

Before the death of Nicholas, his ambassador at Vienna, Prince Alexander Gortchakof, obtained from the allied powers a delay of a fortnight in which to reply to the notification in regard to the Four Guaranties; then, on the 7th of January, he agreed to accept them with the interpretation put upon them by the allies. This seemed a great step taken, but it meant nothing, unless it was a pretext given to Austria for remaining passive. It deceived no one at Paris. A conference was opened at Vienna, March 15, without the concurrence of Prussia, who was unwilling to promise to take any part in the quarrel if the negotiations failed.

The Russian ambassador declared to the conference that Russia would never consent to limit her naval power in the Black Sea. This, in point of fact, annulled the acceptance given two months before, of the note as understood by the allies.

Austria was at the foot of the wall. On this occasion she imitated Prussia and shrank away. At heart, she had but one desire, to drive the Russians from the Danube; she took no interest in fighting to destroy the Russian naval power in the Black Sea. The conference closed, June 4, without achieving anything. Drouyn de Lhuys, the French minister of foreign affairs, whom Napoleon III. thought lacking in firmness towards Austria, had sent in his resignation, and been replaced by Count Walewski, of Polish origin, but supposed to be nearly allied to the Bonaparte family through the first emperor.

Austria, while protesting her attachment to the triple alliance, was really breaking away from it; she dismissed her military reserve, while the Piedmontese troops were joining the French and English. This was ominous, and Count Cavour foresaw the course of coming events.

Napoleon III. did not disguise his dissatisfaction with Austria, in his speech at the opening of the extra legislative session (July 2, 1855). "We are still waiting," he remarked, "for Austria to keep her promises, which rendered our treaty of alliance offensive and defensive alike, should negotiations fail."

The Legislature voted a third loan, — this time, of seven hundred and fifty million francs. Public subscriptions for state loans became more and more a national custom. The number of subscribers exceeded three hundred and sixteen thousand. The amount subscribed was more than thirty-six hundred and fifty-two millions. Foreigners subscribed to the loan to the amount of more than six hundred millions. The Legislature also voted, as on the year before, to issue a call for one hundred and forty thousand men.

Operations went on before Sebastopol with increasing vigor, as the condition of the besieging armies improved; but the great man of war who had charge of the defence displayed the resources of his genius ever more fruitfully as the danger increased. Todleben, seeing the French relieve the English before the Malakof tower, and judging that to be the decisive point, improvised fine outworks to cover that point. The first attack upon these works was unsuccessful (February 23), and he annoyed the assailants by sallies from the direction of the town, where the French had pushed their trenches very near the walls. He opposed their mines with counter-mines, and desperate struggles occurred in the darkness of these subterranean galleries.

April 9 and 10, the besiegers renewed the general bombardment. The effect was terrible, yet it was not decided to attempt an assault. This great uproar only resulted in killing off the Russians and destroying their fortifications, which they were then allowed to rebuild.

The day after the bombardment, the French lost General Bizot of the Engineers, who had conducted the labors of the siege with zeal and ability. He was killed in one of the trenches by a cannon-ball.

Emperor Napoleon was at this time revolving a grand scheme of taking command of the army of the Crimea in person, dreaming of gaining military honors after his political triumphs. He started for London with the empress, to establish personal relations with the queen and her husband, Prince Albert, and with the English ministry. The pleasure of seeing the empire, restored in the person of the nephew of Napoleon, applauded by the English people, played a large part in this journey. Singular sights were witnessed. London did not spare the plaudits on which the Emperor of the French had reckoned, and Queen Victoria with her own hands bestowed upon him the great English order of the Garter, given by the Regent of England to Louis XVIII. as he set out to replace Napoleon I.

The emperor persuaded the English government to adopt his plan for future operations in the Crimea. A few days after his return to France, an Italian, named Pianori, fired a pistol at him twice in the Champs Élysées, missing him both times (April 28). This incident made a deep impression upon him. Every one around him plead with him to abandon his journey to the East, and he yielded, fortunately for the army, which would have been greatly hampered by his presence. He caused enough trouble, as it was, by his letters, pretending to rule the troops from one end of Europe to the other. The submarine cable laid at this time between France and the Black Sea annihilated distance; but with a leader of state like Napoleon III., this cable transmitted more perplexities than useful communications.

Still the emperor rendered one service to the army, when he sent General Pelissier from Africa into the Crimea. With many defects of character, Pelissier united a large measure of energy and activity and the insight of a true military leader. He started out with a brilliant deed, the seizure of a part of the Russian counter-approaches (May 1). Thenceforward the army put their whole hope in him. There were many complications and divisions of opinion in the councils of war between the French commander-in-chief Canrobert, Lord Raglan, and General Niel, who, without holding any special command, was the personal representative of the emperor. Napoleon III., in his letters, merely expressed the ideas suggested to him by General Niel. Canrobert was worn out by these disputes: a fine military administrator, careful of the well-being of his men, he had done genuine service during the awful winter just passed; but with firm courage, he had not the audacious spirit, initiative, and decision required by the situation. He felt keenly aware of it, sent in his resignation of the chief command, and asked to be replaced by Pelissier, becoming himself a simple general of division (May 16). In this he showed a sense of justice and generosity of which few warriors would be capable; history should set it down to his account.

The difficulties which had embarrassed Canrobert were at once renewed for Pelissier. The plan which the emperor had caused to be adopted at London, and upon which he obstinately insisted, really belonged to General Niel,—a man of brilliant mind, but of a very systematic turn, who did not show himself very practical on this occasion. The point in question was the dismemberment of the army, one portion only being retained in front of Sebastopol, the rest to be employed in driving the Russian army out of the Crimea. Pelissier thoroughly disapproved of this plan, feeling assured that the Russian army was in no condition seriously to renew their attack upon the Chersonese, and deeming it as rash as it was vain to seek them out amid the wooded heights and valleys which overspread it; he meant to push the siege with the utmost hostility, and pay no heed to outside affairs. Little accustomed to restraint, he maintained his opinion with a violence which nearly cost him his command. Luckily the minister of war, Marshal Vaillant, interfered, and Pelissier was finally allowed, as he asked, " to act freely." Lord Raglan fully agreed with him.

He acted quickly and forcibly. Between the 22d and 23d of May he carried the Russian outworks in the direction of the town. On the 24th he occupied the valley of the Tchernaïa and the bridge of Traktir across that stream, and drove the Russian outposts back to the heights on the right bank, thus screening the Chersonese from all retaliation.

Outside the Chersonese there was but one point, and that a very distant one, to which an expedition was very necessary, and this was the very thing which the emperor had hitherto prevented. At the precise time that such vigorous measures were being taken before Sebastopol, and on the Tchernaïa, this expedition took place with brilliant success. A body of allied troops, about fifteen thousand in number, embarking on an Anglo-French squadron, landed at Kertch, to the extreme east of the Crimea, May 24. The town of Kertch and the fort of Jéni-Kalé were taken almost without resistance, and the Sea of Azof, that great lake united to the Black Sea by the Straits of Kertch, the old Cimmerian Bosphorus, was opened to French vessels of small draught. All the Russian ships

and military magazines established in and about the Sea of Azof
were captured or destroyed by the allies, the Russian army thus
losing its principal line of supplies, and becoming unable to receive
provisions except by the way of the Isthmus of Pērēkop.   The invasion of the Sea of Azof entailed the abandonment by the Russians of
all the posts which they retained on the boundaries of Circassia, even
the important strongholds of Anapa and Soudjouk-Kalé.   Thus the
fruit of long labor was lost.

In the most painful moments the allied troops had displayed that
constancy so wrongly denied to the French; now confidence and joy
had returned like the sun shining after rain.

Pelissier continued to advance.   After a fresh bombardment (June
6–9), several Russian fortifications were captured and turned against
the town.   The besieged defended themselves valiantly, and the
success of these assaults was dearly bought, but it was considerable.
Pelissier thought that the decisive moment had come.   He resolved
to attack the two main works protecting Karabelnaïa, on June 18,
in concert with Lord Raglan.   The English were to attack the Great
Redan, and the French the Malakof.   Pelissier chose the 18th of
June, desiring to efface the memory of Waterloo by a victory which
French and English were to achieve together upon that bloody
anniversary, hoping thus to fully conciliate the emperor.

This general, who never flattered any one, has been accused on this
occasion of flattering one of Napoleon's weaknesses.   He committed
a still more serious mistake.   In consequence of a quarrel with
the valiant and able General Bosquet, leader of the division ordered
to attack the Malakof, he gave the command of this body to another
general.   The arrival of a new chief at such a time, a stranger
to the troops and unpossessed of their confidence, had very serious
consequences.

The day following a bombardment which lasted through the
17th, the attack began.   Mistakes were made which would probably not have occurred if the leader had not been changed.   One
division attacked too soon, its general was killed; another general met
with the same fate; the Russians resisted with desperate courage;

the assault of the Malakof, despite the heroic efforts of the French, was repulsed.   The English also failed at the Grand Redan.

This check would have been doubly serious if it had led to the fall of Pelissier.   The emperor, for a time, thought of replacing him by General Niel.   Pelissier, in his correspondence with Napoleon III., excused himself with dignity and skill.   The minister of war sustained him, and he retained his office.

The army, however, had not seen the last of its misery; after the winter, came the summer with its scourges.   Cholera reappeared, and scurvy in its train.   Lord Raglan was carried off by cholera, June 28.   He won the sincere esteem of every Frenchman who saw him in action.   He was replaced by General Simpson.

In spite of this renewal of past sufferings, French officers and men thought of nothing but repairing the reverses of June 18. They worked persistently to prepare a new attack.   Men, supplies, and provisions were all abundant.   The minister of war, feeling the necessity of renewing a great portion of the worn-out troops, recalled certain divisions to France and replaced them by others. The English, instead of thus transforming their army, were obliged to re-create regiments which had almost disappeared.   They set to work with ardor.   No one considered that the French and English, masters of the sea, could embark men and materials and send them safely and easily to the Crimea, risking only some very rare maritime disaster.   The Russian troops, on the contrary, had to travel an almost endless distance into the heart of a continent.   With the best possible system there must be great difficulties, great loss of time, and great hardships.   Now the Russian administrative system was the worst in the world; disorder and depredation reigned, high officials speculated disgracefully in the food and clothing intended for the troops, and Nicholas, the much dreaded despot, was the most ill-served of princes.   From this resulted a fearful loss of men: the poor Russian soldiers, exhausted and starved, strewed the interminable roads of the empire with their corpses.   There is no spectacle more heartrending to humanity than that offered by this unhappy nation, so patient and devoted.

Prince Michael Gortchakof, the general commanding the Russian army since Menchikof retired, after the defeat at Eupatoria, felt his powerlessness. His orders from St. Petersburg forced him to risk a final effort to save Sebastopol. He set in motion seventy thousand men, the remnant of the countless levies made in the Crimea, and attacked the allies on the banks of the Tchernaïa. In front of him, to the right, was General La Marmora's Piedmontese corps; to the left, General Herbillon's French troops. He repulsed the Piedmontese and French outposts on the right bank of the Tchernaïa, forced his way across the bridge of Traktir, and attacked the French positions on the Fédioukhine hills on the other side. The French infantry drove the foe down the steep hills, pursued them beyond the Tchernaïa, and the artillery riddled them with shot as they retreated. The attack was no more successful in the valley against another French division, or against the Piedmontese, who occupied Mount Hasfort. Twenty-seven thousand French and Piedmontese sufficed to repel the enemy. The Piedmontese light infantry, the Bersaglieri, greatly distinguished themselves, and Cavour's first object was attained. The Italians had their share in a victory, and Novara began to be wiped from the memory of man (August 16).

The result of the battle of Traktir proved that the assailants were almost at the end of their efforts. A terrible explosion in a powder-magazine, which blew up on the night of August 28, did not put a stop to the work of the trenches, which were now carried, at various points, very close to the enemy's works. The French were within twenty-five yards of the Malakof, so that they would no longer have to traverse a vast exposed place under a shower of shot and shell, in case of a siege.

A final bombardment lasted three whole days, September 5, 6, and 7, being carried on by more than six hundred French guns and nearly two hundred English cannon. Three great Russian ships were burned in the harbor, and the ruin of the city was complete. Between the 17th of August and the 7th of September the garrison had twenty thousand men wounded or disabled.

It was decided that the attack should be general, both upon the

city and Karabelnaïa.   It was agreed to begin at the right, that is,
by the assault from the French, extending from the Malakof to the
Little Redan; then, at the centre, the English were to fall upon the
Great Redan, and finally, at the left, towards the city, the French
were to attack the Central Bastion.   General Bosquet was to command the grand attack on the right.   Under his orders was an officer
who had distinguished himself by his vigor and zeal in the African
campaign, namely, General MacMahon; he was given Canrobert's
command, that general being recalled to France.

There were still fifty thousand men within the fortress, the wreck
of a very large army and navy.   Only four thousand sailors were
left out of eighteen thousand.   The allies were to bring to bear
about forty-six thousand French and eleven thousand English.

On a stormy morning all was made ready, and at noon, on the 8th
of September, Bosquet's corps opened the contest.   The Russians
were taken by surprise, and the first regiment of Zouaves, in
MacMahon's division, entered the Malakof with the greatest ease.

The Little Redan, on the right, was twice taken and lost.   The
French were in the Malakof; but the Russians were not out of it,
and furiously disputed the possession of the terre-pleins and the
tower.   Three French generals were killed and three wounded.
Bosquet was also wounded.   One of the French powder-magazines
exploded in the rear of the attack, but the anxiety caused by this
accident was soon allayed, and both parties held their ground.

On the left, at the sight of the French flag flying from the Malakof, the English flung themselves upon the Great Redan, which
they three times captured and as often lost, the Russians remaining
masters of it.

Towards two o'clock the French attacked the Central Bastion.
After a temporary triumph General Trochu was wounded and
repulsed.   A second attack also failed, two French generals being
killed.

Failure was on every hand save at the Malakof; but that was
the decisive point.   On the side of the city, Sebastopol, terraced
like an amphitheatre, overlooked the fortifications attacked; towards

CAPTURE OF THE MALAKOFF.

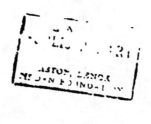

the suburb, Malakof, on the contrary, commanded Karabelnaïa, the harbor, and open bay. The very works of the Russians, and the traverses which they had formed within the Malakof, the post once invaded, assisted the French to complete and retain their conquest. In this hand-to-hand fight, amid shattered timbers and piles of rubbish, the French soldiers, particularly the Zouaves, had a marked advantage over the Russians, being more agile and wary. MacMahon, urging on his whole division, finally chased the Russians from the Malakof. On hearing that the work was undermined, and that he was in danger of being blown up, he replied in these words, since famous : "Here I am, and here I shall remain !" Happily, the train which communicated with the mine was discovered and cut off.

Prince Gortchakof, who had hastened to Sebastopol, brought forward all the forces at his disposal in an effort to reconquer the Malakof, that all-important position. The desperate struggle of the Russians was unavailing against MacMahon's battalions, and Gortchakof recalled the remnants of five divisions, which persisted in hurling themselves into the jaws of death.

The great struggle was at an end. During the night the Russians left Sebastopol by the bridge of rafts, destroying or blowing up everything behind them. They fired or scuttled their ships ; and the Black Sea fleet ceased to exist . Sebastopol was doomed to burn for several months more.

This bloody day cost the Russians nearly thirteen thousand men, the allies losing more than ten thousand.

The debates which preceded the victory were now renewed regarding the use to which it should be turned ; but they were necessarily of a different nature. Pelissier's authority was now most strong, and the emperor acknowledged his brilliant services by sending him a marshal's baton.

The emperor was more eager than ever for a campaign against the Russian army ; it seemed to him that there was no other course to be pursued. Pelissier, not at all dazzled by his great success, persistently declined to go in search of the Russians beyond the line of rocks which divides the Chersonese plain from

the road to Simféropol, the seat of government in the Crimea.
" Our tenacity," he wrote, " will slay the Russians more surely than
any rash attacks." The whole Crimean war was summed up in
these words. It was to the advantage of the allies not to take Sebastopol at the outset; Russia's tremendous, but luckless efforts to
save her great seaport exhausted her far more than was supposed
at Paris.

While leaving the Russian army to their rocks, Pelissier was not
inactive. He joined the English in sending a naval expedition
against Kinbourn, a fortress commanding the gulf in which the
Dnieper and the Boug meet, before Nicolaïef, the second military
port in the Black Sea. The English were the first to use a steam
fleet in the Baltic; the French were first to use iron-plated ships in
the Black Sea. Kinbourn, overwhelmed by shot from the French
vessels, was taken in a few hours (October 19), almost before the
eyes of Alexander II., who was at Nicolaïef. A man doomed to
fatal notoriety first came forward on this occasion; the troops sent
on shore were commanded by General Bazaine !

Pelissier had very marked opinions, not only in regard to special
operations, but in relation to the whole war. His plan would have
been to hold Sebastopol with a strong force, but at the same time
to send the majority of the troops back to France and England. In
this way the basis of the war would be completely changed; it
would become a European instead of an Asiatic war, — war waged
by Poland against Prussia as well as against Russia, with the Austrian alliance.

England would not agree to this radical change ; she was implacable against the Crimea. Pelissier modified his plan without
giving it up; he proposed that the English, combining with the
Turks, should attack the Russian possessions bordering on Persia,
and raise Circassia in revolt. A body of French troops would
guard Sebastopol and the Chersonese plain with the Piedmontese,
and the mass of the French army would return to France, to fit
the country to take a stand against any action Russia might take in
regard to Germany.

Vaillant, the minister of war, replïed that the English would not suffer any separation of the allied troops. The French army, therefore, remained in the Crimea, and was increased rather than reduced, continual reinforcements being sent out, although the imperial guard and another division of infantry were recalled. These troops held a triumphal reception at Paris, December 29, in which there was something beyond mere official show. Paris was touched by the sight of these brave fellows, who had fought so gloriously and suffered so patiently. The people felt as if the grand army had returned, and those most hostile to the empire were delighted at this proof that France had lost none of her warlike qualities.

The Russians, after so many misfortunes, had gained one success during the preceding month. After a prolonged siege, their army of the Caucasus starved out the town of Kars, an important post of Turkey in Asia (November 25). This remote victory, which could in no way affect the course of events, was the very thing that disposed the Russians to yield to their fate. Finding their honor untarnished, and thinking that they should get some direct compensation when they came to negotiate, they decided to solicit peace.

Napoleon's humor seemed to shift in the same direction. The World's Fair, announced three years before as a pledge of peace, took place in the midst of war. Napoleon III. closed it with a speech indicating pacific tendencies. "Europe," he said, "must take her stand. At the point of civilization which we have now reached, public opinion must always carry off the final victory."

Still Napoleon III. would have asked nothing better than to carry out Marshal Pelissier's views by a European war. His overtures to the English government relative to the restoration of Poland were reversed before the retirement of Drouyn de Lhuys, by despatches from that minister to the French ambassador in England. Lord Palmerston firmly refused to agree to them. Napoleon III. also applied to Austria, secretly offering to abandon to her the Danubian provinces of Wallachia and Moldavia, in return for her offensive alliance on the Continent. Austria did not accept. She would never have engaged in a Polish war without the aid and knowledge of England.

From that time forth, Napoleon III. lost his interest for war in the Orient and plotted a reconciliation with Russia. In becoming England's tool, he had hoped to bring the English to serve him in their turn; but while Lord Palmerston made use of other people, he never allowed himself to be used by any one, especially France. This hope gone, Napoleon began to dream of preparing elsewhere the brilliant stroke of policy which no one would help him to carry out in Poland. He thought of Italy, which was nearer at hand, and for which he first fleshed his sword. After Queen Victoria's visit to Paris in August, came King Victor Emanuel in November, with Cavour. The skilful Piedmontese minister felt and seized the opportune moment to act upon the emperor's spirit. When he took leave of Napoleon, the latter used these significant words : " What can we do for Italy ?"

Austria, however, alarmed by the dissatisfaction manifested at Paris, had offered in October to resume the rôle of intermediary with Russia, consenting to go so far as to offer her a new ultimatum. Napoleon III. agreed, as did England ; but at the same time he was working outside of Austria, through the medium of petty German states. His speech at the close of the Exposition had in some sort set neutral nations at work to restore peace. The German states, especially Saxony, spurred on by fear, were consequently negotiating with St. Petersburg.

December 16, an envoy extraordinary from Austria presented at St. Petersburg the ultimatum agreed upon with France and England. The Four Guaranties were rendered more grave: to the total interdiction of maritime armaments in the Black Sea was now added the cession by Russia of that part of Bessarabia lying between the Danube and the Pruth. This strip of territory, inhabited by a population of Roumanian race and tongue, was to be added to the Roumanian province of Wallachia; Russia was to be wholly separated from the Danube. This clause was wholly Austrian in origin. Austria dared not accept the provinces of the Lower Danube; but she wished at least to remove Russia from the mouths of the great stream.

Nothing could have been more difficult for the new Czar and his advisers. Should Russia recede for the first time in many long years? But if the struggle were prolonged, the campaign of 1856 promised the Russians naught save more and greater disasters. The allies were collecting enormous and irresistible forces in the Crimea, which must inevitably crush all that was left of the Russian army. Austria, too, would join the ranks; and in the Baltic, England, which had not ventured to attack Cronstadt in 1854, was now preparing a tremendous expedition against that Sebastopol of the North. She had, the year before, with the help of a French squadron, destroyed Sveaborg, the military port of Finland; and Sweden had now signed a definite treaty with England and France.

Upon the friendly pressure of the King of Prussia, who was much alarmed by the situation, Alexander II. yielded (January 16, 1856), and it was settled that a congress should be held at Paris.

In the state of excitement prevalent in England, where gigantic efforts had been made in view of a decisive campaign, the English people, as well as the government, would vastly have preferred that Russia should not accept the conditions of peace. Nevertheless, when the English Parliament reopened (January 31), the discussion of the address was far more pacific than was expected. All statesmen felt that if the French government desired peace, it was no longer possible to refuse it.

France, whose self-love was flattered by the success of her arms, might have waxed eager over a European war, but by no means wished to continue the struggle in the East.

The Congress of Paris opened February 25th, under the presidency of Count Walewski, French minister of foreign affairs. Russia restored Kars to Turkey, and received back all that had been taken from her; — at Sebastopol, she received nothing but a piece of ground cumbered with smoking ruins and with graves; the English government required even the ruins to be demolished, and not one stone was left standing upon another. France persuaded England to allow the second port in importance in the Black Sea (Nicolaïef), to remain intact with its arsenal and dockyards, on condition that none but light-draught vessels — whose number was limited — were built there.

It was in regard to the cession of territory in Bessarabia that the discussion became most heated : the Russian plenipotentiary, Count Orlof, struggled stoutly for the maintenance of Russia on the northern branch of the Danube on condition of her retiring from the delta of the great stream. Austria proved more stubborn on this point than did the powers who made the war. Russia was forced to yield. Orlof uttered to Cavour on this occasion a remark which a near future was to justify : "This will cost Austria tears of blood."

In reference to this adjustment of boundaries, the question of the consolidation of the two provinces on the Lower Danube, Wallachia and Moldavia, into a single Roumanian state, subject to Turkey, was brought up. In spite of the protests of Austria and Turkey, both opposed to the formation of a Roumanian nationality, it was decided that the wishes of the two peoples should be consulted in regard to their final organization. Their wishes were well known in advance, so that it was the regeneration of a nation, the vanguard of the Gallo-Roman family in the East, which was voted.

During the session of this congress the empress gave birth to a son. This child, reserved for so tragic a doom, was born at the moment of his father's greatest prosperity (March 16, 1856).

Prussia was introduced into the Congress on the 18th of March, after the chief clauses in the treaty were settled, and only in order that she might participate in the renewal of the Convention of 1841, in which she was implicated.

The Ottoman Porte was admitted to the European union; the contracting parties promised to respect the independence and territorial integrity of the Ottoman Empire, and mutually guaranteed the strict observal of this promise. The Ottoman ambassador communicated to the contracting powers a firman from the Sultan, "the spontaneous emanation," as he said, "of his sovereign will, which bettered the condition of his subjects without distinction of religion or race, and which consecrated his solemn intentions towards the Christian peoples of his empire."

This communication forbade the powers the right to interfere, in any case, collectively or separately, with the relations between "his Majesty the Sultan" and his subjects. Thus all the privileges which Russia claimed in Turkey were suppressed, and she also lost the frontier of the Danube, which she had conquered with so much difficulty.

How remote all this seems to-day !

The treaty was signed March 30. The plenipotentiaries repaired in a body to the Tuileries, where Napoleon III. received them with proud satisfaction. France derived no positive advantage from the vast sacrifices which her emperor had exacted from her, but he had gained the power to pose as the disinterested arbiter of European affairs. He had indeed progressed since the days of Strasburg and Boulogne ! The Russian question was settled. Another question was soon to come forward.

March 27, the Piedmontese plenipotentiaries, Cavour and d'Azeglio, presented to the French and English ministers of foreign affairs a note in regard to the situation of Italy in general and the Roman provinces in special, which had been occupied by the Austrians since 1849. Cavour held several long conversations on this point with the emperor and with the English and Russian ministers.

April 8, Count Walewski proposed that the plenipotentiaries should exchange ideas upon various subjects which it would, in his opinion, be well to consider, to prevent fresh complications. He spoke of Greece, where the war in the East had naturally aroused great alarm, and which had been partially occupied by French and English ; he spoke of the Belgian press, whose license must be suppressed in the interests of European order ; he spoke of the necessity of reforming maritime law in time of war ; and finally, he spoke of a subject which stirred the congress deeply, namely, the deplorable condition of the Pontifical States and the Kingdom of Naples. It was amazing indeed to hear the government which sprang from the 2d of December pointing out the consequences of despotism at Rome or Naples. It was a strange fact, but it was an important one, when it resulted in remarks on the disadvantages of a prolonged sojourn of the Austrian troops in the Roman provinces north of the Apennines.

Lively discussions followed between Cavour and the Austrian plenipotentiaries. The French minister had opened the debate. The English minister, Lord Clarendon, took part in it, to support Cavour. The debate produced no material result, but a great moral one; for Cavour was soon enabled to inform the parliament at Turin that "the Italian question was henceforth entered upon the list of European questions."

Cavour went further still in a letter to one of his friends: "In three years," he said, "we shall have war, and a good one!" He was a prophet for his country.

The congress dissolved April 16th, after deciding upon one of the subjects broached by the French minister. The following declaration was announced: "1st, privateering is, and shall continue to be, abolished; 2d, a neutral flag shall protect hostile merchandise, save only such goods as are contraband of war; 3d, neutral merchandise, saving only that which is contraband of war, cannot be seized under the enemy's flag; 4th, blockades, to be obligatory, must be actual."

France and England, at the beginning of the war, had entered upon the path over which the other European powers now followed them. Maritime war lost its character of violence and strange depredation, and returned to the principles accepted, if not always practised, in time of battle.

The evils of war in the Crimea did not cease with its close. While the congress was settling the terms of peace, the French troops were more severely tried in the midst of truce than they would have been had hostilities continued. After a fine autumn, a winter of storms, snow, and frost ensued, even more rigorous than the previous one. During the preceding winter the excitement of danger and the ardor of combat sustained the soldier; now he gave way. The French government did not provide sufficiently for the protection of the troops from inclement weather, and the French, ill-sheltered under tents, or in a kind of loam-coated hut, now suffered far more than the English, who had abundant supplies of everything needed to keep out the cold. A terrible camp fever soon broke out, and thousands fell victims to it, at first in the Crimea, then in the hospitals at Constantinople, to which the sick were sent. Doctors and sisters of charity died with their patients. The English showed their gratitude for the past services of the French, and Protestant sisters of charity came to the aid of Catholic sisters, while Miss Nightingale's name will always be honored in history.

The scourge only ceased with the return of spring; the losses in the allied armies — especially the French — had for two years been frightful. The French counted ninety-five thousand dead, including those who died from the effects of the war up to the end of 1857, but not including the thousands who never recovered their health. Out of this enormous number, scarcely more than ten thousand perished by the enemy's sword.

The English, up to the end of the war, had lost twenty-two thousand men; the Piedmontese, twenty-two hundred; the Turks, about thirty-five thousand. The Russian losses were incalculable; they certainly far exceeded those of all the allied armies put together.

Few wars have been more horribly sanguinary; and yet there was never less hatred between the combatants. In the intervals between the battles, the French and Russian soldier cherished no ill feeling for each other, and when peace was established, visits were exchanged between them, with demonstrations not only of politeness but of friendship, as if no trace of the terrible and recent past lingered in their memory. The Russians were very sensible of the extreme kindness shown to their prisoners in France. Something similar occurred in 1814, but under less striking conditions and in smaller degree.

The Crimea was not fully evacuated until the 5th of July, 1856. Marshal Pelissier, who was the last to return to France, was greeted with enthusiasm. The Crimean conquerors were feasted everywhere, both officially and privately; as after every war, these feasts were celebrated over open graves; but now the graves were out of all proportion to ordinary numbers.

What did France win by her great efforts and her cruel losses? She recovered nothing that was taken from her in 1814 and 1815; but she recovered the glory of her arms in a great war, and the old European coalition, once more formed against her in 1840 in the cause of the Orient, was in the same cause definitely dissolved. This was a considerable gain; but did the man in power know how to profit by it? He had had the English alliance, which Louis Philippe had before him obtained for a time upon less active and less splendid conditions; but already he seemed inclined to change the basis of his foreign policy. Through all his fluctuations a general purpose, if not a plan, was apparent, which might not have been beyond the strength of France if well guided, but which exceeded the personal power of the man who had forced himself upon France. Under the present prosperity the future was big with danger.

FORTRESS OF KARS.

CHAPTER XVII.

SECOND EMPIRE (*continued*). — IDEAS AND CUSTOMS. — PUBLIC WORKS.
— THE LAW FOR GENERAL PROTECTION.

April 16, 1856 to June, 1858.

THE Crimean war was a great war, and yet it produced but a slight effect on the interior situation of France. These remote military operations, which disturbed neither the frontiers nor the merchant service, did not arrest the current of business, manufactures, or speculation. The war merely favored stock jobbing by the abrupt and violent rise and fall created by military or diplomatic tidings. Amid the sterile agitations of the Exchange and of numerous financial associations, whose principal object was to gamble in stocks and pay premiums to their founders, might be seen the gradual increase of useful and productive industries, manufacturing establishments, and railroads. Outside of France, but moved by a feeling which was thoroughly French, and in an interest both national and universal, a private citizen conceived and began to carry out, amid a thousand obstacles, a scheme which would have honored a great government. M. Ferdinand de Lesseps, that diplomat who so patriotically attempted in 1849 to put a stop to the fatal Roman war, appropriated an idea which originated with the school of St. Simon. Enfantin and his followers thought of reopening the canal by which the old Egyptian civilization once united the Mediterranean with the Red Sea, Europe with Asia. It was a question of again opening old roads to the commerce of the world, and shortening the distance between Europe, India, China, and Australia by three thousand odd miles. What others had dreamed of doing, De Lesseps resolved to do. Sentiments very different from those which

produce so many unwholesome schemes caused De Lesseps' grand
plans to be greeted with the utmost sympathy in France. Ever
since the expedition into Egypt, the French had cherished an eager interest in that cradle of civilization, that mysterious land so
triumphantly traversed by the republican troops of France, and
robbed of her secrets by French scientists. The only obstacles
came, for some time, from the nation to which the Suez Canal must
be most profitable; England had a larger interest than any other
nation in drawing nearer to India. The English finally recovered
from their prejudices against the French undertaking, and the heroic perseverance of De Lesseps triumphed over every difficulty.
The great work has now been finished for some time.

What we said just now, in regard to the slight effect produced by
the Crimean war upon domestic matters in France, must in all
probability have ceased to be true if hostilities had been prolonged
beyond the spring of 1856. The crops of grain and silk were bad,
and required the exportation of large sums of money to meet the
deficit; thence resulted a monetary crisis, which would have been
vastly more serious had it been necessary to continue the support of
a great army abroad. The increased price of food, which excited
popular complaint, was not caused solely by scanty crops; there
was another cause in the large cities, which became permanent,
that. is, the increase of taxes, which was connected with the rise
in rents. All this resulted from the destruction and reconstruction
of Paris and other ancient cities, — a regular revolution among
the ediles, to which we shall. presently return; this revolution
necessitated new sources of supply.

To the sufferings caused by a very severe winter, other evils were
added in the spring of 1856, throughout a large part of France.
The Loire, the Allier, the Rhone, the Garonne, and other rivers in
the middle and south, overflowed their banks to a frightful degree.
Parts of Lyons and other cities were submerged and partially destroyed. Still the causes of distress in 1856 did not exercise any
prolonged influence over the economic movement, partly natural,
partly factitious, which stirred the country to its depths.

The changes in Paris, begun before the war, were eagerly hastened on after its close. Napoleon III., while dreaming of vast
schemes abroad, aspired to win a renown unknown to the First Empire, by making a new Paris after Napoleon I., as Augustus and his
successors did with Rome after Cæsar. And he meant to go yet
further. He had found the man whom he needed to carry out such
a task,— M. Haussman, an extraordinarily active man, bold, most
fruitful in the invention and choice of resources, incapable of being
stopped in his onward course by any administrative scruple, and
proceeding, or rather hurrying forward, to reach the goal at any
price and by any road. M. Haussman, under the title of Prefect
of the Seine, was in fact, for several years, prime minister of Paris,
more important and more readily obeyed than any member of the
cabinet, the absolute minister of an absolute monarch.

The work was colossal; it dazzled all the noisy, restless, superficial people, greedy for spectacles and shows, — the cosmopolitan
society for whom a luxurious and superficial Paris was now created,
in accordance with popular taste.

The immensity of the enterprise and the rapidity of its realization, unexampled in history, justly excited surprise; but did they
merit admiration ? Was the work as sensible and useful as it was
amazing ?

Undoubtedly the multiplication of business relations and affairs,
the increasing needs of commerce, and a more and more active
traffic rendered indispensable the enlargement of the principal
streets and the opening of new thoroughfares in Paris; but all
bounds were exceeded: the movement was systematically hastened
on with a lawless impetuosity; the work of a century was accomplished in ten years. This caused not only a tremendous expenditure of money, but also very unfortunate moral and social
phenomena. In the old houses of Paris the various classes of society had each their own floor, and lived side by side and in harmonious relations with one another. In the luxurious buildings of
modern times there was no place for the poor to dwell with the
rich; the workman had to emigrate from the reconstructed streets

and impromptu boulevards, and seek shelter in some distant faubourg or in those suburbs which were speedily annexed to the great
city. This separation of the social groups, this rupture of kindly
relations between families of diverse rank and fortunes, was a sore
evil; even from the manufacturing point of view, it was a mistake
to drive the intelligent and ingenious Parisian citizen, who is
indeed an artist, away from the Louvre and the boulevard, away
from Parisian art and elegance, the source of his inspiration.

Another portion of the working classes seemed to gain greatly by
the increase of building on this great scale; laborers were attracted
from a distance in such numbers as had never before been known.
They received large salaries; but their morals were not improved,
nor were the true interests of social France subserved. Many lost
the habit of going back to their village every winter with the
money earned in Paris to rear up families and cultivate little farms.
The imperial government overstimulated the dangerous tendency
which urges the denizen of the country towards the town, the
dwellers in little towns towards Paris.

As regards the outward aspect of Paris, all will doubtless admit
that the picturesque appearance of the old city should make sacrifices to rapid communication and modern comfort; but here, too,
things were done without limits or bounds. That system of
straight lines was adopted which deprives towns of all individuality, and confounds them in the cold monotony of a single type,
very contrary to the principles of art. We may say, without much
exaggeration, that the Greeks would have regarded it as the work
of barbarians who had studied mathematics, but were ignorant of
the conditions of the beautiful; public hygiene scarcely profited by
the loss of picturesqueness, and was no more gratified than art, by
these endless passages, where there is nothing to break the violence
of the wind.

Buildings utterly lacking in originality, imitated from every
style, rose as if by magic along all these avenues, while old Paris
vanished stone by stone, monument after monument. It seemed as
if this potentate, without past or future, were mad to efface history.

Countless charming and varied relics of old Paris, which might easily have been used in adorning the new city, — cloisters, chapels, colleges, sculptured houses, turrets, and antique ramparts, — fell beneath hammer and axe every hour; unnumbered precious vestiges of the Middle Ages and the Renaissance, hidden within the houses, were only brought to light by the hand of the destroyer to be crushed instantly; things were demolished which could never be replaced.

What we have said of the capital is equally applicable to the greater part of the cities of France; provincial towns were eager to imitate Paris. Ruled by magistrates, the arbitrary choice of the ruling power, these towns ran in debt for foolish structures and exaggerated outlays of every kind. Let one example serve: the residence of the prefect built at Versailles was built on a scale liberal enough to allow it to be used for several years as the palace of the president of the republic.

It is needless to insist upon the moral situation of a country, but lately free, whose domestic policy was so narrow. Business, speculation and pleasure absorbed every thought, at least apparently, except for the distraction of the war, which proved as exciting as any spectacular drama witnessed from afar. No one heeded the legislative chambers; their debates were not printed, and the government was not disposed to allow either body to arouse public attention. The Senate, having shown some tendency to claim the prerogatives of the old House of Lords, was gravely admonished by the *Moniteur* not to exceed its duty (January 11, 1856).

The downfall of liberty affected the intellect as well as the soul. The standard of taste was lowered both in theatrical and in literary matters in general under the influence of the new court and its imitators. Stock-brokers and the women of a doubtful world gave the tone to society. The emperor at times affected to take a stand against the excesses of speculators, and congratulated a talented poet, Ponsard, and a magistrate, Oscar de Vallée, on having attacked them, — the one in a comedy, "Honor and Money"; the other in a book, "The Handlers of Money." But these feeble attempts were futile. Napoleon III. aimed them at his own followers, who heeded him not, and he had not the courage to persevere. Besides, although he had scientific knowledge, he did not really care either for elevated art or serious literature.

But France of the Revolution was not dead. Deep reserves still existed for the future. There were noisy protests from those in exile. Revelations in regard to the 2d of December and its results, indignant tales which could not be published in France, constantly increased outside, and passed through the frontiers in spite of the vigilance of a police system of spies. These were so many flashes of lightning, presaging a fearful clap of thunder, — the book called " Les Chatiments." The genius of Victor Hugo assumed, in this wonderful work, a new and terrible form. The great lyric poet became the great judge; the Latin satirist, Juvenal, quoted from age to age, was now surpassed: to his implacable vigor was added a grandeur of ideas and images unknown to him.

What might be called the literary school of exile not only attacked the 2d of December; it proceeded from effect to cause, and assailed the First Empire in historic and military treatises which bore the names of Edgar Quinet, Charras, and others, and a remarkable reaction, born among these exiles, entered France and took possession of her young men. It was aimed against historic fatalism and a spirit of authority. It was a movement in the opposite direction of the one which, in the time of Louis Philippe, turned the people from liberalism to socialism. The liberal reaction, in its judgment of the past, was carried to excess by many in regard to the history of France. Edgar Quinet exerted the most marked influence in this direction; he was true to himself and to that Protestant philosophy, that proud and lofty individualism, which he had always professed.

Politics thus became contraband, as it were, in that France where despotism refused them a place in open day. French thought, refusing to be stifled, worked in most contradictory directions, and considered all problems anew. A great work on religious philosophy, based on profound meditations, appeared amid these ebbing and flowing tides,—Jean Reynaud's book on " Heaven and Earth."

Here we must look back some twenty years. We have striven
to sum up the great intellectual movement stirring France in the
beginning of Louis Philippe's reign ; we have sketched the various
groups who tried to realize those ideas. None of them succeeded,
although each in its turn, produced in different degrees, a certain
effect upon the French spirit. The St. Simonites, no longer forming
an organized sect, still had considerable influence over public works
and social economy. Fourierism, after futile efforts, died out, leaving few traces behind. The Positivism of Auguste Comte was still
spreading, but it began to divide into various currents. We shall
again have occasion to refer to an illustrious adept who joined
Comte. The New Encyclopedia Group, led by Leroux and Reynaud,
was shattered in its turn, as its parent, St. Simonism, had been.
Pierre Leroux, when he parted from Reynaud, broke all bounds and
lost his balance.

Jean Reynaud, on the contrary, set free from the great work
upon which he had lavished his powers, concentrated the final results of his thought in a broad and distinct total, in the scholarly
work we have just cited. The only collective movement to be
noticed outside of the groups to which we have already alluded
occurred in the bosom of an established religion, in the Protestant
church.

The liberal Protestant school drew its inspiration alike from the
French traditions of Rousseau and from contemporary example in
America. Eminent thinkers and writers, and, at their head, one of
the greatest moralists ever produced by Christianity, one of those
who have most deeply stirred the human soul, Channing, revived
beyond the seas the evangelical spirit and Christian morals. Like
these illustrious Americans, the liberal Protestants of France sim-
plified or cast aside all dogma to cling to its moral significance ; but
at the same time, more than the Americans, they entered into that
historical movement which is one of the essential elements of our
age, and took a prudent advantage of the great works of German
critics upon the formation and phases of Christianity. They offered
a free church and an organized system of worship to those whose

wants were neither met by Catholicism nor by Protestantism called Orthodox.

Liberal Protestantism, represented by a number of most respectable and meritorious men, has lived and thrived among French Protestants, although it has never made any great headway with the masses. Edgar Quinet and many other thinkers regarded it as an attempt to encourage and possibly shelter France in the long storm through which she is passing and which they foresaw.

We must now return to the struggle between the two currents of which we have recently spoken. The counter-current, which opposed all return to the past, was excited by inspirations quite contrary to the essentially theoretic and almost mystical spirit of the sects of 1830; it was, above all, a passionate reaction against the overflowing Jesuitism and hypocrisy of the empire. Public opinion was a prey to vast vacillations; the imperial régime deprived it of all equilibrium. Anti-religious tendencies spread in proportion as the people saw the Catholic church given over to the Jesuits, once more spiritual masters of Pius IX. Intoxicated with their success, the Jesuits were now more irritating and less able, in certain respects, than heretofore. We do not speak of their morals; their casuistry had not changed, as is proved by their books and by certain bishops who unreservedly adopted their maxims; but their policy was modified to the extent of making their attacks upon the spirit of the age less open than previously. They altered the character of Catholic Christianity more and more, to make it their tool, their property. On the one hand, they urged the Pope to destroy every trace of national tradition in the churches, everywhere substituting by force the Roman liturgy for those beautiful antique local liturgies to which former generations had been for ages attached; and on the other hand, they exaggerated the worship of the Virgin until they made it a new religion and threw the divine worship completely into shadow.

Pius IX. had latterly proclaimed a new dogma, the Immaculate Conception, concerning which he consulted the bishops individually, but assembled no council. It declared the Mother of Christ exempt from original sin, and placed her above humanity, as intermediary between God and man. This idea, long argued in the church, had indeed been accepted by the most illustrious theologians of the last centuries, such as Bossuet, for example, although the greatest doctors of the Middle Ages, like St. Bernard, rejected it. The proclamation of the Immaculate Conception was celebrated everywhere with strange solemnity; an image unknown to past generations rose on every hand, on votive columns, church domes, and high altars. It was no longer the Madonna, the mother and child, a representation consecrated by traditional piety and immortalized in art; it was the image of a woman with shining hands, not bearing the infant in her arms, but treading underfoot the world orb.

These novelties would have greatly amazed the old Gallican church; but if they altered the basis, at least they did not lower the form of worship. The same could not be said for the things which accompanied and followed them, — those inventions of devotion recalling paganism, which the Gallican church would have condemned with severity, and one of which, the Sacred Heart, was condemned by one of the most eminent bishops of the last century. The Jesuits replaced Christian spirituality by a species of devout materialism which adored in Jesus Christ, not the spirit, the divine love, but the physical organ, the bloody heart!

Miracles were next required to stir imagination, still capable of being conquered in such fashion. In 1846 two little shepherd boys pretended that they had seen a beautiful lady bathed in light, upon the mountain of Saletto in Dauphiny. She announced that all the crops would rot or wither if the people did not repent, which made a great excitement. Some of the local clergy accepted the "miracle," which the Bishop of Grenoble loudly sanctioned. Other ecclesiastics, struck by the childish details of the story and the more than vulgar language which the children attributed to the vision, rejected the pretended prodigy. Even the Pope at first spoke very scornfully of the affair, and a priest in the diocese of Grenoble accused an ex-nun, named De Lamerlière, of playing the part of the Virgin. This lady brought a suit for libel, but was condemned to pay the costs (1855).

If it were not proved that this lady actually appeared on the mountain, it is at least certain that she boasted of doing so, which may be explained by her eccentricity, which almost amounted to madness.

It may seem as if the new forms of devotion could not have survived these trials and the commentaries upon them. Not so. Saletto triumphed, like the Sacred Heart. The Jesuits saw what profit they could derive from it, and, skilfully aided by the ultramontane press, they imposed Saletto upon the bishops and the Pope. The fame of the spring close by the spot where the vision appeared is widespread.

The Pyrenees soon entered into competition with the Apennines. A few years later (in 1858), a young peasant girl also fancied that she saw a beautiful lady in the hollow of a rock on the bank of the Gare, near Lourdes. Her imagination was fired; she saw vision after vision, and then retired to a convent. Her good faith is not to be doubted; but neither can we doubt that her nervous, sickly temperament predisposed her to hallucinations. The grotto of Lourdes soon attracted as many pilgrims as the fountain of Saletto, and nothing was talked of but visions and miraculous cures. The most striking thing in all these pretended revelations is the poverty of invention and total absence of that mystic poetry which formerly ennobled the aspirations of ecstatics.

Such was the path into which the most ignorant portion of the people were led; such was the pitfall into which stumbled a great part of those upper classes who had compounded with the Jesuits since 1848, and who could not stop their mad career upon the brink of the gulf whither they were urged by dread of progress and intellectual fears. Extreme credulity produced, as was inevitable, extreme negation, the angry negation of those who do not believe in anything because others believe in everything. Doubtless, the people as a whole did not go to this extreme, but the majority of the peasants were as opposed to the Jesuit spirit as the townspeople.

In the lettered classes opposition to ultramontane invasion took various forms. German Hegelianism, a species of negative idealism, ran riot; according to this system, God was but an idea, and man a phenomenon, and the universe was but a series of phenomena in endless succession!

Other groups cast aside all idealism and metaphysics. Side by side with the positivist school, existed the school of independent morals: these were two distinct groups, but closely allied. The followers of the latter school claimed that morals were utterly independent of religion and metaphysics and all conception of man's destiny after death. They were right in maintaining that the moral principle is separable in thought from any other principle, but they erred in failing to see that this was a mere abstraction.

As for positivism, the discords which began, in Comte's lifetime, burst out after his death, in regard to the proper interpretation of his idea and the direction to be given to his school. Comte, as we said elsewhere, desired to found a religion in which God was to be replaced by humanity.

The positivists were soon fortunate enough to be joined by an illustrious scholar and writer, endowed with those literary talents which were denied to their founder. The doctrines of Auguste Comte owe much of their renown to Littré, who clothed them in the eloquent language which he uses with such force and perspicuity. M. Littré shed upon positivism some of the lustre of his personal fame, acquired by so many achievements, from the translation of Hippocrates, which inaugurated his laborious career, to the huge dictionary of the French language by which he crowned it. But all Littré's merits could not impart to positivism what it lacked. This doctrine is condemned not alone by feeling, to which it vainly appeals, but by reason, whose rights it denies by claiming to close the world of ideas to it in the name of experience and phenomenal observation. "Positivism," says Littré, "substitutes the study of the world for the study of man."

Another writer of the first order now appeared: M. Renan's talent was revealed in works where the most brilliant literary style adorned a foundation of broad and bold erudition. Before publishing the book which made his name famous, the "Life of Jesus"

(1863), he had already shown himself to be one of the most richly dowered natures in the literary annals of France. He was at once a learned linguist, a clever and incisive critic, a marvellous artist of varied grades ; he was a historian and a philosopher; he was several great men in one : but were these different minds, and especially the historian and the philosopher, always and everywhere in harmony ?

The historian entered eagerly into the true philosophy of history. A German school, whose chief work was Strauss's " Life of Jesus," desired to destroy all great historic figures, and show nothing in history save the force of things acting independently of human liberty and will, and a sort of unconscious vegetation of society. Edgar Quinet had already stoutly battled with this system, upon the publication of Strauss's book. Renan opposed his own " Life of Jesus" to that of the German scholar, and refuted that dead science by the living science which animates all that it touches, and resuscitates the great figures of the past, instead of dissolving them in a thick fog. Strauss made Jesus a vain shadow; he deprived him of all action, all real life. Renan restored the " Son of Man," living, radiating light and love among the men who yielded to the irresistible power of his person and his word.

Such was Renan the historian. Does the philosopher continue, in the world of ideas, the work accomplished by the historian in the world of facts ?

There, too, he reacts against brutal negations and dry and narrow rationalism ; his religious feeling is expressed in almost mystical forms. Then why does the alluring charm of his narrative and his unequalled portraiture leave behind it so vague and troublous an impression ? Because the life and personality with which the historian endows his historic characters, the philosopher takes away from man considered in himself, in his essence. He rejects, at least impliedly, all affirmations both of positive religion and of positive philosophy. In him we really return to Hegel's negative idealism, according to which man is a phenomenon and God an idea, — a necessary idea, it is true, an idea which pervades and animates the actual world, but not the Supreme *Being*.

The author of the "Life of Jesus" believes in the Son of Man upon earth.   He does not believe, in the words of Jesus, in "Our Father which art in heaven."   Nor does he believe in the personality of man prolonged beyond the earth in heavenly spheres.   And yet, if the being *is* not, if life is an empty dream, what is the use of history?   Is life worth living?

No one has asked this terrible question with greater anxiety than Renan.   He sometimes jests with it to escape from it, but it always seizes hold of him again.   We said that he did not believe in the Father, — he does not believe in the living God, and yet at times he invokes him ; his heart struggles against his abstract conception, and he cries aloud to God.

We might add that a system of philosophy which sees nothing but phenomena about it is something quite inconceivable.   A phenomenon is an act.   There is no act without a being who acts. There was something before the phenomenon which will be after it and which produced it.   Every phenomenon is the manifestation of a being.   If the external man is a phenomenon, like everything which is composite, beneath this apparition lies the real man, the being one and simple, conscious of its own existence, the formative principle of the composite being.

M. Renan's Hegelian idealism and the religious sentiment which he preserved while he suppressed the object of religion, were no more acceptable to the materialists than spiritualism and the doctrine of the indestructibility of individuality.   Materialism spread widely, partly proceeding from a violent reaction against religious bigotry, but there were other causes also.   Philosophical studies began to die out in the latter years of the reign of Louis Philippe, when De Salvandy was at the head of public instruction, and the extraordinary progress of the natural sciences absorbed the majority of active minds, turning them away from metaphysical and moral investigations.   Not content to neglect metaphysics, they denied their existence, as if to get rid of the whole matter, as if the suppression of general ideas — that first philosophy, as Descartes called it, which gave science its principles and methods — could be very advantageous to science.

It is easy to understand how the marvellous progress of physics, of astronomy and physiology, might fascinate an entire generation. By decomposing with the prism the luminous rays of the heavenly bodies, and searching out therein the colors which stand for the various minerals and metals of the earth, we can prove the affinity of composition between our world and spheres remote in the heavens, at immeasurable distances from our solar system. The identity of composition in the universe seems revealed to us, like its infinity.

Nor are the discoveries limited to our earth, less startling to the thinker or less captivating to the mind of the multitude. Electricity annihilates distance; is it not a miracle far beyond any achievement attributed to magic, to receive in Europe a letter from America almost at the moment of its writing? So too spoken words will soon be transmitted, if not to the ends of the earth, at least to very great distances; next, our words and our songs will be stored up and drawn upon at will to echo in the ears of our descendants.

Physiology, the science which studies the human body and the functions of its organs, meantime made similar giant strides in the "Little World," as the old philosophers called man, advancing as rapidly as did astronomy and physics in the "Great World" of the universe.

We have neither time nor ability to detail the great labors and discoveries of the leading French physiologists; the greatest were snatched from us in the prime of life, leaving eminent successors behind them. We will only say that what was essayed with ingenious daring, but without success, by the Germans, Gall and Spurzheim, Frenchmen have realized. They have fixed and localized the functions of the brain, and the different nervous centres governed by the brain, that supreme centre of human life. We cannot do better than refer our readers to the illustrious author of "Experimental Science," and many other immortal works, to Claude Bernard, who has followed to the tomb Paul Broca, the creator of anthropology. In his academic eulogy upon his predecessor, Flourens, Bernard defines the science of all his school.

In the preceding pages we have tried to give the picture of a period important in the world of ideas, a period which still lasts at the time we write; we must now go back to political history, which was destined to pass through many phases before it reached the downfall of the empire.

We have said that the legislative discussions had little interest for the people; it was nevertheless inevitable that some of them should refer to questions of great importance to the future of the nation. The tendency of Napoleon III. was to modify the protective system, and to make commercial relations with foreign countries easier of establishment; as his alliance with England was already less close, and as, however, he was determined to keep up kindly relations with her, he schemed to strengthen by commerce, ties which might be less firm from a political standpoint. The protectionist interest still prevailed in the legislative body as it did in the time of Louis Philippe, and there were loud protests against the acceptance of any more liberal views. But the emperor, having questioned general councils and chambers of commerce, and appointed a special commission to study the subject, announced, through the *Moniteur*, that all prohibitions would be removed on and after July 1, 1861. He thus gave the French manufacturing interest due warning and ample time to prepare for the change. Yet Napoleon III. did not wait until 1861 to go far beyond the scheme of the law of 1856.

During the legislative session of 1856 the Prince Imperial was baptized at Notre Dame with great pomp and ceremony. Pius IX., represented by a Roman Cardinal, was godfather. This intimate alliance with the Pope was to trammel the imperial policy in a matter of great importance.

The session of 1856 – 57 presented certain points worthy of remark. A contingent of one hundred thousand men was voted for the following year, this being twenty thousand more than had been called for on similar occasions before the war. The budget for 1857 exceeded that of 1856 by one hundred and six million francs. The war had increased the annual income by nearly seventy-two million francs.

Great attention was paid to agriculture this year, large sums being devoted to draining swamp lands, etc. A subsidy of fourteen millions was granted for three lines of steamships between France and America, and the railroad between Paris and Lyons was connected with that from Lyons to the Mediterranean. Great scandals now arose on the subject of railroads. M. de Morny, who always had a hand in every speculation, put himself at the head of a company dubbed the Grand Central, which was to build a line from Clermont to Montauban. Stock-jobbers ran the shares up to a high price on the Exchange, before the road was even built; and then the company failed, the road being finally taken up on mutual account by the Orleans and Lyons-Mediterranean companies.

The year 1857 opened with an event which produced a gloomy effect. January 3, the Archbishop of Paris was stabbed, in the church of St. Etienne du Mont, by a derelict and half-crazy priest, called Vergès. As he struck the prelate, he cried, "Down with all goddesses!" which he explained, at his trial, to be an allusion to the Immaculate Conception. Unfortunately Archbishop Sibour was not the last archbishop of Paris who died a tragic death; his predecessor perished in the civil war; his successor was fated to die by an act of nameless barbarity.

The powers of the legislative body elected in 1852, if powers we can call them, expired in 1857. Needless to say that official candidature was immediately practised in its fullest extent by the prefects. Billault, the minister of the interior, issued a circular declaring that "the government considered it just and politic to present for re-election the members of an assembly which had so well seconded the emperor and served the country." He admitted that other candidates might possibly be brought forward; "but if," he added, "enemies of the public peace fancy that they can make this latitude the occasion of a serious protest against our institutions, if they attempt to turn it into an instrument of trouble and scandal, all prefects know their duty, and justice will also sternly execute hers."

The prefects far outdid the minister, and the poor peasants said naïvely, "What is the use of our voting? The government might just as well choose its own deputies!"

The opposition party had no chance to gain the majority from the government, although many protests were made. A newspaper, almost the solitary survivor of the republican press, now acquired a great importance, and worked in a contrary direction. Lively discussions ensued in regard to the line which should be pursued by republicans. Louis Blanc wrote a letter from London, advising them to present themselves for election, and then publicly refuse to take the oath and protest against the empire in the legislative body. The editor of the *Siècle*, ex Deputy Havin, had saved his paper by skilfully worded concessions, and now urged all republicans to enter the legislature to attack the prevailing system and particularly to reclaim public liberty. A committee composed of eminent republican members of the Assemblies of 1848 and 1849 took the same ground, with the proviso that each man should be allowed to decide for himself in the matter of the oath.

The elections took place June 20. The opposition gained five out of the eight deputies from Paris, — Carnot, Goudchaux, Cavaignac, Ollivier, and Darimon; the latter was editor of the *Press*, the rival of the *Siècle*, and had been the assistant of Prudhon. Two republicans were chosen at Lyons and Bordeaux. A struggle would have been almost impossible in the provinces, but a strong minority, often even a majority, sided with the opposition in the large towns.

About the time of the elections the imperial government gained a diplomatic triumph. It prevented the outburst of war between Prussia and Switzerland in regard to the canton of Neufchâtel. This little district, since the treaties of 1815, had been in the peculiar situation of being at once a Swiss canton, member of a federal republic, and a Prussian principality, the royal house of Prussia having reclaimed its ancient rights of feudal heredity to Neufchâtel. The canton was set free from Prussian sovereignty in favor of the revolution of 1848, and in 1856 the royalist party in Neufchâtel unsuccessfully tried a counter-revolution. Switzerland seemed ready to wage a very unequal warfare rather than to give up Neufchâtel, and the Prussian king, at the request of France and the other great powers, finally gave up his claim to his former principality, on condition that the royalist insurgents of 1856 should go scot free.

The latter half of the year 1857 witnessed the death of three illustrious men. July 15, died the poet who celebrated liberty and the great emperor alike, and battled with old monarchy in the name of new France, and clericalism in the name of the *God of all good people*. Béranger's vast popularity was somewhat dimmed after the Empire was restored, on account of that very restoration; the most ardent friends of lost liberty held him responsible, in a greater measure than was just, for what was the fault of France and not of any one man. The people of Paris would nevertheless have followed with sympathy and regret the funeral of the poet whose verses they had so often repeated; but the imperial police, ever suspicious of evil, kept off the crowd by lines of soldiers, and gave a thoroughly official character to the funeral of a man who had held official ceremonies in horror all his life.

Two months later, Daniel Manin, the defender of Venice, died in Paris. The misfortunes of his country and his family broke his heart. He did not live to see the liberation of Italy, for which he did so much by persuading the majority of Italian patriots to rally round Victor Emanuel.

October 28, General Cavaignac joined the melancholy procession. He, too, was carried off by a heart disease,—a fate too common with men who have endured great moral sufferings; his brief political career left a marked impression on the pages of French history.

The legislative session reopened, November 28. One of the five republican deputies for Paris, Cavaignac, was dead; two again refused to take the oath, Carnot and Goudchaux, while Ollivier and Darimon agreed to it. The Lyonnese deputy, Hénon, was elected in 1852, as were Carnot and Goudchaux, and had refused the oath, as they did. He now declared that, his electors having chosen him, not to linger on the threshold of the Assembly, but to cross it, he would accept the formula of the oath, although his opinions were in no way changed.

It seemed as if nothing remarkable would happen in this session, when a tragic event suddenly agitated all minds and made serious changes in the situation.   On the evening of January 14, as the emperor and empress reached the opera-house, three loud explosions were heard.   Three bombs had been fired at the royal carriage. Cries of pain and terror were heard on every hand ; fragments of the shells injured more than one hundred and forty persons, some being fatally wounded.   The emperor's carriage was shattered, and one of the horses killed.   Terrible anxiety pervaded the assembly at the opera, until the emperor and empress appeared in the front of their box ; both had escaped uninjured.

The police arrested four Italians, three of whom proved to be mere subordinate accomplices ; the fourth, Orsini, was a remarkable person in many respects.   His father was killed in 1831, in that insurrection against the Pope in which the elder brother of Napoleon III., as well as he himself, took part.   The son, from his earliest youth, had taken part in all the Italian national conspiracies.   Long a prisoner, sentenced to the galleys for life, then pardoned by Pius IX., he became a member of the Roman Constituent Assembly in 1848 ; captured by the Austrians in the Marches, and imprisoned in the citadel at Mantua, he escaped with marvellous skill and audacity.   Taking refuge in England, he at first hoped that Napoleon III. would set Italy free ; but seeing him ally himself more and more closely with the Pope and with reaction, he resolved to destroy him, as he was an obstacle and not an assistance.   He confided his plan only to the very few agents required for its execution, the affair being managed so secretly that Napoleon III. only escaped by a lucky chance.

The attempt, in its form, recalls that of Fieschi upon Louis Philippe ; but there was, in reality, a vast abyss between the Corsican bandit of 1835 and the Roman conspirator of 1858.   In spite of the horror of a crime which advanced to its end through so many unknown victims, Orsini inspired in all who saw and heard him during his trial an interest which they could not resist.   He acted from impersonal passion and under the impulse of misguided patriot-

ism only. He chose as his lawyer, Jules Favre, who defended him
as he wished to be defended, trying to save, not his head, but his
memory as far as it might be spared. A deep impression was produced on the audience, when Jules Favre, by the emperor's permission, read a letter addressed to the monarch by Orsini. The guilty
man did not ask pardon for himself; he implored the freedom of his
unhappy country, "the constant object of his affection." He did
not go so far as to ask that French blood should be shed for the
Italians, but merely that France should forbid Germany to uphold
Austria "in struggles which may soon come to light. I conjure
your Majesty," he wrote, "to restore to Italy the independence which
her children lost in 1849, through the error of the French [by the
Roman war]. Do not, your Majesty, reject the last prayer of a
patriot upon the steps of the gallows!"

Orsini and his accomplices were condemned to death, February
26. Orsini thanked the emperor for permitting the publication of
his letter, his second epistle being quite as affecting as the first. He
solemnly condemned political assassination, and disclaimed "the
fatal aberration of mind" which led him to plan his crime. He exhorted his countrymen to use no weapons but abnegation, devotion,
unity and virtue, to free their land. As for himself, he offered his
blood as an atonement to the victims of January 24.

The question of a commutation of his punishment was loudly
agitated in imperial circles, and Napoleon III. might have deemed
such clemency politic, if so many victims had not suffered from the
instruments of death directed against his person. Orsini was executed, March 13, with one of his accomplices. He died quietly but
courageously, crying, "Long live Italy! Long live France!"

His death soon bore happy fruits in Italy. His crime had previously borne sad ones for France. In 1801 the First Consul, taking the infernal machine prepared by the royalists as a pretext,
proscribed numbers of republicans. Napoleon III. imitated and
outdid his uncle.

On the reopening of the Legislature, some days after Orsini's attack (January 18), the emperor made a speech which opened with

a splendid picture of the public prosperity, commercial, financial, and religious. "Abroad, our relations with foreign powers were never better; old and new allies [England and Russia] display equal confidence and equal good-will."

The close of the speech ill responded to these pompous premises. Returning to his domestic policy, Napoleon declared that the Empire accepted all that was good of the great principles of 1780, but that unlimited liberty was impossible while a portion of the people persisted in misunderstanding the fundamental basis of the government. "The danger," he added, "whatever may be said, no longer lies in the excessive prerogatives of power, but rather in the absence of repressive laws."

He requested the legislative body to see that "the scandal" of the refusal to take the oath by candidates elect was never repeated, and to pass a law obliging all eligible parties to swear allegiance to the Constitution before standing for office. He then appealed to "the representatives of the country to assist him in searching out means for reducing factious opposition to silence."

The meaning of this threat was soon made clear. February 1, a scheme for a new law was laid before the Legislature: it punished with imprisonment and heavy fines all who should attempt to stir up sedition or insurrection, or who were so much as suspected of such act.

Any one sentenced as guilty of any such crime was liable to be exiled from France. The same precaution for the general safety could be applied to all who were condemned on the occasion of the events of May and June, 1848, or of December, 1851, and whom "important facts seemed to prove again dangerous to public welfare."

A vast number of citizens were thus given over to the most lawless arbitration; the length of the list and the vagueness of the definition allowing of any license. A man might easily be transported simply for having a shot-gun in his possession!

The impression made upon the public was yet more sinister when the name of the man who was to execute this law was made known. One would think that Billault, the minister of the interior, who had

been by turns liberal, republican, and socialist, had given the empire
sufficient proofs of his unscrupulousness. But not so. The most
disreputable of the executors of December 2, General Espinasse, was
sought out; he had continued his odious rôle of the night of the
coup d'état, at home and abroad, and Napoleon III. now made him
minister of the interior, giving him an office which never before fell
to such vile hands (February 7).

The new minister speedily issued a circular letter to the prefects,
declaring that the late frightful attempt to murder the emperor
plainly arose in the bosom of the republican party, etc.

The government knew perfectly well that the republican party
had nothing to do with Orsini's crime; but this calumny seemed
requisite in view of what was to follow.

Morny, who was both president of the Legislature and reporter
of this law, hypocritically protested against the title, "law of suspicion," which the people gave to this strange scheme, and loudly
praised the tolerance and moderation of the government. Émile
Ollivier made his début as a public speaker in opposition to the
scheme, and was joined by some few conservatives, alarmed at this
return to December 2 in time of perfect peace.

Baroche, the president of the council of state, replied by the declaration "that the exaggerated respect paid to the scruples of
jurists and systematic tolerance had brought two successive governments to the revolutions of 1830 and 1848. . . . The Empire will
not imitate such weakness!"

So, then, Charles X. fell because he paid too much respect to the
scruples of legal men! This explanation of the Revolution of 1830
at least had the merit of novelty!

It was not the peculiar arguments of the rhetoricians of the empire that determined the vote, assured in advance to anything which
the ruling powers demanded. Many deputies voted reluctantly and
with blushes; only twenty-four ventured to vote against it; and
when it was carried to the Senate, there was but one dissenting
voice, that of General MacMahon. History should set it down to
his account.

The law was a monstrous one; its execution was even worse.
The new Terror of 1858 was less noisy than that of December 2: as
resistance was impossible, there were no massacres; but the absence
of all struggle and all danger for the persecutors made the persecu-
tion yet more revolting.   Long before the law was presented to the
Legislature, citizens were carried off and sent into exile; after the
law was passed, its executors did not confine themselves to the large
category which gave them such latitude; they might have dispensed
with making a law, but the plan was to compromise the legislative
body in this work of tyranny.

Immediately after the despatch of his circular letter, the new
minister of the interior, "and of the public surety," as he dubbed
himself, summoned all the prefects to Paris.   He received each
separately, and said, "You are prefect of such a department, — so
many arrests!" — "But who shall I arrest?" asked the prefect. —
"Whoever you like!   I have given you the number; the rest is
your affair."

Perhaps it is the most shameful fact in eighty years of revolutions, that so many high officials consented to carry out such orders.
The courageous author of "December 2 in Paris," and "December 2
in the Provinces," M. Eugène Ténot, in connection with Antonin
Dubost, published, before the downfall of Napoleon III., a book upon
"The Men Suspected in 1858," where this ignominious episode of
the Second Empire should be studied in detail.   With a few political opponents still capable of and disposed to action, countless republicans were arrested, who sought nothing but oblivion and were
content to work and be silent.   Old men, invalids, and the mothers
of families were dragged to prison or sent recklessly into exile.
They were taken at hap-hazard, for Espinasse and his delegates must
make up their number.   Out of about two thousand persons arrested, more than four hundred and thirty were sent to Africa,
where they received a wretched subsidy until such time as they
could find work, and those unable to work were left to depend on
their companions, little less wretched than they.

The object of the new Terror was not attained: the opposition party was not stifled, but, on the contrary, it grew in the legislative body, if not in numbers, at least in talent; the Parisian electors filled two of the three empty deputyships with republicans,—Jules Favre, whose admirable plea for Orsini won him popular favor; and Ernest Picard, a young lawyer, whose active and alert intellect and brilliant eloquence predestined him to success on the side of the opposition (April 27 – May 10). Jules Favre and Picard formed, with Ollivier, Hénon, and Darimon, that celebrated bench of "five" who for several years held their ground against almost a whole Assembly.

Amid this quasi-unanimity of the imperialists in the Legislature, there were many members who would have asked nothing better than to put some limits to their devotion, and who did not feel that all was working for the best. The law in regard to discharge from military service came up again during the session of 1858. It was proved that this law had only aggravated the burden of the service to the injury of the people and the benefit of the public treasury; but instead of improving the law, it was made still more onerous by the interdiction of all substitution, save between relations. As usual, there was an effort to resist; then the Assembly yielded. Not all the members of the majority were caught by the painted deception which the emperor waved before them in his opening speech. Some few made an attempt to restore financial equilibrium by suppressing supplementary credit and reducing the ordinary expenses. Deputy Devinck proposed to cut down the expenses of the ministerial department, which had increased eighty million francs in four years. Vain hope! The legislative body could only have rejected the budget of a minister as a whole. This was scarcely likely; so no heed was paid to these suggestions.

The government next presented a law inflicting penalties upon all usurpers of titles of nobility. Napoleon III. had restored the nobility by a decree declaring it to be one of the institutions of the state. A curious discussion ensued on this subject in the Legislature, and the law passed triumphantly.

A law in regard to public works in Paris was then presented.

NEMOURS.

The Louvre was finished and solemnly inaugurated on July 14, 1857,
after which work was begun upon the great roads intersecting Paris
in every direction, at an enormous expense. On this occasion resistance gained ground, the provincial deputies being jealous that
such sums of money should be expended on Paris, and there were
forty-five votes against the law.

Just at this time an incident, not directly political, brought about
the downfall of the strange minister of the interior and of "general
surety." Espinasse had issued a circular inviting all charitable institutions to convert their real estate into government annuities, to the
value of about five hundred million francs, which would only yield
them about 2½ per cent interest. The trustees of the various hospitals were greatly agitated; many resigned, and the clergy, to
whom the empire granted great influence in hospital matters, protested loudly. The emperor yielded, and replaced Espinasse by a
certain magistrate named Delangle (June 14). Perhaps Napoleon
III. even then began to understand, if not the immorality, at least
the absurdity of the new Terror, and willingly took this opportunity
to rid himself of far too compromising a servant.

About the same time (June 24), the emperor created the ministry
of Algeria and its colonies for his cousin, Napoleon Jerome. Although loyal to the empire, Prince Napoleon caused great annoyance by the license of his language, by his anti-clerical and
quasi-revolutionary tirades, and the emperor was not sorry to provide employment for him. The prince's busy spirit soon suggested
innovations which were not unprofitable in that region where there
was so much to be done. French dominion was gradually strengthening and spreading in Algeria. Great Kabylia, into which St.
Arnaud had made but one expedition, had been brought by General
Randon to submit to roads and fortresses in the mountainous region
of Djurdjura. The Kabyles, an energetic and industrious people,
whose customs are more like those of European countries than those
of the Arabs, soon made strong laborers, and patient, excellent soldiers, popular in France under the name of Turcos. France constantly recognized more and more the necessity of attaching these

descendants of ancient African civilization to her cause by equitable treatment.

From this year, 1858, dates the notable increase of French territory in Senegal, due to the military success and skilful administration of Colonel Faidherbe, who thoroughly appreciated the future importance of African settlements.

The two years which had elapsed since the conclusion of peace with Russia had produced no very noteworthy events in France, except the sad and odious episode of the transportations of 1858. As we have said, ever since the beginning of the empire, we must look abroad for the great interests of the epoch, and it is there that great historic events continued to occur. The following chapter will show the origin and outburst of the second war waged by Napoleon III.

CHAPTER XVIII.

SECOND EMPIRE (*continued*). — FOREIGN POLICY OF NAPOLEON III. — ITALIAN WAR. — MAGENTA AND SOLFERINO. — PEACE OF VILLA-FRANCA.

May, 1856, to July, 1859.

AFTER the peace with Russia, Napoleon III. could not continue the Crimean war, nor did he wish to do so, as it gave him but a negative advantage, that of having broken up the old coalition of European monarchies. He now aspired to use the results of this success for the aggrandizement of the empire and the reparation of the reverses of Napoleon I. With this motive, he had recourse to every means and studied every chance; he wavered between the most contradictory opinions and combinations, and still one general idea towered above this confused medley in his mind.

Napoleon I. at St. Helena gave himself up to a retrospective policy; he, who in the day of his power trampled underfoot every nationality and moulded whole peoples like inert matter, after his fall fancied that his only desire had been to arouse and rebuild the nations as the basis of a new Europe.

Louis Napoleon, in his book upon the "Napoleonic Ideas," published in 1839, took this fancy seriously and laid claim to it as his inheritance from his uncle, adding to the principle of nationality the principle of universal suffrage. This idea, single and double, was in the air, and summed up the modern conception of the right of nations: it was great and just. Had this idea been embraced by a statesman of strong and honest conscientiousness, of clear and practical mind, and of a sufficient power of action, it might have regenerated Europe; but all these qualities and faculties were lacking in a man who was deceit itself, who was incapable of giving a definition or of executing anything from a clear head and moral conviction, and who was destined to compromise the best causes when he laid his unsteady hand upon them. The inconsequence and the contradictions which Napoleon III. brought to bear upon the application of the principle which he had seized without comprehending it, were soon but too plainly evident.

We have already shown that the first thought of Napoleon III., was to act in the direction of Poland. Neither Austria nor England lending their sanction, he began to approach Russia and Piedmont, that is, Italy. Moreover, when he sounded Austria, he hoped to settle the Italian question together with the Polish question, by urging Austria towards the Orient.

After the peace, still continuing his attentions to Russia, he tried to keep up his friendly relations with England. In May, 1857, he made overtures to the English minister of foreign affairs, Lord Clarendon, for a close alliance between France, England, and Russia, to the exclusion of Austria. This project was coldly received. The queen's husband, Prince Albert of Saxe-Coburg, a very prudent and thoughtful person, who quietly took a great interest in matters of state, though with great regard to appearances, was much opposed to any change in Europe. He had written to Napoleon III., in April, 1857, dissuading him from his new tendencies, on the occasion of a visit to Paris of the Grand Duke Constantine, brother of the Czar of Russia.

Napoleon III. directed his advances not only to Russia, but to Prussia. After the Russian prince, a Prussian prince came to Paris; this was Frederic William, nephew of the king and son of that Prince William in whose name a Prussian statesman afterwards destroyed the empire of Napoleon III. and built up the German Empire.

Prince Napoleon was sent to Berlin to return this visit to the royal house of Prussia.

It was thought, in imperial circles, that some compensation should be offered England for these continental relations. The Duke de

Persigny, as the former non-commissioned officer Fialin was now called, a great partisan of the English alliance, persuaded Napoleon to make another visit to the Queen of England. Victoria received the emperor and empress at Osborne, in the Isle of Wight (August, 1857). Empress Eugénie became a great favorite with the queen, who appeared greatly charmed with her guests during their few days of intimacy. Napoleon tried to seize this opportunity to touch upon international policy with the queen's husband, and brought up the question of revising the treaties of 1815. Prince Albert protested against it, and the emperor insisted, assuring him that he meant to arrange all contingencies with England.

He however dashed into another scheme, and talked of making great changes not only in Europe, but on the non-European shores of the Mediterranean. He proposed to give Morocco to Spain, Tripoli to the King of Sardinia, Egypt to England, and part of Syria to Austria; then he came back to Europe, and suggested a Scandinavian alliance, the union in a single state of Denmark, Sweden, and Norway, taking Holstein from the King of Denmark to bestow it on Prussia.

Prince Albert replied that Holstein had no desire to become Prussian, and only asked that her union with Schleswig, which had been guaranteed to her, should continue.

This was true of the Germans, but not of the Danes in Schleswig, who would never prefer union with a German duchy to alliance with the Danish kingdom. These words from the husband of the queen proved that he remained a German.

Nor were the overtures of Napoleon III. directly concerning England any better received.

Prince Albert, and also Lord Palmerston, when he learned of the conversation at Osborne, proved little sensible to the offer of Egypt. England, according to Lord Palmerston, had no interest in that country, save as it assured her free passage to India. Lord Palmerston had grown very cold to the ally of England, since the latter had ceased to be content to act as his passive instrument.

The emperor had only half revealed his purpose, and had not explained what he hoped to gain for France. Not only had he kept silent in regard to the frontier of the Rhine; but when he offered positions on the Mediterranean so freely, he never mentioned Tunis, which was plainly, to his thinking, France's portion. It was a singular oversight to let his plans be guessed in this way without giving a word of explanation, and to touch upon everything without going to the root of anything. Napoleon III. was no further advanced when he left England than when he entered it, and he left a disagreeable impression upon the coldly positive spirit of Prince Albert, who saw in him only the stuff for a conspirator, not for a statesman.

The interview with the Queen of England was followed by a meeting with the Emperor of Russia, whom Napoleon joined beyond the Rhine, at the court of Würtemberg, at Stuttgart (September). Every one was cordial, but nothing was settled, although the Russian minister of foreign affairs, Prince Gortchakof, seemed satisfied. A remark attributed to Alexander II. shows that there was a limit to the cordiality displayed at Stuttgart. "He dared to talk to me of Poland!" the Czar is said to have exclaimed.

Meantime England was drawing closer to Prussia; one of Queen Victoria's daughters married that nephew of the King of Prussia who had recently visited Paris.

"The fair days of the English alliance," as a remarkable essay upon diplomatic history expresses it (*Revue des Deux Mondes*), had already passed. Still, Napoleon III. had been a friendly ally to England on an important occasion, the revolt of the Indian Cipayes. In the course of the year 1857 the Indian troops in the service of England revolted almost in a body, and exposed the English government in India to the utmost danger.

In spite of the courage and military skill displayed by the English generals, England would probably have lost the Indian Empire, if the valorous tribe of Sikhs, lately annexed to English India, had joined the insurgents. This warlike tribe of the Upper Indus, whom England had treated most considerately, was faithful to her, and the great Indian insurrection was drowned in rivers of blood. Napoleon III. made not the slightest attempt to benefit by England's trouble.

PALACE OF THE INSTITUTE

The Orsini affair for a moment threw the emperor out of his friendly attitude, and came near bringing about a startling rupture. In the first moment of bewilderment after the attack, the whole official world rang with furious clamors against England, who "allowed all these plots to be hatched in her bosom." This was a strange reproof from men whose master planned his Boulogne expedition in England. And yet the leaders of the great state bodies and the bodies corporate, following in their wake, harped upon this string, regardless of their inconsistency. Some officers even threatened a descent on England. Walewski, the minister of foreign affairs, in less offensive, but still stringent terms, demanded from the British government guaranties against plots on the part of those exiles who had taken refuge in England (January 20, 1858).

Lord Palmerston, unwilling to quarrel, agreed, upon the disavowal of the threat of the military referred to above, to lay a bill before Parliament, punishing as felony (high treason) any plot whose object was the assassination of either an Englishman or a foreigner.

Public opinion in England ran high, and the law was ill received. The House of Commons accepted a motion of blame to the cabinet for failing to reply to the threatening despatch from the French government. Lord Palmerston resigned. Napoleon III. had recovered from his former weakness; he accepted Palmerston's defeat and the withdrawal of the bill, and sent Marshal Pelissier to London as ambassador to settle matters. The conqueror of Sebastopol was well received, and the relations between the two countries once more became friendly (March, 1858).

A diplomatic success during the succeeding summer smoothed the ruffled vanity of Napoleon III. The question of the organization of the principalities of the Danube was left unsettled at the Congress of 1856, and a conference was therefore held by the representatives of the great powers, at Paris, from May to July, 1858. The two principalities, Wallachia and Moldavia, expressed through their assemblies a wish to be united in one state under one prince. Napoleon, who had at first meant to give these countries to Austria to bribe her out of Italy, changed his mind during the Paris Congress, in favor of their liberty and union. Turkey, supported by Austria and England, strove to prevent this union, which would form a Roumanian nation upon the Danube. Russia, from hostility to Austria, sided with France; Prussia imitated Russia; Piedmont, which, following the precedent of 1856, had been asked to join the great powers, also agreed with France. After much discussion they settled upon a singular plan. The two provinces were united, in so much as a legislative committee, chosen half by the Wallachian assembly and half by the Moldavian body, were to make the common laws; each province was, however, to have its own prince and its own assembly.

The Roumanians made skilful use of what was granted them to gain the rest. The two assemblies, Wallachian and Moldavian, agreed to select the same prince, the Roumanian Couza. After much hesitation, the opposing powers yielded, weary of war, and the Roumanian nation was established, to the great displeasure of Austria, which had several thousand Roumanian subjects beyond the Carpathians.

As if to testify that no trace remained of the clouds which obscured the political horizon early in the year, Queen Victoria returned the emperor's visit, at Cherbourg, in August. The queen was received with great pomp on board a French flagship; but on this occasion there was more pomp than real cordiality. Beneath official protestations lurked suspicion and defiance.

The solemn interview at Cherbourg left no result behind. A mysterious conference, unknown to the public, which had occurred at the springs of Plombières the month before, on the contrary, was destined to produce great events. The emperor then formed important projects with King Victor Emanuel's prime minister, Cavour.

As might be expected after the incidents of the Paris Congress, dark clouds were gathering over Italy. The King of Naples, who persisted in his tyranny, had been very unfriendly with France and England ever since the Crimean war. He had then taken sides with Russia in such fashion that but little more was required for the two allies to effect an invasion of Naples. Relations between them were not renewed.

A diplomatic rupture of very different nature occurred soon after the Paris Congress between Austria and Piedmont. Cavour judged that the time for action was at hand, and made great efforts to win France and England to his cause. With the latter government he failed, it being unwilling to infringe upon the treaties of 1815. Lord Palmerston was far less favorably disposed than in 1848. Napoleon III., on the contrary, continued to put forth hopes to the Piedmontese. Cavour established new claims upon him by skilfully aiding his policy in the negotiation just referred to in regard to the provinces of the Danube.

The attack of January 14, 1858, at first seemed as if it must destroy Italian aspirations, and plunge the emperor into reaction abroad as well as at home. It was not so. The attitude and words of Orsini, that unique conspirator, produced a strange effect upon Napoleon; his fatalistic spirit saw in this affair a warning and an order from the lips of Destiny. He ordered Orsini's letters and papers to be published at Paris and Turin.

During the month of May, 1858, Cavour received indirect overtures from Paris in regard to the terms of an alliance between France and Piedmont. Soon after a man in the confidence of the emperor joined the king and the minister at Turin, and settled with them that Cavour was to go, incognito, to Plombières, where the emperor was to take the waters.

Cavour set out, feigning a journey in Switzerland, and reached Plombières secretly, on the 20th of July, unknown even to Walewski, the French minister of foreign affairs. He then agreed, in a tête-à-tête with the emperor, upon a compact between France and Piedmont, or rather Italy. The terms were war with Austria, and the formation of a kingdom in Upper Italy, of about eleven million people; and in return, the cession of Savoy and Nice to France, that is, the restoration of the natural frontier of the Alps. Cavour made haste to return, and went a roundabout way by the right bank of the Rhine to get back to Italy. At Baden, he visited Prince William of Prussia, now regent in consequence of the illness of the king his brother. Shortly after, an Italian envoy, Count Pepoli, a relation of the Bonapartes, was sent to Berlin, to try to draw the Prussian government into the Franco-Piedmontese alliance. These overtures, authorized by Napoleon III., were politely declined by Prussia.

The rest of the year was spent by Piedmont in active preparation, while in France nothing indicated the approach of a great war. This was the usual custom of Napoleon III.; to prevent his enemies from guessing his plans, he avoided taking even the most necessary preparatory steps.

Not until January 1, 1859, was the alarm given to France and Europe. It is said that at his new-year's reception, Napoleon spoke to the Austrian ambassador in terms which presaged a rupture. On the 4th of January the *Constitutionnel* quoted his words: "I regret that our relations with your government are not so friendly as in the past. I beg you will tell the Emperor of Austria that *personal* feelings towards him are quite unchanged."

The blow dealt, the emperor, as usual, tried to weaken its effect. The *Moniteur* came forward to say that "nothing in our diplomatic relations authorizes the fears which alarming reports have tended to create."

These fears were revived when the words uttered by Victor Emanuel at the opening of the Piedmontese Legislature, January 10, were made known. "We cannot," said the king, "remain insensible to the cries of agony which come to us from so many points in Italy."

The king's speech had been communicated to the emperor, and approved — some say, modified — by him.

January 13, Prince Napoleon Jerome started for Turin, where he married, on the 30th, Princess Clotilde, the daughter of Victor Emanuel. The treaty of alliance, verbally agreed upon at Plombières, was signed, January 18, before the marriage contract, and the husband and wife reached Paris, February 4.

The French Legislature opened February 8. The emperor's speech was enigmatical. He said that there were not "sufficient" motives for believing in the war. He hoped that "peace might not be broken"; but his exposition of the "abnormal" condition of Italy was scarcely fitted to confirm the hope.

Napoleon III., for some time to come, continued his system of see-saw in regard to the public. With one hand he issued a pamphlet entitled "Napoleon III. and Italy," which laid down a scheme for Italian national federation without foreign rulers. With the other hand he published in the *Moniteur* a fresh attack upon the people who announced the approach of war, going so far as to claim that it was "impossible for any man of sense to believe such a thing!" At the same time, it is true, the *Moniteur* acknowledged that the emperor had promised to defend Victor Emanuel against all aggressive action on the part of Austria, but nothing more.

Public opinion was greatly divided in France. Financiers, speculators, the clerical party and all the old conservative or reactionary party of 1848 and 1851, with those liberals whom this party had drawn into its ranks, were against the war, — some from opposition to anything that would derange business, some from fear of the consequences which the war might have for the temporal power of the Pope.

The non-reactionary liberals and the republicans themselves were divided into two groups, both of which used serious arguments. The one refused to admit that the power which sprang from December 2 could do anything good either abroad or at home; nothing that it undertook, according to them, could be of any advantage to France or the cause of liberty. The other party believed that a bad government might accidentally accomplish a useful work, and they wished that France, even under the man of December 2, should work abroad in a good cause and for a purpose which, after all, was the same as that of the revolution and modern European justice. They shrank from the thought that the Second Republic, from the misfortune of the times rather than the fault of man, had not been able to do anything for the greatness of France or for European liberty, and they thirsted for action at any cost.

Had the European public known the existence of the secret treaty, they would no longer have doubted that war was at hand; but, with Napoleon's character, nothing was ever very certain, and, as the emperor reserved the right to appoint the time, M. de Cavour still feared that he might retract. England made persistent efforts to prevent conflict; she was, it is true, ill seconded by the other powers. The Russian minister of foreign affairs said plainly to the English ambassador, that if Russia desired peace, she could not regard France and Austria with the same consideration. " With the former," said Prince Gortchakof, " we are on terms of warm cordiality; with the latter, the case is contrary." He concluded by saying that if the peace of Europe were disturbed, Russia was resolved to hold herself free from any pledge.

In view of this attitude on the part of Russia, Prussia did not decide to join England actively; besides, she began to think that a conflict might be profitable. English diplomacy endeavored to persuade Austria to make concessions, but Austria evaded the English suggestions. M. de Cavour, on his side, asked more than Austria could grant, and had no desire that she should accede to his demands. No compromise with foreign domination was possible to him; he must be revenged for Novara or die. He had entire faith in this vengeance, provided the sword was unsheathed.

Certain signs proved to him that Italy, corrected by misfortune, would never renew the errors of 1848; she no longer rashly rejected foreign aid, and without further hesitation, she rallied round the son of Charles Albert. The policy of Cavour and Manin won all hearts and minds; thousands of young men flocked from every part of Italy, to enroll themselves in the Piedmontese army, soon to become the Italian army. The revolutionary hero, Garibaldi, also made terms with Cavour. But nothing could be done until Paris gave the signal.

Negotiations seemed to be renewed. There was great resistance in the circles about the emperor. The empress was opposed to the war; she had not then the political influence which she attained later; but Count Walewski, the minister of foreign affairs, had the same feeling, and the minister of war, Marshal Vaillant, was equally unfavorable.

About the 20th of March, Russia proposed a congress, at the secret instigation of France. Napoleon III. had entered into direct correspondence with Victor Emanuel: he summoned Cavour to Paris, where the Piedmontese minister arrived, March 25. Contrary to his expectation, Cavour was forced to return before anything was settled in regard to the congress, even whether one should be held or no. Austria had no idea of admitting Piedmont, and demanded the disarmament of Piedmont before the opening of the congress. England, with the consent of France, proposed a general laying down of arms and Piedmont's admission to the congress. Cavour accepted with an aching heart; all his plans would be ruined if Austria should agree.

Austria made no reply; she was striving to force Prussia into an alliance with her to act upon the Rhine and Po at one and the same time. Prussia was no better pleased with Austria's proposal than she was with that of France. She had no desire to quarrel with Russia to gratify Austria, and it was for her interest to stand aloof and wait.

Austria, though single-handed, launched out with strange and over-weening pride. She had taken up arms with extreme hostility some months since, and trusted to her military forces. April 23, Cavour received a summons from the Austrian government to lay down his arms within three days. This caused him sincere joy. On the third day he sent his negative answer to an Austrian envoy: "All is over !" he exclaimed; "*Alea jacta est !* (the die is cast)."

Upon the same day, April 26, the French government announced to the Legislature that Piedmont would doubtless be invaded, and that France must respond to the appeal of an allied nation. Two legal projects were presented to the legislative body, — one to increase the contingent of one hundred thousand men to one hundred and forty thousand; the other to authorize a loan of five hundred million francs.

President Morny declared that the emperor had made every effort to avoid war, and strove to allay the popular fears by affirming that, if war was now inevitable, it was at least certain to be local and limited, "especially," he added, "if the German powers are wise enough to see that the question in hand is purely Italian, concealing no scheme of conquest, and breeding no revolutions." He here alluded to the hostile manifestations which had occurred beyond the Rhine since France had shown a disposition to take up arms again.

Émile Ollivier then said, in the name of the republican deputies, that they would gladly aid Italy; but as the object of the war was not clearly defined, they were obliged to take a neutral position. They were unwilling either to pass a vote of complete confidence, or, by rejecting the increase of the contingent, to seem to abandon Italy and side with Austria.

The legislative body, always docile, voted to grant the contingent of one hundred and forty thousand men, amid shouts of, "Long live the Emperor!"

The loan was more seriously discussed. Questions, and even protests from a clerical point of view, were raised in regard to a war which might compromise the temporal power of the Pope. Baroche, president of the State Council, declared that the government would take all measures requisite to insure the papal independence.

Jules Favre made a great speech, in which he agreed with a clerical speaker, that the government was blamable for its failure to consult the mandatories of the country before engaging in war; but at the same time he demanded that the sword of France, once drawn from its scabbard, should not be sheathed until the independence of Italy was secure, and the Austrians were expelled from the peninsula. And he closed by asking the president of the Council of State a decisive question: "If the government of the cardinals be destroyed, must Roman blood be shed anew to restore it?"

Baroche made no reply, but the great problems raised by the Italian war were plain to every eye. The loan was accepted as the contingent had been (April 30).

May 3, the emperor announced to both chambers that Austrian troops had entered Piedmont on the 29th of April, and that this fact placed Austria in a state of war with France. The same day

an imperial proclamation was issued to the people of France, worded
as follows: "Austria has carried matters to such an extreme, that
it becomes requisite for her to rule all territories extending to the
Alps, or for Italy to be free as far as the boundary of the Adriatic.
. . . When France draws her sword, it is not to domineer, but to
liberate."

This was for the friends of nationality. For conservatives and
clericals, Napoleon III. added: " We have no intention of fomenting
disorder in Italy, or of shaking the power of the Holy Father, whom
we restored to his throne."

The startling words which declared Italy free to the Adriatic
produced such an effect that people scarcely noticed the reserve in
regard to the Pope. The Parisians had applauded the regiments as
they set off for Italy, and escorted them to the railway station.
They also applauded the emperor on his departure to join the
army, May 10. This was an event destined to be unparalleled
under the Second Empire. The war was popular with very many,
but whither would it lead ? What was the emperor's plan ?

There were but two logical lines of policy in regard to Italy : the
policy of the men who, like Thiers, demanded that Austria should
merely be prevented from invading Piedmont, but that war should
not be waged for the remodelling of Italy ; and the policy of
those who desired war to the last extreme, that is, until Italy
was able to act fully for herself. The partisans of war rejected all
arguments in favor of the maintenance of the petty Italian states.
Italy, they said, craved unity ; she would attain to it sooner or
later. It would be better that it should come by French aid than in
spite of France and in opposition to her. If it came through France,
Italy would become her ally, their essential interests in Europe
being in accord ; but in this case, despite Italy, the Pope could no
longer be maintained, any more than could the other Italian princes,
and this would entail a rupture with the clerical party.

The words of Napoleon III. had already indicated that he did not
share in this great resolve, and that he wished a very different Italy
from that which the Italians wished.

No sooner had the emperor gone than the rocks became visible upon which the policy that pursued such opposite aims must be wrecked.

Before entering upon the story of the war, we must give some account of the feeling of those powers not engaged in the struggle, who looked on with very varying emotions.

In England the tory ministry, under Lord Derby, was scarcely favorable to France; but public opinion, sympathizing strongly with Italy, would not have allowed the ministry to take sides with Austria, had there been a desire to do so.

Russia, from the beginning of the crisis, had barely disguised her bitter resentment against Austria, and her wish to see that power humbled.

The little German states, on the contrary, loudly declared their aversion to France, and on this point their governments agreed with the people, at least with the ruling classes, the nobility who belonged to the army, the office-holders, and universities. This was a revival of those passions of 1848 which made the Frankfort Assembly vote that soldiers should be sent to aid Austria to retain Milan and Venice in her sway.

Prussia did not give way to these noisy demonstrations; but she prepared to profit by them. She was no longer governed by the dreamy and chimerical Frederic William, whose brain had at last wholly given way, but by his brother William, a man of practical sense and great military skill; who, as regent, revived those traditions of strict discipline in the administration and in the army which had gained Prussia her first triumphs, and which now paved the way for far more extraordinary ones in the near future. The regent had a ministry ably headed by M. de Schleinitz; and a man held high office, who was destined to become minister in a great crisis, and to restore the German Empire for William's benefit: Count Bismarck was now the Prussian ambassador to Russia.

Prussia, at this time, assumed an attitude at once reserved and alert, seeing in the present situation an opportunity to be revenged

for the affronts that she had suffered in 1851. She resumed a
scheme planned in 1854, at the beginning of the Crimean war. The
men who surrounded Frederic William had urged him to make a
secret offer of alliance to England and France, on condition that
Prussia was allowed to found a German federal state, and to hold
command of the German army in case of war. These overtures not
being accepted by England, Frederic William took no further steps,
although his brother, Prince William, urged him to work in concert
with the Western powers, thinking that Prussia must benefit by
sharing in the action.

In 1859 the regent William again attempted to persuade the
German states to place themselves under the military direction of
Prussia, as they were already subject to her commercial guidance.
As early as the latter half of March, Prussia's federal contingent
was armed and equipped, and the desire of the petty states was
granted by a decree from the Diet, ordering the equipment of all
federal contingents; this being before any warlike preparations
had been made in France. The Prussian government represented
this measure as purely defensive.

A month later, Prussia very properly united with England to dissuade Austria from sending her ultimatum to Piedmont; but, war
once declared, Prussia put her whole army upon a warlike footing,
the Prussian legislature eagerly voting the necessary subsidies.
The Prussian government desired, as was said, to labor to restore
peace, being unable to prevent war, and finding it politic to support
its diplomatic action by an armed attitude. The smaller German
states continued to inveigh against France upon every occasion.
When England declared her neutrality, May 13, she informed these
states that if their confederation should attack France without
provocation no assistance need be looked for from England. A fortnight later, a circular from the Russian Minister of Foreign Affairs,
Prince Gortchakof, expressed the same idea even more forcibly. He
severely censured the conduct of Austria, praised that of France,
and blamed the " causeless agitation apparent throughout Germany.
Should the Germanic confederacy assume the offensive against

France, it would contradict the object of its institution, which is purely defensive. In any case the Emperor of Russia will consider only the interests of his country and the dignity of his crown."

The attitude of the great powers at the beginning of the war may therefore be summed up as follows: England simply neutral; Russia neutral, but reserving her freedom of action, and showing herself very favorable to France; Prussia thinking only how to profit by the struggle between France and England to seize the supremacy in Germany.

The sudden resolve which led the Austrian government to send an ultimatum — in point of fact, a declaration of war — was only to be explained by the supposition that Austria had the power and the will to act with electric speed. She had prepared powerful instruments, having by the end of April more than one hundred thousand men upon the Lombardian shore of the Ticino, and reinforcements close by in Lombardo-Venetia; in all, nearly one hundred and eighty thousand soldiers. Piedmont had not more than sixty-odd thousand men, including several thousand Italian volunteers, who were most ardent and zealous, and were commanded by Garibaldi.

France was still unprepared. Her troops were on a peace footing, and, as the emperor himself acknowledged in an order issued June 8, "men, horses, ammunition, and provisions were wanting." He was no better prepared for the breaking out of Italian war than he had been for the breaking out of the war in the Orient. But in the latter case this involved merely a delay; in the former it might cause a disaster. The Austrians were actually ready to march straight to Turin, by masking the stronghold of Alexandria, and to post a vast body of men between the two roads by which the French must come, — the land route by Mont Cenis, and the marine route by way of Genoa. The foe could thus cut the French army into two portions before entering upon any engagement, and render it very difficult and very dangerous for these two divisions to unite with each other, and with the Piedmontese in the rear of Turin. In this way Austria might win the first campaign within a few days.

The Austrian army was commanded by the Hungarian general

Giulay, who had replaced Archduke Maximilian in Lombardo-Venetia. This archduke, reserved for a tragic fate in Mexico, had been sent to Italy to make an attempt to conciliate the people; his brother, Emperor Francis Joseph, recurring to the idea of repression at home and war abroad, then recalled him, and sent Giulay into Italy to assume the part played by Radetzki ten years previous. Giulay had displayed great power as an administrator and organizer in various provincial governments, and was supposed to possess fine military qualities; he had never made war; the event alone could prove of what he was capable.

Instead of crossing the frontier the instant that they received a negative reply from Piedmont, the Austrians remained stationary for two whole days. These two days, which were so important at the opening of the war, were spent by Austria in vain negotiations with England, in the hope of obtaining the neutrality of the eastern shore of the Adriatic, through the intermediation of the English Cabinet.

The Austrian army finally crossed the Ticino between the 30th of April and the 2d of May. Giulay removed his headquarters to Mortara, leaving behind him, to terrify the Italian subjects of Austria, a proclamation decreeing the death penalty for the slightest political offence, such as the mere possession of arms or ammunition! At the same time he issued a promise to the Piedmontese population to restore order and tranquillity, and respect individuals and their property, provided no resistance were made. He assumed that he had come to free the country from the yoke of revolutionists.

These promises were illy kept, and where the inhabitants failed to resist from lack of means, they were equally overwhelmed with requisitions, exactions, and brutalities of every sort.

The Piedmontese did not defend the line of the Ticino; nor did they guard that of the Sesia; they withdrew to a third river, the Dora-Baltea, the last protection of Turin. Giulay, instead of marching forward, tried the ground on his left, to the south of the Po. He attempted to cut off all communication between Alexandria and Genoa. The Piedmontese made a brave resistance. Giulay did not care to fight a serious battle, and having lost four days there, he at last began (May 7) to move upon Turin, by way of Verceil. On May 8, his advance guards were near Biella and Yvrée.

Turin gave up all for lost. The Piedmontese troops had abandoned the line of the Dora, as they had the two previous ones. Giulay had no obstacle before him. Suddenly, instead of continuing his unimpeded march, he stopped short, and his outposts fell •back upon Verceil. Being informed that the "red trousers" had been seen to the south of Turin, at Casale, he feared lest he should be turned and cut off by the French, and the, absence of resistance on the Turin road seemed to him to indicate a trap.

It was true that the French were beginning to arrive from the Upper Alps by way of Suza, and from the sea by way of Genoa; but only in small detachments yet, not only weak in numbers, but destitute of every requisite of a campaign. They had not even a supply of cartridges! Marshal Canrobert, who reached Turin in advance of his troops, advised King Victor Emanuel not to attempt a rash defence upon the Dora, but to abandon Turin and establish himself between the strongholds of Alexandria, Valencia, and Casale, with all his troops, within reach of the French regiments which had been landing at Genoa daily ever since April 24. Two other French regiments straggled into Suza between the 29th of April and the 7th of May. The first division entered Turin, April 30, amid the enthusiastic cheers of the crowd; but these troops, and those that followed them, did not remain in the Piedmontese capital; they were distributed along the road from Alexandria to Casale.

The soldiers landed at Genoa did not enter the plain of Alexandria until after the 7th of May, and in very small parties at first. The forces assembled around Alexandria on the 7th of May were still incapable of serious action, and when Giulay paused on his march, on the 9th, he might easily have entered Turin and cut off the necessary trains of supplies which were coming from the Alps by Suza. He was too timid, and recrossed the Sesia. He was a mass of indecision, variation, and hesitation, when he should have been all promptitude and firmness. His weak conduct made up for Na-

CATHEDRAL OF PALERMO.

poleon's lack of foresight, and gave the French ample time for concentration. A new minister of war, Marshal Randon, had now replaced Marshal Vaillant in France. Randon, who was formerly governor of Algeria, did his best to make up for lost time, and the Piedmontese minister, who brought on the war, M. de Cavour, fed the French troops in the interval. The soldiers were warmly welcomed all along the road from Paris to Marseilles, and from the moment they entered Italy they were almost worshipped by the excited populace.

The French emperor landed at Genoa, May 12. He published a proclamation informing the army that they were to aid a nation to maintain its liberty and free itself from foreign oppression. He recalled the memory of the former Italian army and its victories, adding that "the new Italian army would be worthy of its elder brother."

May 14, Napoleon III. established his headquarters at Alexandria, and on the 15th the French army was almost complete, numbering about one hundred and twenty thousand. The forces of the Franco-Italian allies were therefore almost equal to those of the enemy. On the 17th of May the whole allied army was in line to the south of the Po, on either bank of the Tanaro, the principal southern branch of the Po.

Giulay, having given the French leisure to complete and arrange their forces, decided to assume the offensive on his left, outside the defile of Stradella, a pass where the valley of the Po is compressed between that stream and the Apennines. The Austrian general desired to prevent an attack by the allies upon Placenza. He sent his left wing, under General Stadion, to Voghera, occupied by a French division and a small body of Piedmontese cavalry. An engagement took place between Voghera and Montebello, a name famed in the first Italian war. The French general, Forey, ably seconded by the Piedmontese horse, repulsed the Austrian attack, drove them from Montebello and the neighboring heights, and forced them to retreat. This was a brilliant opening of the campaign. Six thousand French and a few hundred Piedmontese fought against at least fifteen thousand Austrians. General Stadion had supposed himself yielding to much greater numbers (May 20).

This was a sort of reconnoissance of the French positions on the part of Giulay, and his check at Montebello confirmed him in the idea that the principal effort of the French would be brought to bear upon Placenza from the southern bank of the Po.

The plan adopted by the emperor was very different. Napoleon III. had just despatched his cousin, Prince Napoleon Jerome, with a small body of men into Tuscany, where, a revolution having occurred, the grandduke had fled, and a provisory government had been proclaimed. Prince Napoleon was directed to add to his troops such reinforcements as Tuscany might furnish, in order to harass the Austrians on their left flank. It was important to prevent them from turning aside to Genoa; while instead of marching on Placenza, the great allied army moved to the north of the Po, towards the Ticino and the road to Milan. This plan, which involved a long flank march, within reach of the Austrian army, would have been dangerous with an active and clear-sighted opponent; it might succeed with Giulay.

Between the 21st and 24th of May the Piedmontese, who formed the left wing of the French army, began operations to the north of the Po upon the Sesia, and sent several detachments beyond that river. On the extreme left, Garibaldi, with a small body of volunteers, not exceeding three thousand, entered Lombardy, May 23, and called the people to arms. He disconcerted the Austrians by the impetuosity and unexpectedness of his manœuvres, beat the enemy at Varesa, at Como, and roused the whole country from Lake Maggiore to Lake Como; the insurrection even spread into the Valtelline, the valley of the Upper Adda.

The Austrian staff-officers were alarmed at these operations, which seriously imperilled communication with the army of the north; but Giulay persisted in regarding it as a mere diversion. He was informed that the French were gathering their forces on the right of their army, to the south of the Po. This was a manœuvre intended to keep up his illusion, and it proved successful. His only desire

was to cover Stradella, that is, the road to Placenza, and the southern
bank of the Po. Meantime the allied army effected the great flank
movement which had been decided upon, on their left, and proceeded from the south to the north of the Po, by way of Alexandria,
Valencia, and Casale, leaving but one division on the French right
at Tortona. May 30, the Piedmontese crossed the Sesia near Verceil, and captured from the Austrians the positions of Palestro and
the neighboring villages. The Austrians resumed the offensive next
day against Palestro. Just as the Piedmontese were hotly pressed
by the enemy, the 3d Zouaves, commanded by Colonel de Chabron,
hastened to their aid, making one of the grandest charges mentioned in military history. The regiment crossed two small streams,
under a rain of shot and shell, bayoneted every obstacle, captured
or cast into the river a multitude of the enemy, and took eight
cannon, which were sent to Victor Emanuel's headquarters. This
warrior king, stimulated by the heroic deeds which he witnessed,
galloped up to lead on the zouaves, and won the admiration of all
by his ardor and daring. Victor Emanuel gained exceptional popularity among the French troops, whom he loved as much as he
was loved by them.

The same day (May 31), another attack by the Austrians, at a
point not far remote from Palestro, was triumphantly repelled by
General Fanti. The Piedmontese army thus effaced its disaster at
Novara.

The attempt made by an Austrian division to drive the Piedmontese to the other side of the Sesia could not have succeeded in
any case. The great mass of the French army, which continued its
march northward, was already in the rear of the Piedmontese, on
the left bank of the Sesia, aiming for Novara. Giulay still kept the
major part of his army face to face with the French troops at Tortona, not daring to attack them, being unaware of their scanty
numbers.

June 1, the 4th corps of the French army, under General Niel,
drove the Austrians from Novara, which became the base of operations. This division, the 3d corps, under Canrobert, and the greater

part of the Piedmontese, were now in the foremost ranks. The second line was formed by the 2d corps, under General MacMahon, and the Piedmontese troops which fought at Palestro under the king's orders. The imperial guard were held in reserve at Verceil. The 1st corps, under Baraguey d'Hilliers, were on their way from Casale, and the Tortona division had fallen back on Alexandria. Not until the great flank movement was thus near completion were Giulay's eyes opened. The Austrian general, at last undeceived, hastily evacuated Mortara and the right bank of the Ticino, June 2 and 3, to re-enter Lombardy by Placenza. He concentrated his forces on the left bank of the Ticino. A reinforcement was now on the road to him from the Tyrol, and moved towards Magenta, a large borough on the road from Novara to Milan; Magenta became the centre of resistance for the Austrians.

The French movement had described, as it were, the curve of a bow of which the enemy formed the string. Giulay had been deceived too long to alarm the French during this dangerous operation; but it is needless to say that they did not reach Milan without encountering him, he having so little space to traverse to bar their progress. The emperor, however, had hoped to escape. Ignorant in his turn of the movements of the foe, he had planned to furnish his troops with horses at the Ticino, posting his 1st corps upon the road from Mortara to Novara; the 3d and 4th corps upon the Piedmontese bank of the Ticino, opposite Magenta; the 2d corps beyond the Ticino, at Turbigo and Magenta, with the guard as support; and finally, the Piedmontese as a reserve. June 3, the 2d corps (MacMahon's), assisted by a body of light foot from the guard, crossed the Ticino, then a second stream parallel with it, the Naviglio-Grande (Grand Canal), and met with no resistance save at Robecchetto, between Turbigo and Magenta. The Algerian sharpshooters (Turcos) carried the village of Robecchetto at the bayonet's point, with a spirit worthy the zouaves at Palestro. These brave Kabyle mountaineers had already won brilliant laurels in the Crimean war.

The same day, a division of grenadiers, from the guard, arrived

four or five leagues away, towards the southwest, on the other bank
of the Naviglio-Grande. The Austrians had been unsuccessful in
blowing up the chief bridge over the Ticino at San Martino, and the
grenadiers, as well as MacMahon's troops, crossed the river without
difficulty.

The emperor's plan was nevertheless foiled; for the enemy was
before him at Magenta and thereabouts, in large numbers. Giulay
at first intended to attack him in the flank; but an order sent from
Verona by the Austrian emperor forced him to confront the French,
marshalling his men upon the left bank of the Ticino. He massed
as many soldiers as possible about Magenta. The only French
troops in sight of the enemy on the morning of June 14, were the
two divisions of MacMahon's corps on the left, supported by a division of light foot from the guard, twenty-seven thousand in all, and
in the centre, at the decisive point, before the bridge and the village called Ponte Nuovo di Magenta, was a body of grenadiers and
zouaves from the guard, scarcely six thousand in number.

The emperor, who was posted in the rear of the grenadiers at the
bridge of San Martino, on the Ticino, despatched an order to the 3d
and 4th corps, summoning them to hasten to his aid, and calling
upon the Piedmontese at Turbigo to assist MacMahon. He expected these reinforcements to arrive promptly; but the 3d and 4th
corps (under Canrobert and Niel) became mutually entangled; the
marching orders were awkwardly worded, and the roads were
blocked, which greatly delayed the troops. The Piedmontese were
equally dilatory. The emperor, however, had directed MacMahon
to march from Robecchetto upon Magenta, and prepared to support
him by sending his grenadiers in the same direction. MacMahon
started out with his two columns at nine o'clock in the morning.
He informed the emperor that his right column would reach the village of Buffalora, within two kilometers of Ponte Nuovo di Magenta,
by half past two at latest. The left column would be at Magenta at
about half past three. MacMahon left too great a distance between
his two columns; his staff officers pointed out the danger that the
enemy might hurl their forces into the intervening space. To

repair this mistake, he was obliged to send back one of his columns, which had advanced rapidly upon Buffalora, and bring up the other, which was still remote from Magenta. Much time was lost by this manœuvre.

The emperor, at the sound of MacMahon's cannon, which had been firing for an hour in the direction of Buffalora, hurried forward with all the men at his disposal, three regiments of grenadiers and one of zouaves. He even divided this feeble force, sending one regiment of grenadiers to Buffalora to assist MacMahon. The three other regiments attacked the bridge and small village of Ponte Nuovo di Magenta. The enemy, master of the railroad at Milan, occupied a strong position between the stream and a semicircle of hills forming an arc, of which the canal was the chord. The grenadiers and zouaves carried a redoubt which covered a railroad bridge across the canal, then took the first houses in the village, and rushed fearlessly forward on the road to Magenta. They were soon driven back by quadruple or quintuple forces. One of their leaders, the brave General Cler, was killed; still they kept possession of the bridge which they had captured, and made a desperate resistance to the enemy's onslaught. The fate of the battle was to be decided here! The grenadiers of Magenta proved themselves worthy descendants of those of Austerlitz.

They were on the point of defeat! At last, towards half past three, the Picard brigade of Canrobert's 3d corps came in sight. Grenadiers and zouaves, reinforced by these two fresh regiments, eagerly resumed the offensive. The enemy was once more repulsed, but was still much superior in numbers, and the danger was not over. An hour after, a brigade from the 4th corps arrived, with General Niel; then came a third brigade. They pushed boldly on to Magenta, and drove the foe from the semicircle of hills.

MacMahon had at last resumed his movement; he found the village of Buffalora occupied for the moment by the grenadier regiment sent thither by the emperor. The Austrians defending Buffalora, fearing to be caught between two fires, had just left the village; but Giulay ordered a double offensive return both against Mac-

Mahon and against the French right, formed by the newly arrived brigades.

MacMahon displayed great energy in repairing the lost time which had so nearly caused the loss of the battle. He vigorously repulsed the attack of the Austrians, beat them back to Magenta, and followed them thither. Meantime a very lively struggle was raging on the French right. There was a moment of imminent peril. The enemy captured one of the bridges on the extreme French right, and there was an alarming void between the right and left wings.

The bridge was recaptured by General Vinoy and Marshal Canrobert, who brought reinforcements ; the battalions of the 3d and 4th corps came up in disorder, but still they came. The commander of the French artillery, General Augér, filled up the space in the French centre with his batteries of rifled cannon, and his fire broke the Austrian centre. This was the first time that these new long-range cannon had proved effective in an important action. The battle was long and bloody at Magenta, where MacMahon's two columns and a detachment from the French right had entered on three sides at once. At eight in the evening the town was in MacMahon's power. The Piedmontese came up, and Giulay, although he had received successive reinforcements, ordered a retreat.

The French loss exceeded four thousand five hundred men ; that of the Austrians ten thousand, many of whom were prisoners.

We may say that this was a battle of privates, rather than of officers. Neither side had displayed much strategy. The daring of the French soldiers won the victory. Out of one hundred and seventy-eight thousand men at his disposal, Giulay, who had the shorter road to traverse, had only managed to employ sixty-two thousand, and the allied army, now numbering one hundred and eighty-eight thousand men, had not brought more than forty-eight thousand into battle before nightfall.

Giulay halted not far from the field of battle. The greater part of the Austrian forces had not fought. Giulay remained master of his line of retreat to Padua and Placenza, and might be joined on the 5th by two of his corps which had not yet appeared. He at first thought of renewing the contest; but two corps, which had suffered greatly in the struggle, continued their retreat without awaiting his orders. The rest were much shaken, and he felt that he could not resist a fresh attack. June 6, he evacuated Padua and fell back upon the Adda. MacMahon entered Milan, June 7, welcomed by a people mad with joy. Next day, Napoleon III. and Victor Emanuel entered this capital of Lombardy, freed from its tyrants after the eleven years of oppression which had followed its few months of liberty. A thrilling proclamation from the French emperor carried Italian enthusiasm to its utmost height. He declared that he had not come to impose his will upon them, and that his army would put no obstacle in the way of the free manifestation of their legitimate wishes. "Profit," he continued, "by the opportunity now offered you! Your desire for independence, so long expressed, so often deceived, may now be realized if you prove yourselves worthy. Form yourselves into military organization. Take your place beneath the standard of King Victor Emanuel! Be naught but soldiers for to-day; to-morrow you shall be the free citizens of a great country!"

Patriotism everywhere interpreted these words as the promise of the unity of Italy under Victor Emanuel. That very day, June 8th, an Austrian division, which covered the retreat of Giulay, was driven from Melegnano by the 1st French corps, under the orders of Marshal Baraguey d'Hilliers, after a bloody engagement. The town of Melegnano is no other than the famous Marignan of the time of Francis I.

Giulay, meantime, left Placenza, and the Austrian garrisons abandoned Ancona, Bologna, Ferrara, and all the ground which they held in the Papal States. The formation of the 5th corps of French troops in Tuscany, under Prince Napoleon and the Italian general Ulloa, made the enemy fear lest they should be taken on the flank and turned. The 5th corps was then summoned from Tuscany to Parma; the Duchess of Parma, sister of Count Chambord, and the Austrian archduke who reigned at Modena, having fled, as the Grand Duke of Tuscany had previously done.

The allied army resumed its march, June 11, to the north of Milan. On the 12th, it crossed the Adda without resistance. Giulay had with great difficulty restored a semblance of order in his ranks, and had fallen back from the Adda to the Oglio. He made no more attempt to defend the Oglio than the Adda, and never paused till he reached the line of heights beyond the Chiese. Garibaldi had already passed beyond Bergamo with his volunteers, and entered Brescia, followed by the Piedmontese. The headquarters were formed at Brescia, and the allied army reached the Chiese, June 18.

Upon these movements of the allies, Giulay, who had ill responded to what was expected of him, sent in his resignation, and the Emperor of Austria reorganized his forces. Two new corps and a division of cavalry joined the army formerly commanded by Giulay.

Austria had four armies on foot: two in Italy, Emperor Francis Joseph having reinforced and divided Giulay's army; the third army was held in reserve, with its headquarters at Trieste, to watch Hungary, and, if necessary, Russia; the fourth army, the least strong, was the Austrian contingent of the Germanic Confederation, intended to march upon the Rhine, should there be occasion.

The first army was on the shores of the Mincio, under General Wimpffen; the second, under General Schlik, was face to face with the allies on the heights of the Chiese.

The new commanders showed no more fixedness in their plans than had the old one. General Schlik abandoned the heights on the left bank of the Chiese, and the two Austrian armies, joining forces, retired beyond the Mincio, June 20; then, between the 22d and 23d, Francis Joseph sent them across the Mincio again, thus abruptly changing his purpose once more.

The allies had crossed the Chiese on the 21st; but, thanks to the slowness of the movements ordered by Napoleon III., the Austrians were allowed to quietly occupy not only the first line of heights, but a second, running from Lake Garda, stretching from north to south, of which Solferino is the culminating point. Napoleon III. had made it a rule always to march in battle order, that he might be ever ready to repulse an attack, thus disabling himself from rapid progress. His staff never dreamed that they had the whole Austrian army to deal with; it was improbable that the enemy would return to offer fight on this side of the Mincio, — a position less favorable than that of the first heights overlooking the Chiese, and far less advantageous than the quadrilateral, so long prepared by Austria beyond the Mincio.

The Austrians, on their side, had no idea that the majority of the French army had crossed the Chiese. The Austrian emperor's decision was formed by reasons half political, half military. He feared, if he delayed to fight, that he would be involved by the diversions prepared against him in the north, south, and in the direction of the sea. In the north, Garibaldi and the Piedmontese general Cialdini threatened to invade the valley of the Upper Adige, and cut off the Austrian communication with the Tyrol and Friuli. The Franco-Italian corps of Prince Napoleon and General Ulloa, coming from Parma, now arrived on the left flank of the Austrian army; and, finally, a French squadron, with troops to be landed, had just appeared before Venice.

The attitude of Prussia likewise urged Francis Joseph to action. He saw plainly that Prussia's only desire was to profit by the embarrassments of Austria to lay hands on Germany, and he must win a victory for Austria if he would outwit the schemes of the Cabinet at Berlin.

The two armies therefore marched directly towards each other without knowing it; that is, without supposing that their main bodies were about to meet. June 24, the allies took the initiative, and set out before daylight. The Austrians were not ordered to move until late in the morning. Francis Joseph had not all his forces assembled; he had left two corps at a distance, one near the Tyrol, the other on the lower course of the Po. He had upon the battle-field an effective force of one hundred and ninety-eight thousand foot, and more than nineteen thousand horse, of which about one hundred and forty-six thousand foot and seventeen thousand horse were engaged. The allies, still less concentrated, out of about one hundred and seventy-four thousand foot and more than fourteen thousand horse, could not bring to bear more than one hundred and twenty-five thousand foot and scarcely eleven thousand horse.

The scene was now shifted to the stage of the greatest military events of the old Italian war. The French left (the Piedmontese army) marched by Lonato; the French centre, by way of Castiglione. The allied army advanced in four columns; and the great struggle was to be waged upon an extent of four or five leagues, from the southern end of Lake Garda to Castel-Goffredo and Guidizzolo, in the direction of Mantua. The villages of Castel-Goffredo and Medola were soon captured, — the former by the 3d corps (under Canrobert); the second, after a stouter resistance, by the 4th corps (under Niel). Then the 4th corps moved forward upon the plain.

The great battle was now raging on every hand. The superiority of the French rifle-cannon was again shown in the artillery duels with the Austrian batteries. While the French right worked in mid-plain, the centre and left advanced to attack the hills, but with great difficulty and serious loss. On the left, the Piedmontese, too widely scattered over the vast field, struggled manfully against superior forces; driven back several times, they returned stubbornly to the charge, taking and again losing the important position of San Martino.

On the right, Niel's 4th corps was stopped by powerful numbers. The decisive point was at Solferino, in the centre, where the contest was long, desperate, bloody, and full of changes. The 1st corps (Baraguey d'Hilliers's) was stationed there, supported on the right by the 2d corps (MacMahon's). The Austrians, entrenched behind crenulated walls, obstinately defended the tower overlooking the height of Solferino, as well as the cemetery of that town, and a hill covered with cypress. The French lost many men, but the ardor of their troops finally overcame all obstacles. . By half past one all the positions of Solferino were in their hands, together with twenty-two cannon and numerous prisoners.

The imperial guard and 2d corps (MacMahon's) then carried another height beyond Solferino, called Mount Fontana. On the right, Niel's corps (the 4th) had made some progress; but the enemy redoubled their efforts against it. General Niel urgently begged reinforcements from Canrobert, who held the extreme right with the 3d corps. Canrobert, preoccupied by fears that the Austrians might attempt to turn the French by a sally from Mantua, dreaded to part with any of his men, and sent very insufficient help to Niel, which afterwards caused serious trouble between them. Between three and four o'clock, however, when the Austrians, defeated in the centre, made a final attack on the French right, Canrobert decided to co-operate with Niel. It was time. The great numbers massed against Niel were repulsed by the 3d and 4th corps united.

In the centre, the 1st and 2d corps and the guard pushed forward and carried Cavriara, the Austrian emperor's headquarters. Francis Joseph ordered a retreat. A furious tempest of wind and rain put a stop to the battle, and favored the enemy's retreat.

The storm allayed, the Piedmontese captured the village of San Martino, which they had hitherto attacked in vain with sturdy valor, and which the Austrians could no longer retain in their general retreat. The little Piedmontese army had had a severe day of it, and had fought steadily with unequal numbers.

The Austrian loss exceeded twenty-two thousand; that of the allies seventeen thousand. The French lost many more officers than the foe, as often happens when one is constantly acting on the offensive.

To read the official account, one would think that the whole affair took place on a well-arranged chess-board, and that the emperor saw everything, predicted everything, and directed everything. This was far from being the truth. Upon that immense field of battle Napoleon III. was wholly lacking in originating power and quick comprehension. He was incapable of inspiration and spontaneity. If he had any share whatever in the victory, it was as the introducer of rifle-cannon. What we have said of Magenta may be applied with even greater show of reason to Solferino; the battle, so long trembling in the scales, was won by the private soldiers far more than by the generals, especially the general-in-chief.

Next day, the French were quite unfit to pursue the Austrians for lack of food and vehicles. On the false report of an offensive return of the enemy, a singular rout and confusion suddenly occurred in the rear of the army and in the baggage train. The mass of non-combatants, which always follows an army, took to flight helter-skelter, dragging with them or overwhelming everything in their path, even to the ambulances with the wounded. Brave General Auger, commander of the artillery, who had lost his arm in the battle, was thus overthrown with his carriage, and did not survive his injuries. This incident greatly affected the emperor, already overcome by the physical horrors of the battle-field, far more terrible to look upon next day than the fields of Magenta. The allies let six whole days elapse before crossing the Mincio (July 1).

The Austrians had abandoned the line of that river on the 27th of June, and had fallen back on the Adige. They were now at the base of their famous quadrilateral, between the four strongholds of Peschiera, Verona, Legnago, and Mantua. The majority of their army was encamped between Verona and Legnago, holding Peschiera and Mantua with strong garrisons in their front. The French 5th corps rejoined the allied army on the 3d of July. The Austrians centred about Verona. The French decided to take Venice on their right and Peschiera on their left, before attacking Verona. The artillery was to establish its batteries before Peschiera, July 10. A powerful squadron, partly sailing and partly steam vessels, had already posted its advance guard in sight of Venice. The interesting and unfortunate Venetians trembled with joy and quivered with impatience when they saw the tricolored flag beyond the Lido. Fresh reinforcements soon joined the allied army. Success was certain both at Venice and at Peschiera, nor was there any reason to expect much resistance save at Verona.

Just at this time an aide-de-camp of the Russian Emperor arrived at Napoleon III.'s headquarters, with a letter of the utmost importance.

The Russian government at first favored the schemes of Napoleon III. against Austria quite openly. Some weeks after the scene of January 1 at the Tuileries, Prince Gortchakof declared to the English ambassador that Russia could not weigh France and England in the same balance. " I do not say," he added, "that Russia will in no case take part in the fight." If these dispositions on the part of Russia had lasted they would have paralyzed the hostility of the petty German states, and ruined the calculations of Prussia; the Prussian government would not have exposed itself to a rupture at once with France and with Russia; but the tendencies of the Czar were speedily modified. To satisfaction at Austria's defeat, succeeded fear of the consequences of this defeat. Should the war spread further, Napoleon III. would be obliged, as he said himself later on, "to fortify himself frankly with the aid of revolution."

Already the employment of Garibaldi in the Franco-Italian army was most displeasing to Alexander III.; but that did not concern him directly. Now a very different matter came up for discussion and settlement.

The Czar was not free from doubts that Napoleon III. was in secret treaty with Kossuth, the leader of Hungarian revolution in 1848-49. The proud Dictator of Hungary, who in exile still regarded himself as the legitimate head of a national government overthrown by strangers, treated the French Emperor as no more than his own equal. The subject under discussion was the restoration of the revolutionary government of Hungary, and it was certain that if the Franco-Italians were to effect a diversion beyond the Adriatic with Kossuth in their ranks, the Hungarians would rise to a man. Insurrection in Hungary, in the eyes of the Czar, meant revolution in Poland.

Alexander II. was alarmed, and immediately after hearing the news of Solferino, he despatched his aide-de-camp Souwaloff to Napoleon III. with a letter, informing the French Emperor that Russia could not follow France in a war which must needs become both European and revolutionary.

This intervention exercised considerable influence upon the spirit of Napoleon, and was probably decisive with him. Other motives, also, affected the emperor : he was not without apprehension of the revolution which he had called forth, and with which he must presently engage more deeply than ever. The empress and her party eagerly dissuaded him from this purpose by letter. Perhaps also his confidence in himself, as leader of an army, was slightly shaken by the experience of this short campaign. It was difficult for him to be wholly blind to the degree in which he lacked inspiration on the battle-field. Nor had he waited for this experience to equivocate and play a double game. Very soon after his famous phrase, "Italy free to the Adriatic," and during the first military operations before Magenta, this man, compounded of contradictions, had proposed mediation to England through his ambassador, Persigny, and he was quite disposed to renew the dream of certain politicians of 1848, — an Austrian archduke reigning at Venice as independent sovereign, and Lombardy united to Piedmont. July 6, Napoleon III. directed General Fleury, one of the leading spirits of December 2, to bear proposals of armistice to the Austrian Emperor at Verona. These proposals were accepted.

Napoleon III. stopped short when he found that he must needs renounce all hope of the Russian alliance ; Francis Joseph stopped short when he found that he must needs obtain the Prussian alliance. He had already sought this alliance and failed to obtain it, when the fortune of arms still trembled in the balance ; now, being conquered, he knew that it would no longer be refused, but on condition of a fall from the first to the second rank in Germany, or rather the surrender of the Empire of Germany to Prussia.

The advance of the Prussian government in this matter forms a most interesting study. We have given a brief account of it in its first period. After Magenta, Prussia mobilized a great part of her army, thus admitting of an appeal to her *landwehr*. She had not consented to give an assurance of neutrality, and thus follow the example of England and Russia : she claimed that this fact permitted her to play the part of mediator. She continued to restrain the Austrian zeal of the petty German states, flattered Austria with fine

phrases, but refused to give her any written promise in regard to the
guaranty of Austrian possessions in Italy. Prussia was very willing
to offer armed mediation in general terms, reserving to herself the
choice of time, but on the express condition that Austria would
allow her the initiative in all measures to be taken by the Germanic Confederation, and would contract no separate alliance with
any German state.

The Austrian government replied that, Prussia not pledging herself to action, Austria could not renounce her liberty of action in
the domain of German affairs. Prussia was not repelled by this
reserve: she persuaded the Germanic Diet to pass a series of resolutions putting the federal reserves upon a war footing, and conferring on Prussia the chief command of the federal forces, "without
any instructions tracing out or limiting the movements and intentions of Prussia!" Upon these conditions Prussia assumed "the
responsibility of defending the interests of the independence and
dignity of the great German nation."

This occurred upon the eve of Solferino, and it was this which
decided Francis Joseph to risk the battle. Being defeated, if the
war continued, the Austrian Emperor must become, in 1859, the
protégé of Prussia, as he was the *protégé* of Russia in 1849, but
with far worse results for himself and his nation.

It is easy to see why he was so ready to accept the overtures of
Napoleon III.

By the 8th of July an armistice was arranged at Villafranca,
midway between Valeggio and Verona, by the delegates of the three
contending powers. Victor Emanuel was unable to decline entering into the negotiations opened, without consulting him, by his
powerful ally.

Three days later (July 11), the three emperors met at Villafranca.
They held a conference of an hour, where nothing was set down in
writing.

On returning to his headquarters at Valeggio, Napoleon III.
summoned his cousin, Prince Napoleon, and directed him to carry
to the Austrian emperor a rough draught of peace preliminaries,

dictated in accordance with the sentiments expressed during the interview at Villafranca.

By this paper Napoleon III. withdrew his solemn promise that "Italy should be free as far as the Adriatic"; he consented that Venice should remain subject to the Austrian crown. Francis Joseph surrendered Lombardy to the French Emperor, who, "in accordance with the popular wish," bestowed it upon the King of Sardinia. Venice was to form a part of an Italian confederation, of which the Pope was to be honorary president. The two emperors were to exert every effort "short of resorting to arms," to restore the Dukes of Tuscany and Modena to their dominions. The two emperors were also to request the Holy Father to introduce the necessary reforms in his states. An amnesty was to be granted by either party to all persons compromised in the late troubles.

The Emperor of Austria would not allow any mention of "the popular wish," considering it equivalent to a recognition of "revolutionary right"; he refused to forbid officially all "resort to arms," in favor of his Tuscan and Modenese relatives; but this was merely a formal reserve, for he was well assured that France would not interfere, and would not allow Austria to interfere by force in favor of the dispossessed princes. In point of fact, Napoleon III. gave up Venice, and Francis Joseph gave up the Dukes of Tuscany and Modena. There was no serious difficulty save in regard to Lombardy. Francis Joseph, while ceding this province, intended to reserve the two strongholds of Peschiera and Mantua, which were still in his hands.

Prince Napoleon was obliged to refer the question to his cousin. Napoleon III. yielded.

July 12, an imperial proclamation announced to the French army that the bases of peace were established: "The principal object of the war is gained; Italy is to become a nation for the first time."

The emperor went on to speak in pompous terms of Italy, henceforth mistress of her own destiny, who would now unite "all the members of one family in a single body," including Venice, although she was to remain beneath the sway of Austria. He concluded by declaring that the soldiers of France, " who have carried the glory of her arms to so high a pitch, only paused because the struggle was about to assume proportions which no longer comported with the interests which France had at stake in this great war."

What real meaning lay beneath these sonorous words? What impression did the peace of Villafranca make upon that Italy now styled " the mistress of her own destiny," and who still harbored despotic monarchs at Naples and Rome, and a foreign ruler in one of her fairest provinces?

King Victor Emanuel, who concealed beneath the abrupt and open manners of a hunter and soldier the reflective spirit of a politician, repressed his painful doubts, and assured the emperor of his gratitude for what he had done in favor of Italian independence.

Cavour was not bound down by his duty to the ministry as Victor Emanuel was to royalty. He resigned his office; but he was too firm of soul and too clear-sighted not to overcome his first violent emotion with promptitude; he did not hesitate to find speedy means of continuing his interrupted task under other conditions.

At Venice the blow was a fearful one. When her unhappy people saw the flag of freedom fading from her shore with the fleet of France, they felt themselves thrust down, as we may say, remote from light and life, into the gloomy circles of Dante's hell.

Milan and Lombardy wavered between joy at their deliverance and regret that they alone were set free. Throughout the rest of Italy the great national party was overcome with grief and rage. Napoleon III. had urged the Italians on by his dazzling promises; now he stopped them short; the shock was terrible, and an inevitable reaction followed among the populace. Napoleon III. could not fail to observe this, when he traversed Upper Italy on his return to France; he had already greatly compromised the benefit of the immense service which he had rendered Italy, not for himself alone, but unfortunately for France as well.

In France he found a similar state of feeling prevalent. Conservatives and clericals were half content; but the popular sentiment was cruelly disappointed, and this dissatisfaction became indignation in those republicans and patriots who, without forgetting an inexpiable past, had provoked the Italian expedition, and accompanied it with their prayers. Those who had always maintained that nothing good could ever be expected from such a government now applauded their wise prevision.

If men of feeling were enraged, men of reflection and foresight were alarmed.

The previous spring, M. Thiers had said: "They talk of declaring war in April; they will not be ready to begin in August!" This remark cost M. Thiers many a jest. The war, which he declared could not possibly begin before August, was ended in July. And yet M. Thiers was right. The war opened before proper preparations were made; the French must have been beaten; they were not, simply because their adversaries showed themselves even less able than the French government. Others than the Austrians had watched and judged, and now prepared to profit by the errors of France as well as those of Austria.

The Italian war was over, at least for France; but the European crisis had only just begun, brought about by a hand which was fated little by little to lose the power and the capacity to direct it.

The entrance of Napoleon III. into Milan was the culminating point of his reign.

The peace of Villafranca marks the brief pause soon to be followed by decadence and decay.

CHAPTER XIX.

SECOND EMPIRE (*continued*). — RESULTS OF THE ITALIAN WAR. — COMMERCIAL TREATY WITH ENGLAND. — UNION OF SAVOY AND NICE WITH FRANCE. — FORMATION OF THE KINGDOM OF ITALY. — DECREE OF NOVEMBER 24.

July, 1859, to June, 1861.

ON the day after his return to Paris, July 19, the emperor received the great bodies of State at St. Cloud. He affected to speak without reserve in regard to the sudden termination of the war.

"On our arrival outside the walls of Venice," said he, "the struggle was assuming a different character both from a military and a political point of view. . . . . When I began the long and sterile war of sieges, I found myself opposed by Europe in arms, ready either to dispute my success or to aggravate my reverses. . . . . I was forced to prepare for warfare on the Rhine as well as on the Adige. I was forced to make a frank appeal to the memory of the French Revolution as a support. . . . . Can you think that it cost me nothing openly to eliminate from my programme the territory extending from the Mincio to the Adriatic ? . . . . To serve Italian independence, I waged war against the inclination of all Europe. As soon as the fate of France seemed likely to be imperilled, I made peace. Does that prove that our efforts and our sacrifices were all lost ? — No. . . . . The peace which I have just concluded will be fruitful in happy results. The future will reveal them day by day, and ever more for the happiness of Italy, the influence of France, and the repose of Europe."

The explanations — or excuses, as we may call them — presented

CHATEAUBRIAND.

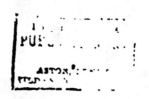

by the emperor to the State bodies, showed that he did not disguise
from himself the unfortunate effect of the treaty of Villafranca;
after such splendid promises, to stop short leaving every problem
unsolved, was to give his adversaries and doubters occasion to recall
the words of the poet, —

> "To be approved, such designs must be carried to their end."

Napoleon III. attempted to act upon popular opinion in various ways.   In order to convince France and Europe that his
government was sufficiently strong to feel no fear of hostile parties,
he granted full and entire amnesty "to all persons condemned for
political crimes or offences, or the object of measures taken in the
interest of public safety."   Another decree annulled the list of
restrictions hitherto given to the press, and which kept all newspapers, the objects of these threatening intimations, in constant danger of arbitrary suppression.

Finally, extraordinary preparations were ordered to celebrate the
return to Paris of the imperial guard and detachments representing
the various divisions of the Italian army.   The splendor of the
skilfully arranged spectacle, the sight of the illustrious wounded,
of French flags pierced by bullets, the procession of banners and
cannon captured from the enemy, once more produced an effect
upon the Parisians, as at the return of the troops from the Crimea,
which might well deceive the emperor; but it was no longer to him
that those popular plaudits were directed, which met his ears on his
departure.

At a banquet given the night before to the chief officers of the
army, Napoleon III. bade them cherish the memory "of the obstacles overcome, the perils avoided, and the imperfections pointed
out; for," he added, " to every warrior memory is science itself."

Neither he nor the men to whom he intrusted the French army
were wise enough to profit by these memories.

Among the exiled republicans there were lively discussions in
regard to the amnesty: should they, or should they not, return to
their country, now that the material obstacle which closed the

frontier to them was removed?   Victor Hugo, Charras, Edgar
Quinet, Schoelcher, Madier de Montjau, Clément Thomas, proudly
and disdainfully protested against the right of the destroyer of legal
order and liberty to pardon the defenders of law and of the right.
They declared that they would never return to France until her
doors were opened to liberty and justice.

" . . . . And should but one remain, let it be me ; "

as Victor Hugo said, in one of his verses modelled in bronze.

Louis Blanc, having decided not to return himself, still admitted
that, in the interest of the republican party, a portion of the proscribed men might and should return to France.

Ledru-Rollin was the only exception to the amnesty, under the
pretext that his was a crime under the common law.   Judgment
had been given against him in a state of contumacy, without any
proof against him, as an accomplice in a plot against the emperor's
life.   Quite disinterested in the matter, he advised his companions
in exile, "banished illegally, illegally recalled," to profit by existing
circumstances.   "Every republican," he wrote, "who returns to
France without degrading himself, is a centre of light and one soldier more ready for the coming day."

The majority of the exiles followed this advice, although they
were well aware of the lack of guaranties which they should find in
France.   They were pardoned for the past; but the law for the
general safety, "the Law of Suspicion," still hung over their future.
The proscribed men returned at their own risk and peril, to contend
with him who had proscribed them, not considering themselves
bound to be grateful because it pleased him to raise the ban in the
interests of his policy.

The imperial government was no more ready to abandon its
means of compression upon printed matter than upon people.   The
daily press imagined that the annulment of all restrictions indicated
the dawn of a gentler era for them.   They were soon undeceived
by a ministerial circular and by a severe note, rapidly followed by
fresh restrictions.

Italian affairs still continued to preoccupy all minds. The disappointment caused by Villafranca was followed by a lively return of interest and fresh attention to events beyond the Alps. People began to see that Villafranca was not the end, but the opening of a second phase of the Italian crisis. Cavour, and all Italy with him, speedily perceived the equivocal nature of the treaty between the two emperors. The Italians knew that Napoleon III. would not use force to restore the fallen princes, nor permit Austria to do so. This was enough to lead them to act boldly. The provisional governments formed by Tuscany, Parma, Modena and Romagna worked with one accord to pave the way for the annexation of their provinces with Piedmont. They displayed an admirable order and harmony, which showed what profit Italy had derived from her rude experience in 1848 and 1849. Traditions of local autonomy and federalist tendencies yielded everywhere to the necessity for union in a single strongly organized body, to resist the stranger still established in formidable positions upon Italian ground. That Tuscany should impose silence on her glorious memories, and renounce her hope of forming an independent state, said everything and promised everything.

The aspect of diplomatic circles upon this great movement was most singular and most complex. Piedmont, under the Ratazzi ministry which had succeeded to the Cavour ministry, had ostensibly abandoned Romagna and the duchies, but let the current run on with hope and joy. England changed her attitude for the third time since the war began. The ministry of Lord Derby, favorable to Austria and ill-disposed towards France and Italy, was forced into neutrality by public opinion. Defeated at the elections, both in regard to foreign and domestic policy, it was replaced in June by a Whig ministry under Lord Palmerston and Lord John Russell. The Whigs therefore came into power as representing a party which, without materially departing from neutrality, still sympathized with the war for Italian independence. The treaty of Villafranca only made this favorable feeling towards Italy more strongly marked, but did not produce the same effect in regard to

France.   English *amour-propre* was wounded that war could be
made and peace achieved without the participation of England, and
the Tory party loudly declared, on the platform and in the newspaper, that the only motive of Napoleon III. in compromising
with Austria was that he might turn against Great Britain.   The
naval preparations of the French were enumerated with emphasis,
their many steam-ships and their preparations for breastplating their
vessels, and protecting them with fenders.   The new ministers put
no faith in the imminent perils proclaimed by their adversaries: they
had no right to complain because peace was made without consulting them; for they had received from Persigny, the French ambassador, a proposal for mediation, to which they had not seen fit to
respond.   They were not disposed to quarrel with France; but they,
nevertheless, ordered "defensive" preparations to calm the anxiety
which had been excited throughout the country: as for Italy, they
decided to put all their diplomacy at the disposal of Italian aspirations, and to urge on the formation of the largest kingdom possible
beyond the Alps.   They hoped to substitute thus, at very little expense, English influence for the French influence acquired at the cost
of so much gold and so much blood, and also to prevent certain Italian provinces from falling to the share of any member or ally of
the Bonaparte family.

   Napoleon III. was in a difficult position, and his attitude was
more puzzling than ever.   He received the agents of Italian provinces cordially, and did not retract the comforting words which he
had uttered to Victor Emanuel when he left him to return to
France: "Now we must see what the Italians can do for themselves."   At the same time, however, he allowed Walewski, his
minister of foreign affairs, to use harsh and discouraging terms to
these same envoys.   September 9, the *Moniteur* published a statement that the greatest concessions would be accorded by Austria to
Venice, on condition that the dispossessed princes were restored
to their thrones.

   This manifestation in the sense of Villafranca seemed to coin-
cide with the raising of the shield of the clerical party in France.

Bologna, Ferrara, and all Romagna refusing to return to papal domination, Pius IX. now broke with the Piedmontese government, and sent his passports to the ambassador of Victor Emmanuel. He refused to listen either to Victor Emmanuel's proposal to rule Romagna as Vicar of the Holy See, or to the request of Napoleon III. that the Holy Father would make "the necessary reforms" in his states. The French bishops, upon this occasion, attacked Napoleon III. with complaints and reproaches. For the first time they assailed that government which had been their ally ever since the 2d of December. Would Napoleon III. yield to the movement of this party, upon which he had hitherto leaned, and thus lose finally all the fruits of his great Italian enterprise?

The duchies and Romagna now sent delegates to Victor Emmanuel to present to him the unanimous desire of their people for annexation to his kingdom. The king, with prudent reserve, accepted the rights which were conferred upon him, in virtue of solemn promises which he was to carry out with the great powers, and especially with the Emperor of the French.

The provinces of Central Italy found no fault with the conditional part of this acceptance, and thenceforth ruled in the name of Victor Emmanuel, "king elect." They completed their military organization, that they might be able to put down any attempt at armed reaction, whether on the part of the dethroned princes or on that of the King of Naples and the Papal troops.

Napoleon III., however, on October 20, wrote to Victor Emmanuel a letter, which, like the plan of September 9, maintained the bases of Villafranca, explained and interpreted as follows: "The honorary presidency of the Pope; the restoration of former sovereigns, 'without foreign intervention,' and excepting the union of the Duchy of Parma with Piedmont; Italian representation, administration, and troops to prevail in Venice; Mantua and Peschiera to become federal fortresses."

Napoleon III. invited Victor Emmanuel to aid him in the development of this plan. The scheme was so chimerical that one can scarcely allow that its author meant it seriously. On Napoleon's part it was expedient in view of the negotiations then drawing to a close at Zurich. The plenipotentiaries of France, Austria, and Piedmont had assembled on that neutral ground to convert the preliminaries of Villafranca into a permanent treaty.

They stumbled across inextricable difficulties, as might readily be supposed. The previously belligerent powers might certainly settle together matters which directly concerned them, such as the situation of Lombardy or Venice; but had they the right to decide upon the organization of all Italy, without consulting the Italian governments foreign to the compact of Villafranca, or those powers which had taken part in the European adjustments of 1815 ?

English diplomacy, although not represented at Zurich, made a great stir in order to promote the referring of the general affairs of Italy to a European Congress. This was the true way in which to deprive France of her preponderance in the question. Yet Napoleon III. did not repulse this scheme, and the negotiations at Zurich resulted merely in the disposal, by a treaty signed November 10, of Lombardy, which was ceded by Austria to France, and by France to Piedmont. As for the rest, France and Austria promised to lend all their influence to bring about the creation of a confederation between the various states of Italy.

The clauses of the federal compact were to be determined by the united representatives of all the Italian states, including Austria ! " The territorial limits of the Italian states which did not originate in the last war, being incapable of change without the concurrence of those powers which presided over their formation and recognized their existence, the rights of the Grand Duke of Tuscany, the Duke of Modena, and the Duke of Parma are expressly reserved."

This implied the meeting of a European congress to regulate all questions left undecided. The European congress was destined to the same fate as the Italian confederacy: it was never to come to pass. While another congress at Paris was pompously proclaimed to Europe, Napoleon III. was arranging a manœuvre which would make that assembly impossible. During the month of December a pamphlet, entitled " The Pope and the Congress," burst upon the

world like a bombshell. It was the work of a well-known publicist,
M. de la Guéronnière, but every one perceived the emperor's ideas
in it. It not only denounced the restoration of Romagna to the
Pope, but, while admitting the necessity of the temporal power of
the Holy Father, it affirmed that the territory of the Papal States
should be reduced to the smallest extent possible, in view of the
absolutely exceptional conditions of his government. The Pope required nothing more than Rome with a suburb of a few thousand
souls.

December 31, Napoleon III. wrote to Pius IX., advising him
plainly to give up his insurgent provinces (Ferrara, Bologna, and
Romagna), and inviting him to request the great powers to preserve the rest of his states for him. The emperor did not go so
far officially as the pamphlet, which had been sent out as an experiment.

Pius IX., who desired neither the presidency of the Italian confederation, nor the reforms which France and even Austria had
demanded of him at Villafranca and Zurich, was still less disposed
to make terms in regard to Romagna.

January 1, 1860, during the official New Year receptions he gave
a violent rating to the commander of the French garrison, General
de Goyon, apropos of the pamphlet, "The Pope and the Congress,"
which he termed an arrant piece of hypocrisy and an ignoble
tissue of contradictions.

Napoleon III. had made up his mind, and this impotent wrath
did not move him. He had recently replaced Walewski, the minister of foreign affairs, who was inimical to Italy, by a distinguished
diplomat, M. Thouvenel, a friend of the Italian cause (January 4,
1860), — a change which was speedily responded to at Turin by
Cavour's resumption of ministerial powers (January 17).

The emperor had determined to consent to the Italian annexations
and to claim the price of his consent. The large compensation
obtained by Piedmont in the place of Venice, which Napoleon III.
had promised her, permitted France in her turn to demand another
annexation, that of Savoy and Nice, conformably to the secret cove-

nants of 1858. The new kingdom of Italy, founded with the aid of France, could not retain provinces which were French in origin, language, and geographical situation.

Napoleon III. foresaw the anger of Europe, and especially of England, when this restoration to France of a portion of her frontiers, wrested from her in 1814, should be accomplished, and this, too, after the emperor had so frequently protested that he had no desire for aggrandizement. He therefore took measures to allay English displeasure.

Under the new Palmerston ministry, as under the Derby ministry, England was already full of uneasiness and jealousy. In Egypt she was striving to hinder the great enterprise of M. de Lesseps; she had persuaded the Ottoman Porte to order the Pacha of Egypt to put a stop to the works undertaken for the piercing of the isthmus of Suez. M. Thouvenel, French ambassador at Constantinople before he was recalled to become minister of foreign affairs, bravely supported M. de Lesseps, and gained the co-operation of the representatives of other great powers against the English embassy. European opinion was unanimous in favor of the reopening of the great roadway of ancient commerce.

The prohibition was removed. Work on the canal was resumed at Damietta and on the Mediterranean, and, on the opposite shore, Port Said was established on the Red Sea. The English public began to blame the groundless opposition of their government, and the future of the Suez Canal was thenceforth secure.

At the other extreme of the Mediterranean, in Morocco, England betrayed an equal lack of confidence. The weak and disorderly government of this African empire either could not or would not prevent the inroads of its subjects across the frontier of the French province of Oran and into territory belonging to Spain upon the Morocco coast. Spain demanded satisfaction, which was refused, upon which she declared war. France, without declaring war against the Emperor of Morocco, sent troops to chastise those tribes which had encroached upon French ground. The English government took alarm at the harmony of action between France and

Spain.   They feared that Gibraltar would be in danger if the Spanish should seize Tangiers and occupy the African shore of the Strait
with the support of France.   The Spanish waged a brief and brilliant campaign ; they gained a battle, and imposed their own terms
on the Emperor of Morocco; but they reassured England by exacting no cession of land.

Napoleon III., on his side, strove to regain English favor by
assisting England more and more actively in an enterprise which
united French and English arms, at the farther end of the world,
in China.   We will speak further of this later on.

The emperor touched English interests still more closely by a
great economic measure.   Towards the close of 1859 he had entered
into negotiations with England for a commercial treaty.   Preliminaries were begun by the French side, in England at first, by the
old St. Simonian, Michael Chevalier, now a leader of the economical
and free-trade party.   The bases were arranged by this secret agent
and Mr. Gladstone, chancellor of the exchequer, assisted by the
famous English economist, Richard Cobden.   After which the affair
was carried on at Paris by Mr. Cobden and the English ambassador,
Lord Cowley, on one side, and on the other by the French minister
of commerce, Rouher, and M. Baroche, minister of foreign affairs
pro tem., until the arrival of Thouvenel.   The minister of finance,
M. Magne, a partisan of the protective system, knew no more of
what was going on than did the public at large.

January 5, 1860, the emperor addressed a letter to M. Achille
Fould, minister of state, setting forth an entire system of political
economy.   He lauded the benefits of free trade, while he acknowledged that, before France developed her foreign trade by exchanging
her produce for that of other countries, she must better her agriculture and liberate her manufactures of every kind from the domestic
obstacles which placed them, in certain respects, in an inferior position.   He then went on to explain what, from his point of view,
should be done to promote agriculture.   As for manufactures, all
duties should be removed from raw material, loans should be granted
to manufacturers to enable them to perfect their stock ; new canals,

highways, and railroads should be completed as rapidly as possible.
The encouragement of commerce by the multiplication of means of
exchange would follow these measures as their natural consequence.
The successive diminution of the tax on commodities of staple consumption. he continued, would then be necessary, as well as the
substitution of protective for prohibitive duties. These improvements, he concluded, might be brought about, on the one hand, by
applying to great public works the sum of one hundred and sixty
million francs left unengaged from the sum total of the loan obtained for the Italian war (Italy had paid back this amount towards
the expenses of France), and, on the other hand, by a provisional
suspension of the sinking fund.

Although this long lucubration contained some commonplaces
and some impractical ideas, the general drift of it was acceptable.
The emperor seemed disposed to proceed prudently in his transformation of the economic system, and in establishing the utility of
commercial treaties with foreign nations, he announced the removal
of no duties save those on raw materials. It is true that this point
opened up a serious question. With the cotton, which France does
not produce, Napoleon III. characterized as raw material wool, then
one of the most important products of what might be called the
rural industry of France, which he would thus surrender unreservedly to competition.

The trade treaty, thus announced, was signed January 23. The
desire to maintain Lord Palmerston's ministry by a commercial
arrangement agreeable to the English people largely contributed
to hasten this result. Palmerston, after all, was worth more to
Napoleon than Lord Derby.

The treaty was in accordance neither with the promises formerly
made by the emperor to the Legislative Chambers, nor the letter of
January 5. It did not go so far as to accept total free trade, but
entered largely upon the path of competition without the preparation promised. Not only were the taxes on what was termed raw
material removed, but a quantity of English manufactured goods
was allowed to enter France in consideration of duties which were

in no case to exceed, for the present, thirty per cent of the value, then, dating from October 1, 1864, twenty-five per cent. Short of this maximum, the French government was at liberty to reduce the duties at will.

England in turn agreed to receive a certain number of French products duty free, and to reduce her duties on French wines. The ships of both nations were to be upon an equal footing. Both powers bound themselves to yield each other mutual profit from any advantage that they might grant to a third power. All this, for England, was subject to the sanction of Parliament; for France, there was no such clause. The dictator of December 2, in his constitution, had assigned himself full power to conclude treaties.

The treaty was valid for ten years, then to continue from year to year, if not disavowed.

After the discussion which took place the year before, upon the occasion of a new tariff law, a lively opposition was now to be expected from the Legislative Body.

The session began on the 1st of March, the emperor opening it with words of peace which confirmed the reduction of the contingent force of one hundred and forty thousand men to one hundred thousand, as well as a large reduction of the effective force already bearing arms. He announced "a number of measures tending to increase the welfare of the working classes, and to multiply commercial relations." The treaty with England he declared was the first step towards this end. He claimed the active support of the Legislature in favor of laws destined to facilitate the application and the advantageous consequences of the treaty, and promised that, in spite of the decrease and suppression of duties, his government would have recourse neither to new taxes nor fresh loans. He closed by an assurance that France had no other desire than to "develop peacefully her vast resources," and by affirming this axiom, — that, the richer and more prosperous a country becomes, the more it contributes to the wealth and prosperity of others.

The discussion of the legal schemes arising from the trade treaty was long and animated. The first scheme related to the tariff on raw material. There was much complaint because the government had brought a fixed and irrevocable treaty to the Chambers, nothing being left to discuss but its practical execution. The commissioners of the government answered the opposition by pointing to the text of the constitution.

Remarkable figures in regard to the increase of French manufactures and export trade under the system just changed were quoted in the course of the debate. In the matter of coal, the production had increased since the Restoration from 9,000,000 hundredweight to 79,000,000; in cast iron, the increase was from 2,000,000 hundredweight in 1826 to 8,500,000 in 1857. French exports, from the amount of 755,000,000 francs in 1847, had risen in 1858 to 1,887,000,000. The question was to know whether the suppression or diminution of duties would cut this progress short, as the protectionists claimed. They were answered by the fact that this great increase did not occur until after the excess of protective duties was diminished. We have quoted figures of general commerce. The special trade of France with England in 1858 had risen to 587,000,000 francs. As for navigation, the ships employed in the merchant service between France and England gauged in 1825 151,000 tons, 84,000 of which were French vessels. In 1858, the ships gauged 2,419,000 tons, of which but 703,000 belonged to France. That country had therefore advanced, but in far less proportion than England.

One of the protectionist orators opposed the emperor with his own words, quoting a passage from the works of Napoleon III., dating from 1842, which treated the theory of free trade as absolutely fatal. M. Pouyer-Quertier, reporter for the committee, eagerly attacked the treaty; but the legal scheme in regard to raw materials was nevertheless accepted by two hundred and forty-nine votes against four. The protectionists did not cast a negative vote, which could not have affected the treaty.

The famous quarrel between the parties of protection and free trade on the subject of the treaty of 1860 was destined to be renewed more than once in the almost periodic crises to which com-

MADAME ADELAIDE.

merce is subject. It was inevitable that this abrupt change of
system should cause much suffering of a certain degree. However,
the great increase of intercourse with England was not to injure
France in the long run, for if the imports were large, so were the
exports. Not only French grape-growers, but stock-raisers as well,
were to send vast supplies to England. Even the manufacturers
of France, by brave and intelligent effort, would finally wage a successful strife in regard to many articles which proved their varied
skill and inventive taste. In fine, the treaty might be blameworthy
in form and for its precipitancy, but not for its tendency, which
was towards progress.

The various laws of application passed in rapid succession. They
related to the purchase of canals; the construction of certain secondary railroads; the beginning of a network of railways in Algiers;
the draining of marshes; work on town and county roads; stocking
certain mountains with timber; diversion to public works of the
funds left from the war loan; and, lastly, loans to manufacturers to
enable them to perfect their stock. This latter scheme was much
contested, as it well might be; it was far from practical, and, if
executed, must necessarily have been done in an insufficient and
arbitrary way.

The passage of the laws resulting from the trade treaty was followed by a very animated debate in regard to the affairs of the city
of Paris. A law was essential to authorize the bonds which the
city, or rather its dictator, M. Haussman, desired to issue to cover
his extraordinary expenses. The gigantic undertaking to create a
new Paris, and the financial burden consequent upon it, alarmed all
provident minds. M. Ernest Picard, with his intelligent good sense
and incisive utterance, made a vigorous attack upon the administration of the prefect of the Seine; but his oratorical success could not
prevent the confirmatory vote which the majority dared not refuse
to yield the emperor. The Legislative Chambers had also passed,
during the previous year, a law doubling the surface extent of the
Paris which formerly was considered so huge! All parishes or parts
of parishes within the circuit of the fortifications were by this law

annexed to the capital. But this was to be expected from the
moment that the fortifications were built. The financial condition,
not merely of Paris but of all France, called for serious consideration. M. Larrabure, a deputy by no means inimical to the imperial
government, drew an honest and far from reassuring picture of the
situation. He showed the constant increase of expenditure and
debt. Within a few years, two thousand two hundred and seventy-
four million francs more than the regular supply had been spent.
The conclusion of Larrabure's speech was that all budgets for eleven
years past would have been discharged in deficit, if recourse had not
been had to extraordinary credit. Moreover, the sinking fund was
not suspended; sums were expended which, in a normal state of
things, would have been set aside each year with the view of redeeming the debt.

Italian affairs excited even more interest in the Legislature than
the trade treaty. Clerical passions waged more violent than protective interests. The emperor, in his opening speech, had complained of the fierce alarm manifested by a portion of the Catholic
world, and their entire oblivion of the services which he had rendered, — he who, single-handed, eleven years since, had maintained
the power of the Holy Father at Rome. These reproaches on the
part of Napoleon III. called forth lively recriminations from the
clerical party in both Chambers. The Senate dared not grant a
favorable reception to the petitions pressed upon its members in
favor of the temporal power; but, in the bosom of the Legislative
Body, many speakers inveighed against the connivance of the government in regard to the annexation of Romagna.

In the same speech which so displeased the clericals, Napoleon
III. expressed his regrets, more or less sincere, that the ideas of
Villafranca had failed of execution.

He acknowledged, in the present situation, having advised Victor
Emmanuel to respond to the desire of the provinces which offered
themselves to him, though with some rather vague reserves as to
the autonomy of Tuscany and the rights of the Holy See to be
respected "in principle." This was the preparation for an important revelation.

"In view of this transformation of Northern Italy, which gives all the Alpine passes to a powerful state, it was my duty," concluded the emperor, "to lay claim to the French side of the mountains. France frankly laid the question before the great powers. She has a right to a guarantee indicated by nature herself."

The English government, although ignorant of the secret agreement of 1858, must have suspected that the Italian annexations would determine the French annexations. Its members, however, displayed as much disappointment and rage as if France's gain were England's loss. The minister of foreign affairs, Lord John Russell, tried to persuade the continental powers to join with England in opposing this modification of the territorial limits of 1815. Although Germany continued to exhibit hatred and anxiety, these overtures were ill received. Prussia would not move in the matter. Austria bitterly replied that she regarded the annexation of Savoy to France in the same light that England had viewed the annexation of Lombardy and Piedmont. Russia had no objection to make to what seemed to her a perfectly fair arrangement between France and Piedmont.

The character of the Whig ministry became worse than that of the Tory ministry which it had so eagerly attacked; its conduct was unjustifiable throughout; for England had not the slightest interest in the question, but the self-love of English statesmen was wounded. They thought themselves outwitted by Napoleon III., who had so loudly protested that he had no idea of enlarging his territory, while he had his secret treaty of 1858 in his pocket. Napoleon III. managed to prove himself wrong in form, although he was right at bottom. His boasted cunning was very ill placed here; honesty would have been a far better policy. If he had made no promises, no one would have had a word to say.

March 25, the *Moniteur* announced that "King Victor Emmanuel consented to the union of Savoy and Nice with France, on condition that he should agree with the French government in regard to the mode of consulting the inhabitants of those provinces without putting any constraint upon their will."

Both provinces voted in the affirmative by an immense majority, Nice on the 15th of April, Savoy on the 22d. Great enthusiasm prevailed in Savoy, where the people remembered their rapturous surrender to France in 1792. There was rather more hesitation at Nice, the birthplace of Garibaldi, and deeply attached to that constitutional liberty not to be found in imperial France.

From the standard of origin, geographical situation, natural interests and relations, the county of Nice, formerly a part of Provence, was quite as French as Savoy. The boundary between France and Italy was originally at the Turbia, beyond Mentone.

The Second Empire thus restored to France a portion of those natural frontiers which the First Republic gave her, and which Napoleon I. lost for her. Napoleon III. yet made her pay dearly for this service!

March 26, the day after that on which the *Moniteur* announced the signing of the treaty between Napoleon III. and Victor Emmanuel, a storm of reproaches burst forth in the English Parliament, which almost amounted to threats. Lord John Russell, who was not used to diplomatic caution, intimated that a European coalition might ensue if similar questions of annexation were renewed.

Coalitions were not so easy of accomplishment in the condition of Europe since the Crimean war, and this was not the danger which France had to dread. In the discussions that followed, the radicals and free-traders, Mr. Bright, Cobden, and their friends, broke with whigs as well as with tories. In point of fact, the English ministry, despite its displeasure, had no wish to break with France, being satisfied with the trade treaty, and desiring French support in China, then in full action. The relations between the two governments had become imbittered; but on neither side was there any thought of a breach.

A paragraph appeared in the *Moniteur*, June 1, protesting against the accusation of aiming at further aggrandizement. A few days later Napoleon III. crossed the frontier on his way to Baden to meet the Prince Regent of Prussia and the leading sovereigns of Germany, who, with the exception of the Emperor of Austria, were then assembled there.   He exerted himself to the utmost to set them at ease in regard to his plans.

Meantime the course of events moved rapidly in Italy.   Victor Emmanuel and Cavour had lost no time in putting the new kingdom upon a constitutional footing, the parliament of Upper Italy taking the place of the Piedmontese parliament at Turin.   This was undoubtedly a great result, but Napoleon III. erred in supposing that the national and unitarian movement in Italy could be arrested midway.   Coming events would surpass not only the expectations of Napoleon III., but the hopes, if not the wishes, of Victor Emmanuel and Cavour.

Had there been a reasonable and liberal government at Naples, a kingdom of Lower Italy might have prolonged its existence more or less, in face of the new kingdom of Upper Italy, with the Pope at Rome between the two.   But the change of rule which had recently occurred in the southern dominion had not brought about any marked improvement.   The young King Francis II., surrounded by his father's counsellors, maintained almost intact the system of terrorism established in the preceding reign; the law of suspicion was still in point of fact the supreme law of Naples and Sicily. Nearly one hundred and eighty thousand names were inscribed upon the police registry, and were subject to supervision as under suspicion.   They comprised almost all the enlightened people of the kingdom.   Since the first of the year, thousands of citizens had been arrested on mere suspicion.   The Swiss soldiers in the service of Naples, who formed the solid nucleus of the army, having revolted, the Neapolitan government strove to replace them with Austrian hirelings.

Sicily was even more severely oppressed than the continental provinces.   Still bleeding from the struggle of 1848 and 1849, she renewed her insurrectionary attempts.   The tricolored flag was hoisted at various points on the island, and the Sicilians uttered an appeal for deliverance to " their brothers " of Upper Italy.

The volunteers of the previous year began to form again in Lombardy, at Genoa and elsewhere.   The fermentation was all pervasive.

The volunteers summoned the hero of the revolutionary war, Garibaldi, who, after Villafranca, was employed in putting Romagna under military organization.

On the night of May 5, Garibaldi left Genoa with a thousand picked men, embarking upon two steamships willingly lent by the company of owners. The Italian government shut their eyes to these preparations, and did not disturb the vessels, which steered for Sicily; only they prevented a scanty detachment, landed on the Tuscan coast by Garibaldi, from entering the Roman provinces. Garibaldi had his eye on both Naples and Rome, but Victor Emmanuel and Cavour would not at any price permit Italy to be exposed to a rupture with the emperor by a *coup de main* at Rome.

Garibaldi landed successfully at Marsala, protected by the connivance of two English ships which hampered the action of Neapolitan vessels sent in pursuit of the volunteers. What next occurred seems more like some romance of chivalry than like history; or, at least, in all modern history the campaign of the "Thousand" recalls nothing but the campaign of Fernando Cortez. The Thousand, reinforced by three or four thousand Sicilians, repulsed all whom they met, reached Palermo in a few days, outwitted by skilful arts of war all attempts to surround them made by the numerous bodies of troops occupying that capital. The Thousand finally entered Palermo, roused the expectant populace to revolt by their single-hearted ardor, and so thoroughly alarmed the twenty-five or thirty thousand soldiers of the King of Naples, that they were forced to capitulate and evacuate the city (May 27–June 6). Garibaldi's heroic flame kindled the soul of an entire nation.

Victor Emmanuel was proclaimed in Palermo and throughout the island. The news from Sicily produced a profound impression all over Europe. The continental powers, who had seemed indifferent to the changes effected in the north and centre of Italy, exhibited great irritation at the attack against the kingdom of Naples. Prussia, far from showing sympathy at the completion of Italian unity, now talked of renewing the triple alliance between Russia, Austria, and Prussia. The Russian minister of foreign affairs, Prince Gor-

tchakof, sent a very decided protest in favor of the Naples Bourbons.
Napoleon III. also protested, but rather in perplexity than in wrath.
The Russian and Prussian manifestoes, however, stopped short at
offering the King of Naples their "moral support." This was not
enough to arrest Garibaldi in his onward course.

The King of Naples, in his distress, resigned himself to beg the
intervention of Napoleon III.; he promised to give his subjects a
constitution, to ally himself with Victor Emmanuel, and proclaimed
every imaginable concession in Naples. " It is too late." Such was
the reply of Napoleon III. to the Neapolitan envoys, whom he sent
back to Turin.

Not that the French emperor viewed with satisfaction the master-
strokes which were destroying all his own combinations. He had
indeed desired the kingdom of Upper Italy; but he by no means
wished for the unity of Italy under Victor Emmanuel. He would
now have been glad to maintain at least the kingdom of Naples
without Sicily. Those about him thought of taking up Napoleonic
traditions once more, and substituting a Murat for the Bourbons. He
had no decided feeling in the matter, but he proposed to England
that they should act together to prevent Garibaldi from crossing
the Straits of Messina and marching on Naples. England did not
consent. The English cabinet had decided to accept Italian unity.

Victor Emmanuel, however, to gratify the emperor, wrote to Garibaldi to dissuade him from crossing the straits. Garibaldi disobeyed,
and effected a descent into Calabria during the first two weeks in
August. The king was quite ready to pardon this lack of obedience, and Cavour applauded the march on Naples in advance, in a
letter to the Italian admiral Persano, who befriended to his utmost
ability the convoy bearing supplies to Garibaldi.

Garibaldi advanced rapidly through the Neapolitan provinces,
stirring to arms Calabria, Campania, and Apulia. One of the first
engagements on the coast of Calabria was marked by the glorious
death of a French lieutenant in the service of the Italian hero, the
former representative of the people, Paul de la Flotte, elected from
Paris in 1850, who had recently joined the Thousand.

King Francis II. felt in no fit state to defend his capital, which he evacuated with his army and retired to Gaeta. Garibaldi entered Naples almost alone, hailed with delight by the whole vast city, including those fiery and fickle lazzaroni so long the support of Bourbon royalty (September 7).

The diplomatic body, for the most part, had followed Francis to Gaeta, but the representatives of England and France remained at Naples. This showed that Napoleon III., as well as the English government, had now decided to accept the union of Upper and Lower Italy in a single kingdom.

Parallel with the startling events of the war, occurred secret political incidents of no less importance. At the time when Cavour applauded the expedition to Naples, there was nevertheless a very serious difference of opinion between him and Garibaldi. The great politician, while desiring the hero's triumph, feared that the latter, who heeded no danger or difficulty, would march straight from Naples to Rome to attack the French garrison. The situation would then become purely revolutionary, and the consequences would be incalculable.

Cavour anxiously considered how to prevent a stroke which might bring on a catastrophe. The condition of the Papal States afforded him the means. Napoleon III. had allowed General Lamoricière, who from republican had turned devout Catholic and legitimist, to assume command of a small Catholic army formed by the Holy Father. The emperor was not ignorant of the grave inconvenience of the occupation of Rome by French troops, and meant to withdraw them when the Pope should have a military force of any permanency at his disposal; but it happened that this little papal army, composed of men of all nations, under the influence of a staff of French legitimists, assumed a guise, not merely counter-revolutionary, but anti-imperialist and distinctly royalist. They set at defiance the French government almost as fully as the new Italian government, to which they addressed rash challenges.

Napoleon III. was therefore very ill disposed towards what was going on at Rome. Cavour made haste to profit by this feeling.

He sent two of the most distinguished men in Italy, Minister Farini and General Cialdini, to seek the emperor at Chambéry, whither he had gone on a visit to his two new provinces of Savoy and Upper Savoy. The Italian envoys represented to Napoleon that their king would lose popularity and soon be swept away by the Italian movement, if he did not take his place at the head of his people to carry on the work of Italian unity. The question was whether the work should be achieved by revolution or by the regular forces of a national monarchy. All that remained to the Pope north of the Apennines, Umbria, and the Marches, was now in a state of insurrection and engaged in struggle with Lamoricière's army. It was impossible to prevent the people of Romagna, Tuscany, and the rest from going to the succor of their neighbors and brothers, and it was equally impossible to put a stop to the purely revolutionary state of the kingdom of Naples, unless the royal Italian army moved towards the Neapolitan provinces and joined them to the kingdom of Italy. To accomplish this it was necessary to seize the Marches and Umbria, passing over the carcass of Lamoricière's army.

Napoleon, after mature reflection, is said to have answered, "*Fate, ma fate presto!*" (Do it, but do it quickly!) This reply has been justly doubted; it is unlike his character. He listened in silence, did not bind himself to anything, but did not dissuade Italy from action. This was all that the king and Cavour required. (End of August.)

The Italian government at first protested against the formation of a "foreign army" in the Roman state; then it demanded the immediate disarmament of the "foreign hirelings." The Pope's minister, Cardinal Antonelli, refused in virulent terms. Cavour addressed a memorandum to the great powers informing them that the royal Italian troops were about to enter Umbria and the Marches to restore order and protect the inhabitants. Rome and her territory would be respected. (September 12.)

Without losing a day, two strong columns of Italians marched forward. September 18, Lamoricière's little army was routed by General Cialdini. Lamoricière withdrew to Ancona, where Cialdini

followed and besieged him. Everything fell to pieces about Lamoricière, and the bold general of African fame, despite all his energy,
was forced to surrender.

Russia and Prussia protested anew, and now supported their protest by the recall of their ambassadors from Turin. Napoleon III.
felt that he could not well avoid doing as much. Victor Emmanuel
and Cavour were but slightly disturbed. They knew that it was a
mere matter of form. The action of the French government was
limited to using the French garrison at Rome, with slight reinforcements, to maintain the two Roman provinces in the south, subject
to the Pope. Viterbo, Orvieto, and other cities had begun by proclaiming Victor Emmanuel, in imitation of their Umbrian neighbors.

Some anxiety was felt in Italy and even in France when it was
known that the emperors of Russia and Austria and the Prince
Regent of Prussia had had an interview at Warsaw (October 21–
26). Was the Holy Alliance to be re-formed? They were soon set
at ease. The French ambassador in Russia notified his government
that the Czar had protested to him that his object was "conciliation
and not coalition." Alexander II. would not grant Austria his aid
to renew the war, nor was Prussia longer inclined that way, especially as Russia had refused her help.

While the monarchs were conferring thus without coming to any
conclusion, the Italian revolution went on, but under royal direction
now. The king's troops entered the papal provinces by land and
sea simultaneously. An offensive return of the army of the King of
Naples, left in possession of the strategic line from Gaeta to Capua,
favored Cavour's plans by detaining Garibaldi on the banks of
the Vulturnus. The volunteers fought brilliantly; but they were
not yet organized with sufficient strength to capture Gaeta or even
Capua, now their foes had finally resolved to defend the last refuge
of Bourbon royalty. The arrival of the Italian regulars solved the
question. The troops of the King of Naples, by one defeat after
another, were driven back upon Gaeta, while throughout the kingdom the people voted for the unity of Italy, one and indivisible,
under Victor Emmanuel.

Following General Cialdini, Victor Emmanuel joined Garibaldi in person. The king entered Naples with the revolutionary hero at his side (November 7). There was far from perfect harmony between them, however. The king felt very sincere sympathy and gratitude towards Garibaldi, but could not permit him to retain that revolutionary dictatorship over the kingdom of Milan which Garibaldi would fain have kept for a time, not from personal ambition, but in the interest of his views regarding Rome. The hero, obliged to pause in his impetuous career, refused the titles, the honors, and the fortune offered him by the king, whose kingdom he had so greatly increased. He withdrew to the little island of Caprera, between Corsica and Sardinia, there to await the moment to liberate Rome and Venice, occupying himself meantime with the cultivation of a few acres of land.

The Italian army had undertaken the siege of Gaeta. Napoleon III., on this occasion, fell back upon fresh contradictions. To make his protests against what he had permitted to take place appear serious, he refused to recognize the blockade of Gaeta, and sent the French fleet to protect that place, forbidding the Italians to attack it by sea. England, to make herself agreeable to Italy at the expense of France, made haste to protest against the refusal to recognize the siege. It was a great blunder to allow the English government this advantage, for the strange situation could not continue long. In January, 1861, Napoleon III., at the instance of Cavour, decided to withdraw his fleet, "from respect," he said, "for the principle of non-intervention." It would have been better to respect it at first, if he was to end there. The ex-King Francis II. was soon after obliged to capitulate, and set sail on a French ship to seek shelter in Rome.

Italy was complete, save for Rome and Venice.

The feeling in France was very various. The world of December and imperialism was greatly astonished, troubled, and embarrassed. The exploits of Garibaldi fired republicans and young people with enthusiasm. Politicians deeply admired Cavour. The ex-liberals allied to the clericals were as disconcerted as the imperialists, and did not conceal their displeasure at these extraordinary novelties which drowned their polished and academic opposition. The clerical party were furious at what they called the emperor's treachery. They exceeded all bounds in their episcopal charges, their pamphlets and papers.

The ruling power still treated the bishops cautiously, but attacked the press savagely. Many papers received official warnings, several were suppressed, notably the famous *Universe*, which, caring little for legitimacy, was the type of lay ultramontanism and held the clergy in tow. Its well-known maxim deprived it of all right to complain: "When I am the weakest," said M. Veuillot to the republican and liberal parties, "I ask you for liberty, because such is your principle; but when I am strongest, I deprive you of it, because it is not mine." A stronger power than his deprived him of it, and a time was yet to come when republicans would cease to admit that any one had a right to demand liberty to destroy liberty.

Amidst these agitations, in view of the intellectual movement excited by the great events occurring abroad, Napoleon III. thought it necessary to do something new at home, and to flatter public opinion by more or less effective concessions.

November 24, 1860, a decree had appeared stating that the Senate and Legislative Body were to vote an annual address in reply to the speech from the crown. The government commissioners, in discussing this address, would give the Chambers all necessary explanations in regard to foreign and domestic policy. The parliamentary reports of the legislative session, drawn up by the authority of the presiding officers, were to be addressed to the whole press. Moreover, the debates were to be printed entire in the official journal, the *Moniteur*. Finally, ministers without departments were to defend all legal schemes before the Chambers in concert with the commissioners from the council of state.

This was a fragment of the old parliamentary system brought forward once more: public affairs discussed in a general way, and legislative debates made public to a certain point, but without parliamentary sanction or ministerial responsibility, without liberty of the press, and with the maintenance of official candidature to the utmost extent.

Thorough imperialists, on the appearance of the decree, felt uneasy in regard to the emperor's "liberalism"; but a circular issued by Persigny, who had recently returned to the ministry of the interior, attested that there was no thought of relaxing the bonds which held the press fast: the warnings given before the decree were alone annulled. A former minister of the interior, the Duke of Padua, had ordered all prefects, in 1859, to draw up secretly a list of those persons under suspicion in the various departments. Persigny preserved these lists, which were to be corrected and altered from time to time according to circumstances. The list for Paris was found intact in 1870.

The legislative session opened February 4, 1861. The emperor's speech announced an evenly balanced budget, although ninety million francs of the receipts had been given up in consequence of the trade treaty. In a statement of the situation published by the government, many explanations were required of matters left unexplained by the emperor. The ninety millions lost were made up by twenty-six millions taken from the sinking fund, by increased taxes, and by the increase of receipts which had set in since peace began, and still the balance of the budget was fictitious; outside of the usual expenditure, distant expeditions to China and elsewhere, to which we shall refer later, had required extraordinary sums.

The Italian question aroused fresh storms. The emperor had been far from explicit; he seemed to blame, for form's sake only, deeds which he had permitted. The clerical party outdid the previous session; they raised a formidable array of bucklers against the Senate. Prince Napoleon, son-in-law of the King of Italy, replied to their first attacks by a great speech, in which he unreservedly upheld revolutionary right against divine right and against the treaties of 1815; he claimed for Italy, Rome, its capital, leaving to the Pope the Vatican and its dependencies, that quarter on the right bank of the Tiber known as the Città Leonina.

A regular tempest ensued in the Senate, so long mute. The ex-minister of the interior, Billault, had great difficulty in obtaining the rejection of two amendments in favor of the temporal power and in gaining permission to refer the question to the imperial wisdom. There was only a majority of seventy-nine against sixty-one.

In the Senate some regard for form was maintained; in the Legislative Body clerical opposition paused at no violence of language. Victor Emmanuel was insulted. "The Italian war," cried Deputy Keller, "is the execution of Orsini's will and testament."

The republicans, the Five, replied by demanding the withdrawal of French troops from Rome. The government observed a just medium; it proceeded between the two contrary amendments which claimed, the one the defence of temporal supremacy by France, the other the evacuation of Rome.

The address was accepted by the Legislative Body by two hundred and thirteen votes against one hundred and thirty-one. Never had such opposition been seen since the restoration of the empire; but the majority of the opponents only rejected the address because the government had shown itself not merely too Italian, but too liberal for their taste ever since the act of November 24.

These harsh discussions had far-reaching echoes among the clergy, and aroused fresh hostile demonstrations. There were some erroneous appeals, some unavailing prosecutions; but a much more serious action, before the close of the year, was the suppression of the central committee of the Society of St. Vincent de Paul. This great association, founded during the July Monarchy, for wholly pious and charitable purposes, had become a powerful weapon in the hands of the clerical party; its branches, spreading throughout France and even into foreign countries, were all subject to a committee of directors which became international. The ruling power broke up this organization, and only allowed the branches to live on condition that all connection between them was dissolved.

Simultaneously with the French legislative session came the opening of the session of the new Italian Parliament, which sprang from the general elections taking place from the Piedmontese Alps to the extreme point of Sicily. M. Cavour had again attempted secret

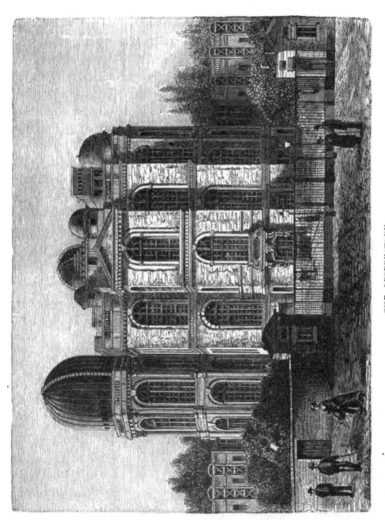

THE OBSERVATORY

negotiations with the Holy Father.   Pius IX., who, despite his hasty
temper, retained a remnant of Italian sentiment, had seemed to
waver for a time; but his minister, Antonelli, placed himself in the
way and broke off everything.   Cavour then declared plainly to the
Parliament that Italy must have Rome for her capital, but that it
could not be entered without the approval of France.   "The Catholic world," he added, "must not deem it the subjection of church
to state.   The independence of the supreme pontiff must not be
decreased thereby."   He explained, on various occasions, what he
understood by the separation of church and state; concordats were
to be suppressed at the same time as the temporal power, and the
church was to be allowed to govern herself as she saw fit, outside of
political authority.   He summed up this conception in the formula:
"A free church in a free state."

He was thinking of gaining Venice as well as Rome, and labored
to cut off Austria for the inevitable hour when the struggle must be
renewed between the Kingdom of Italy and the Austrian Empire in
regard to Venice.   He strove to gain Prussia by pledging her to
repeat in Germany, against the Austrian influence, the deeds of
Piedmont in Italy.   The Prince-Regent of Prussia had recently succeeded his brother under the name of William I. (January 2, 1861).
Cavour sent to him General La Marmora, ex-commander of the
Piedmontese division of the Crimean army.   The Italian negotiator
was well received, but gained no positive result.   Still Cavour was
content for the time being with opening the question.

The new King of Prussia, on his accession, uttered words at once
religious and warlike, as if he felt himself called to play the double
part of soldier and Protestant.   The religious point of view was
afterwards decidedly dominated by the other.

The Prussian Legislature assembling at the same time as the
French and Italian Chambers, an amendment was offered to the
address of the Prussian House of Deputies by the leader of the Left,
M. de Vincke, of the party known as the liberal-nationals.   He affirmed that neither Prussia nor Germany had any interest in thwarting the consolidation of the new state of things in Italy.   Another

deputy, M. de Duncker, declared that the object of the amendment was to turn Italy aside from France, and bring her over to the Prussian alliance.

Minister Schleinitz maintained his reserve, merely saying that the Prussian government could not advise Austria to give up Venice.

The amendment was accepted.

Cavour then opened another negotiation with Napoleon III., from which he hoped to obtain an immediate success. His endeavor was to gain the emperor's recognition of the Kingdom of Italy and the evacuation of Rome by the French troops, on condition that the Pope's safety was secured. The emperor was disposed to accede, in consideration of a promise on the part of the Italian government to prevent any attack on Rome, and on condition of an acknowledgment of the papal right to have an army of Catholic volunteers. The first trial of the system had failed, but still Cavour was undeterred by this difficulty.

The parleys continued at Paris during the dramatic debates of which the Italian Parliament was the scene. A regular political duel was waged between Cavour and Garibaldi. Cavour did ample justice to the liberator of Sicily and Naples, although he dreaded his impetuous outbreaks. The hero was not so fair towards the statesman. Garibaldi had two causes of complaint against Cavour which filled him with bitterness. Born at Nice, of a family of Genoese origin, he could not pardon the head of the ministry for giving his native city to France; nor could he pardon him for stopping him in his march on Rome and Venice, and now for disbanding his army of volunteers by mingling the best elements of it with the regular troops. From the seclusion of his retreat at Caprera, he hurled the most violent protests against the cabinet at Turin. His heart swelling with resentment, he assumed his seat in Parliament at Turin, and, in speaking of the disbandment of the volunteers, he let loose all his wrath against the ministers, accusing them of having exposed Italy to civil war, "to a fratricidal war."

Cavour appeared grander than ever, ruling his temper and explaining with much composure the decisive reasons which had obliged the Italian government to give up Nice as well as Savoy, and not to retain, as a separate organization, an army of volunteers which would seem like a threat of immediate renewal of war in despite of Europe.

Garibaldi's generous soul was not insensible to this grave and noble language. The hero calmed down, though still insisting on the maintenance of the remnant of his southern army. Cavour could not make this concession. Parliament decided in his favor, and Garibaldi, under the personal influence of the king, agreed to a private interview with the minister, and promised not to compromise the government with France nor with Austria. Cavour, on his side, pledged his word to give up neither Venice nor Rome. It was a question of time and means. (April, 1861.)

Cavour gained the day; but he was exhausted by the tremendous efforts of the past two years, by labors and emotions beyond human strength to bear. He was seized with an inflammatory disease at the end of May, and could not assist at the festival which ushered in the Kingdom of Italy by the restoration of the flags to the troops, — a festival which he had promoted, and whose joy was marred by his absence. He died June 6.

The feeling of mourning extended throughout Italy. Cavour had founded his work so well that it could be carried on and completed without him, although he was one of those men who are not to be replaced. His loss was not only a misfortune to Italy, but to France as well. He based his policy upon the French alliance, and the influence which, in the high position he had acquired, he must have exerted over Europe might have warded off great calamities. He was the only man who had any power over the hesitating and yet daring spirit of Napoleon III., and he would never have made other than a good use of it.

Napoleon III. paid his last tribute to this great man by granting to Victor Emmanuel recognition of the Kingdom of Italy, until then uncertain, immediately after his death. England had done the same thing three months before; the smaller states had imitated her example; the great powers now followed, excepting Austria.

The assembly of the scattered portions of Italy in one body, in one state, which, although still incomplete, already numbered twenty-two million inhabitants, — the introduction of this new state among the great European powers, was the most important national event in the history of Europe since the dismemberment of Poland. What would the consequences be to France, the originator of the great deed? France had regained her frontier of the Alps. The rest depended upon the policy to be pursued by her government in regard to the incomplete nation which naturally aspired to perfect itself, and whose interests in Europe were in no way opposed to those of France.

CHAPTER XX.

SECOND EMPIRE (*continued*). — DISTANT EXPEDITIONS. — CHINESE WAR. — ESTABLISHMENT OF COCHIN-CHINA. — EXPEDITION TO SYRIA. — MEXICAN WAR.

1857 to 1867.

THE Second Empire, after its two great European wars, carried on a series of expeditions to the ends of the earth, inspired by the general idea which ruled it, — the desire to occupy public opinion, to divert it from domestic matters, — inspired by various causes and with various views.

Previous to the Italian war, Napoleon III. had already engaged with England in a quarrel with China. This vast and ancient empire, a huge anthill swarming with men, containing a population more than ten times as great as that of France, and several cities twice the size of Paris, attained, about the seventeenth century, its highest degree of power and civilization. Since then it had gradually degenerated; the springs of the huge machine seemed worn out; military ruin was particularly complete. This people, who had invented everything, now carried nothing to completion, and for two centuries past had held aloof from all the progress going on in other parts of the world. Without confessing her inferiority, China feared, and at the same time despised, foreigners, and attempted to close all entrance to her confines both by sea and by land. She deemed herself a world in herself and self-sufficient.

Russia by land, and England by sea, had nevertheless labored persistently to cross the boundaries. The Chinese government did not display the firm determination, and did not obtain the unreserved obedience and loyalty, required for such a voluntary blockade as the vast monarchy desired to impose. Anglo-Indian commerce entered at the southern ports of China. And what a commerce! The steady poisoning of a nation! The English merchants of India, taking advantage of the Chinese love of opium, introduced enormous quantities of this dangerous drug; and the passion, the frenzy of opium drunkenness, invading the country more and more, produced worse ravages among the people than did ever alcohol-drinking among those inhabitants of Western countries most addicted to that vice.

The Chinese government were aroused by the excess of the evil. All the opium stored in Anglo-Indian warehouses at Canton was cast into the sea. A war ensued, in which the Chinese, incapable of withstanding the military and maritime prowess of modern times, were forced to submit to the demands of the English. A treaty, signed at Nankin, August 29, 1842, opened five Chinese ports to English trade. The other maritime nations of Europe and the United States of America claimed and obtained the same privileges (October, 1843).

It was no longer a question of opium only, but of general trade. A commercial and naval treaty was concluded between France and China, September 24, 1844. One of its articles authorized the erection of Christian schools and churches within the limits of the five ports. An edict of the Chinese Emperor empowered native Christians to practise their form of worship within those bounds. As for Catholic missionaries, if they penetrated into the interior of the empire, the Chinese government retained the right to arrest them, but pledged itself to return them to the keeping of their respective consuls. The July Government thus maintained, but to a reasonable extent, its protectorate of Christianity in the Orient, inherited by new France from the old monarchy, which was an influential principle from a political point of view, but also a source of grave embarrassment.

The situation of China, however, grew constantly worse. A great insurrection broke out against the Tartar dynasty, which had for several centuries ruled the Chinese Empire. What was learned in

Europe in regard to the very complex religious and social elements·
at work among the insurgent masses, and the views attributed to
their chief leader seemed prophetic of a total restoration of China,
and excited a lively feeling of expectation. It was illusory; the
revolt of the Taï-Pings was not fated to become organized nor to
found anything whatever; their momentary triumphs, their struggle
of several years' duration, were to result in nothing save ravages and
ruins.

China was a prey at once to civil and foreign war. A new emperor, Irlien-Foung, who ascended the throne in 1850, displayed
much greater hostility to strangers than his father had done. The
French trade treaty was illy fulfilled, and a French missionary was
slain. This was a violation of the agreement by which the Chinese
government bound themselves to do no more than expel missionaries
who should attempt to propagate their faith in the interior of the
empire.

An incident of slight importance, the seizure of a vessel of contested nationality, at the same time renewed the strife between
China and England. The English resumed their hostilities. Admiral Seymour attacked the great seaport town of Canton. The
Chinese, ill provided as they were for war, resisted stubbornly. The
English admiral was finally obliged to abandon an enterprise undertaken with quite insufficient forces (November, 1856–January, 1857).

The peace-loving negotiator of the trade treaty between France
and England, Mr. Cobden, proposed a motion of blame for Lord
Seymour's aggressive act, which was adopted by the House of Commons. Lord Palmerston was obstinate, and, the House having been
dissolved, the electors gave the majority to the warlike minister.
It was decided that England should send five thousand soldiers
with a plenipotentiary. Napoleon III. also resolved to despatch a
plenipotentiary, who should settle matters in concert with the English diplomat. Russia and the United States had their quarrel with
China as well; France and England begged them to join their cause;
but those two states forbade their plenipotentiaries to concur in the
use of force.

Revolt in India delayed the projected operations against China, and confirmed the Chinese government in its resistance.

Nevertheless, in the course of the year, the Canton River was blockaded by the allied squadrons; the French naval division from Indo-China, commanded by Admiral Rigault de Genouilly, had been reinforced and had joined the English. The attack on Canton was renewed at the end of December with more carefully prepared means for action.

Having carried the outposts, the allies entered the city, January 5, 1858, the immense city falling into the hands of five thousand English and from thirteen to fourteen thousand French. Of what avail were matchlocks and bows in the hands of a motley crowd against the perfect weapons and tactics of the French? An arrangement was made with the Russian and American plenipotentiaries in regard to the terms to be made with the Chinese; a small garrison was left at Canton, and the fleet sailed for the gulf of Pé-Tchi-Li, to enter thence the Peï-Ho, the river upon which Pekin, the capital of the empire, is built. May 20, the allies captured the forts on the Peï-Ho, shattered by the shells of the allied fleets, which then re-ascended the river to Tien-Tsin, within three days' march of Pekin.

The Chinese government yielded. Envoys were sent to meet the French plenipotentiaries at Tien-Tsin; the treaty of peace was signed June 27. Russia and America took advantage of French victories without sharing in any save the diplomatic action. Russia was first to obtain a treaty according liberty of worship to all Chinese Christians, and free circulation to missionaries throughout the empire; Russian diplomatic agents who had claims to present were to be admitted temporarily to Pekin.

America, imitating Russia, made similar terms.

The Chinese government persisting in its refusal to receive any permanent embassy at Pekin, France and England yielded the point. Five new ports were opened to foreign trade. The stipulations in regard to Christians were repeated from the Russian treaty. The French in China were to be governed by French laws only. China bound herself to pay a war indemnity.

The settlement was of brief duration. The English, in 1857, opened hostilities for a grievance of very slight importance. In 1859 the war was renewed for a question of etiquette. French and English ambassadors were directed to bear the ratification of the treaty of Tien-Tsin to the Chinese Emperor. It was announced that the envoys would proceed from Tien-Tsin to Pekin. When the English admiral, Hope, preceding the ambassadors whom he was to escort to Tien-Tsin, appeared at the mouth of the Peï-Ho, the Chinese, who had repaired their forts, refused him entrance to the river. The Chinese government did not decline to receive the embassy at Pekin, but would not allow them to travel by the road on which foreign arms had recently defeated the Chinese. The envoys were ordered to proceed by another way. The French and English ambassadors, together with Admiral Hope, declined to submit to this demand, which they regarded as an insult, and decided to open the passage of the Peï-Ho by force. The fortifications on the Peï-Ho had been much improved since the preceding year, and the Chinese artillery was better served. The attack attempted by the English cannoneers was repulsed with considerable loss (June 25, 1859). A French man-of-war and a small body of French troops were also engaged in the skirmish.

When this news reached Europe, the Italian war was over. Napoleon III. desired to give some security to England. He had hitherto been nothing but the auxiliary of the English in China; he was now to assume a more important part, particularly in regard to the army. Besides the question of the English alliance, France had fresh interests in the Upper Orient, and it was necessary that she should maintain her high renown in that region. She had just concluded a treaty with Japan for the first time (October 9, 1858). She had obtained for her merchants the right of residence in the capital, Yeddo, and at Osaka, with freedom to exercise the Christian religion. A French diplomatic agent would henceforth be maintained at Yeddo, and consular agents at several Japanese ports open to French trade, French inhabitants being within the jurisdiction of their consuls.

France had also begun an important settlement in Cochin-China, and hoped to impose a treaty, with cessions of territory, upon the Emperor of Annam, monarch of Cochin-China. France, therefore, must needs have an imposing station in Upper Asia.

Napoleon III. determined to send General Cousin de Montauban with a body of ten thousand men to China. He reached Hong-Kong, February 26, 1860.

The English and French plenipotentiaries sent to Pekin an ultimatum which was declined. The allies then set sail for the north of China, and occupied the island of Chusan, at the mouth of the great Yang-Tse-Kiang in the Yellow Sea (April 21). From Chusan they moved to the gulf of Pé-Tchi-Li, where the troops were landed (May – June). The French soldiers scarcely exceeded eight thousand in number. The English had made a great effort; they had more than twelve thousand soldiers, thirteen hundred of whom were mounted. However, this was a small number to pierce to the heart of this vast empire; but the state of anarchy into which China had fallen favored foreign invasion. The rebel Taï-Pings had captured and sacked several of the chief cities; other great cities on the coast sent deputations to the French and English generals to beg their aid in defending themselves from these devastating hordes.

As in the former expedition, and even more urgently now, the object of the allies was to gain Pekin by Tien-Tsin, and consequently, first of all, to open the Peï-Ho. The Chinese had collected every means of resistance, and a great body of Tartars protected the forts. These descendants of the conquerors of China, to whom the reigning dynasty belonged, were still the military element of the empire. They were driven from their intrenchments by the allied troops; several of the forts were carried by storm; Tartars and Chinese struggled bravely at first, but at the death of their general their weapons dropped from their grasp; the strong positions remaining to them were abandoned or surrendered (August, 1860). The decisive battle of August 21 gave the allies more than five hundred pieces of artillery. On the 26th the allies reached Tien-Tsin by water. The Chinese government, who, before the attack on the Peï-Ho, had put a price on the heads of the allied generals and plenipotentiaries, strove to stop the course of the victors by deceitful negotiations, to gain time to arrange for the defence of Pekin. The allies saw the trap and marched steadily on. The Chinese government then made proposals which seemed more serious. French and English parliamentarians were despatched to the Chinese plenipotentiaries to settle preliminary measures.

These negotiations concealed treason. The Tartar army, assembled outside Pekin, were preparing a surprise for the allied troops. General Montauban and the English general, Grant, warned betimes, abruptly assumed the offensive, turned and routed the masses of cavalry and infantry before them. The Chinese artillery fell into their hands (September 18), but, unfortunately, several French parliamentarians were left in the hands of the enemy and were taken prisoners to Pekin.

The allied generals pursued and attacked the hostile army in the positions to which it had withdrawn. On this occasion the Tartars sustained the reputation for intrepidity attributed to their race. Twenty-five or thirty thousand horsemen, armed with bows and lances, rushed madly upon the little French division, and almost crushed them beneath the weight of numbers, but the French artillery and musketry made bloody ravages among them. The arrival of the English released the French; the Tartar cavalry once swept clear, the infantry (some twenty thousand men) fought nobly; but the inferiority of their arms rendered their numerical superiority useless; they were beaten with great carnage. This was known as the battle of Pa-li-kao, from the name of a bridge over the great canal uniting the Peï-Ho to Pekin. (September 21).

The enemy lost three thousand men, the allies not more than fifty. This says everything for the inequality of their weapons and their skill in using them.

The Chinese Empire, in its lack of organization, could not bring more than between fifty and sixty thousand men to bear against the invaders. Their defeat forced them to reopen negotiations; but still, from an obstinacy which had fatal results, the brother of the Emperor of China, empowered to negotiate, refused to give up in advance the French and English parliamentarians taken contrary to international law. The allies advanced on Pekin with scarcely eight thousand soldiers, half French, half English. They were not more than six kilometers distant from the Chinese capital, and could see its many strange monuments from afar over the long walls of the city. On hearing that the Tartar army had retired to the imperial residence known as the Summer Palace, ten kilometers distant from Pekin, they proceeded thither. Neither the Tartars nor the imperial court expected them. They entered the palace, which was not a single building like Versailles, but besides the principal palace, inhabited by the emperor, comprised a whole series of pavilions, pagodas, and galleries, scattered on the brink of lakes, amidst beautiful gardens stretching as far as the eye could reach. The first who entered this fairy spot were dazzled as if by a vision of the Arabian Nights. In these white marble edifices, with roofs of polished tiles, were stored incalculable riches in precious metals, gems, jade, and other rare stones, silks, enamels, and bronzes; nor was the material value of these treasures in any way equal to the immense interest offered, from a scientific and artistic point of view, by this huge quantity of statues, paintings, vases, carved and lacquered furniture, and ancient manuscripts.

An enlightened prince, the contemporary of Louis XIV., the Emperor Kang-Hi, collected in this place a myriad monuments of Chinese antiquities, the most marvellous specimens of the strange, original, and ingenious art, which marked the most flourishing periods of China, together with documents of incalculable value in relation to Asiatic history. The Chinese people, unlike the Indian races, always had a taste for history.

Those articles which seemed most valuable as curiosities were set aside, by order of the French and English generals, for presentation to the French Emperor and Empress and the English Queen. The rest was given over to a general pillage. What could not be carried off was torn and broken up. Yet worse was to come! When it was known that the French parliamentarians had been treated with odious cruelty to which several had succumbed, the English plenipotentiary, Lord Elgin, and General Grant ordered the burning and entire destruction of the Summer Palace. The French plenipotentiary and general refused to aid in this act of inconceivable barbarism intended as a retaliation for perfidious and barbarous conduct. The deed was nevertheless accomplished. The treasures accumulated for centuries by an ancient civilization were destroyed in a few hours by the representatives of modern European civilization. A strange way indeed to extend progress and teach the Orientals to respect humanity! The Chinese gave the foreigners a name analogous to that title of barbarians scornfully applied by Greeks and Romans to other nations. This was scarcely the way to bring China to feel more kindly towards Europe!

This serious event showed the allies at odds. The English would fain have carried the war to the last extreme and overthrown the Chinese Emperor, who had fled to Tartary. The French plenipotentiary desired peace, and General Montauban refused to enter Pekin by main force, as the English general proposed to do. The Chinese government had offered to pay a heavy indemnity at once to the surviving French and English parliamentarians, and to the family of those who had died in captivity; and had surrendered one of the gates of Pekin to the French troops as a pledge of peaceful intentions. French and English ambassadors went in great pomp to sign the treaties in the capital with the emperor's brother, who was invested with full powers to that effect (October 24–25).

The French left Pekin and soon after China.

This strange and romantic expedition produced no great result for France. The memory of the Summer Palace darkened the history of a campaign otherwise honorable from a military standard. Whether from lack of articles of exchange, or because French merchants have not paid sufficient attention to that region, trade between France and China has not hitherto assumed any considerable dimensions.

Another enterprise, begun at about the same time as the Chinese war, in a country hard by that empire, although less notorious, was destined to be much more significant to France. We refer to the French settlement in Cochin-China.

Of the two Indian peninsulas, the largest, to the west, formerly a subject of dispute between the French and English, had fallen wholly under English rule. The English had also acquired a foothold in the other, the eastern peninsula, by seizing the coast of Burmah and occupying the excellent maritime position of Singapore, which commands the strait between the southern point of the peninsula and the great Indian archipelago. The portion of the eastern peninsula bordering on China forms what is called the Empire of Annam, composed of three divisions, two of which, Cochin-China and Tonkin, were under the direct sway of the head of that empire; the third division, Cambodia, had a vassal king. The natives of these regions are regarded as Indo-Chinese from their affinity with the Chinese. Their government showed the same prejudice for Europeans and the Christian missions as that of China: merciless persecutions marked its course, heedless of any diplomatic remonstrance. Here again French arms were called into play by the missionaries and their complaints.

The missionaries laid great stress, besides their grievances, upon the commercial advantages offered by these countries. Spain, having important interests in Upper Asia through her possession of the Philippine Archipelago, made an arrangement with France against the Annamite government, two Spanish missionaries having recently been beheaded in Cochin-China. A French fleet commanded by Vice-Admiral Rigault de Genouilly, reinforced by a vessel and a few soldiers sent from the Philippines, entered Touran Bay, on the north shore of Cochin-China, August 30, 1858. The forts in the bay were taken with very slight resistance, and occupied by a small body of Franco-Spanish troops. The armament of these forts was better than in China, but the men were either ignorant of the use of their weapons, or unwilling to turn their knowledge to account.

The rainy season interrupted operations, which were resumed early in February, 1859. Hué, the capital of Annam, is situated on the river of the same name, not far from Touran Bay; but the approaches to the town seemed insurmountable. Instead of attacking it, the fleet set sail for the south of Cochin-China, on the confines of Cambodia; it entered the mouth of the Saïgon River, and the troops took possession of all the forts defending the entrance and banks of the stream. Much artillery and a large number of ships fell into the hands of the French, although the Annamites fought more bravely than at Touran. Saïgon, like Touran, is an excellent maritime position, and the surrounding country is highly cultivated. The citadel of Saïgon was blown up; but a fort was kept at the mouth of the river, and a naval subdivision was left at the entrance. The admiral informed the secretary of the navy that Saïgon was destined to become the centre of a vast trade: rice, cotton, sugar, tobacco, cabinet woods, plentiful watercourses, everything was there in abundance. The admiral declared that they must return and remain, as soon as they had sufficient forces.

The troops of the Emperor of Annam vainly strove to drive the French from the posts which they held in Touran Bay and at the entrance of the Saïgon River. In one of these contests they drew up in line against the French soldiers ten war elephants. The hot, damp climate was more to be dreaded by the invaders than the military forces of the Indian monarch, although his army was quite thoroughly organized.

The Chinese war, which absorbed the attention of the French secretary of the navy and the resources of the Upper Orient, delayed the progress of affairs in Cochin-China. Still Saïgon was reoccupied, declared officially to be a French possession, and its harbor, open to all friendly nations, soon began to realize the great commercial advance predicted by the leader of the French expedition.

The Chinese war once ended, the French squadron, reinforced and under the orders of Vice-Admiral Charner, renewed operations in 1861 with three thousand men. The Annamites had built lines of fortifications confining the French in Saïgon. The lines of Ki-Hoa were carried by storm, February 24 – 25, 1861; then the capture of the fortified town of Mytho (April 13) permitted the French to spread through Lower Cochin-China. These victories decided the King of Cambodia to cast off the sovereignty of Annam and place himself under allegiance to France.

A fresh reinforcement of two thousand soldiers then arrived from
France, and an attempt was made to train native troops for service.
This was the first application of the only system which could render
feasible any large settlement.　The citadels of Bien-Hoa and Vinh-
Long fell into the hands of the French soon after (November 21,
1861 – March 22, 1862), and the whole of Southern Cochin-China
was theirs.　The Emperor of Annam, threatened in the North of that
region and even in his capital, Hué, and unable longer to receive
supplies of rice from Lower Cochin-China, decided to negotiate with
Rear-Admiral Bonard, successor to Charner.　By a treaty signed
June 5, 1862, Emperor Tu-Duc promised a war indemnity of twenty-
four million francs, and ceded to France three of the four provinces
which she had conquered in Cochin-China, those of Bien-Hoa, Gia-
ding, and Mytho (a million inhabitants), taking back merely the
province of Vinh-Long.　He also gave up the island of Poulo-Con-
dor, opened to French and Spanish trade in Upper Cochin-China
and Tonkin, the three ports of Touran, Balat, and Quangan, and
granted the French free navigation of the whole course of the Mé-
Kong, or Cambodia River, a strong current of water coming down
from the mountains of Western China and traversing the whole
Empire of Annam.　Religious liberty was accorded to Christians,
and the Emperor of Annam pledged himself to yield no portion of
his territory to any power whatsoever without the consent of France.
Spain had claimed no territorial sessions.

Admiral Bonard organized in a most intelligent manner the native
troops and administration, both of whom performed their duties sat-
isfactorily under French direction.

The acquisition of Cochin-China, like the former one of Algeria,
met with much opposition in France from those averse to colonial
settlements.　Napoleon III. was for a time on the point of almost
wholly abandoning the only one of his distant expeditions which
was really for the interest of France; he came near restoring the
three provinces to the Emperor of Annam in 1864, but did not carry
out this retrograde step which nothing seemed to call for.

France not only retained her new possessions, but was soon forced to exceed their bounds.   The province of Vinh-Long, restored to Annam by France, and the two neighboring provinces of Chaudoc and Hatien, became the centre of brigandage, piracy, and continual aggressions against the French possessions, aggressions alternately excited and disavowed by the Annamite government, which could not resolve to accept either peace or war.   The Governor of French Cochin-China, Vice-Admiral La Grandière, seeing all his complaints were vain, formally demanded the surrender of these three provinces. Upon the refusal of Emperor Tu-Duc, twelve hundred French soldiers and four hundred native troops crossed the frontier and occupied the chief cities of the three provinces without meeting with any resistance.

The inhabitants, set free from brigandage and anarchy, offered no opposition.   The Emperor Tu-Duc negotiated, refused to accept the terms of the French, but did not declare war.

The Annamite government was in a state of disorganization.   In 1869 Tonkin revolted against Tu-Duc.   This country had not been conquered by the Annamite dynasty until 1802, and could not endure its rulers.   Tonkin, far richer and more thickly peopled than Cochin-China (ten millions of inhabitants), abounding in metals of every sort, with a fertile soil and a climate relatively temperate and habitable by Europeans, is contiguous to the best provinces of Western China and the fertile region of the Yun-Nan.   The chief watercourse of Tonkin, the Hong-Kiang, or Red River, flowing from the Yun-Nan, is destined to become a commercial road of far greater importance than the Mé-Kong, or Cambodia River, as soon as Tonkin falls into intelligent hands.   Yun-Nan is a market of fifty or sixty million purchasers.

We can only briefly mention here the events of the epoch whose annals we are now recording.   Two Frenchmen, M. Dupuis, a merchant, and Garnier, a lieutenant in the navy, foresaw the future offered to the national interests of France.   With the aid of the Chinese mandarins of Yun-Nan, who, owing to peculiar circumstances, desired, instead of dreading, relations with Europe, they attempted to open the Red River to French vessels.   The Annamite government opposing the movement, Garnier and Dupuis, with a handful of Frenchmen, drove away the officials and soldiers of Tu-Duc, and took possession of the Lower Tonkin and the whole delta of the Red River, thanks to the hostility of the natives towards the Annamite government.

Emperor Tu-Duc, seeing his empire crumbling about him, acknowledged himself the vassal of France, as the King of Cambodia had done. Lower Tonkin was given back to him, under French supremacy, like the rest; but while the King of Cambodia faithfully observed his engagements towards France, the continual disloyalty of this new vassal, and the impossibility of deriving any advantage from Tonkin and its beautiful river with such an intermediary between France and the natives, rendered inevitable the direct government of Tonkin as well as of Lower Cochin-China by French governors.

It rested with France to prove this some slight compensation for the loss of India which the great Dupleix strove to win for her in the eighteenth century, and at least an equivalent for what Java and the other Sunda islands are to Holland, with the commerce of Western China in addition.

These few words in regard to Indian affairs have led us far beyond the history of the Second Empire. The treaty by which the Emperor of Annam recognized the supremacy of France is dated 1874.

Let us merely add that commercial interests in Indo-China were now united with interests of another sort. Art and history gained a rare discovery by French colonization of those countries. On the borders of Cochin-China and Cambodia, beyond vast forests, on a spot now deserted, called Ang-Kor, were found the ruins of a huge city, the remains of monstrous temples and palaces, acres of walls covered with sculptures recalling and, to say the least, equalling the chief monuments of British India. These were relics of the power of the Khmer nation, which seems to have been a branch of the Aryans of India, and to have imported into this region the Buddhist religion at the period when that faith prevailed in Hindostan.

MONUMENTS OF EGYPT.

The Empire of the Khmers flourished during the early centuries of our middle age. Since its decay Indo-Chinese civilization has degenerated.

While France thus established herself in the Upper Orient, a far other future was growing up for her in the heart of Africa, thanks to the progress which Colonel Faidherbe, a remarkable man, imparted to the French colony of Senegal.

In another quarter of the globe, Oceanica, France had recently acquired New Caledonia, an island well situated between Australia, New Zealand, and the French archipelago of Tahiti. Negus, King of Abyssinia, at last yielded to France the port of Zulla (Adulis of the ancients), at the head of the Red Sea, opposite Aden, — a fine position, from which no advantage had yet been reaped.

In the same year that France entered Pekin, her flags appeared simultaneously at the two extremes of Asia, in Syria and China. Since the peace of 1856 the Ottoman Empire had remained in a state of disorder, unable to profit by the success of the Crimean war to become consolidated, and to remedy the enormous abuses extant. Mussulman fanaticism awoke afresh at the news of the revolt of India against the English. The "true believers" fancied that their numerous Hindoo brothers were about to restore Mussulman rule in Central Asia, and that this would be the signal for a universal destruction of "infidels." Trouble broke out in Syria in the mountains of Lebanon, occupied in part by Catholic Christians of the Latin form, the Maronites, and in part by Druses, — a strange people who are neither Christian, Mohammedan, nor Jew, and who profess an obscure and peculiar religion. The Druses fell upon the Maronites and cruelly sacked their villages with the open connivance of Turkish soldiers and officials. The massacres extended beyond Lebanon as far as the great city of Damascus. The old enemy of France in Algiers, Abd-el-Kader, who lived there in retirement on a pension from the French government, interfered with equal energy and humanity, and rescued a great number of Christians from the fury of the Moslems (May – June, 1860).

Napoleon III. saw what an opportunity this would be to compensate the clergy for Italian matters by protecting the Syrian Christians. The clergy dreamed of making Syria a Catholic kingdom, of restoring the ancient Latin kingdom of Jerusalem. The French government appealed to the other powers, and proposed to England to send an Anglo-French army to re-establish order in Syria.

England agreed reluctantly to permit France to despatch troops, without adding her own, but reinforcing her naval station in that region, and obtaining a promise that the French occupation should not exceed six months. Turkey protested. The other powers quietly looked on. A French division of soldiers landed at Beyrouth (August 16, 1860). The Turks submitted to work with them, though with great lack of sincerity. Some chiefs and a good number of subaltern accomplices were punished; the majority of the ringleaders escaped; France only obtained from the powers the restoration of a previous system by which a Maronite chief governed the whole mountain under the supremacy of the Sultan. The Ottoman Porte agreed to choose a Christian governor for Lebanon, but from another region. An Armenian was selected, and the French departed (March, 1861).

Of the various expeditions to which we have alluded, that to Syria and even that to China were not of much importance to France; nor were the advantageous results of the settlement of Cochin-China as yet very evident, Napoleon III. paying but little heed to that country. These Asiatic operations were no more than diversion to him; but he was very busy with another enterprise which roused him to enthusiasm, an affair of very different significance and destined to have very unfortunate results. The all too famous Mexican question came up for settlement in the year after the Chinese campaign.

To understand the confused and melancholy drama of the Mexican war, the reader must have some notion of the state of that country after its escape from Spanish monarchy.

The national and social conditions of the new republic of Spanish America, and of Mexico in particular, had nothing in common with those of British America, now the United States. Instead of one compact European race, there existed here men of Spanish origin and half-breeds, a cross between Spaniards and Indians, ruling over a much larger number of Indians and natives, that is, ancient Mexican tribes: some of the latter had fallen back into a savage state; many of the others were reduced, under Spanish and half-breed proprietors, to a set of agricultural colonists who might be termed semi-serfs. A very rich and highly immoral clergy; a most ill-disciplined army, whose leaders sometimes combined with the clergy to govern the country, sometimes quarrelled with them; a liberal party who opposed French and American ideas to the retro-grade maxims of the clergy and the dictatorial tendencies of the military leaders, — such were the chief elements of the discordant Mexican society. The army multiplied pronunciamentos and barrack brawls. One government succeeded another in rapid course. A general, Iturbide, crowned himself emperor; he was overthrown; desiring to renew the attempt, he was shot dead. Sometimes popular assemblies ruled, sometimes dictators. There was continual trouble, and political strife afforded a pretext for much brigandage. There was no security for strangers who came to settle or trade in Mexico, and their complaints constantly called forth objections from the various European governments. Under Louis Philippe, far removed as he was from a warlike spirit, in 1839, France was forced to declare war against one of those Mexican dictators to whom we have just alluded, Santa Anna by name. Having gained, lost, and regained the power four or five times, he was not finally overthrown until 1855.

Then appeared a character such as had not been seen before in all the Mexican revolutions. This was the lawyer Benito Juarez, an Indian by birth. Honest, unselfish, energetic, persevering, an ardent patriot, free from the vices so common among his compatriots, he aspired to suppress anarchy, to put an end to the extravagant privileges of clergy and army; he planned to abolish mortmain, which concentrated a fourth, if not a third, of the land in the hands of the clergy. He was the inspirer of a constitution which established the equality of all forms of religious worship and civil condition, and suppressed special jurisdiction in case of privileged persons.

The clerical and military parties united to destroy the constitution in the capital at Mexico by a bold stroke. Juarez, with the National Assembly, withdrew to another city, and civil war continued (1857–58). Miramon, the leader of a band, being proclaimed president at Mexico by some would-be notables, turned everything into money, and concluded two excessively burdensome treaties, — one with Spain, the other with a Swiss banker named Jecker; Miramon accepted thereby, in the name of Mexico, doubtful credits at most exorbitant rates. This affair deserves mention at its outset on account of its results.

Miramon could not long maintain himself in Mexico; the legal government gained the upper hand, and Juarez returned to the capital with the National Assembly.

What course was it for the interest of Mexico, and especially of France, many of whose people were settled in Mexico, to adopt?

The greater part of the French living in Mexico favored Juarez. They were anxious that help should be granted to that government which was making an effort at reorganization, desired time to be given it to regulate its relations with Europe and to pay off its debts to French natives. Unfortunately this feeling did not extend to French official agents, who were closely connected with the clerical party, and had made the mistake of acknowledging that government of adventurers which seized the capital, while the legal power of Juarez was upheld by the great majority of the country. This error, shared moreover by other European representatives, made the position of French agents towards Juarez and the National Mexican Assembly very difficult, — a state of affairs which was greatly aggravated by their malevolent proceedings.

Meantime, Mexican emigrants to Europe were preaching the restoration of monarchy in their country. Napoleon III. was but too well disposed to listen to them; he had long cherished a dream of interposing in the New World, and opposing the Latin race to the Anglo-Saxons, to which scheme many reserves are necessary from an historical point of view; he aspired to found a monarchy in Mexico to arrest the increase of the United States, which had already taken in the Mexican provinces of Texas and California. He did not pretend that he would do Mexico this service for nothing; he intended to demand a province in his turn, namely, Sonora, rich in gold mines. This dream, which floated through his fancy like so many others, assumed consistency in view of the discord in the United States. North and South, abolitionists and slave-holders were rapidly advancing towards that great civil war which broke out before the end of 1861. The man of December 2 had no love for the great American republic, and the prospect of seeing it split asunder delighted him. It seemed strangely to facilitate his intervention in Mexico.

Even before he became emperor, the president prince was largely surrounded by Mexican emigrants, who soon after won the favor of the new empress by flattering her with the prospective glory of restoring religion and monarchy to Mexico. Another influence, exerted from motives not at all akin to politics, strongly urged the emperor in the same direction: we refer to the Duke de Morny. This great promoter of the *coup d'état*, too much given to his own pleasures, too idle to burden himself with ministerial cares, and content to fortify himself in the presidency of the Legislative Body, nevertheless retained his influence over the master who was his handiwork. Always on the watch for lucrative speculations, he was in secret alliance with that Swiss banker, Jecker, who held the great Mexican loan: he had him naturalized as a French citizen, that he might have some ground on which to base his demands.

The next step was to find a monarch for the future monarchy. The Mexican emigrants suggested to Napoleon III. that Austria might furnish the missing man. The Emperor Francis Joseph had a brother, Archduke Maximilian, who was viceroy of Lombardo-Venice some time previous to the Italian war. He had shown amiable intentions in the impossible attempt at reconciling the Italians to Austrian rule. Napoleon III. eagerly entered into the project of sending Maximilian to reign in Mexico; he imagined that Austria would regard this as a sort of compensation for her losses.

Juarez unfortunately furnished the imperial government of France a pretext for its hostility. Being at the end of his resources, he postponed for two years the execution of the treaties by which Mexico appropriated the revenue of her customs to pay her foreign loans (July 17, 1861). France, England, and Spain broke with Mexico. The *Moniteur* published a list of grievances, which added to the action for which Juarez was responsible, — other serious grounds for complaint actually dating back to that pseudo government opposed to Juarez, and recognized by French agents (November, 1861).

The three powers at variance with Mexico were moved by different motives. Spain, as well as Napoleon III., aspired to send a sovereign to Mexico ; but while the latter was thinking of an archduke, the former dreamed of a Spanish prince. Spain was even plotting to work alone, if England and France would take no active measures. As for England, she was opposed to all interference in the domestic policy of Mexico.

The United States strove to prevent the use of force by the European powers, and offered to guarantee the interest on the Mexican debts to the three governments interested, for five years. The English minister of foreign affairs, Lord John Russell, being illdisposed towards the United States, agreed with Napoleon III. in declining the offer. He also drew up a form of treaty between the three powers, stipulating that no one of them should attempt to exert any influence upon the domestic policy of the Mexican Republic. The Spanish government demanded changes, which corresponded with the views of Napoleon III., and Lord John Russell accepted them readily enough.

Article 11 of this compact was accordingly somewhat equivocally worded. The contracting parties pledged themselves, in the use of such coercive measures as were now foreseen, "to exert no influence upon Mexican policy of a nature to injure the just right of the Mexican nation to choose its own form of government." This might be interpreted in the sense of prearranged plebiscites (October 31, 1861).

It was decided that the three powers were to act in concert ; but impatient Spain could not wait. A Spanish squadron, bearing nearly six thousand soldiers, sailed from Cuba, reached Vera Cruz (December 8, 1861), and seized the city without any declaration of war. Only one month later (January 7, 1862), twenty-four hundred French and one thousand English landed at Vera Cruz. The chief command was conferred on the Spanish General Prim, and a manifesto was issued in the name of the three powers. The allies protested that they had no plans for conquest or interference with the Mexican administration. "It is for you," they said, "to put your government upon a firm and lasting basis."

The plenipotentiaries of the three powers conferred together in regard to the terms to be required of Mexico. There were two French plenipotentiaries, — Dubois de Saligny, the French Minister who broke off relations with Juarez, and Rear-Admiral Jurien La Gravière, who commanded the fleet which carried the French troops to Mexico. M. de Saligny, a violent and ungovernable spirit, did his best to embitter the quarrel; it is to him, and not to the admiral, that we must attribute the following ultimatum, drawn up by the French parties: Mexico was to pay France sixty million francs as indemnity for deeds anterior to July 31, 1861, the French plenipotentiaries reserving the right to fix the amount of their claim for later causes at another time. Mexico was also to pay the balance of what was due in virtue of a treaty dated in 1853. Moreover, Mexico was to execute at once the contract made in 1859 between the Mexican government and the firm of Jecker. To guarantee the accomplishment of the pecuniary and other conditions contained in the ultimatum, France was to be allowed to occupy the ports of Vera Cruz and Tampico, with seizure of the customs revenues, to be divided between her and her allies.

The English plenipotentiary, Sir Charles Wilke, loudly protested against the excessive amount of the French indemnity, and especially against the Jecker loan, in which the government of Miramon gave fourteen million francs in treasury bonds for a loan of four millions. The sum total of Jecker's claim amounted to seventy-five millions!

Now, at this time, Jecker had not even been naturalized in France !

The English and Spanish refused to act conjointly upon such conditions. It was settled that each plenipotentiary should put forward the claims of his own government separately.

Although Saligny's only desire was to render all reconciliation impossible, negotiations were begun. Meantime, the troops could not be left exposed to the wasting climate of the Mexican coast. General Prim was directed to make a treaty with the Mexican General Doblado, authorizing the allied troops to occupy a more wholesome situation in the mountains of the interior.

The mood of Spain and the general who represented her had suddenly changed. The projects in regard to Archduke Maximilian had been bruited abroad. In default of an infanta of Spain, General Prim, bold, ambitious, and the husband of a Mexican, had dreamed of the Mexican Empire for himself. Disappointed and utterly unwilling to work for the Austrian, he suddenly became most accommodating. He therefore signed, with the representative of Juarez, preliminaries thus conceived: " The constitutional government of the Mexican Republic having declared to the commissioners of the allied powers that it possesses the necessary elements of power and popular favor to maintain its ground against all intestine revolt, the allies at once enter upon the domain of treaties. Negotiations will be opened at Orizaba. During the negotiations the allied forces will occupy Cordova, Orizaba, and Tetuacan. If the negotiations should unfortunately be broken off, the allied forces will abandon those positions, and return towards Vera Cruz " (February 19, 1862).

The plenipotentiaries accepted this agreement, known as that of La Soledad. When it was proclaimed in Europe, England and Spain approved it. Napoleon III. disavowed it, withdrew from Admiral Jurien La Gravière the full powers with which he was invested, and bestowed them upon Saligny alone (April 8). The emperor laid aside his mask ; he showed that his desire was not to come to terms, but to overthrow the Mexican government at any cost.

The customary mouthpiece of the imperial government in the Legislature, Billault, commented upon the emperor's resolution by emphatic speeches. " There are," he said, " urgent epochs in the life of a nation as of a man, when, let come what will, there can be no compromise with honor or with duty !"

Before the governments could make their intentions known a rupture occurred between their representatives. Almonte, the leader of a band of Mexican emigrants, having come to Vera Cruz to establish a government there under foreign protection, the Spanish and English plenipotentiaries protested against the support afforded to this enterprise by France, and on their part, the French plenipotentiaries declared that they would not treat with the actual government of the republic. Saligny insisted that the troops should march upon Mexico at once. The Spanish and English plenipotentiaries replied that they saw no motive for breaking off negotiations, and that they would quit Mexico with their troops, if the French refused to take part in the conference whose immediate session had been agreed with the Mexican government. They kept their word and departed.

The French had recently received a reinforcement of four or five thousand men, under the orders of General Lorencez. According to the treaty of La Soledad, the French troops were to quit, April 20, the positions conditionally surrendered to them. They began this retrograde movement; then General Lorencez turned back, passing directly over a small Mexican army, and reoccupied Orizaba. He pretended that he was forced to reopen hostilities to protect his sick men who were in danger at Orizaba, where they had been left. Saligny and Almonte assured him that the whole country would hail him as its liberator. He marched straight to Puebla, — an important place, which was to open the road to Mexico for him.

He had been grossly deceived. He was received with shot and shell, was unable to gain possession of the heights which cover the approach to Puebla, and was forced to effect a difficult and dangerous retreat upon Orizaba. He only saved his scanty army by dint of intelligence and energy (May, 1862).

The conduct of the Mexicans towards the French wounded belied the alleged pretext for the breach of the agreement. Juarez had them carefully nursed and then sent them back to their friends.

But let the Mexican government do what it would, the plan of action was already formed at the Tuileries. A sudden attack attempted with a handful of men having failed, Napoleon III. decided to engage all his forces in the contest. General Lorencez, a worthy officer, who had been disgracefully abused, vainly strove to undeceive the emperor, who was more than ever infatuated with Saligny. During the rest of the year and the first months of the next, convoys of troops and supplies were sent off in rapid succession, until the French army in Mexico reached a sum total of more than thirty-eight thousand men and nearly six thousand horses, — an effective force which was maintained at a monstrous, senseless cost. Napoleon III. conferred the chief command upon General Forey ; he addressed a letter to him, in which he frankly broached the famous scheme for the protectorate of " the Latin race " in America, with the intention of preventing the United States from gaining possession of the Gulf of Mexico, and the resolution to establish French influence in Central America (July 3, 1862). This was a strange and very alarming diversion of the great and fundamental interests of France in Europe ! What might not happen at her very door, while she was squandering her gold and her blood in the pursuit of a chimera in the New World ? The result was but too quickly seen !

Public opinion was first roused to anxiety in France, when the rupture of the preliminary treaty of La Soledad was made known, with the consequent departure of the Spanish and English. Of the defenders of the enterprise, one half were the dupes of the other. One worthy man, Michael Chevalier, the economist, was all too mindful on this occasion of the ardent fancies which possessed him in the days of Saint-Simonism ; he fell into the schemes of the emperor in a treatise upon the part to be played by France among the Latin races, — an idea which had a grain of truth, but from which rash and impracticable consequences were deduced. The newspaper *La Patrie*, to gain the partisans of the Italian war, assumed that

Austria would abandon Venice in return for the throne offered to her archduke. The official journals retailed fabulous stories in regard to the triumphal reception supposed to have been offered to French troops by the Mexicans.

All this found little credit with the enlightened public. The most intelligent servants of the empire, and even M. Rouher himself, were, at the outset, greatly opposed to the undertaking. In the Legislative Body the tiny republican group, the famous Five, attacked the expedition in the session which opened early in 1863. Jules Favre took up the financial side of the affair, and pointed out the part played by speculation and private interests. The Legislature, uneasy in reality, feigned approval, and the discussion, as usual, was put down.

Military operations were renewed under General Forey; but that officer did not think it prudent to resume the march on Puebla and Mexico until he was joined by the great body of reinforcements, which arrived in detachments. The Mexicans thus had time to make way for the French, carrying with them all the resources of the country and fortifying themselves in Puebla. The French army suffered alike for want of food and from the climate. Every stay at Vera Cruz and every march from Vera Cruz to the foot of the mountains, at Orizaba, decimated the troops; the naval forces, still close upon the fatal coast, lost even greater numbers; it was in reference to this fact that the cemetery at Vera Cruz was ironically termed "the French garden of acclimatization." The land forces, once in the temperate zone, no longer ran the risk of *vomito negro ;* but the difficulty was to find food. Provisions cost their weight in gold; grain was brought from Havana and the United States. Horses failing, others were purchased at 25,000 francs per head !

As for the natives, they appeared most insensible to the proclamations of Forey, who assured them that no one desired to attack their independence, but to set them free from their oppression, and even to enable them to choose such a government as would suit them best.

The loudly boasted co-operation of the reactionary, clerical, and monarchic party was confined to a handful of men under the orders of an ex-bandit chief named Marquez, who had formerly pillaged, if not massacred, English and French; he was one of the principal authors of the grievances which afforded a pretext for the war.

The attack on Puebla could not be renewed until March. One of the detached forts which protected the town, was carried March 29; but the body of the place was defended with great vigor. The commander of Puebla, General Ortega, very able and very energetic, had made every preparation to convert his city into another Saragossa; fifty churches and convents with thick walls became as many fortresses connected by lines of fosses and barricades. These islets, bristling with artillery, must be attacked, one after the other. These murderous assaults were soon interrupted for lack of sufficient siege artillery and ammunition. General Forey then attempted to reduce the enemy by famine, finding that he could not overcome them by force. He completed the investment of the town; he then detached a division of troops to resist a small Mexican army which was trying to introduce a convoy into the city. The commander of the French division was Marshal Bazaine, who had recently landed in Mexico. Bazaine routed the relief forces (May 8).

The siege artillery and ammunition finally arrived. The besieged could not look for further revictualling; they lacked powder and bread. Ortega made up his mind to surrender. He ordered the guns to be spiked, broke up his rifles, disbanded his soldiers, and yielded himself prisoner with his officers (May 17).

The fate of Puebla decided that of Mexico. Puebla is situated beyond the mountains, on the high and healthy central plain called Anahuac, at the junction of the main roads to Mexico. The capital could not be defended with any chance of success against the army in possession of Puebla. Juarez understood this; he evacuated Mexico, resolving to continue the war everywhere except in the capital, — petty war, if he could not wage war on a grand scale.

General Forey entered Mexico, June 10, amid the plaudits of the reactionists and that part of the populace which always applauds victory. He instituted a government Junta, which delegated the power to a triumvirate composed of two reactionist generals, Almonte and Salas, and the Archbishop of Mexico. The Junta, arbitrarily chosen by the French general, arbitrarily added to its body a certain number of " notables," who constituted themselves a constituent assembly. This assembly decided upon the establishment of a monarchy, and proposed for the throne Archduke Maximilian of Austria (July 10), a deputation being sent to offer him a golden sceptre.

The real authority still remained entirely in the hands of the French general. Saligny himself was subordinate to him; but the malevolent influence of this man overpowered Forey, and led him to belie by his own acts the peaceful and moderate advice which he gave to Mexico in his proclamations. While at Puebla, he had sequestrated the property of all those who bore arms against intervention. He renewed this measure in Mexico. Another decree declared all individuals forming part " of any band of armed malefactors " outlawed ; the members of all such bands were to be judged by a court-martial, whose sentences were without appeal and were to be executed within the twenty-four hours. It is understood that under the title of " malefactors " were confounded all " guerilleros," patriots and bandits alike. After confiscation came proscription ; the men of December 2 were made manifest.

Nor was this all. While all bands were proscribed, one was formed by the very men who proscribed them. Forey formed a counter-guerilla under the command of a French colonel who had brought back a bad reputation from the expedition to China and the Summer Palace, who, in pursuit of the Mexican guerillas, at least rivalled in cruelty and depredations the worst bandit leader. Such practices tended to make this war a school for barbarity and depravity.

Napoleon III., however, began to awake somewhat from his illusions. At the news of the capture of Puebla, he made Forey Marshal of France ; but the fact could not long be hidden from him that the country did not rally, and that the officer who led the invasion had no authority beyond the range of his cannon. He disavowed the extreme measures taken by Forey; he had already determined to recall him to France, being unwilling to leave a marshal in Mexico; but he also recalled Saligny, in regard to whom his eyes were opened somewhat tardily. He then gave the command of the army to Bazaine.

Despatches from the French minister of foreign affairs, Drouyn de Lhuys, shortly before the capture of Puebla, prove that the imperial government would then have renounced its dream of Mexican monarchy and treated with no matter whom, provided it were not Juarez; but, meantime, various events were speedily unfolded to view, and, monarchy once proclaimed in Mexico, Napoleon III. felt himself bound to go on to the end; he plunged obstinately into his fatal scheme, and redoubled his efforts to obtain the acceptance of Maximilian, with whom he had been in treaty for two years back.

The archduke insisted upon two conditions, — the country must submit entirely to him; he must be called to the throne by a legal vote from the people: we have seen how these conditions were fulfilled! On the arrival of the Mexican deputation (October, 1863), Maximilian appeared very uncertain. Several months passed, and Napoleon III. summoned to Paris the archduke and his wife, Princess Carlotta, daughter of King Leopold of Belgium; he succeeded in making Maximilian sign a provisional agreement (March 12, 1864). Nevertheless, upon his return to his residence at Miramar, near Trieste, the archduke's hesitation was renewed. This was because his brother, Emperor Francis Joseph, insisted that if he accepted, he must renounce his eventual claims to the Austrian Empire. His young wife, lively, intelligent and ambitious, eagerly urged him to accept. He finally decided to sign both the renunciation of his archducal rights and a definite treaty with Napoleon III.

The following are the principal clauses: The French troops in Mexico were to be reduced as soon as possible to twenty-five thousand men. They were to leave the Mexican territory as soon as the Emperor of Mexico had organized the necessary troops to replace them. The foreign legion (five thousand men) would remain in Mexico six years after the departure of the other French troops. The expenses of the French expedition, which the Mexican government was to defray, were fixed at two hundred and seventy million francs up to July 1, 1864. From that date the Mexican government would pay to France one thousand francs yearly for each soldier. The Mexican government was to deliver immediately to the French government sixty-six millions on account of the loan (Maximilian had contracted a loan chargeable to Mexico, before accepting the Mexican throne). To reimburse the overplus of the expenses incurred in the war, maintenance of the troops, and indemnities to French subjects, the Mexican government was to pay to France twenty-five millions annually, in hard cash (April 10, 1864). Maximilian thus entered upon his reign with a heavy burden of debt.

By a secret clause, Napoleon III. pledged himself to reduce the French army very gradually; it then consisted of thirty-eight thousand men.

Maximilian set sail with his wife, April 14. The father of the archduchess, King Leopold, on this occasion, for the first time displayed a lack of his habitual prudence by encouraging the enterprise. His paternal ambition for his favorite daughter inspired him with illusions difficult to be understood in so cold and clear-sighted a man.

The new emperor's golden dreams began to fade from the first days of his arrival in the sad city of the *vomito negro*, Vera Cruz. He, however, was well enough received at first by the Indian peasants along his road, their traditions predicting a deliverer coming from the East, and also by the fickle populace of Mexico; but he was immediately forced to face inextricable difficulties. He agreed very ill with the French generals and functionaries, and found no one to uphold him among the Mexicans.

The harmony between the prince, who desired to apply his individual ideas, and the leaders of the foreign power, who were his only support, must have been troubled, with the best will on either side; this good-will did not exist on the part of Marshal Forey's successor. Bazaine, who had proved his military talents as a subordinate, was possessed by an unscrupulous ambition quite out of proportion with his real powers, — an ambition destined one day to destroy him and deal a fearful blow to France.   On his arrival in Mexico, he replaced the hauteur and violence of his predecessor by affected caution; he allied himself with native notabilities; he even entered upon nego-tiations with the hostile chiefs; later on, when he saw that his advances gained him nothing, he returned to the excesses and cruel-ties of the previous period.   Thinking only of the personal advantage to be derived from the situation, he never took into account the interests of the prince whom he was sent to protect.   His selfish calculation annulled the intentions of his under-officers, who would have loyally supported Maximilian.

As for the Mexicans, almost all who were active and capable were with Juarez.   At Paris people believed in the existence of an imagi-nary moderate party, that is to say, one which was neither republican nor ultra-reactionary and clerical.   It was not to be found in Mexico. The old military party was divided and dissolved.   The clerical party, already embroiled with the French, who had declined to surrender everything to its sway, laid claim to all clerical lands, the sole possible resource of the state.   Moreover, the Pope, although refus-ing to come to terms in regard to the sale of clerical property, insisted upon the suppression of freedom of worship, the restoration of convents, the direction of public and private instruction by the clergy, etc.   Maximilian resisted.   He was forced to break with Rome and with the clericals, without gaining the liberals, whom nothing would induce to submit to a foreign monarch.   Much evil might be said of the Mexicans; but it is impossible to deny their spirit of national independence; the sentiments displayed by Spain in 1808, were seen once more among them.

The treasury of the new empire was empty, and its finances were smothered from the start beneath the burden of the liabilities assumed towards England, France, and Spain.   The loan contracted by Maximilian was swallowed up in advance.   The French police and financial functionaries begged by the Mexican Emperor from the French monarch could not remedy such an evil.   Maximilian sent to Paris to try to borrow afresh.   The imperial government came to his aid unreservedly and unscrupulously.   A combination was contrived which blended the former loan with the present one, and which would furnish Mexico with a hundred million francs clear. Ministers Fould and Rouher favored this manœuvre to their utmost ability, as they had favored the previous loan. A deputy named Corta, a member of the Mexican finance committee, gave a most brilliant sketch of the new Mexican Empire, in the French Legislature (April 12, 1865). M. Rouher outdid Corta. Words were followed by deeds: the government treated the Mexican loan, as it were, like a national loan; the offices of the receiver-general became offices for the sale of the Mexican bonds. The participation of the French imperial government forced petty French capitalists into this groundless enterprise; poor little stockholders fancied that these shares were warranted by the government that offered them for sale. No one subscribed in Mexico. Nearly every share was taken in France: the sum total amounted to one hundred and seventy millions; it was almost exclusively the French who had covered the previous loan of about one hundred and two millions.

This loan was not destined to carry Maximilian far; for he never received more than fifty million francs, owing to the deduction of amounts previously due.

The military facts, viewed from a distance, seemed to contradict the administrative and financial distress. A series of triumphs preceded the arrival of Maximilian, and still continued. Bazaine, finding himself at the head of thirty-eight thousand French, to whom he had managed to add twelve or thirteen thousand Mexicans, tolerably equipped, set the army in motion to obtain, according to the style agreed upon, "the adhesion of the various provinces to the imperial government." Several of the principal cities were occupied, including San Luis de Potosi, whither Juarez had transferred his government. Every town attacked was captured, and the ill-organized troops of the Mexican Republic could nowhere withstand the French regiments. They spread, on the one hand, to the Pacific Ocean; on the other, into the northern provinces, where Juarez, intrepid and unshaken, retreated from place to place without yielding the day. A large part of Mexico now obeyed, if not the imperial Mexican government, at least foreign power ; but every one felt that all depended upon the presence of that power, and that if it were withdrawn the Mexican Empire would crumble to dust at once. Bazaine was well aware of this ; and, seeing that Maximilian took no root in the country, he cherished in his turn the dream which allured General Prim for a time. He too married a Mexican, and imagined that he might replace Maximilian, if the latter were forced to abdicate. He was disposed to do everything to disgust him with reigning and treated him as the mere ghost of an emperor. And still the French army, which Bazaine hoped to make his tool, was constantly diminished, not only by battle and disease, but by the departure of regiments now beginning to be recalled to France, conformably to the treaty of Miramar. In April, 1865, Bazaine had not more than twenty-eight thousand French soldiers. True, six thousand Austrian and thirteen hundred Belgian volunteers had joined his ranks ; but these bodies lacked unity, and could not have the solidity of the French.

The republicans, instead of being crushed by so many defeats, renewed a petty warfare on every hand. While the French occupied towns four hundred leagues away from Mexico, the guerillas set to work to cut off communication between that capital and Vera Cruz ; the republicans reoccupied various places in the north, and blockaded several of those which they could not recapture. Maximilian lost his head : not being obeyed or heeded by any one, he at one time had a wild scheme for winning Juarez by offering him the presidency of the Supreme Court ; and again, by some strange folly, allowed himself to be urged into signing a decree relegating to a court-martial "all persons forming a part of any armed band existing without legal authorization" ; all members of such bands to be condemned to capital punishment and executed in twenty-four hours, as was also whoever should connive, in whatsoever fashion, with such bands.

When Maximilian learned that in virtue of his decree two captive generals had been shot, he was terrified at what he had done. The unfortunate man had signed his own death-warrant ! (October 3, 1865.)

VERA CRUZ.

Bazaine, upon the heels of this decree, which he had suggested, forbade the making of prisoners : all persons captured were to be put to death; there would be no exchange of prisoners in the future !

This savage mandate was communicated to the officers without being inscribed upon the order-books. Still it could not be kept secret, any more than could the hangings, shootings, and burnings by which the too notorious counter-guerilla war was marked. On October 28, three weeks after the decree, the American government charged its representative at Paris to call the serious attention of the French imperial government to the "painful sensation which the bloody policy employed in Mexico caused in the United States."

This diplomatic interference was of the utmost importance. For several months Bazaine had felt much uneasiness in regard to the north, — that is, the frontier of the United States. The Americans of the North displayed most unequivocal sympathy for the republicans of Mexico; and Bazaine was daily more alarmed lest surly neutrality should give speedy place to open hostility. What he dreaded, the Mexicans hoped ; and it was this that inspired them with such confidence and courage.

Disgust and depression, on the contrary, filled the hearts of the French, officers and men. Bazaine, wholly occupied with his own mad ambitions and material interests, no longer showed his pristine intelligence and vigor in the field; orders and counter-orders were issued in rapid succession. Letters which have since been published prove the severe judgment of his conduct felt and expressed by the most distinguished officers.

Here we must pause to review the great events which had been going on in the Northern United States ever since the close of 1860, before we can show the decisive influence which those events exercised upon the issue of affairs in Mexico. The United States were no longer united, save in name; there was, in point of fact, a marked opposition of long standing between the Northern and Southern States, which differed essentially in ideas, customs, and interests. The North was democratic, industrial, addicted to navigation; the South, aristocratic, and a producer of tropical commodities, lived by slave labor. In the field of political economy, the North was protectionist, being a nation of manufacturers; the South, free-trader, because it was very important for her people to export her cotton freely. The South, thanks to the leisure which slavery gave her, was far more given to politics than the North; and although very inferior in numbers, the Southern people had hitherto held public office and the reins of government far more frequently than those of the North.

The North at last reacted against this preponderance: the slavery question let loose the dogs of war. Popular feeling in the North, on this point, agreed with popular interest. Aside from political jealousy and manufacturing greed, religious and philosophical principles were brought powerfully to bear; and the men devoted to the abolition of slavery formed a party whose sincerity was incontestable and whose energy was undaunted. The whole world was shaken by the tragic story of John Brown, — that martyr of liberty, hung by slave-owners for preaching the enfranchisement of the blacks. A certain law compelled the confederate States to give up to each other mutually all fugitive slaves. Several of the Northern States refused longer to execute this law, contrary to the public conscience. The quarrel between free-trade and protection at the same time reached a head. One of the Southern States, South Carolina, declared the Union dissolved. Several other States followed Carolina into "secession," and the secessionists formed themselves into the Southern Confederacy (March, 1861). The North would fain have avoided civil war; the South hurried it on, and took the offensive. Two Southern States — Virginia, the home of Washington, and Maryland — refused to be led astray and saved the seat of Congress, the federal city of Washington, by remaining loyal to the Union.

The South, nevertheless, had the advantage at first. Nearly all the officers of the small federal army belonged to her, and she was far better prepared for the war than was the North.

The Northerners were not people to be discouraged by a few defeats. They squandered men and money in Cyclopean efforts unceasingly renewed. They improvised an army; they improvised, with the free help of individuals, an admirable organization for the succor of the wounded and sick of their army. This indomitable nation extemporized war as it extemporized everything. Beaten on shore, the North was still ruler of the sea; she attacked, blockaded, and assailed the Southern coast from that point. September 1, 1862, President Lincoln declared the slaves of the rebels free. The situation, however, was so perilous at the end of 1862 that the president reconsidered this great measure, and made proposals for a compromise which would adjourn the abolition of slavery for a long time. The secessionists refused, hoping to obtain help from abroad. The French minister of foreign affairs, Drouyn de Lhuys, proposed that England and Russia should unite with France to bring about an armistice between "the belligerent parties" in America. This was putting the legal government of the United States upon the same footing with the rebel minority. This step caused lively irritation in the North; and the United States government protested against any attempt at mediation, being well aware that French imperialism and English aristocracy were at heart equally hostile to the cause of the North.

President Lincoln and Congress returned boldly to the scheme for the immediate emancipation of the blacks in rebel States. The Emancipation Act of January 1, 1863, marks one of the great dates of history. This brave resolve was rewarded by brilliant victories in the course of the year 1863. In this campaign the huge long-range guns were employed for the first time by both sides, although they have since been adopted in all countries. Europe learned with amazement that the city of Charleston had been bombarded from a distance of eight and nine miles. It was also about this time that the regular modern school of cavalry was created, — a body of men who no longer aim at breaking through infantry squares, or deciding the fate of battle by a grand charge, but who, by their rapid and remote expeditions, prepare the defeat of the foe by cutting off his communications, carrying off his supplies, and complete their work by harassing his retreat. A people who had hitherto had no army thus renewed and revived the art of war.

In view of the Northern victories, the English government decided to put a stop to such a violation of the rights of nations as the armament of privateers in English ports for the South. The French government also prohibited the building of corsair vessels for the South at Nantes and Bordeaux.

Opinion was divided in a significant manner in France as well as in England. The democracy on both sides of the channel eagerly took part with the North; the English oligarchy and French reaction sided with the South. The attitude of the mass of the English people, on this occasion, was most honorable to them. They suffered cruelly from a crisis in the cotton trade: the governing classes attempted to throw all responsibility upon the Northerners; but the people would not listen to them, and resolutely sympathized with the side which they held to be that of humanity and justice. The French laboring class displayed a similar disinterestedness.

In France, the two parties of North and South had a dramatic opportunity to manifest their feelings. The "Yankee" ship Kearsarge attacked the famous "rebel" privateer, the Alabama, in the British Channel, the latter vessel having done immense injury to the merchant-service of the North. A regular duel ensued in the Cherbourg waters, in sight of numerous spectators, who watched the various phases of the conflict from the top of the sea-wall and the rocks overlooking the harbor. The Kearsarge triumphed, amid the cheers of the French republicans.

Early in 1864 the South seemed lost. She revived temporarily by a desperate effort. A relentless dictatorship converted every inch of ground left her into one vast camp; the Southern government waged a truceless and relentless war, trampling under foot all law, all justice, all humanity. This fierce energy won them a few months of victory. The Northern men, ill-officered, working without unity, underwent a number of partial checks; but a new general-in-chief, Grant, restored the situation. Victory again

QUEEN AMELIA.

perched upon Northern banners in the interior as well as on the sea-coast. The great law which finally set the negroes free was passed January 31, 1865. The work begun in 1864 was finished in 1865. Spring saw the fall of the principal strongholds of the rebels, and the surrender of their skilful leader, Lee. A fanatic partisan of the South chose to avenge the defeat of the slaveholders by assassinating President Lincoln. This crime could not resuscitate a lost cause. Lincoln died triumphant; and the name of the rail-splitter who became the worthy head of a great state, — the name of this strong, simple man, which personifies democracy to every mind, — the name of Lincoln will be forever associated with the abolition of slavery.

The great war of Secession was over, and the United States had its hands free once more. Early in the previous year, at the very time that the South had a return of good fortune, Congress had voted a resolution against the restoration of monarchy in Mexico (April 4, 1864). December 6, Minister Seward despatched a note to this effect to the American representative at Paris. The new president, Johnson, used threatening terms at the opening of Congress, December 4, and sent an envoy extraordinary to Paris, in the person of General Schofield, to demand the evacuation of Mexico within a year. "The American government," said Schofield bluntly, in a despatch to the minister of foreign affairs of Juarez, "desires to aid Napoleon III. to leave Mexico as decently as may be, and to assist him to maintain *that imposture* which consisted in pretending that his army did not return to France simply because the empire [of Mexico] had nothing more to fear." (January 10, 1866.)

Napoleon III. had lost his illusions: he submitted to the affront. At the opening of the Legislative session of 1866, he delivered an address in which every word was a lie (January 22). He assumed that in Mexico "the government founded upon the will of the people was consolidating; that the vanquished and scattered dissenters had no leaders," etc. "I have arranged," he said, "with Emperor Maximilian for the date of the recall of the French troops, that their return may be effected without compromising French interests."

We have seen the truth of the consolidation of the Mexican Empire; it was quite as groundless as the story of the arrangement with Maximilian, for the agent sent to him by Napoleon III., M. Saillard, only started on the 16th of January.

Napoleon III. vainly entreated the United States to prolong the delay which they had granted him. A new and imperious note was despatched, February 22, by Minister Seward. The *Moniteur* was forced to announce the return of the whole French army for the spring of 1867.

Maximilian's awakening was bitter, when the envoy of Napoleon III. informed him that the evacuation was to begin in the following autumn; the pretext was the impossibility that the Emperor of Mexico could continue to pay the troops, according to his promise. Maximilian felt everything crumbling about him. Foreigners sold their lands. The indemnities due to French creditors were no more settled than at the beginning of the intervention. The government officials resigned or went over to the republicans. The Mexican imperial army only existed in seeming. Trouble was renewed between Maximilian and Bazaine. Military defeats ensued. Detachments of the Austrian and Belgian auxiliaries and of the French foreign legion were crushed; great convoys were captured by the republicans, who had recovered the important naval post of Matamoras.

Maximilian attempted to obtain a delay for the departure of the French troops; the French minister of foreign affairs, M. Drouyn de Lhuys, declared that if the Emperor of Mexico refused to accept the terms offered him by M. Saillard, the French government would consider itself freed from every engagement. "I am outwitted!" cried the unfortunate prince; "there was a formal agreement between Napoleon III. and myself, without which I should never have accepted the throne, and which guaranteed me the support of the French troops until the end of the year 1868!"

He was about to sign his abdication; his wife, the Empress Carlotta, snatched the pen from his hands. She set out to make one last effort with Napoleon III. (July, 1866).

She could obtain nothing; to her prayers and tears Napoleon III. replied only by silence. She blazed forth, and summoned him to keep the solemn promises which he had made her husband. " I have done for your husband," he said finally, "all that I can do; I can go no farther!"

She left the room abruptly, exclaiming, " I am rightly punished; the granddaughter of Louis Philippe should never have trusted to a Bonaparte!"

Discord increased constantly in Mexico. The clerical party plotting to seize that faint shadow of power left to Maximilian, the latter ordered the arrest of his ministers, generals, prelates, etc., and then appointed a French general and intendant ministers of war and finance. Upon the warning of the United States minister of foreign affairs that this nomination was of a nature to affect the good relations between the United States and France, Napoleon III. forbade the two French officials to accept.

People at Paris began to suspect the absurd pretensions and treacherous intrigues of Bazaine. Napoleon III., anxious to put an end to them, despatched a trusty man, General Castelnau, with orders to persuade Maximilian to abdicate (September, 1866). Popular indignation was extreme against Bazaine, among all the honest and sensible members of the French army ; it was clear that the man was sacrificing everything to a double prepossession, his pecuniary interest and his extravagant ambition. His dream of gaining acceptance with the Mexicans as emperor was quite as impossible as was the maintenance of Maximilian after the departure of the French, and the pursuit of this dream made him fail in all his duties as leader of the army ; accordingly, each day was marked by some progress of the republicans.

The wretched Emperor of Mexico wavered from scheme to scheme, passed from one extreme to another. He dreamed of vengeance on the man who had deceived him ; he refused to receive the envoy of Napoleon III., then negotiated with him ; then he approached the clericals, accepted their offers, and empowered his official journal to declare that he would retain the power. After which he announced the assembly of a national congress to decide whether the empire should continue or not.

The very day upon which Maximilian took this resolve (December 1), Napoleon III. commanded General Castelnau to send home the French foreign legion and all soldiers or civilians who desired to return to France, as well as the Austrian and Belgian legions, if they wished to do so. Napoleon III. had felt a pressure at home as well as from abroad, from financiers as well as from America. There was a general cry in France : " Let us be done with this !"

As fast as the French troops were withdrawn, the towns returned to the republicans. All hope of reinforcement for Maximilian vanished ; at the demand of the American minister at Vienna, the Austrian Emperor forbade the departure of six thousand recruits for Mexico. The end was at hand. Napoleon III., to shield his self-love to some extent, had attempted to make the United States agree to exclude Juarez from the Mexican presidency. This puerile effort was not taken as serious. The French army evacuated Mexico, February 5, 1867. A sad procession of French families, carrying with them their last resources, followed in its train. The French fleet got under sail from Vera Cruz for France, March 13. She did not take back the thousands of men nor the millions of money devoured by this mad expedition.

The fleet re-entered the port of Toulon, May 5. An order had been sent from Paris that no military honors were to be paid to Bazaine. His disgrace, unfortunately, was not lasting. The emperor had not the courage to break with him permanently.

The French gone, Maximilian strove to hold the field with the inharmonious troops which melted away in his grasp. He was soon driven back to Queretaro, the key of Central Mexico. He there defended himself for two months, then tried to negotiate and to obtain permission to set sail for home. He was unsuccessful. The place was surprised, and the unfortunate prince was forced to give up his sword (May 15, 1867). He was taken before a council of war and condemned to death. The very decree which he had issued against those whom he called rebels was now applied to him. His

defenders and the Prussian minister to Mexico went to Juarez to
beg mercy for him.   The American minister of foreign affairs, Mr.
Seward, informed Juarez that his government desired Maximilian
and his companions to be treated as prisoners of war.   Juarez did
not think it possible to yield to these entreaties.   Maximilian wrote
him a most noble letter, in which he demanded life, not for himself
but for his companions, Generals Miranon and Mejia.   "Let me
suffer alone," he said; "let my blood be the last that is shed!"

The three condemned men fell June 19.   The Empress Carlotta
lost her reason on hearing of her husband's tragic fate.

Public opinion in Europe and America was painfully moved by
the stern rigor of the conqueror; but the responsibility for this
catastrophe rested entirely with the man who urged on and then
abandoned the unfortunate Maximilian in the rash enterprise which
ended so wretchedly.

His punishment was not far off.   The fall of Napoleon III. was
at hand.   It began upon the day when that man, whom unparalleled
good fortune had made the victor over two great European monarchies, was forced to undergo the humiliation of retreating before the
great republic which he had gone forth to challenge in the New
World.   Other events, touching France far more closely, and compromising her far more gravely, foreboded this downfall during the
year 1866.   Before coming to this point, we must rehearse the chief
facts in the history of France and Europe during the Mexican war
and the war of American Secession.

A POPULAR

HISTORY OF FRANCE

FROM 1861 TO 1881.

BY FREDERICK MARTIN.

CHAPTER XXI.

RESULTS OF MEXICAN EXPEDITION. — ISSUES OF FRENCH WARS. — STATE
OF AFFAIRS IN EUROPE. — POLISH INSURRECTION. — PROPOSED CON-
FERENCE. — FAILURE OF PLAN. — SCHLESWIG-HOLSTEIN QUESTION. —
CONVENTION WITH ITALY WITH REGARD TO FRENCH GARRISON IN
ROME. — WAR OF PRUSSIA AND ITALY AGAINST AUSTRIA. — INTER-
VIEW BETWEEN NAPOLEON AND BISMARCK. — POPULAR FEELING. —
THE EMPEROR'S EXPOSITION OF HIS VIEWS. — FAILURE OF CONGRESS.
— LETTER OF THE EMPEROR. — PROGRESS AND RESULTS OF THE WAR.
— NEW POLITICAL CHANGES. — FRANCE AND GERMANY. — EXHIBI-
TION OF 1867. — THE DECAY OF THE EMPEROR. — DIFFICULTIES WITH
GERMANY. — LUXEMBURG QUESTION. — VISIT TO SALZBURG. — ITAL-
IAN ATTACK ON ROME. — FRENCH RESENTMENT. — CONDITION OF
FRANCE. — PROSPECTS OF 1868. — CONSTITUTIONAL CHANGES PRO-
POSED IN LEGISLATURE. — CHANGE OF NEWSPAPER LAWS. — ORGAN-
IZATION OF THE ARMY. — PUBLIC MEETINGS. — PAMPHLET BY THE
EMPEROR. — PROSPECTS OF 1869. — OPPOSITION. — DISPUTE WITH
BELGIUM. — NEW ELECTIONS. — GREAT CONSTITUTIONAL REFORMS:
THEIR TERMS AND THEIR CONSEQUENCES.

THE utter failure of the Mexican project and its terribly tragic
conclusion put an end at once and forever to the great dream
of " the regeneration of the Latin races " in America, the gross result

being that fresh elements of disturbance were called into play, and
new forces, working hard against the stability of the Second Empire.
The great "Latin empire" in America was never to be realized, and
the great Latin empire in Europe was on the verge of those troubles
that were by and by to end in its disastrous downfall. The government whose motto — as the Emperor was never tired of repeating
— was "peace," could only subsist by the "glory" that would accrue through success in war, and even this was denied to it. For
indeed not one of the wars in which the Emperor had engaged, and
in which he and his advisers had so lavishly spent the blood and
treasure of France, had been really successful. The Crimean war
had certainly given temporary stability and popularity to the imperial throne, and brought about an alliance with England, but it
had added heavily to the burdens of the country, and it had not
drawn to the Emperor's side a single one of those leading men
whose adhesion would have been an acquisition to the real strength
of the Empire. The Italian war had caused irritation in Austria; and though it had called forth a united Italy, strong and
free, yet this Italy was unfriendly to France, from the way in which
it conceived its interests to have been sacrificed in the treaty of
Villafranca, as well as on account of the subsequent annexation of
Savoy and Nice. This latter event, too, brought the idea of "natural frontiers" into general prominence, and so raised among the
European powers at large distrust of France, and a constant suspicion of aggressive intentions. The conduct of France in the
Chinese war had introduced a coolness into her relations with
England, while the expeditions in Syria and in Mexico had re-
sulted in the ignominious failure of every one of the purposes for
which they had been undertaken.

Meanwhile, in Europe generally the times were full of trouble
and big with great political changes. In 1863 the French Emperor,
already sufficiently annoyed and perplexed by the state of affairs in
Mexico, and aware that the slightest defeat there would entail dangerous consequences at home, had a further burden of vexation and
anxiety laid on him by the outbreak of an insurrection in Poland.

Ever since 1861 the Russian authorities had been acting towards their Polish subjects with the greatest cruelty; and in 1863 the Poles, unable any longer quietly to bear the arbitrary and oppressive outrage, rose in arms. The insurrection spread widely, and the Russians, especially the forces under the command of General Mouravieff, set to work to stamp it out. This was done in such a ferocious and inhuman manner, and with the connivance and virtual consent of the Prussian government to boot, that the other leading European powers — England, France, and Austria — at once stepped forward to remonstrate with Russia on the bitterness and severity of her repressive measures, and to complain to Prussia of her singular neutrality in the case. The Russian government refused to agree to a general conference, but offered to refer the question to the representatives of Prussia and Austria, the countries among whom the Kingdom of Poland had been divided, and which were therefore, to some extent, concerned parties. Austria rejected this proposal, declining to separate herself from England and France; but as it soon became apparent that England would not go to war on behalf of the Poles, Russia assumed a defiant attitude, and continued a course of policy which almost amounted to the annihilation of the Polish race. This certainly was not a hopeful phase of things, and, though the Emperor tried to throw the entire blame of the failure of the interference on his allies, the feelings of the French people had been too deeply stirred by the cruel proceedings in Poland to acquiesce in any diplomatic arrangement, so that it became absolutely necessary for him to take once more some active step. Political disquiet, too, had showed itself in the results of the summer elections. M. de Persigny, who had attempted to coerce the constituencies, was driven from office, and the issue brought into existence a compact minority, which included a number of eminent statesmen, eager to watch and keen to criticise the conduct of affairs. The situation was difficult. On the one hand there was the alternative of ceasing to remonstrate with the cruel proceedings against Poland, which the national temper would pronounce disgraceful, and probably would not endure; on the other hand, that

of a costly war, which the Emperor clearly saw was an impossible
venture, as there were neither men nor money. The Mexican war
had assumed such proportions as to occupy a very large army, and
the drain of money for it was seriously adding to the already disturbed condition of the finances. In this dilemma the first object
of the Emperor seems to have been to look about for and take
advantage of opportunities to gain time. In an autograph letter,
addressed to the various European courts, and written in a senti-
mental style quite out of keeping with the subject, this apostle of
aggression and of "natural frontiers" proposed that, to secure the
peace of Europe, matters should be referred for adjustment to the
decisions of a congress, which should meet at Paris and deliberate
on European affairs after the model of the famous assembly that
met at Vienna in 1815. The idea was no doubt good; and the
project, had it proved successful, might have caused a fresh outburst of popular enthusiasm in behalf of the Napoleonic dynasty;
for the imagination of a people so fond of "glory," and so devoted
to France as "the grand nation," would have been excited and
pleased by the presence of a representative congress of the nations
of Europe met to settle European destinies within the walls of the
capital.

Had the time been favorable, such a congress might have been
highly successful, and productive of the best results; but the time
was unfavorable. It was from the outset improbable that Russia
would be willing to make concessions; and, though all the European powers but one accepted the proposal, they did so in ways
that showed that the project was fated to prove a failure. Austria
wished for explanations; Prussia talked vaguely of her adherence
to treaties; the Pope expressed a hope that the congress, under the
auspices of the "elder son of the church," would not only restore
his own temporal power, but take measures for the restoration
throughout the world of the supremacy of the Catholic faith. In
fact, the only powers that seemed thoroughly in earnest about the
matter were those that hoped to be enriched at the expense of
their neighbors. We have said that only one power declined to

take any part in the scheme. That power was England; and the
English refusal — especially as Lord Russell's answer was couched
in terms that were undiplomatically outspoken — gave the death-
blow to the proposal. Russia was left at liberty to stamp out the
Polish name and race in any way she pleased, while the French
Emperor's prestige was deeply injured. How keenly he resented
the English refusal was shown in the following year (1864), when
he declined to give effect to his pledges as one of the signatories of
the treaty of 1852, and join England in offering open resistance to
the invasion of Schleswig by Prussia and Austria.

Under Frederick VII., King of Denmark, there had arisen various
disputes as to the rights and privileges of the German subjects in
the German duchies of Schleswig and Holstein. By agreements
entered into, however, in 1850 and 1851, the authority of Frederick
in both duchies had been admitted by Prussia and Austria. In
view of the fact that Frederick was the last of the line of Olden-
burg, and that the dynasty would become extinct at his death, the
great powers thought it desirable to settle the question of the integrity of the Danish monarchy, and by the treaty of London, signed
in 1852, all claims were arranged, and the succession settled on
Prince Christian. Frederick had just commenced a dispute with
Prussia as to the proclamation of a constitution in Holstein, when
he died; and thereupon the old sores opened afresh, and finally war
broke out. England appealed to the great powers to carry out the
treaty of 1852, but all refused; and in this the French Emperor
for his part was no doubt greatly influenced by the vexation he felt
at the pointed refusal of England to agree to his proposed European
conference. He was even said to have encouraged the policy of
Prussia, which availed itself of the situation that had arisen to
promote the unity and independence of the Fatherland. Could he
have foreseen that this was the beginning of that chain of events
which was to raise Germany to a leading place in the affairs of
Europe, and to bring about his own dethronement and exile, his
encouragement and action would have assumed a very different
form.

In September, 1864, the Emperor, under the pretext of rendering the unity of Italy more complete by removing a foreign army from its soil, — but really, in all probability, with the view of courting the fresh favor of the Italians, and at the same time saving money, — entered into a convention with Italy, in which his government pledged itself that the French troops would be withdrawn from Rome in two years, provided the King of Italy, on the other hand, bound himself to abstain from encroachments on the Pope's territory, and to protect it from attacks on the part of others; the Pope to be at liberty to keep up an army for himself, and the capital of Italy to be transferred from Turin to Florence. The withdrawal of the garrison from Rome afforded an opportunity for the reduction of the French army, and as much capital as possible was made of this in proof that the most earnest desire of the French Empire was "peace." The convention with Italy was honorably carried out on both sides; the remnant of the French garrison was withdrawn in 1866, and with it disappeared the last visible sign of the patronage by France of a unified Italy.

In 1866 the troubles which had meanwhile arisen between Prussia and Austria over the administration of the conquered provinces of Schleswig and Holstein came to an open rupture. It was of course the interest of Italy to side with Prussia against Austria, as it afforded her an opportunity of wresting Venetia from the Austrian dominions, and thus making one stride more towards the establishment of the Italian government over the whole peninsula; and so with Prussia Italy sided. What France would do in the circumstances was a question of the first importance, for no one dreamt for a moment that she would play the part of an impartial spectator. An interview which had taken place at Biarritz the previous autumn between Napoleon III. and the Prussian minister, Count Bismarck, brought to mind the secret treaty concluded with Count Cavour before the Italian war. There is little reason to doubt that Bismarck, as the neutrality of France was indispensable, had on this occasion bid so high as to hint at, if not promise, non-interference in the event of France attempting the annexation of

Belgium; and from what subsequently transpired he seems even to have held out hopes of a rectification of the French frontier on the side towards Prussia. Napoleon, still blind to the ambitious aims and growing power of Prussia, took the bait; but the far-seeing among his subjects were inclined to take a very different view of matters, while the mass of the people would, probably, have eagerly accepted an alliance with Austria. Several members of the Legislative Body expressed a strong opposition to the alliance with Germany, especially as it might lead to an increase of Prussian territory. M. Thiers advanced and strongly maintained the idea — the true Napoleonic one — that France could be truly "the great nation" only in proportion as the surrounding states were weak and subdivided. To such criticism in the Legislature the emperor responded by a speech, delivered at Auxerre, in which, after pouring out his sarcasm and contempt on the speakers in the Legislative Body who had opposed his policy, he openly announced his wish to do away with the treaties that had been imposed in 1815, and bring about a new adjustment of power, only stipulating as the condition of the assistance he might give in this task, that, when any foreign state made an addition to its territories, France was to be allowed to add to hers, — of course, necessarily at the expense of some of her neighbors. This violent and most imprudent speech, while it gave direct and open encouragement to Prussia, caused great uneasiness among the other powers, especially Britain, as it was thought that the annexation of Belgium was aimed at. It also defeated the project of a European congress which was afterwards proposed, as Austria at once refused to countenance the discussion of any plan for the alienation or exchange of territory, and it revived again afresh the uneasy feeling that had been produced by the Savoy affair, and by the utterances about the necessity of natural frontiers. The emperor professed to state his own position in a letter to his Minister for Foreign Affairs, dated 11th June, 1866, and described what the minister's course would have been had the proposed congress taken place. In this document it was declared that there was no wish for an increase of territory, provided the balance of power were not disturbed; that there was no wish for an extension of the French frontier unless as an equipoise against territorial aggrandizement elsewhere, or unless one or other of "the neighboring provinces demanded, by freely expressed votes, their annexation to France." Then the letter went on to say that it was his wish that Germany should become more united; that Prussia should have more power in the North; and that Austria, recognizing in regard to Italy the same principle which along with Prussia she had enforced against Denmark, should give up Venice to the Italians; and it concluded with the assurance that it had been agreed by the powers that, no matter how the war resulted, no question "concerning France should be decided without her consent."

It was the fault of Austria that the rupture was rashly precipitated. The imperial army was not ready for action, and the smaller German states which had espoused the Austrian cause were not sufficiently advanced in their preparations. The Prussian arrangements, on the other hand, were all singularly complete. The troops could be brought into the field at once, and they were well armed and well handled. Once war was declared, they struck boldly and fast. The campaign was over in a fortnight, and the Austrians, signally defeated in the battle of Sadowa, made an attempt to procure a cessation of hostilities by surrendering Venetia, not to the King of Italy, but to the Emperor of the French. The Italians indeed had been singularly unsuccessful. They had declared war against Austria at the same time as the Prussians, but had suffered severe defeat at the battle of Custozza, — a defeat, the vexation and disappointment over which were bitterly increased by the surrender of Venetia to the French Emperor instead of to the Italian King. The whole transaction was an Austrian sop to procure Napoleon's intervention, and it may probably have originated in some rash idea of his own. The results were certainly disastrous for him. The irritation it caused in Italy was so strong as to bring about the complete alienation of the Italians from France, which, to say the least of it, was surely not a little ungrateful, for Italy profited by the transfer; and, in spite of all his faults and his selfish policy, the Emperor of France had been one of the best friends of Italian freedom. It did more; it showed Napoleon's total inability to interfere, for immediately on the announcement of the transfer, the Prussians and the Italians both announced their intention of prosecuting the war notwithstanding. Peace was, however, concluded very shortly afterwards, and Prussia was mistress of the whole of Germany. Napoleon, after going through the ceremony of his favorite appeal to popular suffrage, formally handed over Venetia to Italy. As soon as the peace was firmly established, the emperor applied in due form to Prussia for the cession of the coal-field and district of Saarbrück, as part of the price he hoped to receive for his friendly neutrality. The prompt reply, that no part of German territory could be surrendered, and the strength of the power that gave this reply, rendered further discussion unnecessary. In consequence of all this the dissatisfaction in France grew greater. The prestige of the Empire was almost destroyed by the continual failures of the last four years, and fears of German invasion began to be entertained to such an extent that a large increase of the army was proposed at the opening of the sittings of the Legislative Body on the 14th February, 1867.

At the beginning of this session of the Legislature an important political change came into play. In 1860 the right had been granted to the Chamber to discuss the address to the throne. The political situation, however, had now so changed that, in the end of 1866, the Senate voted a law prohibiting the Legislative Body from proposing, or even agitating, any change in the Constitution formulated in 1852, and this was followed up on the 19th January, 1867, by an imperial decree taking away the right of discussing the address, but granting in its place the right of bringing forward interpellations of the government, — the fate of the interpellation being dependent on the will of the majority. One of the earliest of the interpellations was one questioning the legality of the decree of the 19th January; but the government majority was too strong, and a similarly large majority afterwards expressed the approval by the Legislature of the ministerial foreign policy. To

the leading point in M. Rouher's defence of the government, — that
the treaty of Prague had really weakened Germany by cutting it
into three, — Count Bismarck furnished a most cutting and conclusive reply, by publishing the treaties concluded the year before
by Bavaria, Würtemberg, and Baden, agreeing, in the event of
foreign war, to place their respective armies at the disposal of
Prussia.

In spite of all mistakes of government, France was thriving, for,
during the time of the Second Empire, the total value of the exports
and imports had almost doubled; and this year (1867) the material
prosperity of the country was shown in the great Universal Exhibition of Fine Arts and Industry which was opened at Paris on the
1st of April. It was a most imposing mart of nations; and the
number of exhibitors and visitors from all parts of the world was
very large, — the visitors including nearly a hundred imperial and
royal personages, among whom may be mentioned the King of
Prussia, and the Emperors of Russia and Austria. There were great
rejoiçings in Paris, and great official *fêtes* projected; but the official
part of the programme was brought to a sudden conclusion. While
Alexander II. of Russia was returning from a review in company
with Napoleon, an attempt was made on his life by one who had
been a victim of his cruelties in Poland. This incident, followed
as it was by the news of the execution of Maximilian in Mexico,
produced general gloom, and a feeling in some quarters that
amounted to consternation. From this time onward the French
Emperor seemed to lose all nerve. M. Morny, who certainly had
ample opportunities for observation, is recorded to have said, that
"there was no possibility of getting a fixed idea out of Napoleon's
head, or a fixed resolve into it;" but after the death of Maximilian he seems to have become still more irresolute. "As soon as
Fortuna failed him," says Karl Hillebrand, "*Audacia* failed him
too; and without audacity no one wins the favor of the capricious
goddess. The Mexican fiasco, which was due to the success of the
states of North America, — a success as unexpected to many
statesmen as to Napoleon, — made him lose confidence in himself,

and robbed him of the resolution and steadiness of purpose which are the most essential qualities of a statesman. Premature old age, and a disease which always impairs a man's strength of will, did the rest; after Maximilian's death he always acted as though he were feeling his way in the dark,—at one moment advancing, at another retreating,—and so committed all those mistakes which led to the ruin of himself and his nation."

This year (1867) was in many ways an unfortunate one for Napoleon. The utter failure of the Mexican project, followed as it was by the murder of Maximilian, deeply wounded the vanity of the French people; and difficulties with Germany, both before and after, twice almost precipitated the emperor into war, and this he declared afterwards was averted only by his own strong personal resistance to the pressure brought to bear upon him. The first of those difficulties arose out of a secret treaty entered into between Napoleon and the King of Holland, who was grand duke of Luxemburg. Notwithstanding that Luxemburg was nominally a German province, and that its fortified capital was held by a Prussian garrison, the King of Holland had, according to the treaty which was now disclosed, agreed to sell the whole province to France. The North German Parliament at once interposed, and declared, as the exponent of the national determination, that they would allow no German territory to be surrendered, and for some time, as a consequence, France and Prussia were on the brink of war. England and Russia, however, interposed,—Russia being at the time for some purpose of her own interested in cultivating very friendly relations with France,—and offered their good offices in way of mediation. A conference assembled in London to discuss a settlement, and on the 11th May a compromise was effected, by which it was decided that as, on the one hand, Luxemburg had never really formed part of the North German Confederation, and as the occupation of the fortress vested by the treaties of Vienna in the old confederation had lapsed, the Prussian garrison should be withdrawn and the fortifications demolished; and that, on the other hand, the Emperor of France, in consideration of this, should withdraw his claim for completion of the bargain of sale, the King of Holland to remain grand duke of the duchy.

After the death of Maximilian a most imprudent and injudicious visit of Napoleon to the Emperor of Austria at Salzburg again gave rise to fresh rumors of impending hostilities. The journey and the visit were ostensibly undertaken for the purpose of offering sympathy to the Austrian Emperor and condolence with his grief at the untimely fate of his brother; and though this was no doubt true, it is equally certain that it was by no means the whole truth, for there is every reason to believe that there were political schemes involved in the interview, and that the emperor wished to form an Austrian alliance, and to secure some right to intermeddle in German affairs by reviving the French protectorate that formerly existed over some of the smaller German states. The affair, however, came to nothing, and the French official press assiduously protested that it involved no political purposes whatever; it nevertheless called forth from Count Bismarck a circular, in which, after recording with bitter and emphatic pointedness the entirely unpolitical and private nature of the visit, he concluded with the significant hint that it was impossible that France could have intended to interfere in German affairs, as it was well known that no interference in these would ever be brooked by Prussia. The national mortification at such a decided snub had to be appeased in some way, and fortunately at the right moment Italy was discovered to be in a position to be made a scape-goat, and the state of Italian affairs was such as to afford a pretext for interference.

The French garrison had, in accordance with the convention of 1864, been withdrawn from Rome on the 11th December, 1866, and almost immediately after, Garibaldi began to assemble volunteers for the conquest of the remnant of the Papal dominions. He had been making preparations all through summer, and now in September he was ready to commence operations. After attending and speaking at an assembly termed a *Peace* Congress, which had met at Geneva, he proceeded across the Alps to take command of the bands that he had collected on the frontier of the Roman States;

but on his way thither he was prudently arrested by the Italian
authorities, and packed off to Caprera, while Italian troops advanced
to the borders of the Papal dominions to disperse the bands that
awaited his arrival. They, however, proved insufficient for the
purpose, and the volunteers succeeded in forcing their way into
Papal territory. Here was the opportunity France needed, and she
caught at it as a God-send. The King of Italy had failed to carry
out his agreement to protect the territory of the Church from attack.
It was true that the French themselves had been the first to violate
the convention, for the Pope had formed a body of troops who,
though they nominally formed the Papal army and were in the
service of the Pope, were yet in reality French soldiers; and the
French minister of war, Marshal Niel, had, in an official letter,
made a statement which virtually amounted to a confession, that
this Antibes Legion formed a constituent part of the French army.
All this was nothing now. The Italian government, moreover, loyal
to the convention, at once proposed an advance on Rome in order
to protect the city. To this the king, strange to say, refused his
consent, and the ministry immediately resigned. The French government thereupon despatched offhand an expedition to Rome, and
in the engagement at Mentana on the 3d October, the French and
Papal troops inflicted a severe defeat on the volunteers under the
command of Garibaldi, who had meanwhile effected his escape from
Caprera. It was necessary for France to win "glory" somewhere,
and here was the opportunity. The rash and foolish conduct of
Garibaldi undoubtedly brought on a serious crisis, but it might have
passed safely away, had it not been for the excited state of public
feeling in France. A somewhat contemptuous treatment of Italy
by the Minister of Foreign Affairs, the Marquis de Moustier, was
not enough. A statement by M. Thiers, still harping on the old
theme, that the greatness of France depended on the weakness of
the states that surrounded her, and pointing out how the policy of
the Empire was the ruin of this greatness, having been received
in the Legislature with enthusiastic applause, M. Rouher, the prime
minister, unable to resist the tide of popular opinion, plunged into

a series of insulting actions towards Italy, which were as exasperating as they were wanton, and finally committed the French government to the perpetual protection of the territories of the Holy See. The feeling in Italy was almost as strong as it was in France, and from this time the alienation of the two countries may be regarded as complete, though certainly it is the folly of the people, rather than that of the ruler, which must be credited with the result.

The last misfortune of the year was the death, at the age of sixty-seven, of M. Fould, the ablest of the emperor's financial advisers, who was Minister of Finance in the early years of the Empire, and again from 1861 till the beginning of 1867. His loss was much felt; for that an able financier like him was sorely needed is obvious from the facts that the funded debt of France had increased between 1852 and 1864 from almost two hundred and fourteen millions of pounds sterling to nearly four hundred and ninety-three millions, and that from 1854 to 1867 wars alone had involved a debt of about one hundred and five millions of pounds.

At the beginning of 1868 an article in the official paper — the *Moniteur* — reviewed the state of the country and took a highly favorable view of the condition and prospects of France. Everything was peaceful, and " the wisdom of nations and their governments" would no doubt effect an amicable settlement of all questions in dispute. In 1867, France, true to her traditional policy, had been still in the forefront of civilization, and in the Universal Exhibition had symbolized the " ideas of brotherhood and solidarity that are the honor of the age." At home authority and liberty had been found justly balanced, while abroad influence had been exerted "in favor of the peace and general interests of Europe." The support accorded to the Papal throne was given as involving principles of right and justice based on treaties. Thus spoke the official oracle, but the opposition and the opposition papers took a different view of the situation, and circulated a very different report. According to them everything was in a state of disquiet and justified the most gloomy forebodings. Prussia and Russia were pursuing their own ends without regard to treaties or anything else. All signs pointed to a great struggle in which France would have to engage with a host of enemies and few or no allies.

Notwithstanding the usual rumors of war and the threatening tone of the semi-official press, external affairs were in a state of tranquillity throughout the year, and attention was devoted to internal changes proposed by the government. Of these the leading points were the Liberty of the Press, the Organization of the Army, and the Right of Public Meeting, all of which, along with the Budget, gave rise to bitter and stormy debates in the Legislative Body. Greater freedom of the press had been promised by the emperor some time before, and though the promise had never been carried out, yet newspaper prosecutions had been fewer. The forty-second article of the Constitution provided that the only reports of the meetings of the Legislative Body were to be simple copies of the minutes of each sitting, drawn up under the supervision of the president of the Legislature. By a decree of the Senate, passed on the 2d February, 1861, this article was altered, and it was afterwards permissible to publish an abridgment of the debates, drawn up by the secretaries of the body under the superintendence of the president. The publication of any other report rendered the journal in which it appeared liable to prosecution and to a heavy penalty. Early in the year M. Picard brought up in the Legislative Body the case of a number of journals that were under prosecution for inserting articles commenting on these reports. He was supported by Thiers, who maintained that this was an infringement of the right of public discussion. The prime minister, M. Rouher, urged in reply that no right was affected, but what the law was must be settled by the courts rather than the Legislature. The courts decided that the publication of the articles was an infringement of the Constitution, and that the papers were liable to the penalties provided. In addition to the risk of prosecution and fine it had hitherto been necessary to obtain the consent of the government to the establishment of any journal, and the Minister of the Interior and the Prefects had power to give official warnings to any offending paper, and to suspend its publication. In the end of January, however, a bill was introduced by the government, proposing to abolish this permissive right and the power of giving warnings and of suspension, but retaining the system of fines, as well as the regulation that all articles must be signed, and also providing that all convictions should involve temporary deprivation of civil rights. The debates on the provisions of the bill were protracted and agitated, M. Thiers and M. Jules Favre leading the opposition and urging the government to adopt at once the principle of a Free Press. The opposition waxed so strong that at one time the bill was almost abandoned, but in the end the ministry determined to persevere with it; and on the 12th March it passed by a majority of two hundred and forty to one. The one man who voted against it was, however, the able and illustrious Berryer, now an old man of seventy-eight, but still as keen a supporter of the Liberty of the Press as he had been more than fifty·years before, and as determined in his opposition to what he thought wrong, as when, after the fall of Charles X., he was the only one of the Legitimist party who continued a member of the Chamber of Deputies.

The bill for the Organization of the Army had been passed earlier in the session, but not without vigorous opposition in both the Legislative Body and in the Senate. It was urged by the opposition that increase of armaments was a most inconsistent course for an empire whose whole declared policy was "peace." The nations of Europe, it was said, were no longer animated by those feelings of antipathy towards each other which formerly involved them in such bloody strifes, but everywhere there was a sincere conviction of the value of, and a sincere desire for, brotherly intercourse. There was no enemy for France to arm against, and no disposition anywhere to go to war. The non-intervention policy of England was pacific; Austria and Italy were friendly; Russia was too far off; and Prussia had enough and more than enough, to do at home in setting her own house in order. The government, on the other hand, maintained that there was no certainty of peace except in the respect which resulted from thorough readiness for war; that, so far from Europe being in an eminently pacific condition, it was no secret that all the great powers were diligently increasing their armaments; that while under the proposed changes the effective force available for France would be under six hundred thousand men, the proportion she ought to have, as compared with even second-rate German states, should be more than double that number, and that the northern powers could, if they combined together, bring four million of troops into the field against her, while, if ungrateful Italy were to join such a combination, the number would be increased by almost another million; they had money but not men, yet in order to be thoroughly secure it was necessary to have men as well as money. One speaker waxed so outspoken as to express distrust of Prussia, and declare that they must be prepared in case she should swoop down on them as she had already swooped down on Austria, and that no doubt, opportunity offering, she would attempt to secure what she had already claimed in 1815, — all the fortresses on the Saar and Meuse as well as Alsace. The bill was finally carried in the Legislative Body by two hundred votes against sixty, and in the Senate by one hundred and twenty-five votes to one. It was announced during the debate that the whole of the army was to be provided at once with a new and most perfect breech-loading rifle — the Chassepot — which had "done wonders" at Mentana.

The bill authorizing public meetings was introduced in March. By this bill it was provided that a meeting where no political or religious question was to be discussed might be held without authorization, provided it was convened in some "enclosed and covered place," and notice previously given of the place, time, and object of the meeting, such notice being signed by seven inhabitants of the commune where it was to be held "in full possession of their civil and political rights." Political meetings could be held only for electoral purposes, and even then only within stated times; and no one could attend them except the electors and candidates, who were required before being admitted to give their names and addresses

In the same month a pamphlet was published which caused no little sensation, as it was believed to have been inspired, if not written, by the emperor himself. After a narrative of the establishment of the Second Empire, and after recalling how every successive act of the emperor had been approved by the people, it went into a detailed comparison of the careers of the First and Second Empires, and pointed out how, taking act for act and measure for measure all through, there was a perfect analogy, and so agreement in spirit and policy between them. But an incident that took place in August showed with curious pointedness how little the seeming approval of the people was to be relied on as an evidence of popular satisfaction with the Napoleonic Dynasty. The Prince Imperial distributed the prizes to the successful pupils of the university of the Sorbonne. One of these prizes had been gained by the son of General Cavaignac, the emperor's old rival for the presidentship; but this young man, when called by the Minister of Public Instruction, M. Duruy, only rose, and, instead of advancing to receive his prize, immediately sat down again: he would not receive it from the hand of the son of his father's rival. It was an act of gross rudeness; but the loud applause with which it was received by the students was a rather significant revelation of their loyalty towards the emperor. Public opinion was also significantly displayed in connection with the opening of subscriptions for the erection of a monument to an obscure deputy, named Baudin, who fell at the *coup d'état*. Had the government been politic it would have let the matter alone, but instead of this it prosecuted the papers in which the lists of subscriptions appeared, and so drew universal attention to the occurrence, and called forth no inconsiderable amount of indignation. Though the Minister of the Interior, M. Pinard, was removed, and replaced by M. de la Rocquette, it was too late, — the blunder had been committed, and the public would not be persuaded out of the suspicion that the act was done at the instance of the government.

So far as foreign affairs were concerned, everything all through the following year went well. A rupture between Turkey and

Greece was smoothed over by a congress which met at Paris in
the end of January, 1869, and diplomatic relations between the
two countries were re-established. Internal affairs were very quiet.
The emperor's speech at the opening of the Chambers was hopeful.
After alluding to the fact that the bills affecting the press and the
right of public meeting had given rise in some quarters to a certain amount of factious agitation, and a certain fresh outbreak of
ideas that were supposed to be entirely dead, he expressed his
thorough conviction that the nation had the most perfect confidence
in his firmness. The more, he remarked, fickle minds tried to disturb the peace of the nation, the more firm did that peace become.
Commerce was prosperous. The nation, thanks to the Army Bill,
was strong, and all the departments of the public service in effective
order. The "military resources of France" were "on a level with
its destiny in the world." "In this position" they "could loudly
proclaim their desire to maintain peace." Foreign relations were
friendly. Spain was disturbed by revolution, indeed, but there was
no alteration in her friendly relations with France. The prevention
of war between Turkey and Greece by the peaceful deliberations of
the conference might teach them a significant lesson. The people
were staunch in their "faith" and in "affection."

One of the early debates in the Chamber was on an interpellation
about the right of public meeting, and whether meetings at which
the people were incited to "regicide and civil war" should be permitted. The Minister of Justice admitted the danger of those meetings, but said the government were not quite certain whether such
meetings and the theories expressed at them "were not less dangerous when openly discussed than they would be if their expression
were confined to secret societies." They could not see how obscure
these agitators were until they were prosecuted, and then it was only
their association with the sacred name of freedom that invested them
with an interest and influence that did not naturally belong to them.
M. Emile Ollivier, so soon to play such a prominent and tragic part
in the arena of French politics, in vain urged this view of the case
on the government, and reminded them that where silence was im-

posed the result was not necessarily greater security, but often very much the reverse. It is the stoppage of the vent that occasions the volcanic outburst. Vile and shocking as these doctrines were, it might have been better to let their vileness expose itself in the open light of free expression. The expression in action that they were to find in the days of the commune was a worse evil. The interpellation was withdrawn, but it led to the issue of a circular, intimating that the government were determined to make use of their powers to prevent breaches of the law.

An excited state of public feeling that arose about this time against Belgium over some railway questions, passed rapidly away, and about the middle of April the Foreign Minister, the Marquis de Lavalette, was able to give such a satisfactory account of French foreign relations, especially with respect to Germany, that he was loudly cheered from all parts of the Chambers, and M. Thiers and M. Jules Favre expressed their great satisfaction at the statement of the minister.

The Chamber, which had been elected in 1863, fell to be dissolved at the close of this session, and the approach of the elections had caused inquiries to be addressed to the government as to the intimidation of electors and corrupt practices at the elections; but all the answer received was that the government intended to adhere to their former system of official candidates. The Legislative Body broke up on the 26th of April, and active preparations were at once begun for the new elections. Several of the candidates, even some of those who had been opposed to the Empire, were now inclined to adhere to the government. M. Renan protested his motto was "no revolution and no war — progress and liberty." M. Berthe, a republican of the old school, asserted that he had no wish to destroy the Empire. Others were, however, as "irreconcilable" as ever. M. Thiers refused to address the electors. "During the past six years," he said, "I have devoted all my efforts to the achievement of liberty, and the persons who have not been enlightened by my speeches, my acts, and the constancy of my endeavors during the last session will not be so by the explanation of an hour, often consisting only of promises contradicted by acts." M. Henri Rochefort, the notorious editor of *La Lanterne*, did not hesitate openly to announce himself as a Socialist. Signs of a very perturbed state of feeling were everywhere manifest. There were disturbances in almost all the large towns, and in Paris itself crowds paraded the streets singing the Marseillaise and shouting "Vive la République! Vive *la Lanterne!*" The elections showed some gain to the minority. The opposition was especially powerful in good names, and, small as it was, of formidable account, seeing it was composed of men like Thiers, Jules Ferry, Jules Favre, Gambetta, Picard, and Jules Simon.

The action of the press laws had attracted public notice all through the year. The *Moniteur*, which had been for eighty years the official journal of the country, had given offence to the ministry, and had consequently ceased to have any further connection with the government, which authorized the institution of a paper called "The Official Journal of the French Empire," — *Journal Officiel de l'Empire Française,* — and this organ henceforth enjoyed the monopoly of government communications. Further sensation was created by the publication of a letter from M. Seguier, the Procureur-Impérial at Toulouse, intimating his resignation of office "not" as "a voluntary act," but as forced upon him by the reproaches to which he had been subject at the hands of the minister of Justice, on account of his liberal attitude with regard to press prosecutions. "I am," said he, "the victim of my lenient conduct towards the press." In the month of June the excitement over press matters culminated in the trial of Henri Rochefort, editor of *La Lanterne*, — the most scurrilous of all the vile prints that abounded at the time, — on the charge of being concerned in the introduction of that paper into France after it had been forbidden. M. Rochefort was found guilty and sentenced to three years' imprisonment, with loss of civil and political rights, and to pay in addition a fine of ten thousand francs.

Late in July the members of the new legislature were called together in an extraordinary session, for the purpose of verifying the elections; and as soon as they were convened, M. Rouher stood up and announced that they had been summoned merely for this purpose, and that "resolutions and projects . . . . most calculated to realize the wishes of the country," would be submitted at an ordinary session.

Hitherto the government of the Empire had been thoroughly despotic. The ministers had been merely the official representatives of the prerogatives of the emperor, and the chambers had in reality only registered the decrees of the imperial will. There had been no real constitutional government such as exists in Britain. The ministers had been appointed by, and at the pleasure of, the emperor, and were in no way dependent on the majority of the Legislative Body. Now a change was to take place; a change so important — involving as it did the total surrender of the emperor's despotic power — both in its constitutional bearing and its results, that it must be treated of at some length. From 1851 to 1860 Louis Napoleon had been practically autocratic, responsible only to the "people," as he himself put it. In 1860, in prosecution of a policy of "wholesale reform," he suddenly granted to the Legislative Body "publicity of debate, freedom of speech, and a more effective control of the Budget;" and now, in the end of 1869, he was to grant still wider reforms, which were to lead to the constitutional Ollivier government and involve the Empire in the disastrous war with Prussia. All French governments seem somehow to "totter to their fall" the moment they in earnest attempt to become constitutional. The initiation of the new measures which had been shadowed forth in the emperor's letter of the 19th January, 1867, in which, as well as right of public meeting and the freedom of the press, he had promised increased parliamentary power, was, as M. Rouher had intimated, to be reserved for the ordinary session; but it was now resolved to bring them forward at once, and on the 12th of August, a fortnight after the opening of the extraordinary session, the minister read to the Legislative Body a message from the emperor announcing the changes that had been decided on, and that were to be discussed at once, at a meeting of the Senate that had been called for the purpose. It was stated that the changes contemplated were: 1st, that the Legislative Body should have the power of regulating its own proceedings and electing its own *bureaux;* 2d, that amendments should be presented and considered in a more simple manner; 3d, that international treaties with regard to tariffs should be submitted to the Chamber; 4th, that the Budget should be taken in sections so as to give the Legislative Body more control over it; 5th, that the incompatibility existing between the position of deputy and the assumption of certain public functions, particularly those of ministers, should be removed; 6th, that the right of interpellation should be extended. Several of the ministers disapproved very highly of the plan, so much so that Rouher, Duruy, Lavalette, and Baroche resigned office, Bourbeau, Leroux, and Prince de la Tour d'Auvergne being called to their places. M. Rouher became afterwards president of the Senate. Competent observers are agreed that the change was at the time a mistake. The country was not ripe for it. The reform of 1860 had been a success, but it had been carried through by the cool and steady Morny. Morny was gone, and M. Rouher, who seemed to have the full confidence of the emperor, was not enough of a statesman to fill his place.

In the full decree of the Senate, ultimately passed, the principal provisions were that the ministers were responsible and could be impeached only by the Senate. The ministers were to be members of both houses, and had a right to speak when they considered such a course advisable: the meetings of the Senate were to be public, but any five members could demand that the house should resolve into a Secret Committee. The Senate could send back a bill to the Legislative Body for amendment, and any bill thrown out by the Senate could not be again brought forward by the Legislative Body during the same session. Both Chambers were to fix their own internal regulations; the Budget was to be voted by chapters and articles. On the 26th of August M. Devienne brought forward at a meeting of the Senate a long report on the Senate's decree. It pointed out that the frequent changes introduced into the fundamental law gave an appearance of fickleness to a nation that had been often enough subjected to such a charge, but that the emperor seemed desirous to advance in the path of liberty, and to sweep away for the national advantage "the rubbish accumulated by our revolutions. We cannot say," it went on, "what will be the issue of this undertaking. But, whether the result be fortunate or not, history, if she preserves any truth, will declare that Napoleon III. inaugurated alone the liberal movement, not only without constraint, but in the midst of considerable resistance, and under the burden of the discouraging ingratitude which at the outset awaits, among ourselves, the most generous acts of the power existing. The new decree of the Senate has appeared to your committee the wise, opportune, and even necessary continuation of the progress of internal policy undertaken by the emperor; and we therefore propose to you, in principle, to adopt it." It then went on to deal in detail with each of the separate articles of the decree, and to give reasons for their adoption. In dealing with Article 2, which had reference to the responsibility of ministers, it said, "The objection has been made that the dependence of ministers on the emperor and their responsibility before the Chambers were incompatible, and that no good reason could be assigned for introducing two enactments into the same Article. By former constitutions, the person of the sovereign was declared to be above all responsibility, but that legal fiction had been set aside by the emperor, who considered himself responsible to the nation, and, therefore, Article 13 of the Constitution declared, 'The ministers only depend on the head of the state; they are responsible only for what concerns each individually in the affairs of the government; and there is no conjoint responsibility among them.' The emperor, consequently, was alone to be accountable for what was done, and the ministers could only be called on to answer each for his own special acts. It is that state of things which the decree of the Senate desires to put an end to, so that the members of the Cabinet shall be responsible for their acts, not alone individually but collectively. That is the only innovation introduced by the Article, — namely, to enlarge their sphere of responsibility, and to make it collective. The position of the sovereign remains what it was." Speaking of Article 3, which admitted ministers to the Legislative Body, it said, "It completes the political responsibility of ministers before the Chamber, in placing them constantly in presence of the opposition there to be found. . . . . Free governments should be allowed to follow their natural course. In refusing a place to the constitutional opposition, we give a wider scope to subversive passions. We become, without intending it, their accomplices, and with them we compromise the sovereign interest of human societies, — civilization." After recommending for adoption all the proposed Articles, with a few slight alterations, it went on, " We await with confidence the honest execution of these new resolutions, as well as that of all the measures announced in the explanation of reasons presented by the government. This decree of the Senate will have an inevitable influence on the destinies of the country; it is one of the acts that mark their date in the history of a nation. The initiative of laws, rights of amendment, interpellation, order of the day with reasons assigned, the responsibility of ministers, the publicity of your debates, the intervention of the law and of decrees of the Senate in decisions of high interest, — all this both accords and insures considerable changes. Measures of this kind ought to disarm the sincere or simulated distrust of those who represented the direction of the affairs of the country as insufficiently controlled. In presence of such a situation, of a real freedom in speech and in the press, if violence increases instead of subsiding, good citizens will doubtless comprehend that, as there is an hour when they will come forward to aid the public force against riots in the streets, so there is one when they are bound to rise up and combine against the disturbance of the state. Whatever may happen, the legislation of 1852 in all its restrictive points disappears. We ought, however, in justice, to take an inventory of what it has produced for the country. After sixteen years of public peace, it leaves the territory of France enlarged, her income increased by twenty thousand millions, the general commerce tripled; gratuitous primary instruction more than doubled; professional education established; nearly six thousand mutual aid societies founded; *caisses* for the aged, insurances, co-operative societies created; telegraphs; railways; all the elements of prosperity; all the establishments of public assistance augmented in considerable proportions; the most absolute freedom of conscience; religious edifices multiplied; our cities purified; our navy transformed; the maintenance of peace and respect for France supported by one million four hundred thousand soldiers ready to show themselves at the frontier; lastly, the country conducted from a dictatorial government to the most extended constitutional liberty. The generation of 1852 can say to that of 1869, 'This is what I have done. You can do still better if you consolidate the work which I undertook.' If the people whom it is sought to intoxicate with a new sovereignty understand that demagogues are only courtiers whose interested flatteries deceive nations as they once deluded kings, that true friends speak in severe language, then power, whether popular or the reverse, is bound to listen to them, under pain of vacillating and tottering to its fall. The true character of a great and free people is to be on its guard against chimerical promises and dreams of impossible equalities. Confidence in himself, respect for the law, patience in expectation, and calmness in his right, — such are the true qualities of the citizen; such are the features that constitute his own personal dignity and the greatness of his country. If, by virtue of your efforts in sixteen years, France has established herself in that sage and fecund liberty to which the Elect of the nation has conducted her through so many perils; if you shall still hold this torch of political life which we now present, as we held it, propagating light, but never conflagration, then the survivors of that epoch will applaud you and will be happy to say to you, with patriotic emotion and joy, 'You have done better than we.'"

The reading of the report was subsequently followed by a debate which was remarkable for a speech by Prince Napoleon, — the emperor's cousin, — in which he gave expression to political views of a very liberal and advanced nature; but on this occasion the utterance of his sentiments did not seem to give the same offence to the emperor as the democratic speech did which he had delivered at Ajaccio, in May, 1865. Then he was rebuked by a letter of the emperor published in the *Moniteur*, — at that time still the official paper; now he was not rebuked, and from the fact of an interview between him and the emperor the day after he had spoken in the Senate, the inference was drawn that the head of the family was not even offended at his cousin's freedom of speech.

Well might the report say that this Decree would "have an inevitable influence on the destinies of the country," and well might Prince Napoleon ask for more. The emperor had done too much or too little. The radicals, in their unceasing efforts to harass the government and bring it into trouble, had kept constantly "representing the new birth of Germany as the humiliation of France," and done what they could to foster a smouldering hatred for Germany. "The concessions," says Karl Hillebrand, "made by the emperor could only serve the opponents of the Empire, who were henceforth enabled to arouse the general discontent with all the more boldness and violence, and always turned to account the blunders or bad faith of the ministers who were entrusted with the execution of such concessions. Above all, the cry that France had been humiliated by the battle of Sadowa, was employed with obstinate and systematic malice against the man who had allowed Sadowa to be fought. . . . . The contest about the temporal power of the Pope estranged one half of the nation without satisfying the other. The sufferings which the treaty of commerce [with England] had brought on the Northern Departments were another cause of discontent." The emperor had done too much for his own safety. "The train had been laid . . . . meant to destroy the Empire; now it lay there useless, but unhappily not harmless. A single spark . . . . would be sufficient to fire it. The 'responsible' emperor of 1859 might have hindered the train from being laid, or, if it had been laid, might possibly have prevented it from being fired; but the 'irresponsible' emperor of 1870 was powerless. The train did only too well the fearful work for which it had been prepared; but in the fall of the imperial edifice the ground on which it was built was rent asunder and rendered insecure for many years to come. Such another building, if need be, or one resembling it, can be raised again, but what can give back to the cleft and shattered ground the solidity which it had before the catastrophe?" Had the emperor gone farther, and admitted the peace-loving and steady bourgeois to the full amount of power to which they were entitled, they might have given his government strength enough to resist the fanatical outburst of hatred for Germany that led to the war of the coming year. But it was fated to be otherwise, and "the 'irresponsible' monarch, who did not atone for a great fault by an honorable death on the battle-field, ended his days in inglorious exile, as Charles X. and Louis Philippe before him; while his 'responsible' ministers, like those of his predecessor, go where they list in their native land without a blush on their face."

CHAPTER XXII.

POSTPONEMENT OF MEETING OF CHAMBERS. — INTENTIONS OF THE
LEFT. — OPENING OF THE CHAMBERS. — M. ROCHEFORT. — RESIG-
NATION OF MINISTRY. — LETTER OF THE EMPEROR TO M. OLLIVIER.
— NEW MINISTRY. — ASSASSINATION OF VICTOR NOIR. — IMPRIS-
ONMENT OF M. ROCHEFORT. — DISTURBANCES. — PROTECTION AND
FREE TRADE. — DECREE OF THE SENATE CONFIRMING THE CON-
STITUTIONAL CHANGES. — PROPOSED PLÉBISCITE. — MANIFESTO OF
THE EMPEROR. — PLOT AGAINST THE EMPEROR'S LIFE. — RESULT OF
THE PLEBISCITE. — MINISTERIAL CHANGES. — STATE OF NATIONAL
FEELING. — DECEPTIVE REPORTS OF AMBASSADORS. — CONDITION OF
ARMY. — PACIFIC ASSURANCES OF MINISTERS. — FRESH DISTURB-
ANCES. — THE GATHERING OF THE STORM. — AFFAIRS OF SPAIN. —
FRENCH OBJECTION TO PRINCE LEOPOLD OF HOHENZOLLERN. —
FRENCH FEELING AND IMPERIAL NECESSITY. — DIPLOMATIC NEGO-
TIATIONS. — DECLARATION OF WAR. — A GIGANTIC BLUNDER. —
OFFERS OF MEDIATION. — SECRET TREATY ABOUT BELGIUM. — IN-
TENTIONS OF THE EMPEROR. — CONDITION OF THE ARMY. — DISPOSI-
TIONS OF THE GERMANS. — THE BAPTISM OF FIRE. — WEISSENBURG.
— WÖRTH. — SPICHEREN AND FORBACH. — FALL OF THE OLLIVIER
MINISTRY. — MOVEMENTS OF THE EMPEROR AND BAZAINE. — BORNY.
— GRAVELOTTE. — REZONVILLE. — MACMAHON'S MOVEMENTS AND
PLANS. — HIS FAILURE. — SEDAN. — KING WILLIAM'S DESPATCH. —
PROCEEDINGS IN PARIS. — FALL OF THE SECOND EMPIRE. — CHAR-
ACTER OF NAPOLEON III.

THE new session of the Legislature ought to have begun at latest on the 26th October, 1869, but on the 3d of that month a
decree was issued in the official journal, postponing the meeting of

the Chamber till the 29th November. This action on the part of the government at once called forth a violent outburst of indignation from the members of the opposition, and some of the more headstrong of the extreme section of the party openly proclaimed their determination to meet on the 26th October. M. Raspail, in a published letter addressed to the ministry, suggested that the delay was a mere capricious effort to " conserve the idea of personal power," which had under the new *régime* ceased to exist. The leading members, however, of the Left Centre, including MM. Jules Favre, Gambetta, Picard, and Jules Simon, published a document, announcing that they would not meet on the 26th, but that they had "resolved" instead to wait for the actual opening of the session, when they would call " the executive to account for this new insult to the nation." Extensive preparations were made against the chance of any disorder, but the day passed off quietly, public attention having been diverted by the condition of the emperor, who was suffering from an illness so severe that he was for a time unable to transact public business. The illness gave rise to wild rumors of his intention to abdicate, which ceased only on his restoration to health.

In the middle of November a fresh declaration was issued by the members of the Left, in which they intimated their intention of endeavoring to obtain increased liberty of electoral action, extensive alterations of the military law, complete liberty of the press, and power of holding public meetings. Just before the meeting of the Chambers there was a new election for Paris, and the temper of the extreme section of the Republican party was shown by the return among the deputies of M. Henri Rochefort, to whom the emperor had granted a safe conduct during the time of the elections. The emperor had now quite recovered, and was again able to appear in public, and when the Legislature at last met on the appointed day, he opened it in person. In the course of his speech, after referring to the difficulty of securing a peaceful " exercise of liberty," as shown in the recently excited state of public feeling, he made some complimentary allusions to the desire of the Chambers to aid him in the new path he had determined to try. "France desires liberty," he said, "but liberty united with order. For order I will answer. Aid me, gentlemen, to save liberty; and to attain this object let us keep at an equal distance from reaction and revolutionary theories." He then went on to draw attention to the liberal nature of all the measures to be submitted by the ministry: municipal and electoral reform, the development of gratuitous primary instruction, the alteration of succession duties, savings banks, the regulation of infant labor in factories, the consideration of the condition of agriculture, and probable changes in the customs tariff, — all this formed a programme certainly of immense range, and one which, if it had been carried out, would have brought greatly increased prosperity to the country. In reviewing the condition of foreign affairs, he found them everywhere satisfactory. "Sovereigns and nations desire peace, and they are engaged in advancing civilization." He alluded to the Pacific Railroad, the Mont Cenis Tunnel, and the Suez Canal, as signs of progress, and, after referring to the work of the Chambers, concluded as follows: "The more direct participation of the country in its own affairs will constitute for the Empire a fresh source of strength, and the representative assemblies will have henceforth a larger share of responsibility. Let them use it for the promotion of the greatness and prosperity of the nation. May the various shades of opinion disappear when required by the general interest, and may the Chambers prove equally by their enlightenment and their patriotism that France, without again falling into deplorable excesses, is capable of supporting those free institutions which are the honor of civilized countries!"

The first business of the session was the verification of the elections, — a process which had been interrupted by the presentation of the plans for the new constitution, — and some of the debates on this, as well as other matters brought before the Assembly, were, as was to be expected, of a very lively nature. The Republicans were at no pains to conceal their contempt for the emperor, and their desire to overthrow his government. M. Rochefort, in one of his speeches, alluded to Napoleon III. as "the gentleman who walked on the sands of Boulogne, with an eagle on his shoulder and a bit of bacon in his hat," and in another he said, "You have but one fear, — strong government though you pretend to be, — and that fear is the republic. Well, I will tell you, — I am happy to tell you here, — that you are right to fear the republic, for, I am quite convinced, it is near at hand, and it is the republic that will avenge us all." As election after election was discussed, flagrant instances of government interference and manipulation came to light, and the offence thus caused was so great that the ministers were compelled to resign. The Emperor, having accepted their resignation "not without regret," wrote a letter on the 27th December to M. Emile Ollivier, formerly a bitter opponent of the Empire, but a supporter of the liberal measures that had been lately introduced, desiring him to "form a homogeneous cabinet, faithfully representing the majority of the Legislative Body, and resolved to carry out in letter as well as in spirit the decree of the Senate of the 8th September."

By the beginning of 1870, M. Ollivier had succeeded in performing his task, and had organized a ministry representing the opinions of the majority of the Legislative Body, and chosen in the main from the Right Centre or moderate imperialist party, though to some extent also from the Left Centre or moderate liberal ranks, to which M. Ollivier himself belonged. Though the new ministry was fairly conservative in tone, its constitution was yet sufficiently liberal to encourage hopes that the long looked-for era of liberty without license was about to dawn, and the prospects of this at the opening of the Legislature on the 3d January, 1870, were good. The only imperial servant whom the new powers treated with marked disfavor was M. Haussman, the rebuilder and adorner of Paris, the prefect of the Seine ; and he was accordingly dismissed and replaced by M. Chevreau, formerly prefect of the Rhone. This act was strongly objected to by the emperor, but so resolved was he to be guided entirely according to constitutional method, that, when he found the ministers firm, he immediately gave way. Immediately after this constitutional government assumed the direction of affairs, and on the very day of the meeting of the Legislature, the newly repaired vessel of the state was almost shattered by a disturbance brought about through the violent and uncontrollable temper of an obscure and almost disowned member of the Bonaparte family. Prince Pierre Bonaparte, a cousin of the emperor, was a man who had led a very wild and headstrong life, which, as he was an extreme and thorough-going Republican, he had crowned by his marriage with the daughter of a workman of the Faubourg St. Antoine. He was, as may be supposed, by no means a favorite at the Tuileries, and had been pensioned off. A contribution of his to a Corsican paper — the *Avenir de Corse* — on some questions connected with the memory of the first Napoleon, called forth replies from the *Revanche* and from the *Marseillaise*, — a journal edited by Rochefort, — the result of which was that the prince sent a challenge to Rochefort, while at the same time M. Grousset, the Paris correspondent of the *Revanche*, sent two of his friends with a challenge to Prince Pierre. These friends, two journalists, M. de Fonvielle and Victor Noir, were received by the prince in a very violent manner, and a quarrel would seem to have arisen, in which Pierre shot Victor Noir dead. He was at once arrested and conveyed to the Conciergerie, and a decree was issued by the emperor convening the High Court of Justice for his trial. So far, everything that could be done had been done promptly, and the emperor was in no wise responsible for the hot-headed turbulence and violence of his cousin; but the Republicans at once seized the occasion to assail and abuse the emperor and the Bonaparte family. M. Rochefort again rendered himself conspicuous by the outrageous indecency of his attacks. He condemned himself for being " weak enough to imagine that a Bonaparte could be anything else but a murderer." France, he wrote, had been for eighteen years " in the blood-stained hands of these cut-throats, who, not satisfied with mowing down the Republicans with grape-shot in the streets, entice them into filthy snares to kill them within four stone walls." This charge was made in an article in the *Marseillaise*, and in his place in the Legislative Body he declared that " in presence of the crime just committed one knew not whether the country was governed by a Bonaparte or a Borgia." Disturbances

were not unnaturally anticipated at the funeral of Victor Noir, and
extensive preparations were accordingly made for the prompt and
vigorous suppression of any outbreak; but though an immense
crowd of over a hundred thousand persons assembled, they dispersed
quietly enough, on being stopped by a commissary of police, supported by troops, while accompanying M. Rochefort along the
Champs Elysées.

In consequence of the violent articles which still continued to
appear in the *Marseillaise*, the prosecution of M. Rochefort was resolved on; but, as he was a deputy, the consent of the Legislative
Body had to be obtained before this course could be proceeded with.
After debate, the motion for his prosecution was carried by two hundred and twenty-six to thirty-four votes, with the result that he was
in the end condemned to pay a fine of three thousand francs, and
to be imprisoned for six months. He was not, however, deprived of
civil rights, and he did not, therefore, forfeit his seat. He would
no doubt have been much more severely dealt with had the Procureur-
Impérial not moved for the lightest possible sentence. As it was,
his arrest and imprisonment led to an outbreak. A large crowd,
headed by M. Flourens, one of the *Marseillaise* staff, after marching
through some of the streets, shouting " Vive Rochefort," " À bas les
Bonapartes," began to construct barricades, and forcibly to seize
arms, but they were dispersed and the barricades removed by a force
of Sergents de Ville and Guards. For two nights thereafter the
rioting was renewed, but the mobs were always quickly put down
by the authorities; and such a number of arrests was made that the
Conciergerie would hardly hold all the prisoners. The promptitude
of the government had successfully stamped out what might have
become a very formidable disturbance, and the only persons against
whom measures of any severity were employed in the subsequent
trials were the journalists. While a class, composed mainly of
workmen headed by professional agitators, was thus threatening
the public peace in Paris, all the great industrial centres showed
signs of being in a state of ferment and feverish unrest, although a
very large amount of this must be set down to the account of the

intriguing activity of the International Society.   At the large iron
and steel works at Creuzot, belonging to M. Schneider, President of
the Legislative Body, and where nearly ten thousand workmen were
employed, this feeling found expression in a strike, which assumed
such formidable proportions that it could only be suppressed by
calling into action a military force of three thousand men.   Even
after being in this way quenched, the embers of disaffection continued not unnaturally smouldering, and it burst again into flame
in fresh riots in the same place in the month of March.

Ever since 1860, the northern departments had suffered severely
on account of the commercial treaty with England, and had in consequence been in a state of chronic discontent ; and now, in the end
of January, the protectionists, headed by M. Thiers, mustered their
forces for an attack on the measure, as the time was at hand when
the question of its renewal or non-renewal on the old terms fell to
be decided.   The protectionists attacked the treaty on the ground
that it had been concluded on the individual responsibility of the
emperor, and that those most interested had had no voice in the
matter.   To all reasonable people the reply of the government —
that whatever might be the power of the Chambers under the new
constitution, it was, by a decree of the Senate in 1852, undoubtedly
the prerogative of the Emperor in 1860 to make all treaties of commerce as he pleased — was quite conclusive.   M. Thiers, however,
conducted the opposition on general grounds, and basing his argument entirely on Protection lines, pointed out that France was
unable to compete with England, since the latter country possessed
" an abundance of raw material, an immense market, more machinery, cheaper coal, and a greater superiority of production ;" the
chintz printers of Alsace printed on cheap goods brought from England, to such an extent that the commerce of Rouen was ruined,
spinning having decreased by one fourth, weaving by one third,
and engineer work by no less than three fourths ; the linen, wool,
and iron manufactures were suffering from the same causes, and so
was agriculture.   M. Jules Simon advocated free trade, attributed
the suffering state of the different industries to other causes than

commercial treaties, and advanced the proposition that "commercial liberty" was "an indisputable condition of peace; for," said he, "so long as we continue to have an army of revenue officers on the frontier, the fraternity of nations will be impossible. But when peoples shall only be rival traders instead of enemies I defy you to make them fight. By freedom of labor and commerce will be founded the future of liberty, and all war will be at an end." M. de la Roquette took the same view of the causes of depression, and quoted statistics which were contradictory to those of M. Thiers, and the approval of the treaty was secured by the large majority of two hundred and eleven to thirty-two votes.

The trial of Prince Pierre Bonaparte began at Tours on the 21st of March, and the progress of it was watched with intense interest all over the country. The proceedings lasted for six days, and resulted in the acquittal of the prisoner, the jury having brought in a verdict of "not guilty." The disappointment of the liberal party, and especially of the "Irreconcilable" section, was very keen, and was loudly expressed, although, considering the disgraceful nature of the squabble and the character of all the personages concerned, it cannot be said to have been greatly to the credit of the liberals that they took so much of a party concern in its issue.

While the liberal-conservative government was feeling its way forward in a timid and uncertain manner, the emperor was busy elaborating new and startling plans of his own. On the 21st March he addressed a letter to M. Ollivier, in which he stated that he thought it "oppportune under the present circumstances to adopt all the reforms claimed by the constitutional government of the Empire, in order to put an end to the immoderate desire for change which had seized on certain minds, and which disquieted public opinion and created instability." After alluding to the different reforms, he concluded: "I therefore beg you to come to an understanding with your colleagues for the purpose of laying before me the draught of a decree of the Senate to fix invariably the fundamental disposition contained in the *plébiscite* of 1852, to divide the legislative power between the two Chambers, and to restore to the nation that part of the constituent faculty which it had delegated to other hands." This would seem to be a reassertion of the old personal government in a new shape, as was still more obvious in the proposal that followed almost immediately after, the idea of which undoubtedly proceeded from the emperor. This proposal, which was to refer the new constitution to the *plébiscite* of the whole nation, involved neither more nor less than the old theory of the direct responsibility of the emperor to the people. By this move Napoleon once more assumed the conduct of affairs, while his prime minister, whose duty it was to guide the state, looked idly on ; and there is hardly any reason to doubt that the emperor had recourse to an appeal to the people, because he saw the wavering attitude of the government, and dreaded the introduction of changes at the beck of the opposition, which would have been of an unsettling, if not a revolutionary, character. That the popular will would decide as he wished it, his long experience of official manipulation rendered morally certain.

The decree of the Senate was passed, but with an important modification, inspired possibly by Napoleon himself, providing that the emperor was to have power to refer any political question he thought fit to the will of the people by taking a *plébiscite*. There followed immediately thereafter a discussion in the Legislative Body. The debate was long and excited, M. Grévy maintaining on behalf of the opposition that the concessions granted by the decree were verbal rather than real, and that the proposed *plébiscite* was merely a fresh device to confiscate the national sovereignty. In the end an order of the day was adopted by two hundred and twenty-seven votes to forty-three, declaring that "The Legislative Body having heard the declarations of the ministry, and confiding in its devotedness to the imperial and parliamentary government, passes to the order of the day." The first *plébiscite* was to be taken on the question of approval or disapproval of the new constitution. The voting was finally fixed to take place on the 8th of May, and both sides prepared diligently for a full muster of their forces. A small number of deputies and adherents of the left, styling themselves delegates of the people, drew up and issued a manifesto, declaring that the reforms had not gone far enough to satisfy the popular desires, and that the appeal of the ruler to a *plébiscite* was an effort to preserve to himself personal government, and involved the continual threat of a new *coup d'état.* The emperor himself issued a proclamation, setting forth that it was "indispensable that the new constitutional fact should be approved by the people, as were formerly the constitutions of the republic and of the empire." He urged that their approval must always be necessary, and reminded them how for twenty-three years they had constantly supported him by their "co-operation," and rewarded him by their "affection." "Give me," he continued, "another proof of your confidence. By balloting affirmatively you will conjure down the threats of revolution; you will seat order and liberty on a solid basis; and you will render easier for the future the transmission of the crown to my son. Eighteen years ago you were almost unanimous in conferring the most extensive powers on me. Be now, too, as numerous in giving your adhesion to the transformation of the imperial *régime.* . . . . To the request which I address to you to ratify the liberal reforms that have been realized during the last ten years, answer 'Yes.' As to myself, faithful to my origin, I shall imbue myself with your thoughts, fortify myself in your will, and, trusting to Providence, I shall not cease to labor without intermission for the prosperity and greatness of France."

The publication of this letter was almost immediately followed by rumors of the discovery of a plot for the assassination of the emperor. A man of the name of Beaury was arrested by the police, and found to be in possession of compromising documents which connected him with certain schemes of Flourens, who had taken such a leading part in the riots of January. Beaury at once admitted that it had been his intention to shoot the emperor. The police made diligent search for the accomplices, who, however, succeeded in making good their escape, but left behind them traces of their vile purpose in the shape of explosive bombs. The trial of the conspirators was delayed first till July and then till August, at which time it was almost lost sight of in the great events that followed.

The great *plébiscite* was taken on Sunday the 8th May and resulted, in round numbers, in seven million three hundred thousand votes being recorded for the Empire, and only one million five hundred thousand against it. The great imperialist majority came from the peasantry, whereas almost all the large towns — Paris, Lyons, Nantes, Marseilles, Bordeaux, Brest, Cherbourg, Toulon, Angers — voted by considerable majorities the other way, though that in Paris was by no means so large as was expected. Curiously enough all the manufacturing towns of the north, which had suffered so much from the commercial treaty, voted in favor of the Empire; even Rouen, which M. Thiers had so lately described as totally ruined by the imperial free-trade policy, declared for imperialism, though it was only by one vote. The most noteworthy and alarming fact was that the army, always the stronghold of imperialism, had recorded over fifty thousand votes against the Empire; but the majority of these votes were undoubtedly those of men forced into the army under the new Army Bill, and who were dissatisfied with the position into which they had been coerced by it. Preparations had been made on an extensive scale for the immediate suppression of any disturbances that might take place during the voting, and Paris, in particular, had very large bodies of troops drafted into it; but everything passed off quietly, and some small riots that took place in Paris on the two following days were quelled with very little difficulty.

The result of the vote was publicly announced at the Louvre on the 21st May. The pageant attending the ceremony was most imposing, and the emperor's appearance was hailed with loud and prolonged acclamation. The President of the Legislative Body spoke on their behalf, and concluded his speech with the words, " France places the cause of liberty under the protection of your dynasty and of the great bodies of the State." The emperor thanked the nation for this fresh mark of their confidence, and referred to the new possibilities thus afforded for the development and prosperity of the national resources. Changes in the *personnel* of the ministry at once followed, one of which at least caused uneasiness as regarded foreign relations. Count Daru, the Minister of Foreign Affairs, M. Buffet, the Minister of Finance, and M. de Talhouet, the Minister of Public Works, had resigned on the first introduction of the *plébiscite* proposal, and their places were now filled by the Duc de Gramont, M. Mege, and M. Plichon. The retirement of Daru and Buffet considerably weakened the ministry, and the appointment of Gramont, who was noted for his violent hostility to Prussia, led to most disastrous results.

The reopening of the Chambers revealed the fact that at last all parties were tired of the indecision and hesitation of the ministry, due, no doubt, to the inconsistency of its head, M. Ollivier. The Right and Left Centres, any combination of which is always too strong for the other parties, seemed to be merely waiting for their opportunity. The Right Centre, indeed, was almost openly hostile to the ministers, while the Left, broken up into two parties, headed respectively by M. Buffet and M. Ernest Picard, accorded them but a lukewarm support. On the 3d of June the Cabinet was twice defeated. On the following day the ministry demanded what was practically a vote of confidence, and the Right unblushingly told them that they were merely waiting for an opportunity to overthrow their power. The vote of confidence was obtained, but from semi-inspired articles that followed, it was evident that the Cabinet enjoyed the confidence neither of the nation nor of the emperor.

Symptoms of the old enmity towards Prussia began at this time to reappear in a discussion in the Chamber in reference to a convention concluded between Prussia, Italy, and Switzerland, with regard to the St. Gothard railway, but the government utterances were eminently reassuring and fully in accord with the expression of pacific intentions that had been given to Baron Werther, the Prussian ambassador, by Gramont on his accession to office. Still the shadow of coming strife seemed to be constantly enlarging. All classes had keenly felt, and bitterly resented, the humiliating position of France after Sadowa, and all were inspired with a common

animus against Prussia. The foreign minister was a rash man, and
of strongly anti-Prussian sympathies; and far too ready, therefore,
to listen to the reports of the ill-trained and credulous diplomatists
who in the smaller German states accepted the views of the small
section they mingled with as the views of the people at large, and
who never troubled themselves to ascertain the general feeling.
Throughout the minor German states "on the authority of princes,
of prelates, of noblemen, and generally of the society in which
French was commonly spoken, ambassadors and envoys reported to
their government that universal dislike of Prussia was combined
with a disposition to rely on the protection of France. With German literature and journalism, and with the opinions of the great
mass of the community, the representatives of France were utterly
unacquainted, nor could they understand the impotence of provincial jealousies and fashionable antipathies to resist" such an outburst of national enthusiasm as came, when at last Germany was
fairly threatened with invasion. In addition to this, though the
fourth appeal to the people had recorded a large majority in favor
of Napoleon, the votes against him had, since his confirmation in
power in 1852, increased nearly threefold, and the army was evidently so strongly discontented and disaffected, that it might, in
order to restore this chief support of the Napoleonic throne to its
original efficiency, become, at any moment, necessary for the safety
of the dynasty, to set out anew on the path of "glory." M. Thiers
saw the danger of war clearly enough when, in the discussion on the
Army Bill on the 1st and 2d of July, he said, "Prussia requires to
be pacific, in order to attract the south of Germany. We need to be
pacific, in order not to give it her." An attack on German unity
from without was all that Bismarck waited for in order to consolidate
it within, and to give stability to that military system which pressed
so hardly on the people, that it not only gave rise to a strong antipathy to a Prussian alliance in the south, but even sorely taxed the
quiet patience of the north.

The law passed in 1848, prohibiting the princes of the house of
Orleans from entering France, still remained in force, and a petition

which was now presented to the Chamber by the Count de Paris, the Prince de Joinville, the Duke d'Aumale, and the Duke de Chartres, praying for its repeal, and for restoration to "the country they loved," led to a keen debate, and to a farther split in the Left, as two of the leading men of that side took different sides, M. Jules Favre warmly supporting the prayer of the petition, and M. Grévy as warmly opposing it. The result was that the petition was refused by a considerable majority. In the debate on the Army Bill, which was brought forward in the beginning of July, the system established in 1868 was vehemently denounced, on the ground that it was most costly to the nation and oppressive to the people. In the course of the debate the ministers took occasion to repeat their pacific assurances with regard to foreign affairs. M. Ollivier, in particular, was emphatically explicit, when he said that "the government has no uneasiness whatever. At no epoch has the peace of Europe been more assured. Irritating questions nowhere exist. The European cabinets understand that treaties should be maintained. We have developed liberty to assure peace." Yet, notwithstanding this protestation, it is hardly possible to doubt that the resolution to enter upon a quarrel with Prussia at the earliest possible moment had been already taken. Everywhere there was uneasiness. The Budget was unsatisfactory; the summer was so hot and dry that vegetation was almost burned up; Paris was in a very unhealthy condition, the spread of infectious disease being aided probably by the intense heat; the emperor was in bad health; the trial of some members of the International Society, which had attracted attention in connection with the Creuzot riots, was hardly over when another formidable strike took place at Mulhouse, and required the intervention of a large body of soldiers to effect its suppression.

We have seen, then, that on the 2d of July M. Ollivier had declared in the Chamber that "irritating questions nowhere exist," and almost at the same time earnest assurances had been given to the English government to the same effect. Never, said the official representative, had there been in his experience such a lull in foreign affairs. But it was only the calm before the storm, the glimpse of bright sunshine at the edge of the cloud, for only two days later all was changed. On the 4th of July French suscepti- bilities found themselves outraged, and French "public opinion," which one acute observer has defined to be Parisian frivolity, was at a white heat of indignation. We shall now see how this came about.

Spain, tired of an effete and priest-managed government, had, in the end of 1868, risen in rebellion, overthrown the power of Isabella II. and deposed her, and since that time the Spanish throne had been vacant. The nation, adhering to the monarchical form of gov- ernment, was in search of a king, and after a series of quarrels among the leaders of the revolt, who could not make up their minds on whom they were to bestow the power they had obtained, the Provisional Government had at last fixed on the young Duke of Genoa as their future king. The King of Italy, however, refused to allow his nephew to accept, and the beginning of 1870 found Spain still without a settled government. Early in June Marshal Prim announced that at last a suitable candidate for the throne had been found, and it was well known in diplomatic circles, and must have been known to the French government, that this candidate was Prince Leopold of Hohenzollern, brother of the Prince of Rou- mania. They nevertheless offered no objection to the proposal, and showed in no way whatever that the proposal was considered by them objectionable or likely to be distasteful to France. Nor was there any reason why it should be so. True, Leopold was a Prus- sian subject, and a scion of the house of Hohenzollern, but he was of the princely and not the sovereign branch, and was a much nearer kinsman of the emperor himself than of the King of Prussia. His connection with the Prussian royal family amounted to little more than that they had had a common ancestor nearly seven hundred years before, while he was allied to France by his Catholicism and by his descent, on his father's side from the family of Murat, and on his mother's from the family of Beauharnais, to which Napoleon's mother also belonged. When, however, Prince Leopold's

candidature was openly announced in the beginning of July all
these considerations were set aside, and attention wholly concentrated on the fact that the King of Prussia was the head of the
princely house to which Leopold belonged. War on some account
had become a necessity, war with Prussia would be popular, and, if
successful, would seat the Napoleonic dynasty firmly on the throne.
Accordingly it was urged by way of pretext for war, if Prussia
would not give way, that the Hohenzollerns, not content with
threatening France from the north, had determined to place a Prussian on the throne of Spain, so as to be able to threaten her also
from the south. No pretext could have been more frivolous, for it
is perfectly certain that, had France shown any opposition to Leopold on his being first proposed in June, Prim would have abandoned the idea, as he had already yielded to the French emperor's
wishes in the matter of candidates several times before. From the
way in which the French acted all along, it was evident that they
thought themselves ready for the strife, and were determined at all
hazards to force a quarrel on Prussia. The wishes of all the
seven millions of voters who had supported the Empire in the interests of peace were to be sacrificed to win back the affections of
fifty thousand discontented soldiers.

On the 4th of July the *chargé d'affaires* at Berlin called at the
foreign office there to complain of the candidature in question, but
only received for answer the reply that that was a matter with
which the Prussian government had nothing whatever to do. On
the 5th, Baron Werther, the ambassador at Paris, left for Ems,
where the Prussian king then was, that he might have an opportunity of describing fully to him the state of feeling in France.
M. Benedetti, the French ambassador to Germany, also personally
applied to the king for a pledge that Prince Leopold should not be
allowed to go forward with his candidature, but King William replied that it was a matter with which, beyond his sanction as head
of the house of Hohenzollern, he had nothing to do, and in which
he therefore could not interfere. On the 6th of May the Duke de
Gramont was able publicly and officially to gratify his anti-Prussian

proclivities in a speech in the Legislative Body, in which, in a most inflammatory and warlike manner, he declared that France must not look quietly on while another nation destroyed the balance of power by placing one of its princes on the throne of Charles V. He hoped that such a proceeding might still be averted, but should it not, their government would know "how to do its duty without hesitation and without weakness." MM. Jules Favre, Garnier Pagès, Crémieux, and some others of the opposition, alone dared to raise their voices in dissent from such warlike views, but even their sincerity was doubted. It was said that they had been so long accustomed to oppose every act and proposition of the government, that now, however eager they might be to approve, they were unable to overcome the force of habit. The intervention of England even afforded at this supreme moment an opportunity for repentance. Being earnestly pressed by the English government, the King of Prussia gave way in the interests of peace, so far at least as to recommend Prince Leopold to decline the Spanish proposal, and the recommendation was at once respected. M. Ollivier, indeed, told the Legislative Body that the crisis was over, and the emperor himself made the same statement to two of the ambassadors in Paris. But the emperor was not master of the situation. He hesitated, and, had he been the man of 1852, or even of 1860, he would probably have drawn back; but his power was gone. It was urged upon him that the struggle must come some time, and that now, before Germany was further consolidated, was the fitting opportunity. The authorities of the war department declared that everything was ready, both men and material; they were certain that the French chassepot was a superior weapon to the Prussian needle-gun; the Prussians were not prepared; the campaign could not last six weeks. Napoleon yielded to the outcry of the Paris rabble, and though Prussia had given way, and Prince Leopold's candidature was at an end, it was easy enough to offer further provocation in order to bring about a *casus belli*. A fresh demand was therefore made, that the King of Prussia should disavow connection with the candidature of Prince Leopold, not only as the head of the Hohenzollern family, but in his capacity as sovereign, and that he should undertake that the prince's candidature would at no future time be renewed. M. Benedetti at Ems chose the most unfavorable opportunity he could find for presenting these demands, by literally stopping the king while taking exercise in the afternoon in the public gardens. The abrupt demand was answered by an equally abrupt refusal, and orders were given that M. Benedetti should not again be allowed access to his Majesty.

On the 15th of July an explanation was given by M. Ollivier in the Legislative Body, and by Gramont in the Senate. This manifesto, after referring to the expression of feeling in the Chambers on the 6th July as an assurance that the ministry had the support of the Houses, proceeded to detail the course of the negotiations. It dwelt on the moderate nature of the final demand, and the moderate language in which it was couched, as showing that France "had no *arrière pensée*," and was not "seeking a pretext in the Hohenzollern affair." Notwithstanding that the king had refused to give the engagement demanded, such was their desire for peace, that they had not broken off negotiations, and their surprise was therefore great when they learned, the day before, that the king had "sent an aide-de-camp to our ambassador (M. Benedetti), to inform him that he would no longer receive him, and in order to invest this refusal with a·non-ambiguous character his government communicated this officially to the Cabinets of Europe. We learned," it went on, "that at the same time Baron Werther had received orders to take leave of absence, and that Prussia was arming. Under these circumstances we should have forgotten our dignity, and also our prudence, had we attempted more for the sake of conciliation. We have neglected nothing to avoid the war; we shall prepare ourselves to carry on the one offered to us, leaving to each that portion of the responsibility which devolves upon him. Since yesterday we have called out the reserve, and we shall take the necessary measures to guard the interest, and the security, and the honor of France." M. Ollivier added, in words now become historical, that he accepted the challenge of Prussia "with a light heart." In both houses the explanation was received with enthusiasm, and the credit of fifty millions demanded by the Minister of War was at once granted, with but a faint protest from some few members of the Left. On the following Sunday crowds marched about the streets of Paris singing the Marseillaise, and shouting "Vive la guerre!" "À bas la Prusse!" "À Berlin." But it was not to be "à Berlin;" in this case Mohammed was not to go to the mountain, but the mountain was to come to Mohammed, and fall upon him and crush him. As a last effort at reconciliation, Lord Granville urged that both sides should refer the matter to mediation in accordance with the declaration of 1856, but his suggestion was rejected, France replying that the Protocol of Paris was unsuitable to the case, and Prussia maintaining that, as France had taken the initiative in the war she must also take it in accepting mediation. Up to the last moment too, Austria, through Count Beust, did her utmost to dissuade Napoleon from his enterprise. "There is nothing I fear more than a retreat from Prussia," had been the answer. "Look at the enthusiasm for the war all over France; I shall never find it again;" and so, misled by "the statements of an incompetent minister of war," that his army was ready, and by those of "a frivolous minister of foreign affairs," who utterly misinterpreted the feelings of Hanover, Bavaria, and Würtemberg, and counted on Austria as eager to avenge the defeat of Sadowa, Napoleon III. rushed to his fate.

After the formal declaration of war, which took place on the 19th of July, another offer of mediation was made on the 22d by the Pope, fresh in all the new glories of Infallibility. To this ambiguous answers were returned, intimating in most skilful terms of courteous refusal, that his mediation could not be accepted. "God is my witness," said King William, "that neither I nor my people have wished or called for war. We draw the sword in obedience to the sacred duties which God has laid upon sovereigns and nations, to defend the independence and honor of our Fatherland, and we shall be ever ready to lay it down when these blessings have been secured to us. If your Holiness could give me, on behalf of him who has so unexpectedly declared war, the assurance of sincerely peaceful intentions, and securities against the recurrence of a similar attack upon the peace and repose of Europe, I would assuredly not refuse to receive it from the venerable hands of your Holiness."

Disappointment after disappointment met France at the very outset. The remembrance of 1866, on which she had relied so confidently, seemed gone. Austria was firmly neutral, and Hanover, Bavaria, Baden, and Würtemberg, on whose disaffection so much reliance had been placed, at once threw in their lot with Prussia, and were even more eager for the fray than the Prussians themselves. Sudden as the French action had been, Germany at once showed how well she had been prepared. Large supplies were voted by all the states, and the mobilization of the army was immediately begun. On the fast day appointed for prayer for the success of the German arms, the king made a proclamation to the effect that his conscience acquitted him of having provoked this war, and that he was certain of the righteousness of his cause before God. "The struggle before us is serious," he said, "and it will demand heavy sacrifices from my people, and all Germany. But I go forth to it looking to the Omniscient God, and imploring his Almighty support." But at the same time he "kept his powder dry." With remarkable celerity the troops were massed and sent forward, e by the 31st nearly half a million of men were on the frontier.

Not much sympathy was expressed for France anywhere, and inclination to sympathize was entirely removed by the publication by Bismarck of a draft treaty proposed by Napoleon after the war of 1866. It will be remembered that then Count Bismarck had refused to give what he had promised before the commencement of the Austrian war, and, that being so, the French Emperor had tried to get Bismarck's consent to his indemnifying himself by taking possession of Belgium, while he, on his part, was to consent to recognize the union of North and South Germany. The proposal had been put in writing, and Bismarck, while rejecting the plan as giving to Germany nothing but what she had already, while it enriched France, had carefully preserved the paper, no doubt with an eye to future emergencies. The document was indignantly

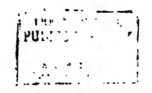

denounced by the French ministers as a forgery, but it was proved that it was throughout in the handwriting of M. Benedetti, the former French ambassador. No doubt Count Bismarck hoped when he sent this secret deed to the *Times* for publication to win by means of it for Germany the moral, if not the active, support of both Belgium and Britain; but if so it failed in its effect, though it caused in both countries a feeling of very painful surprise, a surprise not lessened by the subsequently ascertained fact that the proposal had been again pushed forward by France just on the very eve of the war.

Meanwhile, in France a proclamation to the nation had been issued on the 24th. There were, it said, "solemn moments in the life of peoples when the national honor, violently excited, imposes itself with irresistible force, dominates all interests, and alone takes in hand the destinies of the country. Launched on the path of invasion, Prussia has aroused defiance everywhere, necessitating exaggerated armaments, and turning Europe into a camp where only uncertainty and fear of the morrow reigns. . . . . It only remains to us to confide our destinies to the decision of arms. . . . . We wish to conquer a lasting peace." Preparations had, however, been going on slowly and badly. That splendid army which Marshal Lebœuf had boasted of as in a perfect state of readiness was found to exist mainly on paper. Instead of everything being "ready, ay, more than ready," as he had told Gramont, there was almost no department that was not in confusion. The emperor's plan was to assemble one hundred and fifty thousand men at Metz, one hundred thousand at Strasburg, and fifty thousand at the great camp at Châlons, then to unite the first two armies, and, leaving the third to guard the rear and maintain the communications, to cross the Rhine and march on Berlin, or invade Bavaria and so cut off communication between North and South Germany, it being presumed that the latter, along with Austria, would join the invaders in opposition to the supremacy of Prussia. Had the provisions of the bill of 1868 been carried out, it ought to have been possible to place four hundred thousand troops on the frontier in a fortnight; but the men of the reserves came in slowly, and many of them were found to be totally ignorant of the use of the new breechloader. The commissariat, too, broke down, and there was lack of supplies of every kind. Great hopes were placed on the mitrailleuse, a terrible sort of revolver cannon, which was to scatter its balls among the enemy at the rate of four hundred a minute; but now it was found that the officers and men who had been specially trained in its use had been sent away to other duties, and these guns had to be handled by those who did not know rightly how to use them. "Vast accumulations were piled up in two or three great depôts, whence they could not be rapidly delivered. The transport wagons were stored at one point, their wheels lay elsewhere at a distance, and weeks elapsed before the inopportunely scattered members of those wagons could be recombined." The emperor lingered in Paris till the 28th July, when he started for Metz, having first issued on the 27th a decree appointing the empress regent. Immediately on his arrival he took command of the army, and issued a proclamation to the following effect: —

"Soldiers! I am about to place myself at your head to defend the honor and the soil of the country. You go to fight against one of the best armies of Europe, but others who were quite as worthy were unable to resist your bravery. It will be the same again at the present time. The war which is now commencing will be a long and severe one, since it will have for the scene of its operations places full of fortresses and obstacles; but nothing is too difficult for the soldiers of Africa, the Crimea, Italy, and Mexico. You will again prove what the French army, animated by the sentiment of duty, maintained by discipline, and inspired by love of country, can perform. Whatever road we may take beyond our frontiers we shall find glorious traces of our fathers. We will prove ourselves worthy of them. The whole of France follows you with her ardent wishes, and the eyes of the world are upon you. The fate of liberty and civilization depends upon our success.

"Soldiers! let each one do his duty, and the God of armies will be with us."

Marshal MacMahon, who had taken a prominent part in both
the Crimean and the Italian campaigns, had been recalled from
Algeria, and on his arrival had taken command of the army of Strasburg on the 24th. Marshal Canrobert, another Crimean officer,
was to command the army of Châlons; but alas! at Metz there
were only one hundred thousand men, and at Strasburg only forty
thousand, so that both together fell short of the strength that had
been set down for the Metz army alone; Canrobert had neither
cavalry nor artillery. The only active operations that had as yet
taken place were the destruction of the Prussian end of the bridge
of Kehl on the 22d July, and some skirmishes between the outposts near Saarbrück. The French opportunity of striking a short
sharp blow and cutting Germany in two was over. " If Napoleon
does not cross the Rhine within a fortnight," Von Moltke, the
German commander-in-chief, is reported to have said when war
was declared, " he will never cross it except as a prisoner," and the
precious fortnight thus given had been wasted. The Germans
were taking the initiative vigorously. Their half a million of
soldiers had been pushing forward in three divisions. The first,
advancing on the right by Treves and Sarrelouis, and consisting
of the 1st and 8th North German corps, numbering about sixty
thousand men, was under the command of General von Steinmetz.
The third army occupied the left of the line towards Landau and
Germersheim. It consisted of about one hundred and fifty thousand men, and was formed by the 5th, 6th, and 11th North German corps, with the armies of Bavaria, Würtemberg, and Baden,
under the command of the Crown Prince of Prussia and of General
Blumenthal. The second army, linking the other two together and
advancing in the centre by Mayence and Mannheim towards the
valley of the Moselle, was under the command of Prince Frederick
Charles, the king's nephew, and numbered nearly two hundred thousand men. It was formed by the 2d, 3d, 4th, 7th, 9th, 10th, and
12th North German corps and the Prussian guard. The king,
accompanied by General von Moltke and General von Roon, the
Minister of War, reached Mayence on the 31st July, and assumed

the command of the whole force, but in reality the operations were directed by Von Moltke. The forward roll of this ocean of men now begun was destined to be stopped only once before it reached the walls of Paris.

The war may be said to have fairly begun on the 2d of August, when a large body of French troops, advancing from Metz under the command of the emperor, who was accompanied by the Prince Imperial, crossed the frontier, and drove back the German outposts that occupied the little town of Saarbrück. The engagement was unimportant, for the Germans simply retired before overwhelming numbers, and the emperor made no attempt to cross the river or storm the heights beyond; but, trifling as it was, the result was hailed in France as a great victory. The presence of the Prince Imperial gave an opportunity for a telegram from the emperor to the empress, announcing that young "Louis had received his baptism of fire — baptême de feu." The terms of this announcement were absurdly inflated, and they caused at the time a considerable amount of ridicule. More serious struggles were, however, close at hand. Troops under the command of General Douay had been detached from the left wing of MacMahon's army, and sent to occupy the celebrated line of fortresses about the town of Weissenberg in Alsace. Trusting to the strength of the lines, and careless both in the use of scouting parties and in keeping watch, — points that were characteristic of the French throughout the whole campaign, — this force was surprised at daybreak on the 4th August by a portion of the crown prince's division. Notwithstanding great inferiority in numbers, the French made a gallant stand, but all in vain. The entrenchments were carried at the point of the bayonet, Douay himself was killed, and the French utterly routed. The German king communicated the news of the success to Queen Augusta at Berlin in a telegram couched in a strain of piety peculiar to him, and which has now become almost proverbial. "A brilliant but bloody victory," the message ran, "won to-day, under Fritz's eyes, by the storming of Weissenberg, and of the Gaisberg behind it. Our 5th and 11th corps and two Bavarian army corps fought. The enemy in flight; five hundred unwounded prisoners, a cannon, and the tents in our hands. General of Division Douay killed. On our side General von Kirchbach slightly wounded. Heavy losses in my regiment and the 58th. God be praised for this first glorious deed of arms! May he continue his aid." The crown prince pressed on towards the Vosges, and MacMahon, in order to check the Prussian advance, and by express orders from headquarters, concentrated his whole force — which numbered only forty-five thousand men — in the neighborhood of Wörth, and between that place and Fröschwiller. The movement was a mistake; he was too far from the main body of the army, and reinforcements in sufficient numbers (for those that arrived from General Failly are hardly worth mentioning) had no time to reach him before he was on the 6th attacked by the enormously more numerous army of the crown prince. Skilfully as MacMahon handled his troops, he was outnumbered by more than two to one, and after a gallant resistance for fifteen hours, he was compelled to give way. The defeat became a rout, and had it not been for the determined stand made by some Algerian sharpshooters, and two regiments of cuirassiers, hardly a man would have escaped. As it was, the army became an undisciplined mob, and literally ran away to Châlons, without rallying or making the slightest attempt to defend the rugged passes of the Vosges, which were thus opened for the forward movement of the crown prince, while the whole right wing of the French position was laid bare. The losses in dead and wounded on both sides were about twenty thousand men. Of MacMahon's force there were only about five thousand men left. King William's telegram ran: "What happiness this new victory gained by Fritz! Praise God alone for his favors! Thirty cannon, two eagles, six mitrailleuses, and four thousand prisoners taken. MacMahon was reinforced from the main army. A salute of victory is to be fired." The prisoners were probably more than is here set down, and besides the trophies above mentioned, two railway trains laden with provisions, and MacMahon's carriage, with his baggage and all his papers, fell into the hands of the victors.

While the right wing of the French line had thus been completely annihilated, the centre and left had fared but little better; for on the same date, the 6th August, they had suffered serious disasters in a desperate fight that had been going on all day on the heights of Spicheren, to the west of Saarbrück. Ever since the day of "the baptism of fire," these heights had been occupied by a strong French force under General Frossard. Meanwhile the right and centre lines of advance of the Germans had been converging on this very spot, and on the 6th General Göben, with the advance guard of the German right wing, reached Spicheren, and attacked the French position, which was a very strong one. This time, too, the Germans were inferior in number, though not markedly so. The battle was long and very bloody; for the ground was defended almost inch by inch, and each new position had to be taken at the point of the bayonet. Reinforcements were brought up by train on both sides, and latterly General von Steinmetz came up and took the command of the German army himself. The last stand was made by the French on the almost impregnable heights of Forbach, and when these too were taken, though at a fearful cost of life to the victors, the French army was in full retreat, leaving behind a vast store of provisions and munitions of all kinds.

The French forces were defeated along the whole line, and now, with their right flank bare, they had no choice but to fall back, and a general retreat on the line of the Moselle was decided on, while it was determined that the main body of the army should concentrate round Metz under Marshal Bazaine. Napoleon himself wished, as he relates in a pamphlet afterwards published during his residence at Wilhelmshöhe, to retreat directly on the army of reserve under Marshal Canrobert at Châlons, — which was probably the better plan, — but was prevented by the regency in Paris.

Hitherto Paris had heard of all sorts of imaginary successes; even on the morning of the disasters at Spicheren and Wörth there was a rumor that MacMahon had gained a great victory, and had taken the crown prince prisoner, with twenty-five thousand Prussians; but the truth could be no longer concealed, and it was given to the Parisians in a very brief telegram from the emperor himself: "Marshal MacMahon has lost a battle. General Frossard, on the Saar, has been compelled to fall back. The retreat is being effected in good order. All can be retrieved." Full information was given next day, and at once all Paris clamored for arms, in a perfect frenzy of excitement. The empress hurried to Paris, and issued a proclamation exhorting the people to be united. The city was declared to be in a state of siege, and the Chambers were summoned to meet on the 9th. When they met the place of meeting was surrounded by a dense crowd, who called out to the troops employed to keep them in order, that they ought to be marching to the frontier. Inside, the ministers were greeted with loud shouts for Rochefort and the Republic. Such, indeed, is France, — always running after a cry. Rochefort, a mere noisy demagogue, was to be the new savior of his country! Jules Favre, with more of disgraceful demagogism than dignity, demanded the overthrow, not of the ministry only, but of the Empire also, and proposed that every citizen able to bear arms should receive weapons, and that the National Guards should be reorganized in conformity with the law of 1831. He also suggested the formation of a committee of defence, composed of members of the Assembly. A vote of want of confidence in the ministers was at once carried, and they immediately resigned.

The new ministers were all devoted adherents of the Empire, and Count Palikao, an officer who had seen service in China, and to whom the formation of a cabinet had been entrusted, reserved for himself the post of minister of war. Hereafter things went on as if no emperor existed. Paris was set in order for a siege, and first General Vinoy and then General Trochu appointed to the command of the garrison. A large number of men were at once employed to cut down trees, widen and deepen the ditch, and strengthen the fortifications generally; all Germans were expelled from the city, and National Guards and Mobiles were enrolled to man the defences. At the sitting held on the 11th, Marshal Bazaine was appointed commander-in-chief, the emperor being thus deliberately set aside. There was a loud outcry among the opposition that the interests of the nation were being sacrificed to those of a dynasty, and this was actually the case. Marshal MacMahon had fallen back on Châlons, being joined on the way by the division under General Failly, and had found there the army of reserve under Marshal Canrobert, and large reinforcements that had been sent by the minister of war. All the rest of the army was concentrated under Bazaine at Metz. The two armies united would have numbered over three hundred thousand men, and, notwithstanding all the previous disasters and losses, they might have still been able to retrieve the position, had a moderate garrison been left at Metz, and Bazaine retired with the rest of his forces to join MacMahon. But here again fatal indecision and delay, due to the dynastic reason that the retreat of Bazaine might have been the signal for a revolution in Paris, kept the French paralyzed till it was too late. While Bazaine lingered, the Prussians were active. The king moved his headquarters into French territory to St. Avold, and the army effected a change of front. King William, as soon as he had entered French territory, issued a proclamation to the French inhabitants of the districts occupied by the German armies, informing them that he still desired to live at peace with the French people, that he was fighting against soldiers and not against peaceful citizens, and that all would be well with them so long as they refrained from hostile acts against the German troops.

At last, on the 14th, the emperor left Bazaine for Châlons, and the French retreat continued on the Moselle, but retreat was now too late. Von Moltke was fully alive to the danger of allowing the two French armies to unite, and had determined to keep Bazaine and MacMahon separate, and to defeat them in detail as he had already done with MacMahon and Frossard. Steinmetz proceeded to harass Bazaine's retreat and delay it. There was a battle at Borny on the 14th, which brought about a delay of one day; there was another at Gravelotte on the 16th, and a third at

Rezonville on the 18th, after which Bazaine retired within the shelter of the forts at Metz, and abandoned his communications with MacMahon and with the outer world. These battles are the bloodiest that have been recorded in history, for it is calculated that the losses on both sides during the days from the 14th to the 18th of August could not have been less than one hundred thousand men, killed, wounded, and missing. At Gravelotte, too, it is said that one of the few mistakes made by the Germans during the war occurred, and that the forces of the crown prince ought to have taken Bazaine in the rear at the same time that those of Prince Charles attacked him in front, and thus have effectually hemmed him in.

The emperor reached Châlons on the 16th, and a council of war was immediately held to decide on the plan of action. MacMahon's plan was to retire slowly on Paris, and this was ultimately adopted, and the emperor says in his Wilhelmshöhe pamphlet that it was his own conviction that this was the best thing to do. Here again, however, the evil genius of France, in the shape of dynastic fears, stepped in. The empress and .Palikao declared that the abandonment of Bazaine and a retreat on Paris would be the signal for the outbreak of a revolution, and against the better judgment of all who were in a position to judge rightly another scheme of operations was resolved on.

After Wörth, the Crown Prince of Prussia, having detached the Baden and Bavarian divisions of his army to besiege Strasburg and Phalsburg, had marched westwards by Nancy towards Gravelotte, but not quickly enough to do the work his men had been at first intended for. He was now advancing on Châlons. The new plan forced on MacMahon was to move to the north, take the Prussians in the rear, and forming a junction with Bazaine come down on the army of the crown prince and cause him to retreat for fear of having his communications cut off. On the 21st, the camp at Châlons was broken up and set on fire, and the army moved to Rheims, where MacMahon received despatches from Bazaine informing him of the final defeat at Rezonville, and his intention of

making efforts to break out towards Montmédy. To aid this operation the Châlons army now moved towards Montmédy by Rethel
and Mouzon, and on the 26th had reached Vouziers in the Ar-
dennes. Von Moltke had encouraged the idea that the bulk of
the German army was advancing on Paris, and that the force with
Prince Frederick Charles at Metz was very small; but so secure
was the position there that he was able to detach a strong force
of eighty thousand men to operate under the Crown Prince of Saxony along the valley of the Meuse. The Crown Prince of Prussia,
as soon as he heard of MacMahon's movement, struck across the
country by Grand Pré and Varennes in order to effect a junction
with this army of the Meuse. The French had two days' start,
but, as usual, time was wasted. The junction was effected, and
MacMahon's force was cut off from Paris; for on the 29th the
Prussian cavalry had come up with his rear-guard. Cut off from
Paris, the marshal communicated to Bazaine his intention of falling
back on Mezières, unless he received word from the army of Metz.
On the 30th, General de Failly's division was surprised at Beau-
mont, defeated, and driven into Mouzon, but retreat by the last
remaining path of safety — the road to Mezières — was still open,
till in an evil moment the emperor decided on a concentration about
Sedan; while the Prussians prevented all room for repentance on
the 31st by crossing the Meuse by bridges that the French ought to
have destroyed, and barring the road from Sedan to Mezières. The
French were completely surrounded. At dawn on the 1st of September the closing scene of the emperor's public life began at the
battle of Sedan. Hardly had the strife commenced at the village
of Bazeilles when Marshal MacMahon was so seriously wounded by
a fragment of a shell that he had to be carried off the field, leaving
the chief authority in the hands of his second in command, General
Ducrot, who at once proceeded to make new dispositions of the
troops. These had hardly been carried out when the command was
claimed by General Wimpffen, who had a commission from the
Minister of War empowering him to take the lead in case anything happened to the marshal, and the new leader at once coun-

termanded Ducrot's arrangements. The outlook was forlorn enough apart from the dismay spread by such signs of indecision. By afternoon the battle was over. The French were driven into Sedan in utter confusion, and five hundred pieces of heavy artillery tore up and devastated with shot and shell the whole French position. General Wimpffen offered to cut his way through; but with eighty thousand men, beaten, disordered, and thoroughly demoralized, to oppose to two hundred and forty thousand German troops, ably handled, flushed with victory, and possessing a vastly superior artillery, even this was probably hopeless. The emperor ordered him not to attempt it, but to ask for an armistice instead. He at the same time gave the order that the firing along the whole line should cease, and the white flag be hung out, an order from which both General Wimpffen and General Ducrot dissented. The closing scene was graphically described by the King of Prussia in a letter to his wife. "I ordered," he says, "the firing to cease, and sent Lieutenant-Colonel von Bronsart of the General Staff, with a flag of truce to demand the capitulation of the army and the fortress. . . . . Colonel von Bronsart was admitted, and, on his asking for the commander-in-chief, he was unexpectedly introduced into the presence of the emperor, who wished to give him a letter for myself. When the emperor asked what his message was, and received the answer, 'To demand the surrender of the army and fortress,' he replied, that on this subject he must apply to General de Wimpffen, who had undertaken the command in the place of the wounded General MacMahon, and that he would now send his adjutant-general, Reille, with the letter to myself.

"It was seven o'clock when Reille and Bronsart came to me, the latter a little in advance; and it was first through him that I learnt with certainty the presence of the emperor. You may imagine the impression that this made on all of us, but particularly on myself. Reille sprang from his horse, and gave me the letter of the emperor, adding that he had no other orders. Before I opened the letter I said to him, 'But I demand, as the first condition, that the army lay down its arms.' The letter begins thus:

'Having been unable to die at the head of my troops, I give up my
sword to your Majesty,' leaving all the rest to me. My answer was
that I deplored the manner of our meeting, and begged that a plenipotentiary might be sent with whom we might conclude the capitulation. After I had given the letter to General Reille, I spoke
a few words with him as an old acquaintance, and so this act ended.
I gave Moltke powers to negotiate, and directed Bismarck to remain
behind in case political questions should arise. I then rode to my
carriage and drove here, greeted everywhere along the road with
the loud hurrahs of the trains that were marching up and singing
the National Hymn. It was deeply touching. Candles were
lighted everywhere, so that we were driven through an improvised
illumination. I arrived here [Vendresse, near Sedan] at eleven
o'clock, and drank with those about me to the prosperity of an
army which had accomplished such feats." Well might he say
"feats." The campaign had opened on the 2d of August, and it
was now the eve of the 2d of September. In a month every soldier of the French army not cooped up securely with Bazaine at
Metz was a prisoner in the hands of the Prussians, who had among
their captives now too the fallen chief of the French nation — the
emperor himself.

Never before in French history had a marshal of France, and
such a large body of troops as nearly ninety thousand men, surrendered to an enemy. The emperor left Sedan early on the morning of the 2d of September, and proceeded to the little village of
Donchery, where Bismarck was. The great man of "blood and
iron" met him by the way, and their interview took place in the
garden of a small cottage by the roadside. When Bismarck introduced the question of peace the emperor at once declined to discuss
it, as he had, he said, surrendered as an individual, and had no power
in any way. The control of military and political affairs lay with
the empress as regent, and with the ministry. He then expressed
a wish to see the king. "Moltke and Bismarck," the king's letter
goes on, "appeared at twelve o'clock, with the capitulation duly
signed. At one o'clock I started again with Fritz, and, escorted by

the cavalry and staff, I alighted before the chateau [the chateau of Bellevue, near Fresnoy, close to Sedan], where the emperor came to meet me. The visit lasted a quarter of an hour. We were both much moved at seeing each other again under such circumstances. What my feelings were, — I had seen Napoleon only three years before at the summit of his power, — is more than I can describe." "He was depressed," says the king elsewhere, "but dignified and resigned." Almost immediately after he started for Wilhelmshöhe, a palace near Cassel, formerly the property of the Electors of Hesse-Cassel, and at one time the residence of King Jerome of Westphalia, which had been assigned by the King of Prussia as the residence of his illustrious captive.

The Parisians had been in their usual state of ignorance as to the proceedings of the army, and had had their courage sustained by the promulgation of news of entirely imaginary successes; but as soon as the fatal news of Sedan reached Paris the Minister of War called a meeting of the Legislative Body. The business began about one o'clock, A. M., on the morning of Sunday the 4th of September. Count Palikao at once proceeded with his statement. "Our army," he said, after a few preliminary words, "after heroic efforts, was driven back into Sedan by superior forces. All further resistance having become impossible, it has capitulated, and the emperor has been made prisoner. In the presence of intelligence so serious and so weighty, it would be impossible for the Ministry to enter upon a discussion of the consequences of such events. We therefore ask the Chamber to adjourn the discussion until to-morrow." When the question was put by the president that the house should adjourn, M. Jules Favre interposed, and while he offered no objection to the adjournment of the Chamber, he intimated that he would, on behalf of himself and several of his colleagues, submit to it when, it reassembled, the resolutions that : —

"1. Louis Napoleon Bonaparte and his dynasty are declared to be divested of the powers conferred upon them by the constitution.

"2. A governing commission, consisting of —— members, shall be appointed by the Legislative Body, which commission shall be invested with all the powers of government, and which shall have for its special mission to offer every resistance to invasion, and to expel the enemy from the territory.

" 3. General Trochu is continued in his functions as governor-general of the city of Paris."

After a protest by M. Pinard that they had not the power "to declare a forfeiture of authority," the Chamber adjourned till Sunday, at noon. It had hardly met at this time, when the hall was invaded by a mob, headed by the National Guards, whose duty it was to keep watch and ward outside, who demanded the overthrow of the Imperial dynasty and the proclamation of a republic. Most of the deputies retired, and the extreme left, with the Paris opposition, who remained behind, proceeded to depose the emperor, and thereafter to march to the Hôtel de Ville, with Gambetta at their head, and there to proclaim the Republic. The ministers and the unpopular officials took to flight, and the empress made her escape, by the assistance of Mr. Evans, an American, and of Sir John Burgoyne, to England. The Second Empire was at an end, and from this point Napoleon III. disappears from French history. His character was a complex one. He had great aims, but he failed in their realization; doomed by his action in 1852, he had always bad tools to work with. The publication of the documents found in his bureau shows the dreadful corruption and dishonesty on the part of trusted officials that he was latterly compelled to endure. "Napoleon III.," says one of his keenest critics, "was certainly not French by nature, but his political education remained entirely under the influence of the French ideal of 1789 and 1800. Sparing of speech, but with an inordinate love of writing, he was not endowed with the power of inspiring, convincing, or pleasing his people by his words, whereas his ideas and mode of action were marvellously suited to the average Frenchman. The defectiveness of his early education and the vicissitudes of his life had not been favorable to a harmonious development of his enigmatic nature. . . . . No one understood better than he the needs of the modern world and the national aspirations that characterize our age; and yet there are

few statesmen that did not surpass him in knowledge of men. . . . .
As a prince, he entered on paths which could not but threaten the
common interest of the European monarchies; as a Frenchman, he
showed a sympathy with the just aspirations of other peoples which
his countrymen refused to pardon. . . . . None the less, it is but right
to honor him as a benefactor of Europe and of France, whose name,
set above that of his greater contemporaries, will always mark the
third quarter of this century. . . . . France has to thank him for
nineteen years of rest and security, during which the wealth of the
country was almost doubled. She has to thank him for identifying
the interest of the State with that of the middle classes by means
of the national loans; she has to thank him, lastly, for those economic liberties which freed the hands of commerce and industry.
Far be it from me to hide the dark side of this absolute government,
the miserable tools, worthy only of a Catiline, with which he surrounded himself, and who exercised such an evil influence on French
society; the means, as cruel as they were base, by which the new
régime was founded; the growth of the scandal-mongering papers,
which poisoned the minds of the reading public; the ever-growing
timidity and servility of the officials, and the demoralization of a
portion of the bench. But worse than all were the death-like still-
ness which for nine years lay upon the land, and those wasted millions which brought the public finances into distress. He had much
of the fatalist in him, yet he was always endeavoring to direct the
course of the living powers of history. In moral character he was
one for whom the ideas of right and wrong, mine and thine, do not
seem to have existed, and who shrank neither from perjury nor
bloodshed. Yet he possessed a kindness of heart which won all
those with whom he came in contact, and those royal virtues and
faults of extravagant generosity, ill-timed mercy, unbounded gratitude, and blind audacity, which become a throne so well, even
though they be rather its adornment than its support." Much,
indeed, as we may reprobate the means that he used to raise himself to supreme power, and the manner in which he very often used
the power that he had acquired, it is impossible not to admire him

after his fall. "Dignified in his bearing, and resigned," was the description of him by King William immediately after Sedan, and this remained true of him till his death at Chiselhurst, on the 9th of January, 1873. In the very depths of humiliation and disappointment, the disposition to theatrical display, in which he so much indulged during the whole period of his power and glory, had disappeared, and the real manhood that was in him, and had borne him up so bravely in his early struggles and misfortunes, came once more to the front. "Silent, self-reserved, and self-controlled" in the midst of abuse and calumny, "he neither remonstrated nor recriminated; he did not take the world into the secret of his regrets or remorse;" but returning once more "to England, whose life and people he had always liked, he lived like an English country gentleman, whose shattered health condemns him to retirement and the society of a few intimates. There were attached friends with him when he died, and if constancy could command friends, few men deserved friends better."

CATHEDRAL OF NANTES.

CHAPTER XXIII.

GAMBETTA. — THE GOVERNMENT OF NATIONAL DEFENCE. — THEIR MAN-
IFESTO. — THEIR EXPECTATION OF A TERMINATION OF THE WAR. —
CIRCULAR OF M. JULES FAVRE. — JOURNEY OF M. THIERS. — CIR-
CULAR OF COUNT BISMARCK. — MOVEMENTS OF CROWN PRINCE. —
CONDITION OF FRENCH FORCES. — DELEGATE GOVERNMENT AT TOURS.
STATE OF PARIS. — DIPLOMATIC NEGOTIATIONS. — INTERVIEW BE-
TWEEN M. FAVRE AND COUNT BISMARCK. — CIRCULAR OF COUNT
BISMARCK. — ACTION OF BAZAINE. — DETERMINATION TO REDUCE
PARIS BY FAMINE. — SALLIES FROM PARIS. — GAMBETTA'S APPEAR-
ANCE AT TOURS. — HIS ENERGY. — HIS PROCLAMATION. — NEW
FRENCH ARMY OF THE LOIRE. — PROSPECTS OF THE STRUGGLE. —
IMPERIALIST PLANS OF BAZAINE. — THEIR FAILURE. — FALL OF
METZ. — ITS EFFECT ON THE STATE OF AFFAIRS. — GAMBETTA'S
ANGER. — OUTBREAK OF THE REDS. — RETURN OF M. THIERS. —
HIS NEGOTIATIONS WITH COUNT BISMARCK FOR AN ARMISTICE. —
THEIR FAILURE. — OPERATIONS OF GENERAL D'AURELLE DE PALA-
DINES. — VIGOROUS SORTIE FROM PARIS. — ITS FAILURE. — FAILURE
OF D'AURELLE. — CHANZY'S RETREAT TO LE MANS. — BOMBARD-
MENT OF PARIS. — HARSH MEASURES OF THE GERMANS. — CONDI-
TION OF AFFAIRS AT THE BEGINNING OF 1871. — CAMPAIGN OF
LE MANS. — OPERATIONS OF GENERAL BOURBAKI. — HIS RETREAT.
— FRESH SORTIES FROM PARIS. — RENEWED OUTBREAK OF THE
BELLEVILLE REPUBLICANS. — CAPITULATION OF PARIS. — RETREAT
OF BOURBAKI INTO SWITZERLAND. — WRETCHED CONDITION OF HIS
FORCES.

THIS Gambetta, who had taken such a prominent part in the
proclamation of the Republic, and who had been forcing
himself into notice for a year or two back, was an ardent young

lawyer of some thirty years of age. His eloquence had gained him considerable reputation at the bar, and his appearance as counsel for some of those prosecuted by the government in 1868 procured him such political distinction as was to be obtained from election to the Legislative Body, as one of the Paris deputies who practically constituted the Opposition. He had been elected by the extreme party, he belonged to the "Irreconcilables," and was supposed to hold very advanced opinions; but being stronger headed than many of his coadjutors, he had refrained from any alliance with the tail of the faction. When party feeling ran strong and high over the *plébiscite* he had advocated moderate views, repudiating anarchy, rioting, and violence of every sort, and had declared that it mattered "little to France whether it were governed by this man or that, provided it were well governed," words to be remembered in 1881; for, after playing a leading part in French politics from 1870 onwards, he may now be described as "the man" who rules France, with even evident leanings towards a manipulation of elections and towards autocratic power that would have done no discredit to Napoleon III.

The new government, which took the title of the Government of National Defence, was composed of General Trochu, President; M. Jules Favre, Minister for Foreign Affairs; M. Gambetta, Minister of the Interior; M. Crémieux, Minister of Justice; M. Jules Simon, Minister of Public Instruction; MM. Jules Ferry, Garnier Pagès, Glais Bizoin, Eugène Pelletan, Rochefort, and Emmanuel Arago. It immediately issued a proclamation couched in the histrionic and inflated style that seems to find such favor in the Gallic mind. "Frenchmen!" ran this brilliant state document, which was published on the 5th September, "Frenchmen! the people have disavowed a Chamber which hesitated to save the country when in danger. It has demanded a Republic. The friends of its representatives are not in power but in peril.

"The Republic vanquished the invasion of 1792. The Republic is proclaimed!

"The revolution is accomplished in the name of right and public safety.

" Citizens! watch over the city confided to you. To-morrow you
will be, with the army, avengers of the country."

The new government at once dissolved the Legislative Body,
abolished the Senate, and caused the Republic to be proclaimed in
all the leading cities of France.

The people by whose will this new state of things was brought
about meant rather more than " the three tailors of Tooley Street,"
but meant, after all, little more than the rabble of Paris. Yet excited, and even exultant, as the Paris mob was, it may boast that,
on this occasion at least, the revolution was accomplished without
actual violence.

To the outside world, such a desertion by a nation of its fallen
sovereign in the hour of his necessity and in the midst of his misfortune, as took place in Paris on the 4th of September, 1870,
might well seem matter of shame and dishonor rather than of party
exultation and triumph. With a victorious enemy sweeping everything before him, and fast approaching the very walls of the capital, one would imagine that the fickle Parisians would have had
something else to think of than boast of internal revolution. But
France is nothing, if not inconsistent; and so, after complacently
appropriating to herself all the glories of the successes the emperor
had gained, often against her own will, she now treated him as
responsible for all the disasters of an insane war into which she
had dragged him against his better judgment; and having thus sacrificed to the fates, she went forth with the lightest of hearts to set
up and proclaim a Republic. It is just possible, however, that the
Republican leaders, eager as they professed to be for revenge, and
desirous, as they had ever been, for French "glory" and aggrandizement, imagined that the war might now terminate. The proclamation of King William had set forth that he had assumed the
command of the German armies to repel the aggression of the
Emperor Napoleon, who had made an attack by land and sea on
the German nation, and this was construed into meaning that the
war had been undertaken against the dynasty and not against the
country. Why then, with Napoleon to the wall, should it not now

cease? This was indeed the position taken up by the new Minister for Foreign Affairs, who issued to all the French diplomatic representatives abroad a long circular, detailing at full length the course that had been followed, and defending the action that had been taken by the "population of Paris." There was no word of the national voice of France, but only of the "population of Paris," which "did not wish to perish with the criminal government that was leading France to her ruin," and which had not "pronounced the deposition of Napoleon III. and of his dynasty," but had "registered it in the name of right, justice, and public safety." There was no time to be lost, it went on to say, and the one desire and determination of France was the expulsion of the enemies that were at the gates of the capital. The war had been imposed on France by the Empire and not by the new government; whose leaders had opposed it at first, and still continued to deplore the "human massacres," wherein "were sacrificed the flower of two nations." "On his side," it said elsewhere, "the King of Prussia declared that he made war not against France but against the Imperial dynasty. The dynasty has fallen to the ground. . . . . Does the King of Prussia wish to continue an impious struggle which will be at least as fatal to him as to us? . . . . He is free to assume this responsibility in the face of the world and of history. If it is a challenge, we accept it. We will not cede either an inch of our territory or a stone of our fortresses. . . . . We have a resolute army, well provisioned forts. After the forts we have the ramparts; after the ramparts we have the barricades. Paris can hold out for three months and conquer. If she succumbs, France will start up at her appeal and avenge her. France would continue the struggle, and the aggressor would perish." With the issue of this manifesto, M. Thiers set out for London; and he thereafter visited several of the other European capitals. High hopes would seem to have been entertained by the Government of National Defence that the other European powers would, by their friendly offices, bring about a cessation of hostilities. The English government, indeed, were quite willing to mediate, but they had ascertained that

the Prussians would entertain no proposals in the way of interference.

Since the issue of the King of Prussia's proclamation, indeed,
many things had happened. The early successes of the German
armies had excited intense popular enthusiasm throughout both
North and South Germany; the immediate reunion of all the states
of the Fatherland in one compact whole was at once assured, and
was hailed on all hands as a result that would "make the nation
free and strong." Bavaria and Würtemberg loudly and with one
voice demanded admission to the Bund. The country was quite
determined and unanimous in its resolve that, as it had beaten the
enemy without allies, so it would "conclude a peace without the interference of neutrals." Alsace and Lorraine contained a population of German descent, and though they had been long separated
from their native country, now that there was to be once more
a united Germany, it was necessary that these provinces should be
embraced in it. "Only a peace," it was said, "which brings the
French to a consciousness of their defeat can be lasting; and a false
generosity would be weakness, encouraging new attempts. The
recovery of Alsace and Lorraine is the only guarantee against that
French hankering after German territory which has displayed
itself under every new government." The movement was opposed
only by the social Democrats; and it soon became evident, from a
circular issued by Bismarck in reply to that of M. Jules Favre,
that, in accordance with the opinions of Count Moltke and the
military authorities, the annexation of Strasburg and Metz at all
events had been definitely resolved on. "We cannot," said the
Prussian Prime Minister, evidently with an eye to M. Favre's declaration in reference to the surrender of territory, "believe in the
sincerity of the desire of the present government to make peace so
long as it continues, by its language and its acts at home, to excite
the passions of the people, and to increase the hatred and bitterness
of a population stung by the sufferings of war, and to repudiate in
advance every basis acceptable to Germany as unacceptable by
France." After pointing out that France would have to settle with

Germany alone, and that it would be an act of cruelty to allow her to imagine otherwise, he went on to say that the German terms of peace were quite independent of the question by whom France was to be governed, and the kind of government the French established among themselves. Germany must be protected from French vioence by securer boundaries than those that had hitherto existed. There was no mincing the matter of the cession of territory. "As long as France remains in possession of Strasburg and Metz, so long is its offensive strategically stronger than our defensive power, so far as all South Germany and North Germany on the left bank of the Rhine are concerned. Strasburg in the possession of France is a gate always wide open for attack on South Germany. In the hands of Germany Strasburg and Metz obtain a defensive character. . . . . In rendering it difficult for France, from whose initiative alone hitherto the disturbances of Europe have resulted, to resume the offensive, we at the same time act in the interest of Europe, which is that of peace. From Germany no disturbance of the European peace is to be feared. After having had this war forced upon us, we mean, for our future safety, to demand the price of our mighty efforts."

Meanwhile, the crown prince, having at Sedan crushed the only French army in the field against him, had resumed his interrupted march on Paris along by the valleys of the Marne and the Oise. To oppose the victorious enemy France had still about 420,000 regular troops, but of these nearly 300,000 were cooped up in Metz with Bazaine, and the rest were scattered up and down the country. The raw levies supplied perhaps another 150,000 men, but they were unorganized, untrained, and to a considerable extent unarmed. In Paris itself there were about 30,000 regular troops ; and it was evident that the brunt of the defence would fall on the Mobiles and the National Guards, who had been mustered and armed to the number of about 350,000 men. The garrison was under the command of General Trochu, "a cautious man of strategic science," perhaps a little over cautious, as subsequent events showed ; but he held a difficult post, and his operations must not be rashly judged. The Government of National Defence had hardly time to send MM. Crémieux and Glais Bizoin to Tours, to establish a delegate government there, when General Vinoy was pushed back at Sceaux, and General Ducrot at Meudon, and on the 19th the investment of Paris was complete. The capital was, however, strong and well protected, first by an outlying circle of detached forts which served the purpose of preventing an attacking enemy from approaching the walls of the city itself, and were besides so arranged that several of them would have to be taken before even the bombardment of Paris was possible. The main garrison, too, thus amply protected by the forts, was on its part to render service by constant sallies for the purpose of destroying siege-works directed against the outer line of defence. The movement of MacMahon, which had drawn off the crown prince for a short time, had given a brief respite to Paris, and of this breathing time the utmost advantage had been taken in the way of strengthening the defences. Everything outside the city, between the walls and the forts, and around the forts themselves, likely to afford the slightest shelter to an attacking enemy, — trees, villas, gardens, — all were ruthlessly destroyed, and the roads and railroads were broken up. Inside the city stores of provisions had been laid up, and every preparation made for emergencies.

The chances of European intervention still kept hope alive in the Parisian breast, and M. Jules Favre issued a fresh circular, in which, after admitting the validity of the objection that the government was without regular power, and expressing the desire of those in authority in Paris to have a meeting, if possible, of a duly and freely elected Assembly, he urged that "France, divested of the shroud of the Empire, — free, generous, and ready to immolate herself for right and liberty, — disavowing all political conquests and all violent propaganda, — having no other ambition than to remain mistress of herself, and to develop her moral and material forces, and to work fraternally with her neighbors for the progress of civilization," — having now asked for a cessation of a war which had been begun without her free consent, should have this desire granted so as to make the election of a proper Assembly possible. "Europe," he said further on, "begins to be moved, and sympathy for us is being reawakened." There were some grounds for the hope that the European powers might interfere; for even as early as the end of August, both Italy and Russia — especially Russia — had shown signs of a desire to interpose; and from the first establishment of the new Provisional Government the foreign representatives of France had kept urging on the other European governments, particularly that of England, that there should be a collective note addressed to Germany on behalf of France. So early as the 9th September, M. Favre had, through Lord Lyons, the English ambassador at Paris, put to Count Bismarck the question, "Is Count Bismarck willing to enter into verbal negotiations for an armistice and for a conference upon the conditions of peace, and with whom does he propose to hold this conversation?" Bismarck's answer, forwarded through the English ambassador, did not reach Paris till the 13th, and it shows how fully alive he was to the difficulty of dealing with such a self-elected and mob-supported body as was the Government of National Defence, whose actions the country at large might at any moment refuse to accept or ratify on the ground that it did not represent the nation, and how much, therefore, he appreciated the necessity for the meeting of a properly elected Assembly. He could not, he said, "attach to the overtures of the government now acting in Paris the importance of an overture from the government of France, because it is not yet recognized by France, and the Emperor Napoleon is still formally for foreign powers the bearer of the sovereignty. I answer by the counter-question, What guarantee can the present government, or one of those which will probably follow it, in Paris give that agreements with it would be recognized by France, or even immediately only by the troops at Strasburg and Metz?" M. Favre replied, admitting the justice of Count Bismarck's demand, and offering the political guarantee that the Government of National Defence would without delay call an assembly to ratify the treaty of peace. The military guarantee, he pointed out, was as good as in any regular government, inasmuch as all orders of the war minister were obeyed, and, therefore, there could be no doubt that the arrangements of the armistice would be at once carried out. M. Favre was too impatient to maintain any longer this circuitous mode of communication, and determined to "sacrifice all personal pride and reserve," and go direct to the Prussian headquarters. A preliminary mission of Mr. Malet led to his receiving a pass through the Prussian lines to the headquarters at Ferrières, so that he might ascertain if it were possible to find a basis for the negotiation of an armistice. A difficulty at once arose which made it manifest that all negotiations were as yet hopeless. Count Bismarck expressed his earnest desire to afford facilities for the meeting of a properly constituted Assembly, but he insisted that, before any negotiations for a truce could be carried on, the consent of France to some ultimate alienation of territory (he did not say how much) should be clearly given, and he demanded in addition the immediate surrender of Toul and Strasburg, which were closely besieged, and the admission of the Prussians to the Parisian fort of Mont Valérien. M. Favre indignantly rejected the terms, and, adhering to the tenor of his circular of the 6th September, declared that, while France was willing to pay a large money indemnity for the wrong that had been done by the war against Prussia, she nevertheless would never consent to "cede either an inch of her territory or a stone of her fortresses." The strife was evidently to continue to the bitter end; and advantage was taken of Count Bismarck's position by the Delegate Government at Tours to issue an official proclamation, intimating that Bismarck had announced to M. Favre his intention of reducing France to a second-rate power,—a declaration that led to the transmission of a fresh circular from the Chancellor to the Prussian representatives at foreign courts, at which, after referring in very sarcastic terms to this proclamation as "intended only to impress such circles as are alike unacquainted with the ordinary language of diplomacy, and the geography of France," though it bore the names of Crémieux, Glais Bizoin, and Fourichon, "gentlemen forming part of the government of a great European empire"; he went on to say that M. Favre and he had in their interview never got so far as to "open business-like discussion on terms of peace," and that he had only adhered to the terms intimated in his circular of the 16th September. He pointed out, in conclusion, that the French territory would be still as large as it had been before the annexation of Savoy and Nice; that the loss of seven hundred and fifty thousand inhabitants on a total population of forty-two millions could never affect the standing of France as one of the great powers; and that in drawing M. Favre's attention to these points, he "was far from making any offensive allusion to the consequences of this war as affecting the future position of France in the world." What really passed at the interview it is difficult to say, as the accounts published by M. Favre and by Bismarck vary considerably; but though the Prussian Prime Minister may have been thoroughly sincere in his desire for an armistice, yet there is room for grave doubt as to how far the German authorities were desirous of an armistice before they had forced France to drink the last dregs of the cup of humiliation in compelling the surrender of Paris. Indeed, Bismarck himself said, in a letter to Lord Lyons, "We shall always be ready to enter into negotiations for peace, but not for an armistice;" and the terms of peace would doubtless have included such an entry into Paris as subsequently took place. Be this as it may, he could have certainly but little delicacy in bringing forward the question of the cession of territory with reference to a power that had shown so little hesitation itself in the addition to its dominions of Nice and Savoy, which plainly had been prepared to set aside national feeling in the matter of Belgium, and which had, moreover, had a clearly expressed hankering for a long time back after the possession of as much German territory as would bring its own frontier up to the Rhine. Toul and Strasburg were still holding out, but their surrender was merely a matter of time; and both places yielded within a week after the meeting of the two ministers took place. In both cities the conquerors were received by many of the inhabitants with rejoicing, such was still the love they bore for the Fatherland from which they had been separated for nearly two hundred years.

The only hope for Paris now lay in the aid of an army operating against the encircling Prussians from without, in conjunction with a vigorous sally of the garrison from within; and for this the government had to rely either on the ability of Bazaine to burst through the Prussian forces around Metz, or, failing this, on the capability of the South and East to supply an entirely new army large enough, and in a state of sufficient training, to be able to cope with the invaders. There seemed, indeed, no reason to despair of Bazaine's ability to escape from Metz, for his army was about equal in number to the German force by which he was shut in, and, acting from the inside, he could concentrate his men on a smaller front without exposing his flanks, and thus gain a considerable advantage; but since the fall of the Empire the imperial marshal had been showing a strange lack of energy, pronounced enough to justify suspicion, if not to afford proof, of the treachery for which he was afterwards tried and condemned. He had been hemmed in on the 18th August, from which time till the 31st he made no effort to alter his position, thus allowing the Germans ample time and opportunity, of which they were not slow to avail themselves, to strengthen their positions and to complete their lines of investment. On the 31st, at the time of the battle of Sedan, a sally was made in the direction of St. Barbe, but it does not seem to have been at all of a very vigorous or well-directed nature; and though the French were not finally and completely driven back till the afternoon of the following day, the want of concentration of the troops never left the actual issue at any time in doubt. The news of Sedan and of the overthrow of the Imperial Government reached Metz on the 7th September, and from that time all serious offensive action on the part of the beleaguered army may be said to have ceased; and it soon became evident, notwithstanding the rumors to the contrary effect that were constantly circulating in Paris, that Bazaine was either unable or unwilling to force his way into the field. The question then came to be whether an entirely new army could be organized in time to drive off the investing German force before Paris was compelled to surrender; and to the task of forming this the Provisional Government was now diligently applying itself.

Inside Paris preparations had been made for a bombardment such as that under which Strasburg had been well nigh destroyed; and, with greater care than was displayed there, the greater part of the priceless treasures contained in the art galleries and museums were removed from their places, and put in positions of safety in cellars underground. No such loss as had been sustained by the burning of the Strasburg library was to be allowed to happen. But the expected bombardment had not yet taken place, for the Prussians hesitated before entering on such a work of destruction, and they seemed determined to bring about their end just as they were trying to do at Metz by the slower but not less sure and potent means of famine; and Bismarck, in a fresh circular, issued to the German representatives at foreign courts, drew an appalling picture of what might be the consequences of this method of dealing if it were carried to extremes,— a picture no doubt intended to reach the French government, and to have an effect on its resolutions. After pointing out the recent changes in favor of Germany, brought about by the fall of Toul and Strasburg, he said: "France will have to bear the consequences of the resolution taken by her rulers to engage in a struggle to the last. Her sacrifices will uselessly increase, and the destruction of her social system will be all but inevitable. The commander of the German army regrets his inability to prevent this; but he clearly foresees the results of the resistance recklessly determined upon, and deems it necessary to draw attention to one point in particular,— the condition of Paris. The two more important engagements before the capital, in which . . . . the enemy's troops did not manage to repulse even the front line of the investing army, justify the conclusion that sooner or later Paris must fall. Should the capitulation be put off by the Provisional Government till the want of provisions compels the surrender, terrible consequences will ensue. The absurd destruction of railways, bridges, and canals within a certain distance of Paris has not stayed the progress of the German armies for a moment; but we have only

restored the communications necessary for the military purpose we
have in view, and enough remains demolished to interrupt easy
communication between capital and provinces for a long time to
come.   The German commander will, in the case above mentioned,
find it altogether impossible to provision a population of nearly two
millions for even a single day.   Neither will the neighborhood of
Paris, for a distance of many marches, supply any means of suc-
coring the Parisians, all that there is in it being absolutely necessary for the troops.   Nor shall we be able to remove a portion of
the population by the country roads, as we have no available means
of transport.   The inevitable consequence of this will be that hundreds of thousands will starve.   The French rulers cannot but see
this as clearly as ourselves.   We can only fight out the quarrel
forced upon us, but those who bring on such extreme consequences
will be respousible for them."

Towards the end of September the garrison of Paris made several
sallies on a small scale, probably more for the purpose of accustom-
ing untried troops to the actual feeling of being under fire than
with any more vigorous end in view ; and, though all the time the
drilling and disciplining of the new levies were being actively carried on, the seeming inactivity of the government roused the impatience of the Red Republicans, who, by their clamorous outcry
and rash eagerness for premature action, were causing considerable
trouble in Paris itself, and who in some of the larger towns outside
had openly thrown off their adhesion to the new state of things.
But diplomacy had all the time been busy.   At all the foreign
courts the French diplomatists still kept urging European intervention.   The Great Powers were called upon to " speak to Prussia in
a tone that could not be mistaken, and to take measures to insure
their being listened to," and there were strong appeals to both Italy
and Austria for armed aid.   The general feeling among the Powers
seemed, however, to be in favor of such a cessation of hostilities as
would admit of the election of an Assembly by which France might
make the national will known ; and diplomacy might have succeeded in forcing this view on Prussia when, just at the critical

moment, M. Gambetta made his appearance at the seat of the Provisional Government at Tours.

After Paris was once invested, all ordinary communication with the outside world was cut off, and such news as was procurable was conveyed over the Prussian lines by means of carrier pigeons or balloons, which now first made their appearance as accessories among the appliances of war. One large fixed balloon was used in the city for the purpose of observing the enemy's position; and many were found daring enough to take places in smaller ones, in which, braving the danger of their vehicle being pierced by rifle-balls directed against them as they passed over the investing army, or of its being carried to some place held by the foe, they attempted to make their escape from the besieged city, or to carry communications to the outside world. On the 7th of October, M. Gambetta succeeded in escaping in one of these balloons, and, descending at Amiens, made his way to Tours, bringing with him from the main body of the Government at Paris instructions to the effect that no Assembly was to be elected in the mean time. Stronger willed, stronger headed, more audacious, younger, and more active than the members of the Delegate Government, he at once assumed the position of Minister of War, and became practically *the Government*. While he delivered fiery and extravagant harangues, which excited the utmost enthusiasm among the people throughout the country, he made his acts more than keep pace with his words, and set vigorously to work to bring a new French army into existence. On the 9th he issued a proclamation, the tone of which was admirably calculated to rouse French vanity, and so French spirit. He described the disappointment of the Germans at the sight of the two millions of inhabitants of Paris rallying at once to the Republic instead of quarrelling among themselves, as the invader had expected, and then gave an account of the condition in which he had left Paris. "The Revolution," he said, "found Paris without cannon and without arms. Now four hundred thousand National Guards are armed, one hundred thousand Mobiles have been summoned, and sixty thousand regular troops are assembled. The foundries cast cannon; the women make one million of cartridges daily; the National Guard have two mitrailleurs for each battalion; field-pieces are being made for sorties against the besiegers; the forts are manned by Marines, and are furnished with marvellous artillery, served by the first gunners in the world. Up till now their fire has prevented the enemy from establishing the smallest work." He further narrated that the enceinte was now furnished with three thousand eight hundred cannon, with four hundred rounds of ammunition for each, and that behind the enceinte the barricades — a third line of defence — could be at any moment defended by the Parisians, who had a "genius for street fighting." Paris could be neither captured nor surprised. It could fall only by sedition or famine, and of neither of these was there any danger, for there sedition would not arise, and there was a supply of provisions that would last for months, until an outside army came to their assistance.

Such being the state of Paris, heavy responsibilities lay on those outside. They must "have no other occupation but the war," and they must "accept fraternally the supremacy of Republican power." Nothing was wanting but arms, for all supplies of that sort had been sent to Sedan, Metz, and Strasburg, "as if, one would think, the authors of our disaster, by a last criminal combination, had desired, at their fall, to deprive us of all means of repairing our ruin." Arms were, however, being provided; and all that was needful was that the provinces should arouse themselves, and set to work with courage and hope. "No!" he concluded, "it is not possible that the genius of France will be forevermore obscured; it cannot be that a great nation will let its place in the world be taken from it by an invasion of five hundred thousand men. Up, then, in a mass, and let us die rather than suffer the shame of dismemberment. In the midst of our disasters we have still the sentiment left of French unity and of the indivisibility of the Republic. Paris, surrounded by the enemy, affirms more loudly and more gloriously than ever the immortal device which is dictated to the whole of France: ·' Long live the Republic! Long live France! Long live the Re-

public—one and indivisible!'" Swarms of recruits began to come
in, and those that had been previously trained now proceeded to
take the field. The new army, which was styled the Army of the
Loire, proceeded along the valley of that river towards Paris, but at
Orleans they were met, on the 10th of October, by the Bavarians
under General von der Tann, and driven back; but the Germans
were unable to follow up their success, as no army in sufficient
numbers was available for field operations, and so drill and organization went on at Tours with undiminished diligence without let or
hindrance.

The key to the whole position was still in the hands of Bazaine.
If his efforts to burst out from Metz and make his way to Paris
were feeble and ill-directed, or merely intended to keep up appearances, there could be no doubt of the advantage of even such passive
resistance as his position at Metz afforded; for the Prussian resources were taxed to the utmost to keep up the full strength of the
investing armies at Metz and Paris, and to provide a sufficient
number of men to maintain their communications and keep the
remaining French forces in the North in check. So long as Bazaine
detained over two hundred thousand men under Prince Frederick
Charles about the great fortress in Lorraine, the German troops
available for field service were far too few for operating against the
Army of the Loire, so as to hold it effectively in check, or crush it,
when once it had been properly disciplined and its preparations
brought into a sufficiently forward state to admit of its taking the
field actively and in full force. Had Bazaine but held out for a
week or two longer than he did, the Army of the Loire would undoubtedly have been able to force its way to the relief of Paris,
and the war would have been indefinitely prolonged, or France
would have been able to obtain much more favorable terms than
she eventually did.

In the middle of October, however, the dislike of the Marshal
for, and his disaffection towards, the Republican government, which
have been already alluded to, began to show themselves in a very
open manner. Brooding over the state of affairs, he had hatched

the idea of an Imperial restoration, not in the person of the emperor, the star of whose fortune had set forever, but by means of a meeting of the Senate and Legislature in the North, called by the empress, as still lawfully regent, when the prince imperial would have been placed on the throne, and peace concluded with Germany on Bismarck's own terms. The scheme was so utterly ridiculous, though the exact negotiations have never fully transpired, that one wonders that the German authorities listened for a moment to the proposal; and yet it is certain that they did listen to it, for General Boyer was received on a mission from Metz at the Prussian headquarters at Versailles, and General Bourbaki was allowed to pass from Metz through the Prussian lines, and to proceed to England to obtain the consent of the empress to the plan. The empress refused to have anything to do with it, and Bourbaki, instead of returning to Metz, as he ought to have done, passed through Belgium to Tours, where his offer of service was accepted by M. Gambetta, and he was appointed to the command of an army assembled round Lille, and called the Army of the North. On the 29th of October, almost immediately after the failure of General Bourbaki's mission, Metz surrendered, amid a general outburst of indignation and fury all over France, as well as among the inhabitants of the place itself. Bazaine drove off to join the emperor at Wilhelmshöhe amid a chorus of shouts of "Traitor, coward, sneak, thief," etc., had his carriage windows broken, and had to be rescued by the Prussians from the violence of the crowd. A furious and excited mob gathered in the streets, and had to be dispersed by the soldiery. "All night the sounds of grief, indignation, and terror were kept up. Respectable women ran about the streets, tearing their hair and flinging their bonnets and laces under their feet, wildly crying aloud, 'What will become of our children!'" All discipline was lost; the National Guard refused to lay down their arms; one body of troops vowed they would die rather than yield. "Soldiers, drunk and sober, tumbled hither and thither in irregular groups, with their caps off and their sabres broken, crying, sobbing, and weeping like children." Such was the mutinous condition of the soldiery, and so strong the feeling that they had been betrayed and sold, that it was deemed not only inexpedient but even dangerous to carry out the original terms of the surrender, — namely, that the whole garrison should march out with all the honors of war, — and the whole of the troops were disarmed inside, except the Imperial Guard, which marched out with flags flying and bayonets fixed, and, passing in review before Prince Frederick Charles, laid down their arms at Frescati.

No wonder the rage of France was vehement and loudly expressed. Upon no one did the disaster fall with more crushing effect than on the indefatigable lawyer who governed France outside the walls of Paris, and who, counting on anything but this, nay, relying on the very opposite, was so hard at work establishing new forces for the salvation of Paris and the nation. A week before he had seen, no doubt with complacency, all his new armies — the Army of the Loire, the Northern Army, the Western Army, the Central Army, and the Eastern Army — getting into such an advanced state of preparation that he would soon be able to launch them against the foe, and now in one day all his combinations were placed in jeopardy. A Prussian host of over two hundred thousand men was set free to act against his relieving force, and keep it away from Paris. Well might he give vent to his bitter grief and indignation, as he did in the proclamation that was immediately issued by the Delegate Government at Tours. In it the nation was exhorted to exalt their souls and resolutions against the crushing disasters that had been endured, and to show the world that the French were a great people, " who will not perish, and whose courage rises in the midst even of catastrophes." " A general," it is said, " upon whom France relied even after Mexico, has just deprived the country, when in danger, of more than one hundred thousand of its defenders. Marshal Bazaine has committed treason. He has made himself the agent of the man of Sedan, and the accomplice of the invader; and, disregarding the honor of the army of which he had charge, he surrendered, without even attempting to make a supreme effort, one hundred and twenty-five thousand combatants, twenty thousand wounded, rifles, guns, flags, and the strongest citadel of France — Metz, until now virgin of the contamination of the foreigner." The proclamation assigned the "corrupting power" of the Empire as the cause of all the disasters, and concluded with an exhortation to the nation to remain firm and not lose heart. "Let us firmly hold the glorious flag of Revolution. Our cause is that of justice and right. Europe sees it and feels it. . . . . No illusions! Let us not permit ourselves to languish or to become enervated. But let us prove by deeds that we are willing and able, by our own resources, to maintain our honor, independence, and integrity, — all that makes the country free and proud." Bazaine replied, on the 2d November, in a letter in which he termed the proclamation "a lying lucubration;" and said that M. Gambetta did not seem to be aware of what he was saying, or what was the real position of the Army of Metz; that he (the Marshal) had been unable in spite of his efforts to open communications with the Government at Tours; that an army which had two thousand one hundred and forty officers and forty-two thousand three hundred and fifty men killed and wounded by the enemy's fire could not be an army of traitors, and would not have obeyed a traitor; that only sixty-five thousand real combatants remained, and that, had it not been for the energy and patriotism displayed on all sides, the surrender brought about at length by famine and disorganization would have happened a fortnight sooner than it did. "France," he concluded, "has always been deceived as to our position. I know not why, but the truth will one day prevail. We are conscious of having done our duty."

The Red Republicans had already made two efforts to assert themselves in Paris, one in the end of September, already referred to, and another in the early part of October, both of which had been easily quelled; and the news of this fresh disaster, which soon found its way to Paris, accompanied as it was by the success of the Prussians in the second combat of Le Bourget — a position near St. Denis, from which a sortie of the Paris garrison had dislodged them in the first combat — caused a third and more serious outbreak, the precursor of the ever lamentable outrages of the Com-

mune.   On the 31st of October a crowd of National Guards, headed
by Flourens, of evil notoriety in connection with disturbances,
already described before the beginning of the war, burst into the
Hôtel de Ville and seized the leading members of the government,
including General Trochu and MM. Jules Favre, Garnier Pagès,
and Jules Simon.   M. Ernest Picard, who was also in the building, succeeded, however, in making his escape, and with admirable
coolness and promptitude at once set himself to take most active
measures for restoring order.   Troops were rapidly collected, and
the liberation of General Trochu and M. Jules Simon secured.
Shortly after midnight the large force that had been assembled
about the Hôtel de Ville forced its way in, when the rioters were
easily quelled, and the other members of the government released.
The immediate consequences were an appeal of the government
to a *plébiscite* of the Parisians, which resulted in a majority in
their favor of four hundred and ninety-five thousand three hundred and fifty-eight votes on a total vote of six hundred and twenty
thousand six hundred and thirty-four, and the resignation by
Rochefort of his position in the Ministry.

Diplomacy was still busy.   M. Thiers returned from his visit to
the various European courts without having accomplished his ends,
though about the 18th of October Italy seems to have been
inclined to take active steps.   He had succeeded, however, in
inducing the English government again to bring before the German authorities the question of an armistice, and in prevailing on
the Emperor of Russia to support the application by his personal
appeal.   Austria, Italy, and Spain united with Russia and England
in pressing the matter on Germany, Italy in particular seeming to
be still hankering after more decided measures.   The issue was that
Thiers and Bismarck had a number of interviews between the 3d
and the 6th of November.   The Germans offered "a suspension of
hostilities for twenty-five or twenty-eight days on the basis of
the military *status quo*," the positions of the armies to be those
held by them respectively on the day the truce was signed.   The
time was to be spent in the election of members of a National

Assembly; and Bismarck, so as in no way to prejudge the question of the destiny of Alsace, offered to allow the representation of that province in the Assembly provided there were no electoral agitation. So far both parties were in agreement; but on the fourth point, the question of the revictualling of Paris and other besieged places, divergence arose. To this provision Bismarck refused to agree without some equivalent, as it would have been, to use his own words, to " sacrifice the fruits of all the efforts we had made during two months, and the advantages which we had achieved, and restore the conditions of the struggle to the point at which we found them in the beginning of our investment of Paris." All equivalent was refused, and Bismarck then proposed " a short truce, or that elections should be ordered without a regular Convention being signed for the suspension of hostilities," in which case he "promised free intercourse, and the granting of all facilities consistent with the security of the German armies." This also was declined, and the negotiations were broken off. Prince Frederick Charles was pushing rapidly forward to the scene of active operations, and the French efforts, both within Paris and without, were urged on with redoubled energy. It was seen that there was no hope of European interference, and that France must rely entirely on herself.

Had no fresh German troops been at the moment available, the prospects of some success for France would indeed have been good, for the garrison of Paris had not only secured and strengthened their defences, but they were busy on all sides pushing out new works against the lines of the besiegers, whose scouting and foraging parties were at the same time constantly harassed by the bands of irregular troops which had gathered on the outside. The Army of the Loire, too, now numbering over two hundred thousand men, had been brought into a state of fairly effective organization by the efforts of its commander, General d'Aurelle de Paladines, a strict disciplinarian of the old school, who had seen active service in the Crimea, and was just ready to take the field. On the 9th of November it had advanced in such force as to be able to attack the

German position at Orleans. General von der Tann, who had captured this city nearly a month before, and had been holding it with a very insufficient force, was defeated at Coulmiers, where the French obtained their first success during the war, and was driven back, first to Artenay, and then to Toury, with very heavy losses. The proper plan of D'Aurelle after this would probably have been to hang on the rear of the Bavarians, drive them still farther back, defeat them decisively before more reinforcements could reach them, and be ready to attack fresh troops as they made their appearance, thus dealing with the enemy in detail. As, however, the main object of his advance was the relief of Paris, he thought it better to make a movement to the northwest, towards Chartres and Dreux, while he wasted time in constructing strong intrenchments in the forests north of Orleans. The time thus thrown away was eagerly utilized by the Germans for the concentration of their forces. Reinforcements were despatched from the army around Paris, and Prince Frederick Charles, pressing forward, brought up his forces on the left of Von der Tann's line. On the 27th November D'Aurelle, by a movement concerted with General Trochu, attacked Prince Frederick Charles at Beaune-la-Rolande, and made a desperate effort to force the road to Paris, while on the 30th, at the time when the Army of the Loire, had it succeeded, would have been able to reach a helping hand to them, General Trochu and General Ducrot led a vigorous sortie of the Paris garrison. The fighting was severe, and when night fell the French had driven in the German line at several points, and held possession of the villages of Brie and Champigny.

Thus matters remained over the 1st of December. On the 2d the Saxons surprised and recovered Brie, and the Würtembergers, after a severe struggle, also succeeded in reoccupying Champigny; but the success at both places was brief, for such a terrific fire was opened from the French forts that possession of both of them had to be given up, the German infantry, unsupported by artillery, being unable to face the terrific shower of shells that kept pouring upon them. This was the time when the Army of the Loire, crowned with victory, should have been thundering on the German rear, but, alas, no Army of the Loire was there. In spite of the gallantry and persistence of a portion of D'Aurelle's troops at Beaune-la-Rolande, his raw masses were no match for the veteran Germans, and he had been beaten off. His attacks on the other end of the German line, on the 30th of November and the 1st of December, had had no better fortune, and on the 2d of December he had been driven back on his intrenchments at Orleans. On the 4th Trochu and Ducrot had once more withdrawn their troops across the Marne, and the sortie was at an end. It had failed, owing to Trochu's too "cautious" reliance on the maxim of war, that a besieged garrison must act only in co-operation with a relieving army. The German force in his immediate front during this sally was probably at no time over thirty thousand men, and he had actually in the field against it a body of more than sixty thousand soldiers, which, notwithstanding the forces engaged in feints and other operations elsewhere, might easily in a very short time have been increased to more than double that number. The terrible fire of the forts had thinned the ranks, and, no doubt, in spite of continued previous successes, somewhat affected the *morale* of the enemy, while it had inspired the French troops with hope and confidence,— hope and confidence greatly increased by the news of the previous success of D'Aurelle at Coulmiers; and if Trochu, disregarding the strategic maxims and rules to which he seems to have been a slave (as was to be expected from a man of the legal habit of mind peculiar to "a lawyer who had by accident found himself at St. Cyr and had become a soldier"), had only pressed forward in earnest without thought of a relieving army, he might, in all probability, have forced his way through, and, by threatening the German communications, compelled the siege to be raised. This was not to be; the lack of decision at the critical moment, which had so crippled all the French efforts of the war, both early and late,— alike under the Emperor Napoleon and under the Dictator Gambetta, — once more proved fatal, and the last opportunity,— hazardous no doubt, but still an opportunity,— of relieving Paris was lost. D'Aurelle was driven from his intrenchments on the 4th of December, when Orleans was recaptured by the Germans, and the French army cut in two, one portion retreating to the southeast and the other to the southwest. No sooner was D'Aurelle's failure known at Tours than Gambetta fulminated the usual denunciations against him, and promptly replaced him by General Bourbaki and General Chanzy, who were appointed to command the southeastern and southwestern portions of the army respectively. On the 7th, 8th, 9th, and 10th of December, there was hard fighting between General Chanzy's division and the troops of Prince Frederick Charles, who was advancing on Tours. The French maintained their positions, but, threatened by a flank movement under Prince Louis of Hesse, Chanzy was compelled on the 14th and 15th to retire; and it being no longer necessary to protect Tours, as the Provisional Government had moved its seat to Bordeaux, he turned westward towards Le Mans, where the western army, under the command of General Fiereck, had its headquarters. Tours itself was occupied by the Germans on the 21st, but they retired again almost at once.

The Army of the North, under General Faidherbe, and the Army of the East, under Garibaldi, had meanwhile been carrying on operations against the Prussian forces under General Manteuffel and General Werder, but the fighting had been of a desultory character, and had effected nothing decisive; still all the operations had had a serious effect upon the active strength of the German armies, and it was now found necessary to call out the Landwehr to the number of two hundred thousand men, and to begin to send them to the front.

Another sortie from Paris, which had taken place on the 21st December, and had been directed against Stains, had proved quite ineffectual, but the patience of the German military authorities was exhausted. Possibly when Count Bismarck issued his circular, pointing to famine as the means of inducing the surrender of Paris, he did not calculate on so vigorous a resistance both without and within the walls. Indeed, the determination to reduce Paris by famine seems to have been taken more from a dread lest European

HOTEL DE CLUNY.

opinion should become actively hostile to any attempt to reduce
the city by force of arms than from any feeling of humanity; for
elsewhere, though the soldiers of the Fatherland were kept under
the most rigid discipline, their leaders adopted measures which, in
the majority of instances, fell not a whit short of barbarous outrage.
The burning of the village of Bazeilles, near Sedan, was one of the
most inhuman acts that stain the annals of war; and however
much irritation may have been caused by the attacks of bands of
irregular soldiers, who, under the name of Franc-tireurs, kept up a
sort of guerilla warfare of the most savage kind against outposts
and scouting and foraging parties of the invaders, and however
much they may have been entitled to treat such assailants, when
caught, with severity, they had neither moral nor military right to
treat the general inhabitants in the manner they very often did.
However much the civilized world may be inclined to reprobate
bands of armed men lurking under cover and shooting down their
enemies in cowardly fashion, it certainly will be always inclined
to sympathize with the right of the people of an invaded country
to fight for their homes in open warfare, whether the combatants be
organized or unorganized.   In their efforts to put down this, the
Germans announced their intention, which was rigidly carried out,
of exacting a heavy fine from any place that offered resistance to
occupation by their advancing armies, and their system of " requisi-
tioning " — that is, demanding supplies or anything else they
wished, and taking them without any compensation — prevailed to
a degree and in a manner that made it exactly a system of organized plunder.   Such was the terror that their measures caused in
the earlier part of the war, that one or two troops of their light
cavalry (Uhlans) could ride into almost any town, and obtain its surrender without the slightest resistance.   "At Dourdan," says one
account, " five Prussian Hussars dashed into the railway station,
cut the telegraph wires, and then came to the place, pistol in hand,
and insolently demanded eight hundred rations from the mayor; and
a thousand stupid men stood there on the market-place of Dourdan,
bowing their uncovered heads before five Prussian youths, the old-

est of whom was not thirty! While these five pillagers scoured the adjacent communes, the municipality of Dourdan, with a zeal and activity which had never been shown in favor of our French soldiers, hastened to provide for the requisitions of the following day. Nothing was spared to feed the enemy sumptuously. At St. Arnould, fifty Uhlans condescended to do honor to a banquet served in the market-place. The mayor superintended the waiting, a napkin under his arm."

The news of the fall of Orleans had, when communicated by Count Moltke to the Government of National Defence in Paris, caused fresh discussion of the question of peace; but, on the advice of General Trochu, it was decided to maintain the struggle, as the mere fact of the Germans showing themselves anxious to renew negotiations was a proof that their situation was critical, especially when it was considered that the depth of winter was fast approaching an army poorly sheltered, and in the midst of a hostile country. That the situation towards the end of December, when the fresh levy was called for, and very severe weather set in, was critical cannot be questioned; and when the bombardment was at last decided on, it was no doubt deemed necessary for the very safety of the besieging forces. Large stores of siege materials had been accumulated, and powerful Krupp guns, with their munitions, had been sent to the front by trainfuls at a time. The first position attacked was a work erected on the northeast since the beginning of the siege on Mont Avron. The bombardment began on the 27th December; the defence was reduced to silence the following day, the garrison being unable to stand the heavy cross fire poured in on them from works constructed in ground frozen six inches deep, and carefully masked till the moment they were ready to act; and on the 29th the position was occupied by the Germans, and immediately used as a point of vantage from which to carry on attack against the forts of Rosny and Le Nogent.

Thus gloomily did the year close, which had seen France defeated and humiliated on all hands. The emperor himself was a prisoner, and two large armies, with four marshals, and generals and inferior officers without number, had been forced to yield themselves to the invaders, who had also succeeded in taking possession of a large number of fortified places. Besides Metz and Strasburg, Verdun, Neu Brisach, Thionville, La Fère, Phalsburg, and Montmédy had all passed from the French, and the country was, in spite of the most dogged resistance, practically overrun as far south as Orleans. Paris was beginning to suffer greatly. Food had for long been doled out in quantities far from abundant. Horse-flesh had long been familiar to the Parisians, but now such untried food was resorted to as the flesh of donkeys, cats, dogs, rats, and even mice. Numbers of the animals in the Jardin d'Acclimatation were killed and used as food. "The worst kind of butter cost about ten shillings a pound; a cabbage from one to two shillings. There was no veal. Beef and mutton might be had doled out in very small quantities to those who were content to go and wait patiently for an hour or two till their turn came. Donkey cost from three and sixpence to five shillings a pound; eggs were sixpence each; milk was scarcely to be had." There was, however, still a large supply of horse-flesh, of salt meat, of bread, and of spirits. The death-rate had more than doubled. The Red Republicans were in a state of angry ferment, and the discontent with government action, or rather inaction, was by no means confined to the always turbulent Belleville quarter. The great "plan" of General Trochu had never become apparent, and faith in its practicability, if not in its very existence, had seized on all minds, excepting perhaps that of the General himself. The heavy and useless cannonade from the forts that introduced the new year seemed rather the petulant outburst of disappointed defiance than the sign of grim determination and power of resistance. The superior power of the German fire soon became apparent, and by the 12th of January the forts on the east and south sides of Paris had been silenced, and the works of the besieging armies pushed forward so as to be within range of the city itself, and to be able to pour into it a storm of shot and shell.

Equal want of success followed the French arms elsewhere. The Army of the North, under General Faidherbe, had been severely defeated by the German forces under General Göben. General Chanzy, after his retreat upon Le Mans, had succeeded in reorganizing his forces, and at length fancied himself strong enough to resume the offensive. He accordingly despatched to the Prussian commander at Vendôme a document of a tenor unparalleled in modern warfare, in which he informed the German authorities that they were robbers and devastators, who, having defeated him once, had since persistently lied in the face of Europe, and said that they had always defeated him, and wound up by telling them that his army was now ready. Let the Germans come out and they would settle this quarrel. It is highly improbable that this insolent production had any effect on the plans at the Prussian headquarters; but his challenge was answered by the short but brilliant campaign of Le Mans, which, when we consider that the operations were undertaken in the dead of winter, in a country thoroughly known to the defenders, and that the advance had to be accomplished over roads so covered with ice that the cavalry had to dismount and lead their horses, must certainly be regarded as one of the most splendid achievements of German discipline and perseverance that the whole war affords.

The German army, under the command of Prince Frederick Charles and the Duke of Mecklenburg, that had formerly checkmated and destroyed D'Aurelle's movement to the aid of Paris, began again to advance on the 3d of January. From the 6th to the 12th they were constantly engaged with Chanzy's forces between Vendôme and Le Mans, and notwithstanding the opposition, a country covered with snow, and roads that were sheets of ice, were able to push steadily forward, and at the battle of Le Mans on the 11th and 12th the French were utterly beaten, and fell back on Laval in such confusion that it was certain that the army of investment round Paris would have no more to fear from this quarter for a long time to come.

In his operations Chanzy had not calculated on having to cope with the whole of the German forces in that quarter, for he trusted that General Bourbaki, with the second portion of the former Army

of the Loire, would be able, from the positions he occupied about
Bourges, to keep the left wing under Prince Frederick Charles fully
occupied. Bourbaki had determined on a very bold stroke, and
one which, had it been carried out as skilfully as it was planned,
might even at this supreme moment have materially altered the
state of affairs. Starting on the 5th of January, and succeeding in
giving his movements a secrecy rare in French operations throughout the war, he left a part of his army at Bourges, and marched
eastward with the rest with the intention of cutting off Werder
(who was stationed at Vesoul for the purpose of covering the troops
engaged in the siege of Belfort), pushing him back into the valley
of the Rhine, obtaining command of the Paris and Strasburg railway, and so interrupting the German line of communications. His
troops were, however, ill equipped, and advanced but slowly; and
though he attacked Werder on the 9th, and compelled him to fall
back, he was unable to prevent him from forming a junction with
the besiegers of Belfort under General Treschkow, and such was the
condition of his men that, though they numbered one hundred and
thirty thousand, and were opposed by only about forty thousand
Germans, they were, after three days' fighting — from the 14th to
the 17th of January — compelled to retreat.

At Paris, on the 13th, another sortie had taken place, directed
against Le Bourget, but it was at all times feeble, and resulted
merely in fresh loss of life. It was followed on the 19th by the
most vigorous effort that the garrison had made since Trochu had
thrown away his opportunity in the beginning of December. The
point selected for the effort was on the west side of the city, with
Mont Valérien — the strongest of the Parisian forts — in the centre
of the line of attack. Upwards of one hundred thousand troops were
to act at the different points under the command of Generals Vinoy,
Bellamare, and Ducrot, with Trochu himself to direct the whole
operations. Vinoy's attack was successful, the Prussians were
driven back, and Montretout and St. Cloud were captured. Bellamare, after stiff fighting, was also successful, and effected his junction with Vinoy, but Ducrot suffered a check—only recovered when

the French brought into action a travelling battery, composed of an armor-plated steam-engine furnished with swivel-guns — which ruined the success of the action. The German supports came up, and the garrison was driven back, and by the time darkness set in the investing army had recovered all its lost positions. An application was at once made for an armistice for forty-eight hours, but it was refused without any hesitation, and Trochu resigned the military command into the hands of General Vinoy.

After this crowning disaster the mutterings of Belleville once more passed into action. On the 21st a mob from that quarter forced their way into the prison of Mazas and set free all the political prisoners, including Flourens, who had been placed in confinement for his share in some of the earlier tumults of the Reds since the siege commenced, and the disturbance thus begun terminated in a determined struggle between the mob and detachments of the National Guards. The outbreak was suppressed, but it was the beginning of the end. In spite of a previous reduction of rations, it was now found that the supplies left would hold out only for about a week; and on the 23d M. Jules Favre, sadly changed from the man who announced the determination of France not to cede "an inch of her territory or a stone of her fortresses," once more sought an interview with Count Bismarck. The German Prime Minister still refused to recognize the authority of the Provisional Government, and would only consent to treat as a means of bringing about the meeting of a National Assembly. The negotiations thus begun went on for six days, and on the evening of the 28th the terms of the capitulation of Paris were signed. The armistice was to begin at once at Paris and elsewhere at the end of three days, except in the district about Belfort; it was to last for three weeks; Paris was to pay a contribution of two hundred million francs within a fortnight; the troops of the line and the Mobiles were to be disarmed and interned in Paris as prisoners of war, with the exception of twelve thousand under General Vinoy, who were to retain their arms and maintain order; prisoners were to be exchanged; as soon as the arms were delivered up the city was to be allowed to procure provisions; the forts were to be surrendered, and were to receive Prussian garrisons; the armies in the field (always excepting those near Belfort) were to retain possession of their positions, with a neutral zone intervening between them; an Assembly with full powers was to be summoned to meet at Bordeaux at once. Another stipulation was afterwards made at the particular request of M. Favre, and in spite of the urgent warnings — all too well founded — of Count Bismarck as to the possible danger of the plan, viz., that the National Guard should also retain their arms and undertake the preservation of order in the city. "This," said the German Emperor, "is the first blessed reward of patriotism, heroism, and heavy sacrifices. I thank God for this fresh mercy. May peace soon follow!"

So ended the siege of Paris, and practically the war, for it now only remains to follow the movements of the army on the Swiss frontier under Bourbaki, which had been excepted from the operation of the armistice that the Germans might crown the desperate plight in which it was by reducing it to utter ruin. Bourbaki had no sooner begun his retreat than he was followed by Werder, and also by forces under Manteuffel, which had been specially despatched by Von Moltke to Werder's assistance. The French communications in the direction of Besançon were cut by Manteuffel on the 23d. After two days of inactivity and indecision, of marches and counter-marches, the French attempted to retreat in the direction of Pontarlier, only to find that they had been again outmarched and cut off. Completely hemmed in, they were forced, on the 1st of February, to retreat into Switzerland, where they were disarmed by the Swiss authorities and interned; and we need hardly wonder at their want of success against the foe, however much inferior in numbers, if we consider the relative *morale*, discipline, and equipment of the opponents.

The condition of the French soldiers when they entered Switzerland has been thus described: "Hundreds of poor fellows, their uniforms torn to rags, limped past. The feet and hands of nearly all were frost-bitten, causing the greatest pain. On many a face incipient fever had begun its ravages; many would never march again. In all, the shrunk features and crouching gait told of gnawing hunger, while the deep cough and hoarse voice bore witness to long nights spent on snow and frozen ground. Some had tied bits of wood under their bare feet to protect them from the stones; others wore wooden *sabots;* hundreds had nb socks, and when they had they were merely of thin cotton; others who appeared well shod would show a toeless or heelless boot, the exposed part of the foot, once frozen, being now a wound crusted with dirt. For weeks none had washed, or changed their clothes, or removed their boots. Nothing but hurried march and counter-march. Their hands were blacker than any African's. Some had lost their toes, the limbs of others were so frozen that every movement was agony. The men stated that for three days they had had neither food nor fodder served out to them, and that before that they often got only one loaf between eight men." With such a force as this, and such organization, the wonder is not that Bourbaki did not accomplish more, but that he ever moved at all. It was a second retreat from Moscow.

CHAPTER XXIV.

FEELING OUTSIDE PARIS. — M. GAMBETTA. — HIS BORDEAUX PROCLA-
MATION. — CONFLICT WITH CENTRAL AUTHORITY. — ELECTION OF THE
NATIONAL ASSEMBLY. — ACCESSION OF M. THIERS TO POWER. — THE
TERMS OF PEACE. — PRELIMINARIES RATIFIED BY THE ASSEMBLY. —
DISAFFECTION AMONG THE NATIONAL GUARD AND THE REPUBLI-
CANS. — THE COMMUNE. — THE SECOND SIEGE OF PARIS. — COMMU-
NIST SALLY. — BITTER FEELING BETWEEN THE ARMIES. — CONDUCT
OF SIEGE OPERATIONS. — ROSSEL. — ENTRANCE OF THE VERSAILLES
ARMY INTO PARIS. — EXCESSES OF THE COMMUNE. — RATIFICATION
OF THE TREATY OF PEACE. — OPENING OF THE CHAMBER. — THREAT-
ENED RESIGNATION OF M. THIERS. — SCHEMES OF PARTIES. — ARMY
REORGANIZATION. — FINANCIAL SCHEMES. — THE CONSERVATIVE RE-
PUBLIC. — SUCCESS OF THE NEW LOAN. — OPENING OF THE NEW
SESSION. — FRESH CRISIS. — THE YEAR 1873. — DEATH OF THE EX-
EMPEROR. — LIMITATION OF PRESIDENTIAL POWERS. — FINAL WITH-
DRAWAL OF GERMAN TROOPS. — RESIGNATION OF M. GRÉVY. —
MINISTERIAL CHANGES. — DEFEAT AND RESIGNATION OF M. BUFFET'S
MINISTRY. — RESIGNATION OF M. THIERS. — CAUSES OF HIS FALL. —
ELECTION OF MARSHAL MACMAHON AS PRESIDENT. — INTENTIONS OF
THE MONARCHICAL PARTY. — IMPORTANT DECLARATION OF THE COMTE
DE CHAMBORD.

THAT the struggle of France to cast out the invader who had
fastened on the country such a heavy hand had lasted so long,
was entirely due to the energetic action of M. Gambetta; and,
indeed, had he been able to have his way, the contest would have
been still further prolonged, nay, it would have been maintained so
long as any portion of territory remained unoccupied by the Ger-

mans. Such, too, was the power his strong individuality had acquired
over the minds of the French, that, though his plans failed at every
turn, he never lost the confidence and support of the people. All
the great cities of the South were at one with him when he issued
a proclamation purporting to represent the views of the Delegate
Government at Bordeaux, and denouncing the action of the main
government in no measured terms. " Unknown to us," said he,
" without informing us, and without consulting us, an armistice has
been signed, of which we have but too late learned the guilty
thoughtlessness, which surrenders to the Prussian troops departments occupied by our soldiers, and imposes upon us the obligation
to remain inactive for three weeks in order to convoke a National
Assembly in the sad circumstances in which our country finds itself.
We have demanded an explanation from Paris, and have kept silence
while awaiting the promised arrival of a member of the government . . . . Nobody, however, has come from Paris, and we must
act, and at any price upset the perfidious calculations of the enemies
of France." He also issued a decree that no member of any of the
families that had at any time reigned in France, and that no Minister, Senator, Prefect, or official candidate for a seat in the Legislative Body during the reign of Napoleon III., should be eligible for
election to the new National Assembly. To this objection was
taken by Count Bismarck, and M. Jules Simon was despatched to
Bordeaux to reassert the power of the government proper. Such,
however, was the state of public feeling that M. Simon dared not
show himself in the streets ; and the Paris government, adopting
stronger measures, both issued a decree declaring that Gambetta's
proclamation was " null and void," and that their own former
decrees — which merely excluded members of any family that had
reigned in France from becoming candidates — must be "maintained
in their integrity," and sent MM. Arago, Garnier Pagès, and Eugène
Pelletan to Bordeaux to enforce their authority. M. Gambetta
then gave way and resigned, M. Arago becoming Minister of War.
At the same time the government issued a long official explanation
of the reasons for the surrender of Paris. It gave a detailed account

THE BATTLE OF MONTMIRAIL.

of the sufferings of the city, and the wretched condition to which it had been reduced; of their efforts, when further resistance was vain, to obtain the best possible terms; and then enumerated reasons why the decree issued by the Delegate Government should be set aside. "We regard," it said in concluding, "principles as superior to expedients. We do not wish that the first decree of convocation of the Republican Assembly in 1871 should be an act of mistrust directed against the electors. To them belongs the sovereignty; let them exercise it without weakness, and the country may be saved. The Government of the National Defence regrets then and annuls, if it should be necessary, the decree illegally issued by the Delegation at Bordeaux, and it calls upon all Frenchmen to vote without ostracism for the representatives who may appear to them to be the worthiest of France."

The elections took place all over France in the first week of February, and resulted in the return of an Assembly of a highly conservative nature, although it contained a strong radical minority, sent by the large cities. The disasters up to Sedan had brought discredit on the Imperialists, the disasters since Sedan had brought discredit on the Republicans, and the majority of the Deputies proved to be Legitimists, though the political life of that party had been supposed to be utterly gone. That the majority of the members were worthy of France was apparent from the abuse heaped on them by the anarchists; Flourens describing them as "a collection of bald heads, deaf ears, and eyes which blinked at any ray of sunlight." No French Legislative Body since 1789 had contained so many men of rank and position; and such was the pacific character of the Chamber which met on the 12th of February that the German authorities granted a renewal of the armistice from the 13th to the 24th of the month. As soon as the Assembly was opened the Government of National Defence resigned into its hands the power they held, and declared that it was their intention merely to hold office till successors should be appointed. M. Grévy was appointed President, and on the 17th the Deputies proceeded to appoint a Chief of the Executive Power. Without a single dissentient voice the whole of France turned to one man as the only statesman who was able to fill the post and cope successfully with the difficulties of the position. This was M. Thiers. The veteran statesman accepted the office and selected a ministry, of whom the leading members were M. Dufaure, Minister of Justice; M. Jules Favre, Minister of Foreign Affairs; M. Picard, Minister of the Interior; M. Jules Simon, Minister of Public Instruction; and General Le Flô, Minister of War. Constitutional questions could not be decided upon till peace was concluded, and to the task of settling terms the new government now devoted itself. MM. Thiers, Jules Favre, and Picard were to conduct negotiations, and a committee of fifteen Deputies was appointed to proceed to Paris with them to assist in their deliberations, and share in the responsibility of the peace.

Negotiations were begun on the 22d, and the Germans, wearied by what they considered unnecessary delay in coming to a definite settlement, then announced their intention not to prolong the armistice, if matters were not settled, beyond the 26th. The result was that M. Thiers, wisely seeing that a renewal of the war was a thing not to be thought of, refrained from continuing to attempt the impossible any longer, and determined to accept the terms offered by the Germans, hard and almost intolerable as these were. The preliminaries of peace, which were signed on the 26th of February, were to the effect that the whole of Alsace except Belfort, and a fifth part of Lorraine, including Metz and Thionville, were to be given up to Germany, a delay being granted to admit of the inhabitants of the annexed territories choosing between the two nationalities; France was, in the course of the next three years, to pay to Germany as an indemnity for war expenses the sum of two hundred millions of pounds sterling, with interest at five per cent from the date of the ratification of the treaty; prisoners of war were to be set at liberty; the Germans were to have no rights in the portions of territory not occupied by them; the departments occupied by German troops were to be administered by French officials, who were, however, to be controlled by the

German authorities; the evacuation of territory was to be gradual, and in proportion to the payment of the indemnity; the treaty was to be ratified by the National Assembly, and, immediately after, negotiations for a Treaty of Peace were to be opened at Brussels; a portion of the German army was for three days to occupy a certain part of Paris.

No sooner were the terms known than a cry of indignation arose against the government; excited crowds occupied the streets of Paris, and the National Guards marched about calling for vengeance. But the rage wore itself out. MM. Thiers and Picard issued a proclamation, urging calm self-restraint; all the journals tendered the same advice, and it was determined that during the time of the occupation the city should assume an appearance of deep mourning, and refuse to hold communication with the army of occupation.

The debate in the Assembly on the acceptance of the preliminaries of peace began on the 1st of March and seemed to excite deep emotion throughout the country as well as at Bordeaux, the immediate scene of action; but real debate there could be none. "If you refuse," said the report of the Commission of Assembly sent to Paris to assist the negotiators, "if you refuse to accept these preliminaries, Paris is occupied, and the whole of France will be invaded; and God only knows what disasters will ensue." This was the statement of a fact that was clear enough to the great majority, and the opposition, led by Victor Hugo and Louis Blanc, was useful rather as a safety-valve for public feeling than as being of any real importance. The preliminaries were accepted in a house of six hundred and fifty-three members by a majority of more than five to one. On the 3d of March the German army of occupation — which had been in the assigned part of the city since the 1st — marched off through the Arc de Triomphe, and on the 7th the German headquarters were moved from Versailles. The great Franco-Prussian War was over.

After all the months of bloodshed and disaster that had fallen to the lot of France, it might be imagined that the country would have thankfully accepted the peace that had been obtained, and that all classes would have devoted themselves to the re-establishment of order and to the development of the resources of the country, to meet the fresh burdens that had been imposed on it. This was the proper course, and gladly would the country have adopted it; but before that peace could be attained, the country had yet to suffer from the so-called patriots of the Red Republicans worse outrage than it had endured at the hands of the German invaders.

When the negotiations for the capitulation of Paris were in progress, Count Bismarck had warned M. Favre of the danger of allowing, as he proposed, the National Guard to retain their arms; and the members of the Government of National Defence might themselves have seen the risk they were incurring, had they calmly considered the various *émeutes* that had taken place during the siege, and in which the National Guard had always played such a conspicuous part on the side of disaffection. Now, in the full consciousness of their strength — somewhere about one hundred thousand — and in their possession of a powerful artillery, — for during the German occupation they had, on the pretext of keeping them safe, got a large number of cannon into their hands, — they seemed determined to attempt the revival of the Reign of Terror. Whatever may have been the reasons that influenced the rank and file, — and probably the loss of the pay of a franc and a half per day which they had been receiving during the time of their embodiment was a consideration that weighed powerfully with them, — the designs of the leaders under whom they acted were unquestionably political and revolutionary.

The appointment of General d'Aurelle de Paladines as their commander gave great offence, and on the 9th March an attempt to place the tricolor on the column in the Place de la Bastille instead of the red flag of revolution led to an outbreak. A promise, in the event of the cannon being given up, of the continuance of pay till "ordinary work was resumed," was disregarded, and the dismissal of D'Aurelle and the full recognition of the right of the National Guard to elect its own officers demanded. An effort of the government to seize the cannon in the Place des Vosges failed, and it was now clear enough that more energetic action than negotiations must take place. On the morning of the 18th March a large force of regular troops under Generals Vinoy and Lecomte proceeded to Montmartre and took possession of the guns; but the want of horses for their immediate removal gave time for the Reds to assemble and frustrate the effort, while, worst of all, a large number of the regular troops fraternized with the insurgents. General Lecomte and General Clément Thomas were taken prisoners and almost immediately shot. The outbreak, thus begun, spread rapidly; for, through some unaccountable timidity of the government, the government forces were withdrawn from the city, and the insurgents left free to act as they pleased. They seized General Chanzy at the Orleans railway station, took possession of the Ministry of Justice and the Hôtel de Ville, and threw up barricades round all the revolutionary quarters. The Central Committee of the National Guard, the leading man of which was Assi, a member of the International Society and the organizer of the strike at the Creuzot ironworks, summoned the people of Paris to meet "in their comitia for the communal elections," and declared their intention of resigning their power into the hands of the Commune thus chosen.

The National Assembly removed from Bordeaux and held its sittings at Versailles; but bitter as was the feeling of the majority of the Deputies against the new turbulence, the position of affairs prevented any action from being taken against the insurgents. The removal of General d'Aurelle and the appointment of Admiral Saisset in his place was of no avail. A number of the inhabitants of Paris, styling themselves "Men of Order," attempted to influence affairs by a display of moral force, but they were fired on and dispersed. The Assembly was timid, and apparently quite unable to bring its troops into play. After the fraternization that had already taken place, the military authorities distrusted their forces, and were afraid to lead the soldiers at their command against the National Guard. Through Admiral Saisset concessions were offered, but the demands of the Communists increased with the prospect of obtain-

ing anything. They now modestly demanded that they should su-
persede the Assembly wherever there was any prospect of collision
of power, and be allowed to control the finances; and as a very
natural consequence the negotiations were abandoned. This was
on the 25th March, and on the 26th the Commune was elected, the
victory of the Reds being very easily gained, as hardly any of those
opposed to them voted. Two days afterwards the Commune was
proclaimed at the Hôtel de Ville, the members who had been elected
being seated on a platform in red arm-chairs. The leading man of
the new system was the honest but hot-headed and utopian Delescluze; Cluseret, a man of considerable military genius, who had
led a life of a very wild nature in America, and who was the soul
of the resistance when the actual fighting began, was Delegate of
War; Grousset, of Foreign Affairs; and Rigault, of Public Safety.
The new government applied itself vigorously to changes; conscription was abolished, and the authority of the Versailles government declared " null and void."

Seeing that a desperate struggle must inevitably ensue, a very
large number of the inhabitants of Paris quitted the city, and the
German authorities allowed the prisoners from Metz and Sedan to
return so as to swell the forces at the disposal of M. Thiers. They
also intimated that, in view of the altered circumstances, it might
again become necessary for them to occupy the forts they had
already evacuated. The first shot in the second siege of Paris, in
which Frenchmen were arrayed against Frenchmen, was fired on the
2d April, when a strong division of the Versailles army advanced
against the National Guards posted at Courbevoie, and drove them
into Paris across the Pont de Neuilly. During the ensuing night a
large force of insurgents gathered, and were on the morning of the
3d led in three columns against Versailles. Great hopes had been
placed on the sympathy of the regular troops, but they were doomed
to disappointment. The right wing, advancing by Buzenval, met
in front by General Vinoy and taken on the flank by cavalry under
the Marquis de Gallifet, was dispersed in confusion,—a confusion
seriously increased by the heavy fire poured into their ranks from

Mont Valérien as they returned to Paris. The central column, operating towards Meudon, had no better success, for they broke and retired as soon as they came under fire. The left wing, under General Duval, one of the leading spirits of the Commune, advancing by Châtillon, had some slight success, though this arose more from the forbearance of their opponents than from any exertions of their own; and on the following day they too were, in spite of reinforcements, again driven into Paris across the Pont de Neuilly. The expedition had not only failed, but it had cost the Commune two of its leading men,—Duval, and that Flourens who had already made himself so conspicuous in connection with revolutionary outbreaks under the Empire and the Government of National Defence, —both of whom were taken and promptly shot by the Versailles authorities. The failure and the executions proved so exasperating that the "Commune of Paris" issued a proclamation denouncing the Versailles soldiers as banditti, and the execution of prisoners as murder. "The Government of Versailles," it said, "is acting against the laws of warfare and humanity, and we shall be compelled to make reprisals. . . . . The people, even in its anger, detests bloodshed as it detests civil war, but it is its duty to protect itself against the savage attempts of its enemies, and whatever it may cost it shall be an eye for an eye, a tooth for a tooth." The fate of Generals Clément Thomas and Lecomte not unnaturally suggested the apprehension that this was probably no empty threat; and they had ample means of gratifying their passion for revenge, for they had in their hands a number of leading men, including Darboy, Archbishop of Paris, and M. Bonjean, President of the Court of Cassation, and these—two hundred in all—they proclaimed their intention of holding as hostages.

M. Thiers was still hesitating, and waiting for a force sufficiently powerful to crush all opposition; and in this he was no doubt right, for any success of the Communists, even of the most temporary character, would have proved highly dangerous. The Germans had granted permission to the government to increase their original thirty thousand troops to one hundred and fifty thousand, and prisoners of Metz and Sedan had been pouring steadily back from Germany for this purpose.   On the 8th April Marshal MacMahon took command of the forces at Versailles.   A premature attack on the forts of Issy, Vanves, and Montrouge on the 11th failed, but on the 17th and 19th several of the insurgent positions were carried; on the 25th the bombardment of Issy and Vanves was begun, and from that time onwards operations against the city were carried on with the greatest activity, the insurgents being on all occasions put to the sword in a most merciless manner.   Issy was taken on the 8th May, and Vanves on the 4th, and the *enceinte* laid bare.

Inside Paris all this time there was nothing but jealousy.   To use the words of M. Rochefort, who ought to have been in a position to know the truth, "It is neither dread of the Prussians nor of the shells of M. Thiers which enervates Paris and kills our hopes; it is gaunt suspicion that weighs us down."   First one leader, and then another, was tried, found wanting, and disgraced.   Assi fell and was imprisoned; Delescluze was dismissed from office; Cluseret, who had done such faithful service to the cause by the manner in which he had organized the defence, was also thrown into prison after the capture of Issy, and his place was taken by a young engineer officer named Rossel who had served under Bazaine, who was, according to own statement, drawn into this treason, because he deemed that the government, by making terms with the foe, had lost all claim to his allegiance, and because he imagined that the Revolutionary party could alone bring about the most earnest desire of his heart, — the expulsion of the Prussians from France.   Rossel in turn had hardly been five days in office as Delegate of War when he resigned, intimating in his letter of resignation that, hampered as he was by the weakness of his colleagues of the Commune, he had to withdraw or make himself a dictator.   Delescluze was again chosen to take office and to succeed him, but the accession of a civilian to military power was, amid such divided counsels, but a last resort.

On the 21st May the defenders of the wall at the gate of St. Cloud were driven from their positions by the heavy artillery fire,

INSURRECTION IN ST. MARY'S CLOISTER.

and the besieging army, having become aware of the fact, pushed
forward and secured this entrance to the city; and by the evening
of the 22d there were eighty thousand Versaillists within the walls.
Next day they gained fresh ground, and were ready to re-occupy
the Tuileries and the Hôtel de Ville; but before this was possible
the Communists, mad with despair, had resolved on that series of
outrages against humanity that will make their names detested and
their cause distrusted as long as the story of their crimes stands
recorded in the annals of history. They had already perpetrated
more than one act of vandalism worthy of the severest reprobation
and censure. They had early in May confiscated the funds of the
International Society for Aid to the Wounded in order to provide
pay for their soldiers; on the 12th May, in accordance with a public decree, they had destroyed the private residence of M. Thiers
with all its pictures and books; on the 16th the magnificent column erected in the Place Vendôme in memory of Napoleon I., and
crowned by his statue, was undermined at one side and then pulled
to the ground by means of ropes and utterly destroyed; and now
on the 24th, in the last efforts of despairing rage, bands of men and
women, still more frantic and eager for blood than were those of the
Reign of Terror, rushed through the doomed city. Early in the
morning the Tuileries, the Hôtel de Ville, the Ministry of Finance,
the Palais d'Orsay, and other public and private buildings were
seen to be on fire. The Louvre, too, with all its inestimable treasures, was in flames, and was saved with the greatest difficulty. If
the Commune was to perish, it had clearly resolved that the city
was to perish with it. Men and women marched about in bands
with petroleum, and aided the spread of the conflagration by firing
the city in different places.

Heedless of the flames, the Versailles troops pressed on, eager, if
possible, to save the lives of the two hundred hostages, but, alas, in
vain. A passion for blood had seized on the Commune, and its last
expiring effort was to murder in cold blood, not only a large number of the hostages, but also batches of fresh victims, seized indis-
criminately about the streets by bands of men and women, and

dragged off to instant death. On the 26th Belleville was captured, and on the 27th and 28th the Cemetery of Père la Chaise was the scene of the final struggle, — a struggle of such a desperate nature — for there was no quarter — that, for days after, the air of the district was literally fraught with pestilence. Many of the leaders of the Commune had fallen in the final contest, and all the others who were captured by the Versailles troops during the fighting were at once shot. Of the thirty thousand prisoners who had fallen into the hands of the government, a large number, both men and women, were executed without mercy, and the rest distributed in various prisons to await trial, as also were Rossel, Assi, Grousset, and others, who were captured after the resistance was at an end. Cluseret succeeded in making good his escape. Much as we may deprecate and condemn the severity and ferocity of the executions that stained the immediate triumph of order, some allowance must be made for the feelings of those who had obtained their victory in the midst of the flames or blackened ruins of the French capital.

Of the prisoners, about ten thousand were set free without trial, and the others were sentenced by various courts-martial during the following months and on through the coming year, either to death, transportation, or imprisonment. Rossel, as a soldier who had broken his oath, and Ferré, the instigator of the murder of the hostages, were executed, as was also Verdaguer, the officer in command of the Guards who had murdered Generals Thomas and Lecomte. Rochefort was sentenced to transportation.

During these events at Paris the Assembly at Versailles had on the 18th ratified the Treaty of Peace, which had been signed at Frankfort on the 10th May, and had subsequently shown its monarchical tendencies by the repeal of the laws prohibiting the Bourbons from entering France. The Budget was brought in, and, with a deficit of six hundred millions of francs, besides a deficit of over one thousand millions brought forward from the previous year, did not look very promising; but, on the other hand, a new national loan was readily and largely subscribed, so much so that the government was able to anticipate the dates of payment of the war indemnity, and so to "hasten the deliverance of the country." In the rearrangement of taxation required to meet the fresh burdens of the country, M. Thiers and the Minister of Finance, M. Pouyer-Quertier, showed a hankering after protection by proposing the imposition of taxes on raw material; but these proposals were thrown out. On the 22d July a discussion arose on the position of the Pope, which led to the resignation of M. Jules Favre, who was succeeded by M. Charles Rémusat. In the beginning of September a resolution was passed declaring M. Thiers President of the Republic until the dissolution of the Assembly, with power to appoint his own ministers, and permission to appear from time to time in the Assembly if he saw fit, but only on due notice being given. M. Thiers was very desirous that the Assembly should return to Paris, but a large majority decided on a permanent settlement at Versailles; and at length, on the 17th September, the Deputies adjourned to meet again on the 4th December. Money for the payment of the war indemnity had come in so rapidly that by the end of October only six out of the original thirty-six departments held by the Germans remained in their hands. But the attainment of this must have cost Thiers a hard struggle, for he had, before he could obtain Bismarck's consent to the wished-for change, to grant what was practically free trade to Alsace and German Lorraine; and to such a stubborn protectionist as the French President was this must have been gall and wormwood. He, however, soothed his troubled feelings on the point by giving notice to the English government of the intention to terminate the Treaty of Commerce with England, unless an increase of the duties on cotton and mixed fabrics were agreed to.

The opening of the Chamber on the 4th December was followed by stormy scenes over the admission of the Orleanist Princes to seats in the Assembly, which they were, however, in the end allowed to occupy. M. Thiers's Presidential message, which he read on the 7th, disappointed all parties except the Centre Right and the Centre Left. It announced the intention of the government to annul the Commercial Treaty with England, to propose compulsory service in time of war, and to make an annual levy in time of peace of ninety thousand men chosen by lot. Questions of taxation again came up, and when the year closed it left France trying to face the problem how best to impose taxes so as to raise nearly two hundred and fifty millions of francs of additional revenue.

When the Assembly met after the Christmas recess on the 3d January, fresh discussions on the Budget took place, and the imposition of taxes on raw materials was anew brought forward, and pressed, not only by M. Pouyer-Quertier, but by M. Thiers himself, in a long and — from his point of view — an able speech; but not only was the proposal again strongly opposed in the Chamber itself, but all the great manufacturing towns sent deputies to Versailles to protest earnestly and angrily against the adoption of the proposal. The matter was, after a debate which lasted for eighteen days, referred to a committee, and M. Thiers at once took the course which he had threatened several times before, and which he had always kept hanging over a refractory Assembly, — he next day announced his resignation. There was, however, no statesman of eminence on whom France could so rely, or who could at this moment conduct the affairs of the state with the prestige that belonged to the veteran historian of the First Consulate; and though the Right would probably have gladly accepted a change, and were even prepared to nominate Marshal MacMahon for the vacant post of President, all parties united in urging on M. Thiers his resumption of office, and to this he ultimately assented. The debate on the Treaty of Commerce with England resulted more to his liking, for it was decided by a large majority that "the government be authorized to give notice of withdrawal in convenient time from the treaties with England and Belgium."

Those favorable to the return of the Assembly to Paris, undaunted by the former rejection of the proposal by a very large majority, brought forward a fresh motion on the subject in the beginning of February; but it was again decided against them, and M. Casimir-Périer took advantage of the adverse decision to resign his post as Minister of the Interior, and thus to quit a government with the opinions of whose head he had so little in common. The Assembly, though it claimed constituent powers, had as yet settled nothing as to the form of government. It had found a Republic when it came into existence, and it had indirectly recognized the Republic when it appointed M. Thiers President; but nothing further had been done, and it seemed as if the different parties were yet to have a struggle before the question of the form of government should be considered as settled. The Orleans representatives, the Duc d'Aumale and the Prince de Joinville, had taken their seats in the Assembly, but had not attempted in any way to bring themselves prominently into public notice. The Imperialists formed but a very small party, and were, after the recent fall of the Empire, and under the circumstances that accompanied it, looked on with but little sympathy; still they had not given themselves up to despair. The representative of the elder branch of the Bourbons, the Comte de Chambord, pushed forward his claims to the throne, but in an uncompromising manner that augured but ill for his success. The journals that supported the claims of the rival competitors had been writing so keenly in their favor, and attacking the existing government so violently, that in the end of February it was deemed necessary to take some action to limit their energy, and a bill was accordingly brought in by the new Minister of the Interior, M. Victor Lefranc, to enable the government " to prosecute and punish all attacks in the newspapers upon the rights and authority of the Assembly or the government." This was hailed as a proof that the President had resolved to maintain the Republic; but the note of jubilation was uttered too soon; the bill had not yet passed, and now the reactionary Right were so alarmed that the bill had to be postponed.

On the 4th March the Ministry suffered a heavy loss by the resignation of M. Pouyer-Quertier, who had given offence, and had been so vehemently attacked in the Chamber for his conduct in defending one of the former imperial prefects who had been accused of misapplication of public moneys, that he had no choice left but to quit his post.

After Easter, when the Deputies reassembled, there was a hot debate over the wretched condition of the military resources under the late years of the Empire, and at the outbreak of the war. M. Rouher, with the courage or effrontery that never failed the Imperialists, attempted to defend the Imperial *régime*, but was bitterly assailed by the Duc d'Audiffret Pasquier and by Gambetta. "You men of the light hearts," said the duke, "have we not the right to call out to you in the old phrase, 'Varus, Varus, give us back our legions!' Give us back our legions; give us back the glory of our sires; give us back our provinces!" "If you had arms," said M. Gambetta, "why those hasty contracts? If you had arms, why those forty-eight contracts in four days? If you had not arms, there is but one word,— you were traitors and thieves. . . . . The greatest idea of the last reign which caused all our disasters, and which makes us now bear that Imperial shame on our brow, was Mexico. . . . . Mexico clings to you, Mexico pursues you, Mexico has already executed justice on all those who compromised the honor and grandeur of the country in that detestable adventure. Yes; justice has commenced. It has seized in turn Morny, Jecker, Maximilian, and Napoleon III. It clutches Bazaine; it awaits you."

The great bill of the session, providing for the reorganization of the army, was to have come on immediately after Easter, but it had been delayed in consequence of negotiations which were going on with Germany about the evacuation of territory, and with which the violent language sure to be used when the army question was discussed might have seriously interfered. The bill was at length brought forward on the 27th May, and it was earnestly urged that, as the propositions it embodied had been determined on without regard to politics, and were the result of careful deliberations, they should be accepted without debate. Indeed, debate was very much dreaded, for the general opinion of the Assembly was in favor of compulsory universal short service, while M. Thiers was as strongly in favor of conscription and longer service, and there was considerable fear that there would be another deadlock, and that M. Thiers would resign. A compromise had, however, been arrived at, so that

universal service with certain exceptions was proposed, and the
period of service somewhat lengthened.   Notwithstanding this, the
advice to suppress debate was not adopted, and discussion went
on for three days.   General Trochu insisted strongly that France
should follow the example of Prussia.   The Duc d'Aumale, speaking
for the first time, approved generally of the bill, but while criticising
details pointed out that the late war had shown that no reliance was
to be placed on improvised troops.   The principle being settled, the
details of the bill were considered, and occupied the attention of the
Assembly till the 22d June.

From this time, almost continuously till the end of the session,
the Chamber was busy with financial matters.   The question of the
tax on raw materials again came to the front, for the committee
appointed earlier in the year to deal with the question had suggested
in its room a tax on securities, a tax on mortgages, and a tax on
business transactions, and the Finance Minister declared that even
the tax on raw materials would not give a sufficiently large sum so
long as France was hampered by Commercial Treaties.   M. Thiers,
however, was determined to carry his raw material tax, and by
skilful manipulation of the Budget there was brought out a larger
deficit than was actually the case, and to meet it there was no plan
suggested but an increase of the direct taxes, and of the duty on
salt.   Both of these were so unpopular that they were sure to be
rejected, and thus the President hoped to be able to say, " Well,
you have rejected everything else, you must accept the only remaining plan, and tax raw materials."   The opposition lasted till the 20th
July, when the pressing need of money overcame all scruples, and
the tax on raw materials was accepted.

Considerable discontent had existed for some time in consequence
of M. Thiers' reticence as to his intentions with regard to the form
of government to be adopted.   During the discussion on the Army
Bill the leaders of the Right and Right Centre had had an interview with him on the subject.   The President returned a vague and
unsatisfactory answer, but he now took advantage of one of the
discussions on the taxation question to announce his purpose of

maintaining to the best of his ability a Conservative Republic, a statement which excited vehement outcries of indignation among the Deputies of the Right, but which was received by the Left with cheers.

The new agreement with Germany which had been under discussion between the two governments at Easter was made public in July. It provided for earlier payment of the indemnity and for consequent earlier evacuation of territory by the German troops; and now, in order to provide the money, a fresh loan of three thousand five hundred millions of francs was raised. The result was a most triumphant success for the government. The French subscription alone amounted to twelve times the sum asked, while large amounts would have been taken by England and Germany if necessary. German financiers alone were willing to subscribe more than the whole amount.

After the adjournment of the Assembly in August the French political world became quiet, though the radical party expressed some discontent over the government prohibitions of banquets in celebration of the 4th September — the beginning of the era of the new Republic, — and in celebration of the 22d September — the beginning of the era of the First Republic; but the repose was rudely broken by a speech delivered by M. Gambetta at Grenoble on the 27th September. In it he complained bitterly of the repressive measures that still, under the new reign of liberty, debarred the people from enjoying the right of free public meeting, and declared that " electors and elected should have full liberty for the interchange of ideas." He complained, too, of the character of the present Assembly, and declared for " A new Assembly and new men." " You can do nothing," he said, " with those people at Versailles. We must have a new Assembly and new men, and return to Paris, the head and heart of Republican France." It was this passage, accompanied as it was with the assertion that the government must in future be guided by the wishes of a " lower social stratum," that caused all the alarm, as it was considered to point to an effort to place supremacy in the hands of the laboring and artisan classes.   The Right were at once in arms, and the speech was almost universally censured except by the extreme Republicans. The President himself expressed his disapprobation publicly, and declared that "there were no classes in France, but only the Nation."

The Assembly met on the 12th November, and next day M. Thiers delivered his presidential message, which dealt with finance, with the negotiations for a new Treaty of Commerce with England, and finally with the existence of the Republic and the necessity for the formulation of a proper constitution.   A long and stormy debate over Gambetta's speech at Grenoble terminated in a motion expressing confidence in the government and censure of M. Gambetta; but the government majority had been obtained with difficulty, and once more M. Thiers threatened resignation, but the crisis passed over wher the Right so far abandoned their monarchical desires as to recognize the Republic as the government *de facto* if not *de jure*. Extensive ministerial changes took place at the same time, caused in the first instance by the resignation of the Minister of the Interior, M. Victor Lefranc, who had been censured by the Assembly for receiving petitions in favor of dissolution from the Councils General, whose business is solely with municipal measures, and who are prohibited from taking official part in political matters.   The rest of the session was spent in disputes about the dissolution of the Chamber, and about the constitutional questions of the extent of M. Thiers's power, and the necessity for a Second Chamber, while justice was at last done to the house of Orleans by the passing of a bill restoring the property that had been so shamefully confiscated in 1852.

Hardly had the year 1873 begun when all France was startled by the news of the sudden death of the emperor; but though the Imperialists openly showed their grief, and proclaimed their hopes of the restoration of the Empire with the Prince Imperial as Napoleon IV., and though mass was said for the repose of the soul ot Napoleon III. in many of the churches, the event excited no disturbances.   The party, indeed, professed to be in no wise cast down

or disheartened ; but to outside observers the cause of the Empire
seemed dead in France, and even its constant supporters, the peasantry, to be in favor of a moderate Republic, — for to the peasantry
revolution often means loss or ruin, and they always prefer the
government that is.

The Assembly had met on the 6th January, and the proceedings had hardly begun when the old contest between the President
and the Right was renewed. The leading questions that stood over
from the former year were the extent of M. Thiers's power and the
creation of a Second Chamber. The committee of thirty appointed
to deal with these matters wished to begin with the question of M.
Thiers's relation to the Assembly. Thiers himself wished them to
begin with the question of the Second Chamber, and the battle was
fought from day to day without either party gaining a single advantage. It had been settled by formal resolution before, that M.
Thiers was to address the House only upon occasion, and after giving
due notice; but the influence of the President's voice within the
Chamber was so great that he had practically declined to recognize
this restriction, and had taken part in the debates in the Assembly
as if he had been an ordinary Deputy. Now the committee wished
to draw the line closer about his power, and to fix that his ordinary
mode of communication with the Chamber was to be by written
messages read by one of the ministers, though he might still speak
on special permission being given. But the President declined to
be thus silenced. "If you wish to stop my mouth," said he, "and
make a puppet of me, never, never, will I consent to it, for by consenting I should dishonor myself. If I belonged to those noble
families who have done so much for the country, I might, indeed,
stoop to this and accept the part of Constitutional King; but I, a
petit bourgeois, who by dint of study and labor have arrived at being
what I am, I cannot, I repeat, accept the change of functions which
you propose to me without humiliation and without real shame.
No, no, I will go again before the Assembly. It will hear me; it
will believe me; it will do me justice, and so will the country."
The scheme finally laid before the Assembly was that, (1) The

President should "communicate with the Assembly by messages read by one of the ministers," but he was to be heard at a special sitting when he considered it necessary to speak "in the discussion of laws, after having given notice of his intention by a message;" (2) Laws were to be proclaimed within three days or within a month after their decision by the Assembly, according as they were urgent or not; (3) The President was to have a right to speak on the interpellations on foreign affairs, but on no others unless they involved his direct responsibility; (4) The present Assembly was to settle the question of a Second Chamber, to modify the electoral law, and to provide for the administration of affairs in the interval between the dissolution of the present Chamber and the meeting of the new one.

The debate on the report of the committee was a long one, and the President was strongly pressed to give utterance to his opinions on the form of the future government apart from the present Provisional Republic. M. Thiers, however, declined to make any premature disclosures, and it was not till the 13th March that the bill finally passed, and the Deputies proceeded on the 17th to the much more pleasant task of unanimously ratifying a new convention with Prussia, by which it was agreed that the territory still occupied by the German troops should be evacuated on the 1st July, and that Verdun and the surrounding district — the last places to be released from foreign occupation — should be evacuated on the 4th September; and perhaps there can be no better proof of the real strength of France or of the power and glory to which she may attain under peaceful rule, than the rapidity and ease with which, even after a long and disastrous war, she had in two years paid off the heavy war indemnity imposed by Germany.

Notwithstanding the cheers with which this announcement was received, it was manifest, from the tone of the different sectional leaders, that the freedom of French soil from the tread of the foe would be at once the signal for an outbreak of keen party strife, amid which the government, by no means powerfully supported, would be pretty sure to go to the wall. That they had lost on

critical occasions the support of the dominant Right was evident
from the defeats they were constantly sustaining, and still more so
in the election of a new President of the Assembly in place of
M. Grévy, who had held that office since the opening of the Chamber, but who had resigned on the 4th April in consequence of a
"scene" in which his authority had been defied by one of the
speakers.   The candidate who had the government support was
M. Martel, a member of the Left, but he was set aside by the majority in favor of M. Buffet.   They were defeated also in the elections for a number of vacant seats in the end of April, all the
members returned being Republicans of a more or less extreme
school.

When the Chamber reassembled on the 19th May, after the Easter
recess, M. Thiers announced a change of some of the Ministry.
He tried to please everybody by sacrificing M. de Goulard to please
the Left, and M. Jules Simon to please the Right, and he reaped
for his pains the usual reward of those who prefer expediency to
principle.   Instead of everybody being pleased, nobody was pleased,
and the temper of all parties boded no pleasant times for the ministers
in the conduct of the bill for settling the new constitution, which had
been prepared during the recess and was now brought forward.

The Right refused to allow the bill to be proceeded with until
after the discussion of an interpellation they had brought forward
with reference to the Ministerial changes and the general policy of
the government.   The Left retaliated by demanding the immediate
dissolution of the Chamber.   The debate on the interpellation began
on the 23d May, the attack being led by the Duc de Broglie; and the
ministers having decided that this was a motion dealing with the
general policy of the government, and involving the responsibility of
the President, M. Thiers himself spoke on the 24th.   But the result
was a foregone conclusion.   The Ministry were defeated, and at a
special evening sitting announced their resignation, while M. Buffet read a letter from the President of the Republic announcing
his resignation also.   On a fresh division on the question of accepting the resignation the Right were again victorious, and Marshal

MacMahon, designated as the new President, after some slight hesitation accepted the post and pledged his "word as an honest man
and a soldier" to do his utmost towards "liberating the territory
and restoring moral order throughout the country," as well as towards
maintaining "internal peace and the principles upon which society
rests." Thus fell before the tactics of a reactionary party that certainly did not represent the real mind of France, that brave old
statesman who had been *the* man to whom the whole of France
turned for safety in the troublous times after the fall of Paris, and
who had so manfully worked on behalf of his country from the
time of the winter journey to all the capitals in Europe, undertaken
at the beginning of the siege of Paris in the vain effort to bring
about neutral interference, down to the time of that last convention, by which the invaders agreed to quit French territory long before the time originally fixed. His work was done, and done well.
He had won back for France the confidence of Europe; he had
taught France confidence in herself. In spite of his petulant im-
periousness, his patriotism had about it a nobility and unselfishness
by no means common in French public life, where all is generally
so hollow. Nothing could be more unselfish than the loyalty with
which, setting aside his own opinions, he adhered to the Republic
which had entrusted him with power. Whether he was right or
wrong in maintaining his position so long in the face of the majority,
and in refusing to conform to its wishes, is a question which would
require to be discussed in very wide bearings before any chance of
arriving at the truth would be possible; but that he did maintain
it so long was unquestionably due to the clearness with which he
saw that he was supported by and could rely on the true [public
opinion of France, which was to be found not within the walls of
the Assembly at Versailles, but among all those millions of voters
that upheld the Empire so long as they saw that the Empire was
the only barrier between order and anarchy; and his fall happened as soon as ever this Conservative majority became persuaded
that he was not firm enough to keep down Radicalism.

What the Deputies who overthrew M. Thiers's government really hoped to gain by their action will never be clearly known till the secret political history of the time has been written. That a large party hoped for the restoration of the elder branch of the Bourbons is evident enough from their subsequent actions, though they might have hesitated when they reflected how much the uncompromising attitude of the Comte de Chambord had damaged his chances of success; but it is difficult to see why the Orleanists and Bonapartists should have assisted them. No proper fusion of the Orleanists and Legitimists had taken place, and that the Orleans hopes were themselves vain was clear, inasmuch as, at the last moment, M. Thiers almost triumphed through a threatened disruption of the parties over a proposal that tho Duc d'Aumale should be nominated for the position of President if M. Thiers resigned. The Bonapartists, no doubt, relied on Marshal MacMahon, who had risen to position under the Empire; but though he may have had Imperialist hankerings he was no political Imperialist, and was too honest a man to make use of his position for their purposes. Probably the first wish of all parties was for a change, seeing that a change was the first necessity before any of them could hope for a chance of success in their ulterior plans; after that they were to wait "for something to turn up." What was gained was the constitutional point of an executive representing the wishes of the majority of the Assembly.

This was the point dwelt on by the Marshal in his Presidential message, which was read in the Assembly on the 26th May. "I am," said he, "animated by a sentiment of respect for your wishes, and a desire always scrupulously to execute them. I believe the majority invariably constitutes the law in a parliamentary *régime*, and this is still more the case in the present instance, where, by virtue of the existing laws, the First Magistrate of the Republic is the delegate of the Assembly and the delegate of the law." The leading Ministers were: the Duc de Broglie for Foreign Affairs; M. Ernoul — who had taken a leading part in the debate that preceded the resignation of M. Thiers — for Justice; M. Beulé for the Interior; and M. Magne — an Imperialist — for Finance. In spite

of a number of injudicious acts of the Minister of the Interior in
dismissing several prefects, in attempting to bribe the press, and in
dealing with funerals without religious rites, the government majority not only remained steady but increased; and with the opposition broken and dispirited for want of a recognized leader, the
government passed all their measures, including the Army Organization Bill, and a bill renewing the Treaties of Commerce with
England and Belgium, and abolishing the Raw Material Tax, which
had caused such a storm in the preceding session; for one good result of the change of President and Ministry was the return to a
better trade policy.

No sooner was the Assembly prorogued in the end of July than
a visit of the Comte de Paris to the Comte de Chambord, in which
the latter was formally acknowledged as the " sole representative of
the Monarchical principle in France," showed that the long talked
of fusion of monarchical interests had at last really taken place,
and there was no doubt now that, when the Assembly once more
met, there would be an effort to restore legitimate monarchy, and
place Henry V. on the throne of his ancestors. Whatever were
the opinions of the majority in the Chamber, the country at large
showed its disapproval of the restoration project, for the bye-elec-
tions went against the government. Before the Assembly met,
however, the destined monarch had sealed his fate by addressing, on
the 27th October, a letter to one of the Deputies of the Right who
had taken a leading part in the negotiations with him, taking a firm
and certainly most ridiculous stand on a point that always formed
a leading question in the agreement with him, namely: whether the
national flag of France should be the white banner of the Bourbons or the tricolor. He declared that he could never give up
the white flag, " the standard of Arques and Ivry." Had he given
way on this point he would probably have become sovereign of
France; but France may be thankful for her escape. What could
be the character of a man who would stake the success of his
dynasty on the color of a flag? " All," said one of his supporters,
" is at an end and without hope of a renewal." Nothing more could

be done with the Comte de Chambord; the chance of the Legitimists was over.   All parties, Republicans and all, were agreed that now the only thing to be done was to prolong the powers of Marshal MacMahon, and the points to be settled were merely for how long and under what conditions.

CHATEAU DE CHENONCEAUX.

CHAPTER XXV.

NEW SESSION. — MINISTRY OF THE DUC DE BROGLIE. — THE CONSTITU-
TIONAL QUESTION. — TRIAL OF MARSHAL BAZAINE. — THE SEPTEN-
NATE. — RESIGNATION OF THE MINISTRY. — THE CONSTITUTIONAL
STRUGGLE. — THE BONAPARTISTS. — THE BUDGET. — J'Y SUIS, J'Y
RESTE. — THE EDUCATION BILL. — DEATH OF M. GUIZOT. — PRESI-
DENTIAL MESSAGE. — CONSTITUTION BILL. — PASSING OF THE
ORGANIZATION OF POWERS BILL. — THE SENATE BILL. — THE
SETTLEMENT OF THE CONSTITUTION. — BONAPARTIST CHANCES. —
M. BUFFET'S SECOND MINISTRY. — SCRUTIN DE LISTE OR SCRUTIN
D'ARRONDISSEMENT. — DISSOLUTION OF THE NATIONAL ASSEMBLY.
— THE ELECTIONS. — CHANGE IN M. GAMBETTA'S ACTION. — THE
DUFAURE MINISTRY. — BUDGET COMMITTEE. — THE COMTE DE
MUN. — THE AMNESTY QUESTION. — THE SIMON MINISTRY. — THE
SENATE AND THE BUDGET. — DISMISSAL OF THE MINISTRY. — THE
CRISIS OF THE 16TH MAY. — THE SECOND DE BROGLIE MINISTRY.
— THE MARSHAL'S MESSAGE TO THE CHAMBERS. — ANSWERING
MANIFESTO OF THE LEFT. — DEATH OF M. THIERS. — APPEAL TO
THE COUNTRY. — THE ELECTIONS. — SECOND DUFAURE MINISTRY. —
MACMAHON'S RESIGNATION. — AFFAIRS IN 1878. — THE WADDING-
TON MINISTRY. — THE FREYCINET MINISTRY. — THE FERRY MINIS-
TRY. — M. GAMBETTA AND FRENCH PROSPECTS.

THE Assembly met on the 5th November, and the Presidential
message, which was read by the Duc de Broglie, began with
congratulations on the "complete liberation of the territory," — which
had become an accomplished fact on the 16th September, when
Verdun and the surrounding districts were evacuated by the German troops, — and dwelt on the conservative and peaceful nature

of the government. As soon as business was begun, the Right demanded the prolongation of the Marshal's term of power, the Bonapartists urging, besides, a *plébiscite* on the question as to whether the form of government should be Republican, Imperial, or Monarchical. The Left demanded that the question of the prolongation of powers should be taken along with the bill embodying the new constitution. After a keen and exciting debate, the Assembly, by the unexpectedly large majority of sixty-six, prolonged MacMahon's powers for seven years, and by a majority of forty resolved to appoint by ballot a committee to report on the Constitutional Bill, and the Cabinet was slightly altered to suit the new state of affairs. Among other changes, M. Beulé retired, and the Duc Decazes took office as Foreign Minister, while the Duc de Broglie still kept the leading place as Vice-President of Council.

The last great event of the year was the close of the trial of Marshal Bazaine for surrendering without having destroyed the fortifications of Metz, for not having burned all the colors, and for various other crimes, all amounting to treason. There did not seem much good now in raking up all the scandals of mismanagement connected with the matter, but the government had decided otherwise. The trial lasted from the 6th October till the 10th December, when the Marshal was found guilty and condemned to death, after military degradation; but the sentence was afterwards commuted to twenty years' imprisonment in the Isle of St. Marguerite. But even this did not last long, for in the summer of 1874 he succeeded, with the assistance of his wife and probably of some of the jailers, in making his escape· and from the leniency of the sentences pronounced on his aiders and abettors, the country and the government seemed to be glad to have the matter over.

In the beginning of 1874 the Septennate made its power felt by a law by which the appointment of all Mayors and Deputy-Mayors became vested in the government till the new Municipal Law was passed, a measure which placed in the hands of Ministers probably nearly forty thousand appointments.

Amid all the changes of affairs the hopes of the Imperialists

seemed to be reviving. M. Ollivier, who had quitted France after
his fall, now returned, demanded formal admission to the Academy,
to which he had been elected during his time of office and before
the outbreak of the war, and dared before its Committee to utter
words of eulogy over the deceased emperor; and a large deputation,
headed by M. Rouher and the Duc de Padua, crossed to Chiselhurst
to offer their congratulations to the Prince Imperial on the anniversary of his birth, the 16th of March.

In the end of March there were debates over the proposed
changes in the electoral law, which fixed the age of voters, for reasons connected with the Army Bill, at twenty-five instead of twenty-
one, and required that there should be a term of residence before
the power of voting was acquired, and that the voting should take
place by small electoral districts instead of by departments. The
step, though it was probably taken in the interests of order, was a
reactionary one, and so not likely to escape without keen criticism.
What the Left thought of all the government measures was apparent by the interpellation addressed to the government by the Left,
whether a monarchical restoration, or any attempt to change the
form of government during the next seven years, was to be deemed
contrary to law. The ministers would have secured an easy victory
had not one of the Légitimist deputies, who still, in spite of the
past, adhered to the cause of the Count de Chambord, declared that
he deemed the Septennate but a precursor of restoration. The
government majority was, notwithstanding, sixty; but Marshal
MacMahon deemed it necessary himself to disclaim such an interpretation of his power, and to declare that he "preferred duty to
sentiment." Elections were still going against the government,
and the Left were clamorous for a dissolution, and were loud in
their demands for information as to the ultimate intentions of the
Government of the Septennate.

When the Chamber reassembled after Easter, on the 12th of May,
debate arose as to what business should be taken first, and the Ministry demanding that one course should be taken, announced their
resolve to treat the decision as a vote of confidence or the reverse.

The majority decided against them, and they at once resigned, and with them fell the hopes of Legitimists and Orleanists alike. M. Buffet and the Duc d'Audiffret Pasquier in turn declined to attempt to form a cabinet; M. de Goulard failed, and Marshal MacMahon then became his own Prime Minister, with General de Cissey, the Duc Decazes, and M. Magne to assist him.

The struggle still went on, and the hot debates in the beginning of June were on more than one occasion nearly followed by personal collision between the members of the different factions. The Bonapartists, indeed, seemed to be growing in boldness and in popular favor, and even succeeded in carrying one election against a Republican candidate. The section of the press that supported their cause was outspoken, and there was a wide circulation of Imperial literature in the shape of pamphlets advocating the claims of Napoleon IV., as he was called, and urging an appeal to the people. So much was this the case, and so great was the anxiety, that the head of the state thought it necessary and advisable to speak out, and in an Order of the Day addressed to the Army, he accordingly declared that, the National Assembly having placed in his hands for seven years " the guardianship of order and of public peace," he was determined to " fulfil it to the end, maintaining everywhere the authority of the law and the respect due to it." The declaration was at once replied to by a fresh utterance of the Comte de Chambord, that, though he had hitherto maintained silence, in order not to add to the discord of France, this was no longer possible. "Honor," he said, " imposed on him the duty of an emphatic protest," and he protested, accordingly, against everything but his own restoration and despotic power. The protest led to a motion in the Assembly, that it " resolved energetically to uphold the powers conferred on Marshal MacMahon; " but the government suffered a defeat, and tendered its resignation, which the President declined to accept.

The Left still pressed forward the necessity of going on with the Constitutional Bill, and various schemes and compromises were suggested only to be immediately rejected. All was uncertainty and difficulty, and at this most inopportune moment matters were still more unsettled by the resignation of the able Finance Minister, M. Magne. The Budget prepared by M. Magne had been brought forward towards the end of 1873, and had been accepted with the exception of twenty-eight millions of francs of new taxation. It now became necessary to settle how this was to be made up, and the Assembly and the minister differed on the point, as the Assembly wished the matter to be settled by overturning the arrangement with the Bank of France, and repaying a loan to it in eight instead of six years. M. Magne refused to accept the principle that the bargain with the Bank could be broken at the convenience of the government, and resigned, and his resignation was followed by that of another Bonapartist member of the Cabinet, M. Fourtou.

Defeated on a fresh motion for the definite proclamation of the Republic, brought forward by M. Casimir-Périer, the Left once more brought forward a proposal for a dissolution, and were once more defeated. The warfare was unceasing, but affairs remained just where they were when M. Thiers was driven from office, and so the session closed with the Constitution as far off as ever. The Marshal was still the man of the Malakoff: " J'y suis, j'y reste," — " Here I am, and here I stick."

In the latter part of August the President visited the northwestern provinces, and was everywhere received with favor if not with enthusiasm. This journey was alluded to in the Presidential message, read to the Assembly on the 3d of December, three days after the Deputies had reassembled. In the course of his visit to the departments " he had," he said, " everywhere noticed the manifestation of a love of order, and, with the need of peace and security, the desire that an organization admitted by them to be indispensable should give the power created by the law of the 20th of November the strength it required to fulfil the mission that they had entrusted to it. Unceasingly agitated by the propagation of the most pernicious doctrines, the country asked them to insure the procedure of the government which was to protect it with their assistance, and by measures of wise foresight to guarantee, during that period of sta-

bility which they had promised to France, the regular working of
the public power." He further expressed his hope that they would
come to an agreement on the questions to be discussed, and assured
them that he would not "decline his share of the responsibility."
He had taken power "not to serve the aspirations of any party," but
for "social defence and national recovery," and he called on all good
men to aid him in his task. "It was his duty not to desert the
post in which he had been placed, and to occupy it till the last day
with unchangeable firmness and scrupulous respect for the law."
Such was the message. There was no new announcement, no definite purpose declared, and the Septennate Government and the
Assembly had indeed come to such a pass that the *République
Française* was not far wrong when it said that "the Executive
Power was afraid to speak and the Constituent Power was afraid to
act." Both powers, indeed, seemed afraid to do anything, and the
only business that was taken was a discussion on the state of university education, the arrangements for which were described as of
a most wretchedly inadequate nature. The contest lay between the
clerical and the liberal parties, but the sympathies of the majority,
being reactionary, were of necessity inclined to the clerical view of
matters, and carried everything in favor of that view, and though
the bill dropped out of sight from this time on till the middle of
the following year, it was then passed, and the monopoly so long
enjoyed by the University of France finally abolished.

Far removed from the din and bustle of all this party strife, in
which he had once so loved to move, and in which he had played
so prominent a part, M. Guizot had quietly passed away at his
country seat at Val Richer in Normandy, on the 10th of September.
The old inflexible minister of Louis Philippe had never re-entered
public life since 1848, but none the less had France to mourn for
one of her great ones fallen. He was the last of the Huguenots,
and however blind he was to the signs of the times in the critical
years that preceded 1848, and much as his unbending resistance to
all liberal tendencies may have contributed to bring about the Second Revolution, with the crime and woe of the Second Empire in

its train, his efforts and intentions were always for the good of the country, though it is to be feared that the country was but ill able to appreciate the stern moral principle that formed the basis of his whole life and work.

The Presidential message, which was read to the Chamber on the 6th January, 1875, made a vigorous attempt to cut the knot which was hampering all action, and after declaring that "public opinion would find it difficult to understand further delay," pressed upon the Assembly to proceed first to the discussion of the Bill for the establishment of a Second Chamber, which was "the institution that seemed most imperatively called for," and then to take up the question what was to be the form of government when the Septennate should have expired, or should it terminate "by a decree of Providence" by the Marshal's death before his term of power had ended.

The Assembly, however, refused to accept the government plan as being too ambiguous in its proposals about the importance of the question of future government, and decided by a majority of one hundred and seventy to discuss the points in reverse order, both, however, being made to give place to a fresh instalment of army reorganization. Such a decided ministerial defeat was at once followed by the resignation of the Cabinet; but the President having tried in vain to induce in turn the Duc de Broglie, the Duc d'Audiffret Pasquier, and M. Dufaure to become his leading adviser, was at length forced to fall back on the old ministers, who consented to retain office till the bill settling the constitutional questions was passed. The Army Bill was, after keen discussion of all its points, — for military affairs now always excited strong interest and were diligently attended to, — disposed of by the 20th January, and then the Assembly addressed itself at last in earnest to the Constitution.

Two proposals were brought forward for discussion, each providing for the confirmation of MacMahon's powers, for the exercise of legislative functions by two chambers — the Chamber of Deputies and the Senate — and that in the event of a vacancy in the Presidentship both Chambers should meet in Congress and decide what was to be done. But the motion brought forward by the Right spoke only of the "Executive power," thus maintaining the *status quo*; while that supported by the Left spoke of the "government of the Republic," thus tacitly taking it for granted that the Republican form of government was a fact beyond question or dispute. The point to be settled was the definite assertion of the Republic, or the assertion of an indecision in public feeling, which would leave room for the constant danger of an Imperialist or a Monarchical surprise and a new *coup d'état*. The result was of grave moment, and all parties addressed themselves to the settlement with a vigor, if not always with a dignity, worthy of its importance. Moderate men of different parties urged the necessity of trust in Marshal MacMahon; the Republicans called for the Republic as the only thing that could keep the country permanently secure; the representatives of the Monarchy, separating themselves from the Bonapartists, declared their belief that the Marshal was merely maintaining order till the restoration of the Bourbons was accomplished, and that the proclamation of the Monarchy "was the only means of avoiding the Empire," and "could alone insure the salvation of France." So at least said M. Latour; but M. Jules Favre retorted that this would be "to await a royalty that refused itself to a nation that declined to have it."

The discussion lasted at intervals till the 25th February. The first amendment proposed was one by M. Corne, asserting that "the Government of France is composed of a Senate, a Chamber of Deputies, and a President of the Republic, chief of the Executive power"; but it was rejected by a majority of twenty-four. The next amendment attempted a compromise, but in reality left the matter just where it was before, when it proposed that the government of France should "consist of two Chambers and a President of the Republic, who is eligible for re-election"; and so clear was this that it had to be withdrawn. The third amendment, which was proposed by M. Wallon, and was finally carried, though by a majority of only one vote, was to the effect that "the President of the Republic is elected by an absolute majority of votes by the Senate and Chamber of Deputies united in National Assembly. He is appointed for seven years, and is eligible for re-election." A further amendment by

M. Wallon, providing that the power of dissolving the Chamber
should be granted to the "President of the Republic," instead of
to "Marshal MacMahon," as the bill originally had it, was accepted
by a large majority, and the bill thus amended had to wait for its
third reading till the discussions on the Senate Bill had come to
an end.

The measure providing for the constitution of the Senate had
been introduced on the 25th January, and the debates on it had
been taken alternately with the discussion on the "Organization of
Powers" or Constitutional Bill. The principle of the necessity for
a Second Chamber was accepted by all the sections of the Assembly
except the deputies of extreme opinions. The main question was
how it should be elected, whether by universal suffrage or by definite
nomination; and if the latter was to be the case, what was to be the
principle of nomination. The proposal that it should be elected by
universal suffrage, which emanated from M. Duprat, at one time
endangered the issue of the whole matter; for the scheme was, notwithstanding the manifest absurdity it involved, carried by a majority of twelve. The result was a surprise, — for evidently its
supporters never intended it to be successful, but only to afford
means of factious opposition, — and the Marshal sent a formal message refusing to agree to the amendment, and the third reading of
the bill was rejected by a majority of twenty-three. With matters
in this deadlock a meeting of parties decided on a compromise,
which involved a partial recognition of both the elective and the
nomination systems. Some of the senators were to be elected by
various councils chosen by the people, and others were to be nominated by the Assembly; and with this provision the bill was read for
the third time and became law, while the Organization of Powers
Bill was passed on the following day, the 25th February.

Each bill consisted of nine sections. That relating to the Senate
provided that that body should consist of three hundred members
not under forty years of age, one third of whom were to retire every
three years; should have equal right with the Chamber to deal with
all matters excepting those affecting finance; should form the court

for the trial of the President or ministers who might be impeached, and was to enter, and should enter, on its duties as soon as the National Assembly was dissolved. The Organization Bill dealt with the Chamber of Deputies, with the powers of the President, and with the ministers, the second clause being the celebrated Wallon amendment. The Chamber was to be elected by universal suffrage as settled by the Electoral Law; it was to have the power of proposing to alter the Constitution, though the alteration could only be carried out by a National Assembly formed by both Chambers, and during MacMahon's term of office no revision was possible unless proposed by him. The President was to enforce the laws and make civil and military appointments; to nominate the Council of State; to dissolve the Chamber, with consent of the Senate, at any time; and to be responsible only in case of high treason. The Ministers were to be responsible collectively as well as individually. The last section provided that the Chambers were to sit at Versailles. In whatever light the different sections of the Conservative party may have viewed their adhesion to the new order of things, the long struggle was at last over, though many a peril still remained before the vessel of state reached calm water. The Republic was a recognized fact.

The compromise that was effected over the Senate Bill, as well as at several stages of the Constitution Bill, was largely due to fear of the Bonapartist reaction. The party in the Chamber was compact and well organized, and had in the beginning of the year succeeded in carrying an election against all the other parties in the Department of the Hautes Pyrenées. The success of the Wallon amendment itself had been due to a letter from Marshal Canrobert to the electors of the Department of Lot, refusing to become a candidate for the Assembly, in which he made such allusions to the Empire and the Army as led to the conclusion that there was something more behind. At the moment of the rejection of the Senate Bill, the Imperial reaction was still more apparent in the finding of a jury in an action for libel brought by General Wimpffen against the *Pays*, in which they decided not only that Napoleon III. was not responsible for the disaster of Sedan, but hinted that the real culprits were those Radicals who had opposed the army bills of the late years of the Empire. If more forcible warning of the danger of the country had been needed, it would have been shown in the official inquiry into an election which had taken place in 1873, and in which an Imperialist had been the successful candidate. This report showed that the Imperialists were maintaining in France a full government complete and active down even to a police, and it was well known that there was a powerful minority among the peasantry who still looked with favor on a rule that had given them peace till the Liberals were admitted to a share in the power.

As soon as the Senate and Constitution Bills were passed, the Ministry resigned, and the President confided the formation of a new Ministry to M. Buffet, who became head of the Cabinet and Minister of the Interior, with M. Dufaure as Minister of Justice, and M. Léon Say as Minister of Finance. The former Ministers of War and of Foreign Affairs — General Cissey and the Duc Decazes — took office in the new Ministry, and the Duc d'Audiffret Pasquier succeeded M. Buffet as President of the Assembly.

Hardly had the new Ministry got fairly into working order when there were signs of very hostile feeling shown in Germany in connection with the attention that France was giving to military organization, and the expression of the feeling was of such a nature as to lead to remonstrance with Germany on the part both of England and of Russia. Bismarck, however, showed himself opposed to the warlike tone assumed by some sections of the German press and parliament, and the threats of explosion died away almost as rapidly as they had arisen.

The only constitutional point now to be settled was the question of the elections — Whether was the *scrutin de liste* or the *scrutin d'arrondissement* to be adopted? By the former mode each elector had as many votes as there were Deputies for the department to which he belonged, and he distributed these singly among the Deputies he wished returned; and thus the whole power of election would have practically been placed in the hands of the central party organizations, as each voter would have been compelled to accept the nominations of the party platform without any choice of his own. By the latter mode, each electoral district would select its own representative. The government were strongly in favor of the *scrutin d'arrondissement*, and this was the mode that was ultimately adopted after the Autumn recess, which began on the 4th of August and lasted till the 4th of November.

As soon as the Assembly met, it proceeded, after settling for the time the question of *scrutin de liste* or *scrutin d'arrondissement* in favor of the latter, to pass the electoral law; elected the proportion of senators that fell to be appointed by it (an operation in which the Left, profiting by dissensions in the ranks of their opponents, obtained a great victory), and finally decreed its own dissolution, and fixed the 7th of March, 1876, as the date for the meeting of the new Chambers.

So ended the great Versailles Assembly, which had hoped to restore the Monarchy, and which had ended by establishing the Third Republic. "Though," says a writer in the *Times* summing up its results, "though the Assembly which first met at Bordeaux in the disastrous commencement of 1871 has been guilty of many errors, it will occupy no ignoble place in history. In its number were included, without exception, all the most eminent of living Frenchmen, and it has proved, for the first time since the unfortunate collapse of Louis Philippe, that France is sufficiently enlightened to allow itself to be governed by a parliament. Public order has, since the overthrow of the Commune, been steadily maintained; financial and commercial prosperity has been restored; and successive ministers have stoutly adhered to a prudent and pacific policy in foreign affairs."

The Ministry of M. Buffet was essentially a coalition one, and consisted of hardly reconcilable elements, so that it was utterly unable to agree on the manifesto that it ought to have issued before the appeal to the country; and, in these circumstances, the President, with "the simple directness of a mind trained in camps," took

matters into his own hands and issued a proclamation himself,
which tended greatly to restore confidence in the government, and
was received on all hands with expressions of approbation.   It was
headed "French Republic."   "Frenchmen," said the Marshal, "for
the first time in five years you are summoned to take part in a
general election.   Five years ago you wanted order and peace.   At
the price of the most cruel sacrifices, amid the most terrible trials,
you obtained them.   To-day you still want order and peace.   The
Senators and Deputies you will elect will be bound with the President of the Republic to strive to maintain them.   It will be our
duty to apply together with sincerity the constitutional laws of
which I alone have till 1880 the right of proposing the revision.
After so many agitations, strifes, and misfortunes, repose is necessary to our country, and I think our institutions ought not to be
revised before having been loyally worked.   But to work them as
the safety of France demands, the Conservative and truly Liberal
policy which I have constantly aimed at making prevail is indispensable.   In order to sustain it, I appeal to the union of men who
place the defence of social order, respect for the laws, and devotion
to the country above party recollections, aspirations, and engagements; I invite them all to rally round my government.   Under
the shelter of a strong and respected authority, the sacred rights
which survive all changes of government, and the legitimate interests which every government should protect, must find themselves
in full security.   It is necessary, not only to disarm those who
might disturb that security in the present, but to discourage those
who menace it in the future by anti-social doctrines and revolutionary programmes.   France knows that I never sought nor desired
the power with which I am invested, but she may rely on my exer-
cising it without feebleness; and in order that I may fulfil to the
end the mission which is confided to me, I hope that God will help
me, and that the co-operation of the nation will not be lacking
to me."

The elections resulted in a severe defeat, on all sides, of the
Ministry of M. Buffet, and in the return of a large Republican

majority of what we may term a Conservative nature. This success of the Left was greatly due to the moderate tone of the speeches of all their leading men, including even M. Gambetta, who now first showed signs of the true statesmanlike qualities that were in him. He manifested a seemingly decided desire to abandon that feverish Belleville spirit which had hitherto pervaded all his acts and utterances. Dominating as it did his early political life, it had to a great degree destroyed his influence, and his success in shaking it off has since been rewarded by the increased confidence he has secured. M. Buffet himself failed to secure a seat in the Senate, and though he was proposed as a candidate for the Chamber of Deputies in four places, he was unsuccessful in them all. The elections for the Senate were over by the beginning of February, and resulted in a return of one hundred and forty-eight Republicans, as against one hundred and fifty-three representatives of all the other parties together; but though the Republicans were thus therefore in an actual minority, there was little chance of a steady combination against them of the Legitimists, Ultra-legitimists, Orleanists, and Bonapartists, who constituted the majority. In the first elections for the Chamber of Deputies the Left had a clear majority; for out of the total five hundred and thirty-two seats they won two hundred and ninety-five, a number increased by their success in subsequent elections. The Bonapartists did not fare particularly well, — though they were still formidable, — and even M. Rouher was defeated at Ajaccio by Prince Napoleon, who, following up the radical opinions he had never hesitated giving expression to even under the Empire, had cast in his lot with the Left.

The first result of the elections was of course the resignation of M. Buffet, who was succeeded by M. Dufaure, who became Vice-President of the Council and Minister of Justice. M. Say retained the direction of Finance, and the Duc Decazes that of Foreign Affairs. M. Waddington became Minister of Public Instruction, and there were other changes of less importance.

The new Chamber set vigorously to work. Now that the constitutional question was settled, and the army set in thorough order, attention was devoted to the financial situation, to the usual verification of elections, and to the consideration of a proposal for a general amnesty to those condemned on account of their connection with the Commune. The Budget proposals were fairly satisfactory, and showed a surplus, and such was the prosperity of the country that the surplus *was afterwards largely increased owing to the actual income largely exceeding what had been estimated. A new feature in connection with financial management was the appointment of a Budget Committee for the examination of the sources of revenue and to assist the deliberations of the Ministry, and the renewal of confidence in M. Gambetta was shown by his appointment as President of this body. In his speech in returning thanks, after describing the government of the day as one " giving all security to legitimate interests, a wise, regulated progressive Republic, giving all those guarantees which disorderly minds could alone find insufficient," he described the duty of the Budget Committee to be " to put themselves face to face with realities, to study more nearly the details of the financial system without illusion or precipitation, solely inspired by a spirit of economy, maturity, and wise reform. They were to take care to trust nothing to chance, persuaded that in these delicate matters neither the age nor public opinion could be distanced." The Committee had a difficult task before them. They had both to reform, and, if possible, retrench, — an operation which always requires a very large amount of deliberative power and manipulative skill, and which had now to be accomplished in the face of a system that had grown up through long years of thoroughly unsound financial opinions, and had been based, except with regard to the Imperial commercial treaties, almost entirely on protective principles. As the expenditure increased and additional revenue had to be raised, the method of indirect taxes had constantly been resorted to, — greatly to the disadvantage of French consumers, who were thus strictly prevented from buying in the cheapest market and selling in the dearest, — while direct taxation had been almost totally neglected. The alteration of this burden, which involved a re-valuation of land, was the problem before the Committee at the commencement of its labors.

The system of an Assembly discussing and deciding the validity of the elections of its members is undoubtedly a bad one, as the spirit of temperate judicial impartiality is invariably wanting, and a rampant majority, still excited with the feelings evoked during the newly finished contest, decides everything, not according to the rules of justice, but according to the dictates of party passion. The debates on the elections, which occupied the first weeks of the new Chamber, were not only no exception to, but a strong exemplification of, the evils of the system. The Republican majority showed no regard for anything but their own triumph, and decided every doubtful case in their own favor. The mob rule, which caused the loss of M. Gambetta's election at Avignon, was a fitting case for a powerful assertion of peace and order, but little can be said in defence of their very discreditable arrogance in many other cases. The Pontivy election, where the Comte de Mun, a leading Legitimist, had defeated a Bonapartist candidate, excited keen interest. The Comte was a very eccentric young man, who thought, sincerely enough, that his mission in life was to overthrow the influence of Democratic clubs by Catholic guilds. To this cause he brought a simple but persuasive eloquence, and a manner that was somewhat ludicrous in its dramatic affectation. The opposition to the confirmation was due to the fact that he was a strict churchman, and had been put forward as the coming champion of the clerical party. His opponent was, curiously enough, a churchman, the Abbé Cadoret, but on this occasion he failed to command the support of his brethren, who were all in favor of the Comte. "The Bishop of Vannes gave him his support, the Pope decorated him, the clergy undertook a campaign for him. . . . . The contest was warm, but at the second ballot the Comte de Mun was elected by some hundreds of a majority. The priests intervened, the Bishop mixed himself up in the struggle, the clerical papers were ardent supporters of the layman against the priest. The strife waxed very hot. The return was disputed."

At the sitting at which the case was taken up on the 3d April, the first business was the raising of the State of Siege in Paris, which had now lasted for over four years and a half; and this, though it was by far the more important proceeding, was agreed to without discussion. In his defence the Comte stated that the "real accusations preferred" against him were "the intervention of the Bishop of Vannes and the Archbishop of Paris, and the decoration which it had pleased the Holy Father to bestow on him. This election had," he said, "been considered as a vast conspiracy inspired by the ecclesiastical authorities." In reply to this, he maintained that "the nomination of a priest called for diocesan authority," and that neither the Bishop nor the Archbishop had done more than declare that the Abbé was not supported by them, and that they were as much entitled to express their approval or disapproval of candidates as was Garibaldi, who had given his advice to the electors of some districts. The official reporter on the case denounced the action of the Bishop and Archbishop, on the ground that they were paid officials of the State, and an inquiry was accordingly entered on.

The question of a general amnesty for all those condemned as implicated in the disturbances of 1871 was brought forward by M. Raspail, after the Easter recess in the end of May, and was debated for three days. The proposal was strongly opposed by the government, on whose behalf M. Dufaure made a long and vigorous speech, in which he dwelt with pointed and emphatic severity on the heinous crimes perpetrated by the Commune, and indicated the opinion that a government which had tried only about ten thousand out of the forty thousand persons who were implicated had, for the time, been sufficiently merciful. France had not forgotten the crimes of the Commune. "The wound she received," said he, "is still bleeding. Several years more are still necessary to efface the shocking remembrance of the crimes of the Commune. Clemency has not uttered its last word; but it is not with distinctions of categories that it must be exercised, for categories are always too wide or too narrow. . . . . There are men who, having been culpable, have repented, and whose conduct has become a reparation that ought to be taken into consideration. But these are not categories to introduce into a law. Either you have confidence in the illustrious President of the Republic and his Minister, — then you will leave it to them to select; or you have no confidence, — then seek other ministers. As to those who, free abroad, employ all their activity in cursing their country and exciting hatred against it, or, under the veil of anonymity, speak only of maledictions and reprisals: as for those who preserve all the passions of 1871, they do not accord the amnesty to us; we will not accord it to them." · The reference to categories was in relation to a scheme for the division of the offenders into classes to be pardoned in turn, — a plan said to have been brought forward at the instigation of M. Gambetta, who himself showed further token of his new-born moderation by his absence from the debate. The division showed how hollow and premature was the proposal, for it was supported by only the extreme Radicals, who could, in a house of four hundred and forty-six members, gather no larger a following than the very small minority of fifty-two.

In the Senate the same proposal was brought on somewhat later in the end of May, and supported by Victor Hugo in a speech that lapsed into an elaborate attack on the crimes of the Empire, which were declared to be as bad as or even worse than those of the Commune. "The burning of the Tuileries and the Hôtel de Ville," said he, "was a crime like the violation of the hall of the National Assembly. The massacre of the hostages was a crime just as the massacre of passers-by on the Boulevards was a crime. The deed of the 2d December and the deed of the 18th March throw light on each other. They ought to be judged alike, and if justice is unequal in its decrees it should have reserved all its indulgence for the desperate and feverish population, and all its severity for the adventurer Prince, who, after the Elysée, wanted the Louvre, and who, in stabbing the Republic, stabbed his own oath. The author of the crime died in his bed, after having completed the 2d December by Sedan, treason by incapacity, the overturning of the Republic by the fall of France. As for the accomplices, — Morny, Billault, Magnan, St. Arnaud, Abbatucci, — they have given their names to streets in Paris. Compare with this the execution ground of

FRANKFORT ON THE MAIN.

Satory; 18,984 condemned to transportation and hard labor five thousand leagues from home.   See in what fashion Justice has chastised the 18th March, while it swore allegiance to the crimes of the 2d December."   There was no further discussion, and the minority in favor of the amnesty was much smaller than that which supported it in the Lower Chamber.

A bill introduced by M. Waddington for the repeal of the University Bill of the preceding year, and the restoration of the monopoly of the University of Paris, passed the Chamber of Deputies by a large majority, but was thrown out by the Senate; but as the Ministry had not staked its fate on the passing of the bill, no crisis happened.   The similar rejection of another bill, however, in the special Autumn Session held for the purpose of passing the Budget, led to the resignation of M. Dufaure, and the reconstitution of the Cabinet.

On the 27th June the President had written a letter to the Minister of War requesting him to see that "in future" no prosecution for political offences connected with the troubles of 1871 should be instituted, if it were not "demanded in some way by the unanimous sentiment of all honest people, to whatever opinion they may belong."   "Except these exceptional cases," he said elsewhere, "which it would be difficult for a law to specify beforehand, I think we ought to allow all acts connected with the disastrous insurrection of 1871 to fall into oblivion."   During the Autumn session M. Dufaure had brought in a bill to the same effect, that the future prosecutions should be restricted; and the Chamber had passed the bill, but the Senate threw it out.   The result was contrary to their expectations, for M. Dufaure, driven from power, was replaced by a Ministry headed by M. Jules Simon, and of a much more liberal nature than its predecessors.

The new Premier had hardly assumed the conduct of affairs when the stability of the Cabinet was tried, and again by a conflict with the Senate.   The Budget Committee after diligent work had presented their report, and the Budget, which constituted the chief business of the Session, was passed and sent to the Senate.   It had been provided by the Constitution, that while both Chambers were to have the right of framing and initiating laws, those dealing with finance had to be first "presented to and voted by the Chamber of Deputies." The clause would seem to have been loosely worded, and now the question arose what was the exact meaning of it. The Liberals maintained that the Senate had no power over financial arrangements, but the Conservative majority of the Senate uniting for the nonce, held that, under the section of the Constitution just mentioned, they had equal power with the Chamber of Deputies, except in the matter of priority of discussion. This being so they declined to pass the bill at once as a whole, and maintained their right to deal with it fully in sections, and they were allowed to carry their point. The amendments they had made on some points were adopted by the Chamber, the crisis terminated, and the Senate, appeased by this victory, passed the rest of the Budget without further debate.

Between the meeting of the Chamber on the 9th January, 1877, and the Easter recess, and for a short time afterwards, but little of any importance occurred, unless, in the absence of more exciting matters, party bickerings on the subject of ultramontane influence can be dignified by the name of political business. The strained feelings still existing between France and Germany were exemplified by the expulsion of retired French soldiers from Alsace-Lorraine early in March, and by a speech delivered by Count von Moltke in the German Parliament, in which he dealt with the French military preparations; but the increasing *rapprochement* of the nations was also shown by the mission of the Marquis d'Absac, Marshal MacMahon's adjutant, to present his congratulations to the Emperor of Germany on the celebration of his eightieth birthday, on the 22d March, an act of courtesy which was regarded in Germany with feelings of favor and gratification. The outbreak of war between Russia and Turkey had been followed by a proclamation of French neutrality issued on the 1st May. The Prime Minister, M. Jules Simon, was with moderation and success advancing in the path of his new duties.

All seemed to be going well, when, with a suddenness like thunder
from a clear sky, astonishing to every one except the wire-pullers
behind the scenes, the President on the 16th May addressed a letter
of reproof to M. Favre, which left no course open for him but that
of immediate resignation. Had any doubt existed as to the meaning of the letter, and the intentional sharpness of its tone, it would
have been at once removed by the answer of the Marshal to M.
Simon's tender of his resignation. "I expected it, and I accept it,"
was the reply. The ostensible reason of the reprimand was the
failure of the ministers to speak against certain sections of the
municipal laws and against the repeal of M. Dufaure's Press law,
after the necessity of opposing these had been decided on by the
Cabinet. "The attitude of the head of the Cabinet," said Marshal
MacMahon, "naturally suggests the inquiry whether he retains over
the Chamber the influence necessary to make his own views prevail
An explanation on this point is indispensable, for if I am not responsible like you to the Parliament, I have a responsibility to
France, with which I must now more than ever be preoccupied."
The reason put forward was undoubtedly a mere pretext; and evil
private advice and fear of the extreme Republicans, to whose views
M. Simon was held to show too much favor, were the real causes of
a step as arbitrary as Cromwell's summary expulsion of the Long
Parliament, but lacking that justification in the state of affairs that
made the latter act, however unconstitutional, a benefit to the
nation.

The formation of a new Ministry was entrusted to the Duc de
Broglie, who became Prime Minister and Minister of Justice; M. de
Fourtou, a Bonapartist, was Minister of the Interior; and the Duc
Decazes and General Berthaut, — who had only been kept in office
after the fall of the Dufaure Ministry by the declaration of Marshal MacMahon that his retention was necessary for perfecting the
army reorganization — retained their places as Ministers of Foreign Affairs and of War respectively. The whole matter had been
thoroughly prepared, for they were ready to take office on the 18th.
When the arbitrary procedure of the President became known the

tumult among the Republicans was great, but their leaders coun-
selled them to maintain a moderate attitude, and thus show how
futile were the fears of their opponents. At a private meeting it
was decided to support a motion to the following effect: "The
Chamber, considering that it is incumbent upon it in the present
crisis, in order to accomplish the mandate which it received from
the country, to recall the fact that the preponderance of the Parliamentary power exercised through Ministerial responsibility is the
first condition of the government of the country by the country, —
to establish which was the object of the constitutional laws, — declares that the confidence of the majority will only be enjoyed by a
Cabinet which is free in its action, and resolved to govern in accordance with Republican principles, which can alone secure order
and prosperity at home and abroad," and this motion was proposed
in the Chamber, and was carried by three hundred and fifty-five
votes to one hundred and fifty-four.

The government replied, by reading a message from the President,
that the Cabinets he had chosen at the desire of the majority had
failed in securing the support of a party in favor of " proper ideas,"
being aided only by those whose schemes would "engender disorder
and the degradation of France." "As long," he continued farther
on, "as I am the depositary of power, I shall make use of it to the
whole extent of its legal limits to oppose what I regard as the ruin
of my country. But I am convinced that the country thinks as I
do. It was not the triumph of these theories which it wished at
the last elections. That is not what was announced to it by those
who took advantage of my name, and declared themselves resolved
to sustain my power. . . . . I remain none the less now, as hitherto,
firmly resolved to respect and maintain the institutions which are
the work of the Assembly from which I hold power, and which
have constituted the Republic. Until 1880 I am the only man
who could propose a change. I meditate nothing of the kind. All
my advisers are, like me, determined to work the institutions loyally,
and are incapable of striking any blow at them." While the message was being read the uproar made by the Radicals was an outrage

not only on their boasted moderation, but on decency itself. The
Senate was a very bear-garden. The members of the Left shouted
and howled, and even "left their seats to clench their fists almost
under M. de Broglie's nose." Both Chambers were at once prorogued for four weeks, and the Marshal's declaration that the triumph
of these theories was not what the country wished at the last elections evidently betokened that, at the end of that time, could the
consent of the Senate necessary by the Constitution be obtained,
the Chamber would be dissolved. There was to be no new *coup
d'état :* the Marshal, believing that the majority in the Chamber of
Deputies did not now represent the true opinion of France any more
than it did in the days of M. Thiers's government, had resolved, if
possible, to appeal to the country. His action, though high handed,
was not unconstitutional, for it was expressly declared by law that
he could "choose his own ministers."

In reply to the Marshal's manifesto an answer was drawn up and
published, signed by no less than three hundred and forty-five Deputies. It declared that, notwithstanding the fact that the Chambers
were prorogued evidently with a view to the dissolution of the
Chamber of Deputies, and after the dismissal of a Ministry that
had always commanded a majority, the country would "show by
its coolness, patience, and resolution that an incorrigible minority
cannot wrest from it its own government. However unexpected
this painful trial may be . . . . France will let herself be neither
deceived nor intimidated. She will resist every provocation. . . . .
The trial will not be long. In five months at most France will
speak : the Republic will issue stronger than ever from the popular
urns ; the parties of the past will be finally vanquished ; and France
will be able to face the future with calmness and confidence."

When the Chambers re-assembled on the 16th of June, the Presidential Message, read in the Senate, and again received with loud
outcries, began by announcing that the President wished their assent
to a dissolution of the Chamber of Deputies, and that the ministers
would give the reasons for this wish. He stated plainly his reasons
for dismissing the former ministers. "No Ministry," said he, "could

maintain itself in that Chamber without seeking the alliance, and meeting the conditions of the Radical party. A government bound to such a necessity is no longer master of its own actions. Whatever its personal intentions, it is reduced to serving the ends of those whose support it has accepted, and to paving the way for their accession. It is this to which I would no longer lend myself." After alluding to his regret that the separation of the Chambers was to take place before the Budget had been voted and to the manifesto of the Republican Deputies, he said: "I shall address myself with confidence to the nation. France, like me, desires to maintain intact the institutions which govern us. She desires as much as I that these institutions should not be disfigured by the action of Radicalism. She does not desire that in 1880 — the day when the constitutional laws may be revised — everything should be prepared beforehand for the disorganization of all the moral and material forces of the country. Warned in time, guarding against all misunderstanding and ambiguity, France will, I am sure, do justice to my intention, and will choose for her representatives those who will promise to second me."

An interpellation on the composition of the Cabinet was at once brought forward, and led to a debate, where "the Assembly of the country of elegance and wit, was seen shrieking, hissing, imitating the voice of the speaker, and presenting to the alarmed spectators the picture of a lamentable decadence and unbridled violence." The more important debate on the question of dissolution was begun in the Senate on the 21st of June, and ended the following day, one hundred and fifty members voting in favor of the proposal, and one hundred and twenty against it. The Chamber of Deputies was accordingly dissolved on the 25th, and it was intimated that the new elections were to take place in three months.

Before that time the nation, and particularly that section of it that centred its hopes in the existence of a Conservative Republic, had suffered a great loss. The hand of death had for three years been busy among the public men of France. M. Boulé, M. de Goulard, M. de Rémusat, and M. Casimir-Périer, all former ministers,

CITY HALL OF RHEIMS.

had in turn passed away, but now the country had to mourn for the last of the giants of an earlier political world. On the 3d of September M. Thiers died, at the ripe age of eighty. He was accorded a public funeral, and never perhaps was the respect of a country shown with greater spontaneity than when the remains of " the Liberator of the Territory " were borne to the tomb with " a solemn, dignified, calm homage, magnificent beyond description, and without any of those popular incidents which disquiet the attentive spectator."

The government interfered extensively in the elections, their operations being directed by M. de Fourtou, who had acquired his skill in the conduct of such matters in the time of the Empire, though now he carried the system to a pitch beyond any former effort; but in spite of all their endeavors they succeeded only in reducing the former Republican majority from one hundred and seventy to one hundred and twenty, and the result of the appeal was therefore a defeat. When the new Chamber met on the 7th November M. Grévy was again elected President. The battle of parties began on the 12th, when the Left proposed the appointment of a committee to inquire into all acts of " illegal pressure " at the elections, " to report on the responsibility of their authors whoever they may be," and to propose the resolutions the facts appeared to warrant; and the motion was carried by a majority of one hundred and sixteen. The government were successful in the Senate on the question of an interpellation as to their attitude with regard to this investigation; but notwithstanding this they resigned, and, when the Marshal chose a Ministry outside the Chambers altogether, the situation became still more critical. He was, however, within the letter of the law, for the Constitution made no provision that Ministers should be either Deputies or Senators; but he was evidently violating the spirit of it in relying on a Cabinet that could have no official communication with the Chambers, and the majority, taking advantage of this, passed, by three hundred and twenty-three votes to two hundred and eight, a resolution to " hold no relations with this Ministry," and refused to vote the Budget. Things were in a state of complete deadlock. The President was, as *Punch* represented him, stuck in the mud, "J'y suis, j'y reste," and there was no course open for him but to submit or resign ; and, though M. Gambetta had been condemned to fine and imprisonment for asserting that the President must submit or abdicate, on the ground that this was an insult to the head of the State, the truth of his statement now became such a stubborn fact that Marshal MacMahon was forced to see it. On the 12th of December he did submit, and, turning at last to his true supporters — the moderate Republicans — he once more entrusted the formation of a Cabinet to M. Dufaure, who became President of Council and Minister of Justice. M. Waddington undertook the conduct of Foreign Affairs, and M. Léon Say resumed office as Minister of Finance. The Presidential Message, now countersigned by the Minister of the Interior, and for which the Ministry were responsible, declared that " the end of the crisis" would " be the starting-point of a new era of prosperity in promoting the development of which all the public powers " would " concur." The great struggle which had lasted for almost seven months was over. The contest of the years 1873 and 1874 had established the Republic, that of the summer and autumn of 1877 had settled that the President was necessarily controlled by the Parliamentary majority.

The year 1878 was quiet in all respects as compared with the period of keen struggle that had been going on since the outbreak of the war with Prussia. Parties seemed tired of strife, and now that the victory of Parliamentary control was won, the Republican majority in the Chamber of Deputies — in reality of fairly moderate opinions, however much the blatant clamor of their extreme partisans, at times in danger of being mistaken for the roar of the true lion, may have sometimes caused them to seem otherwise — were able to control and conduct matters pretty much as they liked. Foreign affairs, critical though they were at times in the diplomatic strife that followed the termination of the Russo-Turkish war, were safe in the hands of M. Waddington, who showed himself both prudent and firm. The attention of the country at large was concentrated on the Great Industrial Exhibition of 1878, which was a thorough success, and had surpassed even the gigantic Imperial display of 1867. One result, evidently brought about by the new form of government, was the interest excited among the French people themselves by it, an interest which the Imperial projects could never command.

The action of the Second Chamber had been somewhat factious in the opposition offered to measures approved by the Deputies; but, as one third of the Senate retired at the end of the year, the Senate was, by the new elections, brought more into harmony with the Chamber of Deputies. When the session of 1879 opened, it, however, soon became apparent that the Ministry of M. Dufaure had ceased to command the support of the majority, and their hostility seemed to be directed against the Prime Minister himself, who was deemed not sufficiently liberal in his opinions. The question of confidence was raised on the condition of the Council of State and the magistracy, upon which an attack was made upon ministers by their chief supporters of the Left Centre. The Ministry gave way, but, when they were called on to deal with some army commands that had been held for longer than the specified time, they came into conflict with the President, who refused to give his consent. The ministers stood firm, and on the 30th of January the Marshal resigned. "The Cabinet," he said, "now proposes to me, as regards the great commands, general measures which I deem contrary to the interests of the army, and consequently to those of the country. I cannot subscribe to them. . . . . I accordingly think it my duty to curtail the duration of the trust with which the National Assembly invested me. I resign the Presidency of the Republic. In leaving office, I have the consolation of believing that during the fifty-three years I have devoted to the service of my country as a soldier and as a citizen I have never been guided by other sentiments than those of honor and duty, and perfect devotion to my country." MacMahon's letter was received by the Chambers with perfect silence, and on the afternoon of the same day the Chambers met in congress, and elected M. Jules Grévy President, by the large majority of four hundred and sixty-four votes over his opponent General Chanzy.   M. Dufaure resigned, and M. Gambetta, who had refused to allow himself to be nominated for the Presidency, became President of the Chamber of Deputies.   M. Waddington became Prime Minister, and other changes of less importance took place.   M. de Freycinet became Minister of Works. The new Ministry held much the same line of policy as that of M. Dufaure, and being, therefore, open to the same objections on the part of the Left, existed pretty much on sufferance, and, towards the end of the year, finding themselves placed in an unendurable position, partly from this lack of confidence in their policy, and in immediate connection with a renewal of the agitation for a general amnesty of the Communists, they resigned on the 25th December. The formation of the new Cabinet was entrusted to M. de Freycinet, who became Prime Minister and Minister of Foreign Affairs.   M. Jules Ferry remained Minister of Public Instruction, and the Cabinet as finally constituted was representative of political tendencies of a much more advanced nature than those of their predecessors. It was still, however, too conservative for the majority, who pressed their advanced measures forward eagerly.   The Education Bill was passed after a conflict with the Senate, which rejected a clause dealing with the " unauthorized " religious orders who had engaged in teaching.   A Bill for the regulation of Public Meetings caused dissensions in the Cabinet, and led to ministerial changes.   The amnesty question again brought forward had at last partial success, but not without strife and trouble.   Further quarrels arose over the execution of decrees directed against the Religious Orders, the members of which had been, after the failure of the clause in the Education Bill, proscribed by the government under old laws, and these differences of opinion became so grave that the Cabinet resigned, and was succeeded by a Ministry under the leadership of M. Jules Ferry.

It did not begin its term of office under very favorable auspices, for it resigned very shortly after its formation, in consequence of a defeat on the question of the removability of magistrates.   Resuming office at the urgent request of M. Gambetta, it was again placed in an awkward position by a vote of censure passed in the Senate for harshness in the removal of religious emblems from schools. Many of the complications that beset it arose from the fact that, while M. Jules Ferry was the responsible minister, M. Gambetta was the real leader and minister. At his instigation the government again renewed the plan of *scrutin de liste* which was agitated in 1875, and, getting his own way at last·in the matter of a spirited foreign policy, he is no doubt really responsible for the aggressive and unprovoked war now raging in Tunis over which the Ferry Cabinet secured its last vote of confidence, and which shows that France the Republic, when seized with a fit of earth hunger, is no more given to respect the rights of her neighbors, or loath to acquire a little cheap and tinsel " glory," than was France the Empire.

The vote of confidence was but a precursor to the resignation of the Ministry, for at last M. Gambetta had resolved to assume responsibility as well as power, and he has accordingly acceded to office, and surrounded himself with a Ministry consisting mostly of men young and hitherto untried except in the ranks of journalism. What will be the result ? The question as to whether his recent moderation is the true-born fruit of mellowing experience, or a cunningly devised veil to secure the confidence of the country, is full of import for the future of France. He has given many rash pledges which cannot be fulfilled with safety. Will he cast them behind him, and secure stable power, or will he be but the forerunner of Clémenceau, as he himself was preceded by Dufaure ? Will he forget all about the return of the Chamber to Paris, a rash amnesty of the whole of those implicated in the Commune, the impeachment of those responsible for the crisis of the 16th May, and the general transfer of supreme power to a lower social stratum; and will he be able, forgetting these now that he has come to exercise the full powers of office, still to " keep his friends in Belleville quiet," as he has hitherto done, by letting them " dream of the day " when he is to bring all these things to pass ? It seems for the moment as if he would, but responsibility will ere long be reminded of its old promises, and then, will he be strong enough to break with the past? " Will he be able for a single moment to bear being called what Thiers, when he separated from the incapable politicians of the 'National,' was called, — an epicurean and an upstart (*un ventru et un arrivé*), or even an apostate and a moderantist?" If the Third Republic is to last, it must seek its leaders elsewhere than in Belleville. " It must reject not only the heirs of 1793, but also those of 1791, 1832, 1834, and 1848, to whom Gambetta will always belong, and must look for its leaders among the intellectual successors of Martignac, Casimir-Périer, Thiers, and Dufaure, who have always set the welfare of France above the success of a particular form of government, and sought to make the best of the existing Constitution."

University Press: John Wilson & Son, Cambridge.